Progress without Planning:
The Economic History of Ontario
from Confederation to the
Second World War

THE ONTARIO HISTORICAL STUDIES SERIES

The Ontario Historical Studies Series is a comprehensive history of Ontario from 1791 to the present, which will include several biographies of former premiers, numerous volumes on the economic, social, political, and cultural development of the province, and a general history incorporating the insights and conclusions of the other works in the series. The purpose of the series is to enable general readers and scholars to understand better the distinctive feature of Ontario as one of the principal regions within Canada.

PUBLISHED

J.M.S. Careless, ed *The Pre-Confederation Premiers: Ontario Government Leaders, 1841–1867* (1980)
Charles W. Humphries *'Honest Enough to Be Bold' : The Life and Times of Sir James Pliny Whitney* (1985)
Charles M. Johnston *E.C. Drury: Agrarian Idealist* (1986)
Peter Oliver *G. Howard Ferguson: Ontario Tory* (1977)
A.K. McDougall *John P. Robarts: His Life and Government* (1976)

Christopher Armstrong *The Politics of Federalism: Ontario's Relations with the Federal Government, 1867–1942* (1981)
David Gagan *Hopeful Travellers: Families, Land and Social Change in Mid-Victorian Peel County, Canada West* (1981)
Robert M. Stamp *The Schools of Ontario, 1876–1976* (1982)
K.J. Rea *The Prosperous Years: The Economic History of Ontario, 1939–1975* (1985)
Ian M. Drummond *Progress without Planning: The Economic History of Ontario from Confederation to the Second World War* (1987)

Olga B. Bishop, Barbara I. Irwin, Clara G. Miller, eds *Bibliography of Ontario History, 1867–1976: Cultural, Economic, Political, Social* 2 volumes (1980)
R. Louis Gentilcore and C. Grant Head *Ontario's History in Maps* (1984)
Joseph Schull *Ontario since 1867* (McClelland and Stewart 1978)

IAN M. DRUMMOND
WITH CONTRIBUTIONS BY PETER GEORGE,
KRIS INWOOD, PETER W. SINCLAIR,
AND TOM TRAVES

Progress without Planning: The Economic History of Ontario from Confederation to the Second World War

A project of the
Ontario Historical Studies Series
for the Government of Ontario
Published by University of Toronto Press
Toronto Buffalo London

ISBN 0–8020–2614–1 (cloth)
ISBN 0–8020–6661–5 (paper)

Canadian Cataloguing in Publication Data

Drummond, Ian M., 1933–
  Progress without planning

  (Ontario historical studies series)
  Bibliography: p.
  Includes index.
  ISBN 0-8020-2614-1 (bound). – ISBN 0-8020-6661-5 (pbk.)

  1. Ontario – Economic conditions – 1867–1918.*
  2. Ontario – Economic conditions – 1918–1945.*
  3. Ontario – Industries – History.   I. Title.   II. Series.

HC117.06D78 1987   330.9713'03   c87-093952-1

This book has been published with the assistance of funds provided by the
Government of Ontario through the Ministry of Citizenship and Culture.

Contents

The Ontario Historical Studies Series

For many years the principal theme in English-Canadian historical writing has been the emergence and the consolidation of the Canadian nation. This theme has been developed in uneasy awareness of the persistence and importance of regional interests and identities, but because of the central role of Ontario in the growth of Canada, Ontario has not been seen as a region. Almost unconsciously, historians have equated the history of the province with that of the nation and have depicted the interests of other regions as obstacles to the unity and welfare of Canada.

The creation of the province of Ontario in 1867 was the visible embodiment of a formidable reality, the existence at the core of the new nation of a powerful if disjointed society whose traditions and characteristics differed in many respects from those of the other British North American colonies. The intervening century has not witnessed the assimilation of Ontario to the other regions in Canada; on the contrary it has become a more clearly articulated entity. Within the formal geographical and institutional framework defined so assiduously by Ontario's political leaders, an increasingly intricate web of economic and social interests has been woven and shaped by the dynamic interplay between Toronto and its hinterland. The character of this regional community has been formed in the tension between a rapid adaptation to the processes of modernization and industrialization in modern western society and a reluctance to modify or discard traditional attitudes and values. Not surprisingly, the Ontario outlook is a compound of aggressiveness, conservatism, and the conviction that its values should be the model for the rest of Canada.

From the outset the objective of the Board of Trustees of the series has been to describe and analyse the historical development of Ontario as a distinct region within Canada. The series as planned will include some thirty volumes covering many aspects of the life and work of the province from its original establishment in 1791 as Upper Canada to our own time.

Among these will be biographies of several premiers, numerous works on the growth of the provincial economy, educational institutions, minority groups, and the arts, and a synthesis of the history of Ontario, based upon the contributions of the biographies and thematic studies.

In planning this project, the editors and the board have endeavoured to maintain a reasonable balance between different kinds and areas of historical research and to appoint authors ready to ask new questions about the past and to answer them in accordance with the canons of contemporary scholarship. *Progress without Planning: The Economic History of Ontario from Confederation to the Second World War* is the fifth theme study to be published and the second volume in a projected three-volume economic history of Ontario. It is a comprehensive account of the development of the provincial economy from Confederation to the outbreak of the Second World War. This was a period marked by industrial and agricultural transformation and by major structural changes in the economy. In contrast to the post-1939 years, when governments were expected to shape the course of economic events, the processes examined in this volume were not 'planned or managed by anyone.'

Ian Drummond and his contributors have given us a detailed and very perceptive analysis of a most important phase in the evolution of the Ontario economy. We hope with the author that others will be 'sufficiently inspired or irritated' by it to undertake new research on the economic history of the province.

The editors and the Board of Trustees are grateful to Professor Drummond for undertaking this task.

GOLDWIN FRENCH
PETER OLIVER
JEANNE BECK
MAURICE CARELESS, Chairman of the Board of Trustees

Toronto
20 May 1987

General Preface

The present volume is one of a series of three that will treat the economic development of Ontario from the late eighteenth century until the middle of the 1970s. The first volume, by Douglas McCalla, will cover the period that ends with Confederation. The present volume, the second, deals with the years from Confederation to World War Two. The third volume, K.J. Rea's *The Prosperous Years* (University of Toronto Press, 1985), surveys what most readers will see as the 'modern period.' Taken together, the three volumes are meant to provide a general narrative account of economic developments, as well as an interpretative and analytical comment on them. Because the three authors naturally have chosen to emphasize different elements in their stories, because different sorts of questions properly and naturally emerge as decade follows decade, and partly because there is a parallel evolution in the documentary evidence, both numerical and qualitative, the volumes cannot be conformed to a single mould. Thus, for instance, McCalla must concern himself with settlement and with the role of subsistence production in early Ontario agriculture, while Rea has to give extensive attention to questions of economic policy, which in earlier decades arose in very different forms or not at all. Similarly, the economic history of pre-Confederation Ontario can be written, and perhaps must be written, on the basis of the archival materials, but no one could treat the modern period on such a basis: for the period since 1940 there is little archival documentation, while government statistics and government reports exist in great profusion. Inevitably, the character of the evidence affects the texture of the narrative. In principle, and to some extent in practice, the existing literature has the same effect. But on most topics in Ontario economic history the scholarly literature is remarkably scant, and the popular literature is strikingly uninformative. Thus none of the three authors could proceed by summarizing and synthesizing what others have written about the Ontario economy.

The present volume, like the other two, is written for a wide audience; it tries to supply the sorts of information which one might expect to find in a work of reference and to avoid certain topics about which only other economists and historians would care. In the space and time that were available no one could hope to be comprehensive. The authors have conferred about coverage and the distribution of emphasis, but as each writer has, in the end, made his own choices, the final products must reflect their separate decisions about importance and relevance. Although the three books form part of a single project, and although they will provide a single survey with a considerable unity of content, it is not to be expected that they will be homogeneous.

IAN M. DRUMMOND

Preface

During the past eight years this study has been an absorbing one, not only for the main author and his academic collaborators but for numerous assistants. The basic bibliographical work was begun by Beatrice Saunders and later updated by Bradley Adams and Gail Gorham, who also served as research assistants. Other research assistance was provided by Diane Way, Jack Gibbons, Malcolm Ruby, Bill and Helen Robson, Anne Jamieson, and John Clark. Drafts of some chapters have been read by Robert Bothwell, John English, James Lemon, Donald Kerr, and Bradley Adams; drafts of others have been presented to the Economic History Workshop, University of Toronto, and to the Fourteenth Canadian Quantitative Economic History Conference, which was assisted by a conference grant from the Social Sciences and Humanities Research Council of Canada. Many friends have had to listen to enthusiastic accounts of arguments and evidence, as these gradually emerged from the thicket of research. Much of the original manuscript has been typed and retyped by Kathryn Hough and Pam Bondy, and by the University Secretarial Services. The research has been financed by the Ontario Historical Studies Series, by a most welcome and much-appreciated research grant from the Social Sciences and Humanities Research Council of Canada (410–83–0986), and by the University of Toronto. The book could not have been completed without access to the Spectrix computer installation and its Unix operating system in the Office of the Dean, Faculty of Arts and Science, University of Toronto. The aid of the system's guardians, Linda Lewis and Rod Cherkas, has been especially welcome.

IAN M. DRUMMOND, Toronto, 1986

Appendix C: Tables

Part One:
Overview

1 Introduction

Land, People, and Money: an Economic Anatomy

The new dominion of 1867 was a very different country from the nation that we know. It contained only Nova Scotia, New Brunswick, and the southern portions of present-day Ontario and Quebec. There was no road or rail connection between central Canada and the Maritimes, or between Canada and the more westerly parts of British North America. The dominant metropolis was Montreal, with Toronto very much in second place. There were few cities, and not many large towns. The population was mostly rural and very largely agricultural; although manufacturing was neither new nor feeble, it concerned itself largely with the processing of simple products – the sawing of timber and the grinding of grain. Much production came from the hands of artisans, who generally worked without power assistance. The largest undertaking in the country was the British-owned Grand Trunk Railway, which snaked an uneven single-track line from Sarnia to Rivière du Loup. Water and steam power were in use, but it is likely that most Canadians had never seen a stationary steam engine, although most would probably have seen a railway locomotive.

The dominion government was paramount in the new federation. All the important economic powers, it seemed, had been confided to it; Ottawa, not Toronto, would subsidize railways, build canals, borrow overseas, charter and regulate banks and insurance companies. The provinces could manage the crown lands, but for Ontario that appeared to be a comparatively routine business: while there were crown trees aplenty, interesting minerals had yet to be found in quantity, except for the petroleum of south-western Ontario, which did not belong to the Crown. Provinces could operate schools and welfare systems, but as yet these were seen to be cheap, simple – and largely municipal. The questions of economic policy that would so perplex later Ontario governments[1] had yet to arise. Indeed, the tiny provincial bureaucracy was not equipped to treat any issue of importance. In the decades between 1867 and 1914 things would change. The provincial authorities would acquire new activities, new jurisdictions, and new self-importance.[2] But the process would be gradual. Indeed, in most respects it would not be completed until well after 1945. Meanwhile, in the small dominion of 1867, and for some decades thereafter, the dominion government in Ottawa could be a national government, not just a federal government, acting with an energy and freedom that the Ottawa of the 1980s dare not attempt.

In the first dominion census, that of 1870–1, there seemed to be 1,620,851 people in Ontario.[3] There may actually have been somewhat more, in that the Indian population cannot have been completely enumerated. Nevertheless, the figure serves to remind the reader that although Ontario was by far the largest province in the new dominion, possessing 44 per cent of its population and producing more than half of its output and income, in the whole area of the new province there were fewer people than in Metropolitan Toronto during the 1970s. That population, furthermore, was concentrated in the south-western and eastern parts of the province. The northern and north-western part of present-day Ontario was still little known, and it was almost unsurveyed. There were no incorporated towns or villages north-west of the line Arnprior-Lanark-Gananoque-Orillia-Collingwood. Beyond this line, only a few townships had been surveyed. Northern settlement had not pushed very far, and the exploitation of the northern forest and mineral wealth lay many years in the future. As a mineral producer Ontario was still not very important: its only significant mineral product was petroleum. The forest products industries, however, were of immense importance, producing 25 per cent of the province's industrial output and employing 26 per cent of its industrial workers. This activity was widespread through the southern and eastern parts of the province.

With respect to soils, frost-free periods, and the absence of rocky outcrops, Ontario has relatively little decent agricultural land, most of which had been settled before 1867, although not all the settled acreage had yet been broken to the plough. In effect, Ontario agriculture was confined to the areas south and east of the Canadian Shield, and even in these areas much of the land needed subsoil drainage if it was to be really fertile. As in Quebec and New England, the growing season was not long; the land soon became climatically unrewarding as one moved northward from the Great Lakes.

Then as now, the province was far from homogeneous. There were variations in soil, climate, and degree and type of industrialization. In the settled part of the province one found a comfortable agricultural community where economic diversification had already gone a considerable distance, but where towns and cities were small and few. In 1871, thirteen cities and towns had more than 5,000 residents. These places contained only 10.6 per cent of the population; the rest lived in smaller towns, villages, and the open country. Toronto had 56,092 inhabitants and Ottawa 21,545. Nor had the cities spread far: Ottawa covered less than three square miles and Hamilton less than four, while Toronto spread over 9.3 square miles.

Canada's first census takers divided the population in a way that tells a great deal about the manner in which the social and occupational structure was then viewed. They distinguished six 'classes' – the agricultural, which made up 49 per cent of the work force, the commercial and the domestic, each of which contained 6 per cent, the industrial, which was only 20 per cent, the professional, which was 4 per cent, and the 'unclassed,' which included labourers, packers, pensioners, apprentices, hunters, keepers, messengers, and the 1,567 'gentlemen of leisure' of whom Ontario could boast in 1871.[4] The proportions would be different if all the working but unpaid wives and children had been counted; the point is particularly important in agriculture, where there was at least one working woman in every household, and where many children did unpaid farm labour. Even so, one can easily see why Victorian observers called Ontario an agricultural province. Not only did 89 per cent of the population live in rural areas and in small towns of less than 5,000 souls; 49 per cent of the enumerated work force actually tilled the soil.

Ontario agriculture, like that of the adjacent American states and of the other Canadian provinces, was still essentially a system of family farming, with the family members providing most of the labour. The owner-farmer was typical, the tenant farmer was much less common, and the agricultural labourer was rarer still. In 1871, 83.7 per cent of the 'occupiers of land' tilled their own acres, and 15.9 per cent were tenants, while only 0.4 per cent of the occupiers were described as 'employees.' There were, in addition, wage earners on all three sorts of farm. Some obscurity surrounds the census count for these wage-earning labourers, but it appears that there were more than three farmers for every possible agricultural labourer, and the actual figure may well be four to one.

Although farm people were numerous, professional persons were thin on the ground. There were 1,908 'advocates,' 1,222 accountants, 1,558 doctors, 230 dentists, 6,101 teachers and 53 professors, to which should be added 2,196 ministers of religion and 447 nuns. The clergy and teachers were spread evenly over the settled areas of the province, but the others were not: if lawyers, accountants, doctors, dentists, and professors are added together, 29 per cent are found to be settled in the five large cities. As for provincial and federal civil servants, there were at least 259 'municipal employees,' and 1,177 'government employees,' while a few more folk probably reported themselves in other categories – officers of the court, civil engineers, and so on. Given such numbers, it is hardly surprising that few people went to university. There were 556 persons who declared themselves to be university students, while another 459 said they were students of law and medicine.

In 1870 Ontario's capital goods industries were small and not very important: the only substantial ones were agricultural implements, foundries, and 'machine working.' The great industries were grist-, flour-, and saw-milling; there was, in addition, a wide range of consumer-goods industries, and there were many activities, such as blacksmithing, which serviced transport, the agricultural economy, or both. In industry as a whole, 28 per cent of value added[5] arose from the processing of agricultural products and another 17.5 per cent from the processing of forest products, while 47 per cent came from the production of relatively simple consumer goods. Firewood still provided a significant proportion of the province's heat. What coal was used came from Pennsylvania, and Ontario was a considerable producer of oil, much of which in the early 1870s was exported.

Industrial activity was quite widely dispersed through the settled area, a pattern that was the almost inevitable result of the industrial structure and the heavy reliance on waterpower. There was, however, already some sign of concentration in the five major centres that together produced 24 per cent of the province's industrial output.

Interesting though industry is, it is worth remembering that Ontario was still in large measure an agricultural province, accounting for large proportions of Canada's food production – 84 per cent of the dominion's wheat, 82 per cent of the nation's barley, 52 per cent of the oats, and 91 per cent of the turnips, not to speak of corn or peas. Nor was agriculture ill-equipped, especially in comparison with other provinces. Quebec had more transport vehicles and threshing mills, but in all other respects it was far outdistanced by Ontario. It appears that Ontario must have accounted for all, or almost all, Canada's exports of food products; furthermore, the province contributed importantly to the feeding of other Canadians, especially in Quebec.

In 1870 Ontario might best have been described as an agricultural and artisan economy, not a commercial one, because most of the province's labour, capital, and natural resources were employed in agriculture and in small-scale production. Farmers, furthermore, produced substantial amounts of what later generations would see as industrial or factory products – not only handicrafts but textiles, butter, and cheese. As a user of resources commerce was certainly of small importance, in comparison with these two activities.

It is sometimes suggested that in the later nineteenth century Ontario evolved from a 'commercial society' into an 'industrial society.' There is an element of truth in such a statement, in so far as it relates to the elites, especially in the larger towns. But the statement does reflect a double misunderstanding about the ways in which the Ontario economy actually employed its resources, whether in 1870, in 1900, or in 1941. On the one hand, commerce cannot have mattered much in 1867 as a user of resources: in 1871 only 2.6 per cent of Ontario's gainful workers laboured in trading and financial occupations, while in 1911 the percentage was 8.6 per cent, and in 1941, 10.2 per cent.[6] On the other hand, throughout the period 1867–1941 commerce continued to be of immense importance in the working of Ontario's economy. At Confederation a great deal of agricultural output was consumed by the people who grew it, and another quantity was sold direct by farmers to final consumers, without the intermediation of wholesale or retail traders. Similarly, a high proportion of the artisans and perhaps some small manufacturers sold direct to the final consumers without intermediation. Compared with the situation in later decades retail trade in goods was little developed; farmers purchased few inputs, and the array of consumer goods was as yet quite narrow, while in the nature of things the rural population – 80 per cent of the total – could not be served by a wide range of shops. Nevertheless, there was an important niche for organized trade. Some industry was localized, unable to sell all its output to final buyers. Imports had to be brought to the province, warehoused, and distributed to points of sale through a system of wholesale trade, which, because it handled both consumer goods and intermediate goods that manufacturers and farmers would use for further production, was a significant element in the province's life. In certain towns, such as Toronto, Hamilton, and London, therefore, wholesale trade was very visible, and wholesale traders were local notables.

Similarly, the exporters of the province did not maintain their own external sales networks: farmers, millers, and many although not all lumbermen generally sold their exportable outputs to wholesalers, who would then arrange for exportation. The commerce of exportation, therefore, was equally prominent in the larger towns of the province. Indeed, the same firms often traded in imports and exports, although there was some specialization both by type of trade and by commodity. The wholesale trade made a necessary connection between the producers and final consumers of the province, and the markets of the outside world. It also connected the several parts of the province with one another. Already, however, some manufacturers had begun to bypass the wholesalers. Mail order merchandising was not unknown, although its great days were yet to come.

Commerce, industry, agriculture, lumbering, and household consumption lived in a symbiotic relationship. If agriculture and lumbering had not produced an export surplus, there would have been little for the commercial capitalists to export; conversely, if there had been no wholesale or retail traders, the producers and consumers of the province would have had to spend far more time and money to get the goods, both from abroad and from other parts of the province, which they needed and wanted. Commerce thus made the whole economy of Ontario more productive, and in some respects, by finding and developing export markets, commerce certainly accelerated the development of that economy.

Wholesale trade was both competitive and risky. One kind of risk arose because the distances were great and transport slow, so that prices and markets might change most unpleasantly between the time at which goods were bought and the time at which they were sold. Another sort of risk arose from the fact that the wholesalers often had to give long credit to the retailers to whom they sold and might even have to give such credit to domestic manufacturers from whom they bought. Retailers, in turn, gave credit to purchasers. Farmers were commonly in debt to country stores, while manufacturers usually received extensive credit from their own suppliers, at the same time perhaps giving credit to purchasers. The network of debt was all-pervasive, and the 'turnover of capital' could take quite a long time – almost always a matter of months and in many instances much longer periods. Furthermore, any failure at any point could have wide repercussions, even in the absence of any fundamentally unfavourable turn in commodity markets or money markets themselves. It was easy to enter trade, whether wholesale or retail, precisely because credit was generally easy to find. Thus although the country merchant might have a monopoly with respect to some goods in a small area, there can have been little monopoly power in wholesale trade or in the retail trades of the larger towns.

The commercial system, therefore, was an insecure one, made still more insecure by the fact that wholesale and retail traders were almost always sole proprietorships or unincorporated partnerships. It is sometimes suggested that in 'commercial capitalism' profits were secure and capital turned over quickly. Those who dealt with the commercial capitalists naturally found it tempting to believe such things. But nothing could be further from the truth. The world of the wholesale trader was constantly changing, and the same could be said of retail trade in the larger towns. New firms were constantly appearing, while old firms were constantly vanishing, especially in times of depression such as the mid-1870s or the mid-1890s. Some firms survived, flourished, and grew; others failed dismally. From time to time a merchant would fail and then rise again, either on his own or in partnership with others. In turn, partnerships were often in a state of flux, dissolving and re-forming with variations in the set of partners.

Although the province's financial institutions were as yet small and inexperienced, a reasonably full array had come into existence by 1867. Some chartered banks dated back to the 1850s; others were founded around the time of Confederation, or soon after. In addition there were at least thirty unincorporated 'private banks,' and there were also several 'building societies,' the ancestors of today's trust and loan companies. Life and fire insurance companies were also active, even though most insurance business was written by British and American firms. The only Canadian life insurance company was Canada Life, which, from its Hamilton head office, wrote 831 new policies in the year ending 30 April 1869.[7] Toronto contained a stock exchange, although its life was as yet only flickering.

The building societies concentrated upon mortgage lending, a field proscribed to the chartered banks, which, in turn, concentrated upon the finance of commerce and the provision of working capital – the main sort of finance that Ontario industry required. Indeed, industry seems to have needed rather small amounts of capital, and much of that was circulating funds – the financial counterpart of raw materials, wages, and work in progress. In 1870, for example, the rolling mills reported that they employed a capital of $170,000 to produce output valued at $1.18 million, while spending $849,000 on wages and materials. Their apparent profit, in other words, was almost double their reported capital! The figure is not entirely profit, in that it includes the implicit depreciation allowances that few businesses then calculated. None the less, it is a reasonable approximation to what later national-income accountants would call 'gross business saving.' Data for other industries are similar, suggesting that in general Ontario industry could and did generate large amounts of profit, much of which could be ploughed back, thus financing expansion. In such circumstances there would be little need for external finance, so that unincorporated proprietorships or partnerships would be an appropriate form of business organization. Indeed, the small Toronto Stock Exchange worked chiefly with bank shares, the stocks of the building societies, and government obligations.

When industry in general appears to be highly profitable, the economist would foresee that after 1870 the provincial economy was likely to industrialize: profit would be a spur to expansion and to the entry of new firms. The fate of agriculture would be more difficult to predict from the 1870–1 census data, and as for the energy base, no one could have predicted the emergence of hydroelectricity as a serious alternative not only to water power but to kerosene and to coal. Nor could anyone have guessed about the ways in which falling transport costs and tariff manipulations both in Canada and abroad would affect the evolution of the provincial economy. In the event, Ontario experienced a rapid industrialization and urbanization, a realignment and expansion of agriculture, an explosion of mineral and forestry development in the north, and a transformation of the transportation system and of the energy base. The chapters that follow trace these dramatic changes. First, however, it is necessary briefly to describe the path that will be followed through the thickets of Ontario's economic history.

Growth and Change: a Semi-Theoretical Introduction

There is no right way to describe the economic history of a region such as Ontario. In the literature of economic growth and change one can find many models, and the factual data, both economic and social, can be arranged and selected so as to tell any one of many stories. For twenty years or more, economic historians in North America have been growing more self-conscious about their methodologies. The general reader, furthermore, is entitled to know something about the ways in which the author sees the processes about which he writes. Ever since Marx some economic historians have been inclined to tell their stories as if economic history consisted of some sort of 'Grand March' – from 'feudalism' to 'commercial capitalism,' then on to 'industrial capitalism,' next to 'finance capitalism' and 'monopoly capitalism,' and finally, with a sigh of relief, to 'socialism.' Whatever the general utility of this approach, it is not much help in describing Ontario economic development between 1867 and 1941, if only because capitalism had certainly arrived by 1867, while in 1941 socialism was still far off. Mainstream economic analysis, of the sort that has been extensively developed and refined since Marx's time, is a more helpful guide. It reminds one, first of all, that output, productivity, and living standards may be expected to rise in so far as an economy[8] finds, borrows, and applies helpful technology; discovers and develops new natural resources; accumulates capital in the right industries; and shifts its labour force from one activity to another to seize new opportunities. Without plenty of investment the whole process will come to an end – partly because the economy will be unable to accommodate extra labour or to expand the appropriate sectors, and partly because there is not likely to be enough demand for goods and services. Investment, in other words, creates demands while adjusting the economic structure in such a way that demand becomes ever easier to satisfy. So far as demand is concerned, export markets do just the same thing. But an export boom, in and of itself, does nothing to raise productive capacity, unless local business folk respond by accumulating new plant and by hiring more workers. Finally, for a small region such as Ontario, 'export markets' are as likely to be in other provinces as in other countries.

In Canadian economic historiography there has long been a tradition of emphasizing export markets and of treating regional development – especially the industrial and urban development that characterized Ontario – as entirely derivative. But there is no logical reason why an underpopulated but rich district should not develop on its own. It seems likely that much of Ontario's economic transformation was thus fuelled. Important as export markets doubtless were, especially perhaps in the Prairie 'wheat boom' of the period 1900–13, when transcontinental railways and western development created massive demands for investment goods in other parts of the dominion, the local markets of Ontario and Quebec were certainly of equal or greater importance, especially before 1900 and after 1914. As we shall see in Part 3, it was before 1900 that Ontario's industrial revolution got properly under way, and it was in the 1920s that the province's urban, industrial society may be said to have matured. The 'wheat boom' years can best be seen as an acceleration of a development that had already begun. Furthermore, during those years the provincial economy was stimulated by certain developments, especially those centring on electricity and the automobile industry, which had little or nothing to do with the 'wheat boom.' Urbanization, in turn, provided most of the motive force for the parallel transformation in the province's agriculture, as grain growers turned more of their energy to fodder crops and to livestock. Furthermore, as the province's own population increased, and as living standards rose, there was a growing local market for a widening range of manufactures – and this market, in turn, encouraged new business investment. This propulsive element was not always present: there were periods when living standards did not rise, and there may have been groups for which living standards lagged. But the same might be said of the propulsion from investment and from exports. Here, too, the developmental 'push' was anything but even or steady.

If the existing Canadian literature in history and geography were better balanced, one would not have to stress the distinctions between internal and external sources of growth, specialization, urbanization, and improvement. Regrettably, the literature has a great deal to say about the external forces and very much less about the internal processes of growth and change, leaving the reader to conclude that everything is induced from outside, especially by the impact of foreign marketing possibilities on the domestic economy through the mediation of resource-based 'staple products' – wheat, pine timber, metallic ore, pulpwood.[9] But there are many aspects of Ontario economic development that cannot be conveniently discussed in those terms and do not fit readily into them. Indeed, since Easterbrook and Aitken wrote, several authors have noticed that the course of economic change was somewhat different from what a close reader of Innis might expect.[10] Thus it is neither revolutionary nor novel to see Ontario's economic transformation as in large part self-fuelled, though at times accelerated and stimulated by external developments.

In the interpretation of early Ontario industrialization, much of the most stimulating recent work has come from Marxist historians, especially by those who have a special interest in working-class consciousness. This tendency is hardly surprising. There is little point in studying the working class and the dynamics of Canadian capitalism unless one can convince oneself and others that the working class is large enough to be worth studying and proletarianized enough to have developed class consciousness. For those conditions to be met, 'capitalist relations' have to be widespread. That is, a large proportion of the lower orders has to be working for wages, if at all possible in sizeable steam-powered enterprises. The strength of Marxist analyses, from the viewpoint of the present work, is that they direct attention to two processes: the transfer of labour among activities and among regions, and the accumulation of productive industrial capital. Also, they remind one, at least by implication, that the activities of local businessfolk will, in due course and unless disrupted, transform the economy of a region such as Ontario. Foreign businessfolk and external capital may speed the transformation and may help shape it. But they are not needed to bring it about.

Marxist historiography also, at least by implication although not systematically or explicitly, directs attention to one of the great regularities in modern economic history – the shift of labour out of agriculture and other primary activities, first into manufacturing, and then into an enormous range of service-producing activities – everything from wholesale trade to school-teaching. Non-Marxist economists and historians have also become interested in both components of this pattern.[11] It is now quite clear that everywhere in prosperous lands, such as western Europe, Japan, the United States, and Canada, such shifts have happened, and they are at least the symptom of a broad movement that raises incomes and living standards, not only in urban life but in agriculture also. Marx himself was interested in the first of the shifts but not in the second, and his disciples have generally followed his lead. Marx thought that people would leave agriculture or self-employment only if they were distressed and suffering – 'forced off the land,' their property 'expropriated.' Few people now think that this is the whole story, or even a large part of it: farmers' sons and daughters can decide that life in the city looks attractive, even when life on the farm is, in fact, perfectly tolerable. If one is to construct a balanced picture of economic transformation, one has to attend to the whole process, not just to a part of it.

The interrelated structural changes that accompany this transformation have been much scrutinized in the literature of economic development. Obviously the agricultural sector must be transformed if it is to give up labour without producing mass starvation; in the process, it will become a great deal more productive, and farmers and farm workers are likely to become a great deal better off, at least in the longer run. Also, farmers are likely to spend less of their time in non-agricultural by-employments, such as weaving and carting, and to put more of their effort into strictly agricultural work. Agriculture need not change *before* anything else happens; the two processes of agrarian change and industrialization can occur side by side, as, indeed, they seem to have done in Ontario, especially between 1867 and 1914. But there is more to structural change than agricultural transformation: in addition, the economy must save or borrow enough to accumulate the needed capital goods, not only on the farms and in the factories but in the transportation system and in the urban infrastructure – houses, shops, water supplies, sewerage, even parks, community centres, libraries, and universities. Thus the regional economy cannot reallocate labour without a good deal of what economists call 'capital formation.' But still more accumulation will be needed if full advantage is to be taken of the possibilities both for specialization and for technological progress.

Victorian society, not only in Britain and the United States but also in continental Europe and Canada, was certainly anxious to seize those possibilities: there was an almost universal fascination with progress and with the 'new.' But it is not enough simply to accumulate plant and equipment. Investment must be correctly allocated and efficiently managed and operated; the residents of a region must be willing to work and to change their habits so that the improvement can take place. With respect to changing habits and attitudes, nineteenth-century people, in Ontario as elsewhere, were much more constrained than the people of the late twentieth century. It was no light matter to give up an old job or a familiar group of associates, to strike out on one's own in a new place or a new line of work. Yet people certainly moved around the province, switching jobs and places of residence with considerable freedom.

Given the manifold constraints that Victorian society appears to have placed on individual freedom of action in matters social, cultural, religious, and familial, it is at first sight surprising that in economic matters the Victorian world was not only innovation minded, but essentially unregulated. Not for Ontario or Canada in 1867, or for many decades thereafter, the elaborate network of economic law and regulation that is so familiar in the 1980s.

For Ontario the United States was an important catalyst. The provincial elites of 1867 or of 1900 might have been provincial in another sense, but Torontonians might go to Buffalo for 'dirty weekends,' and they certainly knew what was occurring not only there but in Detroit, Boston, and New York. Farmers, too, might often be aware of developments south of the border. Loyal and British Ontario certainly was: Britain was important to the provincial economy, not only as a market but as a source of information, funds, and workers. Technology and new ideas, however, were far more likely to come from the United States.

In many parts of the world conditions were and are very different, so that extra investment has no pay-off, or a smaller pay-off than might have been expected; in such circumstances living standards are likely to stagnate and may even decline. No one would maintain that in the Ontario economy before 1940 all management was perfect, all labour ideally diligent, or all investment correctly allocated. But the desire to improve and the will to change were certainly present, and on the whole and in a very general way the appropriate actions were taken. If this had not been the case, the process of growth and change could not have produced the favourable effects that, on the whole and in the long run, it did.

It should surprise no one that in a prosperous and expanding economy the financial system should also grow and become more diversified. One observes these patterns in Ontario, as in other regions and countries of the industrializing world, after 1867. Ontario's economic evolution certainly created considerable new demands for finance, although the demands did not grow steadily: during periods of depression, such as the mid-1890s and the 1930s, there was little change in the financial system. The normal condition was otherwise. Apart altogether from business demand, junior governments needed to borrow for capital spending. These outlays had to be in large blocks if they were to be useful: one does not build a school room by room, or an electric system pole by pole over a period of many years. Governments had no profits, no reserves on which to draw, and no inclination to accumulate funds for years before satisfying their electorates' demands. Farmers might borrow in time of need, but they could and did also borrow to improve and develop their holdings. As for manufacturing business, the ploughing-back of profits could cover a substantial part of a business's financial needs, and bank loans could cover much of the rest. But by the late 1890s, when new opportunities appeared, these arrangements were not always good enough: to exploit the new possibilities one would need to make large outlays in sizeable blocks. Hence the need to replace partnerships and proprietorships with limited-liability organizations – companies that could raise money by floating bonds and stocks on the open market, whether in Canada or abroad.

In earlier decades, the network of debt that so often connected producers, consumers, retailers, wholesalers, and British and foreign suppliers could and presumably did create relations of 'dependency.' These might make it difficult for any member of the chain to switch his custom from one supplier to another. The result might be a form of monopoly profit for those who controlled the chain of debt; there would also be a serious barrier to the entry of new firms. But on the other hand, the lender was to some extent the prisoner of the borrower, so that it would be safer to continue a dubious line of credit than to insist on repayment. After 1870 the chain of indebtedness was certainly not a thing of the past, especially in rural areas, where farmers were often in debt to the country storekeepers who might also be the buyers of their surplus produce. The storekeepers, in turn, relied on trade credit from their suppliers. However, with the development of the banking system the chain of credit must have become a good deal more flexible, in that banks and mortgage companies could and did offer alternatives to trade credit. Furthermore, retailers could and did deal with a variety of wholesalers. Dependency relationships, therefore, may sometimes have existed but should not be assumed into existence, nor should their presence be strongly emphasized in the years after 1867.

While the financial structure of Ontario became more internationalized, it also became more centralized, and more specialized as well. These tendencies were interrelated. As Adam Smith pointed out in the eighteenth century, the division of labour is limited by the extent of the market. Specialized financial institutions, such as stockbrokers and bond houses, cannot come into existence until there is enough of the appropriate business to sustain them. The same circumstance would naturally produce a drift of financial businesses to Toronto, and by 1900 that drift was very much in evidence.

Financial evolution was helpful to the process of development because it facilitated the whole process of saving, borrowing, and lending. Admittedly, Ontario did not possess the industrially oriented 'universal banks' that can be found in nineteenth-century Europe, especially in Germany. But the accumulating weight of evidence suggests that this lack was not a problem: industry, in general, seems to have been able to find the finance it needed, partly because so much of it was so profitable, and partly because the banks seem to have been willing to provide much of the working capital that bulked so large for nineteenth-century manufacturers. Also, the financial system developed in a variety of ways that made accumulation easier. Thus it is not apparent[12] that the financial system was somehow biased against industrial development. The mere record of industrial growth, which later chapters survey, would make this charge hard to sustain. The plenitude of domestically owned industrial firms also tends to undermine it, and information about the financial fates of individual firms tends in the same direction.

The question of profitability in wholesale and retail trade is connected with the matter of finance for manufacturing industry. There is now plentiful evidence that traders were not reluctant to invest in manufacturing – that 'commercial capitalists' were not opposed to 'industrial capitalism.' But it seems that commerce did not generate enough retained profit to finance its own expansion simply out of owners' equity. Hence the continuing importance of finance from the banks and from trading partners at home and abroad. The commercial classes were thus naturally anxious to stimulate the development of commercial finance, both at home through the banking system and abroad through the financial markets of Britain and the United States.

The industrial and agricultural transformation of the period was not planned or managed by anyone. This is not to say that governments were uninterested in 'progress,' or that they were unwilling to expedite it. In a variety of ways, as later chapters reveal, they provided encouragement. For manufacturing contributions were made by the protective tariff, government purchasing, municipal grants and tax exemptions, and the policies by which natural resources were supplied to private industry at low cost or no cost. Agricultural transformation also benefited through government-funded research, education, propaganda, and, in the 1920s, from government finance. For some farm products, furthermore, the dominion protective tariff provided help, as did dominion spending on the transport system. Ottawa certainly had a national policy of economic development, which revolved around the transportation system, industrial protection, and western settlement. The provincial authorities, too, may be said to have had a development policy, which centred on urbanization, industrialization, the exploitation of the north, the development of natural resources, and the improvement of agricultural conditions.[13] From time to time, furthermore, a few industries, most importantly the iron and steel industry, benefited from what nowadays would be called an 'industrial strategy' of sectoral encouragement and assistance. The result can certainly be called government intervention – often clumsy, corrupt, and inefficient – but it is hard to see it as government guidance. Nor can one detect the sort of foresighted integration of needs, possibilities, policies, and programs which would nowadays be called planning.

Would things have gone better if governments had been more firmly in charge? Opinions are bound to differ, and assessments will depend partly on one's political outlook – and on the assumptions made about the hypothetical competence of various bureaucracies and politicians, actual and imaginary. If the politicians and the officials are surveyed as they actually were, it is difficult to believe that governments and their officials could have successfully managed much more than they actually did. Indeed, if they had tackled more, perhaps they would simply have lapsed into chaos and confusion. In any event, whatever may be thought of such 'historical counter-factuals,' the actual events are quite clear: from 1867 to 1941 the economic development of Ontario could properly be described as 'progress without planning.'

Arrangement and Organization

Although this work contains an explanatory thread and a considerable amount of interpretative comment, it does not pretend to explain all the developments that it must record if it is to serve its chief function as a work of reference. On many topics in Ontario economic history little explanatory research has been done; on many others there is as yet no scholarly consensus. Nor would it be possible to fill all the gaps at this time or in one book. Thus it is to be hoped that others will be sufficiently inspired or irritated to fill in some of the holes that the present account contains.

Because there is no single hypothesis animating the work, materials have not been selected simply to illustrate or to demonstrate some 'grand theme.' The chapters that follow try to describe and to analyse a complicated process of structural transformation and development that affected the entire provincial economy. For the reader's comfort, all the statistical tables have been grouped in an appendix, and the text has been so designed that it can be read without reference to the tables, which are, none the less, keyed by number to the several chapters. The process of development cannot sensibly be treated decade by decade, nor do changes in government or the rise and decline of political movements make much sense as dividing points. Indeed, in most respects the province's economic development can best be treated as a very long-term process. Hence most of the material is organized by topic, each chapter treating the entire period from Confederation to World War Two. Although there are internal subdivisions within most chapters, only manufacturing is treated in two chapters, according to time period, because for Ontario's industrial revolution the year 1914, marking as it does the end of a 'heroic period' of industrial growth, does form a natural and important point of separation. Material on transport and communication has been distributed between two chapters, one of which treats nineteenth-century activities such as the railways and the canals and the electric novelties of that century, while the other treats the twentieth-century developments in the road systems and in the air.

There are disadvantages to this arrangement. It requires some repetition and cross-referencing. More distressing, the particular character and texture of individual periods – the slump of the 1870s, the electricity boom, the cheese boom, even the Great Depression of the 1930s – cannot always be fully presented in a single passage, even though all the relevant material is included in one chapter or another. But it is in any event difficult for the economic historian, necessarily mired in the details of economic organization, to attain the grand syntheses of the social historian, who can discourse more easily at large. There is also a risk that interconnections will be ignored or inadequately emphasized, although there has been an effort to keep that problem in mind and to write accordingly. Has that effort been successful? The reader must be the judge.

2 *What People Did*

The last chapter outlined a general approach to the structural transformation though which the Ontario economy passed after Confederation. Ideally the observer would like to follow this transformation by tracing the changing contributions and weights of the several industries – agriculture, manufacturing, construction, and the various service activities, such as transportation, wholesale and retail trade, finance, and government and professional service. In later chapters a qualitative picture of these changes will be built up; general information on the composition of output, however, is unavailable. Fortunately the structural transformation can be described and summarized in another way – by examining the changing distribution of the working population among the various occupations and industries. Besides changing the pattern of work, economic evolution interacted with educational development, and it produced a striking change in the weight and significance of wage-work. It also changed the distribution of the populace among the great socio-economic categories of self-employment and wage-work.

The number of gainful workers[1] is reported in table 2.1. It increased more than three-fold in seventy years.[2] It grew especially rapidly in the 1870s and 1880s and in the first thirty years of the twentieth century. In the 1930s, a decade of depression, the rate of growth was comparatively low, and in the 1890s, a decade that also contained a serious through rather briefer depression, the number of gainful workers grew very slowly indeed. It is hardly surprising that the 1901 census results were a disappointment to development-minded Ontarians. In most decades, furthermore, a rising proportion of adult Ontarians were recorded as gainful workers.[3] Only in the the 1890s was this not so, and in other decades this rising involvement in 'gainful labour' made an important contribution to the growth of the working population. The results are especially striking for 1871–91. The same pattern reappears in the first decade of the twentieth century, when much of the upward push comes from working women: their number increased by one-half, while the number of working men rose by only one-eighth.[4] Thereafter, and most notably in the 1920s, there was a pronounced tendency for the number of women workers to rise more rapidly than the number of men workers. Thus in 1891, 13.1 per cent of Ontario's gainful workers were women, while in 1931 the percentage was 18.5 per cent and in 1941, 21.6 per cent. It was not that women were becoming more common in such long-established goods-producing occupations as farm management or iron – and steel-working. Rather, much of the new work was to be found in clerical and sales occupations that were either new or rapidly expanding, and women were very well represented in these. Thus in 1891, for instance, there were 12,000 clerical workers, of whom 2,000 were women, while by 1941 there were 143,000, of whom 75,000 were women. Some of the occupations that were once thought to be characteristically feminine, such as schoolteaching and nursing, were also increasing quite quickly.

It must be admitted that all these figures contain an element of distortion, because Canada's statisticians, like those of most other countries, have always omitted some unpaid family workers – of whom the most important and most numerous are women on farms – from the gainfully employed. But in an agricultural and artisan economy like that of Ontario's at the time of Confederation, almost everyone made a contribution to production at some point in the annual cycle of labour. Only the very young, the very old, the wives and children of prosperous merchants and professional people, and those who could live off property income, were exempt. In towns, furthermore, women often kept animals and cultivated gardens. Thus in earlier decades the effective work-force, and especially the female work-force, was considerably larger than the figures suggest, whereas by 1941 the effective work force was not very much larger than the number of gainful workers: urban children worked little or not at all, while farm wives, though no less numerous than in 1871, were now few in relation to the total population. Indeed, one element of Ontario's economic transformation was the sorting-out of workers from other persons, enabling the historian to define the work-force less ambiguously. This is not to say that if urban women did not work for wages they were more 'leisured' than their sisters on farms. Housework had to be done, and although labour-saving appliances were present in most Ontario urban homes by 1941[5] they simply enabled housewives to maintain higher standards of cleanliness and cooking.[6] But because the national-income statisticians do not include housework in the value of national output, one cannot count housewifery as an occupation.

Occupational Changes and Industrial Patterns

The occupational patterns appear in tables 2.2 and 2.3. It should first be observed that so far as the period 1871–1931 is concerned, Ontario's farms were not being depopulated. The number of farmers and farm workers rose from 1871 to 1891, declined about 10 per cent in the 1890s, and then hovered around the 300,000 mark until the 1930s, when there was another decline of 10 per cent between one census year and another. Thus in absolute terms only the 1890s and the 1930s were times of 'agricultural depopulation' in the province as a whole, although in some regions, counties, and townships the pattern could well have been different. Even the 1930s may be misrepresented by the use of an intercensal comparison: there is plentiful qualitative evidence of a return to the land during the Great Depression of those years, so that there may actually have been an upward fluctuation early in the 1930s, followed by a contraction around the outbreak of war in 1939. In percentage terms, of course, the agriculturists became steadily less important between Confederation and World War Two. It is also virtually certain that in some districts and at some times there was an exodus from non-agricultural work in rural areas, as industry drifted to the larger cities and towns.

In 1871 agriculture was the only significant extractive industry; the other extractive occupations were utterly insignificant, making up only 1.8 per cent of the gainfully occupied. In later decades, especially just after 1901 and in the 1930s, mining became considerably more important than it had been in the nineteenth century. But in the overall pattern of Ontario occupations it remained of little significance, rising to only 1.7 per cent of the total in 1911 and, after some decline in the twenties, to 1.6 per cent in 1941. Thus in 1871 a group of occupations that are primarily concerned with the land and natural resources – agriculture, mining, hunting, fishing, and trapping – made up 51.4 per cent of the gainfully occupied. But this percentage declined steadily, not to say precipitously, touching 21.6 per cent in 1941.

Next consider a group of occupations that are specific to transportation, construction, and manufacturing, including general or common labour outside agriculture. In 1871 this group of occupations contained 34.4 per cent of the gainfully occupied. In the next seventy years the number of such people rose from 150,000 to over 488,000. But the weight of the group, at 33.5 per cent of the gainfully occupied, was almost exactly the same in 1941 as in 1871, although the composition of the category and the character of its work had been transformed in the course of seventy years. In particular, common labourers had become very much less important, and the building trades somewhat more important, while the comparatively

skilled manufacturing occupations had increased their weight significantly.[7] The transport occupations, which we may see as servicing not only the
provincial but the national eonomy, became considerably more weighty
with the development first of the railway and canal systems and then of the
highway network.[8] In 1871 only 8,000 men – 1.8 per cent of the gainfully
occupied – could be identified with transport occupations.[9] Thereafter
these occupations became increasingly important: in 1931 109,000
Ontarians – 8.1 per cent of the province's gainfully occupied – were
working at them.

Even more striking is the rise of employment in the non-mechanized
white-collar occupations – trade and finance, and professional, governmental, domestic, clerical, and personal service. In 1871, 0.4 per cent of
Ontario workers laboured for government, and all the white-collar
occupations together employed only 68,555 persons, or 14.2 per cent of
the gainfully employed. In later decades these figures and percentages rose
dramatically and steadily. By 1921 such workers were more numerous than
farmers and farm workers; by 1941 there were 545,000 such workers –
38.4 per cent of the province's gainfully occupied. Almost 45 per cent of
them were women.

Along with these shifting patterns of production and employment went a
rapid urbanization of the population and the labour force, because most of
the manufacturing occupations and the white-collar occupations and a high
proportion of the transport occupations had to be pursued in urban areas.
Urbanization was a response to the changing pattern of demand for
non-agricultural output. But the process of town-building itself created all
sorts of new non-agricultural work, with implications for the occupational
structure. The cities needed houses, streets, commercial buildings, and
factories, all of which had to be constructed; they also needed, and sooner
or later acquired, a wide range of public utilities and public services that
had to be housed and staffed.

Shifting the focus from occupations to industries, one sees that in the
twentieth century every kind of industrial employment expanded except
that of agriculture, and that the most impressive growth performances were
those of manufacturing and of the various industries that produce
services.[10] The available data are summarized in table 2.4.[11] Some other
industrial groups, such as forestry and mining, showed impressive rates of
growth. But manufacturing employment surpassed even these groups.

None of these industrial and occupational developments was peculiar to
Ontario. As Kuznets and other scholars have shown,[12] the pattern of
occupational change has been broadly the same in all industrializing
countries. Explanations for the pattern, therefore, have to be general and
international, although one may have to inflect them in light of local

peculiarities. In Ontario agriculture, there was specialization and a switch among crops and activities, while mechanization and changes in production patterns allowed each worker to produce more output.[13] In manufacturing and construction, although mechanization and technical progress somewhat reduced the resultant demand for extra labour, the growth of markets in Ontario and elsewhere created a large additional net demand for workers in manufacturing industry and in occupations specific to it. Also in construction, where technological change was slow and where mechanization was uneven in its impact, many more workers were needed decade by decade because of the rising level of physical investment in structures. Hence the rise of employment in manufacturing occupations from 70,000 in 1871 to 321,000 in 1941; hence too the increase in the building trades from 20,000 persons to 78,000.

Simply because the provincial economy was growing, the demand for white-collar staff might be expected to increase in parallel. In 1871 such workers made up 16.1 per cent of the gainfully occupied; applying the same percentage to the gainfully occupied of 1941, we might roughly estimate that at the later date, if there had been no change in employment structure, Ontario would have contained 234,000 white-collar workers instead of the 645,000 it actually did contain at that time. The difference, 411,000, might be taken to represent the joint effect of two forces – rising real productivity in the blue-collar occupations and the much slower pace of technological change in some white-collar occupations, combined with its almost complete absence in others, including some occupations (education, medical services, and many kinds of personal service) where a rise in real income is very likely to produce a more-than-proportional increase in demand for the relevant service. Besides such service occupations, there was an additional group that supplied services not to households but to the productive activities of the economy. Some service occupations, as in law, public administration, trade, finance, and transportation, served both consumers and producers; others, such as the clerical occupations, were purchased only by producers. In the later nineteenth century there were some important technical developments that economized on clerical labour. The telephone, carbon paper, the typewriter, and various systems of filing and forms all enabled the typical clerical worker to do more work per year. Nevertheless, technological progress appears to have been slower in the clerical occupations than in those that produced goods; furthermore, the critical inventions and innovations occurred before 1900, so that in the twentieth century it is difficult to find anything comparable. Furthermore, there was far less opportunity to substitute machinery for direct labour.

In 1871 'commercial clerks' comprised 3.6 per cent of the non-agricultural workers in the province. If technological change had affected both white-collar and blue-collar workers in the same way in later decades, presumably they would have maintained the same proportion. There would then have been just over 42,000 clerks in the province in 1941, whereas in fact there were 140,000. The excess presumably reflects the extent to which technological change had been more labour-saving in the blue-collar activities than in the white-collar ones. As for the occupations that supply services direct to households, on the basis of 1871 patterns there would have been only 35,414 such workers in 1941, whereas in fact there were 392,000. Here we see the joint impact of rising per capita incomes and the absence of much labour-saving technological change in the relevant occupations.

It would seem that the growth of the economy, rising per capita real incomes, and the differential paths of mechanization and technological change in blue-collar and white-collar occupations combined to add 456,000 jobs in the white-collar group. The following complications, however, should be noted. After 1867 Ottawa was the capital of a large and growing dominion, while Toronto, especially after 1900, played a national and international financial role; these special circumstances would tend to increase the number of white-collar jobs in both cities. Furthermore, some proportion of the additional 108,000 jobs that appeared in transport occupations between 1871 and 1941 should be credited to the expansion of Ontario's railway and canal systems to serve a national not simply a provincial constituency.

Education and Class

Different kinds of work demanded new sorts of preparation. Although literacy is useful for all workers, more technical formation may be helpful or necessary for some sorts of non-agricultural blue-collar workers, and a more extended literary education has usually been demanded of most white-collar workers, while professionals normally require some tertiary education, whether in university, college, nursing school, or law school. In 1941 levels of education were still noticeably low in agricultural and some blue-collar occupations, among labourers, and in personal service. But the level rose with white-collar status, through manufacturing, trade, and service workers to the group of professional and recreational service workers wherein most university graduates were to be found. For earlier years such a summary account is not available, but the information about school attendance implies that a slow but steady upgrading of educational level had been under way for a long time.[14] Additional contributions had come from a series of provincial government initiatives beginning with the opening of the Ontario Agricultural College at Guelph in 1874 and the School of Practical Science at Toronto in 1877. In 1894 provincial funding supported a Mining School at Kingston. With the twentieth century funds were provided for secondary technical education[15] and eventually, beginning in 1906, regular grants were made first to the provincial University of Toronto and then, in the 1920s, to Queen's University and the University of Western Ontario. All these efforts, to which one should add the immigration of skilled workers and professional people, tended to raise the average levels of education while diversifying Ontario's work force, perhaps making it more productive and certainly fitting it to the emerging pattern of labour demand. This general congruence was an accident, not a direct result of a conscious government policy, although in the creation of secondary technical education and in providing a more varied mix of tertiary professional opportunities the authorities certainly had the economy very much in mind.

By 1941 wage and salary earners made up 75.1 per cent of the Ontario work force, while non-agricultural employers made up 1.9 per cent. The remainder consisted of farmers, the self-employed, and unpaid family workers. Agriculture was highly capitalized, and so were the self-employed professionals. Earlier data are not available, but in chapter 17 it is shown that compared with 1871, in 1941 there must have been several times as many self-employed folk in wholesale and retail trade, while farmers were slightly more numerous.[16] The growth of the provincial economy had provided opportunities through which a considerable number had been able to establish themselves in self-employment, largely as professionals and in wholesale and retail trade; it had offered wage and salary employment to a very much larger number.

In the process many other changes had occurred. For wage earners hours of work seem to have decreased, and conditions in the workplace had come to be governed by an elaborate code of provincial law and regulation.[17] Far more wage earners had come to work in comparatively large establishments, where the individual worker was likely to be remote from the employer, who, on the other hand, often had less arbitrary power over his workers than the employer of 1871. Some skills had become redundant, and some skilled trades had diminished or passed away; other skilled, semi-skilled, and professional occupations had appeared and grown, so that the balance is as yet hard to strike. For many workers, especially those in the white-collar occupations, working conditions were a great deal more pleasant than they had been seventy years before; for almost all indoor workers premises were now heated, and they were far better lighted than the artisan shops and factory sheds of the late 1860s. In some trades and industries unions provided a modicum of additional security, sometimes combined with social and welfare benefits as well. Although the framework of the welfare state had yet to be erected, there were now dominion-provincial old age pensions and, beginning in 1941, a dominion system of unemployment insurance, linked with the government employment offices that had existed since 1918. To those who attach special virtue to the life of the self-employed farmer or small artisan, the world of 1941 looks quite unattractive compared with that of 1871. But it must none the less be admitted that in all the changes that had affected the workplace and work life since 1871 some things had changed for the better.

Part Two:
The Land and the New Frontiers

3 *Agriculture, 1867–1941*

In 1941, as in 1867, agriculture was Ontario's most important industry. Furthermore, although outstripped by mining and by urban manufacturing and service activities, its record was one of expansion. In 1941 there were more farms and more farmers than in 1871; not only were the farmers more numerous, but they were much more heavily capitalized, far more mechanized, and far better supplied with ancillary power. Farm life, while still not fully penetrated by the devices of the twentieth-century consumer society, had become far more comfortable and convenient: by 1941 the telephone and the radio were widespread, and the dissemination of electricity, with all that it would mean for amenity in farm households, had begun. As for farm production, it was much larger than it had been in 1871 or 1900, and its composition had changed dramatically, emphasizing livestock products and fodder crops, while de-emphasizing wheat. Farm families spent little of their time producing consumer goods, such as textiles, tools, and dairy products, on the farm. But many farms had become part-time occupations, yielding some income to men and women who also worked outside agriculture for much or all of the year. Thus there had been a transformation not only in agricultural output, but in the techniques of production and in the texture of farm life.

This transformation had certainly begun well before Confederation, as the local economy had moved toward mixed farming and away from the wheat monoculture that had once characterized certain districts. By 1867 the farmers of the province, neither peasants nor frontiersmen, had little to learn about buying and selling. In the Ottawa Valley, farming was based on the supplying of the lumber camps, which regularly absorbed large amounts of basic – often very basic – foodstuffs. In southern and south-western Ontario there were local markets in the towns, and there were also export markets, not only in Montreal but in the United States and, from time to time, in Britain. Thus in most of the province's settled districts

the 1850s and 1860s were years of considerable agricultural prosperity.
Partly for that reason, as was shown in chapter 1, Ontario farms were better
equipped than those of Quebec. At Confederation Ontario's farmers, like
its manufacturers, could look upon the future with some confidence. Nor
was such optimism to prove misplaced.

Population, Production, and Living Standards

Ontario's farm population fluctuated, without showing any pronounced
trend: it rose in the later nineteenth century and declined slightly in the
1920s and 1930s. The number of occupied farms followed the same
general course: applying definitions that render the data more or less
comparable from 1891 to 1941, the 1941 census reported[1] that the number
of occupied farms was 172,258 in 1871 and 216,191 in 1891. The
'troubles' of the 1870s and 1880s, which figure so largely in the literature
of agrarian protest, had not prevented the number of farmsteads from
increasing. In the next two decades the number of farms fell a little and then
rose a little, so that in 1911 there were 204,054 occupied farms. The gentle
decline of the next three decades brought the number to 178,204 in 1941.
Thus there were more farmsteads in 1941 than in 1871, although in both
years some of these were only part-time farming operations. Meanwhile,
the average size of farm had been rising – from ninety-three acres in
1871–81 to 125.6 acres in 1941. It follows that the totals for cultivated and
improved acreage were very much larger in 1941 than in the late nineteenth
century, even though there had been some contraction since the 'census
peak year' of 1911.

The approximate stability of the farm population was the result of
out-migration from agriculture. From one viewpoint that out-migration is
an index and measure of agrarian success: the province was able to increase
its agricultural production enormously without much increase in the farm
population. From another viewpoint one might say that Ontario agriculture
was able to avoid the sort of impoverishment that often afflicts rural areas,
by exporting its sons and daughters to rural and urban life outside the
province, and to the growing cities and towns of Ontario itself.

Farming was largely an occupation for the Ontario born, in spite of some
in-migration from Quebec.[2] Also, at least in the twentieth century, it was
an occupation for the middle-aged and the elderly.[3] In these circumstances
it is not surprising that owner-occupancy remained the norm. In 1941, 78.4
per cent of Ontario's farms were wholly owned by their operators, while
another 8.6 per cent were owned in part. The figures for 1871, as was
shown in chapter 1, are not very different. Thus one must suppose that at
least in southern and south-western Ontario most farmers inherited their

holdings, and since the average longevity was rising, while retirement arrangements were incomplete and uncertain at best, the young left the farms and the old stayed on.

Much of the general shape of agricultural change has been made known by McInnis, Isbister, and Lawr,[4] so that in certain respects the following narrative is simply an expansion and extension of their work.[5]

There was, first of all, quite impressive growth in the cultivated area, which rose from 6.5 million acres in 1870 to 9.6 million acres in 1911; even in 1940, after fifteen years of contraction, 9.1 million acres were being cropped.[6] According to the Ontario statistical authorities the actual high point was 1926, when 10.4 million acres were under crop. Besides field crops, farmers used their land for cleared but uncultivated pasture, the quantity of which rose from 2.1 million acres in 1870 to 3 million acres in 1911 and to 3.2 million acres in 1941. There was also a great deal of unimproved 'prairie or natural pasture.' No data are available for early census years, but in 1941 Ontario farmers were using 3.9 million acres in this way. Land was also used in rather small quantities for the cultivation of high-value products that did not count as 'field crops' – for orchards, vineyards, small fruits, vegetables, and flowers. The nineteenth-century censuses produced a single figure of 207,000 such acres for 1871; twentieth-century censuses, organizing the returns differently, report only 174,544 acres in 1941 – much less than in the earlier years of the twentieth century and apparently less than in 1871.[7]

The acreage data can be arranged in three large categories – human food, industrial input, and animal food.[8] This arrangement reveals a striking pattern, which shines through the deficiencies in the data. During the 1870s more and more of the province's acreage was used to produce human food. McInnis has argued[9] that the shift to mixed farming was already under way by the late 1860s, as signalized by the fact that Canada became a net importer of wheat in 1869. He finds a 'mini-wheat boom' in the 1870s, apparently because cattle production became temporarily less profitable than it had been in the 1860s. After 1880–2 the province's farmers devoted less of their acreage to wheat and potatoes, while increases in orchard acreage, though significant until 1911, were not nearly great enough to offset this decline. Industrial inputs show the same sort of declining trend. The production of livestock fodder, however, made ever larger demands on the province's land, in spite of the diminution in oat acreage after World War One. These developments were not peculiar to Ontario; exactly the same pattern was appearing, at the same time or a little later, in the north-eastern United States and in Quebec. Thus between 1880–2 and 1940, the province nearly doubled its allocation of land to the production of livestock fodder, even when no attention is paid to the use of cleared but uncultivated pasture, where some increase can also be detected. The series for cultivated hay and mixed grains are especially striking, and growth in these categories offset the partial withdrawal from some older crops, such as husking corn and roots, after 1900. Soybean production, though begun experimentally in 1893, was of little importance until after 1941.[10]

Wheat developments both summarize and epitomize these changes. The peak acreage was in 1880–2, and from this point the trend was downward in acreage and output, even though yields were slowly rising, partly because farmers were substituting fall wheat for spring wheat. Thus the province was putting a smaller proportion of its cultivated acreage into wheat, which it no longer exported; indeed, a rising proportion of its own needs was being supplied from western Canada, even though its agricultural efficiency, measured by wheat yields per acre, was slowly rising.

Why did wheat acreages decline after 1880–2? A convincing answer would have to be based on farmers' own assertions, very few of which are available. Speculation, therefore, has had to replace evidence, and that speculation has centred on Prairie competition, declining prices, changes in the relative prices of various agricultural products, and variability of prices and yields.

As to the first influence, the argument is plausible but unconvincing. After all, the shift to mixed farming had begun long before the west was settled.[11] Furthermore, Ontario did not stop producing wheat; it simply produced less of it. In the late 1930s and 1940s wheat production was comparable to that of 1861, and was fully 57 per cent of what it had been at the 1882 peak. In so far as Prairie competition was relevant at all, it made its impact by lowering the world price of wheat, thus reducing the price that the Ontario grower could receive either abroad or at home.

As for price movements, the evidence is complicated and much disputed, so that one cannot readily do it justice in a brief summary. In the late nineteenth century all prices fell, but wheat and potato prices dropped much more steeply than the prices of fodder crops. It is hardly surprising, therefore, that land was employed less for the production of wheat and potatoes and more for the production of fodder, where local demand, partly from horses and partly from cattle and other livestock, helped support the prices.

Lawr believes that the movement of wheat prices roughly paralleled the movement of livestock prices, but that farmers moved out of wheat-farming because wheat prices varied more than other prices, exposing farmers to comparatively large amounts of uncertainty. He also notes the attraction of the rising home market, which affected livestock markets much more than grain markets, at least so far as Ontario was concerned. Because Lawr's hypothesis is the sort on which quantitative historians can work, it has sparked a controversy. Marr, who has applied an econometrical test to part of the hypothesis, reaches rather different conclusions: he thinks that the movements in the relative price of wheat were the most important determinants of movements in the crop mix, although movements in relative yields and uncertainties also played a part. But Marr's exercise includes only the prices of fodder and other crops, not the prices of livestock, and it relates only to the crop mix, not to the mix of farm activity as a whole, to which Lawr had directed our attention. Ankli and Millar, applying simpler statistical techniques, conclude that wheat, hay, and clover prices fluctuated much more than oat and barley prices and generally more than cheese and butter prices. They also wonder whether dairy farming actually was more profitable than wheat farming, but they are obliged to conclude that we do not really know.[12] Returning to the fray, Marr and Sinclair report that from 1882 to 1914 wheat prices fell in comparison with oats, hay, and cheese prices, while fluctuating less than cheese prices but more than coarse-grain, hay, and clover prices. After considering variations in yields, they conclude that the mean revenue per acre was somewhat more variable for wheat than for oats, barley, or hay; after econometric manipulation, they conclude that land was allocated to various uses in response to variations in the comparative prices and comparative yields of the various field crops, and that the relation between the wheat prices and the cheese prices was sometimes of importance, but that variability, whether in prices or yields, apparently was not.[13]

It would seem that Lawr has been refuted. But the controversy will doubtless continue. Meanwhile, since historians have perfect hindsight while farmers did not have perfect foresight, there will always be some uncertainty as to whether such statistical and econometrical exercises actually do describe or capture the decision-making of Ontario farmers.

If one broadens one's focus slightly, one may find the remarkable agricultural development of 1870–1900 easier to explain, even though one cannot readily find statistical data with which to illustrate the explanation. As Isbister observes, Ontario farmers normally produced a surplus, in calorific terms, over their own needs, thus establishing the basis for off-farm agricultural marketing, and, in due course, for transformation.[14] Isbister also suggests that the Ontario farmer was much more of a 'man of business' than his counterpart in Quebec, where agrarian change was much slower. Furthermore, during these three decades Ontario's farmers found their local environment transformed by a whole range of developments, some local and some external to the provincial economy. Some of these developments meant a widening of markets; others made it profitable to introduce new crops or to vary the mix of agricultural activities; many, though not all, had the effect of raising the value of owner-occupied land, especially if the farmer could seize the new opportunities. Among the most important new developments were railway building and canal improvement,[15] which opened the provincial market to some imports of human foodstuffs while cheapening the cost of moving such goods from other regions to Ontario and reducing transport costs inside the province. The Ontario population was growing, and, as will be argued in chapter 13, it seems that the average real income per head was rising quite noticeably, especially in the rapidly expanding towns. Ocean freight rates were falling; refrigerated trains and ships were appearing; in Britain real incomes were rising, and the population was hungry for cheese and for bacon. These last two developments were interrelated: cheap pig-feed was hard to come by in the 1870s and 1880s, but the growth of the cheese industry made substantial amounts of whey available.[16] As for Ontarians, they could draw their breadstuffs and potatoes from far away, at least to some extent; not so their meat, cheese, butter, and milk. So far as markets in Britain and Ontario were concerned, it is reasonable to suppose that the increase in the demand for livestock products was more than proportionate to the increase in aggregate real income, while the demand for basic starchy foodstuffs, such as bread and potatoes, would rise less quickly, or even, on a per capita basis, decline. Thus the years before 1900 were the great years for the Ontario cheese trade and for the export trade in bacon. These goods, furthermore, could move across the Atlantic Ocean without expensive refrigeration. For fodder crops, therefore, the local market was bound to be comparatively buoyant. And for oats and hay an additional push came from the growing horse population, not only in Ontario but in Quebec. On the farms of the province, for instance, from 1871 to 1901 the number of horses rose by almost 50 per cent. Other livestock, meanwhile, were increasing in number, and all these animals required food. Natural pasture might suffice for sheep, whose number was falling, but the cattle population, whose number was rising fast, would not be sustained by such unimproved grazing. The population of milch cows rose from 638,759 in 1871 to 1,165,763 in 1901; other cattle increased in number from 764,000 to 1.4 million; the number of swine rose fron under 900,000 to 1.1 million in 1891 and then leapt rapidly upwards in the 1890s, reaching 1.6 million in 1901. The census enumerators first counted poultry in 1891, reporting 8.2 million birds in the province; in 1901 they found 10.5 million. The pressure on the 'fodder base,' to use a Soviet expression from a much later period, was considerable; the result, as reflected in land use and in price movements, has been noted above.

Tobacco provided another and rather different success story. Having collapsed between 1870 and 1880, Ontario's tobacco output revived smartly, and in 1900 the acreage, though still insignificant in the province's land balance, already yielded a remunerative crop. Tobacco culture was strongly localized in the counties where it would be cultivated in the twentieth century: 88.5 per cent of the sown acreage in 1900 lay in Essex county, and the remainder was thinly scattered over twenty-two counties, in fifteen of which there were fewer than ten acres.

In the first decade of the new century agriculture changed little. The cultivated acreage increased, and the structural transformations proceeded. Less and less land was devoted to the production of human food and industrial inputs, in spite of some dramatic developments: tobacco, for instance, quadrupled its acreage between 1900 and 1911, while sugar beet, first introduced with the assistance of a provincial subsidy in 1907, occupied 26.9 thousand acres in 1910. Hungry horses continued to multiply, in spite of the motor car and the truck. According to Ottawa statisticians, oat acreage reached its peak in 1908–9, although there was no pronounced decline until after 1922.

The war dramatically altered the prices of some field crops, and it is hard to avoid the impression that farmers responded by increases in acreage. Wartime exhortations, especially in and after 1917, may have had the same effect.[17] Thus cultivated acreages rose from 9.6 million acres in 1914 to 10.1 million in 1920 – not far below the peak figure of 10.4 million acres that the province's statistical branch recorded for 1926.

New crops, meanwhile, were continuing to appear, and plantings of those recently introduced, such as alfalfa, first recorded in the 1910–11 crop year, were still expanding rapidly. Sugar-beet acreage increased in the 1920s, and tobacco acreage rose more than six-fold between 1910 and 1931. Many older crops, however, absorbed less and less land in the 1920s and 1930s. The acreage of hay and clover also stabilized and then began to decline. The main explanation is obvious enough: horses were on the way out. From a peak of 779,131 in 1915, the farm-horse population fell to 559,863 in 1940.[18] Also the cow population was no longer growing. From 1919 to 1941, and indeed long thereafter, the number of milk cows was approximately stable at 1.1 to 1.2 million, and the number of other sorts of cattle varied little, so that from 1908 until long after 1941 the numbers of milk cows and other cattle fluctuated only between 2.6 and 2.7 million head. The number of sheep, lambs, and hogs also tended to decline after 1914. Thus with a diminishing population of larger livestock, the province's feed-producing crops could not but suffer. Oats and hay were not the only crops to be affected; turnips and other root crops behaved similarly. Matters were made worse by competition from western feed grains and by the development of newer fodder crops such as alfalfa and mixed grains. The offal from sugar-beet processing, which was increasing in amount, could be used for animal feed. Finally, in the late 1920s the corn crop was plagued with disease and infestations.

If the province's cattle had not been eating more, the problems of the feed producers would have been more severe. The data effectively begin only in 1920. From then until World War Two the slaughter weights of cattle, sheep, lambs, hogs, and calves do not appear to have increased much, if at all. Milk output per cow, however, rose by roughly 30 per cent in a quarter-century, and it is hard to believe that the calorific intake of the typical milk cow had not increased more or less in proportion.

What was happening to the milk? The cheddar cheese output was tending to decline, but the output of creamery butter rose almost uninterruptedly; even the depression of the 1930s did not stop the increase. Minor uses – ice cream, concentrated-milk making, and farm-feeding – increased more or less in proportion to output. Farm butter and farm cheese, meanwhile, became decreasingly important, and not much milk was being 'fed on farms,' presumably because there was little change in the province's hog population. Altogether, during the 1920s and 1930s, Ontarians were drinking just over 25 per cent of the milk produced in the province, and the rest was being turned into industrial products of various sorts.

Poultry, meanwhile, proliferated rapidly and consistently from 1900 until 1931. The census enumerators began to count their chickens (and turkeys, geese, and ducks) only in 1891, when they found 8.2 million edible birds in Ontario. In 1931 they found 25.8 million, and in 1941, 24.7 million. Thus the population of poultry, who eat grain but not grass, hay, alfalfa, or sugar-beet pulp, tripled between 1891 and 1941, while between 1911 and 1931 it rose by 78 per cent – much the most rapid increase of any category of livestock. And more eggs were laid – 80 million dozen in 1940, as against 50 million dozen in 1900.

Fruit-growing is of special interest nowadays because so many people are concerned about the regions, such as the Niagara Frontier, where this sort of agriculture has long been concentrated. In acreage terms the orchards of the province contracted from the beginning of the century until 1940. The shrinkage affected many kinds of fruit trees, especially apples, pears, plums, and cherries. By World War Two apple, pear, and plum production was much smaller than it had been at the beginning of the century, while the province was producing substantially more cherries and peaches in 1940 than in 1900. It is natural, in the light of later controversies, to think that the number of fruit trees declined because fertile land was diverted to non-agricultural uses. Such a diversion there certainly was, but other forces may well have been at work. Because of improvements in transportation, a wider range of imported fruits came to be available on a regular basis. Many of these imports, furthermore, could be shipped and consumed throughout the year: there is no closed season on a Jamaican banana or a Hawaiian tinned pineapple. Thus though population and living standards were rising, some kinds of Ontario fruit probably faced more domestic competition in the 1920s and 1930s than in the years before 1900.

As for the vineyards, Ontario's prohibition adventure, which began in 1916,[19] created a special opportunity of a sort that fortunately was rare. 'Native wines' can be traced back at least to the 1871 census, although outputs were pathetically small in the nineteenth centutry. In succeeding decades there were attempts to raise grapes in various parts of Ontario, including improbable regions such as Muskoka. By 1897, when it first surveyed vineyards as such, the Ontario Bureau of Industries could find 11,100 acres, mostly in the Niagara-Welland district and in Essex County. Acreage then declined to 6,600 acres in 1926. However, provincial liquor control created new attractions, because the wineries were allowed to go on selling their product at retail, in bulk, and without attending to its alcoholic content. Presumably as a result, the vineyards began to expand, rising to 15,793 acres in 1933 – not surprisingly, perhaps, the year at which the Great Depression touched bottom, a year when cheap oblivion must have been much in demand. Thereafter acreage fell a little, ending our period at a figure of 14,300 – still a tiny proportion of the province's cultivated acreage, but far larger than the economist's theory of comparative advantage might have led one to expect.

Small fruits, on which data were first gathered in 1909, enjoyed no such artificial protection. Indeed, in local markets they faced the same sort of competition posited in connection with the soft tree fruits. Acreage, none the less, drifted upward, as did outputs, largely because of the strawberry crop, which, in 1940, accounted for more than two-thirds of total output.

As for maple syrup and sugar, the data are not very satisfactory, but they suggest that this activity was the opposite of dynamic, presumably because the process of clearing reduced the stands of readily accessible maple bush.

Until the 1920s, not much is known about market gardening. The census data show considerable expansion during the 1920s, but in 1940–1 the acreage was much the same as in 1930–1. The expansion of the 1920s affected every one of the sixteen separately identified vegetables grown in market gardens; here is surely a reflection of the urbanization and the prosperity of the period. During the decade there was also an increasing commercialization of vegetable production, and even in the 1930s there were increases in the acreages of asparagus, beets, celery, cantaloupes, lettuce, onions, parsnips, rhubarb, and tomatoes. Greenhouses, mean-while, increased their area by 70 per cent in the 1920s, and then stagnated during the 1930s, their luxury produce doubtless affected by the Great Depression. Nurseries also grew in the 1920s and stagnated during the Depression.

It would be pleasant if one could flesh out this statistical account with a more detailed and qualitative narrative. Regrettably, the obvious source for such detail, the local historical literature, is not very helpful. Sometimes, indeed, the local histories are positively misleading, as with Johnson's history of Ontario County.[20] Similarly, concentration on the chronology of rural protest can give a highly distorted impression. The price declines of the years after 1873, for example, doubtless posed problems for the more indebted farmers. Such difficulties are generally blamed for the arrival of the Grange, an activist association of farmers, from the United States in the early 1870s.[21] It can also be argued that the activities of the Patrons of Industry during the early and mid-1890s[22] have something to do with the continuing price decline, and perhaps with the general depression that marked the middle years of that decade. But no one should infer anything about the actual movement of production, earnings, debt, or anything else, from the protestations of organized interest groups, whether on the farms or off them.

Farm Incomes, Living Standards, and Mechanization

Like other Ontarians, the farmers of the province were interested in betterment. This they could seek in various ways. By accumulating machines and consumer durables, and by improving their houses, they could live more comfortably and work less laboriously. They could cultivate more land, raise the yield per acre, change the uses to which land was put, and divert their labour from artisan work to agricultural work to seize the opportunities of specialization and division of labour between country and town. The record shows that they did all those things, and the results in terms of total output and adaptation to changing markets were very impressive indeed, so that in physical terms there was plenty of room for a rise in farm living standards, simply because farm productivity was rising so impressively. Sad to say, until the 1920s it is not possible to trace either mechanization or living standards with any precision. Only in 1926 did the Dominion Bureau of Statistics began to calculate farmers' incomes, thereby making the result of farmers' labour clear at last.

By that time livestock products consistently yielded about three-quarters of farm cash incomes, while crops counted for just under one-quarter, and the share of wheat was tiny – less than 4 per cent of farm income in 1926, and barely 2 per cent in 1940. Fruit, vegetables, and tobacco, meanwhile, yielded a far larger proportion of farm income than one would have expected on the basis of the acreage they used. Besides cash income, farmers received a large income in kind: shelter, some transportation, and considerable amounts of food still came from the farmsteads themselves. In 1926 this kind of income was 25 per cent of total farm income, and in 1940 it was 20 per cent. Even in the mid-1920s little was spent on fertilizer, lime, and supplies for fruit and vegetable cultivation, although such items were becoming more important. Interest, rent, and taxes were rather less onerous than one might have expected from the literature of agrarian protest;[23] Other outlays were much more substantial. Net income, of course, could be determined only by comparing total receipts, in cash and in kind, with total outlays. The result[24] shows how the farm population was faring from 1926 to 1941.

It cannot be too strongly emphasized that the movement of farm prices tells us nothing about farm prosperity, even when these output prices are compared with the prices of farm inputs. Besides these two sets of prices, before one can do the calculation one needs to know about farm artisan work, consumer prices, interest and tax rates, the volumes of the various outputs, the volumes of purchased inputs, and the quantities of farm assets – both producer durables such as tractors and consumer durables such as refrigerators. And even afterwards, if one wants to know how well the 'average farmer' is doing, one has to know how many farmers there were. As was suggested earlier in this chapter, most farms' agricultural outputs appear to have been rising, either for extended periods or throughout the years 1867–1941. Production clearly outstripped the farm population, so that the physical output per farm family must have been growing too. If farm outputs had not been changing, the movement of farm prices would give some idea about money income, and something can sometimes be inferred about the weight of debt. But of course outputs did change, making the debt problem less severe than price movements might suggest. Furthermore, new debts may be incurred, or old ones paid off, so that the weight of old contractual obligations may change, and usually does change, from one period to another. The individual researcher can hardly hope to perform the necessary calculations in a satisfactory way, and of course for Ontario the basic data were not collected by anyone until well into the twentieth century. That is why the present account restricts itself to the years 1926–41 – the period for which official data can be found.

Because they are concentrated on the period of the Great Slump, 1929–33, these data present a most depressing picture. During the late 1920s Ontario farmers were doing quite well, on the average, and the situation was improving from 1926 to 1929. However, in the next three years the situation became very gloomy indeed, so that in 1933 the real net income per occupied farm was less than 40 per cent of what it had been in

1929, while in 1932, on average, an Ontario farm family netted only $147.26 in cash from its farm operations. In total, Ontario farmers were able, even in 1932–3, to pay their taxes, service their debts, and cover their cash outlays for other overheads. But this total conceals a wide variation among individual farms and farmers, and 70 per cent of total farm income in 1932–3 consisted of income in kind. It is hardly surprising that farm acreage declined, or that in 1941 the census-takers found fewer farmers than in 1931. Cattle and sheep herds were reduced, while many farms became idle or abandoned. That was still the case in 1941, even though average real farm income had at last risen above the levels of the late 1920s. By then there were few idle or abandoned farms in the agricultural heartlands of the province, the retrogression being concentrated in the north. That is what one would have expected: a decade of hard times would have had its most painful effects precisely in those regions where agricultural life was hard and uncertain even at the best of times. It is a pity that government policy, by settling the unemployed on these marginal farms, made the problem worse.

Hard though the 1930s had been, Ontario farmers managed to survive the decade with much of their capital stock intact, so that they began the war years with an impressive array of mechanical aids – 17,537 motor trucks, 128,744 automobiles, 35,460 tractors, 796 combine harvesters, 9,094 threshing machines, 32,801 gasoline engines, and 40,137 electric motors.[25] In 1871 the census enumerators found 206,232 'light carriages,' 299,367 'vehicles for transport,' 36,874 'reapers and mowers,' and 46,246 'horse rakes.'[26] It is not sensible to compare one set of numbers with another; what is interesting is the altered technology of cultivation and the changing pattern of rural life that the two lists reflect.

The changing technology had at least two dimensions. One was the choice of power; the other was the introduction of various sorts of machinery, which might be self-propelled, tractor driven, horse drawn, or stationary. Regrettably, from 1871 until 1921 no one counted the machines, motors, or equipment on Ontario farms. Any account, therefore, cannot avoid the anecdotal.

For most of the period 1867–1941 the main source of farm power was the horse. In pioneer days oxen were used for heavy ploughing, threshing, and land clearing, but once the land was ready for cultivation farmers preferred to rely on horses. As was shown above, the number of horses rose, and went on rising, until World War One. Even in 1940–1 there were still several hundred thousand horses on Ontario farms. In 1921, 86.9 per cent of Ontario farms reported at least one horse, and even in 1941, 64.2 per cent did so. Strangely enough, there were always some farms that reported neither horses nor tractors. Some of these were certainly part-time or residential farms. In addition, perhaps there were some farms, especially livestock, tree fruit, and market-gardening establishments, that cultivated nothing or used spades; probably there were also some small farmers who simply hired horse-power from other farmers.

Horses could drive stationary equipment and could thresh, as well as providing traction power. Nevertheless, increasingly horse-power was joined by engine-power – first the stationary engine and the windmill, then the mobile steam engine and the motor car, and finally, during World War One, the tractor. Well before 1900 stationary steam engines were in use on Ontario farms. The steam thresher, for instance, could process 600 to 700 bushels of grain in a day – rather more than most Ontario wheat farmers produced in a year.[27] In August 1877 the first steam threshing machine appeared in Woodbridge; portable steam engines were seen in Peel County during the 1880s.[28] Irwin reports that it was hard to develop sufficiently cheap engines, but that portable units were created and by 1885 were commonplace. The steam engine boom, he thinks, lasted from 1885 until 1912.[29] There were windmills for such activities as pumping, and eventually traction steam engines and portable gasoline engines were also available.[30] By 1910 these gasoline motors, which could be used for pumping and other tasks, were on the market, but they were unreliable and difficult to start, especially in winter. Two local historians[31] believe that between 1910 and 1920 at least half of Glengarry County farmers bought one. However, by 1921 barely 20 per cent of Ontario's farmers owned such motors. Of course the early cars, especially the Ford products, could power some sorts of machinery by the use of take-offs. But they could not be used to pull ploughs or other field machinery. During the nineteenth century there had been experiments with steam traction engines of various kinds, and steam power had certainly been used not only in threshing machines but in field work, although the latter use does not seem to have been very extensive. The machinery was expensive and heavy; given the size of Ontario fields and the condition of Ontario rural roads before 1900, it can hardly have been economical for most farms. Nor could a steam traction engine be used for general transport, as a horse could be.

The automobile changed the balance of advantage that had hitherto favoured the horse, because it could provide faster road transport and could power some farm operations as well. The first gasoline-powered tractors were as unwieldy as the steam traction engines, but with the advent of comparatively light and manoeuvrable equipment in the early 1920s, it was natural for farmers to make the further change if they could afford to do so. In 1921, 29.4 per cent of all Ontario farms possessed at least one car or truck, and 3.5 per cent possessed tractors, which seem first to have appeared in 1917, when the government distributed a good many to speed wartime production.[32] Thereafter the number of tractors increased substantially, so that by 1941, 19.3 per cent of Ontario farms owned at least one tractor, while 76 per cent owned at least one car or truck – a higher figure than in 1931, in spite of the preceding ten-year slump.

The spread of gasoline power in the twentieth century certainly changed the texture of Ontario rural life. Even so, by 1941 there were many Ontario farms that still had little or no mechanical power, whether mobile or stationary. Perhaps a part of the explanation has been provided by two local historians, who report that only in the 1930s were really suitable gasoline engines and pneumatic tractor tires available; they also remind us that the Ferguson hydraulic system, which enormously increased the usefulness of a tractor, appeared only after 1945.[33] In addition, especially in the 1930s, not everyone could find the necessary funds: the capital outlay remained considerable, even though the prices of vehicles, tractors, and gasoline were falling – both absolutely and in comparison with the general price level.

As for the farm machines themselves, one should note the following important developments. First was the proliferation of complicated, increasingly sophisticated horse-powered and horse-drawn machines – horse rakes, hoes, reapers, mowers, binders, and threshing devices of many kinds, which were likely to be stationary.[34] In 1871 there were not many threshing-mills in Ontario, but more than two-thirds of all farms possessed the simpler and cheaper fanning-mills. Horse rakes, reapers, and mowers were surprisingly few in number, suggesting that on the vast majority of Ontario farms the grain crops were still scythed, stooked, and gathered by hand, and that the same was true of hay. Thereafter the comparatively simple machines of the Confederation era were bought, improved, and extensively used. Cream separators appeared in the 1880s and seem to have spread quite rapidly, so that by 1931 66 per cent of the province's farms possessed at least one. Milking machines would save at least as much labour in dairying, but since they were dependent on electric power, it is hardly surprising that even in 1931, when only 16.8 per cent of the province's farms enjoyeded gas or electric light, there were only 4,000 milking machines. Next came what might be called general electrification, a condition that obviously required electricity – produced in a few instances by farmers' own generators, but normally supplied from central generating stations. In 1921 only 6.5 per cent of Ontario's farms were supplied with electricity or gas. In that year the Ontario government made provision to subsidize rural electrification, and thereafter the distribution lines spread, but even in 1941 they had reached only 38 per cent of Ontario's farms. The motor car, indeed, had spread far more widely.

Power, machines, and mechanization certainly lightened the labour of farm life, not only for men but also for women. They may even have raised farm incomes. They also required and reflected a much increased level of agricultural capitalization, not only in the field and in the barn but in the home and in the garage. On Ontario's owner-occupied farms, such a development might itself be taken to reflect farmers' well-being. If the farmer's wife acquires a telephone on the wall and a pump beside the sink, surely she is better off than before – even if her measured income, in cash and in kind, has not risen. In this respect one should observe that although farm equipment had certainly improved since 1871 or since 1921, even by 1940–1 Ontario farms were still comparatively ill equipped with the amenities of twentieth-century life – not only electricity, but running water, flush toilets, electric refrigerators, and the like.[35] In chapter 6 it will be seen that kerosene, the basic fuel for lighting before the age of electricity, was still an important product of the Ontario refining industry, even in 1940–1. Naturally it was in rural areas that most of the kerosene was sold. Wood also maintained most of its ancient popularity as a fuel in Ontario's rural areas. None the less, from 1931 to 1941 some progress was made – piped water, radio, and electric light all became much more common.[36]

One would like to reproduce this analysis of farm prosperity, misery, and amenity for earlier decades – especially for the depressions of the mid-1870s and the mid-1890s. Regrettably, as was observed above, although in a casual way historians know a lot about farm life around Confederation, most of the necessary data to support a more careful description do not exist. A good deal is known about the prices of farm products, something about outputs for 1870 and after 1880, but little or nothing about debt, inputs and costs, and machinery. During the 1880s the Ontario Bureau of Industries did try to study farm costs, but its efforts were unsystematic and were defeated by farmers' unwillingness to fill out questionnaires or even to keep records. The dominion, meanwhile, possessed no proper statistical service for agriculture or for anything else until after 1900.

By combining census data on the average cultivated area with Bureau of Industries' data about average yields, one can construct a 'hypothetical average farm' and say something about its grain output and income from grain for each census year. The result is not at all satisfactory, and experiments with this method produce little, but they do give some indication of a downward drift in real farm cash income *from crops* during the 1880s and 1890s – helping explain, perhaps, the rapid movement into livestock.

At present one cannot do better than draw some tentative inferences from other sorts of information. First of all, it is worth recalling that farm outputs and the stocks of farm animals far outgrew the farm population. Secondly, rural improvement and accumulation of capital did not end in 1867 or 1873. Schools, drainage works, barns, and farmhouses were constructed in such numbers as to challenge any assumptions about general rural impoverishment. Thirdly, one should remember not only the upward trends in the improved acreage, the acreage under crop, and the livestock population but also the increasing number of farm families. The men and women of rural Ontario were not fools, nor were they obliged to stay at work in Ontario agriculture; surely they would not expand the agricultural system with such energy if they expected no gain, and they would not persevere unless adequate returns were reaped. Fourthly, the average farm was cultivating more land and holding more livestock in 1911 than in 1871.

Admittedly, in the 1870s and 1880s Ontario farmers appear to have borrowed a great deal, mostly on mortgage. Indeed, their mortgage needs formed the basis for the remarkable growth of the province's mortgage companies between Confederation and the early 1890s. But although debt can be a sign of trouble, it can also mean that new opportunities are being seized. Furthermore, while some farmers were borrowing others were saving: the mortgage companies and some of the banks found farmers' savings accounts a useful source of funds. Finally, as Easterbrook explains,[37] in the 1890s Ontario's own demand for mortgage credit seems to have diminished quite dramatically, so that the mortgage companies could first reduce their overseas borrowing and then, after 1900, direct a flow of funds from Ontario and overseas to the Canadian prairies.

If Ontario farmers had been facing impoverishment in the later nineteenth century, the above developments would have been very surprising. This is not to say that all was well, that the lot of the typical farmer was always happy or comfortable, or that there were no foreclosures, no unfavourable movements of price, no crop failures, no depressions. All these unpleasant things happened from time to time. But the troubles of particular farmers, or the failures of particular years, need not be generalized, either across the entire farming community or through time. The weight of the indirect evidence is that Ontario agriculture was sufficiently rewarding an occupation to expand and adapt over more than forty years.

Living Standards, Yields, and Prices

One way to do better out of agriculture is to spend less per unit of cultivated land, or per animal – in general, to spend less per task. Some tasks could be mechanized, thus saving labour; in the event, labour-saving technology might not actually reduce costs, but it might save them from rising as rapidly as they would otherwise have risen. In a later chapter it will be suggested that outside Ontario agriculture real wage rates were tending to move upward, while the prices of many manufactured goods were falling, both absolutely and in comparison with agricultural prices. Labour-saving machinery, therefore, was almost bound to look increasingly attractive, if only as a way of controlling outlays while ensuring that farm families, with little help from hired labour, could maintain and expand their cultivated acreages and their herds.

Another way to do better is to raise the output per cropped acre – the yield, or the physical productivity, of the land itself. Agrarian history is full of examples. Better seeds or crop varieties may do the trick. So may manure, fertilizer, underdraining, crop rotation, or insecticides. Better soil preparation through deeper ploughing and harrowing can often be helpful.

Under this heading, it must be admitted, the record of Ontario agriculture is not impressive.[38] For oats and buckwheat yields were tending to decrease; for wheat, barley, and rye, yields were rising, but not very rapidly. Over a sixty-year period, for instance, the yield of spring wheat tended to increase by just over 25 per cent, and the yield of autumn wheat increased only slightly more rapidly, while barley and rye yields rose more slowly.

To the farmer, of course, the long-term trends would be invisible, obscured by the very considerable year-to-year fluctuations in yields. But where yields are not rising quickly, farmers may well experiment with different allocations of the cultivated area, so as to find a more profitable mix of crops or perhaps a more stable and predictable one. Presumably the changing crop patterns may reflect just that sort of adjustment. Prices were also highly variable, and, as was noted above, it has been suggested that farmers may have tried to stabilize their incomes, in the face of fluctuating prices, by changing their crops and their activities.

It might be thought that Ontario's dreary farm productivity performance might reflect the extension of the cultivated area into less rewarding territory in the north and north-west – into one part of what the English economist David Ricardo would have called the 'extensive margin of cultivation.' In fact, the actual shape of development suggests a different pattern.[39] From 1870–1 to 1926, when the cropped acreage reached its peak, the cultivated acreage expanded everywhere. But 65 per cent of the extra cropped land was to be found in the southern counties of the province, and another 20.8 per cent in the eastern districts, which were also long settled; as table 3.13 shows, the contribution of the northern districts and the counties along the southern fringe of the Canadian Shield was only 14 per cent of the new cropped acreage, and only 16 per cent of the extra pasturage. In absolute terms, the new cropland in the southern counties was more than ten times as large as the new cropland in what was called New Ontario. Furthermore, because yields were uniformly greater in the south than in other regions, the extra acreage in the south made a disproportionate contribution to extra output.

From 1926 until 1941 acreages under crop and in pasture fell everywhere except in New Ontario, where the continued expansion of cultivated land made only a small contribution to output, partly because yields were so low and partly because the extra acreage, though not unimpressive in comparison with the base acreage in the district, was of little significance to the province as a whole. Thus it was change in the south, and to a lesser extent to the east, that made the difference so far as outputs and yields were concerned. Perhaps in these areas, too, the Ricardian extensive margin was being encountered as acreages grew in the years before the early 1920s.

Government Policy and Agriculture

Naturally enough, Ontario agriculture received help and encouragement from government, both dominion and provincial. One form of help was research and education; another aimed to make farmers co-operate in ways that would raise their productivity; yet another concerned itself with price-manipulation; still another tried to make some inputs cheaper or easier to obtain.

Although no one in Ottawa or in Toronto would have used the vocabulary of technical economics, it was implicitly recognized that agricultural research and education deserved to be aided because both were valuable to the community at large. Technically, education is partly a 'public good,' and research is almost wholly so. That is, the value of research is properly measured by the total of all benefits to every member of the community; because these pay-offs cannot be appropriated by the persons or groups who do the research, unless government takes a hand too little research will be done. Similarly, although some of the pay-offs from education accrue to the educated, there are other benefits that are more widely spread and that the educated person cannot appropriate. Hence it is sensible for government to subsidize education. In the same way, the dissemination of information about better methods, crops, animals, and so forth would have broad pay-offs that the spreaders of the information could not hope to capture. Again, the information or the distributing of the information can be called a 'public good,' where subsidizing is defensible. Information can be scattered in all sorts of ways – fairs, prize-givings, publications, meetings, and the activities of associations. Finally, certain sorts of land improvement, especially drainage, will be more effective and less costly in relation to the results if they are executed jointly by groups of farmers. Government policies and programs eventually covered all these matters.

In 1867 Ontario inherited from the United Province of Canada an elaborate system of aid for information-spreading. The provincial authorities, after amending the inherited administrative arrangements, began to propagate the good word about 'agriculture and arts.'[40] These measures, and related devices, were used throughout the later years. They were not expensive: in 1871 the provincial government spent $74,000, or 3.9 per cent of its total outlays, on 'agriculture,' and almost all these outlays were for such activities. At first the province did nothing more.

During the early 1870s important new elements were added. The provincial exchequer began to buy the drainage debentures of local governments to encourage collective underdraining. In 1871 the Ontario Agricultural College was adumbrated, and once established at Guelph in 1874, the college became a centre not only for agricultural education but for research and for the dissemination of information. It was an important new departure; for a long time there had been a professor of agriculture at the provincial University of Toronto, but although he possessed experimental plots on the present site of Toronto's Varsity Stadium, he attracted few students. Nor, although he served it in various ways, did the government pay his salary.[41]

Guelph, at first, was not expensive. During the 1870s and 1880s, expenditures averaged $40,000 per year. But these outlays tended to rise, and the work of the college became steadily more sophisticated and useful. A similar pattern was followed by the Ontario Veterinary College, at first a private Toronto institution. Once it had been provincialized in 1908 and moved to Guelph, it also became involved in research to some extent. In due course a lower-level agricultural school was established at Kemptville, where work was concentrated not on research but on teaching and the spreading of information.

The dominion was also spending on agricultural research, though naturally not on agricultural education. The first dominion experimental station was set up at Ottawa in 1886. The Ottawa farm was the centre of the nationwide system of experimental farms that developed subsequently. Within Ontario, a rather smaller station opened in 1909 at Harrow, and a much larger station began to operate at Kapuskasing in 1910. By 1933 there were also sixteen farms where the dominion carried on the work of its 'illustration stations,' which were meant to expose farmers to best-practice agrarian technology.[42] The provincial authorities gradually introduced their own experimental farms that were not linked in any formal way with education. By 1930 there was a horticultural experimental station at Vineland, an experimental farm at Ridgetown, and a demonstration farm at

New Liskeard, where work had begun in 1907.[43] More closely linked with education were the provincial district representatives, of which the first six were appointed in summer 1907. They taught in the high schools but also dealt with farmers, to whom they were meant to disseminate up-to-date information about techniques, crops, and disease control. By 1910 there were fourteen representatives, and the number increased steadily in later years.[44]

Education and research were meant to improve agricultural conditions by helping farmers grow more. Another kind of help could come from improvements in farm prices, especially from tariff protection on the domestic market. Some protection was provided in the nineteenth century and also in the twentieth, but the pattern is hard to summarize both accurately and briefly because of the proliferation of rates and categories.[45] The general twentieth-century tendency, however, can be described as follows. After 1906 the dominion tended to reduce the rates of duty on agricultural goods, thus exposing Ontario farmers to somewhat more competition. In 1930 there was an especially large crop of such reductions, through which the British preferential rate often became zero. These tendencies were apparent with respect to many field crops, fruits, and vegetables. However, in 1930–1 there were sharp increases in duties on beef, butter, cheese, and many canned goods. Tobacco was free of duty intil 1936, when stiff tariffs were imposed. The Canadian-American trade talks of 1935–6 and 1938 occasioned some reductions in food tariffs, but they were hedged carefully about with seasonal qualifications whose effect was to give Ontario producers protection during the season when they needed it most.[46]

Twentieth-century tariff changes, in short, exposed the Ontario grain grower to increased competition, while extending rather higher protective margins, at least some of the time, to those who produced meat, butter, vegetables, and tobacco. Furthermore, the protective margins were maintained comparatively strongly against the Americans, the most relevant direct competitor, even when British Empire goods such as sugar and maize were admitted free, or at comparatively low rates.

The troubles of the 1930s produced many innovations not only in farmers' organizations but in government policy, both dominion and provincial. Mortgage-moratoria helped many farmers to stay on their holdings. A renewal of agricultural co-operation in purchasing, along lines that dated back to 1914, may have helped.[47] More important, in the long run, was the arrival of the marketing board. Originating in the 'white dominions' of the Antipodes, and quickly domesticated in Britain, the board framework of 'compulsory co-operation' proved attractive in Canada also.[48] The Ontario government took the first steps under the milk control legislation of 1934, and in the same year the Dominion Natural Products Marketing Act was passed. Declared *ultra vires* of the dominion, the latter measure was replaced by the Ontario Farm Products Control Act of 1937.[49] By 1940 there were marketing boards for milk, cheese, peaches, asparagus, pears, plums, cherries, and tomatoes. After decades of competing in their own markets and overseas, the farmers of Ontario increasingly demanded protection and encouragement for the cultivation of local opportunities – those provided by the province's own urban markets. In later decades the effectiveness of the boards' arrangements, both for farmers and for the populace at large, would be much discussed. But when one recalls the cash-flow problems of farmers during the 1930s, one can understand why farmers wanted more aid and more regulation than before.

Besides the measures described above, the Ontario government gradually developed a considerable armory of weapons that it deployed in the interest of 'agricultural development.' Expenditures were not always large, but they were unremitting,[50] and they tended to grow. The longest-lived schemes related to colonization roads, immigration, and colonization itself. From 1868 through 1933–4, when the item ceased to be separately identified, the province spent $4 million on immigration and colonization, while from 1868 through 1936–7 it spent $16 million on colonization roads. In addition, from 1911–12 through 1936–7 $66.6 million was spent on northern and north-western Ontario, of which 96.2 per cent was spent on roads. These four items sum to $87.1 million, a figure that is much larger than the $24.6 million that was spent on agricultural education and research from 1871 through 1939–40. When one considers this pattern of spending in relation to the information about stagnating yields and declining acreages in the 1920s and 1930s which was surveyed earlier in this chapter, one has to wonder whether the provincial authorities were allocating their agricultural spending in the most productive way. Much more rational was the subsidizing of the Ontario Hydro rural lines, a scheme that began in 1921. As for the rural development credits that were first provided in the same year and that were withdrawn in the mid-1930s,[51] the output and productivity data suggest that the new money cannot have made much difference: at most, it may have saved farmers a point or two in interest.

Conclusion

This chapter records an impressive achievement in agricultural development. Ontario's farmers were successful, not only in raising output and total productivity but in adapting to changing circumstances and seizing new opportunities. Admittedly, the province's farmers were not very successful at raising the yields per acre of field crops, but in livestock products their record was considerably better, and certainly they were ready to modify the pattern of their productive activities to make the best use of their lands and their talents. In the process they invested massively – in land-clearing, structures, machinery, and, perhaps most important of all, livestock. Acreages rose until the mid-1920s, as did the cultivated land on the typical farm, which also came to hold larger herds of cattle and pigs; the number of horses first rose and then declined, while the number of sheep and lambs declined almost steadily. Farm machinery became more widely distributed and much more sophisticated; farm amenities were improved.

The farmers drew ever more of their incomes from livestock and from local markets, rather than relying on markets in the United States or Britain, although there were periods when the opportunities in the latter helped speed the transformation of the province's agricultural economy. So far as grain is concerned, the province's growing cities drew less of their bread grains from Ontario fields. The gap was filled by imports from the newly settled Canadian west, in a pattern that exemplified the advantages of the interregional division of labour. However, the record for livestock products is very different. Although in the twentieth century the livestock population did not increase particularly quickly, outputs were redirected from external to local markets, while some measures of output per animal were rising. Meanwhile, thanks to the transportation revolution, tropical foodstuffs became more widely available, providing a kind of competition that had hardly been felt in 1870. Declining transport costs had the same general effect. The result, by 1940, was a very complicated interregional and international trade in foodstuffs, a trade that the transport revolution had conditioned and, in large part, created.

Most of the credit for agricultural transformation must go to the farmers. As chapter 18 will show, the financial system contributed to the agricultural transformation, especially before 1890, by raising and transferring mortgage funds from abroad. Governments, both federal and provincial, provided some appropriate assistance, but the provincial authorities, in particular, squandered attention and money on 'extensive projects' in northern and north-western Ontario – projects whose pay-offs, whether measured by outputs or by the living standards of the newly settled farm families, were dismal. Governments also became involved in the provision of cheap credit and, increasingly, in attempts to manage both domestic and external markets.

Ontario agriculture interacted in a complicated way with the urban industrial economy. Because Ontario farmers were already comparatively prosperous in 1867, because they were not immiserized in later decades, and because they were anxious to mechanize their operations and to improve their living arrangements, the farm communities provided an enormous market for local manufacturers. Indeed, at least until World War One they may well have been the single most important such market. Conversely, industry drew upon agriculture for various things – raw materials, savings, and, most important of all, labour. If agriculture had been less adaptable, and if the emerging interregional division of labour had not helped it specialize, the cities would have faced higher prices for basic foodstuffs. Thus the cities would have been less attractive to migrants, whether from rural Ontario or from overseas; the province's population would have grown less quickly, and more native-born Ontarians would have drifted 'south of the border.' A great deal depended, therefore, on the imagination and adaptability of Ontario's farm families.

4 Ontario's Mining Industry, 1870–1940

PETER GEORGE, McMaster University

Ontario's rich endowment of mineral deposits made possible an enormous expansion in the output of metallic minerals from 1870 to 1940. Indeed, it was during this period that Ontario established its position as Canada's major metals-producing province.[1] These minerals played an important role in the northward spread of organized economic activity in the province, and they also provided an important export base for regional development.

This chapter offers a narrative account of developments in the mining industry, concentrating on the three principal non-ferrous metals that were exploited – nickel, which, with copper and the platinum group of metals, is identified with the Sudbury Basin; silver, which, along with cobalt, was produced in Cobalt and the surrounding district; and gold, the product of the rich Porcupine and Kirkland Lake camps and of new mines developed at several locations in north-western Ontario in the 1930s. Some sorts of mineral extraction – iron ore, petroleum, and natural gas – are discussed in later chapters; other varieties, most obviously salt, quarrying, clay, and gravel, are not discussed at all.

The chapter also treats many of the public policy issues that were related to the expansion of mining output. These issues range from the administrative and regulatory conditions affecting the initial discovery of minerals and their later exploitation, through the degree of processing to be done within Ontario, to considerations of provincial revenue and the broad macro-economic effects of mining on the provincial economy.

Annual data that summarize production of the province's major metallic minerals are presented in table 4.1.[2] For nickel physical output and value of production were first reported for 1890; for copper in 1891; and for platinum-group metals in 1902. These metals often occur together, emerging from refineries as joint products. Nickel and copper were the first metals to reach significant levels of production in northern Ontario, and

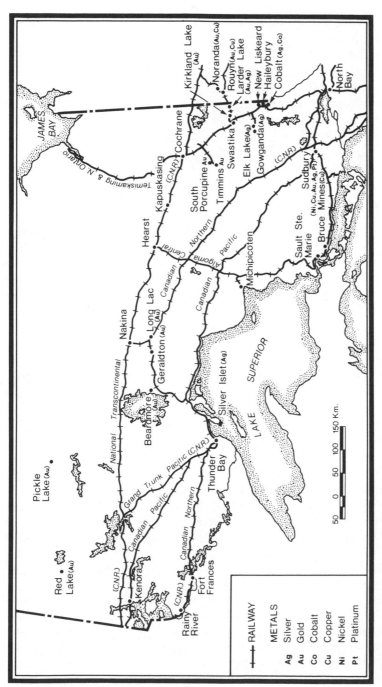

FIGURE 4.1: Locations of Principal Metallic Mineral Mines, Northern Ontario, 1870–1940

they show a steady increase, apart from annual fluctuations, through the period before 1930, with a further rapid rise in the outputs of all three metals in the late 1930s.

Before 1896, gold production is reported only in a fragmentary way. Both the physical output and the value of production series show rapid rates of increase just before World War One, as the Porcupine field was brought into production, and then again in the mid-1920s as the Kirkland Lake mines became fully operational. In the early 1930s there were further significant gains in output and value of production, partly reflecting the increase in the price of gold in 1933–4. The details will appear below. The profitability of gold-mining was affected, to a much greater extent than the profitability of other metal-mining, by these large movements of macro-economic policy. While movements of the exchange rate could also affect profitability in other mining industries, the final price of the other minerals reflected supply and demand, not President Roosevelt's view of what the correct price ought to be.

Silver production is first reported in 1898 and that of its frequent joint product, cobalt, in 1904. Silver production peaked in 1912 as the Cobalt field reached its zenith and then began a slow decline that lasted through the 1930s. The value of cobalt production increased after World War One, and it remained high during the 1920s, partially offsetting the decline in the value of silver mined.

These data clearly indicate that the mining industry grew dramatically, rising from virtually nothing circa 1890 to major importance in the twentieth century. What major events marked this development?[3]

Before 1880 the mining industry was slow to develop.[4] Early discoveries of copper and iron ores in the northern United States, especially in Michigan and Minnesota during the 1840s, gave hope that mining industries would play an important role in Ontario's future. The profitable exploitation of the copper deposits in Michigan, for example, stimulated interest in the north shores of Lakes Huron and Superior; in 1848 the establishment of Bruce Mines led to the first commercial production of copper in Ontario. The mine on Silver Islet, discovered in 1868 near Thunder Bay, drew considerable attention to northern Ontario during the 1870s; some $3 million worth of silver was recovered within a few years. But the mine's collapse in the early 1880s tarnished the image of northern Ontario as a prospect for mining ventures.[5] The discovery of gold near Madoc in Hastings County in 1866 touched off a short-lived boom in eastern Ontario, and a few pockets of gold were discovered in the vicinity of the Lake of the Woods during the late 1870s. But no permanent gold-mining activity was in sight.

As interest in northern Ontario's mining prospects waxed and waned, with periodic discoveries and then often disappointing or short-lived production, the provincial government experimented with a series of mining acts that were intended both to stimulate and to regulate the industry. The emphasis on regulation in the Mining Act of 1864 and in the Gold and Silver Mining Act of 1868 gave way to an encouraging framework in the General Mining Act of 1869. From that year until 1890 the province placed minimal constraints on the location and development of mining properties. The General Mining Act withdrew all previous royalties and reservations on gold and silver production; also, it required neither prior discovery of valuable minerals nor development work before lands could be patented. Indeed, this 'laisser faire' approach was conducive to speculation in mining lands rather than to genuine development of mines, since it created no costs for speculators, who could hold lands without improvement in the hope that values would eventually rise. This feature of the act was to prove a major deficiency in that it ensured the province would fail to participate in the financial gains that promoters would reap from the development of nickel and copper in the Sudbury Basin.

By the early 1880s mining in northern Ontario was viewed with scepticism by prospective miners and promoters. This view was a product of previous disappointments, and of the risks associated with the isolated, rugged terrain of the Canadian Shield. Moreover, the disputes between Ontario and Ottawa over the provincial boundary were settled only by the decisions of the Judicial Committee of the Privy Council in 1884 and 1888.[6] Thus in spite of what hindsight labels generous conditions of access, in 1880 the Shield's mineral resources were still virtually unknown and untouched.

The rapid exploitation of mineral resources after 1880 meant that a great deal more information about the resource base would have to be available to prospectors and mine promoters. These facts were forthcoming partly through the careful and well-publicized research and survey efforts of the Geological Survey of Canada and, after 1891, of the Ontario Bureau of Mines.[7] But the critical ingredient was the building of a number of developmental railways, beginning with the Canadian Pacific Railway. One by-product of the CPR's construction was the discovery of nickel-and copper-bearing ores in the Sudbury Basin in 1883. This project and later subsidized railway-building projects are described below, in chapter 15. The construction of the Temiskiming and Northern Ontario Railway (T&NO) northward from North Bay toward New Liskeard and Haileybury, beginning in 1902, would make possible the discovery and rapid development of the Cobalt silver mines a year later; the pattern would be repeated in the same decade as construction pushed northward towards

Cochrane, as the gold fields in Porcupine and Timmins and shortly afterward in Kirkland Lake, were discovered. Simultaneously, the building of the east-west National Transcontinental was under way, following a direct northerly route from Winnipeg to Quebec. Thus by the beginning of World War One the mineral resource base of northern Ontario was well mapped and accessible through rail transport, and the region's future as a major producer was no longer in doubt.

Nickel and Copper: the Sudbury Basin[8]

The nickel and copper ore ranges near Sudbury surround an oval central depression that is some thirty-seven miles long and seventeen miles wide – the so-called Sudbury Basin, on whose rim the major producing mines are located. The ore body is extremely complex. It contains nickel, copper, and platinum and other rare metals, plus varying amounts of iron, sulphur, silver, and gold. As a result, the processing of these ores has been difficult.

Reports of mineral finds in the area date back to surveys of the mid-1850s. But it was the discovery of copper sulphides in 1883 by a CPR employee during construction west of Sudbury that initiated the development of the nickel and copper mining industry. The discoveries, combined with the promised ease of access via the CPR, led to a prospectors' rush in 1884–5. A series of major ore discoveries along the south rim of the Basin, later to become well-known mines, such as the Murray, Creighton, Copper Cliff, and Stobie, soon followed. Ore bodies on the north rim were not pursued until later in the decade.

The ore-bearing lands were quickly purchased by promoters and speculators, since the land was available for purchase at a nominal price of $1 per acre, without any requirement of discovery or development before transfer of title. The ore deposits were soon acquired by a few groups of speculators, many of whom were based in northern communities such as Pembroke, Ottawa, and Sudbury itself.

One producer – the Canadian Copper Company (CCC), the forerunner of International Nickel – soon emerged to dominate the industry. Canadian Copper was established in 1886 by an American, Samuel J. Ritchie, who had earlier attempted to develop iron ore and railway properties in eastern Ontario and had acquired Sudbury land in 1885. The CCC expanded Ritchie's original holdings and began to work the deposits. Ritchie negotiated a contract with the Orford Copper Company of New Jersey to refine the ore. Copper refining was complicated because the ore contained so much nickel, and the Orford process was developed by Robert Thompson to separate the two metals. The low-grade ores required concentration into nickel-copper matte before shipment to reduce transport costs; CCC heap-roasted ores to burn off the sulphides, and in 1888 the firm began to construct a smelter in Copper Cliff. By 1890 CCC was the Sudbury area's leading mining and smelting firm.

An important matter for any Sudbury mine was access to refining technology and markets. CCC's strong position combined with Orford's ownership of an efficient refining process enabled the firms to expand and dominate the American market for nickel. As information about the steel-hardening properties of nickel was diffused, Ritchie and Thompson were able to capitalize on their political contacts in 1890, thereby obtaining the contracts to supply the US navy with nickel for the tests of nickel-steel armour plate. The success of the tests enhanced the firms' position in the American market, and also brought a rush of prospecting activity and speculation in those crown lands that remained available in Sudbury.

In 1889–91 there were a number of abortive attempts to establish rival firms, among them H.H. Vivian and Company, which mined the Murray deposit, built a local smelter in 1890, and shipped to its refinery in Wales. This firm ceased operations in 1894, and other early rivals also failed, for both financial and technical reasons. It was difficult to gain access to cost-effective refining processes, and the market for nickel was thin and tightly controlled. The grip of CCC and Orford on the American market was strengthened in 1902 when the two firms merged to form International Nickel Company (New Jersey), better known as INCO.[9] The French company, Le Nickel, using New Caledonia ores, had a virtual monopoly in Europe. It was not until the turn of the century that a successful rival firm, Mond Nickel, was established in Sudbury. Mond's refineries were in Wales. Smaller than INCO, Mond produced for the European market and was tolerated by INCO until the two firms merged in 1928. After 1900 the industry expanded rapidly, propelled by pre-war demands for armour plate, and then by the military needs of war itself. By 1913, Sudbury was the major supplier in the world, and INCO was the industry's dominant firm.

Even before 1900 two major issues arose between the Sudbury nickel-mining industry and the provincial government. The province's new Mining Act of 1891 reintroduced royalties on mining, but only for lands patented thereafter; Sudbury properties, having been patented before 1891, were exempt. Thus Queen's Park drew no current revenues from nickel, and it had originally transferred the lands for a mere $1 per acre. The situation was irritating, although not to CCC or INCO. The question of refining also arose. Observers were well aware that because Orford refined in New Jersey, jobs and incomes were created in the United States, not in Sudbury or elsewhere in Ontario. Why could not the refineries relocate? Repeatedly, over a twenty-year period, the Ontario government tried to persuade and even to coerce Orford, and then INCO, to shift them. The wartime emergency finally ended the dispute, and INCO opened a new refinery at Port Colborne in 1918.[10]

In the post-war years there were new uses for nickel, as steel alloys found widespread application in the burgeoning production of consumer durables and semi-durables, not only in Canada but throughout the western world. INCO proposed to capitalize on the situation by developing the large Frood ore body, a property that it shared with Mond. The economic advantages of joint exploitation, and perhaps the desire to control world markets, precipitated the merger of INCO and Mond in 1928. The merger followed shortly after the reorganization of INCO as a Canadian corporation, probably to avoid anti-trust action in the United States because of INCO's monopoly position in the American market. By 1929 INCO (Canada) controlled 90 per cent of the world nickel market. But in 1928 the company did acquiesce in the appearance of Falconbridge Nickel, which mined in the Sudbury Basin while refining at Kristiansand, Norway, directing its output chiefly to the European market. Market-sharing among the major producers, with INCO in a dominant role, continued throughout the 1930s, as armament and rearmament propelled production rapidly upward.[11]

Silver: Cobalt and District[12]

Early attempts at silver production in the vicinity of Thunder Bay in the 1870s and 1880s at Silver Islet and Rabbit Mountain had met with little success. But the discovery of silver in north-eastern Ontario was the first significant find of precious metal in the Canadian Shield. The silver deposits at Cobalt were located as a by-product of railway construction. In the summer of 1903, as the new T&NO line proceeded northward from North Bay, there were two important discoveries at Mile 104, near Long Lake. J. McKinley and E. Darragh staked adjoining claims at the south-east corner of the lake in August, followed by Fred LaRose at the north-west corner in the following month. Other claims were staked later that fall. Many of these early claimants were to sell part or all of their claims to promoters, who financed further development.

When the provincial government became aware of the silver deposits, it withdrew all unclaimed land within ten miles on either side of the railway. In April 1904 the Timiskaming District was declared a Mining Division, and the lands were again opened for prospecting. Even so, prospectors showed limited interest until the winter of 1904–5.

Several mines, the Buffalo, Nipissing, Trethewey, LaRose, and McKinley-Darragh properties among them, began producing in 1904; the first shipments of ore, late that year, helped spread information about the rich ore base, that was now easily accessible by rail. That winter the level of prospecting activity increased greatly, and by the end of 1905 there were sixteen producing mines. At first the refineries were in the United States. But, with the encouragement of the Mineral Refining Bounty Act of 1907 and the pressure of high transport costs, within a few years silver was being processed at several Ontario refineries.

The splendid Cobalt discoveries led the government to take a number of initiatives in administration and regulation and even to make an abortive attempt at public enterprise. In 1905 Queen's Park reserved the Gillies Limit and the unclaimed parts of the beds of Long Lake and Kerr Lake, east of Cobalt, from claim-staking. Once the Limit had been lumbered and a geological survey completed, the government itself tried to exploit the minerals. But few showings were found. Abandoning its plans, the government opened the Limit to public auction in 1909. The rights to the bed of Long Lake were sold for $1.035 million to Cobalt Lake Mining Company and the rights to Kerr Lake to the Crown Reserve Mining Company for $178,500 plus a 10 per cent royalty (eventually exceeding $750,000).[13]

Because the area was covered with dense bush and was still unsurveyed, the early days of the Cobalt camp were marked by frequent disputes over the ownership of claims. One of the most notorious was that between Fred LaRose and M.J. O'Brien, the Ottawa lumber magnate. The government appointed a Special Mining Commission to settle the affair, followed by the appointment of a permanent provincial mining commissioner who could resolve disputes arising from conflicting claims. Moreover, with the establishment of a Mining Division, the provincial authorities began a conscious decentralization in mining-lands administration.

The Cobalt mining field was developed by Canadian capital as well as American, and from the success of Canadian-owned mines came a number of Canadian mining fortunes (e.g., those of M.J. O'Brien and the Timmins brothers) that subsequently were to be sources of risk capital for new silver and gold mines. The opening of local mining exchanges in Cobalt in 1906 and New Liskeard in 1907 also stimulated the participation of local miners and merchants.

Prospecting activity spread out from Cobalt. Silver was discovered in 1907–8 at South Lorrain, some fifteen miles south-east of Cobalt, at Casey Township fifteen miles to the north, and at Elk Lake and Gowganda some fifty-five miles to the north-west. Branch railway lines were built to encourage mining at these places and at Kerr Lake. But by far the most spectacular spin-off from Cobalt was the development of gold-mining at Porcupine, Timmins, and Kirkland Lake – development that depended from the outset on promoters whose capital came from Cobalt mining.

Cobalt began as a camp of small operators, working deposits that were near the surface and that required little capital investment or equipment. It later became necessary to move deeper underground and to invest in ore-treatment processes, so as to increase the quality of metal shipments in the face of high transport costs. To improve the recovery of metals from low-grade ores, mechanical stamp mills and rolling mills were augmented by chemical processes: the cyanide treatment was introduced in 1908, and the selective flotation process began to be used in 1915. Large-scale, capital-intensive operations, relying on hydroelectric power supplied after 1911 by the Northern Ontario Light and Power Company, became increasingly common. These efficient but capital-using techniques were models for hard-rock mining in northern Ontario.[14]

The Cobalt boom was shortlived. The value of silver production peaked in 1912 and sagged noticeably between the wars, even though an increase in the value of cobalt helped offset the declines in silver production. By 1936 only one mine remained in operation. By then most Ontario silver came as a by-product of Sudbury's nickel-copper production, and of gold production at Porcupine, Timmins, and Kirkland Lake. But Cobalt was the critical discovery that changed once and for all the image of the Canadian Shield as an important mining area.

The Gold Fields of Northern Ontario[15]

Gold production has been more widely dispersed across northern Ontario than either silver or nickel-copper. The major centres of production in the north-east, at Porcupine and Kirkland Lake, continued to dominate the province's gold production up to 1940, but new producers emerged in north-western Ontario in the 1930s, in response to the increase in the price of gold.

Until 1914 and again in 1926–9 the price of gold was fixed, because the dominion had adhered to the gold standard, establishing a 'gold content' for the dollar that generated a basic price of $20.67 per ounce, with only a limited possible range of movement above or below that figure. In the United States the price was the same until 1933–4, but when Canada was off the gold standard so that the Canadian dollar floated, as in 1914–26 and after the winter of 1928–9, the Canadian-dollar price of gold could and did vary. Thus the substantial depreciation of the Canadian dollar in the winter of 1931–2 provided some stimulus to gold-mining, further enhanced when, in the course of 1933–4, the American government raised the price of gold from $20.67 per ounce to $35. The dominion goverment, meanwhile, had passed the Gold Export Act of 1932, under which all gold mined in Canada had to be sold to the government at an administered price, which reflected both the American-dollar price and the exchange rate.

Thus the Canadian-dollar price of gold rose from $20.67 per fine troy ounce in 1928 to $23.48 in 1932, $34.50 in 1934, and $35.18 in 1938. The stimulus was especially important because in the early 1930s the general price level was declining, as were the prices of many of the mines' requirements.

New discoveries and transportation improvements interacted. The T&NO was gradually extended to the north, into areas where there had already been periodic prospecting. As early as 1896 E.M. Burwash, a geologist working for the Ontario Bureau of Mines, examined the boundary area between the Districts of Nipissing and Algoma. He was encouraged by the common occurrence of quartz veins with gold tracing, as was W.A. Parks, another geologist, in 1899. The Porcupine area was prospected intermittently in the early 1900s. The first major discovery occurred only in 1909, however, when H.A. Preston and J.A. Wilson staked claims along the 'Golden Stairway' that was to become the Dome Mine. At once there was a large influx of prospectors, including Benny Hollinger, Alex Gillies, and Sandy McIntyre, each of whom staked what would become a major producing mine.

The Porcupine field was located within a confined belt of deposits about twelve miles long by two miles wide. The South Porcupine and Timmins townsites were laid out in 1911, and in 1911–12 the T&NO constructed a branch line, first to the former camp and then to the latter. The early discoveries created the three largest companies – Hollinger, Dome, and McIntyre-Porcupine – that would dominate the area's production throughout the years before World War Two. All three mines were regularly expanded through the acquisition of adjoining properties, and by the construction of large ore-processing facilities. After initially relying on rich ores near the surface, the companies found it necessary to sink deeper shafts, eventually mining lower-grade ores at depths exceeding 5,000 feet. The area also contained other properties of note, such as Preston East Dome, Buffalo Ankerite, Paymaster, Broulan Reef, and Pamour. But there was a high mortality rate among the smaller companies, especially as the capital requirements of efficient mining increased.

Meanwhile, the outward spread of Cobalt prospecting was precipitating another set of gold discoveries. While prospectors were turning northwestwards to the new silver fields at Elk Lake and Gowganda and to the gold fields of the Porcupine, others were searching north and east towards the Quebec border. In 1906 several gold claims were staked at Larder Lake, leading to a mini-rush into the area during the winter of 1906–7. This early enthusiasm was followed by disappointments, and the area lay dormant for many years, until the rise in the gold price in 1933–4 led to the establishment of the Kerr Addison Gold Mines Ltd.

More promising mining properties were to be found closer to the T&NO main line. Gold showings in the neighbourhood of Swastika led prospectors to make a thorough search of the land between the railway and Larder Lake. As early as 1906, some claims were staked on the shores of Kirkland Lake in Teck Township. The ores of the area were unfamiliar to most local prospectors, being composed mainly of porphyry, not quartz, so that these rich formations were not immediately recognizable as goldbearing. Major staking, therefore, was delayed, to begin in earnest only in 1911.

The Kirkland Lake deposits extended some three and a half miles along a narrow front. The principal mines were developed along this fracture, and in the first few years of production they yielded very high-grade ore. Lake Shore Mines Ltd, organized by Harry Oakes in 1914, enjoyed a reputation as Canada's greatest gold mine in the 1930s. The Wright-Hargreaves Mines and the Toburn were also major producers. Other mines in Kirkland Lake included the Teck-Hughes, Sylvanite, Kirkland Lake, and Macassa; located very close together, these seven mines formed the core of the town.[16]

As gold-mining became established in north-eastern Ontario, in the north-western part of the province development was proceeding more slowly. Some small production had occurred there in the 1890s, near the Lake of the Woods. By 1900 many small mines had been brought into production, and some of the larger ones, such as the Sultana, the Mikado, and the Blue Eagle, were paying properties for several years. However, it was not until the 1930s and the rise in the price of gold, that the region increased its production. Several new camps – Red Lake, Pickle Lake, and Long Lac – were then established.

In the Red Lake district, gold was originally found by D.B. Dowling of the Geological Survey of Canada in 1894, and the first claims were staked in 1897. But Red Lake was isolated. Production from the area's low-grade ores was not economic, and the claims were abandoned. After it was surveyed in 1924 by E.L. Bruce, a geologist from the Ontario Bureau of Mines, it was publicized again. The Howey brothers, grubstaked by Haileybury capital and McIntyre-Porcupine interests, staked claims on the shores of Red Lake in 1925. Located on a large but low-grade ore body, Howey Gold Mines Ltd was beset by continuing difficulties, both financial and technological, until $35 gold rendered the firm profitable. Other companies appeared in the 1930s with varying degrees of success.

Unlike Porcupine and Kirkland Lake, the Red Lake field was widely dispersed, and several mines necessarily had their own townsites. The Red Lake development inaugurated bush flying, both to prospect the area and to deliver supplies. Northern Aerial Minerals Exploration, a prospecting firm, was established in 1928, and it was to play a critical role in the discovery of ores both at Red Lake and at Pickle Lake, 100 miles from the railway line, where development began only in 1934.

The third area of gold production in north-western Ontario, the Beardmore-Long Lac field, was a by-product of railway-building. The National Transcontinental line passed through Nakina, and the Canadian Northern line ran from Port Arthur to a point thirty miles south of Nakina before turning south-east towards North Bay. A spur joined the two lines near Nakina. The mines were located along the Canadian Northern route between Lake Nipigon and Long Lac. In 1908 geologists first reported gold showings in this area, and traces were reported near Little Long Lac by Ontario Mines Department geologists in 1916 and confirmed by Geological Survey staff the following year. The discoveries at Beardmore occurred in 1925 and 1929. Then in 1931 a major find was made at Little Long Lac and developed in 1934 by Little Long Lac Gold Mines Ltd. The town of Geraldton became a centre for prospecting and mine-supplying.

Because the principal ore bodies at Porcupine and Kirkland Lake were low-grade and deep lying, the camps required heavy investment. Mines reached depths of more than 5,000 feet at Porcupine and 7,000 feet at Kirkland Lake. Because the ores were complex and railway access was expensive, there was a heavy investment in metal-recovery and concentration processes, ranging from early reliance on stamp mills and cyanidization to later emphasis on concentrators that employed selective flotation. It appears that there were significant economies of large-scale production both in mining and in processing, so that large firms were the most efficient producers in both districts.[17]

Policy Issues in Mining

Throughout the period there was continuing tension between the provincial government's desire to promote mining activity, and its occasional determination to regulate the industry in the public interest and to extract revenue from it. Contrary to what a later mythology would assert, the British North America Act had not given the provinces the 'right to control natural resources.' But it had transferred the crown lands to the provinces, thus allowing governments such as Ontario's to fix whatever terms for access to those lands they might wish to devise – sale price, licence fee, royalty, or whatever. Also, the provinces had been given the power to impose 'direct taxes,' so that they could certainly tax the capitals of mining or corporations, or arrange to share in the profits of mining, if they so wished. The success of the CCC at Sudbury notwithstanding, in the later nineteenth century there was a great deal of frustration with the lack of exploration and production in northern Ontario. Cobalt was to change this situation dramatically. After 1905 there was a sudden surge of interest in mineral resources, and up to World War One far more miners' licences were issued, far more claims recorded, and a great many more mining companies promoted.[18] Thus it became important to devise a pattern of orderly exploitation. But little was known about the mineral resources of the area, nor were serious prospectors and promoters as interested as the authorities would have liked. As the historian H.V. Nelles has so vividly pointed out, a fundamental dilemma confronted the provincial government: how could it draw up regulations that would simultaneously encourage prospecting and mining development and protect the broader society's claim to share in the profits?[19]

Promoting development, securing a 'fair share' of mining profits for the provincial Treasury, preventing unscrupulous practices and unproductive speculation, and encouraging the relocation of refining industries within the province were seemingly competing objectives for the provincial authorities, whether elected or appointed. The mining industry, on the other hand, wanted assured title, speedy dispute-resolution, and adequate' incentives, together with government spending on transport and other infrastructure. The balance shifted back and forth during the period, but something approaching stability was achieved once the Cobalt strike and the later discoveries made the public aware of the possibilities in the northland.

Prior to 1890 the rules for exploration and development[20] on crown lands were liberal – or lax – in the extreme. Earlier attempts to restrict access or to impose provincial royalties and taxes were rescinded in the General Mining Act of 1869. Under this measure any licensed prospector could explore for mineral-bearing ores and, after staking, register his claim with the Department of crown lands in Toronto. Mining locations of 80, 160, or 320 acres could be bought for $1 per acre, for which the buyer obtained title to all mineral rights. There were no requirements of prior discovery of valuable minerals nor of development into a working mine, before the issuance of an ownership-patent. Nor were royalties payable. In fact, the province surrendered all subsequent rights to the resource base, alienating it absolutely – in an environment where neither personal nor corporation incomes were taxed at all.

By the late 1880s, following the developments at Sudbury, reform was clearly needed. Nor had the lax arrangements done much to stimulate development elsewhere in the north. Hence the Ontario government appointed a Royal Commission on Mineral Resources in 1888. Reporting in 1890, the commission brought the potential for industry-government conflict to a head. Taking a pro-industry stance, the commissioners insisted that the government should aid and support the industry, and they advocated only minimal changes in the existing act, although they did suggest that there might be a decrease in the minimum size of claim, proof of the presence of valuable minerals as a condition of staking, and development work before a patent was issued. Such rules would curb the worst speculative excesses. They also asked for a school of mines that could provide training for miners and prospectors, and a provincial bureau of mines that would conduct research and disseminate information about the resource base and mining technique. And they wanted the province to spend more on transportation, especially on railways, with an eye to mining development. Finally, they acknowledged that it was desirable to increase the smelting and refining of metals within Ontario – a concession to the authorities' interest in manufacturing.[21]

Although the commission's report was avowedly pro-industry, the subsequent mining legislation departed significantly from the recommendations. In 1891 a new mining act proposed to extract royalties from mines producing silver, nickel-copper, iron, and other minerals – but only on lands patented after 1891. In 1894 cries from industry led the government to soften the offending clauses. Indeed, in the act of 1900 the government gave up all pretence of collecting royalties and rescinded all remaining reservations of minerals on lands that had passed into private ownership. On the other hand, the government did act to reduce the minimum size of claim, replace the $1 price by a graded price, introduce a system of renewable leases, and require development work before patents would be issued. The Mining Act of 1892 further consolidated these changes.[22]

The provincial authorities also acted to provide more educational and informational assistance to mining. Almost at once the Ontario Bureau of Mines, which was charged with responsibility for geological surveying, education and training, and general regulation and inspection of mines, was established. The bureau opened regional mining offices at Rat Portage (Kenora) in 1897 and at Sudbury in 1900; the first provincial assay office was established in Belleville in 1898. These local offices were meant to help prospectors and miners assess the mineral content of ore samples and to provide technical and geological advice. The bureau also sponsored the formation of the Kingston Mining School, and it arranged for the offering of courses at the School of Practical Science in Toronto, and at summer schools in Copper Cliff, Sudbury, and Rat Portage. After 1903 a provincial geologist was appointed to direct the bureau's research activities, which were always more practical and less scientific than the comparable survey work that the dominion's Geological Survey had long been undertaking. Finally, the bureau published an annual report that outlined all surveys, mining activity, and changes in regulations.[23]

The act of 1897 introduced an important refinement in the form of the requirement of discovery.'[24] An applicant for a mining location or claim was required to show proof that he had discovered a 'valuable mineral' on the property before the claim could be registered. This was to become a crucial feature of the new arrangments, and it certainly stimulated the prospectors, especially after the Cobalt strike, when the policy was strictly enforced.

The Cobalt profits reopened the question of the province's share in the loot from crown lands. Moreover, uncontrolled staking engendered disputes over claims, and caused people to wonder whether there was no more appropriate way for settling disputes and administering regulations. The provincial government began to close lands to staking while it pondered alternatives. Only in April 1904 was this 'freeze' lifted. The next step was to hold a conference with the industry, and the resultant Mining Convention duly assembled at Toronto in 1905. The miners said they wanted a uniform plan of administration, which was subsequently provided under the Mining Act of 1906.[25]

The new act, a major turning point, capitalized on the growing public and professional interest in northern mineral prospects. It tightened up and rearranged the mining regulations, appointed a commissioner to settle disputes, continued miners' licences, and abandoned leaseholds, while maintaining the arrangements under which 'discovery' was a precondition for a claim, and development, for a patent of ownership.[26] Furthermore, the Department of Crown Lands became the Department of Lands, Forests and Mines, with a separate deputy minister for the Mines Division, which would become a separate department in 1918. There was, in addition, further decentralization of administration, speeding the process of claim-registration by relying on local officials who knew their areas, and providing a local means for resolving disputes. The act therefore represented a neat compromise, meeting some of the industry's most pressing concerns with respect to uniformity and speed, while allowing the government to extract some concessions. Thus the basic conditions for regulating the development of the mining sector were in place by 1906, even though the 'discovery' provision would be removed in 1922. Furthermore, in 1907 Queen's Park imposed a mining profit tax.[27]

T.W. Gibson has described the above evolution as an experimental process, based on trial and error;[28] it might also be called an instance of the 'progress without planning' mentioned in chapter 1, above. The government experimented frequently, changing the rules in the hope of increasing the attractiveness of prospecting activity in the north. But the industry's growth was in the end determined by factors exogenous to government mining policy, which served primarly as an impartial and probably relatively efficient allocative and regulatory mechanism once the industry had begun to appreciate the potential riches of the north. Thus, notwith-standing the industry's self-image as a bastion of rugged individualism and private enterprise, mining in northern Ontario proved to be a joint venture linking private enterprise with public policy.[29]

The British North America Act clearly assigned to the province 'all lands, mines, minerals, and royalties due' (clause 109).[30] Provinces could also impose direct taxes (clause 92), a power that Ontario would use, in due course, to tax mining profits.[31] The early experiments with respect to mining land and mining royalties have been described above. Part of the problem in finding a rational base for mine taxation was the belief that mining was a high-risk industry, where risk-bearing justified the possi-bility of high private pay-offs. Another difficulty, prior to 1900, was the province's weak bargaining position: no one was much interested in northern minerals, except around Sudbury. But the Cobalt strikes changed the picture, providing the province with an opportunity to extract more revenue from mining. The result was the tax on mining profits, which was introduced in the Supplementary Revenue Act of 1907. An acreage tax, which had been introduced in 1868 but had produced little revenue, was also continued. Intended as much to speed the development of mining concessions or claims as to produce revenue, it was levied at so low a rate – 2 cents per acre from 1868 to 1877 and in and after 1907 and 1 cent per acre from 1877 to 1907 – that it had no noticeable effect under either heading.

Since the acreage tax was of little account, the province placed major emphasis on the new profits tax, which was levied at a flat rate of 3 per cent on mine profits in excess of $10,000.[32] It would hit both older mines, such as the Sudbury complex, and the newer and prosperous Cobalt properties. Although at first the industry complained that the tax would discourage investment, it later accepted the impost, in the face of persuasive government arguments that the tax was but a small price to pay for the industry's dependence on public investment in railway construction. This was, in fact, a somewhat spurious argument, in that before World War One the T&NO not merely ran a profit and serviced all its own debt out of its revenues, but also attracted a large dominion construction grant. But perhaps the mining industry found it persuasive.

In 1917 there was a substantial change. Following the recommendations of the Royal Ontario Nickel Commission, the flat rate was replaced by a graduated tax on the profits of the nickel and nickel-copper mines, which had been inflated by wartime circumstances. The new rates were 5 per cent on the first $5 million of profits, rising by one percentage point for each additional $5 million. At the same time, the commission having recom-mended a significant rise in the rate of acreage tax, that rate went up to 5 cents per acre – still a much lower rate than in British Columbia.[33] In 1924 the higher rates of 1917 were extended to all mines, and in 1930 the maximum rate was reduced from 7 per cent to 6 per cent on all profits exceeding $5 million.[34]

Table 4.2 summarizes provincial mining revenues from 1891 through 1940. There was a steady flow of revenues from land sales and leases, while revenues from prospecting activity – miners' licences, fees for recording claims – increased quickly after the Cobalt strikes and were at high levels in the late 1920s and during the 1930s. Royalties came from the province's sale of mining rights to the beds of Cobalt and Kerr lakes. The acreage tax was a consistent source of revenue but was dwarfed by the proceeds of the mining profits tax. The sale of provincial goods and services – laboratory, sample, and assay fees; sales of record books, blueprints, and maps – was a minor source of revenue, except in the heyday of the Cobalt boom and during the period of increased exploration activity in the late 1920s and the 1930s. The mining industry found that it could live with the mining profits tax, whose rates were certainly never burdensome. Even so, provincial revenues from mining were small, relative to those from timber dues and bonuses, until the late 1930s.[35] Nor is there any reason to suppose that the provincial exchequer managed to capture all the sums that *logically* were due to it – the full payment that the mining industry could have paid while still earning sufficient profit to attract and hold capital in the industry.

One way to ensure that mining would generate 'downstream' activity in manufacturing would be to impose a manufacturing condition, under which the provincial authorities would require that natural resource assets would be processed and manufactured locally, before export, at least to some extent. The provincial authorities could impose any such 'condition' only on the natural resource outputs from crown lands, as a condition for access to these lands; it could not be applied on privately owned lands. But as the mining areas of northern Ontario were all or almost all crown lands, the idea looked attractive. Furthermore, if the dominion, which could tax and regulate external trade, were willing to impose an export duty on unprocessed natural products, the powers of the national government could be applied to the same end.

During the 1890s the province successfully applied the 'manufacturing condition' first to pine timber in 1898 and then to spruce pulpwood in 1900. Another target was the CCC's nickel operations, which were exporting nickel-copper matte to the Orford works in New Jersey. Not only did Orford have the only efficient process for further refining the matte, but the United States levied a 10 per cent tariff on refined nickel and copper. The Ontario government sought a solution in two ways: first, by trying to interest the owners of alternative processes in the Ontario prospects;

second, by using export duties and bounties to 'persuade' Orford to move its operations to Ontario. Neither policy was effective.

Orford's attitude was doubly irritating because, when CCC was incorporated in 1886, Samuel J. Ritchie promised to locate its refining operations in Canada.[36] His company appears to have tried, during the late 1880s and early 1890s, to obtain a refining process of its own. But its reliance on the Orford process was cemented by the CCC-Orford merger of 1902, which created INCO.

Meanwhile, expressing an increasingly widespread belief that local manufacture and further processing were desirable, in 1890 the Royal Commission on Mineral Resources addressed the question, studying the feasibility of local refining and even of manufacturing nickel-steel – at a time when Ontario produced no steel of any kind.[37] The most enlightened proponents of 'further processing' saw that government might provide financial aid or legislative support as a short-term expedient, analogous to infant-industry protection, so as to get manufacturing industries on a firm footing. Thus as early as 1891 the Ontario government tried to get the imperial authorities to participate in a joint venture that would build a nickel refinery and produce nickel-steel. The United Kingdom was expected to like the idea of assured 'empire supply'; the scheme appealed to Ontario because the local manufactures would have an assured empire market. After a brief review, however, the British admiralty decided that nickel supplies were not a problem, and the proposition lapsed.[38]

Finding that the CCC was still unco-operative and the United States government more protectionist than ever, Ontario pressed for a dominion export tax on nickel and copper mattes, analogous to the tax that had been imposed on logs and pulpwood in 1897. Parliament passed the measure, but as it was never proclaimed, the new law was without effect.[39] Meanwhile, Archibald Blue, the director of the Ontario Bureau of Mines, urged the province to re-open negotiations with London and to press Ottawa for the proclamation of its own new measure. He also wanted Queen's Park to incorporate a new clause into all future land grants, requiring local refining of nickel and copper ores. In November 1899 the province approved these recommendations but did nothing.[40] Again, the province changed tack, opting in the 1900 amendment to the Mines Act for a rebate: there was to be a licence fee of $60 per ton for nickel matte and $50 per ton for copper matte, but these fees would be rebated if the ores were refined in Ontario. Threatened with disallowance by Ottawa, this amendment also was never proclaimed.[41]

In the end both provincial and federal governments backed down in the face of vociferous opposition from the mining industry, especially from CCC, which threatened to withdraw from Sudbury and to move its mining operations to New Caledonia. Provincial and dominion bluff withered in the face of CCC's determined opposition. Not only did Sudbury matte flow south to New Jersey; by 1907 some 70 per cent of the Cobalt silver ores were directed south of the border as well.

In 1907 the provincial authorities decided to try again, but this time with a carrot instead of a stick. Under the Metal Refining Bounty Act they paid a bounty on the refining of nickel, copper, cobalt, and arsenic.[42] The act did not stimulate a change in INCO's practices, because the bounties were too small. But it did promote the establishment of five silver refineries, most of the bounty payments under the act being for the refined cobalt and nickel content of silver ores. In 1917 the act was allowed to lapse.

Ottawa was as exercised by the 'nickel question' as Queen's Park. In 1910 the Standing Committee on Mines and Minerals of the House of Commons studied it. The hearings featured testimony from both sides, including impassioned statements from INCO executives, who claimed that if there were an efficient alternative to the Orford process that could be worked profitably in Ontario they would have adopted it, but that any attempt at 'forced' relocation would precipitate the closure of their Ontario works.[43] The House took no action on the committee's report.

The wartime emergency finally forced a resolution of the lingering dispute. The province's concern for local refining was submerged in widespread public fears that nickel, a strategic war material, was being refined under foreign control. Certainly until the United States entered the war on the allied side late in 1917 there was no legal obstacle that could prevent INCO from selling nickel to the Germans; the only effective obstacle was the British blockade. Public pressure on INCO steadily mounted. In 1915 the Ontario authorities established a Royal Nickel Commission, which reported in 1917 that 'there is nothing to prevent the Hybinette [electrolytic] process being operated as cheaply and efficiently in Ontario as elsewhere.'[44] This was, indeed, the proces that had been proposed in connection with Britain's wartime effort to develop its own mine at Sudbury; the refinery, however, would have been in Norway. By the time the commission reported, INCO had already announced its decision to build a new refinery at Port Colborne. This decision coincided with the revelation that on two occasions during 1916, INCO had shipped nickel from New Jersey to Germany. But the decision also reflected economic factors: eventually the new refinery would replace the old heat-intensive, coal-using Orford process with an electrolytic process that would use cheap Niagara power.

After INCO's Port Colborne refinery had opened in 1918, the controversy over the location of refining ceased to exercise Ontarians. The 'manufacturing condition' passed from public view. But most of INCO's refined nickel was still exported, to be processed still further in foreign lands.

The Economic Impact of Mining

What was the economic impact of the developments that have been described above? Only a partial answer is possible. There is an analytical framework for examining the question, but for the years before 1940 data are few, misleading, or altogether absent. Some conjecture, therefore, cannot be avoided. Nor can the 'social profitability' of Ontario mining be measured as many economists would like – through an estimate of the 'economic rents' that it generated. These rents are defined as 'surplus revenue,' that is to say total receipts minus the costs of purchased inputs and minus the amounts that the capital and labour in the mining industry could have earned if applied elsewhere. Such rents would be approximated by total gross profits in mining, net of depreciation and depletion charges, losses in the industry, and appropriate charges for side-effects such as environmental degradation, sickness, and death attributable to the industry. Sad to say, no one has estimated these rents, and it does not appear feasible to do so.

A sector's economic impact may be categorized as follows.[45] *Direct impacts* are described by data on value of production, employment, capital expenditures, exports, and imports. These data give an impression of the sector's direct contribution, in relation to the contributions of other sectors. Some of these data, particularly employment and value of production, are available for much of the period. *Indirect and induced impacts* are produced in so far as investment, employment, and income are generated elsewhere in the provincial economy by the stimulus that the mining industry provides, either as a supplier of inputs for other industries or as a purchaser of their outputs. Stimuli to produce or invest in input-supplying industries are called backward linkages, and the growth of processing and final-product industries using minerals are called forward linkages. Stimuli may 'leak' into other regional economies, whether in Canada or abroad.

One can also concentrate on the localized impacts of mining, as is done to some extent in chapter 10, below. This sort of focus is a natural one because local impacts are likely to be important, since new mines are often located far from established centres of economic activity. The exploration and development of a mine are associated with major investments in transportation, mine site development, power supply, construction of ore-processing facilities such as smelters, and the development of townsites. Once the mine is in operation, it stimulates supporting services in its community, and there is a general and reasonable presumption that employment in such a community is either directly or indirectly dependent on the local mine or mines.[46] Cobalt, Timmins, and Sudbury are good examples. Mining may also stimulate local production, as of agricultural products and construction timber in the clay belt of northern Ontario.

Moreover, when mines close, as happened at Cobalt during the 1920s and 1930s, the entire regional economy is likely to be dislocated.

The direct effects of mining can be measured by data on the value of production, employment, and wages and salaries. The total value of production for gold, nickel, and copper is found in table 4.1, while table 4.3 contains employment, wages, and salaries data for gold and nickel-copper. All three series reveal the very rapid growth of gold after 1920, with a significant increase in the late 1930s, and of nickel-copper after 1932 as the world began to rearm. The value of silver production declined abruptly with the exhaustion of the Cobalt deposits, and as an employer silver-mining mattered little after World War One. Gold, nickel, and copper were the three major metal-producing industries in Ontario, and, indeed, Ontario produced more that 50 per cent of Canada's metallic-minerals output in 1940. None the less, as table 10.5 reveals, the total output of Ontario mines in 1940 was only 58 per cent of the 1941 manufacturing output of the 'motor cities,' Oshawa and Windsor, and only 19.9 per cent of manufacturing output in the province's four large cities – Toronto, Hamilton, London, and Ottawa. Mining was certainly important. But it was not predominant.

Data on employment and on provincial revenue point in the same direction. It was shown in chapter 2 and in table 2.2 that the employment in mining and quarrying occupations rose from 200 in 1871 to 4,000 in 1901 and to 24,000 in 1941, or from 0.1 per cent of the work force at the first date to 1.6 per cent at the last. This simple measure would suggest that mining cannot have been very important in the whole provincial economy, even after the great discoveries and developments of the twentieth century. Study of the *Public Accounts*, furthermore, suggests that mining never made much of a contribution to provincial government revenue. As chapter 19 reveals, the twentieth-century expansion of government and the beginnings of the provincial welfare state were financed in other ways. If one wants to make the mining industry look especially important, therefore, one must focus on the indirect and induced impacts. Nevertheless, no one would want to deny that the industry grew rapidly, or that in absolute terms it became very important indeed.

Important though the indirect effects would have been, many of the linkages must be left to conjecture. Innis believed that the mining industry would reduce Ontario's dependence on the export of staple commodities, by contributing to a highly integrated, advanced industrial economy.[47] With demand increases – for instance, with the increase in the price of gold in 1931–4, or the role of nickel-steel in rearmament – the production of metals would expand, requiring corresponding increase in capital expenditure for mining and ore-processing, for power and transportation, all of which would have far-reaching consequences for linked secondary industries.[48] Ironically, if Innis were right, a lower-grade ore might be 'better,' because it would require a larger-scale, capital-intensive production process, with greater potential for stimulating the outputs of linked industries. Once ore is recovered from the ground, the sequence of operations through which forward linkages occur would lead from smelting to refining and fabricating and manufacturing of the refined metal into producers' and consumers' goods. In this scheme one is apparently to imagine Ontario in the 1930s becoming the armaments centre not only of the western world but of central Europe as well. Also, presumably, the gold-jewellery industry would move from Italy and New York to Toronto – followed, no doubt, by the diamond-cutting and enamel industries. Naturally enough, things did not happen that way: there were other factors that determined the locations of the metal-consuming industries. In 1940, as in 1914, Ontario manufacturing depended chiefly on imported ores, fuels, and metals – most obviously, on American iron ore, coal, and petroleum.

Weak though these forward linkages proved to be, backward linkages were weaker still. By 1940 most mining properties in northern Ontario had incurred comparatively heavy capital expenditures on the preparation of mining sites, the sinking of shafts, the installing of hoists and pumps, and the constructing of concentrators, and, in some instances, smelters. Table 4.3 presents data on process supplies, fuel, and electricity purchases by the gold – and copper-mining industries for 1937 and 1940. These data crudely approximate a portion of the backward linkages. They indicate that in gold-mining such purchases were roughly 60 per cent of the wage bill, while in nickel-copper they were roughly equal. Similar data for non-ferrous smelting and refining activity, the next stage along in the processing sequence and thus an example of forward linkage, are presented in table 4.4 Although some smelting and refining activity was located in southern Ontario, other major smelters were located in the north, and much of their wage and other input payments were made in that part of the province.

Most studies of the modern mining industry suggest that the indirect and induced effects of mining are on balance about the same as for manufacturing – a little higher for income-generation but, because mining is capital-intensive, a little lower for employment. Also, there is no modern evidence to suggest that mining linkages are particularly strong.[49] On the other hand, there is a widespread perception that mining produces many 'leakages,' because ore and concentrate are so often exported well before end products have been made, because much mining machinery and equipment are imported, and because foreign ownership drains profits into foreign hands. These attributes may well be consistent with economic efficiency but at the same time stand in the way of maximizing income and employment in Ontario, as one can see from the concern about the 'manufacturing condition.' Yet there may be great difficulties in pulling the 'forward-linked activities' into Canada, or into Ontario. Among the problems are market size, industrial organization, capital availability, trade and tariff arrangements. In the early 1970s, for instance, Canada still exported some 70 per cent of its mineral production, most of it in crude form, while importing substantial amounts of fabricated metal products.

Admittedly, it is difficult to obtain a clear picture of mining's indirect and induced effects. Geographers often credit much of Toronto's development to the mining industry, tracing the number of financial businesses, mining companies, and supplier firms that were based there. It is also clear that beginning in the 1890s Toronto was a focus for speculative trading in mining stocks, not only by Ontarians and other Canadians but by the British and Americans as well. However, as later chapters will show, many additional forces were tending to produce an efflorescence of financial and service activities in the provincial capital, especially after 1900. The same is true of areas such as construction and the building of capital equipment.

In 1932 the United States Bureau of Mines reported that for every person directly employed in the mining industry in the United States, some 12.5 persons were indirectly employed in providing supplies, equipment, and transport to the industry.[50] If true for Ontario, this would represent an extremely high employment multiplier; however, because it greatly exceeds the employment multipliers that were estimated for the 1970s it should probably be discounted. Every industry, after all, has an interest in overestimating its indirect effects, thereby exaggerating its 'significance' – and its claims to special treatment. The mining industry was a comparative late-comer to the Ontario scene, and long before it became important, a complicated economy had become established and had embarked upon the process of industrial and commercial development.

On the other hand, evidence of strong local employment effects, especially in adjacent towns, is incontrovertible.[51] Even so, northern Ontario has continued to be highly dependent on primary resource extraction and processing, and much of the attendant derived employment, whether in manufacturing or in the service industries and occupations, has always been in southern Ontario and in the United States.

If the evidence on the strength of linkages is mixed, what about the extent to which their impact within Ontario was diminished by leakages? The greater the proportion of input needs represented by imports, and the greater the proportion of profits remitted abroad, for example, the smaller are the induced local effects. There is good historical evidence, both anecdotal and summary, that foreign investment and imported machinery were important in mining. From early in the period the benefits of American investment, technology, and mining expertise were acknowledged, and Americans played a major role in the first wave of mining devleopment,[52] while at Sudbury British capital was present in the second wave.

During the late nineteenth and early twentieth centuries there was rapid technological change in mining – in deep-mining techniques (first used in Ontario at Silver Islet), in new sources and means of transmitting power (from steam to compressed air to electricity), in drilling and blasting operations (introduction of the diamond drill, machine drilling, and dynamite), in separating and concentrating ore (from stamp mills to roller and ball mills, cyanide processes, and flotation). American engineering and capital provided much of the new technology for Ontario, which was then adapted to local conditions by the mine operators. The rapid diffusion of new technologies was facilitated also by the staffs and the reports of the Geological Survey of Canada and the Ontario Bureau of Mines, and by mining-industry periodicals such as the *Canadian Mining Review*, which began publication in 1883. The diffusion of new technologies contributed greatly to the profitability of mining in Ontario.[53]

As for investment, Americans controlled the nickel-copper industry of Sudbury from its inception, nor was that control significantly lessened when INCO became a Canadian corporation in 1926. The first three successful Cobalt mines – Nipissing, Buffalo, and McKinley-Darragh – were American owned; by 1910 five of the fifteen largest remunerative mines were American, accounting for nearly half of the dividends paid during 1904–10.[54] But the other ten were Canadian and provided the basis for several Canadian mining fortunes, some of which, such as M.J. O'Brien's and the Timmins brothers', permitted Canadians to be principal players in the Porcupine and Kirkland Lake gold fields, wherein US investment was less significant, and which in the 1930s produced more than half of all Ontario's mining output. Cobalt, then, was important both for the emergence of Canadian mining capital and as an example of the leakage that foreign ownership can produce. Later, US capital acquired control of several major gold mines. Even so, the majority of gold and silver shares were in Canadian ownership, while American and British capital continued to dominate the nickel-copper industry before 1940.[55]

In many cases American control led to imports of mining machinery and equipment and frequently also to the establishment of American branch plants in Ontario. This was true, for instance, in the manufacture of both drilling and milling machinery.[56] Since US firms were leaders in the design and manufacture of mining equipment, this activity probably was conducive to efficiency, and of course the branch plants helped convert some leakages into linkages.

Conclusion

Metal-mining on the Canadian Shield played an important role in the opening of Ontario's northern frontier and created much income and wealth within the province. When the members of the Royal Ontario Mining Commission concluded in 1944 that 'the mining industry in Ontario [held] a position of outstanding importance in the economic life of the province,'[57] they may have exaggerated somewhat. Certainly if size, employment, or value of output is the measure, there were larger industries and more important activities. But mining certainly mattered.

Even now, there is much about Ontario mining that remains unknown or obscure. There is still no full-length economic history of the industry. The diffusion and local adaptation of new technologies and the contribution of such local innovations to mine productivity and profitability are as yet only incompletely and imperfectly understood.[58] The study of labour organization and labour relations has just begun.[59] Little is known about occupational health and safety – an important topic, because mining is inherently dangerous and because Ontario's hard-rock mining can cause silicosis, a disease that enabled its victims to claim compensation under the Workmen's Compensation Act only in 1926, twelve years after the act was passed.[60] Nor are there many studies of mining's environmental effects, even though Sudbury's 'moonscape' had been noticed as early as 1890.[61] Thus there is need for more research, and the economic history of Ontario mining is neither a closed book nor a complete one.

5 The North and the North-West: Forestry and Agriculture

PETER W. SINCLAIR, Wilfrid Laurier University

In northern Ontario the rocky Canadian Shield is the predominant geographical feature, the main exception being the lowland of Palaeozoic rocks south and west of Hudson Bay and James Bay. The drainage pattern of the region is generally northward towards James Bay, the major exceptions being the Ottawa Valley and the area of Ontario west of Thunder Bay. Except for the James Bay lowlands, northern Ontario is forested, changing from mixed forest in the south and Ottawa Valley to primarily coniferous forest and eventually, in the north, to tundra.

The development of northern Ontario has been based on the exploitation of its natural resources – minerals, forest products, and agriculture. For all these industries the key element in development has been the transportation system. The northward-flowing tendency of the rivers impeded the opening up of the region, while railway-building, as the last chapter revealed, was the dominant force in stimulating development.

Logs, Lumber, Pulp, and Paper

Forestry had been an important industry in Ontario since the beginning of the nineteenth century, and by the time of Confederation almost 12,000 square miles of pine timber were under licence in Ontario, including virtually all the Ottawa Valley, the Trent River system, and the southern half of the Georgian Bay watershed. The land had not been alienated, but rights to cut timber for specified periods had been sold. After Confederation the province gained control of the crown lands, and undertook to develop its remaining forest reserves.[1] As before, the would-be loggers would be allowed to buy only cutting rights, not the land itself; if the surface was alienated for agricultural purposes, the crown reserved the pine timber for itself, although such arrangements proved almost impossible to enforce.

After 1870, as will be shown more fully in chapter 7, the centre of gravity of the Ontario forest products industry continually shifted to the west and north. This movement was caused by the gradual exhaustion of timber stocks in the more accessible regions,[2] and by the growing importance of the American market, which gradually eclipsed the British in importance. Thus more easterly areas tended to export first to Europe and then to the United States, while the areas developed after 1880 were always oriented primarily towards New York, Chicago, and the Canadian west.

The two major areas developed after Confederation were the Huron-Ottawa tract, which extended from the Ottawa River to northern Georgian Bay and along the north shore of Lake Huron, and the area west and north of Lake Superior running from Thunder Bay to Rainy River and Kenora. The development of the Huron-Ottawa tract began in the early 1870s when the provincial government sold almost 6,000 square miles of timber berths, that is to say cutting rights, on the north shore of Georgian Bay and the shore of Lake Huron between Georgian Bay and the Soo, and subsequently sold almost 3,000 square miles.[3] The pattern of sales is outlined in appendix A.

Logging first began on the northern shore of Georgian Bay, then moved up to Lake Nipissing via the French River, and there was also considerable activity on Manitoulin Island, centred at Little Current. Although the first export-oriented mills were established on the north shore of Lake Huron in the 1860s, most such mills were not constructed until the 1880s, because in the continental recession of the mid-1870s the markets were not receptive. By the late 1880s the towns on the north shore of Lake Huron – Spragge, Algoma Mills, Blind River, and Thessalon – were also coming into prominence. The mills in this region were generally situated near the mouths of rivers for ease of transportation, but the completion of the CPR through northern Ontario in 1885 made it possible for mills to be built near river headwaters, although such mills were not long-lived, apparently becaue they more rapidly depleted local timber.

The north-western portion of the province had a brief flurry of lumbering activity in the 1880s, when the CPR was built from Thunder Bay to Winnipeg, and several mills were set up in Rat Portage (later Kenora). The major increase in logging, however, occurred after 1900 and was spurred by the completion of the Canadian Northern line along Rainy River in 1901 as well as by the rapid settlement of the Canadian prairies after the turn of the century. American interests, particularly Shevlin-Clarke and Backus-Brooke, both from Minnesota, had opened large saw-mills in Fort Frances by 1905. Despite American ownership, these mills found their main markets in the Canadian west, where they faced strong competition, particularly from US timber.

In the 1890s, as noted in the last chapter, much public concern was expressed about the further processing of natural resource products. Would logs be exported unprocessed, or first sawn into lumber within Ontario?[4] This issue was closely related to changes in US tariff policy. With the 1866 abrogation of the Reciprocity Treaty, which had provided free entry to the American market, the United States had imposed a 20 per cent tariff, but saw logs were put on the free list in 1870. In the 1880s there was a specific duty of $2 per thousand board feet, and the dominion government imposed a $1 per thousand board feet export duty on pine saw logs, which was raised to $2 in 1886 and to $3 in 1888. This export duty, historians have long believed, 'induced various Michigan firms to begin sawing in Canada.'[5] In 1890 Canada abolished the export duty, in return for a reduction in the US duty to $1 per thousand board feet. Finally, in 1894 the Americans removed their duty altogether. The move to virtual free trade in lumber, however, led to a noticeable increase in the southward towing of unprocessed Ontario logs to the United States.[6]

In 1897, the US Congress passed the Dingley Tariff, which restored the $2 tariff on imports of sawn lumber. This step was a severe check to the Ontario industry. Since the Dingley Tariff contained a provision for additional duties if Canada imposed export duties on unprocessed logs, the dominion was unwilling to restore its export duty. Instead, the Ontario government, under pressure from lumbermen, imposed the 'manufacturing condition': after 30 April 1898 all saw logs cut on crown land would have to be sawn into lumber within Canada. Despite various court challenges and political pressures, the law was maintained.[7]

Although it is difficult to determine the relative effects of the manufacturing condition, the considerable building boom that affected most regions of Canada in the early twentieth century, and the revival of American demand, the first decade of the new century was one of expansion and prosperity for the Ontario lumber industry. Between 1900 and 1910 the number of establishments increased from 847 to 1,079, while the payrolls grew from $25.6 million to $36.5 million.[8] Production peaked at about 1.8 million board feet in 1911.[9] Despite this decade of expansion, the Ontario industry faced increasing structural problems, including the decline in pine stands, the rapid contraction of the British market, where construction was not buoyant after 1900 and where Russian and Scandinavian competition was intense; the rise in production costs was also a problem. Thus after World War One the provincial industry was stagnant, production never passing 1 million board feet after 1920.[10] In spite of rapidly growing lumber markets and the removal of American duties in 1913, Ontario faced strong competition not only from American suppliers but also from British Columbia.

In the Great Depression of the early 1930s, the entire North American building industry suffered a catastrophic decline, with Canada's lumber production falling to less than half of its pre-war maximum. The fortunes of the Ontario industry mirrored that of the rest of the country. There was some improvement after the 1932 trough, but by 1940 the Ontario industry had still not regained its vitality.[11]

Fortunately for the economy of northern Ontario, the forest products industry did not decline after World War One. Although lumbering was not doing well, the pulp and paper industry, which used spruce rather than the pine on which the lumbermen depended, was expanding very rapidly indeed. The paper industry in Ontario was well established by the time of Confederation, but this early industry was based on the use of rags and straw. The National Policy protective tariffs, introduced in 1879, also stimulated production at Cornwall.[12] But the real growth of the industry came only with the switch from rags to wood pulp as the basic raw material. Output increased rapidly after 1880, and by the end of the decade the chemical sulphite process was introduced to supplement the old mechanical process of converting wood into pulp, although ground-wood pulp was still predominant as late as 1913. The increased production of pulp and paper thus created a market for the spruce and balsam trees that the lumbermen had largely ignored.[13]

Initially, mills were built in southern Ontario, particularly on the Niagara Pensinsula, to be close to markets. Soon the growing importance of pulp wood supplies pulled the industry into the Canadian Shield, first around Kingston and then in the Ottawa Valley. For the location of the industry, water mattered as much as wood; rivers provided a cheap means of moving logs to the mill, an easy waste disposal system, the necessary fluids for the processing, and the potential for hydroelectric power. With the construction of railways, favoured sites were often found where rivers crossed the lines, permitting easy transport of the product.

The major demand factor influencing the Canadian pulp and paper industry was the urban market for newsprint in the United States. The American demand expanded from 1890 to the late 1920s. It was heavily concentrated in the urban markets – Illinois, Michigan, New York, Massachusetts, and Pennsylvania. Although the United States has large supplies of potential pulpwood, the coniferous forests of eastern Canada were close to the markets and generally could produce pulp and paper more cheaply than US mills. As a result, pulp and paper became an export-oriented industry highly dependent on US demand.[14]

As with timber, so with pulpwood: the province did not sell the crown land, but rather sold the rights to cut on each timber limit for a specified period. Except in so far as a hydroelectric plant might form part of a development 'package,' rights to both water power and mining were reserved by the Crown, as was the right to transfer timber limits for settlement. Lumber mills often require only a modest capital investment, but if pulp and paper mills are to be economical they must be large and expensive; such installations naturally have to be treated as long-term investments. To induce a company to make such investments, one had to guarantee secure, long-term access to sufficient pulpwood stocks; no one would accept the system of annual permits to cut that was applied in lumbering. As a result, despite the formal use of tenders, pulp limit agreements were usually negotiated between the provincial government and potential or existing investors. In return for the pulp limits, firms were required to build plants of specified size and to employ minimum work forces. One example is the agreement with the Spanish River Pulp and Paper Company that was signed in September 1899.[15] Under this agreement the firm, which was owned by Marshall J. Dodge of New York City and a number of Ontario businessmen, received the right for twenty-one years to cut named trees sufficient to 'enable the company to work the said pulp and paper mills to their full capacities.' In return the company agreed to pay 20 cents per cord for spruce and 10 cents per cord for other logs, and to erect a mill that would cost no less than $500,000. The annual output would have to be at least 20,000 tons; the average work-force was to be at least 250. Similar conditions were imposed in later agreements, which often also included requirements to buy raw materials within the province. Thus the provincial government tried to use its control of natural resources not only to gain revenues but also to shape the development process and to increase the linkages from natural resource development while reducing the leakages.

In Ontario, as elsewhere in Canada, there was a natural concern that the pulp logs should be converted in the dominion, rather than exported in their raw form. Hence the question of a 'manufacturing condition' for pulpwood. After 1883 the United States charged a paper duty that amounted to 15 per cent ad valorem, while admitting pulp logs free. In 1897 the Dingley Tariff made the duty a specific one and provided for retaliatory levies if Canada were to impose an export duty. After its success with the manufacturing condition on saw logs, and because the policy would circumvent the Dingley Tariff, in 1900 the Ontario government prohibited the export of unmanufactured spruce logs cut from crown land. The prohibition was confirmed in 1902.[16] However, this prohibition did not apply to the cut from private land, so that in 1913 about one-third of the province's pulpwood cut was still being exported.

The imposition of the 'manufacturing condition' was followed by a flurry of mill-planning, but the growth of the industry was initially rather erratic. The first construction was along the north shore of Lake Huron, first at Sault Ste Marie as part of the Clergue industrial complex that is treated in later chapters, and then at Sturgeon Falls and Espanola. By 1905 the Soo mill was closed, and limits at Nipigon, Montreal River, and Keewatin were not developed until after the war, having waited for better markets and financing.[17]

After the war Ontario's pulp industry underwent a rapid expansion. The industry shifted from Lake Huron towards the north-west and into the Clay Belt. Thus Thunder Bay became a major pulp and paper centre, having four mills by 1924, and mills were erected in Nipigon, Kenora, and Dryden. In the Clay Belt, Abitibi Pulp and Power Company erected a large mill at Iroquois Falls, laying the foundation for what was to be a large Canadian-owned firm. Additional mills were erected at Smooth Rock Falls on the CNR and at Haileybury on the Timiskaming and Northern Ontario Railway line (the T&NO). Finally, the Spruce Falls Power and Paper Company was established at Kapuskasing, on the CNR, as the exclusive supplier for the *New York Times*, which owned 49 per cent of the shares in the firm.

The expansion after 1913 closely followed American removal of all duties on newsprint, and considerable emphasis has been given to this factor. More important, however, were the rapid increase in US demand as the newspaper industry expanded, and the increasing cost-advantage of the Canadian producers over their American rivals. Canadian newsprint displaced most of the American product, so that the Canadian industry became almost totally dependent on the American market.[18]

Information on pulp and pulpwood production is not provided in the dominion census or in provincial reports before 1890. In that year the census reported that Ontario's pulpwood production was 114,914 cords. The figure was much the same in 1900, and, indeed, in 1908. By that year Ontario's output was 108,124 cords. Production then surged upward: in 1914 it was three times what it had been six years before, and only a third of the cut came from crown lands. By 1922 total output was almost double the 1914 figure and almost seven times that of 1908.[19]

Despite the rapid expansion of production, the 1920s were difficult years for the industry. The price of newsprint fell steadily from just over $100 per ton in 1921 to $65 per ton in 1926 and $54.30 in 1930. There was also a fall in the rate of capacity utilization in the decade and some evidence of over-expansion.[20]

During this period there was a series of mergers in the industry. Particularly noticeable was the rise of the Abitibi Power and Paper Company (as it was now known). Starting with a single mill at Iroquois Falls, founded in 1912, it grew to be the largest Canadian producer by 1930, with mills at Smooth Rock Falls, Sturgeon Falls, Espanola, and Sault Ste Marie. Much of the acquisition was financed by the sale of bonds and preferred shares, a system of financing that made the firm highly vulnerable should its revenues fall.[21]

The early 1930s were characterized by further decreases in prices, reflecting a contraction in the newsprint market, and a particularly energetic cutthroat competition, as debt-burdened firms fought for sales. As a result, there was a series of defaults and bankruptcies among the pulp companies. Initially there had been attempts to organize voluntary cartels among producers in the late 1920s, but these moves were largely unsuccessful, so that the levels of both prices and production continued to fall. By 1932 the two largest groups in northern Ontario – Abitibi and the American-controlled Backus group – were in receivership. Further attempts were made to organize cartels in Ontario and Quebec to counter price-cutting and to allocate markets. But the cartels met with little success until the two provincial governments stepped in to regulate the industry. Government control meant the end of price-cutting and a slow return to stability in the later 1930s.[22]

Although the pulp and paper industry has not dominated the economy of Ontario to the extent that it has the economies of Quebec and New Brunswick, one cannot readily overestimate its importance to the economy of northern Ontario, not only as employer and as producer, but also as stimulator of urban growth – a theme that is further explored in chapter 10, below. Towns such as Espanola, Sturgeon Falls, Marathon, Dryden, Kapuskasing, Iroquois Falls, Nipigon, and even Thunder Bay were highly dependent on this industry. Overall, the provincial government's forest development policies exemplify what the eminent Canadian economist J.H. Dales called the 'big-economy' obsession of Canadian policy-makers, and what historians such as H.V. Nelles see as the 'promotion' mentality of the Ontario government.[23] The forest resources of Northern Ontario were used to promote maximum investment and employment, with little regard for efficiency, long-term management of the forests them-selves, or protection of the environment. The major purpose was to promote growth of manufacturing industry, based in this instance on the export of comparatively simple manufactured products to the American market. In order to attain these goals the Ontario government was willing to sacrifice revenues and to enter into very close relationships with business interests.

Agriculture in the North and North-West

As in other regions, the forest industry in northern Ontario has been closely associated with agricultural colonization.[24] Settlers followed close behind the lumbermen, finding themselves in a symbiotic relationship with the forest-based manufacturers. On the agricultural side the forest products industry, as well as mining, served to develop local markets for agricultural produce. At least as important were the sale of forest products cut on settlers' lots and settlers' part-time and seasonal work in the lumber industry.

Because the Canadian Shield is so rocky, northern agriculture is almost completely restricted to the areas where glacial action has deposited clay, sand, and other lacustrine materials. This land can be divided into four major categories. The first is a section from Lake Nipissing west to the north shore of Lake Huron, including Manitoulin and St Joseph's islands. The second is made up of the Clay Belt of Timiskaming and Cochrane. The third is the area around Thunder Bay on the west shore of Lake Superior. The fourth is the Rainy River district. There are a few pockets scattered in other areas such as Dryden, and there is also considerable variety within and among the four regions.[25]

After Confederation agriculture and lumbering were spreading into northern Ontario from the east and the south. By the 1870s settlers were advancing into the Muskoka and Parry Sound districts, following on the large sales of timber berths in 1871 and 1872, as the Ontario government opened new townships for settlement. This area was generally rocky, and not well suited to agriculture. The government had greater hopes for the areas around Lake Nipissing west to Sault Ste Marie, and by 1879 it had plans to open townships. Until then no land could be distributed, whether by purchase or under the homestead arrangements of 1868. The difficulties of the lumber industry after 1873 and the lack of railway transport slowed this settlement project, but by 1885 settlers were moving in along the CPR line from Mattawa westward, particularly around Lake Nipissing. By 1887 land was also open around Sudbury and along the north shore of Lake Huron.

In 1890 the provincial government opened eight townships at the head of Lake Timiskaming. This marked the beginning of settlement in the Clay Belt. By 1908 settlers were also moving north into the Cochrane area as the T&NO Railway and the National Transcontinental were constructed through the region. Settlement had also begun early in the 1870s in the Thunder Bay district, near the western end of Lake Superior. After 1892 townships were opened for homesteading in the Rainy River district. In such townships settlers could acquire land by mere occupancy and improvement without having to pay for it; a registration fee would suffice. In the twentieth century the Clay Belt and the north-west received the largest number of settlers, as table 5.1 reveals.

Most settlers in northern Ontario arrived without direct government assistance and took up plots of land as areas became available for settlement. In 1868 the provincial legislature had enacted a Free Grants and Homestead Act, in an attempt to compete with the US homesteading arrangements, thereby drawing immigrants to Ontario and retaining Ontarians within the province. Settlers were required to reside on the land for five years, to clear and cultivate fifteen acres, and to build a house, before a patent transferring ownership to the homesteader could be issued. Naturally this measure could apply only to those parts of the province – the north and north-west – where the land remained in the possession of the Crown; the more attractive land, in the south and east of the province, had long since been alienated and transferred into private ownership. The 1868 act opened townships in Muskoka and Parry Sound to settlement, each farm being 200 acres in extent. In 1878 an additional large parcel of land south and east of Lake Nipissing was opened. Later the system was extended to other portions of Nipissing, Sudbury, and Algoma districts. A similar act was passed for Rainy River in 1886, with even more liberal conditions for the eventual attainment of title.[26]

Land was also offered for sale, including much of the north shore of Lake Nipissing and Lake Huron and some parcels in Thunder Bay. In the Clay Belt there were no free-grant townships, and all lands were sold. Prices varied but were usually 50 cents an acre, paid in instalments, for 160–acre plots, although such lots were reduced to eighty acres in 1925. Settlement conditions similar to those on free-grant lands were also imposed.[27]

Besides these two formal methods of settling on the land, there were many settlers who simply occupied property, particularly in the Nipissing-Algoma region. Many of these squatters quickly stripped the land of its timber and abandoned it – a common practice also on both free and sale land. As a result, the published figures on free grants for north-eastern Ontario are inaccurate guides to the total number of settlers on the land. The figures for the north-west, because of better controls, appear to be more accurate.

The migration to northern Ontario reflected settlers' desire to better their condition, but in each case there were different promptings and different incentives. Furthermore, the pattern of motivation changed with the passage of time. In the period before 1930 and for certain migrants the chief stimulus seems to have been the desire to do well by cutting and selling the standing timber. Changes in transportation costs and especially railway construction affected the pay-off from so doing. The railways directly reduced the cost of transportation, and by stimulating the forest products industries, they provided potential local markets and part-time work. In this respect the T&NO and the National Transcontinental, whose histories are summarized in chapter 15, were particularly important.[28] Until 1930 land was cheap and easily available in northern and north-western Ontario, while the resource industries seemed to provide markets and part-time work. But after 1929, with the onset of the Great Depression of the early 1930s, the motivations changed. A sudden drop in incomes and employment opportunities in the south, coupled with government subsidies for resettlement in the north induced northward migration. This pattern was opposite to that of the pre-1930 years, because it coincided with a dramatic decline in the northern forest-based industries – though not in northern mining – and in the potential to make a living from agriculture. In chapter 3 it was shown that in the province as a whole, agriculture produced inadequate incomes for farmers during the 1930s; in the northern parts of the province this was even more emphatically the case.

Well before the Depression there had been two experiments with government-sponsored settlement. In 1901 the provincial government had issued certificates to Boer War veterans, allowing them to select lots, mainly in the Timiskaming and southern Cochrane districts. Then in 1918 returning soldiers were settled around Kapuskasing, about 100 kilometres west of the town of Cochrane. Neither plan was successful, either in attracting settlers or in holding them.[29]

The first Depression-propelled attempt at directed settlement began in 1932. It was the joint product of soaring unemployment levels and relief costs. For several years the dominion authorities had been encouraging the unemployed to turn to farming; in April 1932 Ottawa convened a joint dominion-provincial conference the aim of which was to reduce relief costs, especially outlays on public works. The result was twofold: the dominion decided to provide direct relief, and it also announced a plan whereby destitute families would receive subsidies if they settled on the land.[30] In effect, the dominion proposed to capitalize the likely direct relief payments to an urban unemployed family, thus providing a lump sum that would place the family on the land. This scheme was conceived primarily as a short-run economizing measure, not a permanent colonization plan.

This Relief Land Settlement Plan, or, as it was usually called, the Gordon Plan, offered a $600 grant to an unemployed relief-receiving family. The grant would be given by the three levels of government. In Ontario about 600 families were sent to previously unsettled land in northern Ontario, since no provision had been made to purchase already cleared land for them. About 320 families went to Cochrane; the rest were scattered in the Thunder Bay, Algoma, and Timiskaming areas.[31]

Such numbers cannot have affected, or reversed, the general 1930s trend towards agricultural depopulation noted in chapter 3, above. The grants were not sufficiently high to support a family for long, and during that decade the prospects for commercial agriculture, as suggested in chapter 3, were dismal. Hence many families soon abandoned the land, moving to local towns or back to southern Ontario, and the press was full of reports of families living in abject misery. When the Liberals took control of the provincial government in 1934, the Lands and Forests Department undertook a study of the plan. Their conclusions were so unfavourable that the plan was ended that very year.[32]

The provincial government also undertook to encourage northern agriculture through an array of expenditures under the Northern and Northwest Development Acts of 1912 and 1915, as documented in table 5.3. Virtually all the expenditures were on road-building – both trunk routes and local systems. Since many trunk roads tended to parallel existing railway lines rather closely, they probably had little impact on transport costs until after World War Two. The local road systems, however, were extremely important, since in summer there was no alternative for most settlers.

Except for the Relief Land Settlement Plan, plus a brief spontaneous flow into rural areas in the early 1930s, few new agricultural settlers moved to northern Ontario after 1930. As can be seen from table 5.2, the number of farm units fell in the areas of older settlement, and rose slightly in some of the newer areas, in the decade from 1930 to 1940. This picture is slightly misleading in that the census definition of a farm lumps part-time and residential farms with commercial operations. In table 5.4 information is provided on the number of abandoned farms, by district; the relatively large number in northern Ontario gives a good indication of the instability of agriculture in the area, compared with Ontario as a whole.

Further indications of the declining state of agriculture in the north can be found in table 5.5, which gives information on the number of farms classed as part-time (more than 50 per cent of the revenue from outside sources), subsistence (more than 50 per cent of the value of farm products consumed on farms), and forest-product-producing farms (majority of revenue from wood products or apiaries). About 51 per cent of the farms in the north were in one of these three categories, compared with 25 per cent for the province as a whole. Many of these farms represent a transition phase between commercial farming and more remunerative alternative activities.

As table 5.6 reveals, most settlers combined the sale of agricultural products with other income-producing activities. Successful farmers generally concentrated on stock-raising, particularly dairy cattle, and on the production of fodder crops – hay, grass, and clover. There were also significant local egg- and poultry-raising enterprises. The two largest sources of non-agricultural income were from the sale of timber and pulpwood from farm lots, and from off-farm wage labour.

The sale of forest products is usually more common on newly settled farms, since the clearing of the land is the first activity that must precede cultivation. The sale of wood provides income in the first year or two, before planting can begin, and it can provide a source of investment capital for the farm. Both the various censuses and the annual reports of the Ontario Department of Lands and Forests provide information on the sale of wood from farms. Before World War One, timber was the most important product, but after 1918 the growth of the pulp and paper industry gave rise to a strong demand for pulpwood. In fact, in many years the recorded cut of pulp logs from settlers' lots exceeded the cut on pulp limits.[33] These figures are almost certainly too high, in that timber and pulpwood cut on private land was exempt from provincial 'manufacturing conditions,' thus giving an incentive to report products as cut on farms so that they could be exported without processing.

As a farm became cleared, farmers turned more towards wage labour to supplement their incomes. The forestry industry was commonly combined with farming because bush work was concentrated in the winter, a season when the farmers' opportunity cost was lowest. Part-time work in construction, government road-building, and other miscellaneous jobs was also common. Settlers in mining districts normally did not combine agriculture with mining, the latter not normally being a part-time occupation.

Something should be said of the activities of what Professor Arthur Lower, the dean of Canadian historians, has called the 'bogus settler' or 'timber pirate.'[34] In the earlier historiography such folk were described as men who obtained plots of land on the pretext of farming, while the actual intention was to cut and sell the timber on the land and then abandon the lot. In addition, Lower allows that some settlers who did intend to farm found themselves drawn into the easy money of timber-stripping. But although both types undoubtedly did exist, to focus on the intentions and characters of the individuals – about whom historians have little direct evidence – tends to obscure the economic nature of the process. People went to northern Ontario with the general intention of making a living; once there, economic opportunities and individual endowments would direct activity into the lines that would produce the greatest private net benefit.

There is scattered evidence from observers that individual settlers allocated more effort to agricultural pursuits when the forest products industry was depressed and less when forestry was buoyant. Furthermore, some settlers specialized in lot-clearing, selling the cleared land to a prospective farmer, and then repeating the process in another location.

Finally, there is evidence that forest products companies deliberately brought some settlers into certain areas, to provide a pool of winter labour.[35]

Thus there is no clear-cut distinction between a 'timber-pirate' and a true settler. Rather, there was a continuum that individuals moved along, according to changing opportunities. The main difference between the failed farmer and the bogus settler is that the latter wasted fewer resources in an unprofitable and fruitless enterprise. The combination of agriculture and forestry was a logical strategy in the initial stages of development, and it was either appropriate or unavoidable given the northern natural resource endowment, but for many settlers it was no more than a transition.

Forestry and agriculture, along with mining, have played the leading roles in the development of northern Ontario. Forest products – first lumber and later pulp and paper – have acted as traditional staple exports. The products were raw materials or semi-finished goods, and the markets lay almost entirely outside the north. Their limitations as a stimulus for development were several: first, they had a tendency towards strong cyclical movements in demand, resulting in rapid changes in production and prices, and thus in employment; second, as was suggested in chapter 4, the nature of the products and the locational disadvantages of northern Ontario led to very few linkages with other economic activities in the region.

The agricultural settlement in northern Ontario is less easy to understand or justify than the growth of extractive industries such as mining and lumbering. The land is of highly variable quality, and the climate makes it marginal for successful agriculture. Also, adequate marketing mechanisms were lacking, while inbound freight could be shipped by rail at comparatively low cost, so that most products could be obtained more cheaply from outside the region, the major exception being perishable dairy products. The fact that agriculture in northern Ontario was extended past the point at which it it was commercially viable should not surprise students of Canadian agricultural history. As the prairie historian V.C. Fowke shows in his study of Canadian agricultural policy, governments typically want agriculture to be larger than strictly commercial considerations would dictate,[36] apparently because agriculture is thought to be the foundation of the economy, something promoting stability and permanence. Thus the developmental assumptions of the period automatically included the subsidy of agricultural settlement as part of a balanced economic expansion. In addition, from time to time northern colonization was a politically useful device for managing certain southern problems, such as returning war veterans or urban unemployment. Agriculture also represented an attempt to diversify the northern economy, rendering that economy less dependent upon mining and forestry. By World War Two, however, it was clear that the future would lie with the latter two industries, and that northern agriculture was a sector in decline.

6 *The Oil and Gas Industry*

Serious oil production in Ontario began in 1858, when the first drilled well in the world was sunk in south-western Ontario. The industry, like that of near-by Pennsylvania, was characterized at first by a multiplicity of small-scale producers and refiners, but refining and distribution eventually became concentrated and, in large part, foreign owned. Similarly, when natural gas production began there was a great deal of small-scale production, but distribution networks from the major fields to the principal markets both in Ontario and abroad were 'natural monopolies' – that is, the volume of business would support one distribution line but not more than one on any particular route. Thus distribution quickly acquired corporate forms appropriate to that economic reality. Both oil and gas reserves were quickly depleted, so that oil imports were important by the turn of the century, while gas production and exports dwindled, and the largest cities of the province were never supplied with Ontario natural gas.

Oil and gas reserves were owned by the people who held title to the land surface, subsoil rights having been transferred along with the surface ownership much earlier in the century throughout the southern part of the province. Thus oil and gas did little for provincial revenue. Indeed, after 1900 the dominion had to provide a subsidy so as to encourage the production of Ontario crude oil. Nor did either level of government possess any coherent policy for distribution or conservation. It is possible that more rational exploitation and more sensible pricing, especially for gas, might have prolonged the lives of some fields, increased their total lifetime outputs, or made it possible to connect cities such as Toronto to the natural gas mains. As for the monopolization of refining and distribution, no attempt was made either to prevent the buying-up of competitors or to enforce divestiture after purchase. When gas supplies began to run short, both provincial and dominion authorities did act to discourage exportation, sequester supplies for domestic users, and hold prices down.

The growth and decline of the industry are traced in table 6.1. Although census years provide figures for 1870 and 1880, there are no census figures for 1890, and the annual data of the Ontario Bureau of Mines are available only from 1891. Oil production rose steadily from very low levels in the late 1850s to just over 900,000 barrels, or 27 million imperial gallons, in the mid-1890s. In this period the oil was used for the production of kerosene and lubricants; the kerosene, in turn, was used for lighting and, to a limited extent, for cooking and even for heating. Oil production began to fall only shortly before the development of motor transport would create a large new demand for gasoline. Thus in 1904 the increasing requirements for petroleum met the downward tendency in production, a tendency that dominion bounty arrangements stayed only temporarily. Even so, 1903 was the last year in which Ontario oil wells produced more crude oil than Ontario refineries processed. Thereafter, until 1935 production declined quite steadily. There was a slight recovery in the late 1930s; even so, in 1940 Ontario's five oil refineries – Imperial, Canadian, British American, McColl Frontenac, and Goodrich – obtained only 1.15 per cent of their refinery throughput from Canadian sources – all in the Petrolia district of south-western Ontario. By then the industry's main products were gasoline and heating oil. Lubricants still mattered, and a good deal of kerosene was still produced, chiefly for lighting in rural areas. But the motor age and the gradual expansion of oil heating had changed the industry: in 1940 there were 225,000 motor vehicles in Ontario, although only 3.9 per cent of urban homes were oil heated.

For natural gas the timing of development was rather different, because production developed and peaked later. But the pattern was the same. There was slow development until after 1900, very rapid expansion until after World War One, an equally dramatic contraction during the 1920s and early 1930s, and then a renewed growth in the late 1930s, which pushed production almost to 60 per cent of the previous peak, which had been reached in 1917. By 1941 output was somewhat less than it had been in 1917, and the future looked anything but bright. Originally popular as an illuminant, natural gas had gradually lost that market to electricity, which also was making inroads in the kitchen, where electric stoves now competed with gas. By 1941, 80 per cent of Ontario urban homes cooked with gas or electricity. Gas heating remained a rarity, although it was more common than fuel oil: in 1941, 5.7 per cent of the urban homes in Ontario were heated with gas, and in addition, some gas was used for process heat in south-western Ontario. Much of the 'gas' that the census reported was manufactured from coal: even in 1941 there was still no natural gas in Toronto, in Ottawa, or anywhere to the north and west of a Hamilton-London-Sarnia line.

Petroleum

In Ontario, as in many other regions, oil seepages first disclosed the presence of underground petroleum. The Indians had long collected seepage oil off the surface of Black Creek in Lambton County. In 1851 the government geologist sent two investigators, who reported gumbeds at Oil Springs. Their report came to the attention of Charles Nelson Tripp, of Woodstock, who with his brother Henry applied for a manufacturing charter. Requested in 1852, the charter was granted in 1854, creating the International Mining and Manufacturing Company, which was meant to produce japanning, varnishes, and asphalt for ship caulking. Regrettably the company had no transport, no knowledge of technology, and little capital. By 1857 Tripp had sold most of his holdings to James Miller Williams.[1]

Williams was a native of New Jersey who had settled in London, Ontario, in 1840. He was a carriage manufacturer. In about 1846 he moved his business to Hamilton, where he began to produce railway cars and equipment. In 1857 he began to drill for oil near Bothwell, but moved his operations to Eniskillen (renamed Petrolea in 1859 and Petrolia in 1874), where in August 1858 he struck oil. The plan was to produce illuminating kerosene. The refinery was first located at Oil Springs, but Williams soon began to ship the crude to Hamilton for refining – in those days, a simple process of distillation. In 1859 he was selling lamp oil at $1 per gallon.[2]

In May 1861 Leonard B. Vaughan, another American and the co-founder of a private bank, drilled the first successful well into rock. The result was a rush of treasure seekers, hundreds of whom came to the Oil Springs-Petrolia region between London and Sarnia. Within three months there were sixty drilled rock wells, yielding forty barrels per day on average.[3] In January 1862 Henry Nixon Shaw brought in the first 'flowing well,' which produced 2000 barrels per day without pumping. Sad to say, thirteen months later this well asphyxiated its discoverer.[4] By August 1861 there were 400 wells at Oil Springs; by April 1862 production was 25,000 barrels per day. However, many of these wells had short lives. By the winter of 1862–3, when Sandford Fleming visited Oil Springs, only two wells were still flowing, the rest having begun to produce salt water instead. There were 100 refineries, with a total capacity of 1,500 barrels a day.[5] After further trouble with water, in 1866 the Oil Springs field shut down.

Transport was a serious problem in these early years. Oil had to be taken by horse-team to the nearest railway shipment point. Originally the crude went on to refineries at Hamilton and Woodstock in barrels. But in 1865 the tank car was invented – at first a horizontal barrel on a wagon frame, and then, in 1866, vertical wooden tanks mounted on flat cars.[6] In spite of these transport problems, in 1862–3 some Canadian oil products were exported to Britain, but regrettably Canadian kerosene smelt offensive, and by 1864 this shortcoming had closed the export markets for the time being. In 1865 the Canada Oil Association, the first price-fixing ring in the industry, began to export 'surpluses' to maintain the domestic price. American markets, too, absorbed a good deal of Canadian crude during the Civil War, when the price of Oil Springs crude rose from 30 cents per barrel in 1862 to $12 per barrel late in 1864. After the war the price fell to $4, then to $2, and then, with the development of the nearby Petrolia field, to 50 cents, at which point the association tried unsuccessfully to take the trade in hand.[7]

At Petrolia oil springs were first reported in 1861. Drilling and digging expanded from these springs. By August 1861 there were sixteen producing wells, and the development continued thereafter. In 1866 the railway reached Petrolia; in 1867 there were large new discoveries, flooding the market and producing a collapse in prices. Even at these much lower prices the industry could survive: by August 1868 there were some eighteen to twenty refineries in the dominion, and at Petrolia there was enough oil in tanks – partly above ground and partly in sunken storage works – to supply Canada for two years. As a result, only fifteen wells were working.[8] In this unstable situation a new price-fixing ring, the Crude Oil Association, was a natural creation. Formed to encourage export, it discriminated between home and export prices, sending 'surplus' oil products to Britain. Fortunately a deodorizing process had been perfected![9] The American market also took some Petrolia output, in spite of a tariff of 20 cents per barrel. Thus by 1869 sixty wells were in production, and 3,000 barrels a week were being refined for export.[10]

Refineries were small, simple, and numerous. In 1870 there were forty in the combine, most of which were located in London. Petrolia's first was built in 1865, and by 1870 it boasted twelve. However, until 1877 the structure of railway freight rates favoured the shipping of crude to London for refining. It was there, in 1870, that Englehart, Guggenheim, and Company built the Siver Star Works, by 1875 the biggest refinery in town. Only in 1877, when the Michigan Central Railroad reached Petrolia, did it become as cheap to ship refined products as to move crude. Refineries then began to move back to the wells; when a fire destroyed his London refinery in 1878, Englehart relocated in Petrolia, which, in 1884, contained nine refineries.[11]

The domestic industry was inclined to overproduction, and the response was combination: in 1873 fifteen Petrolia refiners formed the Home Oil Company, which controlled half the district's production; in 1874 the

Petrolea [sic] Crude Oil and Tanking Company, which controlled the other half, was formed.[12] There were further combinations in 1877, and in 1880 sixteen prominent London and Petrolia oilmen formed Imperial Oil, for which Englehart's works became the centre of operations.[13] The dominion provided help in the form of a protective tariff, which secured the domestic market for the Ontario refiners.

There was still no pipeline from Petrolia to the refining and marketing centres. Following obstructionist tactics in London, whose council feared new fires and explosions, more refineries began to be moved to Petrolia,[14] and when new finds occurred at Oil Springs, they were quickly connected by pipeline to the Petrolia refineries.[15]

Although Imperial Oil had been formed partly to meet American competition, in 1897 it was bought by Standard Oil of New Jersey. Why did this happen? According to one source,[16] Imperial was in difficulties because it could not raise funds for expansion in the prairie kerosene market that it was eager to enter; thus it approached Standard Oil, which already had a distribution system in the Maritimes. This version is not very plausible: kerosene-distributing did not involve large capital outlays, and most of these expenditures represented working capital – precisely the sort Canadian banks were willing to supply. Contemporaries were sceptical also. They observed that Standard began its Canadian incursions quite independently of Imperial, by buying one of the Petrolia refineries. According to this version of the tale, Imperial at first declined to sell out to Standard, which then induced the Laurier government to permit the importation of bulk crude oil in ships and tank cars, thus undercutting the Canadian-based refiners. It is also alleged that Standard, in its customary fashion, obtained from the railways a discriminatory rate that hurt Canadian producers.[17] Such lines of thought suggest that the sale of Imperial was anything but voluntary.

The critical year was 1898. At the beginning of that year there were in Ontario six oil refineries operated by five separate companies. By the end of the second half of the year the business was virtually all in the hands of Imperial of Petrolia and Bushnell of Petrolia and Sarnia. The following year, according to the *Canadian Engineer*, 'it is all one.'[18] Standard then moved the refineries to Sarnia, chiefly so that it could import crude oil, in bulk and cheaply, by tanker, while remaining close to the Petrolia oil wells. It therefore built a pipeline from Petrolia to the lake port. By 1901 all oil refining in Canada was done at Sarnia, the Imperial refinery having been enlarged in 1899 to service the entire national market.

The new monopoly refiner was anything but popular, especially among the small oil producers of Petrolia, even though it seemed to be paying better prices. In 1901, having won the co-operation of independent

American interests, some Petrolia producers set up the Canadian Oil Refining Company. The industry, after all, was not hard to enter: the technology of refining was not complicated, and refiners could and did sell their products to independent wholesalers and dealers. By 1904 the new firm merged with some other Canadian-American interests. In 1908 the company was bought by National Refining of Cleveland, returning to Canadian ownership only many years later.[19]

Production, naturally enough, was far less concentrated than refining or distribution. When the dominion abolished its 5 cents per gallon duty in 1904 and introduced a bounty of 1.5 cents per gallon, there were some 2,000 producing wells in Ontario, and some 400 owners.[20] The bounty was quite substantial, adding nearly 50 per cent to the well-head price of crude. But it ws not enough to preserve self-sufficiency: in 1909 only 45 per cent of refinery throughput came from domestic production. And so high a figure would not be seen again until the 1950s.

By 1914 Ontario still contained only the two refineries – Imperial and Canadian Oil – that had existed a decade before. Thereafter there were new entrants – first, British American in Toronto and Great Lakes at Wallaceburg, then McColl Frontenac in Toronto and Goodrich in Port Credit.[21] Production of refined products, of course, increased by leaps and bounds, chiefly because of the motor car, whose infiltration of provincial life is traced in later chapters. The balance of output accordingly changed, as refineries produced less kerosene and much more gasoline. In 1900 Ontario refineries produced 11.8 million gallons of illuminating oil and 1.5 million gallons of 'benzine and naphtha.' By 1915 the production of illuminating oil had risen to 28.8 million gallons, while 13.5 million gallons of benzine and naphtha were being produced. Kerosene output peaked in 1917, at 40.2 million gallons; in 1940 production was 17.6 million gallons of kerosene and 268.6 million gallons of gasoline. The continued importance of illuminating oil is a reminder that rural Ontario was still largely not electrified at the outbreak of World War Two. Gasoline production quintupled between 1921 and 1940: a testimony to the motor age.

Domestic oil production was very sensitive to market conditions. During the 1920s the low price of crude kept Ontario drilling almost at a standstill; Imperial, meanwhile, became active as a producer not only in Alberta but in Venezuela. The firm continued to buy what Ontario crude there was, but by 1928 most Ontario producers were operating at a loss, pumping only in the hope that things would improve,[22] while the newer refineries worked with crude from the United States. In the first years of the Great Depression that began in 1929 things became worse still, and Imperial paid a premium for Ontario crude so that local producers would stay in operation.[23] When production revived somewhat in the late 1930s, one reason was said to be that prices had risen. But production could not be held at that higher level, while imports continued to increase. Thus by World War Two the Ontario refining industry, which had begun as an important exporter not only to Britain and Europe but to the United States, was little more than a processor of imported raw material – the analogue, in fact, of the textile industry.

Natural Gas

Although several Ontario cities had been supplied with manufactured gas for much of the nineteenth century, before 1890 natural gas was no more than a curiosity and a nuisance for the petroleum industry. Thus the natural gas industry of Ontario did not begin until thirty years after the oil industry was already well established. It sprang from the efforts of the Coste brothers. Born in Amherstburg, Eugene and Denis Coste were educated in France, Egypt, and England. Eugene studied to be a mining engineer and joined the Geological Survey of Canada, leaving it for private practice in 1887; Denis began as a newspaperman.[24]

Thanks to a report on the geology of Ohio that appeared in 1888, Eugene Coste began to wonder whether the Cincinnati incline, which contained gas and oil, might extend under Lake Erie and into Ontario. He formed a syndicate under the name of the Ontario Natural Gas company, and began to drill in Essex County. On 23 January 1889, he struck gas – the first well in Ontario that was able to produce commercial volumes. The Coste company proceeded to drill an additional 100 wells in Essex County, which experienced a gas boom. In 1894 Coste's firm merged with most of the independent producers who had followed his lead, forming the United Gas and Oil Company.

What was to be done with the gas? The most obvious outlets, following the pattern that had developed for manufactured gas in cities, would be lighting and heating. But the local farm and village markets could not absorb the supply. The Windsor gas utility refused to buy Coste's natural product, preferring to continue service with manufactured gas. Nevertheless, in 1894 United Gas laid a pipeline to Windsor and Walkerville, and early in 1895 it extended the pipeline across the river to Detroit. In 1897, furthermore, an old pipeline that had once supplied Detroit from Toledo was reversed, so that Essex County gas supplied not only Detroit but Toledo as well. In July 1900 the exports to Toledo were stopped, but half the production of the Essex field was still being sent to Detroit.[25] In October 1901 the dominion government prohibited the export of Essex gas.[26] Too late: the field was exhausted three years later.

Meanwhile, in 1885, the Port Colborne Gas Light and Fuel Company had successfully drilled for gas 400 yards west of the Welland Canal. The gas was sold for lighting the business section. But only when the Coste brothers took an interest did any extensive development occur. In 1889 the brothers formed another syndicate and successfully drilled 'Coste No. 1.' By 1890 the company, which had become known as Provincial Natural Gas, owned twenty-five wells in the Welland field, and it began to supply Buffalo through a pipeline running east to the Niagara River.[27] There was, it seems, no money for pipelines to more distant Ontario cities, such as Hamilton or Toronto. Meanwhile, other smaller firms began to drill in the Welland area. One such firm was the Erie County Natural Gas Company, a Buffalo concern that wanted to send its output to the United States. Provincial bought Erie and most of the other producers, so that by 1901 it controlled nearly all the Welland field.[28] But it was already difficult to maintain the necessary flow, and in 1894 pumping stations were introduced to keep up the pressure. After 1900 production declined, and export ended in 1903.[29]

New developments occurred in the Haldimand district, where in 1905 a Pittsburgh firm, the Dominion Natural Gas Company, began to drill. It quickly laid a pipe to Hamilton and expanded its production and distribution network until, in 1913, it had 786 producing wells. It also bought gas from small operators. The company supplied Hamilton, Brantford, Galt, St Thomas, and other towns to the south and east of these places.[30]

Other new developments occurred in Tilbury, where Maple City Oil and Gas drilled successfully in summer 1905 and where the Costes' Volcanic Gas and Oil was equally successful in 1906. By 1910 the Tilbury field was supplying Chatham, Windsor, Sarnia, and smaller centres.[31]

In the absence of any useful provincial regulation of the exploitation pattern, it fell to private combinations to conserve gas supplies. Both the Kent and the Welland-Haldimand fields suffered initially from the same problem – many small companies, each anxious to drill as many wells as possible, thus exhausting the gas with undue speed. In the Welland-Haldimand field Dominion Natural Gas solved the problem by 1919, absorbing many small producers and buying the outputs of the remaining small independents. Competitive drilling was thus almost eliminated.[32] In the Tilbury field Volcanic combined with United Fuel and Ridgetown Fuel in 1911, forming Union Natural Gas (still the dominant gas distributor in south-western Ontario) and bringing most of the field under a single control. Union, however, did not control everything; annoyed to be omitted from the Union Gas board, the president of Volcanic proceeded to organize separate companies, which were soon grouped into Southern Ontario Gas. The two firms built pumping stations, drawing off the gas at a faster rate; in 1912 they also built compressor plants.[33]

Spurred by unusually cold winters and by a new industrial demand from war industries, gas output rose by one-third from 1915 to 1917, when it reached its peak of 200 billion cubic feet. There appeared to be a shortage of gas, especially for domestic users. The Ontario legislature passed the Natural Gas Act of 1917, which regulated prices and gave first preference in supply to domestic users, denying gas if necessary to manufacturers and other industries.[34] This measure had the effect of legally overriding existing contracts. Other legislation followed. Meanwhile, serious efforts were made to meter all gas; heretofore, most sales were made at flat monthly or annual fees, which in turn were based on the number of 'burning points.' The gas companies argued that rate regulation plus preference for domestic sales eliminated their profits. But drilling continued through the 1920s, and special efforts were made to increase the flow from old wells. So as to conserve gas the government also provided by regulation in 1919 that new wells must be spaced at least 1,000 feet apart.

During the 1920s industry received no gas, while both retail rates and the number of domestic consumers rose, and total production and domestic consumption tended to fall. In 1924 Dominion Natural Gas began to import some gas from Buffalo, using the old export pipeline.[35] In 1929 it became legal to mix manufactured gas with natural gas. This provision was little used, because the manufactured product was more expensive. Nor was much gas imported.

In 1932–4 output fell back, although the number of domestic consumers still drifted upward. From 1935 to 1940, however, there was a considerable expansion of production. Most new wells were drilled by small companies, which would sign contracts to sell their gas to the large distributing companies. Output rose almost 60 per cent, and once again there was a significant amount of gas available for industrial use; households were taking 72 per cent of Ontario production, and in addition a small amount – less than 1 per cent of total consumption – was imported in the form of 'mixed gas.' After 1940, however, Ontario production and household consumption fell steadily and dramatically; only through an increased use of manufactured gas and imported 'mixed gas' could the companies maintain the level of industrial supply that had been provided in 1939–40 simply from local production. Hence, in December 1940, as a measure to secure industrial supplies in wartime, the Ontario government prohibited the installation of any new natural-gas-burning equipment.

It is reasonably clear that if more foresighted pricing and production policies had been followed in early years, the lifetimes of the gas fields would have been prolonged. Many farmers received free gas; too many users paid flat rates, without metering; in all probability too many wells were drilled too close together; too many wells were exploited by gas-wasting techniques; given the growth of local demand, too much gas was exported. On the other hand, at no time did the producers or the provincial authorities possess the knowledge of reserves, costs, and prices both present and future on which a more appropriate pattern of extraction might have been based. As things were, the area of service was always rather limited, extending from Sarnia through London to Hamilton but not to Toronto. Even London received natural gas only in 1935, when exhaustion of the fields was in sight. Not until the late 1950s would Ottawa and Toronto be served with natural gas. And that gas would come not from Ontario fields but from the Canadian west.

Conclusion

In most respects Ontario's petroleum and natural gas industries had little in common. They were developed and run by different firms, and they grew and declined at different times. The oil industry served as a vehicle for the penetration of Standard Oil into the Canadian economy; the natural gas industry, whose output was more valuable in each succeeding year after 1907, remained largely though not entirely under Canadian ownership and control. In both industries it was in distribution and further processing that concentration was most evident, while production of the oil and gas remained in large part an affair for small business. Especially in the gas industry, however, the exigencies of conservation drew the distributing companies into drilling and management of the wells. Finally, both industries provide plentiful instances of local entrepreneurial vigour: in both it was largely Canadian residents who made the initial investments and who took the initial risks.

Part Three:
The Industrial Revolution in Ontario

7 Ontario's Industrial Revolution, 1867–1914

It was suggested in chapter 1 that soon after Confederation Ontario was poised and ready for rapid industrial development. This chapter and the balance of part 3 trace that development. Because the terrain has yet to be fully explored by scholars, some of the account has to be purely descriptive – a narrative account of what happened. Nevertheless, the general contours of the industrialization can certainly be explained, partly along the lines set out in chapter 1 and partly by a glance at the forces of demand, technical change, and tariff-protection that were operating not only between 1871 and 1914 but in the 1920s as well.

An economy will industrialize comparatively quickly and easily, other things being equal, if the forces of demand are strong enough to induce a supply-response among producers. In this respect Ontario was quite well served before 1914, although there were times when demand slackened painfully. From 1867 to 1873 Canada's exports, railway-building, and house-building all boomed, but from 1873 to 1879 all three sources of demand went into decline. In the next decade, 1879–89, railway-building first expanded dramatically and then fell off, while house-building exploded and exportation rose for two years, then fell for two years, and finally stagnated; in addition, the National Policy tariff-increases that began in 1879 provided some additional protective stimulus to industrial expansion. In 1889 a new export boom began, but both house-building and railway-building contracted considerably, masking the effect of the rising exportation; at the same time, the new technologies of the electrical age began to be applied on a large scale, exerting a new kind of expansionary effect. There was, however, painful recession in the mid-1890s, rather like that of the mid-1870s, although it did not affect all industries to the same extent, or at all. From 1896 to 1913 the export boom continued, and railway – and house-building booms joined forces with it; there was also a broadly based escalation in industrial investment, sparked in part by new technologies, in which the electric and automobile industries played a considerable part.

The reader may wonder about the interrelations among these three 'autonomous' components of demand. Did the export boom cause railway-building? Did the two together cause the fluctuations in house-building, either in Canada as a whole or in Ontario? Regrettably, neither economic analysis nor the available evidence provides a definite answer. Some connections there certainly were. In so far as extra exportation or new railway-building increased the domestic demand for manufactures, it would certainly speed up the growth of cities, thus generating extra demand for houses. However, there are always many other factors at work in determining the timing of house-building. Population pressure alone, in a reasonably prosperous economy, can account for a good deal; so can waves of speculation; so can urban expansion of the manifold sorts that do not depend on linkage from transport or exports. Between 1896 and 1914 the housing boom may be regarded as the reflection of that urbanization that was, in part though not entirely, the reflection of export and investment booms. But for the earlier periods of specially active housing construction, it is hard to see any such connection except in 1867–73. Nor can railway investments be viewed solely or even largely as a reflection of the demand for the transport of exportables. The railway building of the 1880s reflected the construction of the Canadian Pacific Railway, plus competitive expansion among the railway networks in central Canada. Neither sort of activity was induced by the pressure of demand; both created what Innis, Easterbrook, and other 'staples theorists' have taught us to call 'massive excess capacity.' After 1896 railway building was more closely linked with current export volumes and prospects. But Canada built far more miles of track than its exportables were likely to require for many decades to come. Thus railway investments, although connected to export volumes and prospects, could and did develop a life of their own. The same could be said of those other aspects of investment for which at present there are few details.

The period 1870–1914, especially the years after 1900, produced a remarkable structural change in the province's industrial economy, a change so great that it justifies the application of that traditional label, 'industrial revolution.' New capital goods and new consumer goods industries expanded vigorously, while the electrification of the province was properly taken in hand. Indeed, one might say that between 1890 and 1913 the Ontario industrial economy experienced its 'heroic age.' Nor was this transformation effected at the expense of the province's workers, even though conditions in many of the industries, both old and new, were far from salubrious or pleasant.

The Shape of Things

An old tradition talks of much disappointment in the later nineteenth century. The Canadian economy was not developing into a rival of the American, and many of the Canadian-born were emigrating. Nevertheless, the accumulation of evidence now suggests that the performance both of the Canadian and of the Ontarian economies was entirely creditable, even before the mid-1890s. It is time to discard the views of O.D. Skelton[1] and H.A. Innis,[2] concentrating instead on the reality of the economic transformation.

Appendix B discusses some of the perplexities that hover around the statistical data on industrial growth. But whatever their weaknesses, the data show a most impressive growth that continues regularly, although not at the same rate, throughout the post-Confederation decades. Before 1900 there was growth in the 1870s, the 1880s, and the 1890s – especially the 1880s. There is no sign in the data of any extended 'great depression,' although the cyclical downturns of 1873–9 and the early 1890s are naturally not revealed by decennial observations. After 1900 Ontario's industrial economy grew more rapidly than in the 1890s. But the growth rates of the late nineteenth century are not to be treated with scorn. It was once customary to argue, or to assume, that after 1873 Ontario's industrial economy stagnated until the prairie wheat and railway boom of 1896–1913 propelled it onward and upward – perhaps with an assist from the extractive developments in New Ontario, where mining and pulp and paper made rapid progress after 1900. The the real story was rather different, and much more complicated.

Some industries grew more rapidly than others, but expansion was general. Even the oldest industries of the province – milling and forest products – were larger in 1941 than in 1870, at least in terms of the value of their output. Oil refining, pulp and paper, electric light, gas light, and smelting expanded particularly quickly, as did a whole range of capital goods and consumer-durables industries – especially after 1900. It is hardly surprising that this group of industries outgrew the other two groupings by a substantial margin. Within the category of consumer goods industries the success story of butter and cheese is well known, and in the recent past much has been learned about the growth of meat-packing especially in the 1890s. But among the consumer goods industries there are other success stories – baking, factory clothing, factory boots and shoes, canning, hosiery and knitwear, rubber, drugs and medicines – that await their historians. Similarly, in the capital goods grouping a good deal is known about the rather slowly growing agricultural implements industry but almost nothing about the very dynamic machinery and electrical equipment industries.

If one examines the record, one finds that the pattern changes from one decade to another. The long-term growth rates, in other words, give a general impression that can mislead if one is interested in shorter periods of time. In the 1870s and 1880s the capital goods industries did not outgrow the rest of the province's industrial economy; in the period from 1900 until after 1910 they certainly did so, and they surged ahead again during the 1920s only to fall dramatically backward during the 1930s.

It was the rise of labour productivity, sparked by the accumulation of capital, by technological improvement, and by the increasingly diligent and skilful labour force, which provided much of the 'room' for living standards to rise in the long run, not only among manufacturing workers but for other employees and for the self-employed. Because there are elements of approximation in the output and employment data, and because especially before the early 1920s price indices are not very good, one can form only a general impression of these matters. Table 7.18 presents some rough estimates that give some indication of long-term movements. Average output per worker certainly went up, but it rose more slowly in the late nineteenth century than in the twentieth, and the period up to 1929 seems to have been especially conducive to a rise in labour productivity.

For the years before World War One the numbers tell a story of impressive and, apparently, accelerating growth. In forty years the number of industrial workers rose by 174 per cent, the physical volume of output more than quintupled and output per worker very nearly doubled. Although the data cannot detect cyclical slumps that fall between census dates, it is absolutely certain that the province's industrial economy did not stagnate or retrogress for any extended period. These findings are consistent with what was observed in the first chapter: that in 1870 Ontario industry was extremely profitable. They are consistent with the data on occupations that were presented in chapter 2. It should also be noticed that productivity grew rapidly in the 1870s, and then increased dramatically after 1900, when it was a very important source of industrial growth.

To trace the pattern of industrial growth more closely we have removed small firms from the census data for 1870–90 wherever possible and have linked the result with the published census data for 1900 and 1910, arranging them in three categories – capital goods and consumer-durable goods, consumer goods, and those that produce intermediate goods and services. The findings are summarized in tables 7.4 and 7.5. Consumer-durable goods are lumped with capital goods because they are often comparably long-lived and because the same census industries often produced both kinds of output. Indeed, a commodity such as an automobile or a piece of furniture might be one or the other, depending on its final purchaser. As for 'intermediate goods and services,' these consist chiefly of items that were purchased by other firms, either in Canada or abroad. 'Export goods' consists of commodities that were exported wholly or in part. Of course none of the categories is logically airtight. For instance, some electric power and some gas were sold to households; some salt and some buttons were sold to households, and some to industries. Nevertheless, as a description of broad tendencies and broad categories our arrangement is certainly not misleading. What does it say about the industrial growth of Ontario?

First of all, it should be noticed that before 1900 it was the consumer goods industries that made the running, although almost all sorts of output grew. The industrial advance was especially striking in the clothing industry, brewing, musical instruments, and cotton textiles; the woollen industry, however, certainly declined. Several capital goods industries – iron and steel products, furniture making, carriages, boiler-and-engine-making – also recorded impressive advances in output and employment. Thus in twenty years the production of capital goods and consumers durables doubled in current prices, and if these figures are deflated by the DBS general index of iron prices, the 1890 figure is 267 per cent of the 1870 one. The production of consumer goods increased as rapidly, however, so that if the actual figures are deflated by the DBS general wholesale price index, output in 1890 is 266 per cent of output in 1870. If a more appropriate price index were available for consumer goods during this period the gap between the two industry groups would appear much larger. As might be expected, intermediate goods occupied an intermediate position, and the production of export goods, dominated as it was by flour-milling and forest products, expanded impressively while failing to keep pace with the production of consumer goods. Thus the production of lumber products, measured in current prices, grew 129.5 per cent and employment in these industries grew 66 per cent; in flour – and grist-milling the employment grew 25 per cent in twenty years, while production grew by 35 per cent in current prices and by 52 per cent if adjustment is made, using the Michell index, for the fall in the price of grain and flour.

The general impression of the period 1870–90 is as follows. In terms of real output and employment, all three sectors of the Ontario industrial economy were tending to grow, but consumer goods industries were leading the way. Furthermore, only a few new industries were appearing. Among these were fruit and vegetable canning; manufacture of rubber and elastic goods, iron and steel bridges, electrical apparatus, and elevators; and the relatively large-scale production of pumps and windmills. But all these 'new industries' were as yet very small.

In the 1890s growth was very much slower. As before, it was consumer goods production and employment that were growing especially fast. The production of capital goods was also expanding, while the production of intermediate goods and services appears to have lagged behind and the production of export goods actually seems to have fallen, largely because the values of output in flour and grist-milling and in forest products – still the province's largest industries – appears to have fallen substantially. This development, however, is in part a statistical illusion – the result of changing census coverage. For many intermediate goods and services, including electric light, tanning, oil refining, and pulp and paper, the growth-performance was impressive. But such industries were not large enough to have much impact on the performance of the sector in which they have been classified. Among capital goods, however, almost everything grew; the only important declines were registered by carriage-, wagon-, and car-building works, while especially striking advances were made by agricultural implements, electrical apparatus firms, and metal-fabricating enterprises of all kinds. Among the consumer goods industries the advance was almost a general one. The woollens industries certainly contracted, and the clothing industries appear to have done so, but this appearance is almost certainly the result of change in census coverage: because in earlier decades it is hard to draw the lines between the various kinds of tailoring, in this industry the earlier census data have been adjusted to eliminate small establishments, but this adjustment is not very satisfactory. The expansion was particularly notable in the following industries: boots and shoes, baking, butter-and cheese-making, canning, knitwear, printing and publishing, rubber goods, slaughtering, and tobacco processing. Thus the decade was one of broadly based industrial development, largely oriented towards the domestic consumer market but stimulated by continuing domestic capital formation as well.

Ontario's urban and industrial economy depended on imports of fuel – American bituminous and anthracite coal. As J.H. Dales has pointed out, the province was rich in motive power but not in sources of heat. Until 1901 the dominion published data on imports province by province, thereby allowing historians to use coal imports as a proxy measure for the growth and fluctuation of the Ontario economy between 1869 and 1900. The data appear in table 7.6. Between these two dates, Ontario's coal consumption increased more than twenty-five-fold. The results, admittedly, exaggerate the growth of the industrial economy, because during these three decades there was extensive substitution of coal for wood, both in the fuelling of locomotives and in home heating. Also, fluctuations in winter temperatures might affect the figures, especially for anthracite. Nevertheless, the data testify to the size of the province's industrial growth. They also tell something about the cyclical movements. One can clearly detect the recessions of 1875–6 and 1894–5, when both total imports and bituminous imports decline noticeably. The data also show the rapid rise in coke imports after the removal of the tariff in 1895 and after the beginning of coke-smelted iron and steel production late in the 1890s. Coke, however, is a small element of the total, even in 1900.

For the 1890s, where brick and cement production data overlap with coal-import data, the figures show the same cyclical pattern, but the recession in construction that they reveal is longer and more severe. It has long been known that brick production tracks the business cycle quite closely, because of the link between bricks, building, and investment. Thanks to the labours of the Ontario Mines Bureau there are data on Ontario brick production for the entire period 1891–1939 (No data were gathered for 1897 and 1940, but these gaps are not worrisome). The brick data that appear in table 7.7 also testify to the size of the capital goods boom before 1914.

The full series reflect a dramatic pattern of expansion and contraction. The slump of 1893–6 is well documented, as is the remarkable height of the pre-1914 investment boom. From time to time the Bureau of Mines would comment on the swings in building activity that produced the fluctuations in brick output. In 1894, it reported, there was a 'collapse in the building trade.'[3] In 1902 it observed a decided revival in building activity about 1900, which caused renewal of production in many previously idle brickyards.[4] Such remarks are relatively rare: more usually the Bureau would let the data speak for themselves. In the cement industry, whose experience is summarized in table 7.8, no particular cyclical pattern can be detected, but the structural changes are far more dramatic. Output of Portland cement rose almost interruptedly, from 2,000 barrels in 1891, when commercial production began, to 3.8 million barrels in 1913 (barrels of 350 pounds). There were slight retrogressions in 1894 and 1912, but the industry sailed happily through the recessions of the 1890s and 1908–9.

The expansion of both brick and cement industries exemplifies the 'demand linkage' from a high level of investment activity to the development of supplier trades. One can detect a similar development in many of the province's capital goods industries. The recession in both industries during World War One serves as a reminder that the period of hostilities was not a period of growth or prosperity for all segments of the Ontario economy, chiefly because investment, which had fuelled the expansion of the pre-war years, fell off so dramatically.

From 1900 to 1910 it is the extraordinary expansion of the capital goods industries and the consumer durables industries that catches the attention at once. Output grew by 230 per cent, more than tripling in a decade;

employment doubled. In 1900 the motor car industry did not exist, or was too insignificant to be separately identified; in 1910 it employed 2,400 workers and produced $6.3 million worth of cars. The electrical industry increased its output more than six-fold, and its employment almost quadrupled, while the iron, steel, and foundry industries quintupled their production, so that by 1910 they were producing as much as the milling industry, while employing five times as many workers. Employment in this industry grouping was now over 80 per cent of employment in the production of intermediate goods and services; in 1890 the proportion had been just over half. In the consumer goods group, where output doubled and employment increased by over 20 per cent in the first decade of this century, the advance was general. Some industries – boots and shoes, factory clothing, men's shirts and haberdashery, knitwear, patent medicines – tripled their output. The distilleries sextupled theirs, and the rubber industry did nearly as well. Several industries – baking, carpets, coffee and spices, drugs, canning, glove-making, hats, jewellery, musical instruments, printing and publishing, silversmithing, soap-making, tobacco – doubled their outputs in a decade. Regrettably for the growth-performance of the industry group as a whole, four large consumer goods industries – butter- and cheese-making, brewing, textiles and meat-packing – grew much more slowly. Within the intermediate goods and services group the growth was equally broadly based. Milling, forest products, pulp and paper, oil refining, and railway car repair appear to be among the most impressive performers, in part because the enumerators were again counting small grist- and saw-mills. The export goods industries also, were doing respectably, although their overall performance was damped by the relatively slow growth in butter- and cheese-making.

These findings suggest that from 1890 until World War One the Ontario economy was industrializing on the basis of Canada's domestic market. The British market remained open, but the door to the American market was only slightly ajar, and until the abolition of newsprint tariffs just before the war it swung, if anything, more nearly closed. The nation-wide boom in capital formation, so impressive a feature of the period 1896–1914, propelled the province's capital goods industries upward. Further propulsion came from technological progress that stimulated the electrical, paper, and chemical industries, and from special dominion and provincial bounty and subsidy arrangements that assisted smelting and iron- and steel-making. The provincial government's 'manufacturing condition,' which impeded the export of pulpwood, played its part. Thus it was in these years that Canadian General Electric became established, as a venture under sole Canadian ownership after 1892, that Massey-Harris grew by leaps and bounds, that International Harvester came to Canada, that Clergue began his immense Algoma industrial complex, that the Hamilton steel industry was formed and developed on a twentieth-century basis, that Ford of Canada and McLaughlin began to produce cars on a large scale, that great pulp mills began to appear in New Ontario.

Further, these developments were closely interconnected. A building boom meant more business for the province's forest products industries. When the printing and publishing industry was doubling its turnover, no one should be surprised to find that the paper industry did likewise. Also, the growth of the electric power industry, whose turnover increased from just under $1 million in 1900 to $5.6 million in 1910, provided much of the fuel for these developments, while its own expansion produced demand for electrical apparatus – everything from generators to refrigerators.

When the current-dollar data are adjusted, as in table 7.5, to allow for changes in price levels, the picture is broadly the same. The statistical treatment of saw-milling and flour-milling in 1900 continues to influence the results, which are naturally affected in addition by the particular choice of deflator. However, the twentieth-century boom in the production of capital goods and intermediate goods is still very much in evidence, as is the relatively laggard performance of the consumer goods and export goods industries. Also, the effect of deflation is to make the 1890s look very much better, especially with respect to the growth of consumer-goods production. Once more it is clear that in the 1870s, 1880s and 1890s there was no general 'great depression': although growth was not steady, it was in most respects uninterrupted from one decade to another. Again one must remember that the census counts were taken in years that bracketed the general slumps of the mid-1870s and the 1890s.

By 1910 consumer goods amounted to 37 per cent of Ontario's output of manufactures as measured by the census enumerators. Capital goods and consumer durables amounted to 24 per cent, and intermediate goods, 39 per cent. In 1870 the figures, after adjustment to remove many small firms, were 28 per cent and 54 per cent, respectively. These figures summarize the transformation of Ontario into a developing, industrialized, and increasingly sophisticated producer of manufactures: the role of saw-milling and grist-milling, although still significant, had greatly diminished in proportionate terms, while the role of pulp- and paper-making, although already apparent, was as yet very small.

By listing the province's major manufacturing industries one can see, from a different angle, the transformation in its manufacturing activities. Thus in table 7.9 are presented the fifteen largest industries in 1910 and in 1870. Establishments having fewer than five employees are included in 1870 and excluded, except for milling and log and lumber products, in 1910. Only nine industries appear in both lists, and although milling and lumber top both lists, that for 1910 is noticeably more diverse. In 1910 the top fifteen industries produced only 60 per cent of industrial output, as against 81.4 per cent in 1870; both lists contain four capital-goods industries, and both show the close relation between manufactures on the one hand and the products of field and forest on the other.

The list is also a reminder that several of the province's major manufacturing industries received no tariff protection and that others did not need it. Those needing no protection included flour- and lumber-milling, slaughtering and meat-packing, butter and cheese, baking and tanning; all were on an export basis or depended on local markets where transport costs or perishability provided effective shelter. These six industries alone account for 32 per cent of all Ontario's industrial production in 1910. When other such industries are added, the figure rises to 48.3 per cent. When one takes account of the smaller unidentified industries, and of the many small firms in activities such as blacksmithing and tailoring, it is obvious that very much less than half of Ontario's manufacturing industry could be said to have benefited from nominal protection. Further, when account is taken of the reduction of effective rates in comparison with nominal rates, because of the protection of capital goods and of other inputs, the 'effectively protected percentage' must have been lower still. As for the rest, it is obvious that the vast majority must have sold their outputs throughout the dominion more or less in proportion to population and real income per capita. On that basis one would expect that Ontario itself would provide much the largest market for the products of 'protected' industries, and that Quebec must have provided most of the rest.[5] As one goes through the list of Ontario industries, one can identify only a few – agricultural implements, axes and tools, wire fencing, harness and saddlery – of which that general statement may not be true because certain regions, such as western Canada, were more agricultural than Ontario. But in 1910 these four industries produced only 4.5 per cent of all Ontario's industrial output. So much for the argument that through the protective tariff Ontario battened on the other regions.

It must also be remembered that because protection lowered real per capita income in Ontario itself, it somewhat reduced the per capita demand for a wide range of manufactures, most of which were produced within the province. Naturally the politicians and businessmen of the period were not very aware of such repercussions or chose to ignore them.

The Ontario of 1870 contained very few large enterprises of any sort. Indeed, only a small number of businesses were incorporated, and many were proprietorships. Whether size is measured by employment or capitalization, the only really large firm was the Grand Trunk Railway. By 1914 the Ontario economy contained many of the large enterprises that still dominate the provincial economy – sometimes under other names – seventy years later. Among these were Bell Telephone, Ontario Hydro, Massey-Harris, Canadian General Electric, Ford of Canada, Goldie and McCulloch, the Steel Company of Canada (Stelco), Imperial Oil, Canadian Westinghouse, the Canadian Northern Railway, Canadian Cottons, INCO, CCM, Dominion Textiles, Canada Cement, and the ancestors of Canadian Industries Limited, General Motors of Canada, Canada Packers, and Du Pont of Canada. Some of these firms, such as Stelco, Canadian General Electric, CCM, Canadian Northern, Bell, and the textile firms, were Canadian owned and controlled; others, such as Ford, began at the instigation of Canadian entrepreneurs who retained a substantial minority interest; still others, such as Canadian Westinghouse, INCO and the ancestor firms of CIL, began as subsidiaries of American or British businesses.

Big firms appeared for various reasons and in various ways. The market was expanding both at home and abroad; it would have been surprising if many firms had not grown accordingly. Hence, for instance, the William Davies Company of pork packers flourished in the 1890s. As the railway system became more fully developed and cheaper to use, businessmen found it more practicable to exploit economies of scale by building large enterprises on single sites; small firms, meanwhile, lost their 'natural protection.' In some respects technological development may have made large businesses more efficient relative to small ones, but the evidence is conflicting, and most of it is anecdotal or conjectural. In many of the relatively new industries, such as hydroelectricity, telephones, or chemicals, a large installation may have been needed if costs were to be kept down, or if production was to occur at all. But in many lines of work electric motors reduced the size advantage of the large plant and allowed smaller-scale enterprises to produce competitively. Brand-name advertising was effective for certain consumer goods, such as clothing and soap. With the development of the domestic financial system, with improved access to foreign funds, and with municipal subsidization, domestic and foreign entrepreneurs found it increasingly easy to finance a really big plant. In some instances, as in the Clergue promotion at the Soo, the result could be unworkable megalomania. In others, such as the Canadian General Electric works at Peterborough, the result might be substantial scale economies, a wider range of products, or some mixture of the two. Urbanization contributed: because cities and towns were growing fast, businessmen could hope to staff a big plant, assembling large numbers of workers at little direct cost to themselves, simply by local recruitment. There would be no need for the expensive infrastructure of the company town. Finally, the impact of merger and purchase must be considered.

Canada had no anti-combines law until 1889, and the laws of 1889 and thereafter were without effect.[6] Merger, therefore, could occur as and when businessmen wished. Massey and Harris merged in 1891, and in 1891–2 the cotton industry of the dominion was assembled into two great firms. In the late 1890s, under the influence of Toronto financiers, several of Canada's bicycle firms were merged into Canada Cycle and Motor Company, better known as CCM. In 1909–13, spurred at first by cheap and plentiful credit, Toronto and Montreal financiers contrived a spectacular wave of mergers, creating Stelco, Canada Cement, and many other giant concerns.

Many of Ontario's big firms were intended to serve the domestic market. This orientation was obvious with service-producing firms, such as Bell, Toronto Power, and the Canadian Northern Railway. But the large manufacturing firms, such as Canadian General Electric, were oriented wholly or largely towards the domestic market, in which they enjoyed tariff protection. Admittedly there were exceptions. Massey-Harris exported farm implements, and INCO exported most of its production, as did Davies the meat packer. Ford of Canada held a product mandate for the British Empire, though not for the United Kingdom itself. In some of these empire markets Canadian goods enjoyed tariff concessions, and in Canada of course Ford and the other car companies were heavily protected, at least in nominal terms. In absolute terms, therefore, many of the large firms grew because they had a protected market. Conversely, the tariff made it possible for relatively large numbers of small-scale and high-cost firms to survive and grow. Without tariffs some large Ontario firms perhaps would not have existed at all, but other firms would have been larger still.

The average establishment was certainly becoming larger. In 1870 the average employment was 4.6 in all establishments, and 6.5 in those we can identify as the larger ones. For 'census establishments' in 1900 average employment was 25.5 and in 1910, 29.9. In the newer industries the typical establishment was much larger than in older industries or in the province as a whole. Among these were automobiles, railway rolling stock, electrical apparatus, rubber and elastic goods, smelting, and pulp and paper. Thus one explanation for the rising size of establishment is the emergence of new industries in which the typical plant was generally much larger. However, some longer-established industries, such as cottons, woollens, and agricultural implements were moving in the same direction, as were distilling, brewing, boiler-making, and the foundry and machine shop industry. Yet it should not be assumed that there were generally fewer establishments. Between 1890 and 1910, or 1900 and 1910, there was indeed a decline in the numbers of establishments producing bicycles, carriages and wagons, agricultural implements, tobacco-making, washing

machines, breweries, papermaking, and woollens: of these eight industries, the first two were declining ones after 1900. For the other eighteen
industries the number of establishments rose along with average employment, output, and capitalization. Furthermore, several of the industries
that had large establishments in 1910 had shown the same pattern in 1890,
or even earlier. Among these are cars and car works, smelters, cottons,
distilleries, paper mills, agricultural implements, and boiler and engine
works. In all these industries the typical establishment employed many
more workers than in the economy as a whole and substantially more than
the average for 1910.

It should be remembered that an industrial firm might own and operate
two or more establishments, in one or more industries. In 1870 such
practices were unusual; by 1910 they had become somewhat more
common, although it was still usual for a firm to concentrate its activities in
a single industry. Because the census data relate to establishments, not to
firms, they can mislead with respect to 'bigness' or concentration, unless
one is interested only in the single establishment – the entity where wage
earners actually did their work. Hence one must not use the data to draw
any conclusions about concentration or 'market power.' It can only be said
that because of such multiple ownership the Ontario economy was more
concentrated than the data suggest. In addition, however, it should be
noted that the typical Ontario establishment was, even in 1910, a rather
small one. The average industrial establishment had 29.9 employees, was
worth $74,000, and produced $72,000 worth of output. And even in the
large-scale industries, such as agricultural implements, automobiles, cars
and car works, cottons, rubber goods, smelting, and woodpulp, the
average establishment was still relatively small. To the Ontarian of 1870
these new plants would look enormous. To the Ontarian of 1987 they look
modest indeed, although sometimes the new structures of the period can
still impress the architectural historian.

The Capital Goods and Consumer Durables Industries

The theorists of economic transformation[7] and the writers of economic
history teach one to look with special care to the capital goods industries,
because they produce much of the equipment on which an 'industrial
revolution' must depend. In principle, this equipment could be imported;
in practice, every successful industrial transformation has depended, to a
considerable extent, on home-produced machinery and equipment. Ontario's industrial revolution conforms to this general pattern. Generally
speaking, an industrial transformation is accompanied by an increase in the
range and sophistication of the capital goods that an economy produces for

itself. Here, too, the Ontario pattern was in no way unusual. However, if one compares Ontario either with the early industrializers, such as Britain, or with the Third-World industrializers of the mid-twentieth century, such as India, one finds that some capital goods industries and some consumer durables industries were already of importance in the provincial economy well before any transformation could seriously be said to have begun. This fact reflects the structure of the province's agricultural economy and the comparative prosperity of its inhabitants. Among the most important of such industries were those producing agricultural implements and furniture. Both drew heavily on the province's timber stocks; both imported certain important raw materials and components; both depended chiefly on the domestic Canadian market.

As was explained in an earlier section, this study groups capital goods industries with consumer durables industries partly for statistical convenience, and partly because in many instances the same firms produced both types of output. Indeed the same commodity, such as an automobile, may be a consumer durable good if purchased by a household and a capital good if purchased by a business. In 1870 Ontario possessed some important industries of this sort, such as furniture and agricultural implements. Decade by decade the old industries grew, while new industries arrived on the scene. The automobile industry is so important that it has been given a chapter to itself. The other industries are treated in this section.

At the time of Confederation the agricultural implement industry was already well established in Ontario. The typical firm produced a wide range of tools and implements, depending almost entirely on the United States manufacturers for technological innovations, which they produced with or without the formality of licensing.[8] Relying almost totally on the central Canadian market and protected after 1879 by a higher tariff, the industry grew through the 1870s, 1880s, and 1890s. Exports began in 1887–8; Massey and Harris merged in 1891; in 1902 a subsidiary of International Harvester began to build a mammoth plant in Hamilton. Western agricultural development, especially after 1900, created additional markets for the Ontario implement industry. Meanwhile, Massey-Harris was expanding into the United States: in 1910 the firm bought a harvester plant in Batavia, New York.

Looking back from 1987, the reader may find it hard to realize not only that carriage-building was an important industry in nineteenth-century Ontario but that some of the firms were sizeable. There is, furthermore, plentiful evidence of growth before 1900. In the 1890s, for example, McLaughlin of Oshawa expanded its works, and Grey of Chatham was exporting to South Africa. With the benefit of hindsight, such development looks as incongruous as the building of radial electric railways, but it should be remembered that three of the largest carriage-makers – Grey, Tudhope, and McLaughlin – made the transition to auto-building. Indeed, the McLaughlin carriage works that was rebuilt with municipal aid in 1900 is the direct antecedent of General Motors of Canada. Furthermore, Ontario carriage-builders were involved in the creation of the Canadian Ford works. Carriage-building, in short, was not without its dynamic elements.

Both agricultural implement-making and carriage-building drew on artisan skills and on the province's plentiful supplies of hard and soft wood. So did furniture-making, another important nineteenth-century industry. Piano-building and organ-making were well established, producing both for the domestic market and for export. As for non-musical furniture, many large firms were already at work by the 1880s, and the industry expanded its output thereafter, spreading from town to town throughout the southern part of the province.

The metal-using capital goods industries developed not by using local raw materials but by importing iron in various forms, both from the United Kingdom and from the United States. Often local scrap could be re-used; indeed, before 1900 the rolling mills at Toronto and Hamilton worked primarily with such scrap, especially from the railways. Meanwhile, railway-building created considerable though not regular demand for rolling stock, in which wooden upper bodies were attached to metal running gear. The larger railways built much of their own rolling stock and many of their own locomotives, but there was business for the Kingston Locomotive Works, and, sometimes, for other locomotive builders, as well as for car works. The last years of peace, coinciding as they did with a great deal of railway-building, naturally produced a wave of orders for rolling stock. Table 7.10 tells the remarkable story for the year 1912.

The Ontario boat-building industry included many small boat builders that have left little trace in the records, and it also included several more or less specialized large firms, which grew and diversified considerably during this period. The big firms had yards in Toronto, Collingwood, and, after 1904, at Bridgeburg on the Niagara River, and from time to time large steamers were built elsewhere. The growth of lake navigation and the expansion of the canal systems created considerable demand for iron and steel steamships; the Ontario yards met these demands, and in the process they became more technologically sophisticated, as ships increased in size and as engines became more complex.

In the foundry and machinery industries, as in ship-building, ownership and entrepreneurship were almost entirely Canadian before 1914, although there was a noticeable tendency to acquire the rights to manufacture foreign designs, and although immigrants from Britain often made their entrepreneurial marks in the Ontario industry. Among the most important and dynamic firms were the Galt company, Goldie and McCulloch, which had been founded in 1844, and the Dundas firm of Bertram, which had operated under various names since 1852. During the period there was remarkable development in both firms, as new products were added, more sophisticated workmanship attempted, and, at least for Bertram, export markets developed. Other firms, most of them locally owned, were founded, and most of the new firms were successful. The investment boom of 1900–13 naturally provided a good atmosphere for growth.

Although some parts of the electrical equipment industry, which first appeared in the 1880s and boomed in the 1890s and thereafter, had relations with the machinery industries, most of the firms were new foundations. For some time the industry was chiefly concerned with heavy equipment; household appliances would come later, chiefly after 1914. In 1892 Canadian General Electric was formed; wholly Canadian owned, it was a merger of several firms, some of which had been foreign promotions. But it never had the field entirely to itself. Other local and Montreal-based firms were active in the 1890s, and in 1903 the American firm of Westinghouse decided to build a large electrical equipment plant in Hamilton. The building of electric streetcars, also a major development of the 1890s, concerned a wide range of firms, some of which had already been building rolling stock, carriages, or horse-cars.

The bicycle industry, like the electrical equipment industry, boomed during the 1890s. The boom culminated in 1899, when five firms merged into CCM. Sadly for the investors who bought CCM shares, the demand for bicycles fell and did not revive. The company attempted to save itself by diversification: it began to build motor cars. But this business was soon hived off, and the company's future would lie in sporting goods as well as in two- and three-wheelers. Nor would the province's industrial development be fuelled by such slight and simple capital goods.

Intermediate Goods Industries

In a province where construction is important and where the local natural resources provide the basis for construction materials industries, the 'intermediate goods industries' are bound to be significant, especially in times of urbanization and high investment. During this period, furthermore, technological progress created new advantages and new possibilities, first in cement-making and then in woodpulp and paper. On the other hand, depletion of the white-pine forest had gone so far by 1881 that outputs of pine lumber could not be sustained. In one sense the pulp and paper industry was a replacement for the long-established trade in construction-grade timber.

There are many puzzles in the forestry statistics. The decennial censuses contain some data on output; provincial reports on crown lands contain other data; in 1908 the dominion began an annual compilation of forestry statistics. Selecting, compiling, and converting data from these three sources produces tables 7.11 and 7.12.

Since there are no overall output figures for any year before 1900, no convincing statement can be made about the course of total output during the later nineteenth century. Nevertheless, the data do reveal the collapse of the square timber trade. By 1900 the Ottawa Valley had been largely depleted, as had Georgian Bay, which had been opened up only in the early 1870s.[9] Output of square pine had fallen from over 16 million cubic feet to just over one million, while other varieties of square timber, and all sorts of output that could not be classed as 'logs,' had collapsed even more completely. Although the output of square timber from crown lands was sustained remarkably well in the depression of 1873–9, much of this production was sold at unremunerative prices, and much was stockpiled at Quebec to wait for better times. After 1886 production in the Ottawa valley was inconsequential, and in the western region, after 1892 at the latest. Table 7.11 shows how complete the extinction of Ontario's transatlantic timber trade was during the first twenty years of the period 1870–1914. Indeed, by 1900 the census recorded a larger output of square elm than of square pine. By this time more than 60 per cent of the province's square pine came from Nipissing, and another 20 per cent from Bothwell.

Logs for lumber, however, seem to have become immensely more important between 1870 and 1900: certainly in proportionate terms, even though one cannot be sure about the course of output. On crown lands, if the exceptional years 1871 and 1872 are discounted, outputs of logs and dimension lumber were much larger in the mid-1880s than in the late 1860s, and after some retrogression output rose again, to a peak of 955.1 million board feet in 1896. Although the outputs of other woods had been rising for some time, in that year pine lumber was still dominant, accounting for 98.3 per cent of the output from crown lands. The locus of the lumbering industry had shifted by 1900: of that year's output, 63 per cent of the pine came from Nipissing, while another 13 per cent came from Bothwell, 10 per cent from Muskoka and Parry Sound, and a further 10 per cent from Peterborough, Renfrew, and Victoria. In 1870 Nipissing had accounted for only 1.6 per cent of the pine logs and only 8.8 per cent of the square timber that the province then produced.

The oak of 1871, a crop whose significance has often been ignored, came chiefly from the southern parts of the province. Essex, Kent,

Bothwell, Lambton, Middlesex, Norfolk, Haldimand, Monck, and Welland produced 2.6 million cubic feet of square oak – 83 per cent of the province's output. In 1900 oak production was 8.8 million board feet, or 1.7 million cubic feet; the counties that had dominated the production of oak in 1870 now produced only 30 per cent of the province's output.

Just as Ontario's transport system was in part oat-burning, so in 1870 Ontario heated its buildings largely by burning wood. The output of firewood was then 4.5 million cords. In 1880 production was 5.4 million cords, but in 1900 production had fallen to 4 million cords. Doubtless competition from coal and kerosene, and perhaps a rising price for firewood in comparison with other fuels, had produced a substitution against the native product.

The data of table 7.12 reveal the decline of the square timber trade, the much better performance of the log and sawn lumber trade, and the shifting locus of production as the Ottawa valley was logged out, the Belleville district suffered the same fate, and production migrated first to the shores of Lake Huron and then still further afield. One can also see how other softwood lumber became more important, especially after the mid-1890s, with the declining cut of pine. In 1869–70 almost all the reported cut was pine. By 1900, 3.2 per cent of the sawlogs and dimension lumber was other softwood, and by 1913–14 that proportion had risen to 17 per cent. At that time the 'western region,' which had produced only 16 per cent of the cut in 1870, was producing 77 per cent, while the share of the Ottawa Valley had fallen to 20 per cent from 53 per cent. The same sort of thing had happened in the square timber trade.

The data also suggest not only an exhaustion of the ancient pine forests, but a reallocation of activity away from square timber and towards sawn lumber – that is, away from the British market and towards the American and the domestic markets. By the end of the Great Boom, as the minister of lands, forests and mines wrote in 1912, the domestic market had become the dominant one: 'The expansion of our own country and the enormous building boom that is going on ... are such that our lumbermen no longer need look to the u.s. market, our own markets being able to use up most of the lumber taken out at a fairly good price, not only for superior grades as well.'[10] In fact, as the Ottawa data show, 1912 was not as good a year as 1911, while 1913 and 1914 would be progressively worse, as recession spread in North America and as construction fell off, taking lumber prices down as well.[11]

Throughout the period the world of the lumberman was an uncertain one. Production commitments generally had to be made well in advance, and a large cut might have to be stockpiled, or sold at an unattractive price, until times were better. In discussing market conditions the crown lands reports commonly and properly emphasize both 'demand' and 'price.' Current production, therefore, need not match precisely the level of building activity. Nevertheless, so far as sawlogs and dimension lumber were concerned, the movement of output did roughly mirror the movement of the North American building cycle. One may see the effects in the low outputs of 1876–8, again in the mid-1880s, and in 1913–14, when shortages of credit increased the lumbermen's difficulties: 'The great shortage of money compelled a number of lumbermen to shorten up their operations, while others did not open at all. It is not to be expected that there will be an increase in the cutting of the present winter as the financial stringency has not entirely ceased.'[12] Prices also customarily fell in recessions, as in the mid 1870s, the mid 1890s, 1909, and 1914–15. But natural calamities mattered too: snow, or the lack of it, could affect the size of the cut, and problems with runoff could affect its movement along the streams and rivers.

The trends in production help to explain the behaviour of the Ottawa lumber barons, such as J.R. Booth, men who were so noticeably innovative and energetic in the 1890s and thereafter. The future did not lie with local lumbering; it would be necessary to reach farther afield and to try other things. Hence Booth's Canada Atlantic Railway, completed in 1896 to Parry Sound; hence, without doubt, the intense local interest in chemicals, paper, car-building, and hydroelectricity. These long-term trends surely mattered much more than the American tariff developments on which an earlier generation of scholars lavished so much attention.[13]

By the beginning of 1913 Ontario contained six new newsprint paper mills – Dryden, Spanish River, Sturgeon Falls, Sault Ste Marie, International Falls at Fort Frances, and Ontario Paper at Thorold, a site chosen because it had cheap electric power. These six mills had a capacity of 660 tons per day, just over half Canada's national total. In addition, there may have been small outputs from less dramatic new mills, and from additions to old ones.[14] The industry was poised to take advantage of the new opportunities that would follow from the abolition of the American newsprint tariff under the US Reciprocity Act of 26 July, 1911.

Flour-milling, like the pulp and paper industry, was the beneficiary of technological changes that occurred in other countries. At the time of Confederation and for some years thereafter many Ontario mills were converting to new methods, whose effect was to produce better flour, while still relying on millstones and water power.[15] Roller-milling, the development of which began in Switzerland in the 1830s, was perfected in Hungary, where in 1874 porcelain rollers were introduced, thus displacing millstones completely from the milling process.[16] Mixed systems, combining rollers and millstones, were introduced in the province in the

1870s. But all-roller systems were better still. As one scholar explains: 'Roller machines did not demolish the woody hulls of the grain as much as millstones did, did not get as hot, ... required less power, were not dressed as often and required less maintenance. They did 37 per cent more work requiring 47 per cent less power . . . increased the yield per given amount of wheat and made a whiter flour with fewer fragments of hull and germ. Larger mills became possible because rollers required less power, less space, and were more economically run on a large scale.'[17] E.M.B. Snider, who experimented successfully with mixed systems in 1875–7, completed conversion to an all-roller system some time between 1878 and 1881. In 1883 Goldie and McCulloch took out the first Canadian roller-mill patent. Other patents and mechanical improvements followed; the new methods were disseminated quite quickly. But at the same time the output of Ontario's own wheat was tending to fall. The milling industry was increasingly dependent on imports – brought partly from Canada's own western provinces, and partly from the United States – duty free until 1879 and in and after 1880 in bond for exportation. At the same time local mills often continued to mill with stones, concentrating on the production of feed for mixed farming and leaving most flour-milling to the large installations, which, in turn, were increasingly concentrated at points of transshipment, such as the Welland Canal area, or where water power was available in large quantity, such as Kenora.

The flour-milling industry showed a certain tendency towards concentration – but chiefly through new construction, not through merger. W.W. Ogilvie set up a 25,000–barrel mill and an elevator at Fort William in 1899.[18] This giant Canadian firm, founded in 1801, already had mills at Montreal, Winnipeg, Goderich, and Seaforth. In 1902 the business was sold to C.R. Hosmer of Montreal and F.W. Thompson of Winnipeg.[19] In 1903, the Lake of the Woods Milling Company was incorporated to build a large new mill at Rat Portage, where the attraction was Winnipeg River water power.[20] The new company proposed to build one of the biggest mills on the continent, capable of producing 40,000 barrels per day.[21] The machinery would come from Allis-Chalmers of Milwaukee. Less well-located mills, meanwhile, such as those in Peterborough and Ottawa, were being wound up.[22]

Related to the development of the electrical industry, which is surveyed in the next chapter, were certain developments in the chemical trades. With the advent of cheap electric power during the 1890s came the production of calcium carbide, carborundum, and nitrogenous fertilizer, all of which used large amounts of power. The most interesting firm involved in such products was the Willson Carbide Works, which was erected in St Catharines in 1896. Thomas L. Willson had discovered that calcium carbide could produce illuminating gas. In 1897 it was possible to suppose that 'the history of electricity' might be 'repeated in acetylene.'[23] Using his own money, Willson harnessed the power of three locks on the old Welland Canal to generate electricity, which he then applied to lime and coke – or charcoal when he could get it. By mid-1896 the works was exporting large amounts of carbide, chiefly to Germany. Production peaked in 1906–7, but continued to 1914. There were soon hopes for related developments. Rathbun of Deseronto, for instance, possessed immense charcoal kilns, and in 1897 Standard Chemical built another range of charcoal retorts at Fenelon Falls. Besides charcoal, these installations yielded tar and other by-products. The Rathbun firm prospered, and as chapter 11 explains, diversified into iron-making. In 1899 the Bronson family and other Ottawa interests proposed to make calcium carbide in the nation's capital, using 'the very large sawmill premises of Bronson and Weston with its valuable water power.'[24] Regrettably this Bronson carbide enterprise did not make money.

Calcium carbide proved to have other uses: by the application of heat in the presence of nitrogen it would turn into calcium cyanamid, thus fixing the nitrogen in a form that could be ground and used as fertilizer. The process, which consumes a great deal of electricity, was developed in Germany in 1895; the American Cyanamid Company brought the process first to the United States and then, in 1910, to Niagara Falls, Ontario. In 1898 the American Carborundum Company began to produce its patented abrasive material also in Niagara Falls, Ontario.[25] In 1899 the Philadelphia entrepreneur Francis Clergue proposed to use electrolysis to make caustic soda and bleaching powder in his massive Sault Ste Marie industrial complex. Production began in 1902 but ended in 1905: there was severe competition from American suppliers, and the owners claimed that the dominion government refused to put a duty on the competitive imports.[26]

There were hopes for electric refining of metals also. It was thought that the refractory Canadian iron ores might be reduced by electricity.[27] By 1910 there were electric furnaces making ferro-silicon at Welland and the Soo, while the cheap power of DeCew Falls inspired thoughts of electric refining in Hamilton.

The chemical industry was not confined to electro-chemicals; it actually comprised a series of industries, producing a wide range of goods from an equally wide range of inputs. Among the most important for nineteenth-century Ontario were wood, salt, and pyrites; outputs were heavy chemicals, acids, alkalis, and fertilizers.

Wood distillation was a natural outgrowth of the province's forest products industry, and by 1890 it was also interlocked with the production of charcoal, which was, in turn, both an export product and an input for the iron and steel industry. As was noted above, among the leaders in wood distillation were the Rathbun enterprises, which were based in Deseronto.

As for heavy chemicals, it is not yet possible to tell a complete and balanced story of development. The sulphuric acid industry in Brockville and in London has recently been described.[28] Production began in London in 1867, primarily to produce acid for the oil refineries of the city. There was also a firm in Brockville, which built its first plant in 1869, suffered destruction from a cyclone, and lasted until 1884, long after its pyrites deposit was exhausted. The main London firm, the Canada Chemical Manufacturing Company, prospered and expanded for many years, although in 1904 it was forced by competition to close. Other products were developed from time to time. The Brockville firm, for instance, produced superphosphate fertilizer, and hydrochloric and nitric acids. At the turn of the century, as the range of manufacturing industries increased, there were ever more new and varied demands for chemicals. The rubber industry, for instance, absorbed some kinds in large quantities. Regrettably, in 1900 and 1910 the census figures do not separately identify the chemical industry or its components, so that one cannot trace its pre-war expansion systematically. Growth there certainly was, however, so that in 1914 the industry was poised to take advantage of the opportunities that the war would offer.

If the electrical equipment industries and their related chemical industries were full of drama and ingenuity, the brick and cement industries appear boring by comparison. Yet in their growth – especially the growth of the cement trade – there were indeed surprising elements.

The brick industry was widely dispersed, and in the early 1890s its level of sophistication was not high, nor did it require much capital. Large brick works were already established around Toronto and other cities, wherever suitable raw material could be found: bricks, being heavy and inexpensive, cannot support the cost of long-distance transportation. In 1891 the Ontario Bureau of Mines thought there were 257 brickyards; in 1893 it identified 356. Thereafter there was a process of concentration that interacted with the expansion of production. Data are not available for all years, but in 1905 the bureau reported 176 brickyards, and in 1912, 260. Some brick works produced tile and other earthenware artefacts; some firms specialized in the higher-quality wares, such as pressed brick and terra cotta. Some brick works burned wood, and a few seem to have used natural gas, but eventually the normal fuel came to be coal. From time to time the Bureau of Mines remarked on the improvement in brick quality, by which it seems to have meant uniformity of colour and strength. It also noted that the range of face bricks tended to increase and the finish tended to improve, especially after 1900. The results can be seen in the houses and factories of the province. Before 1914 the brick industry also produced appreciable amounts of paving brick. But this product, from which great things had once been hoped, continued to disappoint observers. The quality was variable and often unsatisfactory; brick paving was difficult to lay well or keep even. More interesting, perhaps, was the industry's production of drain tile, in part for agriculture. It will be noticed that outputs of drain tile fluctuated with a distinctive rhythm, reflecting farmers' interest in agricultural improvement and the need for drain tile in urban areas.

The manufacture of 'natural rock cement,' which consisted of ground-up rock and which was sold without any further processing, had a long history in the province. Portland cement, however, was a far better material. Invented in 1824, it consists of various silicates and aluminates of calcium. The cement is prepared by heating chalk or limestone with clay, and grinding the 'clinker' that the heating process yields. Mixed with water, sand, and various aggregates, Portland cement yields the sort of artificial stone that we know as 'concrete.' Ontario first produced the new and better product which arrived only in the 1880s. In 1886 the Rathbun company of Deseronto, which was already a producer of natural cement, began to experiment with Portland cement. Commercial production began in 1891 at Rathbun's Napanee Mills works. Meanwhile, another firm had begun to explore limestone deposits in the Owen Sound area. Seeking advice from British interests in the late 1880s, it soon followed the Rathbuns into commercial production.[29] Thus in 1891 there were two Portland cement works. In 1901 there were four, and in 1913 thirteen works were in production. Many of the works were quite small, and some seem to have used relatively primitive techniques. But there was a noticeable increase in the scale and sophistication of the works as time passed. As for natural rock cement, its three manufacturers also did well through the 1890s, suffering a decline in sales only during 1894–5. However, in 1895 the production of Portland cement exceeded that of natural rock cement, and after peaking in 1901, the output of rock cement fell very quickly. By 1906 only one works survived; in 1908 and thereafter, none was manufactured.

In the great investment boom of 1896–1913, the cement and brick industries could not but grow rapidly. Natural or rock cement was joined by Portland cement, which gradually displaced it. In 1894 the natural cement from Thorold was still widely used for bridge-building throughout the country.[30] But by that year there were Portland cement works at places such as Shallow Lake, and the Rathbun cement works around Napanee were being enlarged. By 1897 the Owen Sound Portland Cement Company and the Rathbuns were supplying large quantities of cement across Canada,[31] and both firms were expanding once again.[32] Meanwhile, the manager of the Don Valley Brick Works claimed that his plant was the largest and most efficient in North America, employing some eighty men and producing in 1898 more than 10 million bricks.[33] From 1893 to 1897 the province's output of natural cement rose from 55,323 barrels to 84,670 barrels, and the production of Portland cement climbed from 30,580 barrels to 96,825 barrels.[34] In 1899 American interests set up a new cement company at Dry Lake, Ontario, and the Owen Sound company expanded further in 1899 and in 1900, when another company was established at Lakefield. In the following years expansion was general, and large new firms were located in places such as Ottawa and Durham, where the world's largest rotary mill was erected.[35] By 1905 the Ottawa Public Works Department was specifying Canadian cement.[36] By that year there was concern about competition and low prices, at least in the United States, but in Ontario expansion continued apace. In 1906 there were twelve producing plants, and another two were under construction; from 1900 to 1906 the production of natural rock cement fell from 125,428 barrels to 8,473 barrels, while that of Portland cement rose without interruption from 306,726 barrels to 1,598,815 barrels.[37] Growth continued in later years, although some firms had financial problems.

In 1909 came the 'Great Cement Merger' – a $30 million combination with a capacity to produce 4.5 million barrels – 1.5 million more than Canada's consumption.[38] The new Canada Cement Company absorbed five Ontario and three Quebec firms, and also one works in Alberta. Eleven Ontario firms remained outside the merger, but their capacities were relatively small, so that the new colossus accounted for the bulk of the province's cement output. Further, at the time of the merger three of the independent firms were idle, and two operated for only part of the year. The merger was floated off at a time of weak prices. The average ex-factory price of Ontario Portland cement had fallen from $2.50 per barrel in 1891 to $1.20 per barrel in 1908. During 1909 the price rose to $1.27, but then the decline was resumed, until in 1915 cement sold for $1.05 per barrel. The *Canadian Engineer* estimated that cement cost 70 cents per barrel to make, and another 70 cents to distribute; 'for the last year,' however, 'prices of cement have been below that figure – thirty and forty per cent below, but it was well known that in some cases it was being sold below cost.'[39] There can be no doubt that one purpose of the merger was to introduce 'order' and thereby ensure profitability for an increasingly heavily capitalized industry. But in 1910, to the discomfiture of the new company, the price of the product continued to fall, and the mills operated only at 57.6 per cent of capacity.[40] Yet Canada's production continued to rise through 1910, 1911, and 1912, and the domestic industry now supplied the bulk of domestic consumption.

By 1913 there were twenty-four Portland cement plants in the country, of which fifteen were in Ontario.[41] Since 1893 Canada's cement production had increased eighty-three-fold, and Ontario's production was 1902 per cent of its 1891 total. The industry was riding on the back of the nation-wide capital investment boom. Indeed, during 1913 the congestion on the railway lines from Ontario westward was so acute that the dominion halved the duty on cement, between 1 June and 31 October, so that American mills could more readily help supply western demand. This was one industry where, for the time being, western demand was indeed crucial. But for the cement industry the pre-war years were the last halcyon ones.

Some Consumer Goods Industries

The capital goods industries provided much of the glamour and excitement of the years before 1914. They were the 'high-technology industries' of the period, and if anybody had imagined an industrial strategy for Ontario they would doubtless have been at the centre of it. Some intermediate goods industries also had glamour. The meteoric rise of the Portland cement industry and its combination into a mammoth enterprise produced a dramatic story. The pulp and paper industry, although its great days of expansion still lay in the future, was off to an excellent start. The iron and steel industry also by 1914 had become firmly established on the Ontario scene. Saw-milling continued, although its thriving days were past.

Few of the consumer goods industries that fed and clothed the people not only of the province but of much of the nation produced much drama. But it should be remembered that they were of large and increasing importance in the life of the province, especially in cities such as Toronto. By 1890 the shoe and clothing trades were moving rapidly from artisan to factory organization. The advent of immigration from central Europe speeded this process but did not cause it; the basic machines had been available for some time, electric power increased the advantages of factory-style production, as did the growth of population, while rising real incomes provided a growing domestic market that businessmen were quick to exploit. Similarly, the bakers, the confectioners, the brewers, and the distillers saw wider prospects, although for the latter two industries the increasing strength of the prohibitionist interest posed a threat for the future, while falling per capita consumption of beverage alcohol restrained growth up to 1900. The great boom industry of the late nineteenth century, butter- and cheese-making, still comprised 1,248 establishments and 2,450 employees. By 1900 the golden days of exportation would soon be past: the domestic market would absorb more of the cheese output, and growing urban markets would absorb more of the province's milk.

As yet there is little detailed knowledge about consumer goods industries such as shoes, clothing, cigars and cigarette-making, food-processing, printing, or publishing. Developments in these trades, important though they were in the growing cities, have only begun to attract historians' attention. However, pork-packing is one such industry about which a great deal is now known. As the historian Michael Bliss has shown,[42] drama and excitement can be found even in the processing of pigs. Bliss's spirited and detailed account treats the progress of William Davies, who arrived from Britain in 1854, set up a special plant for meat curing and smoking in 1861, and built a much larger packing plant in 1874. As Bliss explains: 'In 1875 he [Davies] processed about 30,000 hogs, two-thirds of which were exported to England. A dozen years later, in 1887, he slaughtered 63,500 hogs, and in 1886 more than 80,000, a volume greater than all other packers in Ontario combined.'[43] Unable to buy enough lean hogs in Ontario, in the late 1880s Davies was dependent chiefly on Chicago animals.[44] In the early 1890s the supply conditions changed, partly because of Davies's own activities as propagandist and breeder. Thus in 1893 the company packed more than 95,000 Canadian hogs and no American ones. Other firms quickly began to pack and to export. However, both experimentation and meticulous attention were needed for success; without the greatest care, the pork would 'taint.' Meanwhile, Canadian bacon could do well in Britain only because Canadian packers could buy hogs more cheaply than European packers. Joseph Flavelle, who joined the firm at the founder's invitation, quickly acted to replace dry-salting with 'pickle,' an innovation that produced a better product, and 'pumping' of brine, a process that reduced costs. The Davies company stood ready to buy every hog on offer in Toronto.

As the quality of Davies's pack improved, so did its competitive position in the British market, and its killings rose accordingly: in 1899 the company packed 446,000 hogs.[45] It was by then the largest pork-packing firm in the British Empire, employing some 300 workers. Thereafter, in standard textbook fashion, competition raised the price of Ontario hogs while lowering the British price of Canadian bacon. By 1914, Bliss argues, Canadian bacon was no longer competitive with Danish in the British market; 'in 1913 the Canadian trade was one-tenth of the Danish.'[46] Meanwhile, however, the domestic market had mushroomed.

Pigs, dairying, and butter and cheese production were interlocked because it was customary to feed pigs with whey and other offals from the cheese press and the churn. Farm families followed this procedure, as did the emerging rural cheese factories. If the late nineteenth century witnessed the triumph of the Ontario pig, it also saw the triumphant advance first of the factory cheese and then of the factory butter-mould.

Although butter had been produced on Ontario farms since the first settlers arrived, the development of a commercial butter industry depended on the discovery of a simple and accurate way of measuring butterfat, and of some sort of quality-control.[47] The first prerequisite was satisfied by developments carried out in the United States during the late 1880s; the second was assisted by the development of 'creameries,' each of which processed the butter from several farms, and by the introduction of the mechanical 'cream separator,' which speeded the separation of milk from cream. Workable separators were devised in Europe during the 1870s, and were quickly adopted in Ontario; factory-style creameries came to Quebec in 1873 and to Ontario no later than 1875. Butter exports were tending to decline, however, falling from 19 million pounds in 1872 to less than 2 million pounds in 1888–9.

Although cold storage was perhaps of little significance for a North Atlantic trade in butter, such facilities within central Canada were certainly important: much butter was preserved with salt, yet rancid butter was common. Cold storage became available in Montreal in 1894, and in 1895 the dominion government authorities began to arrange for 'regular ice-car services for butter over stated routes' to Montreal. In addition, the dominion dairy commissioner developed plans for small cold storage facilities, and from 1896 to 1931 the government provided a grant for each such installation. Small mechanical refrigerating machines became available for this use soon after 1900. In 1895, meanwhile, the dominion government installed ice-cooled insulated chambers in six transatlantic steamships. In 1896 another four steamers were thus equipped, and in 1897 fourteen. The policy lapsed about 1900, but, we are told, 'from that time all new ships of the regular lines coming to the St Lawrence have been fully equipped with refrigerated space.'[48] In 1907, furthermore, the dominion provided subsidies for the construction of public cold storage warehouses. Although large cities such as Toronto already had such installations, smaller cities and towns did not; the dominion's new subsidy policy helped make cold storage facilities much more widely available.

By 1914, therefore, there was little risk that Ontario butter would have to be sold as lubricating oil or grease. Exports, furthermore, revived dramatically around the turn of the century, rising from 5.8 million pounds in 1896 to 34 million in 1906. Thereafter, however, they quickly fell away, and the nation began to import large quantities of butter. The technological improvements of the late nineteenth century had quickly generated a new export market, but that market had proved temporary; although there would again be large net exports in 1915–27, export volumes would never again rise to the levels of 1905–6.

The cheese industry developed earlier and with less dependence on technological improvement and quality control. However, the importation of the 'factory cheese system' from New York State to Oxford County, in 1864, was of immense importance. The basic technology was the same as had been used for farm cheese-making, but the factories did employ 'labour saving devices,'[49] so that farm production dwindled. Some cheese factories were proprietary businesses, while others were co-operatives. Much of the agricultural area, including the eastern section of the province and the Ottawa valley, became well populated with cheese factories, although facilities for cheese-making did not spread very much within the Niagara Peninsula, in the south-west, or in the northern counties of Old Ontario. In due course there were better sources of rennet, better storage arrangements including ice-cooled storage at Ingersoll in 1886, and refrigeration at Montreal in 1894. The development of an export trade did not wait upon such improvements. Cheese exports rose from six million pounds in 1868 to 80 million pounds in 1885, 155 million pounds in 1894, and 234 million pounds in 1904, the peak year for cheese exports.[50] In that year, it is thought, home consumption might have been 17 million pounds, so that 89 per cent of Canada's cheese production was going abroad.[51] Although production in Quebec was significant, most of that exportation seems to have come from Ontario. In 1904 New Zealand sent only 9 million pounds of cheese to Britain, and Canada supplied 95 per cent of Britain's cheese imports 'of the same type.' Thereafter Canada's exports fell away, but even in 1914 the dominion still exported 144 million pounds of cheese. Domestic consumption, meanwhile, presumably was larger than in 1904.

Most Canadian cheese was cheddar. However, Canadian cheese makers enjoyed the dubious honour of inventing 'process cheese,' wherein additives and grinding are used to change texture and flavour. Well before World War One, A.F. McLaren of Ingersoll was marketing 'McLaren's Imperial'; J.C. Kraft, a Canadian, developed his own form of process cheese, buying out the McLaren company and setting up the Kraft-McLaren Cheese Company in 1921.[52]

To supplement this qualitative picture of the importation and spread of new methods in the dairy industries a quantitative picture is desirable. The available data are summarized in table 7.13, wherein the most striking feature is the retreat of farm cheese production in the face of factory production. The laggard development of 'butter factories,' or creameries, is also apparent. Indeed, although the growth of farm butter production is less dramatic than the expansion of factory cheese production, it is far from negligible.[53]

What of the volume of cheese production? Applying the price indices that appear to be the most suitable,[54] it becomes apparent that the census data really do say that in the 1870s the outputs of the cheese factories really did triple, and that from 1870 to 1900 the increase was nearly eight-fold, while from 1900 to 1910 output declined by about 10 per cent. On the other hand, the production of factory butter sextupled between 1880 and 1900 and increased another 70 per cent from 1900 to 1910. If the factory cheese industry was one of the province's spectacular performers from 1870 to 1900, from 1880 to 1910 the factory butter industry was performing almost as well.

It is generally thought that the exportation of cheese declined partly because of competition from New Zealand and Denmark and partly because the growing domestic markets within Canada demanded not only more cheese but also, and more importantly, ever larger quantities of milk. A study of the butter data suggests that demand for butter may have played a part also. As was seen in chapter 3, after 1919 the number of Ontario cows did not rise, although the average yield per cow was drifting upward. Milk, however, could become a popular urban food only if the public believed that it was safe to drink milk. That belief, in turn, required first of all an improvement in delivery systems and secondly the spread of pasteurization. It was also necessary to devise systems of shipment, so that farm milk could reach cities. That step was taken first – well before 1900. However, 'This milk was delivered to customers without treatment of any kind until the close of the nineteenth century.' Nor was it generally bottled.[55]

Although in Denmark and Switzerland there had been hygienic systems of milk distribution since the late 1870s, none was introduced in Canada until 1900, when the City Dairy opened in Toronto and the Ottawa Dairy in the capital. Both provided for regular daily delivery of bottled milk – an important matter when neither retail stores nor households generally possessed refrigeration. The Ottawa Dairy began to pasteurize its milk in 1906, and in 1915, after the practice had gradually spread, Toronto required that milk be pasteurized except where the producing herds could be certified as disease-free.[56] One effect, one must suppose, was a reduction in tuberculosis, diphtheria, scarlet fever, typhoid, and various other communicable diseases. Another effect was surely to encourage the consumption of fluid milk. A third was to reduce the number of cows in city backyards and sheds.

Condensed milk was first produced by Gail Borden in New York State during 1853, and malted milk was invented by William Horlick of Wisconsin in 1883. In Canada condensed milk was first produced in Nova Scotia, but south-western Ontario soon became the locus for most of the country's production. Milk powder was first made at Brownville in 1904. By 1912 Canada was producing 12 million pounds of condensed milk and exporting 4.4 million pounds; most of this trade originated in Ontario.

Conclusion

Ontario's industrial revolution was remarkably wide ranging. Through pork-packing, factory cheese, and factory butter it was close to the soil. Through saw-milling, pulp, and paper, it was linked with the great forest industries of the province. Its flour-milling industry changed from a processor of the local wheat to a processor of prairie grain and a producer of animal fodder, altering its scale and location in the process. Although the industrial transformation was well under way before electricity was adopted, the subsequent development of hydro power came to mean a great deal not only for the domestic and industrial consumer, but also for the manufacturing firms that produced capital goods and consumer durable goods. Although by 1914 the arrival of the automobile had not particularly affected the province's road system, it was already influencing the manu-facturing industries in a variety of ways, and, as car ownership spread into rural areas, the structure of farm life changed as well. Nor was industrial growth entirely of an 'extensive' kind. Even after 1900, when so much of the nation's output was being accumulated, labour productivity was rising rapidly enough to propel living standards upward, at least on the average and in general. This is not to deny that for many urban workers conditions in 1913 or 1914 were anything but comfortable. None the less, for many people they do appear to have been improving, and certainly they were good enough to attract migrants, both from rural Ontario and from outside the province.

Besides the labour that flowed to Ontario from overseas, the province's industrial revolution depended to some extent on external sources of capital, managerial skill, and entrepreneurial talent. This fact should surprise nobody: the small Ontario economy of 1870 or 1880 could not and did not contain enough reserves of capacity to transform itself without supplementation from abroad. The new products and new techniques came almost exclusively from elsewhere – partly from overseas and partly from the United States. In observing the inflows of capital funds, labour, and managerial and entrepreneurial talent, one should not fall into the error of assuming that local supplies were wanting, or that some sort of structural failure is reflected in the fact that inputs flowed from abroad. In fact, the province contained many entrepreneurs, considerable thrift, and a great deal of risk-taking. Nor did the importation of technology represent some sort of failure. Ontario was a small element in the developing industrial economy of the western world, and other regions were not only larger but more industrialized and much better equipped with the human resources and the institutions that could generate new products and new methods. To some extent the Ontario economy was responding to stimuli from abroad – to new and attractive market possibilities. But many of the stimuli were local, as were many of the market-opportunities.

During the period that has been examined in this chapter the Ontario economy acquired a recognizably 'modern' form. Cities and industries grew apace, both before 1890 and after 1900. Many familiar firms and industries made their appearance for the first time, while some older-established trades became much less significant both for the province's industry and for its entire economy. Hydroelectricity appeared to supplement the province's energy base, reducing its dependence on the importation of coal. Heavy industry, capital goods industries, and the characteristic consumer durables industries of twentieth-century life all blossomed impressively. So far as consumer goods were concerned, Ontario's principal markets were still within its own boundaries and in Quebec. The same was true, although to a lesser extent, of its capital goods trades, where, especially after the mid-1890s, the nation-wide investment boom created new cyclically fluctuating markets for iron, steel, rolling stock, cement, bricks, and agricultural implements. The province was an important exporter of manufactures: automobiles, agricultural machinery, sawmill products, pulp and paper, processed meat, flour, and smelter products were among the goods that flowed from its factories to non-Canadian lands. As for the domestic market, the protective tariff helped direct Canadian demand from foreign suppliers to Ontario factories. At the same time, it attracted not only an increasing flow of components, spare parts, and capital goods, but also additional amounts of direct investment, especially, though not exclusively, from the United States. The effects of this long economic expansion are still clearly marked on the landscape – in the Victorian streets and town centres that date from 1890 or earlier, and in the large areas of Edwardian housing that represent the urban expansion of 1896–1913. During the 1920s and 1930s further industrialization and urbanization would take place, but there would be nothing as dramatic as the transformation that occurred before 1914.

8 The Electrification of Ontario

In the industrial transformation of the province, the electrical industries played an enormously important part, especially in the 1890s and thereafter. This major and massive technological change rested upon a group of crucial inventions that were all made elsewhere, in the 1870s and 1880s, but they were quickly domesticated in the province.

In 1870 Ontario industry was propelled very largely by water power. Grist-mills, saw-mills, fulling-mills, textile-mills, and foundry installations all depended on falling water to turn wheels, drive hammers, and pump air through bellows. Power sites were widely distributed through the settled areas of the province, and since the demands for the services of industries such as milling were very largely local, the geographical pattern of production was naturally a scattered one, in that both power sources and other inputs, such as logs and unmilled grain, were dispersed. Well before 1867 there had been a noticeable tendency for one sort of mill to be joined by others, so that a village might first possess a saw-mill, then a grist-mill, then perhaps a woollen-mill, and even a foundry. Furthermore, the mill sites and mill buildings were often converted from one use to another, or supplementary lines of work might be jointly accommodated under the original roof. Local owners and managers owned and operated these firms. In a few places, such as Dundas and Gananoque, water powers were so attractive that they produced a genuine sense of industrialization; Gananoque, for instance, was sometimes called 'the Birmingham of Canada,' because its water powers produced such a wide range of metal goods. In Ottawa the waterfalls of the Rideau and Ottawa rivers powered numerous saw-mills and grist-mills.

Dependence on water power, however, was not universal even in 1870. Some industrial centres, such as Hamilton and Berlin, possessed none. Indeed, during the 1860s most Berlin factories were steam propelled. Although there had been mills on the River Thames at London at one time, the city's industrial development was based on steam not on water power. In Toronto there were mills on the Don and Humber rivers, but by 1870 it was already clear that most new industries would be sited in parts of the city where water power was not available.

As time passed, during the 1870s and 1880s, there was certainly a change in the 'fuel balance,' although one cannot document this change statistically. Small-town mills were very inclined to catch fire, and if the local agricultural and forest economies no longer required their services, they were not rebuilt. Deforestation probably produced variations in stream flow that would make some mills uneconomic, even when their services were still in demand. On the other hand, there were improvements in water wheel design, of which the turbine water wheel, which made better use of whatever water was available, was the most important. However, boiler and steam engine design was becoming even more efficient, so that the 'steam cities,' such as Berlin, London, Toronto, and Hamilton, could and did develop as industrial centres without relying on water power. Thanks to the development of the southern Ontario railway system and to the improvement in cross-lake transportation, American coal could be laid down at more Ontario points on favourable terms. It is also reasonable to suppose that although many small mills were allowed to continue in service as long as they could be operated, when replacement was needed, water would give way to steam power. That is to say, so long as the mills were operable in a physical sense, and so long as they earned enough to cover direct operating costs, they would remain in operation; replacement, however, would often be with a later technology, in so far as replacement occurred at all. Thus overshot and undershot wheels gave way to turbine wheels, and water power in general gave way to steam. Nevertheless, the transition to steam was by no means complete when a still-newer technology, that of electricity, appeared on the scene.

The Beginnings of Electrification

If there were any electric light plants in 1881, the census takers did not manage to record them. It appears that hydroelectric power was first used in Ontario in 1882, to light an Ottawa mill. Thereafter, decade by decade, they reported on 'electric works,' under one label or another, until with the Dominion Bureau of Statistics annual data began to appear. Table 8.1 presents the best statistical picture that the census can yield for the period 1880–1915. When interpreting the table, two things must be remembered. When electrical generating plant was incorporated into the equipment of another business, such as a tannery or a chemical works – a common arrangement before 1910, especially in the 1890s – that plant is not included in the tabulation. Secondly, the price per unit of electric power was tending to fall, especially after 1900. The real value of output – or volume of output – therefore rose even more rapidly than the table suggests.

The 1891 census reported the number of establishments in each census district. The result is interesting, in that it gives some idea of the extent to which electric power was available by that time. There was still no plant in Ottawa, although some local mills were already generating their own power. Hamilton reported four plants and Toronto two; there were two plants in each of six constituencies and one in each of a further thirty-one. Cornwall, Kingston, London, Perth, Peterborough, Prescott, and Renfrew were serviced. These early plants were small, and their distribution systems were small scale and local. In some instances pre-existing water power sites powered the generators, but dynamos might be coupled to steam engines, which in turn were normally fuelled by American coal. The electric power itself, in turn, was sold in the immediate locality.

At first, electric power was of interest almost entirely in connection with lighting.[1] In 1882 the *Canadian Manufacturer* reported that the following year the new Welland Canal would be lit by electricity throughout its length.[2] On 13 April 1883, the Edison electric light was first introduced into Canada to light the mills of Canada Cotton Manufacturing Co. at Cornwall. All the equipment, which operated at 110 volts, was made in Hamilton.[3] In this as in all other early installations the factory had its own dynamo, which was driven by a steam engine. Electric street lighting was installed soon after, appearing in Hamilton in 1883; as the wires quickly spread up and down the streets of urban Ontario it became possible to connect those businesses who would not use enough power to justify a self-contained installation. Peterborough, where electric power was first available by mid-1884, was among the first Ontario towns to possess electric light. The dynamo was placed in an old mill,[4] and the Royal Electric Company of Montreal supplied the equipment. Toronto's first installation, designed and operated by J.J. Wright, was begun in spring 1883.[5] In the 1880s, and indeed in the 1890s, it was usual for companies to charge by the individual light – incandescent bulb and / or arc – just as the gas light companies had generally charged by the burner. Cities paid for street lighting in this way, as did private and commercial consumers of power. Larger firms, however, continued to install their own dynamos. Often having spare capacity, by 1890 they were proceeding to install electric motors as well as electric light; also, by 1890 the electrification of street railways had begun.[6]

As the electricity-generating industry grew, the dominion took steps to inspect the installations, levying fees based on the number of arc and incandescent lamps connected by each company. The result, starting with the fiscal year 1895–6, is an annual series of data that reports the number of installations and the number of each sort of lamp. Until the end of 1912–13, these data are available company by company; they appear in table 8.2. For 1901 they are more comprehensive than the census returns, which do not include all the very small installations that were so common, especially in small towns and villages. Even so, these data are not a perfect measure of the growth of the industry, because they take no account of electric motive power, and because they include installations that were parts of other businesses. They do, however, testify to the rapidity with which the industry grew, and to the explosive growth that followed the introduction of hydroelectric power in Toronto, Hamilton, and much of south-central Ontario in the years after 1898.

These Inland Revenue returns, specifying as they do the identity of every firm and the place of its activity, can be used to describe the structure of the emerging industry. At the beginning, in 1894–6, very few firms were publicly owned – only twelve in 1895–6, almost all located in small towns or villages. In a few places, electric service was interlocked with other businesses – in Walkerville, with distilling; in Owen Sound, with manufacturing; in Gravenhurst, with 'trading'; in Brantford and Woodstock, with street railways; in Gananoque, with water supply; in Simcoe, Chatham, St Thomas, Stratford, Berlin, and Galt, with gas. Thanks to the prevalence of the franchising system, very few places had two supplying companies, and no place had more than two. In Renfrew, A.W. Wright competed with Mackay and Guest; in Smiths Falls, also, there were two supplier companies. But in Toronto and Perth, competition was only apparent: each city had one firm for arc lighting and another for incandescent lighting. In the larger cities substantial enterprises had already appeared – the London Electric Light Company, the Ottawa Electric Company, the Toronto Incandescent Light Company, the Hamilton Electric Light Company. In other centres, too, there were considerable medium-sized businesses. But in many of the 141 places where electricity was produced for sale, the supplier-enterprises were very small, and many of these firms appear to have been proprietorships rather than incorporated companies. Indeed, some were so very small that they must have been by-employments for their owners, who would run a generator, light a few municipal arc lights, and perhaps sell small amounts of current for incandescent lamps. Such an enterprise was J. & W. McMaster, of Ridgetown, with forty-four arc lights and ten incandescents. Thus, although electricity was being generated in some remarkably small places, in such villages and hamlets it was rarely available in quantity. Nor was it distributed to the countryside.

Perhaps some farmers had their own generators, but no one knows how many.

The local histories give some additional glimpses of electrification, especially in the early stages. The village of Orangeville acquired an electrical company in 1882. The idea was to use scrap wood from a planing mill and coffin factory to generate steam for an electric dynamo. There was no power for industry until long afterward; the small, unsatisfactory, and frequently bankrupt Orangeville installation barely sufficed for lighting. In 1886, the Gilmour saw-mills at Trenton began to produce hydroelectric power for the town. Similarly, at Cornwall, in 1887 the canal was tapped for hydroelectric power, although it appears that at first the power was used only for lighting. In 1889 Oakville acquired electric lighting, thanks to a generator that was powered by a steam threshing machine. In 1890 the Maple Leaf Rubber Company of Port Dalhousie began to use its fourteen-foot head of water to generate electricity, which it supplied to the townsfolk. At St Catharines, from 1884 onward, there were hydroelectric plants, which supplied small businesses and the town street-lighting system; in 1887, to supply the continent's first regular electric streetcar service, the old Welland Canal was tapped for hydroelectric power. Similarly at Brantford, where the Grand River drops thirty-three feet in twelve miles, Mr Alfred Watts installed an electric dynamo in the mid-1880s, and in 1894 electricity for motive power was first supplied. With connection to the DeCew Falls system of Hamilton Cataract Power in 1908, there was a sharp fall in Brantford's electricity rates. In Dundas, a local hydroelectricity company began to operate in 1895. And in Fergus, by 1900, a local doctor owned an electricity plant.

As time passed, the structure of the industry changed, although by 1914 it was still remarkably individualistic and small-scale. More and more municipalities were taking over pre-existing electric plants, or installing new ones. By 1911–12 there were sixty-eight municipal power plants in the province; in 1903 there had been only thirty-seven. Furthermore, there was a perceptible tendency for the medium-sized cities to join the ranks of the villages and small towns where the municipal power movement had begun. In terms of generating capacity, the greatest advance of the municipal movement occurred in Ottawa, where in 1906 the city took over the Consumers' Electric Company, thereafter operating and developing its own system in competition with the Ottawa Electric Company. In 1911–12 Ottawa Electric supplied almost three times as many light bulbs as the city's system, but in 1906–7 it had supplied more than four times as many. In London and Hamilton private power companies still reigned supreme. The ancestor of the Hamilton Electric Light and Power Company, which supplied 108,900 bulbs in 1912–13, supplied 8,000 bulbs in 1895–6. In

Toronto, the incandescent company supplied 30,000 bulbs in 1895–6, whereas its successor, the Toronto Electric Light Company, supplied half a million in 1912–13. Regrettably, because the competing Toronto municipal system owned no generators of its own, the Inland Revenue officials noted its existence in their 1912–13 report without reporting the size of its network, which, although still smaller than that of Toronto Electric, was growing quickly.

It was because the large firms of Toronto, Hamilton, London, and Ottawa, and the smaller firms of many medium-sized cities had yet to extend their transmission lines at all widely that there was still so much scope for small-scale enterprise, whether public or private, in the smaller towns and villages of the province. Nor had the provincially owned Hydro-Electric Commission yet made much of an impact on this situation. In 1914 it still generated very little power of its own, and its distribution system was still little more than a Y of trunk lines, connecting Niagara Falls with Toronto and London. Its impact on the province as a whole and the extension of its service to rural areas would be matters for the future.

Because at first it was thought to be difficult or impossible to transmit electricity over any great distance, hydroelectric power was developed more slowly than might have been expected. In the late 1880s there was a tendency to adumbrate great engineering schemes that would bring water to the larger cities and generate power there. Georgian Bay water was to come to Toronto and Lake Erie or Grand River water to Hamilton.[7] Nothing came of these plans. But in 1890 the Cataract Construction Company, usually identified with W.B. Rankine of New York, began to build tunnels and power houses on the American side of Niagara Falls. The company at first planned to supply Buffalo, twenty-two miles away; if that great distance could be spanned, it would extend its service to Rochester, sixty miles distant. The *Canadian Engineer* observed, 'This will be the longest distance to which the electric current will have been conveyed on a commercial scale, and the demonstration of its feasibility will at once settle the question as to whether electric power can be conveyed on a large scale to Hamilton and Toronto from the Canadian side of Niagara.'[8]

Unhindered by problems of long-distance transmission, hydro power developed in Ottawa far more rapidly than elsewhere. Although in 1880 there was no electric installation, by 1900 the city possessed more electric bulbs than Toronto and almost as many as Montreal – a tribute to the cheapness and reliability of the hydro service. The Chaudière Falls provided a drop of thirty feet, and were said in 1902 to have the potential to develop 50,000 horsepower at low water. Within a forty-five-mile radius there were said to be sites with a potential of 500,000 horsepower.[9] Because there were many owners of water power, several installations were put up, annoying engineers while satisfying such capitalists as Booth, Ahearn, Clemow, and Bronson. In 1900 nearly all the powerhouses and mills around the Chaudière burned down; even after rebuilding there were still several separate installations. One belonged to the Ottawa Street Railway, which in 1891 had begun to operate a regular service of electric streetcars. Another belonged to the Bronson Carbide Company. There was also the Ottawa Electric Company, which operated not only a hydroelectric plant but also a steam auxiliary station for itself and for the streetcar company.[10] Booth and Eddy generated their own power, and still other installations served Hull.

In the Ottawa developments the great timber magnates, especially Booth and Bronson, played an important role. So did Thomas Ahearn and Warren Soper, who began respectively as a telegraph messenger and a cash boy. In the early 1880s they formed a partnership as electrical engineers and contractors, building many long-distance telegraph lines, including the CPR telegraph system from ocean to ocean. In 1891 they created the Ottawa Electric Railway Company and equipped it with its own generating station. Ahearn, Soper, and Bronson became allied, first with one another and then with associates such as Francis Clemow and Robert Blackburn; the group of local entrepreneurs quickly came to control the street railways, the local gas enterprises, and much of the electric generating capacity of the Ottawa area. Hydroelectric power, however, was not enough of an attraction to pull much new industry to the national capital.

On the Niagara frontier development took a different course.[11] In 1892 the American Rankine syndicate, under the name of Canadian Niagara Power Company, leased the water powers on the Canadian side of the falls from the Queen Victoria Niagara Falls Park Commission, which wanted some money to beautify its holdings. The lease was for 100 years; it gave almost complete monopoly power to the company, which was obligated only to pay a small fixed annual fee, to start work by May 1897, to produce at least 25,000 hoursepower by November 1898, and to supply at least half of its power to Canadian buyers. The Canadian side was thought to be more attractive for power purposes. By 1895 the company had paid $87,500 in fees but had yet to begin work on the Canadian side; on the American side the parent firm supplied its first power on 2 July 1895. So far as Canada was concerned, moreover, the Rankine syndicate appeared to be obstructionist. In 1896 the Welland Power and Supply Company of St Catharines proposed to generate 300,000 horsepower by taking water from the Welland River and tipping it over the escarpment; Rankine refused to allow the company to draw the necessary water.[12]

Fortunately for the promoters of the Cataract Power Company of Hamilton, Rankine was unable to thwart their plan to draw water from the

Welland Canal and bring it down the escarpment near DeCew Falls.[13] At first there would be 4,000 to 5,000 horsepower, but as much as 60,000 horspower could be generated at that site.[14] The power would have to move some thirty-five miles from the dynamos to Hamilton. No such long-distance transmission had as yet been attempted, but the problem was solved by engineers from the Royal Electric Company of Montreal and Toronto. Beside the Welland Canal the Willson Carbide Works was generating its own hydro power.

In 1897 the Canadian Niagara Power Company, still having done no work on the Canadian side, applied for an extension. Yet on 25 August 1898 the Hamilton Cataract group opened its power plant near DeCew Falls, the entire project having been constructed in ten months and twenty days.[15] Hamilton received its first regular supply on 23 October 1898. No wonder it was thought that the Rankine syndicate was delaying unduly! In December 1898 the Ontario government referred the question of the Rankine franchise to the High Court of Justice. In October 1899 it issued a new franchise, which obligated the Canadian Niagara Power Company to supply power to Toronto. In 1900 the company promised to do so by July 1, 1903.[16] Only in 1899 had the company begun to bore test holes for its proposed tunnel;[17] in 1902, although work had progressed, the installation was not complete or usable.[18]

Under the new franchise arrangements the Rankine syndicate had lost its monopoly control. Two firms, one based in Buffalo and the other in Toronto, quickly secured permission to undertake projects. In 1900 the new Ontario Power Company obtained access to the water power, and in 1902 it began its works, which were designed to take water from the Welland River and bring it down the cliff at the Horseshoe Falls on the Canadian side. At the same time a group of Toronto capitalists applied for a company charter and approached the Niagara Park commissioners. The group was a strong one – William Mackenzie, Fred Nicholls, S.G. Beatty, and H.M. Pellatt of Toronto and James Ross of Montreal. On 29 January 1903 its franchise was secured. At this point the company was called the Toronto and Niagara Power Company. It proposed to generate 125,000 horsepower, while Ontario Power proposed to produce 150,000 horsepower at first and another 150,000 in due course, and Canadian Niagara Power planned for 100,000. By September 1904 Toronto and Niagara had begun to build their steel transmission line. In view of the ties of ownership and community of interest, it is hardly surprising to find that a 'large part' of the metal work was coming from the Canada Foundry Company of Toronto,[19] a subsidiary of Canadian General Electric, which Nicholls controlled. At Niagara itself the actual execution of the Toronto and Niagara Company's works was entrusted to the Electrical Development

Company of Ontario – 'a company composed chiefly of the same shareholders ... of whom Frederick Nicholls, of Toronto, is perhaps best known to electrical men.'[20]

Ontario Power put its first turbine to work on 1 July 1905, by which time the Canadian Niagara installation was substantially completed, and work was well advanced on the Electrical Development Company site. In 1905 that firm received permission to double its output, and agreed to furnish electricity to the towns and cities of western Ontario at prices fixed by the lieutenant-governor-in-council.

The Coming of Ontario Hydro

Before the new firms had begun construction, Ontario businessmen had begun to agitate for some share in Niagara's output of hydroelectricity. On 11 February 1902, a group of Waterloo businessmen met to discuss the question of 'cheap power to manufacturers.'[21] The leader of the gathering was E.W.B. Snider, a prominent miller and manufacturer. He suggested that the smaller cities should band together for electric purposes, perhaps in collaboration with Toronto, which was already trying to erect a municipal transmission line to Niagara. At this stage it was not clear whether the best idea was to entice the power companies into the transmission business, for the towns to develop their own power and transmit it, or for the provincial government to develop and sell the power to the towns, many of which already owned their own public utilities. Municipal eagerness was increased by the 'coal famine' of 1902, when strikes in the American mines threatened the factories of Ontario with fuel shortages. In autumn 1902 Snider met Premier George Ross, who was happy to see the cities and towns construct a transmission system, but who himself was not prepared to act. Support, meanwhile, was increasing: since the Toronto power syndicate was unpopular, Toronto businessmen became active in the movement. Pressed by an energetic delegation, in 1903 Ross introduced legislation to provide for an Ontario Power Commission, which would conduct feasibility studies with an eye to the production and transmission of power under municipal auspices. Snider became the chairman of the commission.

The new Conservative administration of James Whitney, taking office in 1905, was believed to be more sympathetic to the public power interests, and more critical of the 'Niagara monopolists,' than the outgoing Liberal government. It should also be noticed that the Ross government was terrified of debt, whereas, as chapter 19 will show, the Whitney government seemed almost to be eager to borrow. The difference was crucial: to transmit hydroelectric power over long distances and to generate it under public auspices would demand plenty of capital. Soon after taking office, Whitney annulled a contract that Ross had accepted, under which the Electrical Development Company would have held all the remaining rights at Niagara.[22] Adam Beck, the mayor of London, called for a provincial commission to formulate a hydroelectric policy; Whitney set up such a commission on 5 July 1905, installing Beck as chairman. In spring 1906, Beck's commission recommended a publicly owned distribution system. The earlier Snider commission favoured a municipal co-operative distribution network, which would buy power from the private companies at the falls. Beck's commission also proposed that the private companies should go on generating power, but under regulation. The Electrical Development Company most reluctantly revealed that it proposed to charge between $25 and $35 per horsepower in Toronto, while the Ontario Power Company was charging between $12.50 and $12.75 on the two sides of Niagara Falls. Whitney proceeded to set up a permanent Hydro-Electric Commission, under Beck's chairmanship. The new body, quickly nicknamed Ontario Hydro, would regulate the private utility companies and would distribute power; it was armed with powers of expropriation, but Whitney took some care to ensure that British capitalists, who were financing not only the Electrical Development Company but also the province (which was borrowing on the capital markets for the first time), would not take fright. The American-owned Ontario Power Company was willing to co-operate with the commission; the Toronto-based Electrical Development Company was not, and took great trouble to change the government's mind. But in Toronto and in at least twelve other Ontario cities, rate-payers endorsed the idea of municipal distribution. In April 1907 the commission signed a contract with the Ontario Power Company.[23] And in spring 1907 the legislature made it possible for Toronto to erect its own distribution system without having to acquire the Toronto Electric Light Company.

Not surprisingly, the Electrical Development Company, its works unfinished and its bonds unsalable, 'tottered on the brink of collapse.'[24] It was rescued by William Mackenzie, who devised the Toronto Power Company as a holding entity that would consolidate the several interlocked electric enterprises. 'The object of all this maneuvering,' Nelles writes, 'was to permit the Toronto Railway Company to guarantee a sufficient number of Electrical Development Company bonds to complete its works.'[25] In August 1908 a contract for the construction of the commission distribution system was signed; after frantic efforts to block the commission's plans, Mackenzie was obliged to persevere with his own transmission line to Toronto.

Even without access to the hydroelectricity of Niagara, the Toronto

Electric Light Company, though violently unpopular, could claim to have served the public well. From its foundation in 1884 until 1908 its paid up capital rose from $175,000 to $3,385,477.29, while its rates appeared to have fallen quite dramatically. In 1884 it had charged the city $226.30 per street light per year; in 1908 it charged $69.35. It also appeared to be charging less per kilowatt hour than the average of large North American cities. In Ottawa and Orillia, electricity was substantially cheaper than in Toronto.[26] But these smaller cities had hydro, and in 1908 Toronto still did not. Niagara electricity reached Berlin over Ontario Hydro lines early in October 1910 and Toronto only in 1911.

At first the municipal Hydro-Electric Commission and Toronto Electric Light co-existed. The city built its own distribution system and used 'its' power to light streets and public buildings and to operate its pumping stations. As it had contracted to take more power from Niagara than it needed for municipal purposes, it had plenty of power to sell, undercutting the Company from 30 to 40 per cent.[27] Neither municipal nor provincial Hydro yet generated any electricity; they bought power from the Ontario Power Company at Niagara.

Construction work had proceeded more slowly and more expensively than anybody had foreseen. By 1911 Canadian Niagara generators were rated at 62,500 horsepower, and the Electrical Development Company's dynamos were rated at 50,000. The latter firm had raised $10 million in mortgage bonds and had spent $12.6 million at Niagara and $3.6 million on the Niagara-Toronto transmission line; it had an accrued net loss and had paid its bond interest only with difficulty. Indeed, in 1908, having spent $8 million without having finished the plant, it found the remaining $2 million in bonds 'almost unsalable on account of misconceptions as to the effects of Government-owned power projects.'[28] Mackenzie had saved the project by organizing the Toronto Power Company to lease both the Electrical Development Company and the transmission company, ordinary share-holders' equity being written down by half.

In 1901 there were 196 electricity-generating plants in Ontario, as against 50 in Quebec; the province was using 6,830 arc lamps and 384,496 incandescent bulbs. In Toronto alone there were 80,000 incandescent lamps, and Ottawa had just as many. By 1904 Ontario contained 205 plants and nearly 600,000 light bulbs, of which 170,000 were in Toronto and 112,000 in Ottawa. As table 8.2 reveals, this sort of growth continued in later years.

The Ontario electrical scene contained far too much activity for us to survey in full detail. However, Francis Clergue's development of hydro power at the Soo and the Kaministiquia Power Company's project at the Lakehead should be acknowledged. Clergue began the Soo power development in the late 1890s, first on the Ontario side and then on the American. The original plan was to use the power chiefly for metallurgy and for the production of calcium carbide, which did indeed become established at the Soo. Pulp production was also envisaged. The plans grew more grandiose; in 1902 it was expected that Clergue's new dam would furnish power second only to that of Niagara Falls. He was also said to be planning to develop the Kakabeka Falls, near Port Arthur.[29] Whatever the truth of these rumours, Clergue's financial collapse precluded any extension of his empire to the Lakehead, where the Kaministiquia Power Company bought Kakabeka Falls from the province. In December 1906 it began to transmit power over eighteen miles to the Lakehead. This was a much smaller project than the Niagara ones: by 1913 its generating capacity was only 15,000 horsepower. But it was of great importance for its region, where it supplied power to Ontario Hydro for Port Arthur and served Fort William direct.[30]

Most of the power companies during the period 1895–1914 were funded by important issues of long-term bonds, both in Canada and abroad. Faced with very large initial capital outlays and enjoying little or nothing by way of cash flow from other lines of activity, they had no choice. Admittedly, in Toronto the Mackenzie interests could and did provide some capital funds from their other businesses, and they could ensure that their associated banks and insurance companies would take up some of the new bonds. Similarly in Ottawa the Booths and the Bronsons had timber profits that could be directed into the electrical businesses, and perhaps Ahearn and Soper earned enough by means of contracting to do a little of the same. Nevertheless, the larger firms could not avoid some recourse to the open market. And the sums were very large. Consider the Electrical Development Company, which raised $8 million in bonds between 1903 and 1908. In 1903 the province of Ontario had no funded debt at all; in 1908 the deposit liabilities of Canada's chartered banks were $664 million. There can be no doubt that these private electrical projects were very large indeed and that they imposed considerable demands not only on the province's construction and engineering industries but on the national financial fabric.

It is no wonder that some financial recklessness occurred, especially in Toronto and at the Soo. The political arguments of the early twentieth century were much concerned with 'power monopoly' as opposed to 'power for the people,' and the press delighted in exposing the misdoings of the Coxes, Mackenzies, and Nichollses. There is no doubt that such men were anxious to do well, or very well, out of the new opportunities. It is also quite clear that from time to time they cut corners.[31] However, they were local entrepreneurs, grappling with engineering and financial problems of an unprecedented size and complexity. If large-scale hydroelectric projects were to be completed, very large amounts of capital would have to be mobilized. When the Toronto entrepreneurial group began its labours, the provincial government was rather ostentatiously uninterested, and it is difficult to believe that a municipal power system would have undertaken the development at the falls; what Toronto might well have got would be a municipal steam plant, providing service 'at cost' – a rather high cost, compared with the cost of Niagara power. The fact was that the Ontario capitalists undertook an important job of work, one that would serve the citizens of the province as well as themselves. That in the course of their undertakings they irritated those same citizens into taking over much of the responsibility is, perhaps, an example of serendipity in economic history.

The electric power industry was expanding with remarkable speed. Everything was in its favour. Economic growth was increasing the demand for power, especially perhaps for electric power. Technological progress continued to reduce the costs of construction and equipment, while rendering that equipment more reliable. In some markets, such as Toronto and Ottawa, the advent of competition and the breakdown of restrictive practices ensured that the full gains from cost-reductions would be passed on to the public; in some other markets, the combination of Niagara transmission lines and municipal ownership had the same effect. Thus it is no wonder that the production of Niagara power increased dramatically.

Once its system of distribution lines was nearing completion, Ontario Hydro began to acquire its own generating plant. The major developments occurred after 1914, when Hydro first bought one of the Niagara plants, then built the enormous Chippewa installation at Niagara, and finally began to buy up the plants of the surviving private generating companies, not only at Niagara but elsewhere. However, the first two installations were made before World War One. In 1913 Hydro opened a plant at Wasdell Falls on the Severn River, the first plant designed and constructed by it. Meanwhile, at Eugenia in the county of Grey, a rather larger installation was in prospect. The Eugenia site had first been exploited in 1895, when William Hogg set up a 40 horsepower plant, using a twenty-foot head, to run a chopping mill and to light Eugenia and Flesherton. He also tried to interest the Toronto Railway Company, arguing that a really large installation would transmit power to Toronto. The Mackenzie interests, not surprisingly, did not find the proposal enticing. But in 1905 a Toronto syndicate led by Cawthra Mulock did buy the Eugenia site and arranged for engineering studies. Encouraged by these reports, the syndicate did some engineering work, constructed tunnels, and arranged for local franchises. However, Ontario Hydro having been set up, the syndicate saw little prospect of raising large sums on attractive terms and decided to wait until Ontario Hydro would buy them out. Negotiations to this end were undertaken in 1912; in 1914 the commission bought the Eugenia site; late in 1915, its installation complete, it could supply up to 4,500 horsepower in hydroelectric power. Local municipalities were quickly connected; among these was Durham, an important milling and furniture-making centre which had possessed electric street lighting since 1890. It would be some time, however, before such local Hydro networks would be connected to the larger Niagara-based grid.

Later Developments

After 1914 electrification proceeded apace, tracing a path that had clearly been adumbrated before that time. Ontario Hydro expanded greatly. Its transmission lines spread ever more widely, and with a subsidy from the provincial government it began to extend service into rural areas, producing the effects on rural life described in chapter 3. It also became a major producer of hydroelectric power, partly by constructing its own immense works at Niagara and partly by the purchase of private installations at Niagara and elsewhere. But even in 1941 Ontario's electrical system remained a 'mixed' one. Toronto and some other districts that were served from Niagara also enjoyed the dubious advantage of twenty-five-cycle alternating current. This local peculiarity lasted until the 1950s, when its flickering lights and specialized equipment finally vanished. Other parts of the province had long enjoyed the sixty-cycle current that was the North American standard. But if currents were mixed before 1941, so were patterns of ownership. Ontario Hydro was still a large purchaser of privately generated power, not only from Ontario firms but also from generating stations in Quebec. In some areas, furthermore, private power companies continued not only to generate power but also to distribute it. Almost everywhere, by 1941, hydroelectricity had driven out the old thermal installations; nuclear energy had yet to be harnessed.

9 *Manufacturing, 1914–41*

By 1914 the heroic days of Ontario's manufacturing development had already occurred. The Great Boom had ended in 1913, and a cyclical downturn had begun. Not merely had the province's economic balance shifted from countryside to town and from agriculture to industry; the province's cities and towns now possessed a wide range of sophisticated industries, oriented both to consumers and to producers and exploiting a substantial part of the remarkable technological progress that had been so marked a feature of development in the United States and western Europe between the mid-1880s and the outbreak of war. This is not to say that nothing interesting happened after 1914. A few new industries appeared, and some others grew with remarkable speed, especially during the prosperous years of the mid- and late 1920s. But compared with the period from the mid-1890s to the outbreak of World War One the industrial economy grew more slowly and more predictably, with far fewer surprises. And in 1929 the onset of the Great Depression brought development to an end for almost a decade.

This chapter traces the development of manufacturing during a quarter century in which the dominant characteristics were not so much technological change and massive investment but war and the business cycle. The former was a new phenomenon so far as Ontario industry was concerned, and both the world wars started at times when the Ontario economy was depressed. The business cycle was not new, but now that Ontario was more industrialized than in 1871, it mattered a great deal more. As before 1914, cyclical disturbances came mainly from outside – the fluctuations in export trade and in Canada-wide levels of investment, in which Ontario itself played a considerable but not a dominant part. The foreign environment, furthermore, now mattered in new ways. Ontario's automobile industry was heavily dependent on British Empire markets, so that prosperity, depression, and tariff policy in far-off places such as New Zealand and

India would make a real difference to its fate. And the American market mattered much more than before World War One. Ontario's paper industry, one of the boom trades of the post-1914 years, depended wholly on the United States for its export sales. Much of Ontario's nickel and non-ferrous metal also went to the United States, which, by 1920, was Canada's largest single export market – a position it maintained during most of the 1920s.

Because Canada's statistical services improved so greatly after 1914[1] one can treat these years 1914–41 in a narrative fashion that was not possible before 1914. This kind of treatment is appropriate, indeed essential, in that the years after 1914 were dominated by comparatively short-lived economic fluctuations – the serious slump of 1913–15, the far-from-universal wartime boom of 1915–20, the deep slump of the early 1920s, the comforting prosperity of the later 1920s, the alarming economic collapse of 1929–33, and the halting and incomplete recovery that carried Ontario's manufacturing industries to 1939, and to the outbreak of yet another world war.

If one wants to understand the large movements of the industrial economy one can properly concentrate, as in chapter 7, on the development of exports and of domestic investment; devoting less attention to technological change,[2] because such changes mattered much less for Ontario in the 1920s and 1930s than in the years before 1914.

The War and the Post-War Slump

The outbreak of war did not at once stimulate Canada's export trade, which declined in real terms from 1914 to 1915. Then there was a great change: the volume of exports doubled in two years, and the value of exports in 1918 was more than four times what it had been in 1913. These developments had a potent indirect effect on Ontario's manufacturing industry, but the direct effect was powerful too; paper, non-ferrous metals, vehicles, and various iron and steel products were important elements in the export growth, and in these industries Ontario accounted for all or much of Canada's total production. It was wartime demand that accounted for most of the growth in the province's exports of iron, steel, nickel, and a wide range of manufactures. It was American demand, stimulated by the abolition of the American newsprint tariff, that accounted for the growth of the province's pulp and paper industry; in 1910 production had risen to $55 million, and the nation as a whole exported 89 per cent of its newsprint production. Nickel exports also rose a great deal; further, under the stress of war the dominion and provincial authorities were able to force International Nickel to set up a refinery at Port Colborne. Smelting, therefore, expanded production from $13 million in 1910 to $21 million in

1915; even after peace in 1919 Ontario's smelters produced $31 million worth of output. The war also stimulated a revival of Ontario's transatlantic food-export trades, which had been quiescent or declining before 1914. The bacon, butter, and cheese trades found newly active markets in Britain; prices and volumes rose considerably[3] – indeed, in the eyes of some observers, scandalously.

Because it asked respondents to distinguish between 'general trade'and 'war trade,' the 1916 postal census gives a graphic idea of the importance which war work was already acquiring. The year 1915 was not a prosperous one. Total reported employment was less in 1915 than in 1910. Yet already 9.5 per cent of Ontario industrial production was said to be 'war trade.' Inside the grouping of thirty-two industries that produced 86 per cent of all the province's 'war goods,' a clear pattern can be detected. Table 9.1 summarizes the industrial data. The province's heavy industries and capital goods industries were deeply involved, doing almost half of the 'war trade' and in many cases depending on war demand for a remarkably large percentage of their wartime sales. The textile clothing and leather trades were also deeply involved because their work was needed to equip a citizen army and its transport. They did about one-third of the province's 'war trade.' The food industries, however, were apparently of little account in the province's war effort; although they certainly helped to feed the overseas allies, such orders and shipments were presumably not counted as 'war trade' unless the respondents could identify them as destined to feed the troops in camps and trenches.

As for 'general trade,' in some of the capital goods and heavy industries the level of demand in 1915 was no higher than it had been in 1910. The investment wave of the Great Boom having passed over the province's economy, many of these industries had more capacity than they would have known what to do with, in the absence of wartime demand for boilers and engines, railway equipment, electrical apparatus, explosives, and the like.

The postal census contained no entry for 'munitions'; although it did report a small 'lock and gunsmithing' industry, its tabulations reflect the fact that the war effort of the province's manufacturing industry is distributed over many industries in accordance with the relevant peacetime outputs of these industries. Nor was there as yet a serious aircraft industry, although in Toronto Curtiss Aircraft, which was set up in 1916, did produce a few aeroplanes. Indeed, by the end of the war Curtiss, together with its successor, Canadian Aeroplanes Ltd, had made 3,000 in all.

The export boom did not survive the end of the war. Export volumes and values both declined precipitously to a trough in 1922, at which time export values were only 71 per cent higher than in 1913 and export volumes only 15 per cent higher. As the capacity of Canada's export industries had grown considerably in the interim, the margin of excess capacity was much larger in 1922 than it had been before the war. Ontario's manufacturing industries could not escape the multiplier effects of this contraction. The collapse was especially severe for non-ferrous metals and also for iron and steel products, whose export value did not return to the 1919–20 levels until 1940. Exports of wood and paper products, as a group, also declined in volume and value terms, but exports of newsprint expanded by 73 per cent in the face of the general trading difficulties. This development, which saw the value of Ontario's pulp and paper output rise from $55 million in 1919 to $83 million in 1922, helped cushion the effect of the slump on the Ontario regional economy and partly explains the fact that although the value of Ontario manufacturing output fell from 1920 to 1922, the volume of that output remained approximately constant from 1919 through 1921 and rose slightly in 1922. Further cushioning came from the behaviour of housing investment, both in Canada as a whole and within the province.[4]

In a quite direct way, all this activity of building and subdividing meant orders for Ontario's intermediate and capital goods industries; indirectly, through multiplier effects, it generated more demand for manufactures in general; even more indirectly, burgeoning cities and subdivisions combined with new provincial programs of road improvement to create growing markets for Ontario's motor industry. The output of trucks and buses fell considerably in 1921–2 but recovered even more impressively in 1923;[5] provincial spending on roads and bridges rose steadily from 1918 through 1923. Railway investment, however, behaved in an annoyingly pro-cyclical fashion, increasing the expansionary pressure in 1918–20 and the depressionary forces in 1921–5. These contractionary forces were transmitted to Ontario's capital goods industries, as table 9.2 shows. So far as foundry and machine shop products are concerned, the decline was probably less than these numbers suggest, because the definition of the industry seems to have become narrower between 1919 and 1922. Nevertheless, even when these redefinitions are taken into account there is still a dramatic decline. The electrical industries, buoyed up by the nation-wide electrification, seem to have ridden through the slump with little trouble. The iron-using industries, however, were by 1922 suffering the direct and indirect effects of recession on all fronts – house building, exportation, and investment in railways and in new plant and equipment. Construction and house building in Ontario did not provide enough of a cushion for these industries.

Expansion in the 1920s

Before the various kinds of investment had reached their lowest levels,

Canadian exports had begun to recover. Although there were slight retrogressions in 1925 and 1927, from the trough year of 1922 to the peak year of 1928 the general tendency was strongly upward, both in terms of volume and in terms of value. Assisted by preferential tariff-arrangements in Britain, Australia, New Zealand, the West Indies, and some other empire countries, and by what would now be called 'world product mandating' inside firms such as Ford, Ontario's automobile exports increased greatly. By 1928, as chapter 12 explains, well over 30 per cent of car production was being exported, and 60 per cent of Canada's car registrations were in Ontario and Quebec: the new industry thus depended mainly on markets in central Canada and abroad. Employment in Ontario's auto industry had increased by 122 per cent since 1922, and the value of the industry's output had increased from $84 million to $162 million. Canada's exports of newsprint had increased from 932 million tons in 1922 to 1,911 million in 1928, and the country's production had increased even more rapidly. Hence employment in pulp and paper firms grew in six years from 8,542 to 10,993; in 1929 employment expanded still more, to 11,023. Non-ferrous metals exports grew strongly both in volume and in value between 1922 and 1926; they then suffered a sharp retrogression in 1927 but grew once more in 1928–9, so that by 1929 Ontario's non-ferrous metals smelting industry employed 3,400 people and sold $49 million of output.

From a low point in the calendar year 1921 (or in the fiscal year ending 31 March 1922), the value of Canada's exports rose 67 per cent to the 1928 peak. The value of national exports of agricultural and animal products rose only 17 per cent, the value of exports of forest products rose 38 per cent, the value of exports of iron and steel products rose 150 per cent, and the value of non-ferrous metals and products rose by 233 per cent. These three groups of exports came largely though not entirely from Ontario factories.

Canada's export expansion of the 1920s, therefore, was focused to some extent on Ontario's manufacturing industries, which were benefiting directly from the growth of markets not only in the United States but also in Britain and elsewhere in the commonwealth and empire. The expansion of exports was accompanied, and very much exceeded, by the expansion of domestic investment. Buckley's annual estimates of construction work rise from $692 million in 1924 to a peak of $1,046 million in 1929.[6] From 1924–5 to 1929, export values rose by only $12 million and in real terms exports declined; obviously, therefore, most of the expansionary forces were coming from domestic investment, especially in non-residential construction, machinery and equipment, and non-farm inventories.

Within Ontario, the direct impact of this investment demand can be seen in the expansion of industries such as primary iron and steel, hardware, electrical apparatus, foundries, and machinery, all of which grew between 1926 and 1929. In the machinery industry the value of output doubled in three years, and employment increased 41 per cent. In electrical apparatus output went up by 83 per cent, and employment rose by 42 per cent. In primary iron and steel employment and the value of output roughly doubled.

On the other hand, for Canadian agriculture the late 1920s were not years of great prosperity, and those Ontario industries that depended on farm buyers or farm suppliers were not expanding very much, or at all. In agricultural implements, production and employment increased by about 50 per cent between 1924 and 1926 but grew very little between 1926 and 1929 – three years in which Ontario's meat-packing industry was actually contracting. The butter and cheese industry showed the same pattern of growth between 1924 and 1926, followed by stagnation until the end of the decade. In flour-milling both employment and output tended to contract throughout the decade: both employment and the value of output were considerably larger in 1919 than in 1929.

One aspect of the investment-fuelled expansion was the new importance of consumer durables – the motor car and the newly widened array of household appliances, most of which were falling in price. Of the range of industries that were stimulated, only the radio industry was genuinely new; all the others had existed in Ontario before 1914. Nor were the new technologies developed to any extent within the province; product designs came largely from the United States, as did production technologies, although adaptation was often needed to produce the comparatively small quantities that the Canadian and the export markets demanded.

In the expanding auto, tire, appliance, and electrical industries the scale of plant was generally larger, and the foreign-owned enterprise was more prominent, than Ontario had seen before. A few large firms, such as McLaughlin and Canadian General Electric, moved from Canadian to American ownership. Canadian-owned firms, such as Moffatt and the other components of General Steel Wares, also expanded rapidly to meet the new demands. Efforts were made to set up new Canadian-owned firms, such as the Rugby car company, or the Rogers Majestic radio manufacturing company. If some of these Canadian-owned efforts were unsuccessful and some were small, the same could be said of many of the foreign-owned branch plants.

During the 1920s there was little concern about the volume of American direct investment. Such investment, whether arising from take-overs of existing businesses or from new initiatives, was recognized to be increasing, for a wide variety of reasons. In pulp, paper, and mining, a company would have to come to Ontario if it wished to use the province's natural resources. In many lines of manufacturing, it was convenient to operate within Canada so as to get behind the dominion's wall of protective tariffs or to gain access to British Empire markets whose governments charged preferentially low rates on goods from other empire countries, such as Canada. If one intended to operate a branch plant in Canada at all, Ontario was for most firms the logical place to settle. It offered the same locational advantages as the industrial heartland of the United States. English was spoken, and the bureaucratic and legal systems were somewhat more predictable than those of Quebec, where, in addition, population was smaller, per capita incomes were lower, and labour was not always so experienced. Unions and town governments generally welcomed such plants, which meant a broader tax base and seemed to mean more jobs. There was, in any event, no fear that the American firms were squeezing out the locally owned ones: these were developing mightily, often with the assistance of licensed technologies from the United States.

In the nation as a whole the iron and steel industry was not buoyant. The volume of steel ingots and castings did not return to the 1918 level until 1940, and the volume of pig iron production was almost equally sluggish, rising above the 1919 level only in 1928–9 and never again returning to the 1929 level. The series for hot rolled iron and iron bars begins in 1920: output was below the 1920 level until 1940. As chapter 11 reveals, this depressing national picture was bound to have an effect on the Ontario industry that was so large a proportion of the nation's. It is no wonder that Stelco had little need for loans or new shares from the time of its foundation until after World War Two, or that developments at Algoma were so uncertain.[7]

A business that did well in the 1920s was the Beach Foundry of Ottawa. Established in 1894 by Benson C. Beach with two assistants in Winchester, Ontario, the firm at first produced the 'Beach longwood box stove.' By the turn of the century it was making a full line of cast-iron ranges, and in 1902 it introduced its first steel coal-and-wood range. In 1903 it was incorporated, and thereafter its expansion continued, but even so, the firm had difficulty in keeping up with demand. In 1914 Beach moved his business to Ottawa. The firm was still specialized, and rather small: in 1915 its turnover was only $55,031. But by 1920 the value of its sales had quintupled, and it suffered only slightly in the recession of 1921. In 1922 a new plant was built, and later in the decade it was considerably expanded. In the next two years, Beach began to produce first gas and then electric ranges, and furnaces also appeared in his product line; the production of refrigerators was contemplated, although not until the mid-1930s did the company actually make any. Warehouses and retail stores were spread far and wide across the country; in the late 1920s Beach even began to export. Meanwhile, the company had begun to purchase technology, under licence, from American firms. In 1928 sales were just over $900,000 – more than fifteen times what they had been when the company moved to Ottawa from Winchester.[8]

Although the late 1920s can properly be seen as an era of large plants, it is possible to exaggerate the 'bigness' of the decade. The automobile industry comprised eleven establishments, with average employment of 1,376 men and average output of $15 million, or about 17,000 units per plant. Few other industries approached the average size of the establishments in the motor industry. In electrical apparatus and supplies there were 101 establishments, with average output of less than $1 million. The machinery industry contained 120 establishments, the automobile supplies industry forty-two, the woollen cloth industry twenty-nine, the cotton cloth industry fourteen. There were thirty-six breweries and eight distilleries; the average brewery sold $0.5 million worth of beer a year, and the typical distillery marketed $2.6 million dollars' worth of spirits. The nine oil refineries each produced an average of $4 million, while employing an average of 260 workers.

For the Ontario economy the economic development of the 1920s was partly derived from the nation-wide investment boom, partly reflected the continent-wide – indeed, world-wide – development of certain consumer-durables industries, and to a lesser extent depended on success in the exportation of automobiles, pulp, paper, nickel, and other non-ferrous metals. Technological progress made an important contribution to the reduction of costs of production in several industries, most importantly in the consumer-durables trades, thereby widening markets and raising living standards. But Canada was still in large part an agricultural nation: in 1921, 33 per cent of the labour force worked in agriculture, and even in 1931 the proportion was still 29 per cent. And agriculture was not particularly prosperous. In a sense the prosperity of the late 1920s was more broadly based than the boom of the pre-1913 years, because it was not closely involved with railway-building: railways are inconvenient stimuli, because they involve very large outlays in short periods of time, followed by long periods in which nothing much need be done. Railway-building was still important in the late 1920s. Indeed, in 1929 the railways spent more on construction and repair than they had spent in 1913. But other components of investment had become much larger than before the war, and so had the export trade, where the expansion since 1921–2 had more than offset the contraction of 1917–18 – 1921–2. Nevertheless, if the nation's export trade were to contract or if its investment effort were to flag, Ontario's industrial economy would suffer severely. Early in 1929 the former occurred and later in 1929 the latter.

In the 1920s and 1930s no one regularly counted the unemployed. Since the end of the war there had been a system of federal-provincial labour exchanges, but naturally registration was not compulsory, and there was no system of unemployment insurance that could generate administrative data on 'claimants.' The Dominion Bureau of Statistics later produced annual estimates of the national labour force, its principal components, and the number of unemployed. These estimates cover 1926 and every later year. If the estimated number of unemployed are related to the estimated non-agricultural labour force, it can seen that in 1927–8 something very close to full employment must have existed. Averaging the two years together and attributing none of the unemployment to agriculture, one finds that only 2.7 per cent of the non-agricultural labour force appears to have been unemployed. In 1929, however, economic growth failed to keep pace with the growth of the labour force, so that non-agricultural employment stagnated and 4.6 per cent of the non-agricultural labour force was unemployed. This was the beginning of the slide into depression: in each subsequent year the number rose until in 1933, 37.7 per cent of Canada's non-agricultural labour force was unemployed.

The Great Depression of the Early 1930s

The contraction of the Canadian economy between 1928–9 and 1933 is a classic example of what economists call the multiplier-accelerator process working in a downward direction, and it has been analysed in these terms by Safarian.[9] Reflecting the problems in overseas markets and the selling and stockpiling policies of the western wheat pools, Canada's exports of agricultural products fell in 1929, in terms both of volume and value. The effect on Ontario's industrial economy was negative, but because domestic investment and other export volumes and values were still rising, Ontario's industrial economy could, in 1929, continue to expand the value of its output, its real output, and its employment. However, with the onset of general contraction both in the United States and in Britain and Europe, all other categories of export began to slide downward in value and volume terms. Generally this process can be observed in 1930, although in one case – non-ferrous metals – the decline in volume was delayed until 1931. In Ontario, therefore, during 1930 this industry showed almost no decline in the value of production and even produced a small increase in employment. But by 1930 the downward slide in Canada's pulp and paper exports was being precisely translated into a contraction of Ontario's pulp and paper industry. From peak to trough the volume of Canada's exports fell 27 per cent, the volume of the nation's paper and wood products exports fell 40 per cent, and the volume of non-ferrous metals exports fell 37 per cent. Nor was it unimportant that Ontario's exports of such goods went chiefly to the United States, the country where the slump was especially deep and especially long, and where the even more protective tariff measures of 1930–1 were often very painful for Canada. As for the empire markets that took Ontario's auto and farm machinery exports, these too were very hard hit.

Table 9.3 gives information about the contraction of some Canadian export markets for which the goods came wholly or mostly from Ontario. The numbers, especially if compared with information on production in Ontario, are dramatic. In 1929 it seems that the Ontario motor industry was exporting over one-quarter of its output; from fiscal 1929–30 to 1932, export values fell by 90 per cent, and this shrinkage accounts for over 25 per cent of the decline in industry sales. The agricultural implement industry, which exported almost half its output in 1929, saw export values fall by 90 per cent, with dramatic effects on the scale of its production and employment. The Ontario paper industry contracted its sales by $41 million; Canada's exports of pulp and paper fell by $92.2 million. Exports of rubber footwear and tires fell by 69 per cent, or some $19 million, while sales of Ontario's rubber industry dropped by $43 million, so that 44 per cent of the contraction followed on a decline in export sales. The machinery industry, which had been exporting less than one-sixth of its output in 1929, saw its exports fall by 60 per cent – painful, but less dramatic in its impact on domestic output because the industry had depended less extensively on export demand. The depressing story can be prolonged. Although butter exports fluctuated, cheese exports fell. In 1929 Ontario's production of butter and cheese was just about triple Canada's exports of these goods, most of which must have come from Ontario; the contraction in export sales equals almost half of the contraction in the province's butter and cheese production. By fiscal 1933–4 market prospects improved for nickel, and the British Empire's network of preferential trade agreements, concluded at Ottawa in 1932, had re-created something of an export market for Ontario meats, cars, and parts, while the repeal of American prohibition produced a large increase in Ontario whisky sales, as did the retreat from semi-prohibition in Canada itself.

These comparisons are meant to emphasize that the collapse of Canada's export trade in 1929–33 had a direct effect, not just an indirect effect, on the prosperity of Ontario manufacturing, which did not live simply by serving the Canadian domestic market. Large and important components of the province's manufacturing economy were already on an export basis by 1929; markets in the United States, Britain, and the empire were of direct importance to these industries. Slump abroad, therefore, meant a new kind of slump at home.

Nor were the troubles of Ontario manufacturing simply a reflection of drought and price-collapse in the Prairie wheat economy. Besides depending on export markets, the provincial manufacturing industries also depended heavily on the amounts that Canadians were willing to spend on consumer durables, plant, equipment, and structures of all kinds, as well as on inventories. In the slump of 1929–33 Canadians bought much less under all these headings. In terms of 1971 prices, inventory-accumulation went from $390 million in 1929 to minus $253 million in 1931, a turn-around equal to 4 per cent of 1928's gross national expenditure. The economy continued to deplete its inventories in 1932 and 1933. As the economy was using more than it was producing, production and employment were bound to be depressed. However, other kinds of investment declined too. The volume of gross business fixed capital formation fell by 78 per cent between 1929 and 1933. Residential construction fell by 74 per cent from its 1928 peak to 1933; between 1929 and 1933 non-residential construction fell by 81 per cent, and the volume of investment in machinery and equipment fell by 80 per cent, with predictably disastrous effects on Ontario's heavy industries. Table 9.4 summarizes some of what happened. Because of the sharp increases in dominion tariff rates that occurred in 1930–2, Ontario's heavy industries won a larger share of the smaller domestic market, and so they did not have to shrink as much as that market had shrunk. The shrinkage, none the less, was dramatic and very painful, not only for employees but for employers as well.

The contraction of the early 1930s appears to have been unprecedented. Although one cannot trace the year-to-year fluctuations in industrial output and employment during the slumps of the 1870s and the 1890s, it is generally thought that they were much less severe than the slump of the 1930s, and it is certain that they were much less prolonged. From 1929 to 1933, the real gross output of Ontario manufacturing fell by 37 per cent, and employment fell by 32 per cent; measured in current prices, the value of output declined by 52.5 per cent. Almost all industries suffered, although in general the consumer goods industries suffered much less, because spending on non-durable consumer goods was much better sustained than spending on capital goods and consumer durable goods. The output of bread, biscuits, and confectionery fell by 38 per cent in terms of current prices. In the clothing trades, employment fell by 34 per cent, in hosiery and knit goods by 21 per cent, in slaughtering and meat packing by 11 per cent. The drink makers, however, were affected disproportionately, for reasons that are hard to fathom. By 1932 distilling had vanished from the list of Ontario's forty leading industries, not to reappear until 1936, at which time it employed slightly fewer workers than in 1929 but produced, in terms of value, 43 per cent less. Nation-wide, sales of proof spirits did not regain the 1929 level until 1958, although beer production passed the 1929 level in 1937 and has stayed well above it ever since.

Among many of Ontario's capital goods and consumer durables industries, production all but collapsed. Canada's output of railway cars fell to thirty-one in 1933–34, and the national output of locomotives fell to zero. Washing machine production fell by about 42 per cent, stove production fell 61 per cent, the volume of pig iron production and the value of farm implements and parts fell 87 per cent. Rail production fell 88 per cent. Admittedly, a few consumer durables did surprisingly well. The production of mechanical refrigerators nearly quintupled between 1929 and 1932, and the production downturn in 1933 was, in percentage terms, a very mild one; in 1934 production surged ahead again, so that by 1942 Canada was producing fifteen times as many refrigerators as in 1929. Radios, also, did quite well. Production did not peak until 1931, in which year the nation's output was nearly double what it had been in 1929; between 1931 and 1933 production fell by 61 per cent, but in 1934 there was an impressive recovery, so that by 1937 Canada was producing almost as many radios as in 1931 and almost twice as many as in 1929. As Ontario was the centre for most of Canada's appliance and radio industry, the buoyant performance of refrigerator and radio sales provided a cushion for a few Ontario businesses. But the cushion was not very substantial: in 1933, Canada's production of radios and refrigerators was valued at only $6.3 million – less than 0.7 per cent of Ontario's own industrial output.

The motor industry and its suppliers suffered dramatically, and their troubles may be seen as a symbol and summary of the difficulties in which the heavy industries found themselves. The rubber industry, heavily dependent on motorists' and car-makers' demand, was also hard hit. In the province's automobile supplies industry the values of output fell by 60 per cent, although employment declined only 18 per cent.

Some of the intermediate goods industries did rather better, even though the nine Ontario industries that can be identified and placed in this category both in 1929 and 1933 showed a 46 per cent decline in the value of output and a 30 per cent decline in employment between these two years. The national output of wheat flour was quite well sustained by comparison, falling 25 per cent between 1929 and 1933. In Ontario the value of output from the milling industry fell by one-half, but employment fell only 16 per cent. Because of the new protective measures of the Bennett government Canada's output of basic cotton textiles actually rose considerably from 1930 to 1933, although in Ontario the industry's employment fell by 7 per cent and the value of its output by 18 per cent. In the woollens industry, which also received a great deal of extra protection, Canada's output rose steadily from 1930 through the lean years; thus it is not surprising that in Ontario's woollens industry employment was 24 per cent higher in 1933 than it had been in 1929. But domestic protection could not help those industries that produced for a world market. Ontario's saw-milling industries were so badly hit that like the agricultural implements industries they vanished from the list of the province's forty largest industries, not to return until 1934, when their total employment was less than one-third of what it had been in 1929. Canada's volume of pulp production fell 34 per cent, and its volume of paper production fell 30 per cent, between 1929 and 1933. In Ontario employment fell by 30.6 per cent, and the value of the industry's output went down by 50 per cent. No wonder that the pulp and paper industry was having trouble in servicing its borrowings, or that the overcapitalization and overexpansion of the industry symbolized the Depression to some professional observers at the time.

Recovery

After the slough of despond in 1932–3, recovery came, but its progress was halting and uneven. From 1933 to 1937 the real output of Ontario manufacturing rose 71 per cent and employment rose 43 per cent. Real output in 1937 was 8 per cent higher than in 1929, but employment was still 2 per cent lower; indeed, employment was lower than it had been in 1917, even after the data for that early year have been adjusted to be comparable with the data for the late 1930s. In 1938 real output fell 8 per cent and employment fell 3 per cent, but in 1939 there was a renewal of recovery, so that real output again passed the 1929 level; in 1940 employment at long last did likewise, so that from 1938 to 1941 real output rose 59 per cent, and employment rose 51 per cent, effectively eliminating unemployment. For the owners of the manufacturing firms, prosperity returned: in 1941 more than half of value added remained after the payment of salaries and wages, and this amount, from which interest and depreciation would have to be paid, represented 33 per cent of reported capital – a much higher proportion than in the depth of the slump.

   Although the recovery was broadly based, in certain industries renewal and expansion were especially striking. Car, truck, and bus production rose from just over 50,000 units in 1932 and 1933 to 187,252 units in 1937 and to 264,919 units in 1941, by which time two-thirds of the units were trucks and buses. Tire production grew 72 per cent between 1933 and 1941. Canada's steel production rose 613 per cent, and in the Ontario industry employment increased by 392 per cent. By 1941 the aircraft industry, with output of $32 million and employment of 7,405, was

Ontario's seventeenth-largest in terms of gross output – well ahead of such old-time stalwarts of the provincial economy as agricultural implements, men's clothing, and furniture. From 1933 to 1941 the province's electrical equipment industry almost tripled its employment and more than tripled the value of its output; during the same period Canada's stove and washing machine outputs more than doubled, radio output more than tripled, and the output of mechanical refrigerators more than quadrupled, but in 1941 the national output of these three appliances was valued at only 21 per cent of Ontario's output of electrical apparatus and supplies, in which heavy electrical equipment therefore continued to predominate. By 1941 Ontario's general machinery output was almost six times what it had been in 1933, and employment in this industry had almost tripled; having shed almost half its workers between 1929 and 1933, by 1941 the province's machinery industry was almost double the size it had been in 1929, whether one measures by employment or by the value of output. Among the capital goods industries that can be identified both in 1929 and 1941 (including railway rolling stock and aircraft only in 1941), the value of output increased by 63 per cent and employment increased by 49 per cent; if rolling stock and aircraft are dropped from the 1941 figures it can be seen that output rose by 46 per cent in terms of current prices, which were slightly lower in 1929 than in 1941; the real output of the capital goods industries, therefore, grew by roughly 31 per cent, while employment grew 25 per cent between 1929 and 1941.

In the consumer goods industries the Ontario pattern is rather different. Thirteen consumer goods industries can be identified both in 1933 and in 1941; between the two dates these industries' employment grew 55 per cent, while the value of their output grew 171 per cent; during the same period, a group of six capital goods industries experienced 432 per cent growth in the value of output, and 164 per cent extra employment. As one might be expected, with the recovery from a very deep depression the demand for capital goods, which had fallen much more catastrophically than the demand for consumer goods, naturally revived more strongly; by 1941, furthermore, wartime demands were providing additional and special impetus. In the twelve consumer goods industries that can be observed both in 1929 and in 1941, employment rose 29 per cent and the value of output rose 50 per cent in terms of current prices, or by 56 per cent in real terms. From the beginning of the Great Depression to its end, in other words, the production of consumer goods seems to have grown more rapidly than the production of capital goods and consumer durables, in spite of the special pressure from wartime demand in the last three years of the period 1929–41; employment also grew more quickly in the consumer goods industries than in the heavy industries. But in both sectors real productivity per worker rose considerably and at roughly the same rate, 147 per cent, and the value of output rose 159 per cent; in the heavy chemicals industries employment increased 110 per cent, while the value of output increased 72 per cent and volume increased 75 per cent; the brass and copper industry doubled its employment and the value of its output. In the pulp and paper industry employment went down by 9 per cent between 1929 and 1941, while the value of production increased only 22 per cent and the volume of output went up by only some 26 per cent.[10]

Only with respect to the smelting of non-ferrous metals can any close connection be seen between the province's own natural resources and the expansion of manufacturing industry during the 1930s. In the slump of 1929–33 the smelting industry certainly suffered: employment fell 31 per cent, and the value of output fell 11 per cent, although the relevant price level[11] fell so dramatically that the apparent volume of production actually went up by 37 per cent! From 1933 to 1941 employment increased by 160 per cent, so that in 1941 it was 94 per cent higher than it had been in 1929. The value of output rose 292 per cent, and the volume rose 224 per cent, so that between 1929 and 1941 the volume of output from Ontario's non-ferrous smelters rose 347 per cent. This single industry accounts for 39 per cent of the increase in the value of output from our ten intermediate goods industries between 1929 and 1941. It accounts also for 17 per cent of the extra employment in this group. But 46.5 per cent of the extra employment, and 22 per cent of the extra value of output, originated in the primary iron and steel industry, while 9 per cent of the extra output and 22 per cent of the extra employment came from the cotton and woollen industries.

These comparisons may seem unfair in that they do not cover Ontario saw-mill and wood-processing industries, because the 1933 and 1941 censuses of manufacturing include these industries in total production and employment without giving any specific information about them. However, from the published data one can infer that in 1941 the outputs of the 'sawmill industry' and the planing industries were each less than $24,027,982. But in 1929 each earned substantially more than $24 million, and the prices of their outputs were lower in 1941 than in 1929.[12] The great days of the Ontario saw-mill industry were now long in the past.

In the circumstances of the 1930s it was obviously impossible for capital goods industries and heavy industry generally to revive. Personal expenditure, however, had been better sustained in the slump, and it rose far faster and farther than investment spending. The volume of personal expenditure fell only 18 per cent between 1929 and 1933; it then rose steadily to 1937, at which time it was almost as large as in 1929; after a small retrocession in 1938 it resumed its upward movement in 1939–41, in which year it was 16 per cent higher than in 1929. The effect was obvious in Ontario's consumer goods industries, most of which by 1939 were larger, both in terms of output and in terms of employment, than they had been in 1929. By 1941 war-ordering had affected some of them, such as the clothing trades, and the reduction of British exports had presumably helped these and other industries in the domestic market, which Canada's tariff reductions of the mid – and late 1930s had opened somewhat more widely to American and British competition. The consumer durables industries gained also: in 1939 the automobile industry was still smaller than it had been in 1929, but Ontario's electrical apparatus industry was a good deal larger in terms of employment, and apparently in terms of the volume of output; the value of production was still somewhat lower than it had been at the end of the 1920s.

What lay behind the surprising strength of consumer demand in the 1930s? It is obvious that Canadian households did not reduce their spending in step with the declines in their earnings; they reduced their rates of saving, or consumed their savings, and as they became more prosperous they energetically tried to spend themselves back to the living standards of the late 1920s. However, underlying this household behaviour is the performance of industry itself. Real output per worker was rising, and so were real average annual earnings. The gains from productivity growth, which continued to be reaped during the 1930s, were in large part passed on to the workers, in spite of mass unemployment.

As for Ontario's own export products, the volume and value of non-ferrous metals exports moved up almost uninterruptedly from 1932 to 1941, by which time export values had quintupled and volumes had quadrupled. Wood and paper products followed the same pattern, although the rates of recovery were rather lower. The volume of non-ferrous metals exports reached the 1929 level in 1934 and went on growing; the volume of forest products exports reached the 1929 figure in 1936 and continued to climb. Exports of iron and steel products, which include automobiles and machinery, were much slower and more erratic: the 1929 volume of export sales was not reached until 1940.

Hence it is easy to explain the impressive recovery of Ontario's non-ferrous metal smelting and refining, where employment and output were already above the 1929 levels by 1934, and where, in 1941, employment was almost double what it had been in 1929, while output was 250 per cent higher. Industrial recovery and rearmament abroad naturally created a growing world demand for nickel and for other non-ferrous metals, while the price realignments and devaluations of the early 1930s stimulated the production of gold. For Ontario's pulp and paper industry economic revival in the United States produced renewed demand.

However, the industry was so overcapitalized or overexpanded in relation to depression-level demand that price competition continued to be severe. In 1929 a ton of newsprint was worth $55.34; in 1933, $33.11; in 1937, $34.41; and in 1941, $45.15.[13] If these prices are used to perform a rough deflation of the data on the value of output from Ontario's pulp and paper industry, the physical output of that industry seems to have been about the same in 1929 and in 1941. Employment, however, was lower: presumably the mills had been forced to become more efficient.

The actual outbreak of war did not at once create new opportunities for Ontario heavy industry. Federal spending was slow to rise; provincial and local governments spent much more than Ottawa, even in 1939, at which time the dominion spent only 3 per cent more on material and supplies than it had spent in 1938. In 1940–1, however, the situation changed very quickly. Provincial and local governments reduced their capital spending, while the dominion enormously increased its outlays not only on military pay and allowances but also on material and supplies: federal outlays on goods and non-labour services rose from $103 million in 1939 to $697 million in 1941. Given the proportionate size of the Ontario economy and its industrialized profile, the result was a large injection of new spending. Since private consumption, business investment, and exports also rose, almost all the new federal spending was a net direct addition to the demand for the output of the country's manufacturing industry, and given the distribution of that industry, the majority of that extra demand must have flowed to Ontario. Military pay and allowances, which increased from $32 million in 1939 to $386 million in 1941, also represented additional demand in that civilian employment increased also. Although some of that new military pay may have been saved, and although it circulated through the economic fabric much more covertly than new government procurement, indirectly it helped create extra demand for Ontario manufacturers.

These new federal outlays were large relative to Canada's economy and even larger relative to Ontario's manufacturing industry. The result was a considerable push to production, employment, sales, and profits. Furthermore, there were other expansionary forces at work. In 1939 Canada's gross national product was $5,621 million, and Ontario's manufacturers produced $1,746 million worth of output. Between 1939 and 1941 federal government spending on goods and services went up by $977 million, gross national product went up by $2,661 million, and Ontario's industrial output went up by $1,376 million. Total fixed investment went up by $409 million; exports, moreover, rose by $1,019 million, and total commodity exports increased by $696 million, of which fully 70 per cent consisted of the commodity groupings – wood products and paper, iron and its products, non-ferrous metals and products, and miscellaneous products –

that were of special interest to Ontario manufacturers. With so many expansionary forces working simultaneously, it is hardly surprising that for the province's manufacturing industry the last two years of the period were times of unexampled prosperity.

Conclusion

The period 1914–41 is in many respects a paradoxical one. Outputs, unemployment, and living standards fluctuated dramatically, but the data do not suffice to reveal any sort of a trend in unemployment, and for output, employment, and standards of living among manufacturing workers, trends were strongly upward. In these years, especially in the later 1920s and at the end of the 1930s, an industrial economy was consolidated. Indeed, as was seen above in chapters 2 and 3, during the 1930s the agricultural population actually shrank, not only in proportionate terms but in absolute amount. Manufacturing industry had established itself at the the centre of the province's economic life. Or so it seemed. Yet as chapter 2 revealed, many kinds of service or white-collar employment were growing very fast indeed, and many of these occupations provided decent living standards and a degree of job security to which the assembly-line workers and the craftsmen could not aspire. Hopes and expectations naturally rested on 'goods production,' especially on manufacturing. Yet perhaps it was in the service trades that the future of the province was eventually to be found.

10 *The Development of Industrial Cities*

Centred as it was on the development of manufacturing and service industries, the economic growth of Ontario naturally produced a considerable urbanization as well. The shaping of the cities was very largely a matter for the private enterprise of land-owner and speculative subdivider and builder. Government made no serious effort to shape urban growth. Water, sanitary sewers, and pavements were provided, but often rather late in the day. Building codes and inspections gradually came to ensure certain minimum standards of physical soundness. Largely under the influence of anti-fire regulations, brick construction gradually and incompletely displaced frame. In Ottawa, after 1900 some steps were taken on the road towards civic beautification. Almost all cities maintained some parks and playgrounds, although by 1914 such provision often seemed inadequate, ill-located, or both. Thus it was by good fortune, not good planning, that Ontario cities avoided the severe and dramatic degradation that has so often accompanied urbanization. Overcrowding, filth, and misery there certainly were, especially in Toronto and Hamilton. Yet conditions might have been a great deal worse.

One must begin by describing 'urbanization' itself. Up to and including the census of 1941, Canadian statisticians counted as 'urban' all incorporated places, regardless of size. For our period, therefore, intercensal comparisons of raw census data are in a sense legitimate, but every census includes as 'urban' some people whom common sense would not treat in that way, and excludes as 'rural' some people who lived on the unincorporated fringes of cities and towns.[1]

During the period 1891–1941 the population of Canada increased from 3.7 million to 11.5 million, and the population of Ontario grew from 1.6 million to 3.8 million. On the basis of the 1941 definition, 19.6 per cent of Canada's population and 22 per cent of Ontario's was urban in 1871. For 1931 the figures are 53.7 per cent and 61 per cent, and for 1941 they are

54.3 per cent and 62 per cent. Urbanization in Ontario seems to have continued, without intermission, decade by decade. The data are summarized in table 10.1.

On a slightly narrower definition, which excludes those who lived in incorporated cities, towns, and villages having 1000 inhabitants or fewer, 20.6 per cent of Ontario's people were urban in 1871. The percentage rose to 27.1 per cent in 1881, 35 per cent in 1891, 40.3 per cent in 1901, and 49.5 per cent in 1911.

So far as industry was concerned, urbanization meant a concentration of industrial activity in cities – especially in the larger ones. In 1870 the five large cities – Hamilton, Kingston, London, Ottawa, and Toronto – provided 23.6 per cent of the province's industrial employment and produced 24.5 per cent of its industrial output. By 1910 they accounted for 43 per cent of output and 44 per cent of industrial employment. In a few towns, such as Kingston, Belleville, Brockville, and Cornwall, relatively little had happened. Indeed, Kingston's industrial employment peaked in 1890, although its industrial output in 1910 was 300 per cent of the 1870 output. But in other large centres the development had been dramatic. The most impressive performance had been in Toronto, which accounted for 11 per cent of industrial employment and 11.9 per cent of industrial output in 1870; by 1910 its share had risen to 26.3 per cent of output and 27.3 per cent of industrial employment. The industrial growth of Toronto, where industrial employment increased by 595 per cent and industrial output by 1026 per cent in forty years, is certainly the most dramatic. Other cities and towns, however, also performed with éclat. In Hamilton industrial employment rose by 369 per cent, in Ottawa by 197 per cent, and in London by 309 per cent. Outputs, naturally, rose by still higher percentages. Furthermore, many smaller centres emerged as significant industrial producers. Among these were Berlin, Brantford, Galt, Guelph, Oshawa, Peterborough, St Catharines, St Thomas, Sarnia, Stratford, Windsor, and Woodstock. For 1870 industrial production of these cities was not reported separately. In 1880 they produced output valued at $13.2 million – 8.4 per cent of Ontario's industrial production. In 1910 their output was worth $80.5 million – 13.8 per cent of industrial production.

Industrial activity was becoming increasingly urbanized because the character of that activity was changing. In 1870 a small group of small-town and rural industries – blacksmithing, milling, and saw-milling – accounted for 37 per cent of the province's industrial output. In 1910 blacksmithing had been almost eliminated from the industrial census by the narrowing of the census-taker's net; although both saw-milling and flour-milling had increased dramatically, as producers of output and employers of labour they had grown less rapidly than the province's industrial economy, so that in 1910 these three old rural industries accounted for only 16.8 per cent of industrial output. It is doubtful if the addition of blacksmithing on the same statistical basis as in 1870 would have raised this percentage significantly.

The statistical record takes on more life if it is supplemented by descriptions of developments in the various major cities – Toronto, Hamilton, Ottawa, and some of the smaller centres. All aspects of urban development, even in the larger cities, cannot be described here. Fortunately, a series of studies of Canadian cities will soon provide comprehensive accounts.[2] Toronto, Ottawa, and Hamilton have already been treated. Therefore, the present chapter will attempt only a survey of developments in building, transport, and manufacturing industry in so far as these appear to have shaped the several urban economies.

The Big Cities

Before 1914 Toronto grew both in area and in population. Population rose from 56,000 in 1871 to 181,000 in 1891, 208, 000 in 1901, and 376,000 in 1911.[3] The city gained a rail connection with the CPR at North Bay in 1886, and after 1903 the Temiskaming and Northern Ontario Railway gradually extended its hinterland into the rich mining areas in New Ontario. Through merger and absorption Toronto lost control of its privately owned hinterland railways, and its timber and grain export trades gradually fell away. As a centre of wholesale and retail trade and of finance, however, its importance steadily increased, while its manufacturing industry grew decade by decade.

The eminent geographer Jacob Spelt[4] has asked whether the growth of Toronto was at the expense of other Ontario centres. He concludes that in general it was not. The critical years for Toronto, Spelt shows, occurred between 1850 and 1880. Of utmost importance was the existence of a separate and direct access to the seaboard, via New York. Toronto could and did become established as a direct importer and direct exporter, bypassing the St Lawrence canal system and the Grand Trunk. Other Lake Ontario ports, such as Whitby, Cobourg, Port Credit, and Oakville, had at one time possessed reasonable hopes of growth on the basis of a similar export-import pattern. Cobourg and Port Hope, indeed, built 'tapline' railways to the interior just as Toronto and Hamilton did. But Toronto succeeded, through merger and through superior financial acumen, in constructing and maintaining a much better tributary rail network. Further, in the late 1860s and 1870s it established itself as a significant financial centre, replacing the Bank of Upper Canada with new foundations and absorbing some of the regional banks, as is described below in chapter 18.

Wholesaling and manufacturing, attracted by the rail network and increasingly dependent on it, were drawn to Toronto. By 1881 there were 390 commercial travellers based in Toronto, eight in Cobourg, and four in Port Hope.[5]

Increasingly, more and more industry, commerce, and finance would be drawn to this focus of the rail transport system; where rail service was inadequate or altogether absent, towns grew slowly, stagnated, or declined. Something of the sort can be detected in Kingston, which had little agricultural hinterland and not much by way of railway communication to the interior. Admittedly, the transshipment of grain generated some activity. But little grain from Ontario or the American states was moving to Montreal by canal. It is true that around 1880 Kingston possessed a shipyard, an engine works that employed 350 people, a cotton-mill that employed 200, and factories that made musical instruments and steam engines. But the city had some locational disadvantages, and few obvious advantages.[6]

Spelt distinguishes between 'propelling' activities, which sell goods and services outside a city or town, and 'service' activities, which sell only within the built-up area where they are settled and within a small tributary district. He concludes that in 1881 'the sawmill settlements on and near the Shield were probably the only places in which propelling industries played a dominant part' in the growth of urban places.[7] Toronto and Kingston, he thinks, were 'in 1881 still predominantly service centres.' But as he admits, the distinction is impossible to draw in any really conclusive way, nor could he precisely measure either activity.[8] Without 'exports' no urban place can grow, if only because it must buy food and raw materials.

Not everything was concentrated in Toronto, even along the shore of Lake Ontario between Kingston and Hamilton. Oshawa was emerging as an important producer of carriages and agricultural implements. Joseph Hall had set up a farm machinery factory there in 1858. In 1878, G. McLaughlin moved to Oshawa and began to produce carriages. In Cobourg there was a woollen-mill, and also a car and locomotive works that employed 175. Belleville had a large locomotive shop and a factory. Trenton and Deseronto had enormous lumber mills, as did Peterborough. Spelt gives other examples. Of the smaller lakeshore centres only Oshawa had a bright industrial future, although industry would certainly grow and flourish in many of the smaller centres. Massey's departure from Newcastle is often thought to be symbolic. The Massey firm produced Canada's first mowing machine (1852), its first self-rake reaper (1863), and, in 1879, the Massey harvester. But in 1879 the company moved to Toronto.[9]

One need not enter into the debates among theoreticians as to whether

Toronto's situation in 1870 was 'really' industrial capitalism, or whether the elements of artisanship, the 'manufactury,' and various 'pre-capitalist formations' were still present in inconveniently large amounts. Kealey's research[10] allows us to observe that by 1870 there were plenty of steam-powered plants, a great deal of very old-fashioned 'putting-out,' and many 'manufactories' where large numbers of more or less skilled wage-earners worked for employers with little or no assistance from mechanical power. In 1870 Toronto employed 2,879 steam horsepower, of which 31 per cent was in metal-working and another 28.7 per cent was in woodworking, brewing, and distilling. There was almost no steam power in 'the clothing and shoe industries – Toronto's largest employers,' probably because the technology of steam power was only rarely compatible with the production of such items. Kealey explains that by 1871 Toronto's capital goods industries were already producing many items – rerolled rails, stoves, locomotives, car wheels, boilers, foundry items, engines and other machines.[11] He argues[12] that in 1870 'fully 70 per cent of Toronto workers in 1871 worked in shops or factories employing over 30 men and women.' This statement is correct so far as one restricts one's attention to what Kealey calls 'factories,' and what the census called 'establishments.' As a statement about workers in general it is incorrect, ignoring not only the professional, domestic, commercial, and other workers who were more numerous than the industrial workers but also those workers who were employed in large non-industrial enterprises, such as the railways and the gas works.

Nor is it altogether clear, as Kealey tells us, that 'increasing concentration of capital. . .was taking place in Toronto between 1871 and 1891.'[13] For Marxists such a development would be important because it would serve to demonstrate that by 1892 'Toronto stood poised on the brink of the next stage of economic development – monopoly capitalism.'[14] In fact, there are no data on the size distribution of Toronto businesses for 1880 and 1890; therefore no one can know whether or not concentration was increasing. Large enterprises were appearing, and without question capital was being accumulated, and the number of employees was rising fast. But so was the number of establishments – a crude measure of concentration, but one of the few that can be devised, and the main one that Marx himself had in mind.

Marx described the 'centralization' of control over capital as 'concentration of capitals *already formed*, destruction of their individual independence, expropriation of capitalist by capitalist, transformation of many small into few large capitals.'[15] Little of that sort of thing can be detected in the data. In distilling, the number of establishments falls from two to one; in all others the number of establishments increases. Further, the increase is often substantial – from thirty-six to thirty-eight in machine and foundry products, from eighty-nine to 680 in garments, from seven to sixty-eight in furniture. If one turns to average employment and average output in each industry, one gets results that are equally inconsistent with the hypothesis of 'concentration.' Admittedly, there are some increases – in machinery and foundry products, garments, brewing, tin and sheet iron, musical instruments, carriage-making. But even in 1890 some of these industries were not really very concentrated. In carriage-making, for instance, the average Toronto firm employed 10.4 people, and produced output to the value of $11,200. In tin and sheet iron, average employment was nine, and average output $14,000. It is really hard to see such industries as 'concentrated,' on any definition, with thirty establishments in the former and fifty-three in the latter! Or what of the 680 establishments in the garment industries, or the 149 boot and shoe 'factories'? Each with an average of five employees and with average annual output of $7,800? Many such places were tiny artisan workshops co-existing perhaps with much larger enterprises. But by that very token, 'concentration' in Marx's own sense had not arrived.

As Toronto's industries grew, and as other elements of its economic base expanded more or less parallel with manufacturing industry, the city experienced a series of construction booms, each of which added street upon street of characteristic Victorian and Edwardian frontages – tall, narrow, pointy, generally built either as semi-detached 'doubles' or in short rows. The physical expansion of the city was shaped by the pre-existing pattern of land holdings, which had been largely based on comparatively long and narrow tracts, each of which could then be subdivided to yield several parallel streets. The timing of the expansion, however, was controlled by speculative builders and subdividers.

Although there are few published data on nineteenth-century building activity, Buckley has found and published figures for Toronto that stretch back to 1886.[16] Also, Buckley's findings can be used to illustrate a national building cycle. He finds[17] very large increases in building during the first five years after Confederation, stagnation and slump from 1871 until 1880, enormous expansion to 1889, retrogression until 1896, and then an immense boom that, with a slight interruption in 1907–8, continued until 1912. Toronto data show the same wave-like pattern: permits per capita rise by 59 per cent in the great housing boom of the late 1880s, fall by 61 per cent between 1889 and 1897, then rise by 964 per cent to their 1911 peak.[18] Data on subdivisions, land transfers, and brick production seem to confirm this impression.[19]

Urban historians have taught economic historians to look for connections between urban transit systems and the development of cities – both the geographical spread and the timing of physical growth. For Ontario, before 1914, the approach is especially interesting, because no government agency was planning the growth of any city. The geographer Peter Goheen[20] observes the joint impact of street railways and intercity railways on Toronto's physical layout. The intercity railways produced a loss of amenity along the waterfront where much industry and a great deal of warehousing were tending to concentrate, and increasingly there were new concentrations of industry along the rail lines, especially to the west of the city. Toronto's street railways, Goheen believes, were essential in the production of a large and diverse city where the various kinds of land use – industry, commerce, upper class residential districts, and working class housing – became ever more clearly distinct. Goheen also believes that to some extent, in the 1880s, Toronto's horse-drawn street railway system was built ahead of settlement, especially to the east of the Don; he reminds us of the significance of street railways for the northern thrust of the city up Yonge Street and for the filling-up of the city's north-west quadrant – south of St Clair Avenue and east of High Park – during the 1890s. The historian Maurice Careless agrees[21] that the new electric system 'facilitated traffic movements after 1891.'

The original Toronto Street Railway Company operated its horse-car system under a franchise of 1861, which expired in 1891. After a brief interlude of municipal operation the city awarded a thirty-year franchise to a new company, the Toronto Railway Company, which was a project of the local entrepreneur, William Mackenzie. The new firm was required to electrify the system, which it duly did. Electric interurban lines, meanwhile, were being constructed under separate managements, to the north, north-west, west, and east. These lines did not run into the downtown area; indeed, they did not always make physical contact with the streetcar system. Mackenzie and Donald Mann acquired control over these suburban and interurban 'radial lines' in 1904, but they did not integrate their several acquisitions. Nor were they willing to expand their streetcar system beyond the city's 1891 boundaries. This reluctance was a considerable inconvenience, since between 1905 and 1914 the city's area was doubled, from seventeen to thirty-five square miles, by a series of annexations – North Rosedale, Deer Park, Moore Park, North Toronto. In 1911 the Judicial Committee of the Privy Council ruled in favour of the company; the city responded by building its own lines in the annexed areas. The municipal lines, however, did not form an integrated system, nor did they extend into open country, although they, like some of the Toronto Railway Company lines, did serve areas that were still being filled with houses.

In the area of the 1891 city, passengers could ride anywhere for a single fare. Beyond these boundaries, riders would face at least one transfer and at least two fares if they wished to reach the central city or to cross it. Suburban development tended to align itself along the suburban 'radial' routes – north Yonge Street, the Weston Road, the Lakeshore, and Kingston Road. But the inconvenience of the system and its extra cost, which produced something akin to the 'zone fares' that were common in Europe, probably imposed a certain restraint on urban sprawl. This is not to say that housing was never built in advance of demand, or that the physical expansion of the city proceeded layer on layer, in an orderly fashion, like the accretion of rings around a tree trunk. Especially in the boom of the 1880s, and after 1900, there was a substantial amount of discontinuous building, much of it speculative, and some concern about the cost of extending services over a territory that to the Victorians appeared to be large and loosely settled. In the street plans of the period the pattern, or lack of pattern, can be clearly detected. But the transit system limited the possibility of 'sprawl,' and filling-in was rapid and complete. The result was a city of narrow frontages and well-filled lots.

No industrial city has ever been altogether salubrious, especially when viewed by public health enthusiasts and those who dislike the physical symptoms of low wages and low productivity. Toronto, by 1914, was no exception. In two areas, Cabbagetown near the stinking mouth of the Don River and 'The Ward' to the west of the city hall, there was serious congestion.[22] Also, to the east of the Don River there were conditions that middle-class observers found distressing. Would some sort of public housing be a useful palliative? After much study and many recriminations, in 1912 a group of financiers formed the Toronto Housing Company, and in 1913 the provincial legislature provided that a city could guarantee bond issues for limited-dividend housing companies. The Toronto Housing Company then borrowed $850,000 and raised another $100,000 by selling stock to 166 shareholders. By the end of that year it had built 242 moderate-rent apartments and bought three further parcels of land.[23] But it built no more, and of course its two projects, though valuable, could not and did not eradicate substandard housing. Reformers were especially distressed by the ill-serviced and ill-constructed shack-towns which, by 1907, already ringed the city. As the *Globe* reported, 'There is scarcely a terminating car line in the city but taps the shacklands, and in the early hours of the day brings hundreds of its fathers, sons, brothers – and even women – down to the daily toil.'[24] A more recent account[25] writes of 'shacks covered with tar and paper ... in several outlying areas ... One of the largest stretched west from Poplar Plains Road between Davenport Road and St Clair Avenue West.' But as the city already stretched far to east, west, and north of this district, it cannot really be called 'outlying.' And it was well-served by the inner-city streetcar system.

Normal North American practice would have extended the streetcar lines, carried the interurban cars downtown, and probably integrated the two sorts of transit. It has been suggested[26] that Mackenzie refused to follow this normal North American practice in Toronto precisely because he wanted to collect two fares. This line of thought, which was familiar at the time, did not make the entrepreneur particularly popular. But as D.F. Davis has observed[27] the company probably behaved quite sensibly in trying to maximize its profits or at least to maintain them. Unlike most North American transit companies of the period, the Toronto Railway Company (TRC) itself was not embroiled in land speculation or complex promotional schemes. Mackenzie saved his speculative enthusiasms for his Canadian Northern Railway and for other ventures, such as Niagara power. Indeed, it may well be that he needed the profits of the TRC to help with the creation of the Electrical Development Company and the Canadian Northern, and that the financial troubles of these enterprises may have increased his willingness, in 1913, to sell his street railway enterprise to the city. Even so, although the TRC was more profitable than the general run of street railway companies, whose lines were generally extended too far and too fast – 'to their technological as opposed to economic limits' making them 'loss leaders for the real estate industry,'[28] – the company was not particularly profitable at any time. Davis argues that the TRC may have managed to earn something like 10 per cent on capital. He says, 'To its dying day, it was the atypical street railway in that it served no greater end than its own profitability.'[29] But in so doing the TRC helped give Toronto its characteristic shape.

It is now possible to write about Hamilton in much the same detail as Toronto. Not only has a serious municipal history been published,[30] but the numerous writings on labour history in Hamilton are very helpful indeed. For Ottawa there is no equally comprehensive body of published research. Fortunately, the Ottawa urban economy was a simple one, especially when compared with Hamilton's or Toronto's, and in fact a good deal is known about it.

According to the labour historian Bryan Palmer, 'By the early 1870s, when Hamilton first attained the reputation it would vigorously defend in later years as "The Birmingham of Canada", the transition to the final stage of capitalist development, what Marx referred to as modern industry, was completed.'[31] The number of steam-powered factories had been rising quite rapidly. Among the major enterprises were Wanzer's, Wilson's, and Bowman and Gardner's sewing machine factories, employing a total of 513 workers. There was also a very large cotton mill. Besides the three sewing machine factories Palmer mentions Copp Bros Foundry, MacPherson's Boot and Shoe works, the Hamilton Rolling Mills, and the local plant of the Gurney stove company, which also operated in Toronto and elsewhere. Indeed, by the 1880s there were several stove foundries in Hamilton and many other iron products were produced there as well.[32] But it cannot be correct to assert, as Palmer does, that trades such as shoemaking, blacksmithing, butchering, and baking 'struggled to survive.'[33] After all, Hamilton's human and horse populations were both rising, and except for shoemaking, the trades that served men and beasts had not been much affected by labour-displacing technological change.

After 1879 the National Policy, according to Palmer, produced 'unprecedented industrial expansion in the early 1880s,'[34] although other factors, as chapter 7 argues, were certainly at work in Hamilton as elsewhere in the province. Nevertheless, the National Policy did have some obvious direct effects in Hamilton: in 1879 it caused a group of American businessmen to lease from the Great Western Railway the rolling mills that had been idle since 1872.[35] The result was the Ontario Rolling Mills Company. In 1887, following a further tariff increase, a large screw company moved from Dundas to a new and larger site in Hamilton, where it received tax concessions. The Ontario Tack Company was erected in the city in 1885.[36] Then in 1893, work began on a modern iron and steel works.[37] Westinghouse Air Brake soon followed, and, after the turn of the century, so did International Harvester.

Well before 1890 there was already apparent a tendency for large Hamilton enterprises to concentrate along the lakeshore, fringing the south edge of Hamilton Harbour and extending into it on newly filled land. By 1900 there was a grouping of iron and steel works, air brake manufacturers, chemical works, and the like. Why did such activities cluster in Hamilton? The available explanations, which emphasize transport costs, market locations, and comparatively cheap supplies of imported raw materials, such as coal, are suggestive if not wholly satisfying. It is certainly worth remembering that from 1898 onward, thanks to the private development of the DeCew Falls hydroelectric site, Hamilton had the cheapest electric power of any important North American city. This fact doubtless helped Hamilton share in the Great Boom after 1900. But the city was already an important industrial centre in 1880, and during the ensuing decade its industrial output more than doubled, with no help from cheap hydroelectric power. On the other hand, after 1900 its industrial output grew more rapidly than that of any large Ontario town, including Toronto. Thus in the Great Boom electric power may well have mattered.

The population of Hamilton grew from 27,000 in 1871 to 82,000 in 1911. By 1921 half of all Hamilton dwellings were owner-occupied; in

1871 the figure had been only 25 per cent. Horse-cars began to operate in 1877. In 1892 the Dominion Power Company acquired the street railway, electrified it the next year, and acquired and built an extensive network of radials, with lines into downtown Hamilton. But from 1900 to 1911 the street railway was unable to pay a dividend, a fact which suggests that the system had been extended too far. The two incline railways that climbed Hamilton Mountain were constructed in 1895 and 1900. Although at least one of the inclines could carry trolley cars, the incline railways were not fully integrated with the ordinary transit system; the Mountain dwellers, therefore, could face at least one transfer if they were to travel downtown by public transit.[38] The localization of heavy industry along the eastern end of the bay-shore presumably increased the demand for urban transit services. On the other hand, as industry concentrated in that district, working-class housing clustered nearby.

It is natural, in the late twentieth century, to suppose that Ottawa grew because it was the seat of the dominion government. But there were only 300 civil servants in 1871, and only 4,585 in 1911. The geographer George Nader has claimed that 'from Confederation to the First World War the continued growth of the Ottawa economy was dependent more on industrial development than on governmental functions.'[39] On the other hand, Ottawa's lumber industries were anything but buoyant. Thus by 1910–11 the city's industrial workers were only twice as numerous as its civil servants – a far smaller proportion than at Confederation.

Ottawa industry was spread out – partly in Hull, partly at the Chaudière Falls, partly at the mouth of the Rideau River and in New Edinburgh. Water power, the original locational factor, determined this pattern; the advent of cheap Chaudière hydroelectricity did not change the situation. In 1896 a cement dam was built at the Chaudière to replace the timber and earth dam of 1868, largely at the instigation of the lumbermen and the street railway and utility interests. Although some smaller mills failed during the depression of the 1890s, while the Great Fire of 1900 eliminated most of the remaining mills in the Chaudière area, the new industries were not numerous, and they were located at or very near the sites of the old. Further, to a striking extent they were controlled by the same old Ottawa entrepreneurs, especially the Eddy firm, the Bronsons, the McKay Estate, and the Booth interests – all family firms that had done well in the lumber trade. Nor did the pulp and paper industry, with E.B. Eddy's erection of a mechanical pulp and paper mill in 1886 and a chemical paper plant in 1889, change the location of industry. The Booth pulp mill followed in 1904.

Ottawa's street railways dated from 1866. Indeed, that eminent

'philosopher of railroads,' T.C. Keefer, was president of the Ottawa City
Passenger Railway Company, which ran horse-cars in summer and sleighs
in winter. It has been suggested that after electrification, which began in
1891 with the formation of the competing Ottawa Electric Street Railway
Company, the Ottawa system may have been as conservative as Toronto's.
Yet route-planning did have some effect on the shaping of the city. New
lines were pushed down Bank Street into Ottawa South, a short distance
beyond the built-up area. To the east, a line was run out the Montreal Road,
so that the townsfolk could visit the cemeteries and picnic in them. From
1893 there was a woodsy line to Rockcliffe Park, operating on a private
right of way and providing for the residential development of the McKay
Estate, which T.C. Keefer managed. The most dramatic development,
however, happened to the west: in 1900 the street railway pushed a
double-track line, on nine miles of private right of way, to the village and
park of Britannia Beach.

These transit adventures did not quickly or dramatically change the
shape of the national capital, where population was growing rather slowly
– from 21,500 in 1871 to 87,000 in 1911 – and where the twentieth-
century housing boom was later and more gentle than in Hamilton or in
Toronto. Like Hamilton, the Ottawa of 1914 was still a rather small place.
But in due course the adventurous extensions to east and west began to be
reflected in housing patterns: Ottawa had always been a rather elongated
urban place, and the streetcar made it more so. The east-west axis,
following the streetcar lines, was far longer than the north-south axis, and
the westerly prolongation was far longer than the eastern. Moreover, the
lines in Hull and the interurban radial line to Aylmer were separate
systems; although there were direct connections to central Ottawa, the
result was in some respects analogous to that in Toronto.

Smaller Centres

If our knowledge of economic developments in the largest cities seems
incomplete, for the other industrializing areas – the Windsor frontier,
London, the Grand River Valley, Brantford, Kitchener-Waterloo, even
Oshawa – it is even less satisfactory. Interesting work, however, is under
way. The industrialization of Berlin (today's Kitchener) has recently been
studied,[40] and work has been done on the development of turbine and
woollen manufacture in the small towns of Meaford and Almonte.[41] As
such studies accumulate, our knowledge of the province's industrialization
will be much enriched. At this point, a complete and balanced account
cannot be assembled, even if space were adequate for the task. Yet the
numerous local histories, though uneven in quality and inconsistent in

coverage, cast some light on developments outside the large cities. What follows depends heavily on such work.

Some Ontario towns originated as ports, but almost all these also possessed, or soon acquired, saw-mills and grist-mills as well. The concentration of functions was a natural one, in that the ports were generally at river mouths from which in early years the chief export products were wheat, flour, and lumber. Kingston, Goderich, Oakville, Trenton, and Port Credit were such places; some managed the transition to industry with ease, while others changed with difficulty or not at all. Thus the adventures of the lake ports were anything but certain or easy, given their initial dependence on the export of products for which neither production nor vent was certain. The development of the canal ports, Welland, Cornwall, Dunnville, and Port Dalhousie, was rather more regular, because these places could offer not only dockage for transshipped cargoes but also water power and, increasingly, cheap supplies of inputs that arrived by water. St Catharines, Port Colborne, and Welland might be regarded as port towns, although for all three centres the canal mattered more as a power source than as a generator of port traffic. In a sense Dundas, standing as it did at the head of navigation on the Desjardins Canal, might also be called a port. But the growth of the city's industry was attributable to the water powers of the district. Furthermore, in spite of the mighty development of the Bertram works, the city did not really thrive as an industrial centre, and the construction of a tiny steam railway between Dundas and Hamilton had, by 1890, pointed the way to the city's future as a bedroom suburb.

Other places developed simply on the basis of local water power, with little or no port activity. Among such places were Strathroy, Durham, Elora, Georgetown, St Marys, Stratford, Guelph, Brantford, Paris, Peterborough, and Gananoque. The latter place developed such an array of metal-working firms that it competed with Hamilton for the the title, 'Birmingham of Canada.' All such places began as milling sites for lumber, wheat, or both, but after Confederation they developed in very different ways. Furniture manufacture became widespread. So did knitting-mills. Thus, for instance, in 1870 Penman's began to knit at Paris. Peterborough continued to rely on saw-milling until well after 1870, but new and much more sophisticated manufacturing plants moved to the town in the early 1890s.

Water power alone was not always enough to produce industrial growth. At Niagara Falls there was very little industrial development until 1904, when the first hydroelectric power was produced on the Canadian side. Nor did all parts of southern Ontario share equally, or at all, in the province's industrial revolution. Some of the old port towns stagnated or declined between 1870 and 1914, or even long after. In villages and small towns that had depended on waterpowered saw-milling, grist-milling, and foundry work, one could frequently observe a local, small-scale process of 'deindustrialization,' often assisted by devastating fires. The local histories frequently describe such fires, which repeatedly destroyed entire mills. Where prospects remained good, insurance adequate, or municipal assistance forthcoming, as in Oshawa, rebuilding could and did occur; where insurance was inadequate or prospects poor, it did not. The results could be spectacular. In Strathroy, for instance, all the main factories burned to the ground between 1884 and 1894; none was rebuilt, and the town's population fell from 5,000 to 2,000 in that decade.[42]

Where such events occurred, it could be difficult for local businessfolk to seize new opportunities, even when the necessary scale of the prospective enterprises might be within local grasp. And where disasters did not destroy the local capitalists, scale might still be formidably large. But the picture remains a mixed one. In Ottawa and Deseronto[43] the timber entrepreneurs had no difficulty in taking advantage of the new opportunities. In Peterborough the local lumber magnates were less robust, although no one could find sloth in entrepreneurs such as George Cox. In Niagara Falls there were no capitalists to speak of, and the new, technologically advanced, gigantic factories spilled over from American parent firms often located on the opposite bank of the Niagara River. In Berlin the local burghers were delighted to attract a branch of US Rubber, an enormous enterprise that it may be supposed they could neither finance nor manage without effecting an undesirable disengagement from their own thriving businesses. In London the oil-refining trade did a great deal to develop the city in the 1860s, and even after the refineries had passed into foreign ownership during the 1890s, the city's remaining great industries – the McClary stove works, the Leonard foundry and engine works, the Carling, Dimond, and Labatt breweries, the Empire Brass Company, and the many cigar and shoe manufacturers – remained in local ownership and control.[44] Only the very large Grand Trunk shops, which had come to London in the early 1890s, might be regarded as a instance of foreign ownership and control. Thus in the smaller centres of the province, as in the larger cities, a varied mixture of local initiative and external direct investment can be observed.

After 1890 there was some urban development in the parts of the province north and west of Lake Nipissing. Some places developed simply as divisional points on the expanding railway system, and as transshipment points where goods moved from rail to water. Where water power was available, as at Kenora and Thunder Bay, some industrial development could follow. The most spectacular transition from transshipment point to industrial city occurred at Sault Ste Marie, where the American entrepreneur Francis Clergue erected a hydroelectric station, an iron and steel works, and a complex of industrial plants. Population rose from 2,400 in 1891 to 11,000 in 1911; industrial production rose from $100,000 to $1 million. Clergue soon overreached himself, and, as explained in chapter 11, his shaky empire collapsed in financial disarray. But the plants and industries he had promoted survived, and most of them flourished – sooner or later.[45]

The development of Sudbury, which began in the 1880s, was very different. Indeed, Sudbury was Ontario's first important example of the genus 'mining town,' something of which the province would see much more after the Cobalt silver discoveries of 1903. With the construction of the T&NO Railway and with the extension of prospecting in New Ontario, other mining towns appeared. Further urban development in the north, at Kapuskasing, Dryden, Iroquois Falls, Smooth Rock Falls, and Espanola, would have to await the development of local hydroelectric sources, and the removal of the American newsprint tariff, a change legislated in 1911 but effected only in 1913.

Developments after 1914

With population growth after 1914 came further geographical expansion. Central cities grew, both in population and in area. Satellite towns appeared and grew – Eastview, Rockcliffe Park, Forest Hill, East York, Leaside, Mimico, Long Branch, New Toronto, Port Credit. To some extent urban growth shaped the transport system, but the former was not much influenced by the latter except perhaps in Ottawa, where the streetcar network had been built ahead of demand and where no new lines were laid down between 1914 and the abandonment of the system in the 1950s. In Toronto, with the municipal take-over of the private street railway and radial lines in 1921, a policy of modest development and integration was adopted, but the system was not built in advance of demand, and the more far-flung radial railways were gradually abandoned, even though some of the radial lines were integrated into the streetcar system. Some commuters rode the steam railways, but commuter services did not appear. In all the larger cities that kept their streetcars, motor buses came into use as supplementary carriers to serve new suburbs, and road networks around the large cities were dramatically improved in the 1930s, but neither development produced a genuine American-style suburban sprawl. Deeply though the motor car had penetrated the fabric of Ontario society, because that society was comparatively poor the car was less common in the cities of the province than in American centres of comparable size, and Ontario's city streets were often narrow, congested, and difficult for cars. Suburban buses often provided slow and infrequent service, and almost always involved transfers: extra fares, furthermore, were frequently exacted. Thus the larger Ontario cities continued to present the closely built appearance that they had acquired before 1914. To anyone who has seen Calgary or Vancouver, the difference will be apparent at once.

After 1914 the most striking demographic developments centred upon the motor cities – Oshawa and the Windsor area – and the populated places of the Ontario north. By 1941 there were 132,000 people in Oshawa and Windsor; in 1901 there had been under 20,000. The northern centres – Cobalt, Cochrane, Copper Cliff, Dryden, Kenora, New Liskeard, Rainy River, Sioux Lookout, Sturgeon Falls, Sudbury, and Timmins – had grown from 12,450 people to 104,742, of whom more than 60 per cent lived in the Timmins and Sudbury areas. Admittedly this group is heterogeneous. Cobalt, Haileybury, and Rainy River were larger in 1911 than in 1941. It was the pulp and paper, gold, and nickel towns that grew with especial speed. Thus between 1901 and 1941 Sudbury's population increased from 2,027 people to 32,203, that of Timmins grew from zero to 28,790, and Dryden from 140 to 1,641. By 1941 Sudbury and Timmins were larger than Oshawa, although neither was more than one-third the size of Windsor. But, while in percentage terms the large Ontario cities grew more slowly in the 1920s than between 1900 and 1914, in absolute terms the growth of Toronto, Hamilton, and London was almost as great in the latter period as in the former, and a high proportion of the extra population was supported by the new industrial jobs that, at least for the time being, created jobs in construction and in the many industries that produced components for the building industry. It is remarkable that the 'staple theorists' of the 1920s – Mackintosh and Innis – seem to have been unaware of the urban and industrial growth taking place round about them.

Table 10.2 brings together data on population, and on employment and output in manufacturing during the twentieth century. Population figures relate to the 1941 boundaries in all years; the data on industrial activity follow the census definitions in each year and so are not precisely comparable one with another, but the discontinuities are not sufficiently serious to make the table misleading.

It has not been possible to assemble comprehensive data on manufacturing in the northern centres, partly because the Dominion Bureau of Statistics was not allowed to publish any figures that could reveal the activities of any single firm. However, it is reasonably clear that except in the pulp towns, manufacturing activity in the north was not enormous even at the end of our period. Table 10.3, which summarizes all the information on northern manufacturing that the bureau ever published for 1939, shows that total employment in manufacturing in these five northern centres was much smaller than in Cornwall or Welland, and slightly smaller than in New Toronto.

The motor cities grew more rapidly than the older large industrial centres – Ottawa, London, Hamilton, and Toronto. But the province's industry was still remarkably concentrated around the western end of Lake Ontario. In 1900 Toronto and Hamilton accounted for 31 per cent of Ontario's industrial output and Ottawa and London for another 7 per cent. In 1929, 39 per cent of the province's manufactures came from Toronto and Hamilton, while only 4 per cent came from London and Ottawa. In 1941 the figures are 33 per cent for Toronto and Hamilton and 4 per cent for Ottawa and London, at which time the motor cities, which were insignificant in 1900, produced 13 per cent of the province's manufactures.

The expansion of the motor industry is obvious when the growth of Oshawa and the Windsor area is examined. Some motor cars were assembled elsewhere, as in Toronto, St Catharines, and Leaside, but the industry was concentrated in these two areas. That growth is even more striking if the years up to the peak of 1929 are surveyed, when industrial employment in the two motor cities was fourteen times what it had been in 1900, and more than three times what it had been in 1919. From 1900 to 1929 the value of industrial output in the two areas increased eighty-three-fold, from 1919 to 1929 more than four-fold, and from 1900 to 1941, 152–fold.

The growth was not uninterrupted. Employment and output fell in 1924, and the data clearly show a decline in output and employment around Windsor for 1927, the year in which the Ford Motor Company was switching from Model T to Model A. The slump of the 1930s, also, was especially severe for Oshawa and Windsor: industrial employment fell from 23,827 to 13,597, and the value of production to less than $66 million. In 1939 both output and employment were still somewhat smaller than they had been in 1929. But in 1941 industrial employment was almost 39,000, and the value of manufactures was almost $400 million. The rise of the motor car had created two new foci for Ontario's industrial growth.

Ottawa, where industrial employment grew only 44 per cent in forty years, suffered from the failing of saw-milling and grist-milling, together with the shift of paper-making to the other side of the Ottawa River. Although London contained no obvious dynamic industry, it outgrew Ottawa in industrial employment and output, though not in population: the burgeoning of the central civil service in the 1920s provided a new stimulus for growth in the capital of the dominion. The nation's capital was turning into white-collar heaven: already by 1921 it contained 10,376 officials, compared with 5,841 industrial workers. Toronto presumably suffered from the hard times that befell the agricultural implements industry, and Hamilton from the difficulties of the iron and steel trades, especially in the 1930s. On the other hand, both cities were stimulated, directly and indirectly, by the growth of the motor industry and by the extremely rapid expansion of the electrical equipment trades. Much of Canadian Westinghouse was in Hamilton. Although Canadian General Electric operated in Peterborough and elsewhere in Ontario, it had large Toronto plants as well. Toronto manufacturing, moreover, retained the diversity that characterized it both before 1900 and after 1945.

Conclusion

In the smaller cities and in many of the towns, as in the larger cities of the province, urbanization and industrialization went hand in hand with electrification, not only of light and factory work but of local transit. Streetcar systems had appeared everywhere, even in quite small centres such as Cornwall. Electric radial railways had often formed local networks, as in the Grand Valley and around London. These electric systems must have had some significance for urban growth and industrialization, if only because they allowed new factories to draw workers, both skilled and unskilled, from larger areas, thus reducing the degree of congestion and 'disamenity' that industrialization might otherwise have imposed. Also, of course, streetcars and radials saved the workers' time, increasing the amount of leisure in a typical work-week, and facilitating the workers' social, cultural, and organizational endeavours. So far as the smaller cities are concerned, the impact of transit on factory location and housing has yet to be studied.

One should also observe the geographical centralization that accompanied industrialization. The old Ontario industries – milling, lumbering, foundries – were small-town or rural activities, especially in so far as they used water power; it will be recalled that Ottawa was the only sizeable town to possess large water power resources. The newer types of industry, especially after 1890, tended to use steam or electric power; to that extent they were 'footloose' in a way that the older industries had not been. They could still be drawn to places where power was plentiful and cheap; hence the concentration of chemical and other industries that appeared at Niagara Falls after 1904; hence too the intense interest, at places such as Berlin and London, in hydroelectric power from Niagara. With the construction of the Ontario Hydro grid, comparatively cheap electric power became available in the larger towns on attractive terms, throughout a large area of south-central Ontario; distance from the Falls, however, was still a cost-raising factor, and it is interesting to note that Hydro's first generating plants, at Eugenia and Wasdell Falls, were meant to serve parts of the province that could not be economically reached from Niagara. But long before these generating stations came into operation, the industrial base in their service areas had vanished, almost without trace.

11 *The Iron and Steel Industry*

KRIS INWOOD, University of Guelph

It is convenient to divide the early history of Ontario's primary iron industry into three phases. In the first phase, which ended only in the 1890s, demand grew but there was no effective supply response. In the second phase, which lasted from the early 1890s until World War One, demand continued to grow, while there was considerable investment in productive capacity; the expansion was paralleled and perhaps spurred by changes in transportation costs and by increasingly supportive public policy. In the third phase, which lasted from 1913 to 1939, demand stagnated and its composition changed; the number of firms in the industry declined, and survivors adjusted to the new environment in various ways reflecting their individual circumstances. The chapter, which concentrates its attention on the first two phases, is organized accordingly. It begins by defining the primary iron industry.

Throughout the years 1870–1939 the first stage of iron and steel production was the smelting of iron ore and coal in a blast furnace to produce pig iron. Pig iron, in turn, could be cast into desired shapes in a foundry, puddled into wrought iron, or converted to steel. Wrought iron and steel are low-carbon and fibrous metals with considerable tensile strength; they are rolled, machined or otherwise reworked to produce structural pieces, hardware, railway iron and machinery. Cast iron is a higher-carbon metal with compressive rather than tensile strength; although more brittle, cast iron will take a much more intricate shape. In 1870 most pig iron was puddled or cast. By the end of the period almost all pig iron was converted to steel and rolled in integrated iron and steel works encompassing the blast furnace, steel furnace and rolling mill. The focus of this chapter is the operation of blast and steel furnaces with accompanying mills.

Early Days

Although the primary iron industry was unable to secure a permanent place in the Ontario economy until the 1890s, several blast furnaces before 1850 used locally supplied iron ore and charcoal to smelt pig iron. The furnaces were located at Olinda and Normandale in western Ontario, Madoc in central Ontario, and Lyndhurst in eastern Ontario.[1] None of these furnaces survived into the second half of the century. Unsuccessful attempts to smelt elsewhere were also made, the most important of these sited at Marmora. At Marmora a large iron-works was owned by a succession of companies involving some of the most important capitalists in early Canada.[2] The Marmora iron works produced little except during the 1820s to fulfil a military contract, which probably was let to assist the fledgling industrial enterprise. In spite of repeated attempts to revive production at Marmora and elsewhere in the province, Ontario ceased to produce iron by the 1850s.[3]

The demand for metal continued to grow, as evidenced by the fast growth of secondary iron firms reworking iron to supply a wide variety of capital goods.[4] Machine shops, foundries and rolling mills used iron and steel to produce agricultural implements, hardware, rolling stock, stoves, engines, machinery, structural metal and so on. Because firms located on the St Lawrence River and lower Great Lakes dominated Canadian capital goods production, the demand for primary iron was easily accessible to an Ontario furnace. Metal demand growth was particularly strong during the railway investment boom of the late 1840s and 1850s.[5] The disappearance of early iron furnaces in the face of these favourable demand conditions suggests a supply impediment to growth.

Throughout the following half-century investors and government officials tried without success to revive the primary iron industry in Ontario. Attention was attracted for several reasons. Ontario had many small deposits of iron ore and considerable forest reserves to supply wood fuel for a blast furnace. Indeed, between 1850 and 1890 Ontario exported iron ore, wood and charcoal to the United States. Moreover, the necessary transportation facilities were available; by the early 1880s several railways and canals connected the iron ore and forest region of central Ontario with the harbours and industrial centres along Lake Ontario. Additional track could have been laid at minimal cost if these lines were somehow inadequate.

Not surprisingly, investors showed considerable interest in iron production during the strong economic growth of the early 1870s and again during the early 1880s. Interest intensified when the Canadian government committed itself to a national policy of industrial promotion in 1879. Literally dozens of iron mines were explored in central and eastern Ontario during the 1880s.[6] In several cases investors went so far as to begin construction. On the Burnt River in Victoria County a blast furnace was constructed although never used.[7] At Sharbot Lake and Deseronto by-product recovery kilns with a capacity to supply low-cost charcoal for a blast furnace were built during the 1880s.[8] These projects were abandoned before iron production was able to begin, although a later attempt at Deseronto was more successful (see below).

Several attempts to enter iron production were halted at an even more preliminary stage of development. These efforts may be presumed to represent a lesser commitment of resources individually, although collectively the record during the 1880s is impressive. There was active interest in the establishment of iron works in Kingston and in its hinterland defined by the Kingston and Pembroke Railway and the Rideau Canal. Port Hope and Belleville also attracted potential investors; indeed, Belleville was the focus of three separate groups in 1882. Ottawa had hosted three separate groups in 1880. Would-be iron companies frequently discussed the erection of a blast furnace in Toronto.

The lakeshore sites west of Kingston were to be supplied with central Ontario ores drawn along one or more of a number of possible railways. The same iron mines and railways also inspired plans to erect blast furnaces in the back-country – principally in the old Marmora-Madoc smelting region and in upper Victoria County. Several active and important members of the Canadian financial and merchant elite supported the iron companies, the railway companies, or both.[9] Very clearly, the iron industry was not languishing for lack of interest. Indeed, the persistence of some promoters was remarkable.

One energetic fellow attempted to arouse interest in smelting at three locations – Trois-Rivières, Belleville, and the Rideau Canal – all in the same year. Another aspiring industrialist, Charles Pusey, purchased a six-mile stretch of railway in central Ontario during the 1860s and began to promote the idea of iron manufacture. Little came of his efforts. In 1880 Pusey worked six central Ontario mines and prospected others, but no blast furnace was erected. Ten years later he was still trying to attract support for smelting in the Bancroft area.

Another illustration is afforded by Edward Haycock, who in 1872 came across an abandoned iron mine while hunting quail with his son.[10] Haycock immediately turned his mind to iron production; the Ottawa Iron and Steel Manufacturing Company was organized to erect four Catalan forges.[11] At this time, the international price of iron was high and rising. No doubt Haycock was also aware that the Canadian government soon would be purchasing a large quantity of iron for railway construction. Haycock had a grandiose scheme to erect a large iron and steel works, which would be financed by a mortgage from the Ontario Bank and investment by James Skead and the MacLaren family. Skead's wealth had been earned in the timber trade; he also made use of credit from the Union Bank of Lower Canada at this time. The MacLarens were important timber traders, active in the Bank of Ottawa and inclined to invest in iron manufacturing.[12] Haycock did not add to the wealth of Skead or the MacLarens. The Catalan-forge installations produced only briefly during 1874 and 1875, and never expanded, although as late as 1883 Haycock again tried to raise capital in England to sustain further metallurgical adventures.

Sam Ritchie was no less persistent than Pusey or Haycock. Ritchie's first major iron project centred on the Coe Hill mine in upper Hastings County[13]; and he and his supporters incurred considerable expense in building a railway from Lake Ontario.[14] Unfortunately, the ore contained more sulphur than had been anticipated. Ritchie persevered. He and his backers, including the MacLarens, negotiated to use a magnetic separator for ore purification. Because separation was costly, the purified ore was expensive; nevertheless, it may have been hoped that the inventor's name, Thomas Edison, would gain the company a sympathetic hearing with new investors.[15] Ritchie's belief in the weakness of investors for new technology led to another proposal in 1889 involving the Sudbury copper-nickel deposits, which were then being developed for the first time. Ritchie proposed to extend the Central Ontario Railway from Coe Hill to Sudbury and to erect copper and iron smelting works at different locations along the line.[16]

Ritchie was formulating his copper-iron scheme at the same time as an English researcher announced that nickel could be alloyed with steel to produce a new metal of military significance.[17] The Sudbury ore happened to contain considerable nickel, which hitherto had been regarded as a nuisance in the otherwise valuable copper ore. Ritchie quickly changed the focus of his proposal from copper-iron to nickel-steel. The new scheme was superficially similar to one developed later by Bethlehem Steel, which used Cuban nickel-iron ores in the manufacture of nickel-steel.[18] Ritchie's plans came to nought because he lacked control of the valuable nickel deposits and his iron deposit turned out to be unsuitable metallurgically.[19]

Local investors provided some support for these iron-making proposals and would have given more had the prospects been more attractive. The failure to establish production was not the result of inadequate internal transportation or lack of interest by Canadian investors. Rather, projects were abandoned because of transportation costs on imported inputs, the small size of the domestic market, and the limitations of Ontario's natural resources. The province was not well endowed with the natural resources needed for iron-making. The small size of many ore deposits precluded an increase in labour productivity comparable to that experienced at American mines.[20] Even the best Ontario mines soon experienced diminishing returns in the form of rising costs, declining quality, or both. Indeed, the ore's quality was often poor.[21] Much of it was a dense magnetite and difficult to smelt; in any case the presence of harmful impurities such as phosphorus, sulphur, titanium and silicon ruled out an exclusive reliance on local ores. Although undependable by itself, Ontario ore could be mixed in some small proportion with better-quality ores; hence Ontario ore was exported to American furnaces having access to other ores.[22] Even this activity disappeared in the late 1880s as iron ore prices fell dramatically; marginal mining districts such as central Ontario simply ceased to produce at this time.

A second important resource was coal. Ontario has no suitable coal; the closest Canadian source is in the Atlantic region. Moreover, maritime coal was costly to extract and poor in quality. High-quality coal from American mines was closer to hand, but even these mines were hundreds of miles away. Imported coal was made more expensive after 1879 by a 60 cent per ton import duty designed to increase the revenue of Nova Scotia coal companies.

Resource weakness was exacerbated by the small size of domestic market relative to the scale of output needed to produce efficiently; the market size handicap was aggravated by quality variation and transportation costs. The entire Canadian iron market would not have been available to a single blast furnace because many types of iron existed and a single furnace typically produced only one or perhaps two kinds. A single firm making radiators, for example, required the purchase of five different types of pig iron.[23] Transportation costs also eroded the effective size of market; furnaces at Buffalo and Detroit, for example, inevitably captured some of the market that otherwise would have been available to a firm situated in eastern or northern Ontario.

Deseronto, Hamilton, and the Soo

Before 1850 an iron works could be small and also efficient; isolated furnaces produced at low enough cost to service a local market. After 1850 the market expanded, but the size of an efficient iron and steel works also grew as a result of technological change.[24] Although the small domestic market and resource inadequacy dissuaded investors from realizing their plans for iron manufacture during the 1870s and 1880s, several new plants were built or begun during the 1890s. In 1891 blast furnaces were built at Ferrona, Nova Scotia and Radnor, Quebec. The Hamilton blast furnace followed in 1894–5. In 1898 blast furnaces were built in Ontario at Deseronto and Midland. In 1899 the Hamilton company erected a steel works and expanded its blast furnace, while the Pictou County firm planned a blast furnace expansion, and the planning for large steel works at Sault Ste Marie and Sydney began. Several factors account for this new appeal to investors.

One development, of course, was the continued growth of Canadian metal consumption, which was rapid between 1870 and 1890.[25] However, market growth cannot provide a complete explanation. If it were simply a matter of the Canadian market, becoming large enough to admit an efficient scale of operation, and if several plants were built during the 1890s, then the output of at least one plant could have been absorbed earlier. In fact, the decade of the 1890s was a period of slow growth in secondary iron production and hence in the demand for primary iron.[26] This is a curious decade for the efficiencies of large-scale production to be realized for the first time. It is true that the demand for metal increased dramatically after 1900, as was seen above in chapter 7.[27] Nevertheless, the most important new iron and steel plants in Ontario, as elsewhere in Canada, were either built or planned before the onset of the boom.[28] As important as was market growth, it was not the only influence favouring the revival of iron production in Ontario.

Another favourable influence was the decline in transportation costs. Technological change caused a dramatic decline in freight rates by rail and water, especially over long distances.[29] The freight cost of assembling raw materials diminished further between 1870 and 1900 because fuel efficiency and the quality of ore improved.[30] For Canadian firms the transport cost of importing ore and coal fell relative to the freight cost of importing finished iron and steel.[31] The result was a reduction in the transport cost handicap of production in Ontario with American iron ore and coal.

Some degree of transportation handicap did persist. The freight bill on raw materials for production in Ontario continued to exceed the freight cost of importing finished metal.[32] Fortunately additional encouragement became available. In 1879 the dominion government began the more or less systematic practice of protecting domestic industries by means of an import tariff and other measures. The tariff was intended to raise the price in Canada at which goods produced in other countries would compete with Canadian-made goods. The size and nature of the tariff varied with an industry's circumstance; the tariff on pig iron was not large in 1879, for two reasons. First, it was not obvious that pig iron could be produced profitably even if the industry were heavily tariffed. Second, primary iron was purchased by manufacturers competing with imported machinery and equipment. Hence the tariff raised input prices and reduced the profits of domestic capital goods makers, who not suprisingly lobbied against the imposition of a primary iron tariff.[33] Likewise, merchants importing foreign iron opposed a measure that would diminish their trade.

Nevertheless, a more substantial iron tariff retained its appeal for politicians and the public. Iron and steel production contributed dynamically to British and American economic growth in the nineteenth century, and some people believed that it would contribute as well to Canadian national power and wealth: 'Canada can never be great till she makes her own iron. The iron makers in all ages have been masters of the world; the iron importers have always been weak and dependent.'[34] The iron lobby also gained ground as the market and transportation devlopments noted above reduced the handicap for domestic production. The evolution of the iron tariff was in this sense a result as well as a cause of economic change. Barring strong opposition from metal consumers the government appears to have been willing to supply protection as demanded by credible investors in iron and steel: 'Steel rails will for the moment not be touched, although when home works get ready to go into the trade, they will probably be taken care of.'[35] This 1887 prediction later proved correct; when Canadian steel works began rolling rails after 1900, they were supported handsomely by tariffs, subsidies, and other measures.

A more protective tariff also may have been intended to placate Nova Scotians threatening to secede from Canada, since the iron industry was expected to expand most vigorously in the coal and iron ore region of Nova Scotia.[36] The tariff increase also may have been desired for the increase in revenue that would become available to the federal government.[37]

The first step to increased protection for iron production was the introduction in 1884 of a direct subsidy to makers of pig iron; the subsidy would stimulate production as effectively as a tariff without raising the price of pig iron. The subsidy was followed in 1887 by a sharp increase in the iron tariff; the new Canadian finance minister, Charles Tupper, surprised even the iron lobby with this change.[38] The 'Tupper tariff' of 1887 finally gave the iron industry enough protection to offset the vestigial disadvantages of transportation costs and market size.[39] An 1894 increase in the tariff on scrap wrought-iron and the extension in 1897 of production subsidies to iron made with imported ore further increased the rate of protection. Nevertheless, uncertainty about its permanence undermined the effectiveness of government policy.

The business community worried that the policy of industrial promotion could be altered or removed as easily and unexpectedly as it had been introduced.[40] The government that introduced the National Policy had been Conservative. What would happen if Conservative policy shifted or the Liberal party eventually gained control of the government? This uncertainty was removed only after the Liberals won the federal election of

1896. Investors and potential investors in iron and steel were greatly relieved that the Liberals, although they had campaigned for freer trade, preserved the National Policy rather than abandoning it. Confidence in the durability of government support was strengthened; as a result the efficacy of public policy increased, even though the apparent level of protection did not change markedly.

The industry responded enthusiastically to the enhancement of government support. During the early 1890s a blast furnace was built at Hamilton. After a recession in mid-decade the Hamilton firm expanded; by 1900 new plants were built or under construction at Deseronto, Sault Ste Marie, and Midland. By 1913 additional blast furnaces had been erected at Port Colborne, Parry Sound, Thunder Bay, and Hamilton. Data describing the annual outputs of the furnaces appear in tables 11.1, 11.2, and 11.3. An examination of the Deseronto, Hamilton and Sault Ste Marie firms will illustrate the diversity of this industrial expansion.

One firm to enter production during the 1890s was the Deseronto Iron Company. In 1898 the Rathbuns, a family of lumber merchants and industrialists whom we have encountered in earlier chapters, joined with the former owners of an abandoned Detroit iron-works and other interests to erect a blast furnace at Deseronto, where the Rathbun saw-mill was situated. The blast furnace was built in 1898 with a small municipal subsidy;[41] production began the following year.

This blast furnace was fired by charcoal rather than coal or coke. Until the eighteenth century all iron smelting had used charcoal or wood as its fuel. Learning how to substitute coal or coke for charcoal was an important technological advance during Britain's early Industrial Revolution.[42] By the 1750s iron could be produced more cheaply with coal or coke in Great Britain.[43] Subsequent improvements in the quality and cost of coke iron further imperilled charcoal iron manufacture, which began to decline in Great Britain during the eighteenth century, and by the mid-nineteenth century in western Europe and the eastern seaboard of North America.[44]

In Canada, however, wood was cheaper and metallurgical coal more expensive. Here charcoal smelting was able to survive by securing a specialized market, reducing the price paid for charcoal and improving productivity at the blast furnace.[45] The Deseronto furnace doubled labour productivity and almost doubled fuel productivity from that of Canadian charcoal furnaces twenty-five years earlier.[46] This productivity growth was the result of improvements in the quality of raw materials and changes in the technology of smelting.

The Deseronto blast furnace was taller and thinner and was injected with oxygen at greater pressure and temperature than had been the practice previously in Canada.[47] These modifications accelerated the smelting process. Because iron was produced at a much faster rate, effective use of the new technique required a large scale of production. This fact probably delayed its introduction into Canada, where charcoal iron consumption during the 1880s had not been sufficient to absorb the output of even one modern charcoal furnace.[48] The cost of iron production was reduced further by a decline in the price of charcoal, which was $5 per ton at Marmora during the 1820s, $6.50 at Londonderry, Nova Scotia during the 1850s, $7.50 to $8 during the 1870s at Londonderry and St Maurice, Quebec, and only $4.36 per ton at Deseronto in 1900.[49]

At Deseronto inexpensive waste wood was available from the nearby Rathbun lumber mills, which drew from the surviving forests of central Ontario by an elaborate network of railways and rivers. Fuel costs were reduced further by manufacturing charcoal in kilns that captured gas and liquid released from the wood during carbonization.[50] At Deseronto the first by-product recovery kilns were erected during the early 1880s; later in the decade and early in the 1890s the Rathbuns expressed interest in iron smelting. Before the Deseronto furnace was built locally made charcoal had to be shipped to blast furnaces in Quebec and Michigan. The by-product gas and liquid were distilled in a preliminary way at the kiln to produce marketable acetate of lime and methyl alcohol. Further refining yielded formaldehyde, acetone, acetic acid, and their derivatives. By 1910 nearly half of the firm's revenue derived from chemical products.

The iron produced at Deseronto with charcoal fuel had distinctive metallurgical properties that were valuable in certain applications. An extremely hard surface could be imparted to charcoal iron castings in a special process called 'chilling'; this characteristic was valuable for railway car wheels and the rolls used in rolling mills.[51] Chilled wheel foundries tended to be larger than the other foundries; by 1890 Ontario wheel foundries were located at Hamilton, St Thomas, and soon after at Fort William.[52]

A second special application was in the manufacture of malleable castings, which had unusual tensile strength for their weight.[53] Their uses included lightweight but intricately shaped machinery pieces for moving vehicles such as agricultural implements and railway rolling stock. Malleable iron foundries, which could be rather small, existed at Guelph, Toronto, Hamilton, Oshawa, Whitby, Merrickville, Walkerville, and Smiths Falls in 1890; additional malleable foundries were built at Hamilton, Toronto, Galt, St Catharines, Brantford and possibly Brockville in the following few years.[54]

The Deseronto Iron Company, which later was reorganized as the Standard Chemical Company, the Standard Iron Company, and the Standard Iron, Chemical and Lumber Company, expanded quickly to meet the enormous growth in Canadian demand for railway rolling stock and agricultural implements. By 1913 the firm had established half a dozen charcoal kilns through central Ontario and Quebec as well as chemical refineries in Montreal, England, and Germany. In the same year a new blast furnace was built at Parry Sound.

As it turned out, 1913 was not a good year for the company to incur new capital expenditures. Metal consumption diminished dramatically in a serious recession. Even worse, the demand derived from investment in agriculture and railways failed to recover during World War One. The war effort consumed large quantities of iron, but munitions and other war-related sources of demand placed no special value on the unique properties of charcoal iron.

The wartime chemical market, by contrast, was more favourable to the company. Wood chemicals were in strong demand for the manufacture of explosives; indeed, Britain's War Office soon purchased directly or indirectly the entire chemical output of the company.[55] The wartime chemical expansion made available increasing quantities of charcoal. In 1917, however, the blast furnace began to substitute coke for charcoal; two years later the company permanently abandoned the manufacture of iron.

Iron production at Deseronto disappeared because charcoal smelting became a more expensive way to manufacture iron.[56] The data presented in table 11.1 permit some analysis of manufacturing costs. Production at a coke furnace in Hamilton serves as a benchmark for comparison. Coke smelting continued to be profitable at Hamilton; charcoal smelting at Deseronto evidently was not.[57] The cost data help one understand why.

Raw material and labour costs comprised about 85 per cent of all costs of iron production.[58] Capital and miscellaneous costs accounted for the remaining 15 per cent. Between 1899 and 1916 material and labour costs per ton of pig iron declined slightly at Hamilton but nearly doubled at Deseronto. The increasing relative cost of raw materials and labour doomed the Deseronto blast furnace. Several input price and productivity developments account for the relative cost change.

One important influence was the stagnation of labour productivity at Deseronto in contrast to a considerable increase at the coke furnace. Second, the price of ore rose slightly at Deseronto and declined at Hamilton. At the same time the quality of ore, reflected in its productivity, deteriorated much more at the former site. Finally, and most importantly, the price of Deseronto charcoal relative to that of coke at Hamilton increased, while fuel needs per ton of iron rose at Deseronto and fell at Hamilton.

The price of charcoal rose because of the limited availability of woodland and a demand for fuel that increased enormously during the early twentieth-century growth spurt of the Canadian economy. Charcoal consumption in central Canada almost tripled between 1900 and 1910 as Canada changed from being a net importer during the 1890s to a net exporter after 1910.[59] Most of the increase derived from charcoal use in filtration, ammunition, and non-metallurgical fuel use.[60] The expansion of demand, which accelerated during the war, raised the price of charcoal and freed the chemical producer from a dependence upon iron furnaces to absorb its charcoal.

The prospects for charcoal smelting were also impaired by the laggard improvement in fuel and labour productivity. There was a limit to the perfectability of charcoal furnaces, which apparently could not share further in technical change and the economies of larger-scale production. The ore price and productivity developments are more difficult to explain; possibly the company's fundamental weakness for other reasons compounded the difficulty of procuring ore on favourable terms. Whatever the precise balance of market and technical influences, it is hardly surprising that the Deseronto blast furnace was blown out permanently in 1919, even as the Hamilton iron and steel company continued to expand steadily and profitably.

In Hamilton, as in other Canadian cities, large-scale iron- and steel-making (as opposed to further processing of imports and reprocessing of scrap metal) began in the 1890s. In 1893 a group of American capitalists accepted the Hamilton city council's offer of long-term tax exemptions, a free site of seventy-five acres of land, and a large cash bonus.[61] The American investors withdrew, reportedly because federal subsidies were tied to the use of Ontario ores of doubtful quality;[62] they were replaced by Hamilton merchants and banking interests, stockbrokers from Toronto, and individuals active in Hamilton foundries and other secondary iron firms.[63] The Hamilton furnace finally was completed in December 1895.

In spite of its initial difficulties the company, known successively as the Hamilton Blast Furnace Company, the Hamilton Steel and Iron Company, and the Steel Company of Canada, or Stelco, expanded steadily. In 1899 it merged with the Ontario Rolling Mills, which had located in Hamilton to reroll scrap metal in response to the early National Policy tariffs. Immediately after this merger the blast furnace was expanded and steel furnaces were erected.[64] Another blast furnace was built in 1907; the firm gradually increased its steel-making capacity and installed equipment to mechanize the handling of materials.[65] New rolling-mill facilities were built after the firm merged in 1910 with most of the important rolling-mill companies in southern Ontario and Quebec.[66] Electric motors drove machinery for the new plant, which was completed in 1913; much of the electrical equipment was produced in Hamilton by the Westinghouse

Company.[67] During the war the firm purchased coal mines in the United States and erected a by-product recovery coke oven, new steel furnaces, equipment to manufacture munitions, and a plate mill.

The Hamilton firm was able to expand because it enjoyed several advantages. One was the choice of smelting with coke, which helped minimize production cost. As we have seen, the price of coke did not rise as quickly as the price of charcoal, and the coke furnace's input productivity was enhanced by expanding the scale of production and improving its techniques.

A second source of strength was the firm's location at Hamilton, which minimized the cost of transporting raw materials to the furnace and the finished product to market.[68] Iron ore came from Lake Superior to Lake Erie by water; coal was brought by rail from Pennsylvania.

Most important was the proximity of many companies processing iron and steel. A very large share of Canadian secondary iron and steel production was situated in the urban centres of southern and south-western Ontario. Hamilton itself had been for some time an important centre for iron foundries and rolling stock manufacture.[69] An even wider array of metal manufacturers located in the city during the first two decades of Confederation: the Canada Pipe Foundry, Hamilton Bridge and Tool Company, the Spence file factory, the Ontario Rolling Mill, Hamilton Iron Forging Company, the Ontario Tack Company, and the Canada Screw Company, among others.[70] The concentration of metal manufacturing in southern and southwestern Ontario, particularly in Hamilton, helps explain the success of the Hamilton blast furnace.

Further advantages of the Hamilton firm were the markets that it served and the integration within one company of blast furnaces, steel furnaces, and bar- and finishing-mills. The blast furnace produced pig iron, which could be sold directly to foundries for use in iron castings. Alternatively, the company might convert the pig iron into wrought-iron or steel ingots to be rolled and rerolled into bars, rods, and other useful shapes. The rolled metal was processed further in the manufacture of wire, nails, railway fastenings, hardware of all kinds, light structural metal, and specialized machinery pieces. Stelco was distinctive among Canadian firms because it did not depend largely on purchasing by railways, which accounted for a substantial but quite changeable portion of domestic iron and steel consumption.[71]

Diversification of the firm's final product enhanced stability; if the market for one product line was depressed, metal might be diverted to another. In addition, because various stages of the production process were integrated under one management, material flows could be co-ordinated to permit continuous operation of the equipment and minimization of inventory requirements. The cost of rolling was especially sensitive to continuity of operation.[72] The manager of one steel company observed: 'It is necessary to operate our mill fully if we are to operate it at all. If we run only single shift the cost of our rods goes up by dollars and not cents. We can't run short time because we can't give our men continuous employment.'[73]

Stelco's steel-rolling capacity reflected the changing composition of metal demand. Formerly ferric metal had been sold as pig iron to foundries or as bar iron to machine shops. By the 1890s, however, a large and increasing share of ferric metal was converted to steel and then rolled.[74] A typical steel company rerolled steel billets ('semi-finished' steel) to produce rails, pipes, rods from which wire and hardware were fashioned, structural steel for the construction trades, or sheets used in the fabrication of automobiles, cans, and appliances.[75] The demand for rails and structural steel was unstable because it depended on the construction trades. In any case, high-volume structural and rail mills could not operate efficiently in the small Canadian market (with the exception of rail mills during the early twentieth century railway and wheat boom). With its substantial rod and sheet capacity the Hamilton-based firm chose to serve the fastest-growing and most stable sources of ferric metal demand.

Although most of their iron was converted to steel and then rolled, the Hamilton blast furnaces nevertheless remained the basis of Stelco production. A majority of the cost of producing steel blooms and bars was incurred in the operation of the blast furnace.[76] If its blast furnaces were not profitable, a steel company would be certain to encounter difficulties. It is clear that the Hamilton blast furnace was profitable. The market value of a ton of Hamilton pig iron at the turn of the century was $0.75 greater than its material and labour costs.[77] In addition the firm received cash subsidies of $3 per ton from the provincial and dominion governments.[78] The combined margin of $3.75 ensured that the Hamilton blast furnace would be fundamentally profitable, since capital and miscellaneous costs are unlikely to have exceeded $2 per ton.[79]

This profitability survived through changing circumstances. The provincial and federal governments gradually reduced and then eliminated direct cash subsidies, although the indirect benefits of tariff and non-tariff restrictions on imports continued to be enjoyed. The decline in subsidies was offset by a substantial increase in the margin of market value over costs. Between 1906 and 1910 the value of pig iron at the Hamilton furnace regularly exceeded material and labour costs by more than $2 per ton, even during the recession of 1908.[80] Later, during the difficult years of recession and war, 1913–16, the blast furnace still managed to win an average margin over material and labour costs of $3 per ton.

The company continued to be profitable through the 1920s and 1930s. Dividends were paid and bonds retired even during the worst years of the Great Depression.[81] In part this reflected the firm's low operating costs, since labour productivity continued to improve during the 1920s.[82] As well, the market for light steel products served by Stelco did not suffer the same catastrophic decline during the Great Depression as did the market for heavy rolled pieces that were used in construction and heavy equipment.[83] The favourable demand and supply conditions allowed the firm to increase its share of Canadian steel ingot production from 10 per cent in 1910 to 17 per cent in 1918 and then 45 per cent in 1932.[84] The rise in market share softened the impact of the depression as total Canadian steel production in 1932 fell to its lowest level since 1904.[85]

Not surprisingly the firm was encouraged to invest in larger and more modern machinery and buildings, and to expand working capital. The funds to effect this expansion were found in operating revenue, an increase in outstanding indebtedness (bonds, mortgages, and short-term loans), and retained earnings (profits net of bond, mortgage, and dividend payments).

The company's annual reports indicate the sources of finance for its large-scale expansion and modernization in the period 1911–14. No stock was issued. Instead, annual expenditures of about $500,000 on 'repair, maintenance and improvement' were financed from operating revenue; this practice continued even when revenue declined during the difficult years of 1913–14. Moreover the company disbursed as dividend payments only one-third of its disposable profits; the remainder was retained for investment.[86] Its outstanding debt also increased; Canadian financial institutions and investors were particularly helpful in loaning these funds.[87] Debt expansion and retained earnings appear to have provided about $7 million during the period 1911–14; the two sources were roughly equal in importance although the share of retained earnings declined somewhat during the recession years of 1913–16.[88]

The company's expansion required labour as well as capital, even though its labour needs were reduced and simplified through the introduction of labour-saving machinery.[89] The company's work-force, which had numbered 1,500 in 1908, rose to 6,700 by 1913.[90] Labour was recruited in nearby American industrial centres; also, there was considerable reliance on immigrants recently arrived in North America. The average wage per day in the blast furnace department rose from $1.66 in 1895 to $5.59 in 1920.[91] Although this increase of 240 per cent is best regarded as an approximation, it compares favourably with the Bertram-Percy estimates of an 165 per cent increase in the average national wage and a 128 per cent cost of living increase for the same period.[92] Moreover, the firm attempted to retain its workers with modern labour relations practices such as benefit schemes with a long-term horizon and the use of internal promotions to fill the more attractive jobs.[93] In spite of these efforts, the Hamilton firm experienced considerable labour turnover and many strikes in its early years.[94]

As a business enterprise Stelco's success was marred only by a bitter record of management-labour relations. The firm continued to prosper even during World War One and through most of the interwar period. The same could not be said of the Lake Superior Corporation located in Sault Ste Marie (and indeed, it would be difficult to imagine an iron and steel company more unlike Stelco).

The Lake Superior Corporation (LSC) produced its first steel early in 1902;[95] it faced bankruptcy the following year. Between 1904 and 1908 the firm was able to operate only because the provincial government guaranteed payments to both capital and labour employed by the firm.[96] During the war the company, by then known as the Algoma Steel Corporation, again faced reorganization after failing to pay its bond holders.[97] During the 1920s the firm's affairs were a 'financial quagmire,' with losses averaging $400,000 per year.[98] During the 1930s the threat of bankruptcy again loomed large until the company was reorganized in 1935.[99] No dividends were paid during the firm's first thirty-five years, and bond payments were suspended several times.[100]

Two questions arise. First, why was iron and steel manufacture at the Soo unprofitable? Second, how could the company get underway and then continue in the face of these financial difficulties? The first question turns out to be rather easy to answer; the second is more difficult.

The Lake Superior Corporation began as a canal and hydroelectric conglomerate exploiting the drop in water level between Lake Superior and Lake Huron. In 1898 the firm began experiments to produce nickel-steel and sulphuric acid from sulphur-bearing nickel-iron ore in the Sudbury region.[101] The idea was similar to that of Sam Ritchie a decade earlier (see above) with the added features of using LSC hydroelectric power and supplying sulphuric acid to the LSC pulp mill. Ferro-nickel matte would be made available for smelting with an admixture of richer iron ore in order to produce nickel-steel.

During 1899 the company announced that a large deposit of high-quality iron ore had been discovered conveniently nearby at Michipicoten, near the present town of Wawa; the deposit was developed as the Helen Mine.[102] By the end of the year plans were being laid for a large iron and steel works at the Soo;[103] the first steel was poured in 1902.

The defects of this grandiose scheme did not become known until after considerable money had been invested and a large number of immigrants were lured by the promise of employment to settle at the Soo. The nickel-steel scheme turned out to be technically infeasible and the Sudbury ores worthless.[104] Ore from the Helen Mine was poor in quality[105] and limited in quantity:[106] the mine closed in 1917 after producing only 10 per cent of the amount promised in 1900. Only 13 per cent of the ore used by the LSC during its first ten years came from the Helen Mine.[107] Local supplies of hardwood were to be used in the manufacture of charcoal for the LSC blast furnaces, but the Soo region lacked sufficient stands of hardwood to produce the necessary charcoal.[108] After a brief experiment with charcoal in 1905 the furnaces relied exclusively upon coke fuel.

Because local resources were inadequate, most of the ore and all the coal had to be imported. Unfortunately, the location of the plant made little sense if local ore, fuel, and hydroelectricity were not used.[109] The plant's distance from the sources of fuel, scrap, and skilled labour and from the markets for finished steel imposed a heavy transportation cost burden.[110] Because of these handicaps the LSC blast furnaces won an average margin over material and labour costs between 1913 and 1920 of only $1.50 compared with almost $5 at Stelco for the same period.[111]

The rest of the company's plant was equally unimpressive. The first steel furnaces and rolling mill were purchased second-hand; they had been obsolete when built in 1888 and were used no more than a few months in 1899 before being moved to the Soo.[112] Nevertheless, this equipment served to create the appearance of an imposing industrial capacity quickly and inexpensively.

The LSC produced very little other than steel rails. The advantage of this market lay in the assistance afforded by government subsidies and tariffs, stiff anti-dumping legislation, direct government purchase of rails for publicly owned railways (in some cases without public tender), and a requirement that publicly subsidized railways (which was almost all of them) purchase rails domestically if they were available.[113]

The LSC rail mill absorbed almost the entire steel output of the company. Annual capacity of this mill was about 360,000 net tons, an amount typical of heavy rail mills at the turn of the century and an amount actually produced in 1913. Unfortunately, that was the only year in which rail production exceeded 300,000 tons. Between 1906 and 1913 annual mill output averaged 227,000 tons; between 1914 and 1920 the annnual average fell to 133,000 tons.[114] The steel furnaces and rolling-mills operated somewhat under capacity between 1904 and 1913 and even more so in subsequent years.[115]

The inability to make more complete use of its equipment was not the result of another producer besting the LSC for control of the rail market. On the contrary, the LSC accounted for 60–65 per cent of Canadian heavy rail output in 1906–13 and 70–75 per cent in 1914–20; the sole competition was the troubled Dominion Iron and Steel Corporation (DISC) located at Sydney, Nova Scotia. As noted in tables 11.3 through 11.4, DISC and a second firm, the Nova Scotia Steel and Coal Company, experienced a steady decline in their share of Canadian production. This was because the coal and iron ore available in Nova Scotia were increasingly expensive to mine and rather poor in quality.[116]

A more fundamental problem for the LSC was the small size and instability of Canadian rail demand. Annual Canadian rail needs during the 1880s averaged 100,000 net tons, rising to 440,000 tons in the decade immediately preceding World War One.[117] In the latter period Canadian consumption was sufficient to support one rail-mill at an efficient scale of operation. Unfortunately, rail consumption declined to an annual average of 270,000 tons during the 1920s and dropped again to 220,000 tons during the 1930s.[118] Not surprisingly, the LSC shared with DISC the burden of a shrinking market.

The LSC attempted with little success to diversify into the production of tubes, railway fishplates, rolling stock, merchant bars, light structural material, and other lines in order to utilize the steel works more fully. Although interested from an early date in the rolling of heavy structural materials, the company was unwilling to invest in the necessary facilities.[119] In this the Soo firm showed sensible if uncharacteristic restraint; the Canadian market for heavy structural metal was not large enough to sustain domestic production on an economical basis.[120]

The company did manage to diversify in one respect after 1914; it supplied large quantities of steel to the war effort.[121] Between 1914 and 1918 Canadian steel capacity more than doubled to meet the British demand for shell steel; by 1916 Canadian firms were supplying between a quarter and a third of British artillery needs.[122] Between 1915 and 1918 an average 490,000 tons of steel annually were used for shell production; total Canadian steel ingot production averaged 960,000 tons per year 1911–14 and 1.46 million tons 1915–18.[123] In these years the war effort, directly and indirectly, must have consumed more than half of all Canadian iron and steel output. The LSC, with a larger steel capacity than any other Canadian firm, was a major beneficiary of this important demand.[124] Unfortunately for the LSC, the demand for artillery shells did not survive the transition to peace-time.

The LSC's drive to diversify was handicapped by an inability to compete except in markets characterized by feeble domestic competition and some significant dependence of consumers upon the government, as with the railway and munitions industries. Possibly the company could have produced structural steel if a substantial tariff had been created as the LSC requested.[125] The government undoubtedly refused to provide a structural steel tariff because consumers of structural steel would have been handicapped unfairly if they were forced to purchase from a structural mill that was in an inappropriate location, such as at the Soo, and operating inefficiently in the small Canadian market.

The LSC, like the Sydney mills in Nova Scotia, tried and failed to diversify into the market for steel wire rods, which were used in all kinds of hardware manufacture. The market for steel rods, like those for structural shapes used in construction and sheets used in automobiles and appliances, continued to expand during the interwar period. Hence Canadian wire rod production managed to triple between 1909 and 1913 and 1935 and 1939, while rail production declined by 75 per cent in the same interval.[126] In the case of wire rods, the obstacle to LSC's growth was direct competition with a more efficient supplier: Stelco.

The peculiar financial structure of the LSC is also alleged to have impeded the firm's diversification; Donald Eldon defines this conventional view:[127] 'Diversification was only possible to a limited extent on account of financial difficulties, and yet the only possible solution of financial difficulties was diversification. The financial stalemate appeared quite early in the firm's history. Because of a lack of confidence in the company's stocks financing relied almost entirely upon short term loans and bonds secured by the physical assets of the steel company.'[128] This resulting obligation to make annual payments to bond holders later limited the firm's flexibility and absorbed internal funds that otherwise might have been reinvested. A program of diversification almost inevitably would have involved new investors prepared to commit fresh funds. The new investors would have been expected to guarantee payments to the old bond-holders in addition to obtaining a return on the new funds. Unfortunately, given the firm's locational, market, and resource handicaps, it was hard to believe that earnings would improve enough to respect the legitimate interests of past investors and still pay a return to new funds.

If the LSC had been more profitable in the first place, the burden of maintaining bond payments would have been more manageable, and the returns to investment in diversification more attractive. The LSC eventually was reorganized during the 1930s with a controversial scheme that eliminated the necessity for annual payments to any investor in the firm during its first thirty-five years.[129] This scheme probably could not have been implemented if it had not been for the depressed economic climate of the 1930s and the non-pecuniary goals of James Dunn, who effected the reorganization and assumed control of the firm in 1935.[130]

Freed of the burden of its past, the Lake Superior Corporation finally was in a position to finance changes to utilize the steel plant more fully. A sheet- and tin-plate mill was erected to serve the growing market for flat rolled metal, especially that used in the manufacture of tin cans.[131] Unfortunately, the new mill was an 'unmitigated disaster' and closed in 1942.[132]

A weak resource base, inappropriate location, and early mismanagement explain much of the firm's failure to become profitable before World War Two. Complicating burdens were the small size of domestic market relative to an efficient scale of operation in the heavy rolled trades and a financial structure that reflected the firm's serious operational handicaps. All these factors contributed to the numerous and sometimes spectacular problems of the Lake Superior Corporation. It is more difficult to explain how the firm managed to obtain financing in the first place and to survive through thirty-five years of more or less unprofitable operation.

The initial financing would have been much more difficult to obtain had there not been an extraordinary boom in industrial securities between 1899 and 1902.[133] For the first time North American investors demanded industrial securities in large volume. Several spectacular steel industry mergers in the United States and a sharp rise in iron and steel prices focused the particular attention of investors upon new steel companies such as the LSC.

The prospect for LSC profitability must have been difficult to assess. Between 1894 and 1903 the company expanded, diversified, and in this process attracted a supply of funds for investment. In retrospect, one can doubt if any of its activities was profitable; at the time, however, this would have been difficult to assess as long as the flow of new funds offset any losses in established activities.[134] As well, the LSC's subsidiary firms purchased a considerable amount from each other; the failure to earn a net profit on commerce with firms not part of the conglomerate would have been difficult to discern during the period of expansion.

The LSC's corporate structure and pattern of growth were the handiwork of Francis H. Clergue, until 1903 the firm's American promoter. His reckless ambition, legendary powers of persuasion, and metallurgical ignorance contributed to the establishment of the Soo steel works – and to its failure.[135] 'He is fatally optimistic ... He is a royal entertainer, and a great spender – a right good fellow, in fact – and we are all sorry that his schemes have always failed.'[136] Although Clergue's contribution was influential and idiosyncratic, it was conditioned by a fortuitous set of circumstances: the first great boom in industrial securities, the discovery of a small deposit of low-grade iron ore at Michipicoten, the strategic significance of nickel-steel, his company's insatiable demand for new capital, and government commitments to northern development and the iron and steel industry.

There can be little doubt that the visible hand of public policy served as midwife and handmaiden to steel-making at the Soo. The provincial and federal governments made available subsidies and tariffs (supported by anti-dumping legislation), guarantees of payments to both capital and labour, a Canadian-content requirement for purchasing by federally subsidized railways, government contracts to purchase rails at a rather high price even before the plant was built, legislation permitting the controversial 1935 reorganization, and so on.[137]

Government support had its limits, of course, but they reflected the LSC's fundamental weakness and the legitimate interests of consumers and more efficient steel producers, rather than a lack of will on the part of public authorities.[138] To some extent, government assistance was motivated by a belief that iron and steel production was an essential ingredient in economic growth. More particularly there was a visible public commitment to the development of northern Ontario, in which region the Lake Superior Corporation loomed large.[139] It was plausible to claim that if disaster should overtake this company, it would be impossible to secure any further capital for the development of what was known as 'New Ontario' for many years to come.[140] By 1903 government officials had committed their political capital to regional and industrial development policies that were alarmingly dependent upon the survival of the LSC. As a result, further efforts to sustain the firm were attractive politically even if rather less so financially.[141]

Steel-making at the Soo was not, or at any rate not simply, an economic response to general market forces. Unmistakable in the story of the LSC is the presence of what the economic historian Fritz Redlich calls a unique, non-repetitive component that makes the historical process as a whole a unique process.[142] Production at Deseronto and Hamilton, by contrast, can be explained more straightforwardly as the rational response of investors to market demand, input prices, and available technology.

The evolution of these firms reflects differing capacities for adjustment to input price fluctuations, changes in the composition of metal demand and a general deceleration in the growth of metal consumption between 1913 and 1939. After two decades of activity the Deseronto charcoal furnace disappeared as quietly and as sensibly as it had appeared. Production at Hamilton prospered and expanded in all manner of circumstance. Steel-making at the Soo began as an adventurous enterprise, and continued to be a troubled one.

Some Smaller Firms

Other firms were active in the province; their annual output of pig iron is reported in the tables for this chapter. At Midland a blast furnace was erected in 1899 by the Canada Iron Furnace Company, which controlled a chain of wheel and pipe foundries, a Montreal heavy-metal importing house, and charcoal iron smelting in Quebec.[143] The company had investigated a move to southern Ontario during the early 1890s.[144] A site at Midland on Georgian Bay attracted the firm because of convenient water access, a local supply of wood in the old saw-milling town, and a cash subsidy from the municipality.[145] At first, it was intended that the furnace use charcoal; but the charcoal kilns were never used, because wood proved to be more expensive than anticipated.[146] A close relationship developed with the LSC, which sold Helen ore to Midland, purchased Midland pig iron, and contributed 40 per cent of the capital for the Midland works.[147]

The Midland furnace failed to survive the period of excess capacity in the iron market during the 1920s, a fate also encountered by the Port Colborne blast furnace of the Canadian Furnace Company, a subsidiary of an American firm.[148] A blast furnace at Port Arthur fared even worse. The Port Arthur furnace produced only briefly between 1907 and 1911.[149] The furnace used iron ore discovered during the 1880s, which together with a handsome municipal bonus provided the basis for various plans to smelt at the Lakehead between 1890 and 1905. In the latter year the Canadian Northern Railway and related interests began erection of the iron works, which did not go into blast until two years later.[150] The ore quickly proved to be inadequate in quality, but the railway interests continued to plan for even larger-scale production, presumably with alternate sources of ore, in Toronto and at Port Arthur.[151]

The municipality of Collingwood also offered a cash subsidy to secure the building of a plant, which operated even more briefly than the Port Arthur one. Although the Cramp Steel Company erected steel furnaces and rolling-mills at Collingwood between 1900 and 1903, there is no record of any production even after a reorganization in 1904 as the Northern Iron and Steel Company.[152] After sitting idle for several years, the Collingwood steel furnaces were fired briefly during World War One to produce shell.[153] Even this very limited record of production was more than the US Steel Corporation could muster. The giant American firm took an interest in a plan for smelting during 1905; by the beginning of 1907 land was purchased near Windsor, but as late as 1913 the company seemed more interested in propagating rumours than in erecting a steel plant.[154] US Steel operated wire and tinplate mills at this site between 1930 and 1932 before selling the land to the troubled Dominion Steel and Coal Company of Cape Breton, which never managed to build a iron and steel works there.[155]

Although Collingwood and Windsor were singularly unproductive sites, firms elsewhere managed to smelt steel. Large-scale production at Hamilton and the Soo was discussed above. By 1907 smaller-scale works at Ottawa, Owen Sound, and Welland were casting steel into specialized shapes as well as producing ingot steel.[156] The Owen Sound foundry of William Kennedy and Sons appears to have been the first in Ontario to remain in business for several years. Steel founding had been attempted previously in London, Niagara, and Toronto.[157] Because a steel foundry typically was rather small, production was possible in the small Canadian market; nevertheless, quality control problems impeded the early development of steel-casting here as elsewhere in North America.[158]

These foundries did not smelt their own pig iron, perhaps because of the small scale of their operations. Typically, they used open hearth furnaces to cast machinery pieces, projectiles, wheels, shafting, railway hardware, and mill rolls; the castings could be forged, welded, or rolled.[159] Like the malleable and chilled iron foundries mentioned above, steel foundries served a specialized and growing market. New steel foundries appeared by 1920; several in the Welland area used electric furnaces to produce specialty steels along with ferro-alloys. The dominion government continued research into the production of steel in electric furnaces, which had been started by the LSC. Although dismissed by industry sources as a 'wild goose chase,' the government's commitment led it to pay cash subsidies to electric steel producers in 1907. In spite of this assistance, electric steel remained largely a specialty trade.[160]

DOFASCO

The larger steel foundries produced ingots for general consumption as well as the more specialized castings. The most important of the ingot producers was the Dominion Steel Foundry Company, organized in 1913 and amalgamated with the Hamilton Steel Wheel Company in 1917 to form the Dominion Foundries and Steel Limited, or DOFASCO.[161] DOFASCO located in Hamilton because of that city's easy access to sources of scrap metal and to its principal market, railway workshops. During the war DOFASCO produced large quantities of shell steel and presumably also benefited from the excess supply of scrap metal generated by munitions manufacturers. The appearance and early growth of DOFASCO is recorded in the tabular data describing steel ingot production (table 11.3).

DOFASCO, like nearby Stelco, has been able to expand and survive to this day. So has the LSC, which is now known as the Algoma Steel Corporation. Other firms were less fortunate. The experience of Ontario's iron companies conveys something of the rich diversity of the province's industrial evolution. Almost without exception, the firms producing iron and steel began as part of an investment wave that transformed the Canadian industry between 1890 and 1920. Since its beginnings the primary iron industry has been remarkably successful; as is indicated in the tables, Ontario's iron output increased from nothing during the 1870s and 1880s to half of the Canadian total on the eve of World War One. The Ontario share rose further to reach two-thirds of Canadian output during the 1920s and 1930s. The expansion of the province's iron industry was a response to the various influences outlined in this chapter.

12 The Development of the Ontario Automobile Industry to 1939

TOM TRAVES, York University

In chapters 7 and 8 the automobile industry was seen to be of great importance for Ontario's economic development both before and after 1914. Chapters 16, 17, and 19 examine its significance for the province's transport system, its retail trading network, and its fiscal arrangements. The present chapter treats the industry itself, though not the full social effect of the automobile in the 'age of auto-industrialization,'[1] nor all its interconnections with the other sectors of the provincial economy. A definitive answer to the question of interconnection cannot be provided without the use of an 'input-output' table – a statistical device that traces the linkages among all the industries of the provincial economy. For the years before 1941 no such table exists. The data in table 12.1, however, may suggest something about the kind and the scope of the linkages. Today it is frequently claimed that one in every ten Ontario jobs is auto-related; similar claims were advanced before World War Two.[2] The statistics presented in chapters 2 and 17 suggest that this fraction is probably too large, even when full account is taken of the jobs in oil refining, gasoline, and auto sales and service before World War Two. But no one doubts that for Ontario's economy, the automobile mattered.

Foundation

From its earliest days in Canada, nearly all the industry's parts and assembly plants were located in Ontario. By 1939, the province contained 91 per cent of the capital in Canada's auto industry, and 95 per cent of its workers; 95 per cent of the industry's output was produced in Ontario, which contained an even higher percentage of the parts industry.[3] In large measure that geographical pattern can be explained by market considerations. Imported components came from plants that were located primarily in adjacent states.[4] The branch plant character[5] of the large firms, plus the dependence on imported components that characterized the smaller firms also, was thus of central importance. For those components that were produced in Canada, Ontario's usual locational advantages – augmented in the twentieth century by cheap hydro power – were at work. Also, Ontario contained more than 49 per cent of Canada's vehicle registrations in 1915, 47.3 per cent in 1925, 48 per cent in 1935, and 47 per cent in 1940.[6] Another 15 per cent of the vehicles were in Quebec in 1940, while, in the late 1920s, more than 38 per cent of the annual output was being sent abroad – not to the United States but overseas, in worldwide markets throughout the British Empire. Finally, all the individual Canadian entrepreneurs who established the leading concerns, both branch plant and autonomous, had operated other manufacturing plants in the region before entering the automobile business. Certainly Oshawa owes its prominence to such considerations.

The dominant firms in the industry, the Ford Motor Company of Canada and the ancestor of General Motors of Canada, were established in the first decade of the twentieth century. While the creation of such concerns bears witness to the emerging superiority of American industry as a source of design and components, in one important respect these cases depart significantly from the pattern that Mira Wilkins and Frank Hill found generally to describe the global expansion of American industry: 'The evolution was from the export of an American-made article, to the exportation of a branch of the business, to augmentation of the investment, to assembly and then to full foreign manufacture.'[7] The Canadian case differs to the extent that it was local businessmen who took the initiative in pursuing the foreign connection.

Ford Motors established a Canadian branch when it was still a new and tiny American enterprise, in response to the entreaties of Gordon M. McGregor, a Walkerville carriage maker, who wanted to diversify into the new industry.[8] Ford had actually crossed the border in August 1903, when the sixth car the company built was exported to Toronto, but no thought was then given to manufacturing in Canada. In 1904 McGregor approached Henry Ford and persuaded him to sign a licensing and patent agreement that became the basis of Ford of Canada. The 35 per cent Canadian tariff on automobile imports, the apparent strength of the Canadian market, and McGregor's promise to finance the branch operation personally apparently determined Ford's decision. On 17 August 1904 Ford became incorporated in Canada, under provincial charter, with a capitalization of $125,000, of which $56,250 represented real assets. Twenty-eight Canadian shareholders, including McGregor, C.M. Walker of the Hiram Walker brewing family, a Walkerville banker, a physician, and an auto dealer, provided 60 per cent of the invested capital, but the

Ford Motor Company of Michigan received 50 per cent of the new firm's authorized shares. In exchange, Ford agreed to furnish his Canadian branch with the necessary patents, plans, drawings, and specifications to build a Ford car. The Americans also agreed, for a fee, to provide advice on general operating problems. For its part, the Canadian firm received the sole right to manufacture and sell Ford products in Canada and the then-existing British Empire, including India, Malaya, South Africa, New Zealand, and Australia. Gordon McGregor became the new company's general manager and secretary, John S. Gray, president of American Ford, assumed a similar position in the branch, and Henry Ford became vice-president. Operations began at once.

General Motors of Canada owed its origins, in part, to an engineer's attack of pleurisy.[9] R.S. McLaughlin, son and partner of one of Canada's largest carriage makers, persuaded his father and brother in 1905 that they ought to consider an alliance with an American auto maker. After personally testing out a number of American-built cars and touring their producers' factories, McLaughlin initiated active negotiations with W.C. Durant, a major American carriage- and wagon-maker, who had recently acquired control of the Buick Motor Car Company and had built it into the largest American auto manufacturer. McLaughlin wanted access to the excellent Buick engine, but when he failed at first to reach a satisfactory financial arrangement with Durant, he and his brother decided to build their own motor. They hired an American engineer, built him a first-class machine shop, ordered a number of moving parts from a Cleveland firm, and worked out plans to do their own engine castings. Everything was ready to produce the company's first 100 cars, when the engineer became severely ill with pleurisy and work in his shop came to a dead halt. In desperation, McLaughlin wired Durant again and asked to borrow one of his engineers. Instead, Durant himself arrived in Oshawa, the negotiations to use the Buick engine started anew, and this time they reached a successful conclusion. In 1907 the McLaughlin Motor Car Company signed a fifteen-year agreement with Buick to use its engines and a few other parts in a McLaughlin-built-and-designed body. Eight years later, the McLaughlins struck a similar deal with Durant's Chevrolet Company. Ownership of the new Canadian auto producer was divided between the McLaughlin family, with 7,000 shares, and Buick (absorbed by Durant's General Motors Corporation in 1908), with 5,000.[10] Nearly half a century later R.S. McLaughlin reflected on these events and their implications for the Canadian industry.

I have heard people regret that the coincidence of an engineer falling ill should have put an end to the project to produce an all-Canadian car. I may say that any regret on my part is tempered by the hard facts of the automobile industry, by the very great probability that if our engineer Arthur Milbrath had not become ill and we had proceeded with our plan to make our own cars, we almost certainly would have taken a header; and once having failed in our first effort we might never had got back into the automobile business ... Even with the Buick connection we had to be lucky to succeed. We just happened to pick a car that was destined to make good. I have often wondered why some cars succeeded and some failed. One of the strangest facts about the automobile business in North America is that in its fifty-odd years no fewer than 2,400 different makers have manufactured and offered cars for sale ... and today you can count on the fingers of two hands the car manufacturers who have survived.[11]

The experience of numerous other Canadian auto makers confirms McLaughlin's speculation that success was unpredictable. For example, a year after the Oshawa manufacturer had set out on his new course, one of his competitors in the carriage business, J.B. Tudhope of Orillia, also launched himself in the auto business after touring the American producers and choosing the air-cooled McIntyre engine. The Tudhope-McIntyre sold well, but Tudhope's Orillia plant burned to the ground in 1909 and he decided to switch allegiance to the Everitt 30, an American machine built by a former carriage worker from Chatham, Ontario. Tudhope installed the 782 jigs and dies needed to manufacture the Everitt in Canada, and when the American firm sold out to Studebaker Brothers in 1911, the now-orphaned Canadian plant tried to press on alone with a modified version of its original design. By the time war broke out in 1914, Tudhope could no longer compete against the lower-priced, improved American models that crowded the market, so he decided finally to abandon the auto business. In 1915, when the McLaughlins secured their Chevrolet connection, Tudhope bought their carriage works.[12]

Other Canadian branch operations also suffered from the vagaries of their parents' fortunes. The Russell Motor Car Company began production in 1908, using the Knight sleeve-valve engine, a British design that for a brief period appeared to overcome the problem of engine knock associated with primitive fuels and valve defects in the standard 'poppet-valve' engines.[13] Russell was a spin-off from the 1899 merger of five bicycle producers into CCM. In this respect, as well as in its use of a British engine, Russell differed from the standard Canadian operation, which usually had evolved from the carriage and wagon trade. In the United States and Britain, bicycle makers quite commonly turned to auto production, for such manufacturers had already learned to master the large-volume precision machine work and the necessary techniques of industrial organization that later became familiar features of the automobile industry.

(Thus the Dodge brothers, for example, started out as bicycle builders in Canada before moving to the United States to start again in the new line.)[14]

Russell's initial success was most impressive. Within four years of starting production, the firm's work-force doubled in size to 1,200 men. But disaster struck in 1913 when the company lost access to the Knight engine and had to start building its own production facilities. This transition took time and cost Russell dearly. Even though the company recovered and actually built an improved motor the days of the sleeve-valve engine were numbered because its poppet-valve competitor, which also used far less oil, had been improved. By the outbreak of war, Russell's engine was essentially obsolete, and in 1916 the Canadian firm sold out to Willys-Overland of Toledo, Ohio, which was the only major American firm to use a similar engine design. This arrangement provided Russell with a new lease on life, but eventually Willys-Overland also called it a day, stopping Canadian production in 1933.

Gray-Dort Motors Limited of Chatham also experienced a match-like existence, burning brightly for a brief period and then expiring quickly.[15] The Gray family began business in 1853 making wagons and bobsleds, but they caught the auto bug early, Robert Gray being one of the original investors in Ford of Canada. This connection led to an auto dealership, and by 1908 the Grays had also secured a contract to supply Ford with auto bodies, which in those days were wood-framed and carriage-like. In 1915 the Grays decided to strike out on their own. They initiated a partnership with Josiah Dallas Dort, who had entered the auto business in Michigan after first enjoying great success with his partner in the wagon trade, W.C. Durant. Dort supplied the engines and transmissions, while the Grays built the bodies. The Gray-Dort did very well in Canada. Branch offices were established from Toronto to Vancouver, the company managed to penetrate some export markets, and by 1921 Gray-Dort employed 760 men to produce 9,000 cars. Its American partner, however, suffered serious financial setbacks, and in 1921 the aging J.D. Dort decided to close up shop. Once again, a successful Canadian firm found itself orphaned as its supply of American parts disappeared. Within three years Gray-Dort too had to close the doors of its 15.1–acre plant.

No Canadian automobile producer succeeded without an effective American partner. Why? There were, to be sure, attempts made to build an 'all-Canadian car.' Table 12.2 provides a surprisingly long list of Ontario auto makers who tried. As early as 1867 Canadian artisans had built a functional steam-powered car, and later in the century others experimented successfully with gasoline and electrically powered vehicles. But the transition to mass production proved impossible. A relatively small, dispersed market, a primitive road system, and a hostile climate, not to mention the constantly evolving technology of the automobile itself, made the auto industry in Canada a very risky proposition indeed. By contrast, if a Canadian manufacturer gained assess to an effective American source of technology and components, he stood a much better chance of success. This was especially important to the former carriage makers who dominated the Canadian industry since they possessed no exceptional engineering knowledge that they could use to form the basis of an independent centre of production. As William Gray explained in 1924, on the eve of the collapse of his Gray-Dort Motors:

The trend ... of the past few years has been toward price reduction, and price reduction can only take place through volumes, that is the result of highly specialized and large organizations ... This in Canada is particularly true, where the problems of distribution are so severe on account of the tremendous distance over which a product must be scattered to meet the market of a small population ... Altogether, in round figures, before the smallest type of motor car company can be instituted that is going to start out with any kind of successful production programme at all, they have to at least invest in the neighbourhood of a million dollars, just in equipment alone, and then you would still have your engineering problems to solve. That is why the successful companies of Canada found it necessary to affiliate themselves with American interests, because with our small and limited outputs it is impossible to carry the tremendous overhead of engineering expenses. [It] is simply a problem that we must face until we have more population.[16]

Certainly the McLaughlins of General Motors accepted the logic of this argument. In 1918, as their fifteen-year agreement with Buick neared its end, the McLaughlins, who had no male heirs wanting to remain in the business, decided to sell out to their American partners rather than risk competition on their own. 'There were hundreds, almost thousands of newly formed car companies in the US failing and going by the board,' recalled R.S. McLaughlin many years later. 'I could see the inside of the cup and I knew what it meant.' Shortly thereafter GM merged the Canadian Buick and Chevrolet operations into the newly created General Motors of Canada Ltd; R.S. McLaughlin continued as president of this firm and sat on the American board for many years.[17]

A suitable American connection provided an innovative Canadian entrepreneur with a distinct competitive edge. Even the McLaughlins were prepared to scrap plans for their own engines in order to gain what they perceived to be technological security and the financial benefits that came with it. Moreover, technological dependence, at this time, did not involve managerial dependence, so that the Canadian entrepreneurs apparently felt no tension among their goals of autonomy, profits, and security. From an individual perspective, which was the only one actually considered, partnership with Americans made good business sense. It is only when such behaviour is considered in the aggregate, and from a structural perspective, that some later observers have claimed these individual decisions possess negative connotations.[18]

Table 12.3 provides a list of American-owned auto makers who operated in Ontario at one time or another. It will be noted that many firms had very short lives and that others seem to have been enticed into Canada by the dominion tariff increases of the early 1930s and perhaps by the prospect of access to empire markets on preferential terms – a prospect that became much more significant in the early 1930s than it had been before. The large and successful firms – Ford, Studebaker, Willys, General Motors, Chrysler – were also the firms that were large and long lived in the United States.

Expansion

While the fortunes of individual firms varied tremendously, the industry as a whole grew very rapidly in Canada before the Great Depression of the 1930s. By the 1920s the Canadian industry was the second largest in the world, and its export sales, on a per capita basis, surpassed even those of the United States.[19] In most respects, however, Canadian manufacturers operated as regional producers in a continental industry, producing the same models as their American parents and using technology that was derived from south of the border. Canadian producers followed the production and marketing patterns established by their parent firms. Canadian consumers, too, behaved like Americans and responded to the same forces; automobiles were becoming cheaper and better, while there were more good roads on which they could be driven. Most North American producers oriented themselves to a mass market for cheap, reliable cars, so that by 1921, 74 per cent of all Canadian new car sales cost less than $1,000 – still no small sum, given Canadian incomes, but not hopelessly out of reach, as the growth of the industry attests.[20] As table 12.5 illustrates, most such vehicles were sold to farmers and small businessmen.[21]

Lower prices were the key to the mass market, and improved production methods and designs brought costs down steadily. One important element was standardization and interchangeability of parts, a development that dramatically reduced the need for skilled craftsmen in the auto factories themselves. Another was Henry Ford's moving assembly line, first installed in 1913. The 'line' was shortly applied in Canada, with the same machines and techniques, and similar results.[22] As early as 1913 the Canadian branch had managed to reduce its skilled work force to 6 per cent of the total, the rest being semi-skilled operators of pre-set machines. A decade later the company employed as many electrically powered machines as men.[23] These changes in production techniques had profound consequences for labour relations in the industry, a point discussed later, but they did serve to reduce costs, so that prices fell, while sales and total employment rose impressively, as table 12.4 reveals. The first Model T touring car sold for $1,150 in 1909, then fell to $650 in 1914 after the assembly line was in place, declined again to $495 at the end of World War One, and finally dropped to $415 in 1926, when the Model T enjoyed its best and last year on the Canadian market.[24]

As cars became cheaper, they also got better. The improved comfort and convenience of the automobile helped sales, as did technical improvements that made them easier to drive. The electric starter, shock absorbers, four-wheel brakes, and inflatable tires that were easy to change all contributed to a less complicated and smoother ride. The development of higher-compression engines, the shift from four-to six-cylinder motors, and the introduction of lead-based anti-knock fluids all led to to more powerful and efficient cars.[25] Another significant development, especially for Canadians, was the wider availability of closed models. As late as 1922, only 20 per cent of all the passenger cars produced in Canada were closed. However, with the introduction of hydraulic body presses that could turn out body panels in volume and continuous electric welding techniques that allowed factories to assemble different body sections quickly and cheaply, closed models soon challenged open touring cars not only in quality but in price. By 1925 closed models accounted for 40 per cent of Canadian production, and all-weather driving became a more realistic prospect.[26] Finally, buyers quickly took to the wide range of colour choices available after the introduction in 1923 of the lacquer spray Duco paint that General Motors and Dupont jointly developed. Ford's basic black enamel finish had already cut the number of painting operations to two, and reduced drying time to just a few hours, but because the process demanded a baking heat of 400°F, it could be applied only to all-metal components, such as fenders, running boards, and the like. The Duco process reduced painting and drying time from thirty days to three.[27] The result was a reduction in costs and an enhancement of aesthetic appeal.

Finally, car sales improved because the gradual development of local and intercity road networks made extended driving more feasible. So far as Ontario is concerned, these developments are traced in chapters 16 and 19 below; in other provinces and in some of the Canadian industry's overseas markets, roads improved less rapidly than in Ontario, but improvements there certainly were. Between 1923 and 1928, as new car sales tripled, surfaced road mileage in Canada increased by 35 per cent. In 1935 roughly one-quarter of all non-urban roads, by mileage, were surfaced, a big change from 1928, when only one-sixth were so improved. Revenues for vehicle licences and gasoline taxes were everywhere being directed to road improvement.[28] Provincial governments were no doubt responding not only to the growing importance of the automobile in society but to pressure from lobbying groups, and to the opportunities for patronage inherent in highway-building. Even so, road guides and automobile enthusiasts frequently complained about the primitive conditions they faced. A Ford sales manager, for example, reported that he had driven his car 'down to the hubs in ooze,' and, reasonably enough, he concluded that such conditions hurt sales.[29]

The Canadian market was important, but, as table 12.4 reveals, the export market also bulked large. Because the United Kingdom granted a substantial tariff preference to empire goods in 1919 and because of a network of trade agreements and unilateral concessions elsewhere in the empire, in many though not all empire markets lower tariffs were charged on Canadian cars than on American.[30] American auto makers tried to seize on that advantage by scheduling their imperial exports from Canada. In 1921, for example, General Motors moved its export headquarters to Oshawa and handed over the imperial market to the Canadian division. Ford had done the same in 1904, although it had reserved the United Kingdom, where it later set up another subsidiary. Subsequently, empire markets accounted for more than 80 per cent of Canadian auto exports.[31] These sales were crucial to the Canadian industry. In the 1920s exports accounted for about 50 per cent of Ford's total production, 40 per cent of that of General Motors, and 25 per cent of that of Chrysler.[32] Such exports provided many benefits for Canadian producers. They allowed longer production runs, thereby reducing costs, and they smoothed out production cycles, because in the southern hemisphere sales tended to peak during Canada's winter doldrums; even after deducting the cost of imported components, they provided some net receipts of foreign exchange from export sales.[33]

Understandably, the Canadian companies sought vigorously to develop these overseas markets. Ford led the way by creating twelve Ford of Canada branch assembly plants in South Africa, India, Malaya, and Australia. There was even, by 1939, a Ford branch plant in Burnaby, British Columbia, whose output was aimed partly at overseas markets. By 1926 Ford had invested nearly $6 million in such operations. But it was hard for Canadian producers to retain their empire business, so that they usually quoted the lower American wholesale prices, not the higher

Canadian ones, as the basis of their export price structure. The dominion government helped, too: it allowed Canadian producers to claim a 99 per cent drawback of tariffs and sales taxes that had been paid on imported American parts, provided that these parts were intended for re-export, whether assembled or not. The ultimate effect was most striking. For instance, in 1924, when US production was nearly twenty-four times the Canadian, Canadian exports amounted to nearly one-third of American.[34]

The Canadian industry appreciated the dominion's efforts to aid export campaigns through tariff drawbacks and trade treaties,[35] but it took less kindly to a major government initiative of 1926 that was meant to reduce domestic prices and increase Canadian content through a series of tariff changes.[36] Ottawa's action reflected less a concern for the place of the auto industry in the economy, and more a sharply tuned sensitivity to increasing nationalist sentiments and a very strong feeling across the country that the auto makers had taken advantage of the high tariffs to inflate prices and profits. As a result, in April 1926 the government announced that for cars valued at not more than $1,200 – 75 per cent of the Canadian market – the general tariff rate would be cut from 35 to 20 per cent. On higher-priced cars the duty henceforth would be 27.5 per cent. The duties on parts were not to be reduced, but henceforth those companies that produced or purchased 50 per cent of the value of their finished cars in Canada would be eligible for a 25 per cent drawback on all the duties they had paid on account of parts and materials. This was the 'Canadian content concession,' a provision that eventually other countries would copy, or would convert into a 'content requirement.'

These proposals were applauded by most businessmen and by all regions of the country, but the auto makers and the parts producers mounted a heated campaign to force their withdrawal. Complaining that they would no longer be able to do business, the auto makers lobbied, placed newspaper advertisements, and encouraged their workers to protest. Only Ford, Chevrolet, and Willys-Overland could at that point hope to qualify for the drawback. The parts makers argued that the auto makers would simply reduce their purchase prices for parts, thus passing the tariff cuts along to them; despite the Canadian content provisions, the auto makers would force them to cut their prices or to take a smaller share of the market.[37]

These efforts failed to move the government completely off its course, but the pressure did produce three significant amendments that ultimately reconciled the industry to change. First of all, the government agreed to repeal its excise tax of 5 per cent on lower-priced cars and 10 per cent on the more expensive vehicles if a company met the Canadian content standards. This concession actually increased the protective margin, making it 26 per cent on the lower-priced cars. Second, the government decided to apply the Canadian content provisions with some delay, and in stages: until April 1927 the standard was to be 40 per cent, and 50 per cent only thereafter. Thus the smaller firms would have time to work on improving their 'content performance.' Finally, the government accepted the industry's proposal whereby the drawback would be based on total output, not on individual models. This change allowed firms to build up credits on their largest-selling lines, while continuing to produce smaller runs of other cars, usually higher-priced models, that had Canadian content.[38]

The new tariff provisions made a considerable difference. Consumer prices certainly fell: in 1928 a Dominion Bureau of Statistics study estimated that prices had dropped approximately 10 per cent since 1926. How much of that decrease should be attributed to the tariff-change can never be ascertained for certain, but some effect there had certainly been. The auto-parts makers seem to have done extremely well out of the changes, in that their production grew far more rapidly than the production of cars, which increased from 102,000 vehicles in 1926 to 205,000 in 1929. But there was a black cloud on the horizon. As many smaller American manufacturers began to take advantage of mass production techniques, their prices fell, so that they became better able to penetrate the less well-protected Canadian market. Between 1925 and 1929 the imports' market share jumped from 14.3 to 21.8 per cent. This competition represented a serious problem for the local industry, since, despite a doubling of its production, it was still using only 66 per cent of its total capacity.[39]

A fundamental change in the basic character of the continental industry during these years strongly conditioned the Ontario producers' strategy and capacity to respond to import competition. During the industry's first two decades, while the North American mass market developed, the low-priced basic Model T swept the field. By 1926, 15 million had been produced in the United States and 750,000 in Canada. But by the early 1920s the US market for really cheap and crude vehicles was becoming saturated. When purchasers bought replacements for their first car or for their second, they often wanted something better than the 'Tin Lizzie.' This change offered new market possibilities, which Ford's competitors, especially General Motors with its aspiration to provide 'a car for every purse and purpose,' were quick to seize. By 1927 Ford executives could read the writing on the wall, and they abruptly shut down all their plants, worldwide, beginning a costly retooling to produce the new 'Model A.' Because the somewhat poorer Canadian purchasers were still comparatively attached to the Model T – indeed, Ford of Canada enjoyed its best year in 1926 – this move may not have been appropriate for the Canadian scene.

Certainly it hit Ford of Canada particularly hard. While the Model A was eventually a success, the 1927 shut-down created a marketing vacuum that allowed GM finally to take the lead. From 1920 to 1926 Ford had claimed 43.4 per cent of the Canadian market, while GM captured 25.1 per cent. During the remaining years of the decade GM surged ahead, with 32.1 per cent of total sales as against 23.2 per cent for Ford.[40]

As imports increased, the Ontario producers lobbied the dominion government to give them further tariff protection. The industry argued that the Customs Department should base the value for duty on retail prices rather than the wholesale rates the Americans charged their local dealers. Since the standard discount rate was about 30 per cent, this proposal amounted to a demand for an increase in the rate of duty of about 6 per cent. Ford went one step further. The company argued that the 'Drawback and Excise Tax Exemption [established in 1926] should operate as an inducement to promote ... manufacturing in Canada.' Since Ford had long since attained a Canadian-content figure of 75 per cent, the firm now advocated that the exemption level should rise from 50 to 60 per cent. They also pressed the government to abolish duty drawbacks for more expensive models. Both proposals were aimed not at Ford's foreign competition but at other domestic producers who had been steadily encroaching on Ford's market share.[41]

At first Ottawa was loath to accede to these requests, but the electoral victory of Bennett's protectionist Conservatives in 1930 and the impact of the Great Depression soon produced a more sympathetic response. Industry complaints during record years of prosperity were one thing; the Great Depression was something else. Outputs and work-forces were falling fast, and the industry's excess capacity was rising.[42] Despite strong opposition from the import dealers' association, in February 1931 the government finally announced the long-awaited tariff revisions. By order-in-council the cabinet fixed a 20 per cent maximum discount, for valuation purposes, on the list price in the country of origin. This was rather less new protection than the industry had requested, but nevertheless in board rooms and beer parlours the changes were heartily welcomed; auto buyers, among them impoverished farmers and struggling small business-folk, would have less cause to rejoice. Later in the year, the duty on cars valued from $1,200 to $2,100 rose to 30 per cent, and on cars of higher value the duty henceforth was to be 40 per cent. Lower-priced cars continued to pay the 20 per cent duty established in 1926, but on the new and higher basis of valuation fixed earlier in the year.

The impact of these changes was felt immediately. Imports, which had averaged about 20 per cent of total sales in 1929 and 1930, dropped to just 8.1 per cent in 1931 and 1932. By the end of 1932 imports held only 2.8 per cent of the domestic market. What is more, four of the leading American exporters of the 1920s – Nash, Hudson, Graham-Paige, and Packard – had established manufacturing and assembly operations in Ontario by 1932.[43]

Depression

During the 1930s production and employment levels failed to regain the record heights that were established at the end of the 1920s. Between 1929 and 1932 vehicular output fell 77 per cent, and the industry utilized only some 15 per cent of its productive potential. Employment fell by 54 per cent. In this period this industry contracted more than the economy as a whole, but as the deferred demand from the slump years built up and as the export picture improved, the automobile producers enjoyed a more rapid recovery than other industries. Between 1933 and 1937 the gross value of motor vehicle production increased 220 per cent, a much better performance than most manufacturing industries could show. Despite the rebound in sales, many companies failed, while others withdrew from the Canadian market. The picture is complicated because a company might leave Canada following the collapse of its American parent, or it might close its Canadian branch plant while continuing production in the United States, supplying Canada from the parent establishment. Among the companies that chose the latter course were Graham-Paige, Willys-Overland, Studebaker, Hudson, and Packard.[44]

Because the industry was in such difficulties, because trade and tariff policy were much debated in the early 1930s, and because there was an ongoing chorous of complaints about Canadian-American price differentials, in 1935 the dominion government asked the Tariff Board to investigate the automobile industry. Before the board completed its investigations in 1936, the government signed the Canada-United States Trade Agreement, which granted American manufacturers most-favoured-nation status. This meant that American manufacturers would henceforth pay the lower, intermediate-tariff rates, rather than the higher, general rates that had applied heretofore. As a result, the rate of duty on automobiles valued at less than $1,200 dropped to 17.5 per cent, while on those valued at more than $1,200 but less than $2,100 the rate was to be 22.5 per cent and on more expensive vehicles 30 per cent. The Tariff Board had no choice but to accept these new rates, but it recommended additional changes, primarily in response to the presentations of the car makers and the parts producers.[45]

Following the board report, the 5 per cent excise was replaced by a special 3 per cent import tax that lasted until 1939. Also, the administratively complicated duty drawback system was repealed, and a system of 'conditional free entry' was set up. There were two conditions under which foreign parts could enter Canada duty free. If the parts were of a 'class or kind not made in Canada,' no duty was charged provided that the manufacturer qualified under new content regulations, which varied from 40 per cent of total factory cost to 60 per cent, depending on factory output. In 1938 the latter figure was raised to 65 per cent. For commercial vehicles the content standard was 40 per cent. Finally, for most parts the tariff rate was 17.5 per cent, although for some the duty was 25 per cent.

Once again, as in 1926, the major tariff changes had a striking effect. Branch plants of low or uncertain profitability, such as those recently established by Studebaker, Hudson, and Packard, were shut down; the parent companies could now serve their small Canadian markets more cheaply from the United States. Secondly, with less protection and fewer branch plants, imports increased, rising from 8.6 per cent of Canadian sales in 1936 to 19.2 per cent by 1939. Finally, the new content regulations pressed the big auto makers to increase their local purchases. The three largest firms – GM, Ford, and Chrysler – therefore increased their Canadian input from 55 per cent of total cost in 1934 to 67.4 per cent in 1938. The Ontario parts industry benefited accordingly; Canadian consumers suffered from the additional indirect protection that the content regulations provided. In 1934 the parts makers enjoyed sales of more than $61 million, and employed an average of 12,500 workers, of whom 91.5 per cent worked in Ontario. Five years later, it is estimated that sales exceeded the record 1929 level of $105 million, and the industry employed an average of 18,000 men and women. When World War Two broke out, the parts makers were well situated to produce defence items for the government.[46]

Production and profit levels improved, especially after 1934, and the job picture brightened as well, but under the relentless pressure of mass unemployment elsewhere money wages continued to lag well behind pre-depression levels. By 1937 the Oshawa auto workers were prepared to take action to rectify this situation. General Motors, which had recently imposed five successive wage cuts despite record profits, provided the precipitating factor when, on 15 February, they announced a speed-up on the assembly line: production, hereafter, was to move not at twenty-seven units per hour, but at thirty-two.[47] Seven weeks later the recently created United Auto Workers of America – the UAW – led GM's 4,000 Oshawa workers out on strike.

The Oshawa strike was certainly not the first expression of labour unrest in automotive history. But it represented the first successful attempt to establish industrial unionism – union organization based not on a craft, such as moulding or carpentry, but on an industry, such as coal-mining or car-assembly – in the mass production industries that dominated the province's economic structure. Why was this sort of unionism not established earlier? Undoubtedly high wages were one factor that militated against unionism. In 1925, for instance, auto workers earned $1,577 per year compared with an average in Canadian manufacturing of $971. But as John Manley points out, this was not the whole story.[48] Assembly-line techniques, which required only easily replaceable assembly-line workers, made it impossible to bargain on the basis of indispensible skills, and highly seasonal production schedules further weakened the auto workers' relative position in the labour market, where, in any event, unionization had made little progress. In addition, the auto companies capitalized on this weakness by developing industrial relations policies that emphasized the atomization of the work-force. At Ford, 94 per cent of the work force was semi-skilled at best, and most jobs on the assembly line could be mastered in a single shift. Ford also recruited its employees from a wide variety of ethnic groups, so that interethnic rivalries weakened organizing drives, and the company ensured compliance with its strict behavioural rules by a continuous system of close supervision. General Motors, by contrast, tried to use corporate welfare policies – medical and dental insurance, sick benefits, company mortgages, a savings and investment fund, sports clubs, and musical societies – to emphasize its concern for the welfare, and hence the productivity, of its work-force. Finally, in contrast to Ford's glorification of the assembly line, GM stressed the traditional artisanship and craft skills that its employees brought to the job – although the progressive degradation of job skills was just as obvious in Oshawa as it was in Windsor.

Corporate policies could stall unionization but could not prevent labour unrest and sporadic organizing drives.[49] In 1928, after a decade free from strife, eight brief strikes broke out. Over the next nine years the industry was disrupted periodically by minor local outbreaks, but no union organization persisted. Interunion squabbles and the fierce hostility of the companies, who repeatedly fired union organizers, discouraged the efforts to organize. However, in the winter of 1936–7 the UAW did manage to establish two locals in the Canadian parts industry, and when the union won a major victory in GM's main American plant, the tide turned.

The Oshawa strike, which began on 8 April 1937, ended a month-long period of organizing and company-union discussion in which GM tried to avoid the formal recognition of the UAW, but during which the UAW signed up 4,000 members.[50] Negotiations were complicated by the fact that Ontario Premier Mitchell Hepburn intervened, urging a fanatical resistance against the Committee for Industrial Organization (CIO), with which the UAW was affiliated. He feared that other CIO unions would succeed in organizing the province's resource industries. Once the strike began, Hepburn effectively took over negotiations from GM, and against much good advice he resisted an agreement, despite the willingness of the company and union to settle, because he feared the CIO and the UAW. In fact, the strike was largely a local affair; the UAW provided a key organizer and a lot of publicity and emotional support, but the strike was won on the basis of local organization and the workers' desire in what had suddenly become a union town to stand up to company domination. After fifteen days the strike finally ended with an agreement between 'General Motors Company of Canada and the employees of the company at Oshawa.' In symbolic terms the UAW had failed to win recognition; in fact, it gained the first lasting union contract in the industry. Ford succumbed to the UAW in 1941, and thereafter the rest of the industry was soon unionized.[51]

When war broke out in 1939, the industry soon shifted to war production. An initial order for gun tractors was followed by a flood of commonwealth orders for military vehicles. In 1942 civilian production was suspended, but it had been curtailed some time before. Output and employment quickly climbed to levels never before attained.[52] Only months before the war began, the Tariff Board had once again reviewed the industry's progress. The board concluded that in 1936 the industry made a net contribution to Canada of at least $41.4 million – roughly 0.8 per cent of Canada's national output. The rationale behind the board's calculations made little economic sense, but the exercise created an aura of 'scientific' support for its conclusion that the tariff regulations underpinning existing branch plant operations were 'good business' for Canada. Whether Canadian consumers agreed with the necessity of paying higher prices for American cars built in Canada is doubtful, but the thousands of semi-skilled workers who found their livelihoods in the automotive industry – over 16,000 in 1929, over 14,000 in 1939, and more than 21,000 in 1942–44 – were bound to see things differently.[53] So were the parts manufacturers, many of them Canadian owned, who had battened on the protection that the tariff and the 'Canadian-content' arrangements provided. And so were the car makers themselves – a potent lobby, and as this chapter has shown, an often-successful one.

13 *Labour and Capital*

Although the process of industrialization is worth studying for its own sake, there is little reason to rejoice in it or to celebrate it unless it can be shown to have helped improve the general conditions of life, at least in the long run. Most economists would deduce that this is likely to be the case: they would say that the process of industrialization is bound to be accompanied by an improvement in technological knowledge, and by an increase in capital per worker, so that the output per worker is bound to rise, and that the forces of competition will tend to transfer the larger part of this extra productivity to the workers themselves, in the form of higher real wages, sooner or later. The general tendency of economic historiography, however, does not speak with so single a voice, partly because so many economic historians have assumed, or have been anxious to prove, the contrary. Admittedly, among those who are really knowledgeable about living conditions in western Europe, Japan, North America, or the Antipodes before the age of industrialization, there are not many who would maintain that things are now worse than they once were. Nevertheless, there is a well-established tradition of 'nay-saying' with respect to workers' living standards during industrial transformations.

The pessimists' story can have several elements. It may or may not be said that real wages or real earnings actually declined. Indeed, that assertion is no longer a possible one, in that the most recent scholarship on the British Industrial Revolution has shown conclusively that they did not.[1] But the pessimists' response will be, 'That does not matter, because there are qualitative elements' – the miseries of urban existence as opposed to the pleasures of rural life; the subordination of wage-earning status as against the splendid autonomy of self-employment in cowshed or artisan workshop; the surrender of control over the pace of work as against the right to regulate one's own work and to manage one's own workplace; craft, skill, autonomy, and self-respect as against 'de-skilling.' It may even be asserted, in the end, that although workers may have become better off both quantitatively and qualitatively, they have lost in so far as capitalists make off with a larger *proportion* of wealth than before. The name for this interesting phenomenon is 'relative immiserization.'

Whatever the evidence may be – and on some of the above topics no evidence can ever be marshalled in a conclusive way – some purely intellectual confusion is commonly at work. The optimists have been known to assert what has to be demonstrated – an upward movement in real wage rates without deterioration in the quality of life sufficient to offset that improvement. Among the pessimists, it is sometimes supposed that the capitalists cannot gain – as they manifestly did between 1871 and 1940 – unless someone else loses. But that is a fallacy. If the economy is growing, if skill and capital are accumulating, and if technological knowledge is improving, it is possible in principle for everyone to gain. It is also often assumed that whatever capitalists may *do*, the *intention* or the *effect* of the action must be to hurt the workers. But that is also not necessarily so. Mechanization, for instance, may displace or 'de-skill' some workers, while at the same time reducing total costs and paying higher real wages to those who are left, perhaps at the same time generating demands for new skills and making cheaper the final product, thus distributing benefits to all the community.

Mortality and Amenity

Death rates and housing conditions are often used to give some indirect impression about living standards. With respect to longevity and mortality, there is no information that is specific to particular groups, such as wage earners in factories. But because most Ontarians were workers – farmers, artisans, employees – life expectancy and mortality can perhaps be an indirect measure of well-being. The nineteenth-century data are not as good as the scholar might wish,[2] but something can be gleaned from them. The Dominion Bureau of Statistics later calculated that, among all Canadians, life expectancy at age twenty had risen slightly during the years of Ontario's industrial revolution, although for the more elderly the reverse had been the case.[3] Ontario's own registrar-general recorded a considerable decline in death rates from 1871 to World War One. The crude death rate, adjusted by the registrar to allow for reporting defects, was twenty-one per thousand in 1871, and the figure was the same in the counties of Carleton, Wentworth, and York. From 1882 to 1888 the average rate for the whole province was 11.3 per thousand, although in Toronto it still averaged 21.3, in Hamilton, 17.9, and in Ottawa, 27.4; in the late 1870s Toronto recorded a slightly lower rate than in the 1880s,

Ottawa a considerably lower rate, and Hamilton much the same. Thereafter there was an irregular but dramatic improvement: in 1914 Toronto recorded a death rate of 11.7 per thousand, Hamilton a figure of 11.4, and Ottawa – still a comparatively unhealthy place – a figure of 17.3. The same pattern appears in other cities and towns, so that by World War One all these places were more salubrious than they were soon after Confederation, and very much more wholesome than they had been in the 1880s, or even in 1906. For the province as a whole there was a further fall in the death rate during the 1890s, when the figure averaged eleven per thousand, considerable retrogression in the years 1900–10, and then renewed improvement just before the war. The average death rate in 1912–14 was 12.3 per thousand – a little higher than in the 1880s, when reporting was certainly less thorough, but apparently very much lower than in the early 1870s.[4]

It is difficult to reconcile these data with any assertion of general impoverishment or immiserization; indeed, in so far as they reveal falling death rates in the cities and rising life expectancy among the young they suggest that things were, on the whole and in the long run, getting better. The same impression can be garnered, in a rather different way, from the available information about medical personnel,[5] and from the dominion housing census of 1941,[6] which enquired about a wide range of 'modern amenities' – central heating, running water, flush toilets, and so on. Again it is hard to reconcile the data with any hypothesis of general impoverishment.

The facts are summarized in table 13.1. In 1941 70 per cent of urban Ontarians possessed central heating, compared with 19 per cent of farm dwellers. Ninety per cent of the urbanized had a radio, 76 per cent had refrigeration, 91 per cent had flush toilets, 84 per cent had private or shared baths or showers, 94 per cent had inside running water, and 98 per cent had electric light, 80 per cent cooked either with electricity or with gas, 57 per cent had telephone service, 45 per cent had vacuum cleaners, and 43 per cent had automobiles. These figures, of course, are far below the saturation levels that would be attained after World War Two. But they are very much higher, except with respect to automobile ownership, than the contemporary figures for rural areas, which, in matters such as heating, plumbing, and lighting, might be taken to represent the common living standards of nineteenth-century Ontario, whether rural or urban. Even though there are no organized tabulations for earlier years, it must be concluded that the standards of urban amenity had been dramatically upgraded in the decades before 1941.

Nor does housing seem to have been particularly crowded. In 1941 only 3.6 per cent of urban Ontarians lived in a dwelling that had fewer than three rooms. Most dwellings were far larger; the median dwelling had six rooms, and 86 per cent had five rooms or more; 80 per cent of urban dwellings, furthermore, contained five persons or fewer, and only 6.7 per cent of all dwellings contained eight persons or more.[7] No one would claim that all Ontarians lived comfortably or conveniently, even in 1941. Nevertheless, these figures suggest that town-dwellers were neither crowded nor ill-housed.

Wages and Earnings

The foundations for the level of comfort and amenity recorded in 1941 were begun decades before. Table 13.2 presents some estimates of the movement in money earnings and real earnings in Ontario industry between 1870 and 1914.[8] It seems that real earnings rose dramatically, although this is not to say that earnings were 'high' on any absolute scale, much less that working conditions were 'good': there is plentiful evidence that they were not. Nevertheless it is worth recording that in the 1870s and 1880s real earnings seem to have risen by at least 1 per cent per year in the former decade, and by at least 2.7 per cent per year in the latter. During the 1880s the Ontario Bureau of Industries made some effort to measure earnings and living costs among Ontario workers. The seven survey years are too few to establish any sort of a trend, but the data do suggest that on average Ontario workers earned a 'surplus' over their living costs.[9] These data also suggest that many of the working people of the province may well have been coping quite comfortably with the stresses and strains of advancing industrialism.[10] People who can spend less than half of their income on food, and from 23 per cent to 29 per cent of their incomes on clothing, are nowhere near the poverty line. The numerous boarders seem to have been much the best off, in terms of 'surplus,' but householders were, on the average, not uncomfortable.[11]

In the 1890s average annual wages per industrial worker rose by $40, or 13 per cent, while the available measures of the consumer price level appear to have fallen by at least 2 per cent, and the actual consumer price level certainly fell more steeply. Real earnings obviously must have risen, although the increase was very gradual – probably less than 1.5 per cent per year. After 1900 labour productivity rose, as did the money earnings per worker. What happened to prices is harder to summarize,[12] and so it is quite possible to get different results for the period of the Great Boom, depending on the price index used. If the Bertram-Percy index is employed, an increase of 1.7 per cent per year is shown, a result broadly consistent with Bertram-Percy's results for Canada-wide real hourly wage rates but quite inconsistent with Piva's conclusions for Toronto, and with the previous conclusions of the dominion Cost of Living Enquiry.[13] There are many possible sources for the divergences,[14] and with respect to living standards during the Great Boom of 1900–13 it must be said that no one yet knows enough to reach a firm conclusion. But it is hard to see how standards could have fallen, and for some occupations, at least, there is substantial evidence that living standards rose, although of course this does not mean that workers lived comfortable or secure lives. Illness, old age, and unemployment, both cyclical and seasonal, were alarming problems for many working people, aginst which the governments of the day had made few provisions. Municipal relief was available, but there was no government social insurance. Nor were real earnings generally ample, if measured by the scales of the 1970s and 1980s. However, nothing is gained by applying such a modern scale or by using a 'definition of the poverty line' based on the earnings that would suffice for one wage-earner to support four dependents in a six-room house with inside plumbing, while allowing the household to eat ten pounds of meat per week.[15] Many workers were unmarried people who boarded in others' homes. In 1886–7, for instance, 40.6 per cent of all respondent workers were boarders, while 18 per cent owned their own houses; the balance were householding tenants.[16] Boarders' outlays were naturally much less than those of tenants and owners. And what can be said of living standards among a working class in which 30 per cent of all householders were home-owners?

The data get better after 1914, and it is clear that the general tendency in real earnings and real wages continued upward, yet because of war and depression the course of development was anything but smooth and untroubled. Whether earlier decades, including as they did the slumps of the mid-1870s and early 1890s, were less troubled than the 1920s and 1930s it is impossible to say. But in the Ontario economy of 1914–41 the fluctuations of the industrial economy mattered much more than before 1900, simply because that industrial system was now so much larger in comparison with the provincial economy as a whole. Conversely, industry's success in accumulating capital and raising real earnings provided a much greater leverage in the entire provincial economy, while periods of industrial slump and unemployment were proportionately more painful than in the agrarian economy of the 1870s, because a higher proportion of the population now worked for wages – and because cyclical fluctuations were much more likely to hit the capital goods industries than the burgeoning service trades.

In manufacturing, employment apparently declined in 1913–15, recovered and expanded to 1917, changed little from 1917 to 1920, then slumped again to 1924, and moved up steadily until 1929, from which peak the world depression carried it down by 32 per cent to the distressing – indeed, almost disastrous – level of 1932–3. Recovery thereafter was slow, and there was a renewed retrogression in 1938–9, so that it was only in 1940, after the outbreak of war, that manufacturing employment in Ontario rose to about the 1929 level. During the ensuing dramatic expansion of 1941 there were jobs not only for the unemployed but for those who had never worked before. There was, furthermore, an increase in work for women, although the massive wartime growth of the female work-force was yet to come.

Real earnings in manufacturing followed a somewhat similar path, but the fluctuations were far less dramatic, and real earnings normally turned upward or downward with a slightly different timing and much less sharply. Indeed, although real earnings fell between 1930 and the depth of the slump, at no time in the depressed 1930s were they below the level of 1929, which, in turn, was a good deal higher than in the mid-1920s or before. Money wages, as Keynesian economists would expect, were sticky in a downward direction, even in the face of considerable unemployment, so that movements in living costs could produce some surprising effects on real wage rates and earnings. However, there were also periods, such as the late 1920s and the period 1939–41, when employment and real earnings in manufacturing could and did rise together.

A comparison of 1941 with 1917 shows that average real earnings in manufacturing had risen quite impressively,[17] although naturally there was not improvement in every single year. One also finds that the slump of the 1930s had made remarkably little difference to the upward movement of real earnings. If the old Dominion Bureau of Statistics cost-of-living index is used, in which 1935–9 = 100, average annual real earnings were $828 in 1917, $1,028 in 1929, $1,169 in 1939, and $1,305 in 1941. Thus average real earnings rose 58 per cent in twenty-four years, and the typical industrial worker of 1941 was very much better off than the worker of 1917 or 1929. For those who had jobs, real earnings moved almost uninterruptedly upward through the Great Depression. Hence, in large part, the findings of the 1941 census with respect to housing and urban amenities.

Mechanization, Capitalization, and Living Standards

The movements of real earnings are certainly dominated in the long run by long-term movements in technological change and in the accumulation of human and physical capital. In the process it is to be expected that capitalists will not suffer – rather the reverse. If expected rates of return had not been attractive enough, the improvements described could not have taken place. Because growth involved and required the accumulation of new capital, to prevent capitalist disappointments total profits would have to grow too – though not necessarily at the same rate. Furthermore, during periods of investment-propelled boom, such as the first thirteen years of the twentieth century, the economist would expect profits to be especially buoyant. This statement is not a deduction from any sort of exploitation hypothesis, nor has it anything to do with investment incentives, for which *expected* profits, not realized or recorded profits, are what matter. Rather, it is a deduction from contemporary economists' understanding of the processes that determine the level of national income and its division among classes.[18] Something of the result can be seen in the data of table 13.4.

As time passed, Ontario capitalists certainly accumulated more manufacturing capital. According to the census, 'total capital invested' was $37.9 million in 1870, while in 1910 it was $595.4 million, so that the ratio between reported capital and reported output had risen from 0.33 to 1.03. In the course of the industrial revolution, if one is to believe that the census figures mean anything at all, Ontario industry had to accumulate $567.5 million in additional private capital – most of it, in spite of striking instances of external investment, Ontario owned. Over the same period, and with the same qualification as to the meaning of the capital data, the capital per worker also rose, from $434 per employee in 1871 to $1,048 per employee in 1890 and $2,493 in 1910. Because problems of valuation and definition are so severe with respect to capital, these numbers do not deserve a great deal of respect. Nevertheless they do illustrate, in broad outline, the trend that was under way. To raise industrial output, employment, and output per worker, Ontario had to accumulate considerable industrial capital. Also, the process was under way throughout the period with which this book is concerned; it was not confined to the boom years after 1900.[19]

After 1914 the process continued. From 1917 to 1941 the census of manufacturing reported an increase of $700 million in the capitalization of Ontario manufacturing.[20] There was an increase in most years, although not in all the years of the early 1930s. The apparent capital per employee rose from $3,865 in 1917 to $4,991 in 1941,[21] increasing regularly but not uninterruptedly. One may take these numbers to imply a considerable increase in the quantity of machinery and equipment at the disposal of the typical worker. The rise in capital per worker, interacting with technological change both embodied and disembodied and with the increasing skill of the labour force, must increase the typical worker's physical output. Indeed, in some periods, such as the mid- and late 1920s, when consumer prices changed remarkably little, these forces presumably determined the movement of real earnings. But in the early 1930s new investment virtually ceased, so that the effect of technological progress remained *in potentio*, and it was the movements of money wages and consumer prices that controlled the movement of real wages at a time when, because of under-utilization of plant, real output per worker was falling. When underlying conditions improved and demand and investment revived, as in 1936–7 and 1940–1, real earnings could move ahead very rapidly even though unemployment remained high, and consumer prices were rising; new technology could to some extent be applied through new investment, while old plant and equipment could be more fully utilized – often for the first time in a decade or longer. The living standards of 1940–1, therefore, should be seen as the cumulative result of processes that had been at work for many decades and that the Great Depression of the 1930s had short-circuited only temporarily, and only in part.

14 *Protecting the Workers*

The new industries and the growing cities of the late nineteenth century could be unpleasant places to work. Wages and working conditions were often unsatisfactory, and hours were generally long. In the 1880s two dominion royal commissions[1] traced the distressing results; more recently, Canadian social historians have begun to study the various dimensions of working-class misery and discontent.[2] But just as the economy was industrializing, governments and workers were working jointly and separately to improve the conditions among the province's wage-earners. Governments were acting, through regulation and legislation, while the workers were acting also, through unionization in its many forms.

At Confederation no one had given much thought to the place of labour in the new federal system. The provinces were to be responsible for property, civil rights, and any residual matters of a 'purely local nature,' including the management of the municipalities. With the passsage of time governments found it necessary to take cognizance of many labour matters – first of all, the status of trade unions; then the management of trade disputes; next, working conditions in factories, shops, and mines; finally, the regulation of wages and hours of work. None of these matters had been on the legislators' agenda in 1867; almost all had appeared by 1890. For some decades both levels of government were involved in giving status to unions and in helping resolve trade disputes; it was far from clear, even in the early 1880s, whether dominion or province might have the power to regulate working conditions.

The Framework of Law and Regulation

As the labour historian Eugene Forsey explains, long before Confederation there had been some unions in Ontario, although few had lasted very long.[3] Nevertheless, at Confederation the 'union movement' still faced certain legal obstacles that only dominion action could remove. In the early 1870s it was still possible to regard any trade union as a criminal conspiracy. Furthermore, strikers could be haled before the criminal courts for breach of contract under a variety of 'master and servant' measures. Dominion action to remove these deterrents occurred between 1872 and 1878.[4] However, the changes gave no positive encouragement to union activity, nor were employers required to recognize unions, to bargain collectively, or to treat in good faith. There were no arrangements for expediting the bargaining process, for choosing or 'certifying' a legally authorized bargaining agent, or for the arbitration of disputes – all key elements in Canada's present-day labour codes. Indeed, there would be no general action on these matters until World War Two, when, once again, the dominion would take the initiative.

Nevertheless, the provincial legislature did take early steps to provide for some elements of arbitration. The Ontario Trades Arbitration Act of 1873 established an early and voluntary form of conciliation. Special meetings of master and workmen could be summoned to set up arbitration boards.[5] But very little use was made of this statute. As a contemporary observed, it was 'practically worthless,' inasmuch as it contained a proviso that under it 'there shall be no authority to fix wage rates.'[6] This obvious defect was remedied only in 1890.

Without repealing the 1873 measure, in 1894 the Ontario legislature passed the Ontario Trades Disputes Act, a statute that survived without amendment of consequence until 1932, at which time the province delegated its activities as conciliator and arbitrator to the dominion, more or less incidentally repealing the Act of 1894. On the request of either or both parties to an industrial dispute there could be a Council of Conciliation, with representatives of the disputants; there was also provision for a Council of Arbitration that could be set up in the first instance, or if the parties had failed to agree at the conciliation stage. The parties could agree in advance to accept the arbitrators' award, which would then be binding.[7] In 1902 a provision was added under which civil servants could promote a settlement by visiting the scene of trouble *before* a strike or lock-out had occurred, in order to mediate.[8]

In 1907 the dominion's Industrial Disputes Investigation Act, or IDIA, brought Ottawa onto the stage with respect to disputes in public utilities and coal mines. Also, unlike the provincial measure of 1894, the IDIA made conciliation compulsory in these industries, prohibiting strikes until some time after conciliation. But in 1910, doubtless to protect its own jurisdiction, Ontario re-enacted the measures of 1894–1902.[9] Thus until the Judicial Committee of the Privy Council declared the IDIA *ultra vires* of the dominion in 1925, the principles of the old provincial statutes could be applied everywhere except in railways, other public utilities, and transport services, where the dominion measure provided the legal framework. In 1927 the dominion redefined the scope of the IDIA, so that it would cover businesses that were under the legislative authority of parliament; there was also provision by which a province could opt in, making the act's writ run in disputes that would otherwise have been under provincial jurisdiction. In 1932 Ontario did just this.[10] Thus in the 1930s the principles of compulsory conciliation and cooling-off applied over most of Ontario's non-agricultural economy, but nothing had as yet been done to encourage or protect union organization as such.[11] The province, however, did take some cognizance of unions' existence. Legislation of 1874 and 1894 provided for the creation of benevolent, provident, and friendly societies – including unions – as incorporated bodies that could hold property.[12] But this was facilitation, not active encouragement or protection.

In other directions the province's statute law gradually evolved to give some protection for the status, freedom, and earnings of employees. In 1873 the Ontario Master and Servant Act and the Mechanic's Lien Act were passed.[13] In 1885, 1891, 1895, and 1896 there were measures giving certain priority to wage-claims, and in later years such measures were extended and repeated in various statutes.[14] In 1886 a rather attenuated form of workmen's compensation was enacted,[15] and the arrangements were somewhat liberalized in 1899.[16] But only in 1914 did the province bring the workmen's compensation arrangements into line with those of more advanced jurisdictions by creating a fund, a board, and a right to compensation without the need to sue in the courts.[17] On the other hand, in the industries that the act enumerated the injured employee lost the right to bring an independent action against his employer; the board's payments were to be the only compensation. In later years the legislature adjusted the scheme of 1914 in various ways, but the principle of administrative adjudication outside the courts was now established, as was the principle that employers would have to find the money for compensation. What is noticeable is that Ontario acted so long after some American states and several European nations had shown the way.[18]

As for industrial standards and working conditions, in the late 1870s it was still not clear which level of government was responsible, and the labour organizations were pressing for a dominion Factory Act of the kind first adopted in the United Kingdom some decades before. There seems to have been no suggestion in any quarter that there might be constitutional objections.[19] Indeed, in 1882 a factory bill was introduced into the Senate, only to be withdrawn in the face of employer opposition. In 1884 there were revised dominion bills, but apparently for the same reason they were not proceeded with. In 1885 Prime Minister John A. Macdonald said that his government was considering a fourth bill, but it never brought one forward.[20] Thus it was left to the Ontario Legislature to take some initiative, and in 1884, many years after the imperial Parliament had first passed a factory act, Ontario acquired one of its own. The new measure,[21] which was proclaimed only in 1886, provided for a single inspector and charged him with the inspection of factories in 121 separately identified industries – everything from sugar to window-blind-making. It is no wonder that for several years the new measure was little enforced. Four years later the legislature made similar provisions for shops,[22] and in 1889 the coverage of the Factory Act was much extended.[23] Later amendments changed the arrangements in detail but not in principle, and all the protective arrangements were codified and amended from time to time, so that the Factory Act of 1884 slowly and gradually evolved into the Factory, Shop, and Office Building Act of 1932.[24] In due course there was much better provision for inspection and enforcement.

Paralleling the factory and shops legislation was the provincial mining code, which made increasingly elaborate provision for protecting the health and safety of miners while completely failing for many years to regulate their hours of work. In most respects the exfoliating code can be seen as the direct descendant of the rules adopted early in the 1890s, but in the course of thirty years the rules became far more extensive, more precise, and therefore more enforceable. Inspectors, by 1930, had acquired a good deal of power to require the rectification of anything dangerous, defective, or illegal; they could even close a mine.[25] Thus in the course of the twentieth century there was a reasonably systematic development of the province's mining code. In 1900 the provisions were general and incomplete, and there was only a rudimentary mechanism for enforcement. By 1930 the province possessed a full-blown safety code for the mines, with rigorous provisions for the exclusion of young workers and for the limitation of underground work. Also, by 1930 there was a proper mining inspectorate.

The description of this evolution is not meant to imply that all the laws' provisions were observed, or that nothing more could have been or should have been done. To enforce the increasingly complicated law was expensive. And so was compliance with it. No one should be surprised to find employers cutting corners, ignoring directives, or using their political influence to prevent or delay the enactment of still more restrictive and costly rules. As for mining, in particular, since it is inherently a dangerous activity, no one should be surprised to find that workers died in the mines, or that working people were often far from satisfied with the mines' safety arrangements and amenities. Nevertheless, the development of the safety code is quite striking, and there is no doubt that it gradually and eventually made the mines and factories of Ontario far safer than they would otherwise have been.

As with health and safety, so with wages: the dominion's authority faded, while provincial authority gradually came to be recognized as paramount, except in wartime. Before 1914 there seems to have been little demand for the fixing of minimum wages, except in relation to governments' own contracts. But in 1917 a Dominion Government Industrial Conference recommended that in the several provinces there should be minimum wage rates for women and girls, and that wage-rates should be co-ordinated. At the end of World War One there were proposals for a dominion minimum-wage system, but these would probably have come to constitutional grief even if Ottawa had wanted to act on them. It remained for Ontario's farmer-labour government to provide a minimum-wage law.[26] The measure covered only women and girls, and it was a very gentle statute, appearing to follow rather than lead the market forces that fixed the rates for various kinds of work. In 1921 the Ontario Minimum Wage Board began its labours.[27] In 1922 it received the power to fix hours of work as well as wage rates; gradually it constructed a network of maximum hours and minimum wages, but they were differentiated by trade and by place of employment. There would be no general minimum-wage floor until long after World War Two.

The gradual development of the 1920s culminated in the Industrial Standards Act of 1935. This remarkable measure, which is still on the statute books, although much amended and in large part superseded, may be seen in various lights. From one angle it appears to be an importation of the American arrangements embedded in Roosevelt's National Industrial Recovery Act, one of the key elements in the early New Deal. Certainly there were many similarities. From a second angle the Ontario measure might be regarded as an effort to prevent or retard the growth of ordinary unionism by providing other channels through which masters and men could settle wages and working conditions. From a third angle it must be admitted that the Act seems to envisage a society organized along 'corporatist' lines, that is, where the appropriate decision-making bodies are collectivities of employers and employees. These ideas were commonplace at the time. They had been much canvassed in Roman Catholic social thought and in part embodied in the actual institutions of Mussolini's Italy; soon they would appear in Franco's Spain. The parallel is striking, although no doubt Ontario's legislators were unaware of it.

The act provided that the minister of labour might, on petition of employers or employees in any industry, convene a conference on the labour situation and labour practices in that industry. Such a conference could agree on schedules of wages, hours, or both, and these schedules would have the force of law. The minister might investigate any partnership or association that he might believe was being used to evade the act, and he could define and redefine zones in various industries within which conferences could be held and regulations framed.[28] During the fiscal year 1935–6 the Minimum Wage Board began to operate the Industrial Standards arrangements. Its orders covered both men and women. They were highly specific, applying to groups such as common construction labourers in Windsor, bricklayers in Ottawa, and barbers in Kirkland Lake. There was a perceptible tendency to concentrate on the service occupations, where unionization was often impractical, and on the construction trades, where the act's minima might help underpin a very long-lived tradition of craft unionism. In the next few years the legislature proceeded to extend the coverage of the act, and to establish that the board could 'establish minimum wages and maximum hours for any or all employees.'[29]

The optimistic might have hoped that through labour-management consultation, problems of wages and hours could be settled amicably and without conflict. In fact, the period 1935–7 was one of considerable labour unrest in Ontario, a period when unionization was making substantial advances and when the basis for a later pattern of labour-management relations was being laid. However attractive the consultative and conciliatory apparatus might have seemed to another generation or in another place, by 1935 industrial development had gone too for for any system of joint consultation to obviate the demand for union organization and recognition.

Unions and Unionization

There is a natural tendency, especially given the character of a secondary literature that still concentrates largely upon individual unions and upon heroic strikes that the workers generally lose, to exaggerate the significance – whether economic or social – of the union movement in the period 1867–1941, especially before 1900. Union membership seems never to have been a large proportion of the province's non-agricultural labour force, so that there was generally little likelihood of an Ontario worker being involved in a labour dispute. Nor were unions often the victors in their battles with managements. Indeed it is apparent that most questions of wages and working conditions must have been settled outside the framework of confrontation, collective bargaining, and arbitration that unions hoped to erect.

Economists generally argue that, whatever the utility of unions in giving workers self-respect and control over the workplace, they can affect wages and working conditions only when certain conditions are met. It is reasonably clear that in industrializing Ontario these conditions were rarely satisfied, and that therefore the reluctance of the work-force to form stable unions may have reflected a realistic assessment of the pay-off from union membership; it may not simply have been the result of fear, or a reaction to the hostility with which most employers regarded unions and unionists. Before 1914 it was easy for employers to draw workers from rural life, from the United States, from Britain, or from Europe. Few industrial occupations required the kinds of skill, or the extended preparation, that would give unions some control over the supply of labour, and in many such occupations there was always the possibility of bringing in skilled workers from Britain or from the United States. If workers became obstreperous, it was all too easy for an employer to turn out his entire labour force and start again with new workers who, in many lines, would soon be as efficient as the old. There is plentiful evidence from the 1880s, and later, of employers who did exactly this.

Where unions *were* long-lived, and where they appear to have had some success in raising wages, controlling the pace of work and other conditions at the workplace, or reducing hours of work with no loss of wages, there were necessary technical skills that workers had to possess and over which unions managed to acquire some control. The obvious examples are the typographical unions and the unions in the skilled building trades. In such cases, too, it was to be expected that local unions would reach out and affiliate with unions in other cities and countries to control the interregional movement of the relevant skills. It is also plausible to suppose, as Heron[30] and others have suggested with respect to the Hamilton iron and steel workers, that employers might manage the character of mechanization and technical change to reduce or eliminate the workers' power by getting rid of the need for their skills. As yet, however, there is little or no evidence as to employers' *motivation* or *intention*: owners and managers might have simply been trying to reduce costs or standardize quality, so that 'de-skilling' would then be a byproduct of mechanization, not a reason for it.

Although no membership data are available, the industrial boom that followed Confederation was certainly accompanied by a renewal of union organization, judging at least from the information on new unions and on inter-union groupings – municipal and national. In 1872 a Nine-Hour League was formed, and strikes were fought in pursuit of the fifty-four-hour week. But the depression of the 1870s seems to have killed most unions. With the economic recovery of the late 1870s there was renewed vigour in the labour movement. Many traditional craft locals, each organizing a particular variety of craftsman or artisan, were formed. Also, a new kind of union, the Knights of Labour, appeared in Ontario, and for a few years in the 1880s the Ontario Bureau of Industries gathered data about union memberships. The materials are of varying quality. Such usable information as can be winnowed from the bureau reports is summarized in table 14.1. In a general way the table does show the expansion of union and strike activity that occurred in the mid-1880s, and it also shows the growth of the Knights of Labour, while revealing that the increase in union activity was by no means confined to the Knights. Furthermore the quantitative information, especially when supplemented by the narrative accounts in the bureau reports, makes it clear that the wave of unionization receded in the latter years of the decade, and that it had not returned before the depression of the 1890s.

For labour historians[31] the most interesting aspect of the 1880s has proved to be the rise and decline of the Knights of Labour. The Knights came to Canada from the United States in 1875, but the first local assembly, at Hamilton, was soon moribund; the order really took hold in 1881–2. There followed a surge of organization, so that by 1886 there were 'pretty certainly 206 Canadian assemblies,' of which 159 were in Ontario.[32] The Knights constituted themselves as a secret society, and they were willing to organize anybody and everybody, either in general-membership assemblies or in craft-based groupings that resembled traditional unions. The order did not enjoy using the strike weapon, although it was certainly willing to employ it on occasion and to step in and lead when other groups had gone on strike. It is generally agreed that the Knights were prominent in most of the major strikes during the 1880s and in the early 1890s as well – the telegraphers' strike of 1882, the Toronto Street Railway strike of 1886, the several cotton-mill strikes at Cornwall and Merriton, and the great Ottawa lumber strike of 1891. It has even been said that because the class and factory system had arrived in Ontario 'forcefully and unambiguously for the first time,' the Knights were able to forge 'a movement culture of opposition.'[33] Scholars seem to agree in suggesting that the peak membership, reached in the mid-1880s, was between 14,000 and 16,000.[34] Using the figures from tables 2.1 and 2.2, and interpolating, one can produce an estimate of Ontario's non-agricultural work-force in 1886: the figure is 360,000. Thus no more than 4.4 per cent of that work force can possibly have been members of the Knights, and when it is remembered that some of the membership was in other provinces, the percentage becomes smaller still,[35] although in some localities the figure was certainly much higher, at least for short periods of time.[36] After the 1886 peak the Knights clearly diminished, both in membership and in numbers of assemblies, although there were temporary recoveries in places such as Ottawa. Forsey thinks that by 1888 there were only 10,151 Knights in Canada, and certainly there were fewer in later years; by 1897–8 there were only four surviving local assemblies.[37]

For the ordinary unions, although not for the Knights of Labour, the expansion of the 1880s continued through the 1890s. The locals were concentrated in the large industrial towns but also spread outside them, so that by 1903 Forsey finds locals of the large us-based craft unions – the so-called internationals – in at least 103 Ontario places.[38] New unions were being set up; old unions were acquiring new locals. In addition, there were locals that were not attached to the internationals and usually not to any Canada-wide union. When the Ontario Bureau of Labour set out to survey unions in 1902 it found only three Knights of Labour assemblies; 97 per cent of all the bureau's respondents were craft unions. Most of the reporting unions had been formed after 1899, although twenty-six went back to the 1880s and three to the 1840s and 1850s. A total membership of 16,477 was reported, of which 47 per cent was in Toronto and 9 per cent in Hamilton. This figure represents only 3.6 per cent of the province's non-agricultural work force as of 1901, but inasmuch as Forsey found more locals than the bureau did, there may be some underreporting in the bureau data. The typical local was quite small – somewhere between eleven and 100 members. Eleven locals claimed to have ten members or less, and one had only three, although one claimed a membership of 1,000, and another claimed 700.[39]

With the the creation of the dominion Department of Labour in 1900, more reliable data on unions and memberships become available. These are summarized in table 14.2. The dominion believed that it had counted all the unions, but it knew that it had not counted all the members, because some locals did not report membership, although the non-reporting fraction diminished dramatically through time. Thus it is somewhat disconcerting to find that the membership data were normally used, by the Labour Department and by others, to trace without adjustment the growth and development of Canadian unionism. A great deal of the apparent union growth after 1900 is simply an improvement in reporting practices. Therefore, for present purposes the data have been adjusted to eliminate the effect of differential underreporting.[40] In all the statements and comparisons that follow, the adjusted data will be used.

During the first forty years of the twentieth century, as during the last thirty years of the nineteenth, unionism and unions must have been marginal to the life and work of most Ontarians. Nor did unionism much increase its penetration of the work-force during these decades – at least, not in any long-run or sustained fashion. In 1911, 8.4 per cent of the province's non-agricultural work-force belonged to unions. There were some dramatic membership booms, and in peak periods, such as 1914 and 1919–20, unionization was certainly more extensive than in the census years. But union membership was as likely to go down as up; there were sharp retrogressions during slumps – the early years of World War One, the early 1920s, the early 1930s. Thus although 12.2 per cent of the non-agricultural work-force belonged to unions in 1921, for 1931 the percentage is only 6.4 per cent. The prosperity of the late 1920s had its echo effect on unionization, but by 1933 there were fewer unionists than there had been in 1912. Thereafter matters improved, with a dramatic peak in 1937. The advances of 1936–7 are often credited to the active organizing drive of the new unions, associated with the American Committee for Industrial Organization (the CIO), which tried to organize all the blue-collar workers in a particular plant, firm or industry, rather than restricting itself to particular crafts or skills. As was shown in chapters 12 and 13, for cities such as Oshawa the effect was certainly dramatic. But the advance was broadly based, affecting many industries and cities. Thus by 1940–1, after decades of fluctuation around a gently rising trend, there were slightly more than twice as many Ontario unionists as there had been in 1911. Yet even then, no more than 10.5 per cent of the province's non-farm workers were members. Since 1911 the increase in union coverage had been anything but great, although some development there had certainly been.

The data on strikes, which begin in 1888, suggest that if unions had any significance at all in late nineteenth-century Ontario that significance must have been almost entirely psychological and social, except perhaps for the members of a very few highly organized trades. Thereafter the situation became rather different. There were far more strikes recorded after 1900, and although there were fluctuations from year to year, the tranquillity that employers had enjoyed during the 1890s never returned. There were peaks of strike activity in 1919–20, 1928–9, and 1936–7 – precisely the times when the numbers of unionists were rising, and rising fast. But although unions became more numerous and in certain years strikes became more frequent, it is very hard to detect any upward trend in the number of days lost through strike action: the series shows enormous year-to-year fluctuations, but no longer-run direction of movement. Furthermore, if this measure of strike activity is compared with the number of non-agricultural workers, it can be seen that with the passage of time Ontarians were steadily *less* likely to lose work days to strike action.[41]

This is not to say there were no dramatic and significant strikes – events that have left their marks on the collective consciousness of the working class (or so we are told)[42] and in the statistics of strike activity.[43] Yet in the data it is hard to see any general trend either towards union organization or towards militancy. In absolute terms unions and their members became more numerous, but relative to the non-agricultural labour force neither union membership nor strike activity became much more significant. What this fact signifies is hard to say. A right-wing observer might conclude that there was no sustained long-run mass demand for unions, unionization, or strike activity in Ontario. A left-wing observer might conclude that the persecutions and manipulations of the capitalist class prevented the objectively necessary rise of working-class organization. Both left-wing and right-wing observers would probably agree that eventually the government made the difference: its active encouragement of union organization and membership combined with the definite benefits to be derived therefrom in the new legal environment of the post-1939 years unleashed a growth of union organization and union membership that pushed indices of membership to much higher levels after 1941. In other words, it is reasonable to suppose that without the active encouragement and protection of the state, union activity would not have become as important as it has become, although it might well have become more important than it was in the 1920s and 1930s.

It is sometimes suggested, or implied, that ordinary working people gained nothing from Ontario's industrialization until, in the late 1930s and thereafter, the large and energetic industrial unions came along to fight for their interests. But the data of earlier chapters appear to show that living standards had been drifting upward long before unionization was at all important. In so far as one might want to credit unions with an improvement in living standards – itself an uncertain proposition – one surely would not want to do so when only 10 per cent of the relevant work-force belongs to unions, and when, throughout most of the preceding seventy years, the percentage of union members was clearly much lower. The data of this chapter, therefore, reinforce an earlier conclusion: as far as workers' living standards were rising, the most important explanations must be found in technological improvement, more skill, more education, better organization not of the workers but of the workplaces, and increasing capital per worker – the elements that most economists and economic historians would choose to stress.

Unions do not exist simply to go on strike, and at least in more recent times many unions have made important contributions to the welfare and self-respect of their members without striking at all. But where employers are not obliged to recognize unions or to bargain with them, such peaceful contributions may well be more infrequent and less significant than in the much more regulated system of labour relations with which Ontarians have become familiar since 1940. Yet the data do serve to remind us that the history of unions in Ontario had better not be the history of strikes, however dramatic, traumatic, or heroic some of these strikes may have been. If all

Ontario unions did for their workers was to defend their interests by manning the barricades, the unions cannot have made much difference to anything or anybody.

It would be interesting to know more about how British migration, which was substantial until the early 1930s, affected labour organization and working-class culture in Ontario. Coming as they did from a society wherein trade unionism was far better developed, the British might have been expected to have played an important role in the development of Ontario unionism and in the refining of local techniques for controlling the nature and pace of unionists' work. Although this subject definitely needs to be researched anew, the secondary literature conveys the impression that Ontario unionism developed almost wholly on American models and hardly at all on British ones, even though a few local branches of British unions were indeed set up. But one wonders, for instance, whether the consolidation of Ontario unionism from the 1880s to the 1930s has anything to do with the application, conscious or unconscious, of models from Britain. Or did craft unionism follow logically and, as it were, inevitably from the need of the craftsman to control his workplace? It is often said that Canadian unionism followed the craft model because the American Federation of Labour (A), extending its tentacles into Canada after the turn of the century, forced Canadian unionism into this mould, using the Trades and Labour Congress of Canada as its surrogate. Craft unionism certainly was what the A favoured, financed, and helped organize. But as the data show, craft unionism was the dominant element in Canadian unionism long before the A made its appearance.

The above puzzles are matters for the labour historians and the social historians. The relations among unionization, union pressure, and the gradual development of government schemes for protecting the workers are subjects for the political historian. Between 1919 and 1941 several general measures of social amelioration – mothers' allowances, old age pensions, public housing, dominion-provincial labour exchanges, and finally unemployment insurance – were of great interest to working people, perhaps just as interesting as the regulatory measures surveyed earlier in this chapter. It is sometimes suggested that such developments are, or must be, the result either of union pressure or of the urgings of the organized political left, with which, for many purposes, the unions are often linked. However, it is difficult for the economic historian to distinguish between the lobbying activities of the unions, on the one hand, and the general tendencies towards reform and pressure for it, on the other. The distinction is especially important when it is recognized that only a small proportion of the population was unionized, and that the union leaders could not always, or often, deliver the vote. Doubtless all the above influences were present, and it is the task of the political historian to sort them out to locate the pressures that produced 'reform.' What is striking, however, is the lack of correlation between the halting, stumbling, and irregular progress of union organization and the slow but much more regular development of reform legislation in Ontario during the twentieth century.

One may also wonder whether there is any systematic relationship between the pattern of unionization, strikes, and the ebb and flow of union membership, and the data on the movements of real earnings, employment, and unemployment, some of which were examined in the preceding chapter. Here one can do more than observe some obvious parallels. The expansion of union activity in the 1880s does not seem to coincide with immiserization, while the slumps of 1921–2 and 1929–33 do coincide with collapses in union membership and strike activity, doubtless because people were afraid of unemployment. Also in both of these periods, and even more so in the 1930s, many workers may have recognized that so long as they had jobs, they were comparatively well off, and some may have noticed that their living standards were actually rising in the face of depression. At such times there would be little incentive to organize or strike. Some of the same considerations might explain the comparatively small amount of union activity in the mid – and late 1920s. The number of jobs was increasing, and living standards were rising, while employers were in general opposed to union organization. Why rock the boat? Certainly in the late 1920s there were some interesting strikes and some new attempts at union organization.[44] But such occurrences were exceptional, and they did not get very far. On the other hand, the years 1918–20 saw a remarkable peak in unionization and in strike activity, and it is hard not to connect these things with the inflationary experience of those years, even though it was only in 1920 that money earnings in manufacturing failed to keep pace with prices.

The mid- and late 1930s, however, present a problem for any simple economic interpretation of union activity. Unemployment was still high, and many of the industries in which the new industrial unionism was specially interested were still comparatively depressed. But the number of jobs was increasing, and for the average worker who had a job, living standards had never been higher, although he may not have realized that this was so. Did some workers act on the assumption that in a time of recovery unionization might make some progress? Did such attitudes provide the soil into which the organizing activity of the CIO, the United Auto Workers, and the other new industrial unions could plant some sort of root? And is it the fact of recovery that makes the late 1930s different, in this respect at least, from the late 1920s, when it would have been hard to prophesy a bright future for Ontario unionism?

Part Four:
Transportation, Communication, Trade,
and Finance

15 The Older Means of Transport and Communication: Rail, Water, and the Early Electric Media

Transport and communications were fundamental to the economic transformation that has been traced in earlier chapters. Before 1914 development centred on the railways and on the Great Lakes-St Lawrence system of waterways, together with the canals that were meant to improve that system. The electric media – the telegraph and the telephone – also made contributions to economic development, chiefly because they transmitted information and instructions speedily and cheaply.

Transport Patterns

At Confederation, and for some time after, there were three main patterns in the movement of commodities through and within Ontario. The Grand Trunk Railway provided an east-west axis through the settled parts of the province, and the Great Western Railway, in the southern districts, strengthened this east-west orientation. There was a great deal of traffic across the lower Great Lakes, especially Erie and Ontario, but along the lakes and up or down the St Lawrence River traffic had not developed as the early canal builders had hoped, partly because of competition from railways and from American canals but largely because the great bulk traffic that would later predominate on that route did not yet exist. Much more important were the south-north movement of American coal and the north-south movements of Canadian lumber and grain. On both sides of the lower lakes there were many little ports through which such cargoes moved. On the Canadian side, goods might well reach these ports by water. Lumber also moved down the Ottawa River to Montreal. Imports came either by rail or by water to major wholesaling points – primarily to Toronto and Hamilton – from which they fanned out over the southern and south-western parts of the province, using a network of railways that dated from the 1850s and were to a considerable extent locally owned, even though most of the finance for their construction had been raised in Britain. There were similar tap-line railways from some of the smaller lake ports, such as Cobourg and Whitby. These short local lines had been built to accommodate local traffic – 'up' freight that consisted largely of manufactures and 'down' freight that was mostly lumber and grain. Some goods also came by rail over the Niagara Frontier from the United States. The British-owned Grand Trunk, although certainly interested in short-haul local business, had been conceived as a long-haul through line – a link between Montreal and the Atlantic ports and with Ontario and the American mid-west. The canal development of pre-Confederation days had had the same aim; so far as the American mid-west was concerned, neither canal nor railway development had as yet met with much success, chiefly because charges were lower and service was better on the American side of the border.

Between 1867 and 1914, thanks to the economic development of the Great Lakes area and of the Canadian prairies, Ontario's transport system had to cope not only with enormously increased volumes of freight, but with new or much-changed patterns of movement. To a large extent these novelties centred upon the long-distance movement of cheap and bulky goods – especially western wheat, Minnesota iron ore, Pennsylvania coal, and both American and Canadian petroleum. Transport development, in turn, both anticipated such demands and adapted to them. Thus the rail lines from the Prairies to the Lakehead were built largely in advance of demand, while the Great Lakes water transport system was adapted and improved more or less in step with that demand. In northern Ontario, after 1900, some developmental lines were built, specifically to open up remote areas for farming and mining. Other northern lines, built to serve large national purposes, had the incidental effect of disclosing exploitable resources, not only of the forest but also of the mine. In southern and south-western Ontario, meanwhile, the rail network grew more dense, and a new east-west main line appeared in this part of the province when the Canadian Pacific Railway chose to challenge the Grand Trunk on its home ground. Branch and tributary lines were much elaborated, partly for reasons of competition. The interchange of goods and people was much facilitated, because there were more lines and because rates were falling both absolutely and in comparison with the general price level. To explain this decline one must consider not only competition but also technical progress in railway operation, improvements in railway management, and even the increasing volume of freight and passenger traffic, a development that allowed the lines to use their capacity more fully. Toronto and Hamilton continued to be the main loci for the distribution of manufactures, but as more cities and towns produced such goods, patterns of interchange became more complicated, both within southern Ontario and across the country. By 1886 the province was exporting manufactures by rail to the Maritime provinces and to the Canadian north-west. As western settlement proceeded, especially after 1900, the latter movement grew quickly. But since most Canadians still lived in central Canada, it was in and around there that most manufactures – and most railway passengers – circulated. The same was true of electric messages, whether transmitted by telegraph or by telephone.

The development of transport illustrates the lack of genuine planning to which allusion was made in chapter 1. Transport was largely, but not entirely, controlled by the dominion. There was not much co-ordination between the two levels of government and even less between the development of rail and water systems. Some facilities, such as the rail bridges through northern Ontario, were over-built; others, such as the Great Lakes canal improvements, were sometimes laggard and almost always ill co-ordinated.

In rail transport, during the 1870s there was a revival of the local initiative that had been so marked a feature of the 1850s. Local elites in Toronto, Hamilton, and some of the smaller lakeside centres could and did promote short lines. Their efforts helped produce a much denser rail network in south-western Ontario, but of course that was not their intention. Their motives, indeed, were mixed. Some promoters hoped to draw traffic and business to the 'home town'; some hoped to tap sources of primary products, especially lumber, or to raise the value of hinterland acres, thus producing capital gains; some hoped to gain from activities such as contracting, stock-jobbing, and the other promotional activities that revolved around nineteenth-century railways; it seems that few expected to gain simply by drawing modest dividends from the transport of people and goods.

National initiatives soon became important, with the construction of the Canadian Pacific main line, and with the competitive response of the Grand Trunk. The results, by 1890, were as follows: the network in southern and south-western Ontario had become closer still; a transcontinental main line stretched across Ontario from the Quebec border to Ottawa and North Bay, Sudbury, the Lakehead, and the Manitoba border; most of the locally owned short lines had come under the control of the CPR and the Grand Trunk.[1]

Following a lull in the 1890s, the new century saw a burst of railway expansion, which carried the province's railway mileage to a new peak. In this movement there was again a variety of participants: government subsidies continued, but both the dominion and the Ontario governments played significant promotional roles. In Ottawa the Laurier government was anxious to garner votes, to service the western grain economy, and to give some benefits to its Toronto business supporters; in Queen's Park, the Ross and Whitney governments were eager to develop northern and north-western Ontario. The result was two-fold: Ontario acquired a sketchy network of 'development lines,' built in advance of traffic, and stretching over the northern parts of the province; Toronto magnates constructed and operated their very own transcontinental railway line, the Canadian Northern Railway.[2] In the settled areas of the south and south-west the great national railway developments of 1900–14 made comparatively little difference, although the Canadian Northern did build and purchase some trunk and branch lines, while the CPR and the Grand Trunk continued to improve and extend their systems. The rail network, therefore, became denser. Paralleling these large national developments, but in no way co-ordinated with them, was the spread of electric rail transport – first in cities and towns, and then, through 'radial' lines, outside them.

The system of water transport, meanwhile, was developing with a temporal logic of its own. The dominion government was in charge of navigable waterways; all canal works were its publicly operated projects. But ships were privately owned, and there was, from time to time, acute competition not only with American ships but with American canals. The ships grew in number and changed in character for various reasons: the changing dimensions of the canal locks; the realization that an oddly shaped 'laker' design was both safe and efficient under Great Lakes conditions; the worldwide developments in areas such as steel-hull construction and engine design; the enormous growth of traffic in cheap, heavy, bulky goods, such as grain, iron ore, coal, and petroleum. As for the canal developments of the period, scholars have yet to scrutinize the timing of Ottawa's decisions, but the following elements are supposed to have been present: the desire to provide political patronage; competition with American facilities; the pressure of demand from shipping, both current and prospective.

The Railways

By the time of Confederation the railways of Ontario had amassed a dismal financial record. They were in a sorry state, both financially and physically. No one was earning much from railway operation: the Grand Trunk and the Great Western had been kept from bankruptcy only by special intercessory legislation, and few of the locally owned feeder lines were in better shape. The lines had been unevenly graded and lightly constructed, with insufficient ballast and with iron rails that quickly wore out, providing work for the rerolling-mills in Toronto and Hamilton but involving added cost for the proprietors.

The gauges, furthermore, were a mess. Governed by Canadian legislation of 1852 and with the eager acquiescence of the Grand Trunk, most Ontario railways had been built on the 'broad gauge' of five feet six inches. As American lines used the 'standard gauge' of four feet eight and a half inches, trains could not readily move between Ontario and neighbouring states, whether by the suspension bridge across the Niagara River or by car-ferry across the unbridged rivers at Windsor and Sarnia. Expedients could be and were devised. On some lines, but not on all, the Grand Trunk and Great Western had laid down a third rail so that cars of both gauges could travel. The Grand Trunk also used many freight cars with adjustable axles, and the railway company was even prepared to change the wheels under loaded cars. But these expedients, costly and uncertain, did not obviate transshipment of freight. Further problems arose because a few Ontario lines had been built to a narrow gauge of three feet six inches. Thus within Ontario, as at the riverine frontiers, transshipment was necessary.

By 1870 it was clear to the business community that the inherited network was not satisfactory. Fortunately, with economic growth came a willingness to spend on improvements, which, in turn, made it possible for the lines to carry more traffic. Passenger service, too, was improving: in 1870 the Grand Trunk began to run Pullman 'palace cars.' New bridges were built at Buffalo in 1873 and at Niagara in 1883; at Sarnia and Windsor car-ferries would carry the traffic until tunnels were completed in 1891 and 1910, respectively.[3] To help with construction costs on new lines, provincial grants became available. The politics of the relevant legislation and the mixture of lobbying and log-rolling that must have accompanied it have yet to attract historians' attention. But it is clear that in the early 1870s the Ontario government was moving on several fronts to encourage development; railway-building in the settled districts was bound to seem useful in that connection, and certainly both farmers and townsfolk were eager for new lines. As for the gauge problem, in 1872 the Grand Trunk began to convert its main line to standard gauge, and other tributary railways followed its example in the 1870s. As lines were altered, old rolling stock had to be converted or scrapped and replaced. To some extent the companies seized the opportunity to replace the elderly locomotives once bought in the United Kingdom with new and more powerful designs – some locally made, but many imported from the United States. This embodiment of technological progress helped make the railways more efficient; competition, not only within Ontario but from American lines, ensured that at least some of the gains would be passed on to shippers in the form of lower rates. For farmers, the result was a higher price for marketed output than would otherwise have been received, combined with a lower price for purchased inputs and consumer goods; such an improvement in the terms of trade would sooner or later translate itself into a higher value for farm land – – compared with the value of that land in the absence of railway improvement. For townsfolk, lower railway rates meant some mixture of cheaper food, a wider domestic market, and, at least in some instances, more competition from imported manufactured goods.

The completion of the Intercolonial Railway line to the Maritimes seems to have made little difference in Ontario: in due course there would be Intercolonial orders for the Kingston locomotive works, but the Maritime market was a small one, nor was Maritime competition very significant in central Canada. With the advent of the Canadian Pacific, however, a new phase began. In the first instance, some Ontario contractors did well out of the project, which they helped build. With the completion of the Winnipeg-Lakehead line, Manitoba grain began to arrive at the Lakehead, where it took to water; the first such shipments occurred in 1883, and they increased rapidly thereafter, as Manitoba settlement proceeded. The new north-western market, in turn, bought Ontario manufactures, which moved westward over the CPR main line. Admittedly, that market grew slowly: in 1891 its population was only 7 per cent of the population in central Canada, and even in 1901 it was just short of 11 per cent. Even so, this was a net addition to demand, and it boded well for the future. Finally, in the very process of construction the CPR laid bare the nickel-silver-copper deposits at Sudbury, where production began in the mid-1880s.[4]

Of great importance to southern and south-western Ontario was the challenge by the new company. To prevent the Canadian Pacific from developing its own traffic-gathering network, the Grand Trunk busily absorbed as many Ontario railways as it could. Thus the Northern and Northwestern, the Midland, and many other lines that had been owned in Ontario and managed from Hamilton, Peterborough, and Toronto came to be owned in Britain and managed from Montreal. The Great Western Railway, too, was absorbed into the Grand Trunk system. But the Canadian Pacific was also anxious to buy up companies, and its acquisitions effected the same transfers of ownership and control. Also, the Canadian Pacific found it necessary to build its own lines through southern Ontario – first from its main line to Toronto, then on to Windsor and around Lake Ontario to Buffalo. To the annoyance of the Grand Trunk, Ottawa subsidized these new railway projects, apparently because the Grand Trunk was unpopular and because competition was desirable on general grounds. Also, it may well have been thought that there was now enough traffic to justify a duplication of main or trunk lines.

During the 1880s and 1890s there were qualitative improvements in the system. The Grand Trunk, for example, began to double-track its Toronto-Montreal main line in 1887 and finished the task in 1903. Gradually, too, it fitted all its rolling stock with automatic couplings and air brakes. Meanwhile, rail rates drifted still further downward, and the railways themselves, with their ancillary services, bulked ever larger in the provincial economy. In 1871 there were 1,930 railway employees; in 1891 there were 12,870, and in 1911, 36,700. In their own shops the railways did an ever-increasing volume of maintenance, repair, and even new construction of locomotives and other rolling stock.[5] Entire towns revolved around the railways, either as divisional points or as centres for overhaul, repair, and construction. In addition, there was a striking growth of firms and industries that serviced the railways. As yet Canada produced no steel rails, and once Ontario railways abandoned wood fuel, they burned American coal, since neither British nor Maritime coal could be landed in most parts of Ontario at a competitive price. But there was plenty of construction work to be done, and many components had to be bought locally. Westinghouse Air Brake, for example, set up a Hamilton factory – one of the first really large 'multinational branch plants' – to serve the Canadian railway market.

A new stage in railway development began in 1897, when William Mackenzie and Donald Mann, two Toronto businessmen who had begun their promotional careers as railway contractors in Manitoba, took control of a company that was meant to build a line from Winnipeg to Port Arthur – in direct competition with the CPR. Aided by federal and provincial subsidies and guarantees, and with generous help from the Canadian Bank of Commerce, the two promoters quickly expanded their system, extending the railway from a local line in Manitoba to the continent-spanning Canadian Northern Railway. From one viewpoint the rise of Mackenzie and Mann symbolizes the rise of Toronto, and its financial strength in comparison with that of Montreal, in the twenty years before World War One. From another viewpoint it reveals the close links that evolved between Toronto's financial institutions and the city's entrepreneurs. As the historian T.D. Regehr has examined the complicated financial arrangements,[6] these need not be described in any detail. It is enough to note that in their capacity as contractors Mackenzie and Mann could and did borrow from the Bank of Commerce to finance the construction of the railway that they owned, and that everyone knew they owned. Essentially the bank financed the contractors in the belief that the railway would eventually be able to sell bonds, thus allowing first the contractors and secondly the bank to be paid. The bank, in turn, became heavily involved in the overseas marketing of the railway's bonds, and when the London bond market became unresponsive in 1913–14, the bank was obliged to continue its advances lest the railway project collapse. By the end of 1916 the bank's advances totalled over $28 million – an amount that far exceeded its own capital.[7]

Ontario entrepreneurs and financiers were not directly involved in the other new transcontinental line, the National Transcontinental Railway and the Grand Trunk Pacific Railway, a joint project of the dominion authorities and the Grand Trunk that had the effect of opening certain areas of northern Ontario for the mining and forestry industries.[8] But the Ontario government did take a direct interest in the construction of two development lines – the Algoma Central and Hudson's Bay Railway, and the Temiskaming and Northern Ontario Railway. The former was a privately owned line that began with the promotional activities of Francis Clergue, the Philadelphian responsible for industrial development in and around the Soo.[9] In 1898 Clergue bought an ore deposit that would later become the Helen Mine, and in 1899 he incorporated the Algoma Central, which was to run from the mine to the Soo. In 1900 the Ontario government gave a land grant, complete with timber and mineral rights, on the understanding that the railway would bring in 1,000 settlers a year. But Clergue ran out of money in 1903. After complicated financial adventures the line was completed in 1914 to the new National Transcontinental main line. Traffic did not materialize, and so by 1916 the line was in receivership, where it stayed until 1959.[10] For the government-owned Temiskaming and Northern Ontario the financial record appears brighter. Responding to the hopes of Toronto politicians and business people that Ontario could acquire a new agricultural frontier, in 1899 Premier George Ross sent survey parties into the Timiskaming District, and in 1901 he decided to build colonization roads and also a railway from North Bay to New Liskeard. Construction began in 1902, and in 1903, just as mineral wealth was discovered, the line reached Cobalt. By 1909 it reached the National Transcontinental at New Liskeard. After World War One branches were extended, largely to tap heavily mineralized areas; in 1931–2, partly to make work during the Great Depression, the line was continued to Moosonee – the Hudson's Bay post on Hudson Bay that had been its announced goal since 1905.[11]

In explaining this outburst of early twentieth-century railway building, Canada's historians normally stress the political, personal, and sectional pressures to which the politicians were responding, both on Parliament Hill and in Queen's Park. Without ignoring these elements, the economic historian turns his attention to other causal forces. The prairie wheat crops were growing, and the 1901 harvest had been especially large; there was more grain than the CPR could move on its lightly built single-track line across north-western Ontario to the Lakehead. Interest rates, a very large element in railway construction costs, were lower than they had ever been. Both Britain and North America were awash with capital funds, which were looking for profitable or at least plausible outlets. In 1903 the dominion could borrow at 3 per cent, and the railways, aided by federal or provincial guarantees, paid very little more. Money was flowing into the dominion savings bank system, and Ottawa could, for the time being, issue more paper money without new enabling legislation. The dominion was running budget surpluses, and Ontario's revenues were buoyant too: between 1901 and 1904 the province's revenue from succession duties had increased 37 per cent, and from natural resources, 75 per cent, while it still had no net debt.[12] What better time to go adventuring with large new projects?

Provincial spending and assistance were essentially supplements to dominion aid, but Queen's Park did make some contribution to the remarkable increase in Ontario's railway mileage, which rose from 6,605 in mid-1901 to an all-time peak of 11,320 in mid-1916.[13] Thereafter the mileage fell a little, although even at the end of 1939 it was still 10,570.

The Canals and Lakes

For railways, the weight and the ballasting of the rails combined with the gauge of the track and the signalling system to influence the volume of freight that a line could carry. For canals, and therefore for the St Lawrence-Great Lakes system, a similar role was played by locks and by controlling depth. Long before Confederation, the Rideau Canal had been completed from Ottawa to Kingston, but its locks were small and numerous, while its depth was not great. The St Lawrence canals were also shallow: their controlling depth was nine feet. The Welland Canal had the same depth, and at Sault Ste Marie there was a canal on the American side with a depth of eleven and a half feet. By 1870 it was realized that the canals probably were too shallow, and did not have large enough locks, to handle the growth of trade. The dominion's Canal Commission recommended that the Welland and St Lawrence canals should be rebuilt, with much larger locks and with a depth of twelve feet. This target was later revised to fourteen feet, and the Welland was indeed rebuilt to this depth. But it was not finished until 1887, and the St Lawrence canals were not completed until 1904. Nor were they deepened further until the building of the St Lawrence Seaway in the 1950s. As for the Welland, reconstruction to sea-going standards began in 1913, but was completed only in 1933.

The Canal Commission also wanted a Canadian lock at the Soo. In 1870–1 the American government proceeded to build a very large Soo lock; there followed a kind of lock-building competition. In 1888–95 the

Canadians built a still larger lock, and in 1896 the Americans topped the Canadian effort with a lock that was shorter, but wider and deeper. In 1919 the Americans opened a yet more capacious lock – almost big enough for ocean-going ships, although, of course, these could not pass up the St Lawrence and Welland canals into Lake Erie.

Meanwhile other canal projects were discussed, and some were actually pursued. The Ottawa-Rideau arrangements were maintained, and from time to time, especially during the boom of 1900–13, there were suggestions for a great new canal from Ottawa to Georgian Bay via Lake Nipissing and French River.[14] The Murray Canal was built at the north end of Prince Edward County, and the Severn-Trent navigation was much improved and extended. But these systems carried little traffic. In 1890, for instance, Trent freight was only 2.4 per cent of Welland freight, and the Rideau waterway carried only 11.2 per cent as much freight as the Welland. Unfortunately for these canal systems, with the exhaustion of local timber resources one kind of traffic diminished, while the poverty of the local soils prevented another kind from arising.

The effect of the Great Lakes-St Lawrence improvements was to compartmentalize the navigation. Until the opening of the new Welland Canal in 1933, the upper lakes constituted one system, while the Welland, Lake Ontario, and the St Lawrence canals defined others. Only relatively small boats could pass from Montreal to the head of the lakes, or vice versa. Hence, for through traffic from west to east or east to west, complicated patterns of transshipment had to be developed. The iron ore of Minnesota could pass directly to Lake Erie without trouble, as could Canada's Prairie wheat. Yet the grain became involved in the most complicated patterns. Grain and flour were put on the water as soon as possible and shippers tended to stick to water transport because it was cheaper than rail. The Georgian Bay ports – Collingwood, Owen Sound, Port McNicoll, Midland, Depot Harbour – were commonly used transshipment points. But some grain went to Buffalo, continuing to seaboard by the American Erie Canal, and more was transshipped at Port Colborne for the trip to Montreal. After the completion of the Welland Canal improvements in 1933 this was not necessary, but the large boats still could not traverse the St Lawrence canals; hence there were huge transshipment elevators at Kingston and Cornwall. Finally, some small boats did make the entire through trip between Montreal and the Lakehead.

The depths of the American canal system also affected the patterns, as did the tolls – or lack thereof. Because the Erie Canal had only a seven-foot draft in its upper reaches, after the deepening of the St Lawrence canals in 1904 Montreal captured much of the transit trade in American grain that it had sought since the 1840s. The American Soo canal had originally charged no tolls, nor did the new Canadian canal of 1895. On the Erie Canal, tolls were abolished in 1883. Canada responded by rebating most of the tolls on the Welland and St Lawrence, and in 1885 the United States retaliated by imposing a toll at the Soo on any ship that was destined for a Canadian port. The result was a stand-off: Canada abolished its rebates, the Americans abolished their Soo tolls, and Canada decided to build its own Soo canal. In 1903, following representations from the Dominion Maritime Association, the dominion abolished all tolls and tonnage taxes on the Welland and St Lawrence systems. Thereafter, until the opening of the St Lawrence Seaway in 1959 there were no tolls anywhere from the lakehead to Montreal and New York. In that the navigable waterways and canals were expensive to maintain and to build, it follows that the dominion was subsidizing lake transport. Probably it had no real choice, given the complicated possibilities for Canadian-American acrimony and the limited scope for intergovernmental cooperation.

By the 1880s one could detect a certain division of labour between rail and water transport. This situation would survive, with little change, for many decades. Grain was placed on shipboard as soon as possible but had to use rail to the Lakehead, or in winter, or when the water routes were too congested. Other heavy, cheap, bulky goods – iron ore, lumber, coal, crude and refined petroleum – did likewise. Thus in 1892, 77 per cent of the Welland traffic consisted of flour, wheat, corn, lumber, and coal, and in 1939, 75 per cent of the traffic through Canadian canals consisted of the following raw materials and crude products: wheat, flour, gasoline, petroleum, paper, pulpwood, coal, coke, and iron ore. The economic development of the province somewhat changed the commodity mix of the canal traffic; it did not alter its basic character.

How much shipping was based in Ontario ports? The data show a surprisingly rapid growth in Ontario tonnage between 1874 and 1881, then stagnation until 1899, at which time tonnage began a sustained and rapid rise that lasted to 1916, so that in the latter year Ontario tonnage was nearly 250 per cent of what it had been in the former. In the nineteenth century the average tonnage per vessel tended to fall, but in the twentieth century it almost quadrupled, chiefly because ever-larger freighters were being built to operate on the enlarged canals. Thus the average tonnage was 139 in 1874, 88 in 1900, and 303 in 1939.[15]

As for the ships themselves, the lake trade began in the nineteenth century with small wooden ships. Schooners, for instance, transported timber and grain southward and returned with American coal. The advent of the specialized 'laker' – the motorized steel-hulled bulk carrier – gradually changed the whole shape of shipping on the lakes. For the lumber trade, where the ports of collection were small and often remote from railways, the sailing schooner survived well into the twentieth century. Thus the transition to steel steamships took a very long time. Only in 1890 were there more steam than sailing ships on the Welland Canal, and even in 1903, more sailing ships than steam ships traversed the St Lawrence canal system. The sailing ships of the 1860s could generally carry 300 to 700 long tons of cargo. Steam barges arrived in the 1860s. In 1869, at Cleveland, the first recognizable 'laker' was launched. The ship was a wooden propeller steamer that drew only 11.5 feet, but its shape was that of the future: the cabin and pilot-house were far forward, the engine room was far aft, and there was a long, continuous, open cargo hold that could carry 1,200 tons of iron ore. Such purpose-built bulk carriers became increasingly common. In 1886 the first steel-hulled 'laker' was launched, and as the locks became larger, so did the lakers, their hulls precisely designed to pass the maximum cargo through the locks. The first laker was 211 feet long; the first 600-foot carrier was launched in 1907, and ships of that size became the standard after World War One. Between 1899 and 1930 more than 420 bulk carriers were built on the Great Lakes.

The ownership picture is complicated in detail but the line of evolution is straightforward and familiar. Initially every ship was the private property of an individual or a partnership, but the great railway companies soon acquired their own vessels. Lesser railways followed suit, as did the great land-based businesses – iron, steel, coal, and other industrial firms, which built and operated vessels just as they would soon buy and run their own trucks. This development seems to have been well underway by 1900. Francis Clergue's Lake Superior Corporation was a leader. By that time, furthermore, a large part of the 'common carrier' business on the lakes had been gathered into the bosom of the firms that were to become Canada Steamship Lines of Montreal. The oldest component of this firm was founded in 1845, and the enterprise grew quite steadily by expansion and merger. In 1913, when it adopted its present name, it contained at least nine and possibly ten steamship companies. It later acquired at least five more. Some of the firms it absorbed, such as the Northern Navigation Company, themselves were long-lived enterprises that had also grown through merger. Thus as Ontario shipping became more heavily capitalized and more technologically sophisticated, it also came to be controlled by a small number of very large firms.

As on land, so also on water: until the twentieth century had begun, both the dominion and the province placed their faith in competition to control the prices that common carriers would charge. In 1903 the dominion reluctantly began to regulate railway rates through the Board of Railway Commissioners. But only in 1923 did the board acquire any regulatory powers with respect to shipping rates. Regulation, however, mattered much less for shipping than for the railways: except for the grain trade, if a shipper thought he was being quoted an unfair price he could simply buy his own ship. As this chapter has shown, many industrial companies did just this.

Electric Communication: Telegraphy, Telephony, and the Streetcar

In Canada telegraphy dates from 1846, when T.D. Harris began to build a line from Toronto to Niagara. In 1847 the Montreal Telegraph Company began its operations, soon elaborating a network that connected most Canadian centres. By 1868 there were landline connections to New York and other American centres, although the first workable transatlantic cables were completed only in 1886. In 1868 a second major firm, Dominion Telegraph of Toronto, began operations, but in 1880 the two firms were merged into the Great North West Telegraph Company. Thereafter, the Canadian Pacific Telegraph system provided an alternative service, and the Canadian Northern and the T&NO began to do likewise early in the twentieth century.

The telephone was invented by Alexander Graham Bell of Brantford, Ontario, and in the application of the new invention Ontario did not lag behind the United States. In autumn 1877 a line was run from Prime Minister Alexander Mackenzie's Ottawa office to Rideau Hall. The first telephone exchange in the British Empire was set up in Hamilton in 1878, and in the same year Toronto acquired its first outside overhead line, connecting Osgoode Hall with three law offices. Hamilton and Dundas were wired together in 1879. When the Boston master mariner C.F. Sise arrived in Montreal in 1880 to set up the Bell Telephone Company of Canada, there were already several dozen telephone companies in the country; furthermore, the old-established telegraph firms had begun to supply telephone service, although they had been reluctant to take up Mr Bell's own ideas.[16]

Incorporated by the dominion and based in Montreal, Bell was set up in 1880 to take over all the relevant patents, to build and sell equipment, to develop a system of intercity trunk lines, and to acquire or build local telephone systems in the larger cities and towns. Like its American parent, Bell aimed at control so extensive and thoroughgoing that its enemies would call it a monopoly, although it never provided all the telephone service nor made all the equipment. By the end of 1880 it had made several acquisitions, including local systems in Windsor, Hamilton, London, Ottawa, Guelph, Brantford, St Thomas, and Cornwall. At that time it had 2,100 subscribers in all parts of the country. The next year it had 3,100; by 1884 it was operating in Toronto, where in 1889, with 16,550 subscribers, it began to construct underground conduits, and in 1891 it set up a second exchange to service the Toronto east end. The loss of its patent protection in 1885 proved to be no deterrent. By 1893 Bell had exclusive contracts with all the larger cities and towns of Ontario; by 1904 there were 66,160 subscribers, of whom 12,832 were in Toronto and eighty-five were in Winona. By then Bell also had arrangements for the interchange of business with thirty-one Canadian firms, of which twenty-four appear to have been in Ontario.[17]

The Bell system was far from popular, especially in small centres and rural areas. Bell was reluctant to tolerate competition from parallel telephone systems, and would use predatory pricing to force competitors out of business. In smaller and more isolated centres its service was sometimes inadequate, and its rates naturally occasioned criticism, partly because competitors sometimes appeared to be cheaper, and partly because the company was manifestly profitable. Bell was fond of exclusive contracts with railway companies – arrangements by which only Bell could install phones in railway stations. Only in 1902 was Bell required to provide service to anyone who wanted a telephone, even in those areas where it had run lines and established exchanges. Only after 1908 were its rates regulated in any general or thoroughgoing way, and for some time it seemed that the dominion Board of Railway Commissioners simply endorsed the rates that Bell proposed.

Bell sometimes appeared reluctant to extend services to small villages and to farms, although there were parts of the province, such as the Niagara District, where Bell rural service certainly did exist. The result was an efflorescence of very small telephone enterprises, in which local physicians sometimes played a leading role. Telephone technology was still developing and changing with great speed. It was still possible to connect a small number of rural phones on a single line and to operate the result with a system of code rings, forgoing both switchboard and operator. It was often physically impossible to connect such simple arrangements to the more complicated Bell system. The Select Committee of 1905 found one rural system whose switchboard was housed in a physician's house and operated in her spare moments by his wife's companion.

Thus by 1913 Ontario contained 370 separately organized telephone enterprises, of which Bell was only one.[18] By that date there were 175,506 telephone installations in the province. Development thereafter was well chronicled and rapid. In 1929 there were 509,000 telephones, and in 1939, 629,000. The number of companies also grew: in 1925 there were 625. But the dominant position of 'Ma Bell' was clearly established, resting on a monopoly of the long-distance lines and on the supply of services in the larger cities and towns.

It is easy to criticize the behaviour of Bell, especially if one views matters from a populist perspective, as many Ontarians had come to do by 1900.[19] But there was a certain logic to the company's proceedings, and it is possible to argue that they served the community as well as the shareholders. In nineteenth-century Canada governments were neither ready nor willing to determine the standards of telephone service or to ensure that the various instruments could communicate with one another; Bell's 'monopolistic' proceedings can be viewed as an attempt to do just that. Similarly, it was and is wasteful to have parallel and duplicative telephone networks in any particular district, especially if the two networks do not communicate with one another, and if each tries to offer service to every potential subscriber. It would not have been sensible if two or three telephone systems each had bedecked the same Toronto or Ottawa streets with their overhead wires or their conduits. One may imagine a regulatory system in which companies bid competitively for local franchises. Something of the sort did happen, at least from time to time, with respect to street railway systems. But no one proposed it for telephones, and indeed, until well into the twentieth century, Bell's dominion charter of incorporation seemed to mean that it could set up shop wherever it liked. Conversely, there was no orderly mechanism through which Bell and its competitors could compete, except by predatory pricing and other sorts of 'dirty tricks.' The result was not always edifying, but, given the legal framework and the lack of statutory regulation, it was understandable. And given this situation, the outcome was not self-evidently contrary to the public interest.

The telephone was an instrument of business, a means of entertainment, and a great saver of time. Both to householder and to businessman, time is money, and, once the telephone had been invented, the new device came to seem increasingly valuable, not only as a time-saver but in other directions too: it meant fewer messenger boys and less correspondence. Furthermore, the value of a single telephone increases dramatically as the number of telephones rises: there are more businesses and more people whom one can call. Indeed, this point illustrates the wastefulness of local competition in telephone service. Admittedly, in the absence of technological change, a growing system becomes a more expensive one, and the costs rise much more than proportionately to the increase in subscribers. Householders and businesses might or might not have been willing to pay higher charges as the scope of the system grew. Fortunately, technological progress was tending to lower the cost of the service while improving its quality and range. Thus Ontarians were offered a service whose benefits were large and increasing in comparison with its price and whose price, in turn, was falling in comparison not only with earnings but with the prices of goods and services in general. A more potent recipe for growth could hardly be imagined.

While the electric telephone was becoming a widespread though not universal feature of late nineteenth-century Ontario life, the same thing was happening to another electric invention – the streetcar. In some Ontario cities and towns there had been horse car lines since well before Confederation.[20] The electrification of such lines began in the late 1880s, replacing underfoot horse-droppings with overhead wires. Cities, operating under provincial legislation, devised franchises, which were necessary because the streetcar companies used municipal property – the streets. By 1915 there were thirteen street railways in Ontario. The largest was the Toronto Street Railway, with sixty-two miles of track. Ottawa and London each had about twenty-five miles, while Hamilton had more than thirty. There were sizeable systems on the Detroit River frontier and at Thunder Bay, and smaller ones in Berlin and Waterloo, Cornwall, Kingston, Oshawa, Sarnia, and St Thomas.[21] Meanwhile, paralleling the electrification and extension of city systems were the first suburban and intercity electric railways – what the Americans and British Columbians would call 'interurbans' and Ontarians would call 'radials.' The first ran seven miles, from St Catharines to Thorold. In 1889 a two-mile line was laid up the side of Yonge Street from the edge of Toronto into the countryside, and in the 1890s it was extended to Newmarket. Later it would reach Lake Simcoe. Other lines ran outward from Toronto, Hamilton, and London, and stretched up and down the Grand Valley and the Windsor shore of the St Clair River. By 1915 mileage had reached 385.5.

Surburbanites used the radials, but so did farmers, villagers, and business travellers. Although built chiefly for passenger service, most radials would also carry small parcels, and many, such as the Hamilton, Grimsby, and Beamsville Company, hauled freight cars as well. After 1900 the lines were better graded and the cars more heavily constructed; often the newer lines ran not on the roadsides but on their own rights of way, like 'real railways.' Eminent capitalist promoters, such as William Mackenzie of Toronto and the magnates of Hamilton, were actively involved in the radial lines. Indeed, interurban development in the first fifteen years of this century is one among many testimonies to the entrepreneurial vigour of Ontario businessmen, especially in Hamilton and Toronto.[22] In this respect, radial development is part of the electrification story which was examined in chapter 8 above.

The economic significance of the streetcar and the radial railway may seem to be slight. Their construction absorbed capital funds, both domestic and external, but few lines were strikingly profitable; for Canada as a whole, for instance, interurban lines earned only 3.9 per cent on capital in

1914. And although the radials helped some commuters, farmers, holiday-makers, and day-trippers, nowhere did they produce the sort of suburban dispersion that had followed on suburban railway-building and electrification around London, England, and some large American cities. But just as the telephone integrated the growing cities more tightly and completely, so did the new electric transport. This effect, impossible to quantify, at least for the years before 1914, should none the less not be ignored.

16 Roads, Airways, and Airwaves: Changing Modes of Communication in the Twentieth Century

In the twentieth century three quite novel means of communication emerged – the modern paved highway, the airplane, and the radio wave. In earlier chapters it was suggested that these new technologies had implications for industrial development, not only before 1914 but in the 1920s and thereafter. Roads and radio also changed the texture of rural life. Roads and airplanes, furthermore, affected the pace and character of new development, especially in Ontario's northland. Yet because roads, airplanes, and radios did not much affect the costs of the several inputs in the more closely settled parts of the province, or change the pattern of interregional and international competition, none had the profound effects on economic structure that followed from the exploitation of those older technologies, the railway and the canal. Nor did they accelerate the doing of business in the way that the telegraph and the telephone did. In later years the airplane would certainly do so, and the impact could be noticed in the early years of World War Two. But before 1939, except in certain remote areas, that impact was still slight.

Road Transport

This section is chiefly concerned with trunk road transport outside cities and towns, although in tracing the 'age of the motor car' one cannot avoid giving some attention to cars and trucks in towns. The story is almost entirely concerned with developments during the twentieth century, when motor transport and all-weather pavement came to Ontario. Nevertheless, there are some important nineteenth-century elements in the story, and these cannot be omitted.

From before Confederation Ontario inherited a few ill-maintained trunk roads – Yonge Street, Dundas Street, King Street – that stretched for considerable distances and had once been of importance both for passenger traffic and for freight. Their utility, however, had diminished with the construction of the railway system. There were also local roads, no better maintained, that served rural areas. The intersections of roads often defined and located the villages, and even the larger centres. Both local roads and trunk roads were locally maintained, largely by compulsory 'statute labour.' The work was often badly done and badly supervised, but nobody cared particularly. Road traffic was almost entirely local; in winter, ice and snow provided excellent surfaces for sleighs; the horse and the ox could cope with road conditions that would later defeat the two-wheel-drive motor vehicle.

Besides these local arrangements there was a pre-Confederation provision, continued after 1867, by which the provincial authorities would spend on 'colonization roads' in areas that were being opened up for settlement. In some regions, such as Haliburton and Muskoka, the late nineteenth-century story of these roads is a gloomy one. The roads were often poorly constructed; frequently they opened up land that proved unsuitable for agriculture. It sometimes seemed as if only the timber interests gained from such provincial expenditures. But fortunately the outlays were never very great.

Another pre-Confederation provision was for private toll roads. Joint stock companies could be formed to take over and maintain stretches of road, or to build new ones, sometimes without the formal acquiescence of the 'host' municipality. Many of the decent interurban road surfaces in nineteenth-century Ontario seem to have been laid as toll roads in the first instance. It has proved impossible to discover just how many toll roads Ontario contained at various times, or where they were located. But the flow of provincial legislation after 1867[1] suggests that there were always a certain number of toll roads, that they were generally local projects, and that their maintenance was a continuing problem and an ever-present source of dispute. No one should be surprised if this was so: local traffic on local roads can rarely have generated enough revenue to make careful and regular maintenance worthwhile to the owners. Fortunately, after the new century had begun, the provincial government took an interest in road-building, and this interest quickly rendered the toll-road idea otiose, although some tollroads did survive into the 1920s.

At Confederation, and long afterward, most urban roads were unpaved. Streetcars made a difference, because the car companies were generally required partially to pave the streets they used. After 1878, when the first bicycle reached Canada from England, bicyclists exerted considerable pressure for road improvement. By the beginning of 1895 there were more than ninety bicycle shops in Toronto, and they had already sold more than 18,000 bicycles.[2]

Outside the cities and towns there were perceptible signs of change in the 1890s and early in the new century. The Ontario Good Roads Association was founded in 1894, and in 1900 Ontario abolished statute labour, putting road-making in professional hands. In 1901 the government began to pay one-third of the cost of road-works that were executed to a suitable standard. But as yet there was little need for good roads outside towns, even though farmers were often eager for better local roads. The first gasoline-powered car came to Canada only in 1898, and in 1904 there were only 535 motor vehicles in the province.[3]

The act of 1901, generally called the 'good roads act,' provided $1 million for road improvements. This was a major change: from Confederation until that time the provincial authorities had spent an average of only $106,000 per year on colonization roads and had made no other appropriations for road works, although they had paid for some bridges. County councils were to designate the roads to be improved, but if they did not act or if too many municipalities were recalcitrant, individual municipalities could improve their own roads, with the same one-third subsidy from the province. In the next sixteen years this framework of grants in aid to counties and municipalities was extended and developed in various ways. There was even provision in 1912 for the receipt of dominion highway subsidies, although it does not appear that any were paid at that time.[4] But the legal and ideological framework had one defect: although the 'good roads act' could provide for the improvement of rural and local roads within each county, it made no provision for through roads of any length. The need would soon be pressing: by 1914 there were 35,357 motor vehicles in the province. Hence to provide for a paved concrete road between Toronto and Hamilton the province had to establish a Toronto and Hamilton Highway Commission with power to impose levies on towns and cities and to spend provincial funds as well.[5] Since this procedure was obviously clumsy and confusing, in 1915 a new Ontario Highways Act was passed, which created a Department of Highways, authorized the lieutenant-governor-in-council to designate any route a 'main road' on petition of local municipalities, and erected a board of trustees for each such route, the province contributing up to $4,000 per mile or 40 per cent of the cost, whichever was less.[6] This arrangement for 'main roads,' however, could only be a stopgap measure, requiring as it did a quite unreasonable degree of co-ordination among the municipalities that would have to petition the lieutenant-governor-in-council. Nor was it reasonable to suppose that any group of municipalities would agree to create a 'main road' if the principal beneficiaries would be travellers from other and more remote centres. In Ontario, as in all other jurisdictions, a central highway initiative was bound to appear.

In 1917 'an act to provide for a provincial highway system,' better known as the Provincial Highway Act, was passed. The act's preamble is a neat summary of the change in attitude: it says that highways that connect centres of population would be 'of general benefit to the inhabitants of Ontario,' and that it would be 'unjust and unfair that the cost of providing for such traffic should be borne wholly by the municipalities through that the [highways] would pass.'[7] The minister of highways could acquire, and his department could control and maintain, any highway or system of highways. The province would pay for construction and maintenance, although the municipalities would have to pay the province 30 per cent of its outlays. The main roads of Ontario had been, in effect, 'provincialized.'

During the 1920s the framework of financing and subsidy was changed many times. From 1920 until 1936 the Highways Department was free to spend all the motor licence fees and all gasoline revenues; municipal and dominion contributions were also to be paid to the department, and there were, in addition, ad hoc grants from general provincial revenue. Some interest and sinking fund payments had to be covered out of these funds, but in essence the province had set aside very considerable monies simply to pay for highway improvements. While these arrangements lasted, they helped ensure that the revenue from motoring would be spent on the roads. Dominion subsidies were not insignificant. In the 1920s Ottawa paid $5.9 million towards a trans-Canada highway. In the 1930s, as part of dominion-provincial relief work, there were further such payments.

Meanwhile, under legislation of 1911 and later measures special provision was made for roadbuilding in the northern and north-western areas of the province. These outlays began in 1912 and developed rapidly in the 1920s. They were managed by the Department of Northern Development until 1937, at which time the Department of Highways acquired the responsibility for northern roads. Altogether, $66 million was spent between 1912 and 1936. A skeleton of 'trunk roads' was constructed in the northern parts of Ontario, although even in 1940 it was still not possible to drive from east to west across the province. As was observed in chapter 5, there was also some attempt to encourage northern settlement and development with local road systems.

The provincial highway system began very modestly. In the early reports of the Highways Department one detects a gradual process of 'assuming' control of township and county roads to define one trunk route across the province, with spurs to places such as Ottawa and Niagara Falls. Thus in 1917 there were 45.7 miles of provincial highway; but in 1920 the mileage was already 1,200, and thereafter the total rose fairly steadily. The 'King's Highway' label was adopted in 1930.

Although many of the photos that decorate the early *Reports* were doubtless chosen to illustrate the splendid contribution that the department's efforts were making, it does appear that many of these 'main arteries' were in appalling condition when the province took them over. A few were described as 'old macadam,' and these may once have been toll roads. But others resembled nothing so much as long, narrow ploughed fields. What was required first, the deputy minister and his officials repeatedly explained, was minimum essential repair, so that the roads would actually be fit for traffic, followed by grading, draining, and perhaps gravelling or even macadamizing in the old British sense – the making of a surface by compacting layers of stones of various sizes. There was much preaching of the value of rolling and the virtue of 'the drag.' In 1920, the department's engineers still believed, 'It would seem possible that good gravel roads would provide at small expenditure an ideal surface for many years to come.'[8] But in that very year regular and extensive paving began, and by 1922 it was well under way. At the end of 1929, when there were 2,438 miles of provincial highway, 75 per cent of the mileage was hard-surfaced in one way or another.

By the mid-1930s it was obvious that in Ontario, as in the many other jurisdictions that had built new highways during the 1920s, road-building had created new problems without always solving or ameliorating the old ones. Certainly, rural roads had improved beyond measure. But within and outside cities, traffic had grown at least as rapidly as the capacity of the road system. Indeed, it might be argued that if roads had not been improved so much, Ontarians would not have bought so many cars. Thus by 1939 congestion was often worse than it had been in 1919. Problems were naturally most acute inside the large cities, where little had as yet been done to expand the carrying capacities of the Victorian street systems. In addition, the growth of intercity passenger and freight traffic created problems on a few lengths of Ontario's two-lane paved highways. Around the large cities and even far outside them the efficiency of new roads was often reduced, swiftly and dramatically, by 'ribbon development' – strips of housing, factories, and businesses of various kinds, all opening onto the newly paved or widened road. There were really only two possibilities. The province might restrict the use of private motor vehicles, especially cars. Or it might embark on a modernization of its road system while restricting access to the newly modernized roads. No one seems to have been prepared to contemplate the former course of action; hence the provincial authorities set their feet, however tentatively, on the other path – following a route that other jurisdictions, especially Germany and the United States, had already begun to take.

In 1933 the provincial authorities began to modernize anew. Their approach was very gradual: there was no suggestion that major new arteries would eventually be built, and the emphasis was on 'dual highways,' where medians and shrubberies separate the lanes of traffic but where there is no thoroughgoing management of traffic, and where there are still many level crossings. In 1936 work began on a dual 'Middle Road' between Toronto and Burlington, and similar projects were begun on short stretches near Stratford, to the east of Toronto, near Woodstock, and westward from Brockville. A new 'Niagara Falls highway' was started; it would meet the Middle Road by means of a 'semi-clover leaf' – the first such device in Canada. The Middle Road was in use in 1937, and at the time of the royal visit in early summer 1939 the entire Toronto-Niagara artery was named the Queen Elizabeth Way. The extension to Fort Erie was still under construction.

In 1939 Ontario boasted some 72,000 miles of highway – provincial, county, and township roads. Of these, 5,000 miles were hard-surfaced, 50,000 miles were gravel or stone, and 17,000 were earth – some graded, and presumably some not. The province had come a long way since 1917, when the Toronto-Hamilton concrete highway, a stretch of thirty-six miles, had been opened. In 1939 the province contained 683,000 motor vehicles – 29 per cent more than in 1933. Gasoline consumption, also, had risen 50 per cent since that year of deep depression.[9]

The provincial authorities moved early to license and tax vehicles; they were much more reluctant to license or tax drivers, except for chauffeurs, for whom licences were required under legislation of 1908. Perhaps it was believed that because so much traffic was rural and so many drivers were farmers, the risk of collision was slight and the work of licensing owner-drivers was not justified. Whatever the reason, it was only in 1927 that such licences were required: in that year some 444,000 were issued, along with some 65,000 chauffeurs' licences, most of which were renewals. More than 15 per cent of all Ontarians, regardless of age, were licensed drivers.

Even in 1939 long-distance driving was still remarkably rare, although by that time paved roads spanned the province from east to west and extended from the south some distance into the north. In the tabulations of the Highways Department traffic censuses[10] one detects a pronounced concentration of traffic around Toronto and in what Ontarians of a later generation would call the Golden Horseshoe. In northern and north-western Ontario the incomplete and unpaved trunk road system followed the railway lines, largely duplicating their routes. Furthermore, it was as yet impossible to keep all main roads open in winter.

Nor had the road network yet much affected the location of industry and commerce. There was 'ribbon development,' but there were no shopping plazas and no suburban industrial parks; few industrial sites depended solely on road transport, nor was the rural landscape littered with 'deserted villages' whose decay could be blamed on the motor car. Ontario's summer 'cottage culture' antedated the automobile, but the car and the road improvements of the interwar years certainly helped that culture to grow. Thanks to its liquor laws and its unattractive public catering, Ontario had few of the suburban roadhouses and restaurants that were features of the period in Britain and the United States. Even the 'drive-in restaurant,' already a fact of Vancouver life, had made little impression on Ontario by 1939.

Yet motor transport had certainly made a difference to the province. In cities it spread congestion and atmospheric pollution, banished horse manure, and created problems for electric streetcars and radial railways. It reduced the demand for oats, both in towns and on farms. The car increased the distance over which commuting made sense, somewhat encouraging the tendency of cities and towns to sprawl. In the process, it created capital gains for some farmers, or for other speculators who were lucky enough to buy suburban farm land at the right time. For farmers, factory-owners, and merchants, trucks meant more reliable and faster transport over short distances; for householders, cars really did bring a sort of freedom – an independence from streetcar and railway schedules.

For electric traction, the motor age was anything but pleasant. The expansion of electric street railways and the development of radials effectively ended with World War One. Before the war Sir Adam Beck, the chairman of Ontario Hydro, tried to promote radials, and he continued to do so in the 1920s, but the 1920s and 1930s were decades of abandonment, complete or partial. The Toronto lines were partially merged with the Toronto Transit Commission's streetcar system after the city acquired Sir William Mackenzie's properties in 1921. But the longer lines were abandoned one by one. As for city streetcars, there was little new development except in Toronto, where the TTC produced an integrated system without significantly extending the network, except insofar as it incorporated parts of the radials. In Ottawa no new lines were constructed from World War One to the abandonment of streetcar transport in the 1950s. In general, even in Toronto, where new transit lines were needed, the operators bought buses. Furthermore, as intercity roads improved longer-distance bus travel became commonplace: it was slow, but it was also inexpensive. By 1939 the future of electric traction appeared uncertain indeed.

Airways and Airwaves in the Twentieth Century

Until well after World War Two, civil aviation mattered little to most

Ontarians, except some dwellers in isolated northern districts. In 1920 Canada's first commercial bush flights were logged in Manitoba, and such commercial aviation quickly spread not only to northern Quebec but to northern and north-western Ontario, where, as chapter 4 revealed, during the 1920s and 1930s it made some contribution not only to exploration but to the provisioning of mine sites. But the bush-flying businesses were small, ill-financed, and unstable. When the dominion post office began to offer air mail service in the winter of 1927–8, post office business was a useful supplement to their more routine commercial work. Sad to say, in the depth of the Great Depression R.B. Bennett's dominion government felt obliged to save money by dropping most of its air mail arrangements. Thus, for instance, the Toronto-Montreal service, which had begun in 1928, was gone by 1934. Furthermore, with the improvement of northern road systems and the extension of railway branch lines, there was less freight for the bush pilots to move. Longer-distance services, whether for passengers or for mail, would require massive airfield improvement – something that the dominion took in hand only in 1936, when Mackenzie King's new Liberal government began to develop what it called the 'Trans-Canada Airway.'

In 1936–7 Ontario contained nine 'municipal air harbours,' as the *Canada Year Book* called civil air fields. None was in Toronto. There were no dominion civil aerodromes anywhere in Ontario, although the dominion had some military installations, and had already built civil facilities near Montreal with an eye to north-south and transatlantic traffic, not only by airplane but by dirigible. However, in 1937 things were already beginning to change: Trans-Canada Airlines (TCA) was incorporated as a dominion crown corporation, and serious work on the Trans-Canada Airway was well in hand. The dominion built some airfields, and subsidized others that were in municipal control. Thus in 1939 the Toronto Island Airport was in operation, and in October 1938 TCA began to fly an express service that linked Montreal, Toronto, and Vancouver. In that year Ontario recorded 59,170 air passengers plus 10 million tons of freight and almost 300,000 tons of mail; with the creation of TCA, serious and regular air mail service became a fact of Ontario life, although it did not connect the province's southern cities with one another.

When war broke out, the numbers of civil passengers and freight soon fell to the levels of 1937, or to even lower levels. But the weight of mail increased several-fold: under war conditions the speed of transcontinental air mail was immensely valuable.[11]

Radio broadcasting, like aviation, is a twentieth-century development, and its impact on Ontario life and work was as great as the impact of the motor car, even though its strictly economic significance, as user of resources or as producer of services, was still slight in 1940. Before World War One radio was used entirely as a form of long-distance wireless telegraphy, especially in connection with shipping. In Canada, experimental broadcasting began in 1919, when Canadian Marconi began transmissions in Montreal. Regular broadcasting started the same year and quickly spread. By September 1922 there were twenty-three commercial licences in Ontario, and twelve in Toronto, where Station CFCA began[12] under the auspices of the *Toronto Star*. In 1923 Canadian National Railways began to operate promotional stations, and in 1924 it had outlets in Toronto and Ottawa. Since there were few broadcast channels for any one city – usually only one, and never more than two – the channels had to be shared. Nevertheless, in the mid-1920s many stations appeared. Rogers Majestic, a radio manufacturer, had one. So did battery manufacturers, department stores, car dealers, newspapers, and entrepreneurs of all kinds. Many stations were little more than promotional engines for their owners' businesses. In 1933 there were eighteen stations in Ontario, and in 1936 there were twenty-six. With the creation of the Canadian Radio Broadcasting Commission (CRBC) in 1933 the dominion government began to elaborate a system of 'national broadcasting' whose main production centres would inevitably be Montreal and Toronto. The dominion also created the Canadian Broadcasting Corporation (CBC) in 1936, thereby accelerating this development, and the CBC soon provided, for the first time, a high-powered signal that blanketed the more closely settled parts of the province. Provincial government initiatives in broadcasting were more than thirty years in the future.[13] Television, though operating by 1938 in Britain and the United States, had yet to reach Canada.

During the early years of broadcasting, in the 1920s, when neither level of government had taken any interest in the new radio medium, broadcasting was chaotic and confusing. Radio waves and radio stations, unlike the television stations of today, could and did jostle messily together on a single wave band, where signals might well interfere with one another. At first, because there was only one wave length in each city, local stations would have to share the time. Thus some early stations operated for only a few hours a week, and many – the so-called 'phantom' stations – owned no transmitting equipment, relying on other firms' transmitters. The early stations came and went with great frequency. Toronto was allocated a second band in 1925, but for some years there was no serious intergovernmental attempt to allocate wave lengths among the various North American nations, so that until the 1930s Ontario broadcasters and listeners often had to cope with interference from American stations, and even from Mexico.

Nevertheless, the number of receiving sets rose dramatically – from zero in 1919 to 521,000 in 1940.[14] At first the receivers were awkward, and, unless home-made, they were expensive. Later they became much simpler, more reliable, and cheaper, although even in 1939 the purchase of a radio was a significant outlay for most Ontario families. Still, it was one that most of them were willing to make: in 1941 there was a radio for every fourteen inhabitants in the province, and the majority of farm families possessed a receiver, many or most of them battery powered.

Why did broadcasting develop so fast? For the listener a receiving set, once bought and licensed, provided entertainment that was increasingly varied and almost entirely free: only batteries or hydro power, plus tubes and occasional repairs, would have to be paid for. During the day the entertainment could be enjoyed along with other activities, thus costing nothing even in terms of time. And for many Ontarians, especially in smaller towns and on the farms, an evening radio broadcast was not very likely to displace other activities, there being so few to displace. It was in the 1930s that Canadian traditions such as 'Hockey Night in Canada,' with Foster Hewitt transmitting live from Maple Leaf Gardens, and 'The Happy Gang,' with a daily transmission of cheerful singers and burbly ballads, became established. There was uplift too: the CNR stations and their successors, the CRBC and the CBC, carried plays and symphony concerts.

For the broadcasters, once sponsored advertising became established in the early 1920s, a station licence could appear to be a licence to print money. In fact, in the early days that was not always so: audiences and advertising revenues were often disappointing, especially in smaller centres. Yet broadcasting licences were cheap, the capital cost of a small station was not very high, and the medium was glamorous, even – or perhaps especially – in places such as Wingham or Smiths Falls.

17 The Revolution in Ontario Commerce

If the changes in industrial organization and production appear dramatic, the changes in commercial organization are equally so. It is generally said that in the larger towns, such as Toronto and Hamilton, in the late nineteenth century there was an evolution from 'commerce' to 'industry and finance.'[1] As observed in chapter 1, that sort of statement tells something about elites and rather less about economic structure. It ignores, most obviously, the rising elite of retail trade, as exemplified by Robert Simpson and Timothy Eaton. It also directs attention away from the fact that in the large cities, as elsewhere in the province, during the last thirty years of the nineteenth century considerable commercial development took place under a variety of headings. On the other hand, the statement does serve as a reminder that in the urban elites of 1900 the industrial and financial families were far more numerous and prominent, in comparison with the wholesaling families, than they had been in 1870. Indeed, at that earlier date the financial figures often had the closest of links with the mercantile interests, especially in wholesale trade, while at the end of the century the industrial-financial nexus is of much greater moment, wholesalers having become at once less prominent and more numerous.

Yet commerce, defined as the circulating and distributing of goods, was far more important in 1900 than it had been in 1870. The volume of trade was a great deal larger, and the march of urbanization and industrialization had made more of the populace dependent on that circulation. The volume of wholesale trade must have increased dramatically, though whether Toronto was pulling ahead of Montreal, its great competitor, there is no way of knowing. As an employer, commerce certainly increased in absolute and proportionate importance. Women, furthermore, finding their ways into the paid labour force, often did so by clerking in shops, both large and small. Here, as so often, it is not always appropriate to concentrate upon the elites, or on the blue-collar factory occupations.

At Confederation little development in retail trade could yet be detected. Shops, of course, existed, and in Toronto it was customary to talk of the glories of King Street as if that rough provincial thoroughfare was Bond Street or the rue de la Paix. Some long-established dry-goods stores had begun the evolution that would eventually turn several of the larger firms into department stores. But as yet this had not happened in Ontario. Nor had chain stores or cheap multiple shops, such as Woolworth, yet appeared on the Ontario scene. In Toronto and the other larger towns there were many small shops, almost always unincorporated businesses under the direct management of their owners, and often selling a wide range of goods, there being little chance of a living for a specialized merchant. The towns were small, and their buying power per capita was far less than it would later be. In villages and hamlets there were general stores. The retail trade in fresh foodstuffs, however, largely bypassed these retail traders, both in towns and in the country, leaving the grocery trade to deal in a narrow range of foodstuffs – biscuits, sugar, coffee, tea, spices, baking powder, and similar durable items, as well as spirits and wine. Farmers brought their own goods to market, or sold them to local traders who might also sell them locally. Butter and cheese passed through the wholesale trading system, which presumably supplied some such goods in towns. Milk, however, was chiefly sold by those who owned their own cows, so that the supply in towns was uncertain both in quality and in quantity. Retail traders carried textiles, but much clothing was home made, and 'bespoke tailoring,' where the artisan took the order and sold direct to the customer, was common. The same was true for shoemaking, although factory-made shoes and boots were certainly on the retail market.

From the commercial directories of the immediate post-Confederation years one can garner certain impressions about the character of retail trade outside the major cities. In the more remote counties, such as Victoria and Glengarry, villages of comparable size had fewer commercial establishments than in more central counties, such as Waterloo. There were many general agents who also worked for local businesses, such as saw-mills or manufacturers. In the villages, storekeepers were often postmasters and sometimes farmers as well; in such places, probably because occupations were less specialized, people were much less specific about their work than in towns. Partnerships, especially fraternal partnerships, were common in storekeeping, hotelkeeping, butchering, dressmaking, and the millinery trade. Members of a family were often in business together. Shoemakers were remarkably common. In most towns and villages there seem to have been at least two shoemakers to every store. Hotels, too, were everywhere, and were certainly as numerous as stores. It was only in the larger centres –

those having more than 500 citizens – that there were marked signs of specialized retail trade – glassware, crockery, boots, shoes, and so on. In the villages with populations of less than 500 it was rare to find anyone with only one occupation. Thus barristers were also notaries public and insurance agents; storekeepers were also postmasters; lumber merchants owned saw-mills, and grain merchants, grist-mills. In really small places – those with fewer than 200 people – most of the residents were farmers or labourers, one of whom was usually the town merchant. Furthermore, the smaller the place, the stronger the impression that the local general store was both a buyer and a seller.

It may be doubted whether any country general store could be regarded as 'typical', but the inventory of one such establishment will give some idea of the texture of Ontario commerce early in our period. In March 1880 Henry Elliott's general store at Hampton, a small village near Brooklin, held an inventory that was valued at $1,802.95. There were stocks of cloth, canvas, patterns, articles of clothing, trimmings, notions, boots, rubbers, locks, door knobs and other hardware, knives, mouse traps, cutlery, jewellery, combs, farm tools, nails, seeds, glue, borax, camphor, various farming chemicals, drugs, paper, books, and envelopes.[2] Elliott was also an agent for sewing machines, pianos, and organs, which he was quite prepared to sell on the instalment plan. Furthermore, he took subscriptions for newspapers, and he lent money. As he explained in an advertisement, he was in a position to provide mortgage funds at 6 per cent; he would place funds for others, and he was an insurance agent.[3] This was the sort of country general store that could, and presumably sometimes did, evolve into a private bank.

With the growth of turnover that accompanied the expansion of the provincial economy, successful merchants could expect an increase in total profits, even if profit per dollar of turnover was not rising. With the gradual spread of the limited liability company in the last decades of the century, it became possible for the larger firms to separate company capital from the assets of the proprietors, so that these family assets might be protected even if the business fell on hard times. Indeed, nineteenth-century observers often suspected that this was the main reason for adopting the limited-liability form. But because it was easy to enter wholesale and retail trade, competitive forces must have kept down the profit per dollar of turnover. Liabilities, furthermore, could and probably often did rise as fast as assets, or faster. And most small traders, especially small retail traders, probably did rather badly, perhaps earning only enough to keep themselves in business. The success stories, such as Eaton, Simpson, Freiman, Ogilvie, or Northway, are spectacular. But there is no reason to suppose that they are typical.

Commerce, Competition, and the Emergence of the Department Store after 1867

Between Confederation and World War One there were many changes in the pattern of trade. Wholesalers found new opportunities in the new dominion; at the same time, new retailing arrangements were tending to bypass them to some extent, and in retrospect one can see that some of the newer consumer goods would be marketed without the intervention of the old-line wholesalers: manufacturers themselves would do some of the wholesalers' work, and new specialized wholesaling firms would come into existence. As for the newer capital goods, it was neither necessary or practical to sell them through wholesale channels. Thus light bulbs might or might not pass through wholesalers, but electrical generators would be most unlikely to do so. The changing pattern of industrial production would therefore in due course affect the wholesaler's role. But before 1890 there was no marked shift either towards capital goods or towards the new consumer goods of the 'second industrial revolution;' much more relevant was the continued industrialization of Canada itself, a process that widened the range of locally available manufactures, probably reducing the proportionate need to distribute imports. Nor did the wholesalers maintain control over the province's export trade. Some of Ontario's saw-millers had already dealt direct with American distributors; this pattern continued and appears to have increased. In the rise of the cheese and butter export trades, admittedly, there were new opportunities for intermediation because the markets were far away and the producers many and small. But meat packers, such as the William Davies Company, generally dealt direct with their British agents. It is to be supposed that, with the changes in the pattern of Ontario's own agricultural production and the growth of the province's city markets, there must have been a larger amount of intraprovincial intermediation, linking farmers with retail shops. But this development is very hard to trace. Wholesale grocers certainly proliferated, but it seems that they dealt exclusively in 'dry groceries.' At the same time, as flour milling became increasingly concentrated in large enterprises on a few sites, much of the trade must have dealt directly with overseas buyers, so that a diminishing proportion of the milled flour presumably went through wholesalers' hands. In general, the drift towards bigness diminished the wholesaler's role, because manufacturers could more readily carry on the necessary functions 'in house.' At the same time, developments in retail trade both increased and diminished the wholesaler's role. On the one hand, there was a proliferation of shops – small proprietorships that would certainly still find it convenient to draw supplies and credit from the wholesale trade. And as the wholesalers sent out ever-larger platoons of travelling salesmen, this convenience was further increased; indeed, by the early 1890s it was rare for the retailer to visit the city where his wholesalers did their business, because the travelling salesman could and did handle most of the things that had once needed personal contact. But on the other hand, the emergent department stores tended increasingly to buy direct, bypassing the wholesalers; the growth of mail-order buying, furthermore, bypassed not only the wholesaler but the small retailer as well.

In groceries at least, wholesale trading expanded considerably between Confederation and the mid-1890s. At Confederation there were said to be only two or three wholesale grocers in Toronto, whereas by the early 1890s there were a dozen, plus many brokers who carried stock. In the course of that quarter-century some Toronto wholesalers had begun to specialize in one or two commodities, so that by 1894 many firms were not carrying anything like a full grocery line. At Confederation London had only three wholesale firms of all sorts, while by the early 1890s there were 'scores', including five wholesale grocery houses. Hamilton, which in 1870 was locked in competition with Toronto for the Ontario trade, still possessed sizeable wholesale grocery firms in the 1890s, which traded not only in Ontario but across the Prairies to the Rockies and to British Columbia.[4]

The distinguished historian Maurice Careless has explained how the province's rail network, constructed in the 1850s and later expanded, tended to focus trade on Toronto, expanding the city's hinterland and creating a large field for the city's importers, exporters, and financiers. The subsequent development of that network, especially in the 1870s and 1880s, made it possible to shorten the terms of credit, and allowed retailers to work with smaller stocks.[5] Hence by 1890 the Dominion Wholesale Grocers' Guild was able to reduce the terms of credit and the discounts for cash payment. Retailers raged, tried to find alternative sources of supply – and, presumably, paid when they had to.[6] Retail grocers, meanwhile, had begun to combine in some districts, asking wholesalers not to supply competing local merchants who did not join local associations.[7]

After Confederation, and especially after the tariff increases of 1879, Toronto wholesalers enjoyed broader trading horizons. Industrialization in Central Canada, the tariff, and railways to east and west, enabled them to sell goods not only on the prairies but in the Maritime provinces as well.[8] In the 1870s, following a Montreal lead from the previous decade, they began to employ travelling salesmen; by the 1880s Toronto's 'drummers' were to be seen on the Prairies and in Atlantic Canada. Toronto's export trade was less buoyant than the city's import and distribution trade: the grain trade was falling away, and lumber exports were increasingly finding other routes to their final markets in the United States, while crops such as barley generally moved south across the lakes from lesser ports, such as Picton. Nevertheless, business was thriving for the merchants of the Queen City. Concentrated on lower Yonge Street at Confederation, in the early 1870s the wholesale houses spread westward to Simcoe Street.[9] Yet some sectors of the wholesale trade were faring less well. The historian Brenda Newall reports[10] that the city contained twenty-seven wholesale dry-goods firms in 1871, forty in 1881, and only twenty-eight in 1891.

In Hamilton, during the last quarter of the nineteenth century a transition occurred: new industrial elites joined the old commercial ones, and the character of wholesale trade was affected by changing patterns of circulation. But in the city, which had no stock exchange and which was losing some of its financial businesses to Toronto, there were few rising financial magnates to match the industrial ones. Yet Hamilton 'clung to a historic function as a wholesale distribution centre for groceries, dry goods, and hardware.' The central business district remained on James Street and around Gore Park, its drawing power assisted by the streetcar and radial railway networks. But the urban historian John Weaver reports that in spite of Hamilton's rapid expansion, its business district changed less than those of Toronto, Montreal, or Vancouver.[11] As in Toronto, local dry goods stores grew into department stores. But in the dry-goods trades Hamilton had no retail entrepreneurs as dynamic as Eaton or Simpson.

Ottawa, at Confederation, may have had some role in the supplying of lumber camps, but it was not much of a wholesaling centre, having little by way of settled or prosperous hinterland and existing as it did in Montreal's shadow. Its retail commerce was already centred on Rideau Street and around By Ward Market, with an extension along Sparks Street close to the horse-car line. As the town and its streetcar network spread, so did the shopping district, but the centre remained where it had been in 1867, and when department stores appeared, they faced one another across Rideau Street, where almost every Ottawa streetcar was routed. Furthermore, Ottawa retailing was slow to change: the Ogilvie firm began as a dry-goods store well before Confederation, but evolved only gradually into a local department store, while the Freiman business, founded in 1892 as a furniture store, did not become a proper department store until after the turn of the century.

In Toronto the situation was very different. At Confederation the city's retail stores, though widely distributed throughout the built-up area, already evinced a certain concentration along King Street, especially to the east of Yonge Street. On that stretch of road were to be found those long-established dry-goods emporia – Dunn, Murray, Walker, Thompson – that were to become the city's first department stores. During the next quarter century retail trade developed rapidly, and there was a considerable shift of location, as shops spread westward along Queen Street to Spadina Avenue while a new fashionable district established itself on Yonge between Queen and Dundas Streets. Newall reports that in 1871 there were seventy-one dry-goods retailers in Toronto, in 1881, 131, and in 1891, 119. Evidently the slump of the 1870s had not impeded the growth of retailing. The businesses of 1871, however, rarely lingered: of the 119 companies that operated in 1891, only eleven had been established before 1871, and all the others were more recent creations.[12]

The Emergence of the Department Store in the Nineteenth Century

Although some retail shops had operated on a cash basis in 1867, the normal practice of the nineteenth century, both on the frontier and in metropolitan centres, was 'long credit to an established clientele.' Further, retail prices were often a matter of bargaining; pre-fixed prices were as yet anything but universal. Hence the importance of the practices that Timothy Eaton followed in his new Toronto establishment, opened on Yonge near Queen Street in 1869. Eaton had been a Toronto retailer before moving to St Marys, from which he returned to the provincial capital. The Yonge Street location was not fashionable at first, but Eaton pulled business to his shop with money-back guarantees and fixed prices, while selling for cash only. In 1872 Robert Simpson copied the Eaton move, shifting his shop from Newmarket to Queen and Yonge. He adopted similar merchandising methods. The two dry-goods and clothing firms then expanded in parallel, and in remarkably similar ways. By 1875 Eaton had fourteen employees, and in 1881, 150. In 1883 the firm moved into a new four-storey block, serviced with elevators. Soon there were weekly 'Bargain Days'; in 1907 escalators were installed. Simpson built a large new store in 1894, following a fire, and after another blaze the firm rebuilt in still more splendid style in 1895. Further expanded in later years, that 'gay nineties' structure remains the Simpson flagship store.[13] Facing trouble from wholesalers, Eaton set up his own wholesale firm so that he could buy directly in Britain.[14] In 1893 Eaton opened his own order office in London, England; in 1899 he did the same in Paris, using the fact to good effect in his advertising; other buying offices, in New York, Manchester, Belfast, Leicester, and Yokohama and Kobe, would be established in the new century.[15] Simpson's development was much the same.

In the world of Toronto retailing, Eaton and Simpson were late-comers. Newall[16] has demonstrated how much longer-established dry-goods businesses evolved into department stores, so that, of the six such stores in 1891, five had existed as dry-goods firms in 1871. The Eaton company itself began to manufacture only in 1890, assembling muslin underwear with eight sewing machines.[17] But in 1897, following some years of price-cutting that the depression of the early and mid-1890s presumably accentuated, the Mammoth Store and Walker both failed, and the dominance of Eaton and Simpson was assured.

Ordinary grocers and dry-goods retailers hated the department stores. Among the former there was a widespread concern lest the 'departmentals' practise loss-leader selling, reckless advertising, or both. But after the failures of the mid-1890s, the grocery trade thought that the survivors were 'doing business in a steadier, straighter way.' Retailers meanwhile adjusted, partly by switching more of their business to a cash basis and partly by narrowing their margins.[18]

Mail-order business generated another set of worries. Eaton produced his first catalogue in 1884, and Simpson soon followed. Effective mail-order selling was assisted by the improvements in rail service and in the postal network. For the big stores catalogue selling had many advantages. It was useful to inventory control, because one could list an item and then arrange for production only as orders came in.[19] Also, of course, mail-order business meant larger turnover. The significance of this element is underlined by the fact that until 1909–11 neither Eaton nor Simpson segregated retail from mail-order stocks.[20] Naturally mail-order merchandising meant new and painful competition for small-town and country merchants, because the two great stores were often able to buy, or even to manufacture, at lower prices. In addition, the catalogues could offer a far wider and often more up-to-date array of merchandise than the small retail stores. Thus the mail-order business grew rapidly, assisted by an increasingly speedy and reliable rail delivery system, and by the catalogues' ability to bring more or less high-fashion goods to small towns and farms. The Eaton mail-order business was so successful that in 1903 it had to move into its own building; until the 1920s, furthermore, the Eaton family concentrated upon the mail-order business, not attempting to develop a large chain of retail outlets.[21]

Outside Toronto the 1890s saw the creation of many so-called department stores, which often survived into the new century, although presumably in the smaller centres they cannot have stocked a wide range of goods. More interesting business stories could be told about significant firms such as Freiman and Ogilvie in Ottawa, or the Arcade in Hamilton. Regrettably, these companies have yet to attract their historians, nor do the archival collections tell us much about them.[22]

For central-city department stores the technological changes of the late nineteenth century must have enhanced drawing power, while making really large stores a good deal more workable. Thus it is impossible to imagine a sizeable department store without elevators, or without good artificial light, whether gas or electric. Telephone ordering further increased the outreach of the stores, especially into middle-class families, and in 1885 both Eaton's and Simpson's began to take orders by telephone, Toronto having acquired its first exchange in 1879. Thanks to electric streetcars and radial railways, by 1900 the central shopping districts could draw clients from an ever-growing hinterland, and thanks to the big stores' efficient delivery systems, purchases could arrive almost as speedily as purchasers. Before 1914 cars were few and women drivers fewer. But within the range of the streetcar or the radial car, department store competition was genuinely formidable, and other retailers were anything but happy about it. Indeed, the collapse of a 'departmental' would be reported with glee, and both municipal and provincial legislators often considered measures that would clip their competitive wings.[23] Furthermore, the mail-order system carried that competition far into the countryside. Other outlets, none the less, continued to expand. With the joint development of chain merchandising and motoring after 1900 new competitive situations would arise to which the 'departmentals' themselves would have to adjust.

Variety Stores and Department Stores in the Twentieth Century

If the department store and the mail-order catalogue are the great success stories of the late nineteenth century so far as marketing is concerned, chain merchandising is the success story of the early twentieth century, especially of the 1920s. In this story the department stores were involved to some extent, and the marketing of many products, old and new, was affected. But as the next section reveals, the real drama was found in the food trades. Thus it is best to see the further development of the department stores as an extension of their nineteenth-century evolution.

American or American-style variety stores form part of the twentieth-century story. They have many similarities to department stores, although they operate on a much smaller scale. In Ontario, and in Canada, the earliest seems to have been S.H. Knox, a company that opened a Toronto store in 1897. In 1908 another American variety chain, E.P. Charlton, opened in Canada. In 1911 the American parents of these two chains were merged with Woolworth, adopting the Woolworth name for the thirty-two Canadian outlets, mostly in Ontario, which came into the merger. By 1933 there were 136 Woolworth outlets in Canada, with sales of $15.3 million and with a net return on capital of 26.71 per cent.[24] Metropolitan Stores, incorporated in Canada only in 1920, had about forty-nine Canadian outlets by 1933, and most of them were in Ontario.[25] Kresge opened its first Canadian store, in Kitchener, only in May 1929, but by 1933 there were forty-four Kresge stores, from Quebec to British Columbia.[26] In 1928 Zeller's Limited was organized in London, Ontario, to operate a chain of 'five and dime stores' in competition with the three large American chains, all firms with which Walter P. Zeller had formerly worked. A few months later, before the Zeller chain had expanded outside London itself, an American holding company bought the firm and set about extending it.[27]

Paralleling the development of the variety stores was the twentieth-century growth of the great department stores. Until the 1920s, Eaton and Simpson branches were few. In 1905 the Robert Simpson Company, aided by funds from the Bank of Commerce, bought Murphy's department store in Montreal.[28] It also made gradual and modest acquisition of manufacturing firms, the largest being bought in 1913, and buying agencies were opened in Paris and London. But by 1912 the firm was in financial difficulties, owing $2 million to the bank and another $1 million to trade creditors: it was necessary to sell bonds and preferred shares in London[29] – and perhaps to be cautious about more expansion for the time being. Eaton also set up its first branch, in Winnipeg, in 1905. But Sir John Craig Eaton, who took over the family business in 1907, seems to have been more interested in the mail-order business. Perhaps it is not surprising, then, that it was he who opened the company's first local mail-order office, at Oakville, in 1916. A few others followed. The logic of this operation was impeccable: the post office had ceased to deliver parcels to farms, but at local offices the farmers could place orders in person, and collect their goods, the items having been delivered from Eaton's Toronto warehouses. Sir John Eaton also pioneered the self-service 'grocerteria' [sic], as it was called at first. In 1917 he opened one in his Winnipeg store and soon afterward did the same in Toronto.[30] Major chain development, however, would have to await Sir John's departure.

On Sir John's death in 1922 Robert Young Eaton took over the firm. Almost at once there was a rapid expansion of Eaton retailing. A Montreal store was acquired in 1925, and a store in Regina was opened in 1926. More groceterias were established. Some were acquired with the absorption of the Canadian Department Stores, but many more were new foundations. By 1931 there were forty-four Eaton groceterias in Ontario, including those in the small department stores; in all Canada, by 1934, there were seventy-two, of which fifty-seven were entirely separate from other Eaton stores.[31] These figures did not include the grocery and groceteria departments in the large stores such as that in Toronto. New order offices also sprang up: in 1926–9, there were 100 across the dominion. In 1927 the first Eaton Ontario branch department store appeared in Hamilton. In 1928 Eaton bought the Canadian Department Stores, a bankrupt merger of 1926 that had twenty-one rather small outlets, all but one in Ontario, including centres such as Ottawa. In 1929 stores were opened in Saskatoon, Calgary, and Edmonton. Eaton also established several Teco department stores in various centres outside Ontario. And in 1927 it began to develop its large new College Street site, where, in 1930, it opened the first element in the immense and lavish merchandising palace that it hoped to complete at some later time.

The growth of the Eaton business was spectacular, especially if viewed from a long perspective. Assets rose from $885,000 in 1891, the year of incorporation, to $107.7 million in 1931.[32] Sales rose from $1.6 million in 1891 to $125 million in 1921 and to $172 million in 1931.[33] By 1933 the Toronto stores provided 26.2 per cent of the turnover, the mail-order business another 26.8 per cent, the chain operations of groceterias, smaller department stores, and the like, 10.4 per cent; the rest of the business was done at the department stores in Montreal and in the west.[34] The expansion of the late 1920s seemed to create financial strains. In 1929 Eaton was obliged to borrow for the first time. It created the T. Eaton Realty Company, which issued $12 million in first-mortgage bonds;[35] the firm also raised $12 million in preferred shares, which were held within the Eaton family.[36]

The Robert Simpson Company was less adventurous. It never tried to set up a network of smaller retail stores, as Eaton did in the 1920s; it restricted its expansion to the construction of large downtown stores, and even in 1938 it had such stores only in Toronto, Montreal, Regina, and Halifax,[37] the latter two being no more than retail salesrooms in the catalogue order offices. By 1934, furthermore, there were thirty-five Ontario catalogue order offices and 'merchant agents', and 101 mail order selling departments nationwide. But the Toronto retail store still dominated the business: in the year ending 27 January 1915 it contributed 59 per cent of the Simpson firm's turnover, and in the year ending 3 January 1934, 63 per cent of a turnover that had increased 160 per cent in the intervening nineteen years.[38] In Michael Bliss's biography of Sir Joseph Flavelle, who had bought into the Simpson business in 1898 and who controlled it from 1920 to 1929, there is some suggestion that the aging tycoon had become unwilling to take large risks.[39] In 1920 there was a chance to merge with the Hudson's Bay Company, but Flavelle rejected the opportunity. Later in the decade Simpson decided not to follow Eaton to College Street or to branch all over the province. But the business remained attractive. In the late 1920s there were several American offers of purchase, and when, in 1929, C.L. Burton and the stockbroker H.J. Gundy bought out Flavelle and his associates, they had no trouble raising $10 million from the Toronto banks.[40] Nor did Gundy find it difficult to sell millions of dollars' worth of bonds and stocks to the public.

In the euphoric atmosphere of the late 1920s it was easy to exaggerate the profit-possibilities of expansion, and doubtless in later decades the Eaton family must have regretted the unwieldy commitment to the College Street store, which traded at a loss in the early 1930s. Indeed, so did the whole Eaton empire – groceterias, College Street, mail-order, Canadian Department Stores, and so on.[41] Simpson's did rather better than Eaton's in the slump: gross of depreciation the firm ran at a profit throughout the bad years of the early 1930s, although it did not cover depreciation in 1932 and although its mail-order division was not profitable from 1929 at least through 1933.[42] Perhaps there was something to be said for caution. None the less, one can see why chain department stores on the new Eaton model looked more sensible and attractive after 1919 than before 1914. Farmers, who were buying more cars and driving them on much improved roads, were far more mobile in the 1920s than before 1914. Meanwhile, the array of 'new' consumer goods was expanding very rapidly, and many country storekeepers would probably not have wanted to stock the new goods, if only because sales would be unpredictable, small, or both.

Even in the 1930s there were still new opportunities to be seized. At first it may seem paradoxical to find new outlets appearing in these times of trouble, but there were pockets of cheer. Thus one finds Eaton opening a new store in the gold-mining city of Kirkland Lake. And it is worth remembering that by the end of the decade there were 20 per cent more cars on the province's roads than there had been in 1929, while a whole range of consumer durable goods, such as radios, refrigerators, and electric stoves, had become much more common during the depression decade. There was money around, for those who could seize it from the consumer. Also, there were some really new technological possibilities to be exploited even in the 1930s – the frozen food display cabinet, the glassine package for meat, and, most important of all, the supermarket.

The Rise of Chain Retailing

It is safe to say that in 1867 Ontario contained no chain stores. There were still only a few at the turn of the century. Among these were the retail clothing stores of Grafton and John Northway. Grafton began in 1853 as a dry-goods and mens' clothing store in Dundas. The first branch was established in 1889; by 1905 there were six branches, plus the Dundas head office. The firm did a little manufacturing but bought most of its stock.[43] As for John Northway, the English-born entrepreneur had begun by opening a Tillsonburg tailoring shop in 1873. By 1900 Northway operated at least five stores and a manufacturing plant that made coats and suits; he was importing textiles direct from Britain, and in 1903 he opened his first

Toronto store.[44] Fifteen retail meat markets were operated by the William Davies Company, a rapidly expanding network in the Toronto area: by 1904 there were forty Davies stores in Ontario, and the firm was contemplating a Montreal operation.[45] There was also the three-shop grouping of the Hamilton grocer William Carroll, who had opened his first store in 1893 and who is said to have pioneered 'cash-and-carry' marketing of groceries.[46] These early firms were not self-service, nor did they have large floor areas. They grew by multiplication, propelled by entrepreneurial initiative, the ploughing-back of profits, and the power of bulk buying, doubtless assisted by bank credit. After all, what sort of loan could more readily be self-liquidating than the loan secured on retail stock in trade?

By 1914 food retailing had still not changed very much, except in certain technological respects – meat slicers, more prepackaged goods, the beginnings of refrigeration. Perhaps the most interesting development had been the advent of pure-milk dairying, with door-to-door deliveries, in the larger centres. Although cash-and-carry had made some inroads by 1914, retailers still normally gave credit, and in the cities and towns they generally delivered. Indeed, delivery had become more common with the spread of telephone ordering, an important development of the years between 1890 and 1914. The motor car was being used to make deliveries, although horse-traction and bicycle power were still much more common.[47] But the impact of other technological innovations was being felt: cash registers, computing scales, typewriters, coffee grinders, cheese cutters, and electric lights were proliferating.[48]

With the last years of the war, change came fast. First of all, cash-and-carry selling began to spread, partly because during the war it had become difficult to maintain delivery systems. Stores seized the opportunity to shed the costs of delivery. Carroll's of Hamilton, which had always operated on this basis, was expanding: in 1920 Carroll had eighteen stores, deriving, as he himself explained, advantages from this aspect of his business and from efficiencies in buying and warehousing.[49] He could often buy direct from manufacturers and often could so so on specially favourable terms. Arnold Brothers, who operated four stores in Toronto, also operated on the cash-and-carry basis; furthermore, unlike most grocery stores, they sold meat and fish as well.[50] The William Davies Company now operated thirty-eight stores in the Toronto area, another eleven elsewhere in Ontario, and sixteen in Montreal. From its Hull packing house, Matthews-Blackwell operated one retail butcher shop in Hull and thirteen in Ottawa.[51] These old-established chains would expand later: for instance, in 1923 Carroll had forty-six outlets and was enlarging his warehouses.

The wholesale grocers were continuing the battle for monopoly control that they had been waging since the setting-up of the Wholesale Grocers' Guild in 1883. Although the dominion's pre-war attempt at anti-combines action had not been successful, the old guild had lapsed about 1913. But its successor, the Wholesale Grocers of Ontario (WGO), pursued the old tactics with the old weapons. It did not try to fix retail prices, but it worked hard to ensure that manufacturers would sell only to wholesalers, not to retailers or to co-operatives; its main weapon was the boycott. Of some eighty wholesale grocers in the province in 1919, seventy-two or seventy-three belonged to the grouping. The direct result of its activity was trouble for the United Farmers of Ontario (UFO), whose co-operative had to buy its own wholesale grocery firm to acquire supplies from manufacturers. Similarly, when some sixty Toronto retailers formed the York Trading Company (YTC) as a wholesale grocery firm, the WGO was extremely reluctant to admit the YTC to membership, arguing that the new firm was 'not really' a wholesale grocer at all.[52]

The links in the chains of distribution were already numerous, and the structure could be complicated. Butter, cheese, and other farm produce might be bought direct from the farmers, even by quite large enterprises, which might also buy from creameries, as the Davies company did. As for the smaller corner stores, perhaps a Dundas Street grocer was typical: he reported that a Richmond Hill farmer provided him with supplies, coming down with the goods on the radial railway. It was common for farmers to sell livestock to drovers, who in turn brought the live animals to the stockyards, where they were sold, usually through commission merchants, and bought either by retail butchers or by packing companies; the slaughtering, in turn, was a matter for specialist abattoirs. In the Ottawa Valley the 'travellers' of the Matthews-Blackwell packing house visited each town weekly, calling on each butcher. But although most retail butchers bought from the packing houses some bought direct from farmers, and by 1919 the UFO had its own commission agent in Toronto's Union Stockyards, the intention being to bypass the drovers. There was also a UFO retail store that sold farm produce, butter, and eggs. But it did not sell more cheaply than ordinary retail stores, and E.C. Drury argued that it should not: 'There is no reason why we should ... you should not expect philanthropy in a business concern.'[53]

The information on margins, profits, and turnovers at the end of World War One is fragmentary at best, and one cannot be sure how representative the figures are. The William Davies Company reported that in its retail stores the cost of doing business, not including the costs of goods sold, was 27.5 per cent of turnover. The Matthews-Blackwell Company reported a net profit of 2 to 3 per cent on turnover – a much higher figure than today's supermarket chains can generally show. H.C. Beckett, a wholesale grocer from Hamilton who had an annual turnover of $2 million, a year-end inventory of $300,000, a capital of $400,000, and over twenty 'travellers' on the road, reported that the cost of his business was about 10 per cent of turnover. As for retail trade, matters are confused, because many proprietors paid themselves a salary, counting profits only after deducting that amount, while others did not, and comparatively few seem to have charged themselves interest on their own capital, or rent on any shop and residential properties that they might own and use. A high-class Toronto grocer who kept two horses and a Ford for delivery in Rosedale reported a net profit of 20 per cent on gross turnover of $66,000; an Avenue Road grocer who also served the carriage trade reported a turnover of $90,000, and kept four delivery wagons, but said he had made no profit for the past two years; a small corner grocer on Dundas Street, who lived above the shop, earned $2,000 on a turnover of $28,000, and charged himself no rent.[54]

It would be unwise to place too much credence in these fragmentary and incoherent reports. Nonetheless, they seem to carry certain implications with respect to the prospects in retail grocery selling. First of all, wholesalers were obliged to maintain considerable numbers of travellers; indeed, they argued that it was this service that induced manufacturers to sell through them, because the costs of direct sale would be higher – an argument that assumes that each manufacturer would have to maintain his own platoon of travellers. But of course a chain merchandiser needs no travellers: he simply supplies his own shops from his own warehouse; manufacturers can sell direct to the warehouse at very little cost. Second, the gross margins in wholesaling were considerable – certainly large enough to suggest that one might do well by 'cutting out the middleman.' Third, retail trade was anything but unprofitable; new retail outlets, whether chain or independent, might confidently be predicted on the basis of the reportage of the preceding paragraph. Finally, the position of the wholesaler, especially in the grocery trades, was entrenched merely because the retail trade was so fragmented; it was that fragmentation that gave the wholesaler a cost advantage from the manufacturer's viewpoint. Anything that changed the organization of retail trade would at once affect the manufacturer's cost calculation. Thus it is interesting to note that although the Davies and Matthews-Blackwell stores did not always buy from their parent packing houses, they did not buy from wholesalers either.

Although chain retailing had begun to affect the food trades before 1919, the real transformation began in that year and is closely associated with Dominion and Loblaw's. In this transformation Loblaw's, although adhering closely to American models, may properly be given pride of place.

Theodore P. Loblaw began work with the Toronto grocer W.C. Cork at 400 King Street East, in 1889. In 1894 he moved to another store, which Cork bought in 1896. Loblaw became a partner in 1898 and sole owner in 1900, while Cork began again. In 1910 Loblaw began to assemble his chain, which at first was neither cash-and-carry nor self-serve. Having failed in an attempt to bring together his own buying group of independents, he opened a second store so as to gain economies of large scale.[55] In 1918 he converted his stores to cash-and-carry. The change required him to buy specially heavy paper bags, and perhaps it cost him some customers, but one manager reported that the business had not suffered. People would take things home in baby carriages, and there was 'a plentiful supply of small boys with sleighs to handle the heavier articles.'[56] In 1919, when he had sixteen stores, he was taken over by F.E. Robson, a grocery broker, who in turn sold out to the group that was launching Dominion Stores – a firm that was substantially American-owned but managed and directed in Canada. Loblaw became the Toronto manager for the United Farmers of Ontario. At that time, having visited several American cities and having seen the self-service system in operation, he decided to introduce it to Toronto; late in 1919, associating himself yet again with W.C. Cork, he opened his first 'grocerteria' while at first retaining his connection with the UFO. Cork reported the results: a sharp reduction in the necessary staff, and economies from buying in large quantities. There was, he admitted, as yet no practicable way to handle bread, milk, and certain other perishables, and there was some concern about the quality of self-serve fruit and vegetables. Yet by December there were already almost a dozen 'grocerterias' in Toronto, and Cork was sure they had 'come to stay.'[57]

Meanwhile, the new owners of the old Loblaw chain were making rapid progress. Having become Dominion Stores, they were opening one or two new outlets a week. The first Dominion store was opened on 23 May 1919, and Robson shortly sold the old Loblaw outlets to Dominion, which had begun with only two stores of its own. By 1925 there were 354 Dominion stores, and in 1931, 575. Loblaw's expansion was less rapid, partly because he aimed to have larger stores, with extreme standardization of the kind that Piggly Wiggly had pioneered in the United States and Safeway and Piggly Wiggly were bringing to western Canada. By 1925 there were twenty-nine Loblaw grocerterias, and in 1929, eighty-seven in Ontario and another seventy-eight or more in New York State. Dominion was expanding by merger and by purchase, as well as through the opening of its own new branches. In December 1929 it bought a small chain of stores in Ottawa, and two years later there were rumours that it would absorb Stop and Shop (formerly Arnold's). The full merger did not take place, but Dominion did buy twelve Stop and Shop outlets.[58] In 1929 there was discussion of a Dominion-Loblaw merger. The two firms signed an agreement to form a new holding company, close the Dominion warehouse, and jointly compete with A&P. The merger fell through, however, because of the stock market collapse of autumn 1929.[59]

Meanwhile, old chains expanded and new ones appeared. By 1929 there were ninety-seven Carroll outlets, with a turnover of $2.8 million, and 160 Stop and Shop stores with a turnover of a $8 million.[60] A&P, which had been well established in the United States by 1920, launched itself in Ontario in 1928, and in 1929 it had seventy-seven stores in the province; its national turnover was $9 million from 200 stores. These chains, like Dominion, were not self-service, and offered delivery, although most of their business was cash-and-carry.[61]

Besides the chain stores that were corporations under single ownerships, there were the buying groups, which associated independent retailers with one another, and with wholesalers and jobbers, in a variety of ways. The first appeared in the 1890s as an answer to department store competition, and they were not restricted to food retailing, where they expanded partly in response to the corporate food chains, and partly as a way to avoid the evil ministrations of the wholesale grocers. By the mid-1920s there were large and effective buying groups in such commodities as hardware and shoes; indeed, the firms that came together to form the Canadian Department Stores had earlier been members of a single buying group. Sometimes a wholesaler or jobber might take the initiative in forming a group of associated retailers; sometimes the retailers themselves might take the initiative, either setting up their own wholesalers or signing a contract with one or more wholesalers. To make matters still more complicated, some buying groups were local, while others were province-wide or even national in their coverage; some specialized in areas such as groceries, while others dealt in other goods as well.[62]

It is obvious that in a general way the chain food stores, whether corporate or buying group, were riding the wave of expansion that characterized the mid- and later 1920s. One way to gauge their success is simply to note the rapidity of their growth; another is to observe the ease with which they could finance their expansion. Internally generated funds, it seems, could do much: in 1920 Carroll reported that one needed only $5,000 cash to run a 'normal average grocery store.'[63] In terms of expansion, therefore, a little retained profit could go a long way. As for external funding, share issues were few, and seem to have been taken up without difficulty, largely by the existing shareholders of the corporate chains. All these developments continued into the Great Depression and, indeed, long afterward.

Meanwhile, in 1933 the first stores called 'supermarkets' appeared.

They were in Toronto, and at first they were spartan operations with minimum fittings and furnishings – 'no frills' retail warehouses. Among the first were Carload Groceteria and Power Self-Service Grocery. Dominion and Loblaw's, however, moved in the same direction, responding to competition: by January 1939 three-quarters of all Loblaw's stores were of supermarket type.[64] And in the process Loblaw's grew and grew: in 1938 its turnover was $24 million while Dominion's was only $19.5 million, almost exactly the reverse of the situation that had existed in 1929–30. The T. Eaton Company, too, was moving toward gigantism: it reduced the number of its Ontario outlets from forty-one in 1929 to sixteen in 1938, and the total turnover of its grocery business seems to have diminished more than proportionately, while in 1936 it opened a huge 'Foodateria' in the basement of its Toronto store.[65]

Co-operative retailing, so popular in Europe at this time, was tried, but with little success. In 1908, for instance, the Brantford Co-operative Association began to sell groceries. It was quickly followed by others— at least eleven in the following two years and more thereafter. These experiments were various. But most of the early experiments failed. The most ambitious co-operative project was that of the UFO, who founded a co-operative in 1914. Beginning with a turnover of $33,000, the co-operative expanded quite smartly, and when T.P. Loblaw became general manager in 1919, it was decided to set up local branches. By 1920 there were forty in all. But Loblaw left in 1920, and in the slump of 1920–1 the retail outlets did not do very well. All the branches had to be liquidated, at a cost of $300,000 to the central co-operative.[66] The last United Farmers retail store closed in October 1922,[67] although in the late 1930s the central farmers' co-op began to distribute tractors and a wide range of electrical appliances.[68] Co-operative buying, in which independent retailers grouped themselves together, had considerably more success.[69]

Chains, of course, were not restricted to the food trades, and in other lines chain development began well before 1914. George Tamblyn opened his first drug store in Toronto in 1904, and his first branch in 1907; three more followed in 1908–9. In 1905 the Drug Trading Company Ltd was formed as a buying group to service the Independent Druggists' Alliance, which by the early 1930s numbered 935 stores.[70] Laura Secord began its operations in 1913, and although Hunt's Candy was incorporated only in 1919, the business antedated that year.[71] Still, as in the food trades, really dramatic changes would come only after 1919. In many lines of marketing there was considerable development during the 1920s – with results that architectural historians have sometimes called the 'homogenization of Main Street,' because in general the chains used standardized designs for their store fronts and often for their interiors as well.

In the clothing trades, as in food retailing, 1919 was a year of profit, worry, and change. E.R. Fisher, the Ottawa men's haberdasher whose business had been founded in 1905, reported a gross margin of 27.23 per cent and a net profit of 7.61 per cent on a turnover of $140,000. None the less, Fisher fulminated against the competition of a chain tailor, whose garments he said were badly made, not tailored at all, and simply steamed into a semblance of shape: 'Did you ever see a man who repeated [one of these orders]? ... I am selling suits, and they are selling rags. I have repeaters and they do not.' But as in the food trades there was scope to bypass the middleman: in 1919 Galt Brothers, a wholesale cloth dealer, said that their gross trading margin was 25 per cent. And although a Hamilton coal merchant claimed to make only 1.7 per cent on turnover, that narrow margin yielded 17 per cent on capital, while an Ottawa shoe retailer reported a net profit of $2,619 on a turnover of $52,000 and on an 'investment' of $19,000. Profits, it seemed, could be made in retailing, and the chain merchandisers were quick to seize them.[72] Many familiar names were already well established and expanding fast during the 1920s – Tamblyn, Metropolitan Stores, Zeller, Liggett, Owl Drug, Laura Secord, Dack, Agnew-Surpass, Hunt, Murray, Honey Dew, and of course the chains of service stations – Imperial, British American, McColl-Frontenac. The brothers A.J. and John Billes opened the first Canadian Tire store in 1922, and in 1934 they began to look for associate dealers – locally-owned enterprises that would use the firm's logo and sell its line of goods. This early example of franchising was highly successful: by 1939 there were seventy-one such dealerships, mostly in Ontario and in the Maritimes. Bata did not yet operate in Canada: the Czech refugee industrialist would not arrive in Frankford, Ontario, until 1939.

During the 1920s there were also some interesting instances of vertical integration, in which manufacturers acquired the firms that processed or distributed their outputs. Thus in the 1920s the milling companies began to buy bakeries. The first to do so was Maple Leaf, which acquired control of Canada Bread in 1922. In 1928–30, Lake of the Woods and Ogilvie did likewise, and so did Western Canada Flour Mills. The result was a noticeable but not complete control of further processing. In Toronto, by 1933, 55 per cent of all the bakers' bread was made in miller-controlled bakeries; in Hamilton the percentage was only 32 per cent, but in Ottawa it was 65 per cent.[73]

The chains' idea was to eliminate the middleman by servicing their branches from their own warehouses. Perhaps, as contemporaries sometimes observed, some such form of mass distribution was needed to fill the gap that might otherwise have yawned between mass production and mass consumption;[74] it should be remembered that although there had been brand names and brand advertising before World War One, the 1920s certainly saw a transformation in the scale both of branding and of promotion. The chain movement changed the face of retailing, as independents cleaned up their stores, paid closer attention to management, and priced their goods more carefully.[75] Ordinary food wholesalers meanwhile merged, and lost power and influence.[76] The result was a major shake-out in the province's distributive trades. It has been suggested that the origin was the pressure from the expanding department stores in the late nineteenth century.[77] But the real spur for chain development was felt only after 1919, especially through the competition resulting from the growth of the great proprietary food chains, particularly Loblaw's and Dominion, and later in the 1920s the A&P. Meanwhile, as was noted above, independent grocers responded by grouping themselves into buying groups, with standardized store fronts and some specialized branding and packaging.

What was the result? Did the chains drive out the independents? Did wholesalers become extinct? What about department stores in relation to the new chain grocery enterprises? Perhaps to its own surprise, the Royal Commission on Price Spreads discovered that in the textile trades the role of the chain merchandisers was still surprisingly modest. In 1933 the primary cotton textile industry sold 58.3 per cent of its output to manufacturers, 18.3 per cent to wholesalers and jobbers, only 14.9 per cent to department and chain stores, and 8.5 per cent to other types of retail traders.[78] As for hosiery, in 1933 the chains took 12.5 per cent of output, the department stores and mail order houses 25.3 per cent, and the wholesalers 17.4 per cent; almost all the rest went directly to independent wholesalers and to consumers.[79] These figures, of course, are no more than an indication; so far as market shares and numbers of sellers are concerned, the last section of this chapter will present a fuller answer. First, however, it is necessary to survey the drink trades.

The Drink Trades: Taverns, Hotels, Bottle Shops, and Other Watering Places

The drink trades are of special interest for many reasons. First of all, at Confederation they were among the most widespread and most successful of Ontario's retail businesses. Second, because the trades were licensed and regulated there are reasonably good statistical data with which their fates can be traced. Third, because 'beverage alcohol' was a focus for reformist agitation and prohibitionist sentiment, government policy mattered much more for the drink trades than for most other economic activities in the province. From almost all viewpoints, therefore, the drink trades are *sui generis* – certainly odd enough to deserve their own section in this narrative.

In 1871, according to *Lovell's Directory*, there were in Ontario 2,756 hotels and inns, of which sixty-one had associated stores. There were, in addition, 759 taverns and saloons, and ninety-three retail shops that claimed to sell liquor – a considerable understatement, since, though most retail food stores sold drink, few shops included the relevant tag in their directory descriptions. The total size of the drink-trading network was thus at least 3,608 retail establishments, in a year when there were about 2,926 country general stores, about 1,691 grocery stores, about 1,073 butcher shops, and about 1,131 stores that sold apparel.[80] There is no information about turnover, but in comparison with other retail trading networks the beverage business had more outlets than any other sort of retail trade in the province. Scanning the directory entries for towns and villages, one finds that hotels were at least as common as stores. In addition, in the 1870s the province's grocery wholesalers normally sold drink as well,[81] so that the drink trades were even larger than they might seem if only the retail networks are examined.

The directory categories are not precisely the same as those that the licensing authorities used. Yet the licensing series, which begins in 1874, confirms the impression given by the directory entries. In 1874 there were in Ontario 4,793 'licensed taverns', a figure that presumably includes all the licensed hotel premises, and in addition there were 1,307 shops licensed to sell beverage alcohol. Adding the small numbers of wholesale and vessel licences one gets a total of 6,185 points of sale – a remarkable figure for a province of only 1.6 million people of all ages in 1871. There were, in fact, 262 Ontarians per licence, and some 338 Ontarians per tavern. This was the well-watered soil on which the flower of the temperance movement would shortly bloom. In the circumstances, its growth should surprise nobody.

In the drink trades, as in many other matters, there was at first some confusion as to which level of government could do what. The dominion could and did provide for local prohibition, but the province distributed the licences for wholesale and retail trade; furthermore, by 1900 it was clear that the provincial legislature, if it wished, could prohibit the sale and consumption of alcoholic drink, though not its manufacture, anywhere in Ontario. The result was a changing patchwork of 'dry' and 'wet.' In 1877–9, eleven Ontario counties were 'dry,' in whole or in part, under an 1864 statute of the province of Canada. The cities in these counties, however, were all 'wet.' With the passing of the new Canada Temperance Act in 1878 the situation changed, although some 'dry' areas certainly continued. In the 1880s there was a renewed wave of county-wide prohibition, this time under the new Dominion Act, but again inapplicable within the cities of the province. In addition, under 'local option' arrangements, much smaller areas could again vote for local prohibition. By the beginning of 1916, 357 municipalities of all sorts – townships, villages, towns, and cities – had done so.[82] These municipalities, naturally enough, received no licences, whether for hotels, taverns, or shops. But although it was illegal to sell the evil stuff in a 'dry' area, it was not illegal to drink it in such places.

Agitation for prohibition was of course continual, and after 1890 it grew shriller, so that the drink trade was under increasing pressure. By that time grocery wholesalers had generally withdrawn from the trade, and the number of wholesale licences had fallen from a peak of 147 in 1876 to only twenty-one in 1891. Temperance agitation was one reason for the withdrawal of the wholesalers, and another was the growth of general grocery business, such that wholesalers could specialize in it. Yet another reason was a change in pricing: by ordering ten barrels of liquor at a time, a retailer could buy on the same terms as a wholesaler, and there was nothing to prevent several retailers from clubbing together and then dividing the ten barrels that they had jointly ordered. Those wholesalers who continued in the trade were said to specialize in the more exclusive imported liquors, eschewing the local product.[83]

It is apparent that the drink trades were not 'growth industries.' From 1874 to 1915 the number of licensed taverns declined from 4,793 to 1,224, or by 75 per cent. As for those shops licensed to sell spirits, wine, or beer by the bottle, the decline is even more sharp – 84 per cent. The years during which county prohibition was widespread, in the 1870s and again in the 1880s, show especially sharp declines. But even when these perturbations are set aside, the downward drift remains. The same pattern, a diminishing number of outlets, appears in every city and in every county.

This contraction of the retail trade matched the decline of per capita consumption, which, in so far as spirits and wine were concerned, was so marked a feature of the later nineteenth century. As official statistics reveal,[84] per capita consumption was falling, and falling fast. In 1874 spirits consumption was just under two gallons per head. In 1898 it was barely half a gallon, and even in 1911–13 it barely passed the one-gallon level. Over the same period per capita wine consumption fell by more than two-thirds, and even in 1913–14 it was less than half what it had been in the early 1870s. Per capita beer consumption, however, increased several-fold. Like that of spirits, beer consumption fell away in the late 1870s, but by 1913–14 it had risen to more than double the level of the mid-1870s.

These data are quite suggestive. Those for the last quarter of the nineteenth century cause one to suspect either a very marked change in relative prices, for which there seems to be no satisfactory evidence, or a very deep-running change in consumer preferences – a change that expressed itself both at the cash desk and at the ballot box. Other things being equal, such a change would surely create room for other sorts of consumer purchases, and thus for other industries and for other sorts of retail marketing. Of course the data might also be thought to reflect a general impoverishment, but other evidence suggests that no such thing occurred. After 1900, however, there is a drift back to the bottle. Whether one looks at wine, beer, or spirits, per capita consumption was unequivocally rising. Admittedly the per-capita consumption data apply to the entire dominion, but there is no reason to doubt that they apply with fair accuracy to Ontario. The upward drift is hard to reconcile with any hypothesis of general impoverishment, but it may have implications for the efficiency of the work-force, just as the 'temperance decades' of the late nineteenth century may imply more diligent and efficient hands. On the other hand, since people were tending to drink more – and the data were widely publicized – it is easy to understand why the professional temperance forces became ever more angry and ever more vocal. It must have seemed that the decades of persuasion, propaganda, and legislative effort might not, after all, be paying off.

At the time of World War One came renewed temperance propaganda, further reductions in the number of licensed premises, substantial declines in per capita consumption, and, in 1916, a form of general, province-wide prohibition. The Ontario Temperance Act, which took effect on 7 September 1916, did not prohibit the production, warehousing, transport, or consumption of beverage alcohol.[85] But ordinary citizens could buy beverage alcohol within the province only on a doctor's prescription, only for medical reasons, and only in bottle. No alcohol was to be sold by the glass, nor could it be consumed on the premises of the vendors. For the convenience of the public there were to be 'Standard Hotels,' designated by the authorities and endowed with semi-monopoly over the sale of 'all non-intoxicating drinks and beverages, cigars, cigarettes, and tobacco'; the hotels could also conduct an 'ice cream shop or general restaurant or cafe without further licence.'[86] It should be noted that the Standard Hotels could not sell wine or beer, although they could sell 'near-beer' – a malt beverage of very low alcohol content, so weak that it was not defined as beverage alcohol at all. Soon after the introduction of prohibition, some 1,372 Standard Hotels were believed to be in operation. As for the Ontario wineries, they were allowed to sell their product with little restriction, but only in lots of five gallons or more. At first there was nothing to prevent anyone from buying alcohol outside the province, and evidently many of the more prosperous did so, although during the brief period of dominion prohibition their style must have been cramped somewhat. But in 1920 the provincial legislature stopped the relevant bolt-hole; it was now illegal to transport 'liquor' for sale in Ontario.[87]

At first, most points of sale were pharmacies. By February 1918 there were some 1,250 of these. In addition there were four 'licensed vendors,' and only these could sell in bottles of more than six ounces. By early 1919 there were seven such vendors, and in June 1919 the provincial government took them over from their private owners, thus establishing 'Government Dispensaries' – two in Toronto and one in each of Hamilton, London, Windsor, Kingston, and Ottawa. In 1921 an eighth dispensary was opened in Fort William. The dispensaries sold liquor in large bottles across the counter, and carried on a considerable mail-order business. All their retail business was supported by doctors' prescriptions. They also supplied druggists, whose number was multiplying rapidly in the face of this new opportunity. In the first full year of the dispensaries' operation their turnover was $3.36 million, and their net profit was $860,000 – dramatic proof of the money that was to be made in the drink trade, even under close restriction. There were, in addition, some fifty native wine producers who could sell their product in bulk. The authorities soon began to monitor the prescribing practices of physicians, and they were worried by the proliferation of druggists. Originally club licences were not to be issued, but in 1925 it became legal for 'any club' to receive a vendor's permit, thus clearing the way for the efflorescence of the Canadian Legion, and perhaps giving the Orange Order a new lease of life.

The 1926 election brought a retreat from prohibition, and on 1 June 1927 new arrangements, which present-day Ontarians would find familiar, came into effect. Wine, beer, and spirits could now be bought without prescription, but only by licensed purchasers, and only from authorized vendors – the government stores of the Liquor Control Board (LCBO), brewers' warehouses, and native wine producers. On 'opening day' there were sixteen LCBO stores; by the end of 1927 there were eighty-six, and also eighty-six brewers' warehouses and some fifty vendors of native wines. Thus the number of stores was rising sharply, as was the turnover. In 1931–2 there were 124 LCBO stores, with a turnover of $45.8 million, and 102 brewers' warehouses, as well as forty-nine wineries. The number of consumer-licences was now over 368,000. For the first two years of the new system, licences were not required for the purchase of native wine. But with the discovery that much of this 'wine', which the statute did not define precisely, had an alcohol content of 27 per cent or more, permits were required, starting in 1929–30.

There was still no provision for the sale of any 'liquor,' which meant any beverage possessing more than 2.5 per cent alcohol, by the glass, although 'near-beer' was allowed, thus providing the first stones in the foundation for the 'beer parlour' or 'beverage room.' In 1934 the law was amended in a most important way. Now there was provision for the sale of wine and beer by the glass, though only in certain carefully defined circumstances. These goods could be sold 'in standard hotels, and in such other premises as the regulations may provide and define.'[88] Beer was only to be sold in places 'to which the sale, serving, and consumption of beer shall be restricted and defined.' Wine was to be sold only for consumption with meals. There were specific provisions for licensing veterans' clubs and union halls. There could be no 'bars or counters' over which wine or beer might be served; all patrons were to be seated decorously, at tables. Finally, 'light beer' of less than 2.5 per cent alcohol was still not to count as 'liquor.'

The new arrangements had a dramatic effect on the hotel industry. In 1871 the province contained 2,756 hotels, in 1930, 1,604, and in 1941, 1,762; during the 1930s the number of rooms and other units of accommodation rose from 39,052 to 45,504.[89] In 1930, naturally, the hotels drew no revenue from 'liquor,' because they were not allowed to sell it. Although some hotels made something by selling near-beer, this watery product has never been popular in Canada, and the dominion's statisticians did not separately identify it. 'Other sources,' which must contain any near-beer receipts, amount to only 14.1 per cent of the hotels' total gross revenue in 1930. By 1941, however, 60.1 per cent of all hotel revenue in Ontario came from beer and wine – almost all of it from beer. Thus the 'beverage rooms,' or beer parlours, were floating the hotel industry back to a prosperity that it cannot have enjoyed since 1916. Of course not all hotels were licensed, and 'motor courts,' 'motor hotels,' and 'motels,' which were beginning to appear in resort areas and on city outskirts during the 1930s, were especially likely not to be.

The retail trade in wine and spirits remained firmly under the control of the provincial liquor control board, which also licensed the hotels. Government liquor revenues fell off perceptibly in the early years of the Great Depression but then rebounded strongly, reaching $12.2 million by 1940–1. Beer consumption moved up smartly, rising from 21.6 million gallons in 1935–6 to 31.3 million in 1940–1. The consumption of imported wine and spirits, which were not much affected by the new regulations, did not show any pronounced trend. Indeed, even in 1940–1 Ontario was consuming only 60,000 gallons of imported wines, only 300,000 gallons of imported spirits, and only 1.2 million gallons of domestic spirits. Native wine consumption, however, had moved up considerably, rising from 1.4 million gallons in 1936–7 to 2 million in 1940–1.[90] In 1941, 130 LCBO stores produced a turnover of $33 million, while 136 brewers' warehouses received $20 million, and forty-nine wine stores, $2.5 million.[91] These figures may be compared with the 211 'shops' of 1915, or with the 1,307 'shops' of 1874.

The pattern of consumption continued to change. Drinkers were still shifting towards beer. In 1941, per capita beer consumption in Ontario was 8.26 gallons, while on the average each Ontarian consumed 0.54 gallons of wine and .296 gallons of spirits.[92] Thus there had been a continuing and very perceptible shift not only towards beer but also towards wine – hardly surprising, given the concessionary terms on which the Ontario local product was marketed, and the heavy 'fortification' that made Ontario pseudo-port and so-called sherry the cheapest routes to oblivion. It is symptomatic that in 1939, imported wine was less than 3 per cent of Ontario's wine consumption.[93]

The Ontario version of the 'great experiment' had a variety of unintended side-effects. First and most obviously, it transferred much of the drink trade into public ownership and created monopoly gains for those who received beverage-room licences during the 1930s and thereafter, for the native wine industry, and for those growers who produced the grapes on which that industry rested. Second, the mixture of temperance licensing, prohibition, and control restricted the field for small business and for individual endeavour in the retail drink trades. It would, admittedly, be hard to argue that Ontarians 'really needed' the number of retail drink outlets that existed in the early 1870s. Further, if one is right to suspect that there was a genuine change in tastes during the late nineteenth century, the trade would have contracted, or would have grown comparatively slowly, in any event. Urbanization, by concentrating the population, might also have been expected to reduce the ratio between population and watering places. Yet in many places the small bar or bottle shop has been a way by which the small man or woman could climb from wage-earning status to self-employment. In Ontario this path was first narrowed and then altogether closed. At best the result must have been to divert much talent into other lines of retail trade; at worst, it must have meant discouragement and frustration for many would-be entrepreneurs. Finally, restrictive licensing plus government monopoly naturally created opportunities for patronage, and these should not be ignored. Doubtless in addition there were more profound social and cultural effects; it is even possible that the experiment was worth what it cost. But the mandate of the economic historian does not extend to a consideration of these larger questions.

Conclusion: Old Trades and New Trading

This final section assembles statistical material from 1870 and 1871 and from the official census tabulations of 1923, 1930, and 1941, in the hope that these materials will serve to summarize and illuminate the process of change. For the nineteenth century, official data hardly exist, although the decennial censuses did record some relevant information about trades such as blacksmithing – trades that later statisticians would treat not as manufacturing or as industry but as 'retail services.' To fill in the many gaps that the census leaves, this section relies not only upon the 1870–1 census but upon province-wide data from a standard business directory for 1871. Early directories yield little more than a count of establishments, and they also pose serious problems of identification and definition before their information can be compared with the counts from the special Dominion Bureau of Statistics tabulation of 1923, which is thought to cover only two-thirds of the province's retail and wholesale establishments, or with the much more detailed, sophisticated, and comprehensive data for 1930 and 1941, when the distributive trades were examined in the course of decennial census-taking. Because the problems of comparability and coverage are so great, it seems better to embed the statistics in descriptive prose, rather than to present them in tabular forms that could easily mislead.[94]

First of all, thanks to economic growth and urbanization, the number of retail merchandising outlets clearly grew, and grew dramatically, from 1870–1 to the 1930s. In 1871, from directory entries, we can definitely identify 8,655 retail establishments, not including hotels, taverns, and establishments separately counted by the census. To this figure should probably be added the 851 merchants and dealers in general merchandise and the 661 dealers in tinsmithing, tinware, and stoves, as well as the 6,950 establishments in blacksmithing, boot and shoemaking, dressmaking, saddle- and harness-making, and tailoring, so that the total number of retail merchandising establishments in 1870–1 might be something like 17,117. In 1923 the incomplete census enumerated 21,892 separate retail establishments; in 1930 the census counted 43,045, and in 1941, 47,055. Obviously, the trend towards combination earlier described had not reduced the number of separate outlets; indeed, the reverse took place.

To these merchandising outlets must be added the places that sold services. In 1870–1 Ontario contained few of them, except for the 2,779 hotels, inns, and temperance houses, and the 759 saloons and taverns, which Lovell identified, and another 453 very miscellaneous establishments listed either by Lovell or by the census enumerators. There were, for example, three bowling alleys, three cleaners, ninety-seven photographic galleries, sixty-five laundries, two clock and watch repairers, 250 barbers and hairdressers – and exactly one theatre. To these figures should be added certain census categories – the 2,894 blacksmiths, the 1,965 boot-

and shoemakers, and the 676 harness-makers, all of whom presumably did some repair work. Altogether, and excluding hotels and taverns, there were something like 5,988 purveyors of services in 1870–1.[95] In 1930 there were 15,566 purveyors of retail services, and in 1941, 17,612. There were still 1,145 blacksmiths and shoers of horses and 178 harness repair shops in 1941, and in 1930 there were two legitimate theatres – not much growth since 1871! But in 1930 there were 324 motion picture theatres, and in 1941, 412. Nor had billiard and pool halls diminished: by 1941 they numbered 426, compared with three in 1871.

As for hotels and other licensed premises, the story was told in the last section and need only be summarized here. Lovell finds 3,538 such places in 1871, and at the beginning of the provincial licensing series in 1874 there were 4,793 'taverns,' a figure that presumably includes all the hotels. In 1941 Ontario contained 1,762 hotels, not all of which were licensed; there were no other licensed premises.

When one examines the 1930 and 1941 censuses in detail, one is struck by the enormous array of retail services, most of them the creations of the twentieth century, which the entrepreneurs of Ontario were then offering. In 1941, 606 establishments provided business services such as advertising and sign painting. There were 9,405 establishments providing personal services, including 3,165 barber shops and 2,106 beauty parlours; in 1870–1, as we saw above, there were only 250 barbers and hairdressers. In 1941 shoe-repair shops, in large part the successors to the 3,391 boot- and shoemakers of 1870–1, numbered 1,644, while cleaners and dyers numbered 937 – a far cry from the three that can be identified for 1871. Photography had expanded considerably – from ninety-seven establishments in 1870–1 to 378 in 1941. Undertaking had boomed, rising from no identifiable establishments in 1871 to 319 in 1930 and 445 in 1941. In fact, with the exception of undertaking, the great majority of the establishments in the repair and service group looked after commodities that had not existed in 1871 and that were still very rare or nonexistent at the end of the nineteenth century. In 1941 there were 3,559 establishments purveying repairs and services, not counting shoe repair shops. Of this total, 1,323 were concerned with blacksmithing and horse-coping, and another 291 repaired watches and jewellery; the remaining 2,236 establishments were concerned almost exclusively with electrical and automotive work.

Thus with the decline of the old service trades the new trades had boomed. Furthermore, the new service establishments, like the old, were still largely the preserve of the 'small man': chain operation was rare, and the establishments were still small. In 1941 the average turnover in the repair and service group was $3,969, while for retail service as a whole the figure was $6,434, and there were 12,226 unsalaried proprietors, plus many thousands who paid themselves a salary as well as sharing in profits.

For retail merchandise trade, of course, the picture is much more mixed, because of the rise of department stores and chain stores, two categories that did not exist in 1870–1. Country general stores were still numerous: there were 2,662 in 1930, and 2,350 in 1941, with an average turnover of $18,840 per store. In 1871 there were certainly 2,926 country general stores, and in addition there were 851 dealers in general merchandise, so that for comparative purposes the total might be 3,777. Whatever the correct figure for 1871, the total undoubtedly declined over the following seventy years. The decline, however, was probably less than many people, especially those worried by the largely mythic 'agricultural depopulation,' would have expected.

Food retailing, propelled by population growth, urbanization, and rising per capita real incomes, had expanded significantly. The development of pre-packaged and branded food products may also have played some part. In 1871 there were certainly 3,674 food shops, in 1930, 14,263, and in 1941, 14,019, with an average turnover of $22,440 per establishment. The 1930 and 1941 figures exclude those bakeries and dairies that reported to the census of manufacturing. In 1871 there were 747 bakers and nineteen dealers in dairy products within the total for food-retailing, while the 1870–1 census records the existence of 385 bakers, all or almost all of whom had a retail business; in 1941 there were 293 'bakery products stores' and 114 'dairy products stores,' not including the baking and dairying establishments that were defined as industrial. Thus even here, in spite of the intrusion of the factory, growth can be seen, especially when it is remembered that by 1941 such products were also being sold in various types of grocery store, including the new supermarkets.

For clothing and shoes the story is complicated in a similar way by the drift of production into factories after 1871. In 1870, according to the census, there were 473 dressmaking and millinery establishments, and 942 tailoring and clothing establishments, most of which presumably undertook a mixture of production and retail sale. There were also, according to *Lovell's Directory*, 118 clothing stores that are not subsumed under these categories, plus 39 identifiable boot and shoe stores, to which should presumably be added most or all of the census figure for boot- and shoemaking establishments: 1,965. Thus in 1870–1 there were some 3,537 apparel establishments, of which 3,380 were a 'pre-industrial' mixture of handicraft production and retail sale, while 157 were retail shops of a more 'modern' type. In 1930 the province contained 3,702 clothing stores and 782 shoe stores, so that the total of 4,484 is 27 per cent larger than our total for 1870–1; in 1941 there were 4,280 apparel shops and 788 shoe stores, and the total, 5,068, is 43 per cent larger than our 1870–1 figure. Thus, although production and sale had become separated long before 1930, there were far more retail outlets than there had been, and so far as employees and entrepreneurs were concerned, the movement towards factory work and wage labour was more than offset by the expansion in retail selling.

The statistics for the department stores and variety stores are confusing because they include order offices and mail-order businesses. In 1941 Ontario contained 247 'department stores and mail order houses or offices.' Their sales amounted to only 10.8 per cent of total provincial merchandise turnover, even though they included all the extra-provincial mail-order business of Eaton and Simpson. Even the raw percentage, however, is probably smaller than most observers would have expected. The same might be said of the general merchandise and variety stores, such as Woolworth and Kresge. In 1941 there were 1,005 such establishments in the province, but they did only 3.9 per cent of the retail business.

What of the wholesalers? So prominent at Confederation, especially in Toronto and Hamilton, the tribe of wholesalers might have been expected to vanish, or to dwindle markedly, during the transformation of merchandising that followed the development first of department stores and then of chain stores. In fact, nothing of the sort seems to have happened.

The directory count for 1871 reveals 430 'general agents and brokers' and 2,723 merchants and dealers, not including the 851 'general merchants.' In total, therefore, there might appear to have been as many as 3,153 wholesalers, but the actual figure must be a great deal less – something more than 430, but perhaps not a great deal more. Lovell reports 206 dealers in dry goods and apparel including 57 in dry-goods, 154 who dealt in groceries including tea, 151 who dealt in hardware, and only 7 identified wholesalers of tobacco and its products – a total of 518 establishments. The incomplete census of 1923 reports 1,120 wholesalers in Ontario, but this is evidently a serious under-count, as can be seen when the 1923 figure is compared with that for 1930, a year for which the census detected 2,004 'wholesalers proper' and 3,938 wholesalers in total, the difference consisting of manufacturers' sales branches, petroleum bulk stations, agents and brokers, and assemblers of primary products, such as farm goods and lumber. The larger figure, therefore, is the one that ought to be compared with the 1871 count: the comparison shows that the number of wholesalers had grown by 25 per cent in sixty years, in spite of all the changes in retail trading practice, even if one bases one's comparison on the unreasonable 1871 figure of 3,153; if one uses 518, the total of identified wholesalers as enumerated above, one gets a seven-fold increase.

The 1923 census, in spite of its inadequacies, did include tabulations that showed just how regionally concentrated wholesaling still was. Toronto reported 552 wholesalers, Hamilton sixty, Ottawa fifty-three, and London twenty-eight, while another ninety-one were scattered among Windsor, Brantford, Kitchener, Kingston, the Soo, Peterborough, and Fort William, leaving only 336 for the rest of the province. In this respect, at least, little had changed since 1871: wholesaling was still an activity for the larger centres, and pre-eminently for Toronto.

The expansion of wholesaling continued through the 1930s. In 1941 Ontario contained 6,244 wholesalers, and 3,539 'wholesalers proper.' In 1941 there were 1,534 wholesale food dealers of various kinds; in 1871 663 merchants and dealers who dealt in farm and food products can be identified. In these trades the growth of wholesaling had not been proportionate to the growth of the provincial economy, doubtless because of the changes in merchandising, yet expansion there had certainly been. Similarly, in 1941 there were 416 wholesalers, agents, and brokers who dealt in dry goods and apparel, of which only 41 dealt in shoes; in 1871 there had been 206, of which 137 dealt in shoes, and only fifty-seven in 'drygoods and fancy goods.' This comparison serves to emphasize that in the 1871 figure there are many who were not really wholesalers, especially among those who dealt in boots and shoes. But even if this problem is not taken into account, the data suggest a considerable expansion of soft-goods wholesaling, in spite of the department and chain stores.

Of course the chains did make a difference, even though it is not detectable until 1930, when, of the 43,045 retail merchandising establishments, 3,269 belonged to chains and another 1,746 to buying groups, while 36,760 were independent and another 1,270 were of other types. As was shown above, there might have been 17,117 retail merchandising establishments in 1870–1; obviously, therefore, the number of independent establishments had considerably more than doubled, in spite of the chains. Furthermore, even though 65 per cent of the buying group outlets and 74 per cent of the chain outlets dealt in foodstuffs, in 1930 there were still 9,395 food stores – more than double the count for 1871.

During the 1930s, while the chains and buying groups reduced the number of their food outlets, the independents proliferated, so that by 1941 the province contained 9,716 outlets that sold meat and groceries in various combinations – a larger total than in 1930. Of the 47,055 stores in the province 38,391, or 92.5 per cent, were 'single-store independents,' while 4.8 per cent belonged to'voluntary chains,' more conventionally called buying groups, and only 7.2 per cent were chain stores, a category that included the department stores. The remainder were 'other types' – a few industrial stores and leased departments or concessions. However. the

chains enjoyed 21 per cent of the sales, and the voluntary buying groups
4.1 per cent. Among grocery stores that did not sell meat, chains did 20.4
per cent of the business – substantially less than they had done in 1930;
voluntary chains, with 12.8 per cent of the turnover, also had less of the
business than in 1930. But the grocery group as a whole was doing less
business than in 1930 – $89 million as against $98 million – while the
'combination stores', which sold both meat and groceries, had almost
doubled their turnover in a decade, reaching $142 million in 1941. In this
category the chains had 55.7 per cent of the business in 1941, compared
with 41.3 per cent of a much smaller total in 1930, while the share of the
buying groups had fallen from 12.6 per cent to 6 per cent. Among meats
and seafood markets, the chains had only 8.9 per cent of the business, and
the buying groups had only another 0.1 per cent. But if the three categories
of food merchandising are aggregated it can be seen that in 1941 the
chains had 38.3 per cent of the business, and the buying groups had another
7.6 per cent. The age of the supermarket had only begun; in particular,
comparatively few chain outlets had parking lots, and none was located in
suburban shopping plazas, which did not yet exist. But the shape of the
future was already adumbrated in the food-merchandising patterns of the
early 1940s.

For other types of good there is not much sign of a common pattern.
Among variety stores, chains did 90 per cent of the business in 1941;
among filling stations, only 11.7 per cent, compared with 30 per cent in
1930. The figure for filling stations is surprisingly low, but it reflects the
fact that the census classification is based on ownership. Thus if Imperial
Oil, for example, gave franchises to dealers but did not own or manage the
filling stations, these stations appear as 'independent businesses' – logical
enough from one standpoint, but not in terms of the visual impact of the
omnipresent and standardized Imperial Esso station designs, colour
schemes, and logos. In the clothing trades the independents did just over 80
per cent of the business, but in shoe-merchandising the chains were making
rapid progress, having raised their total turnover from $3.4 million in 1930
to $8.8 million in 1941 and their share of the turnover from 21.5 per cent in
the former year to 43.4 per cent in the latter, a development that perhaps
reflected the arrival of the Batas in 1939. Among drug stores, the chains
had 20.4 per cent of the turnover in 1930 and 20.8 per cent in 1941. In
lumber, building material, and furniture the chains were of little importance, handling 11.8 per cent of the lumber turnover and 15.9 per cent of
the furniture turnover in 1941. The day of Beaver Lumber and Canadian
Tire had dawned. The chains handled 30 per cent of the turnover in
household appliances and radio merchandise; here one surely sees the
influence of the department stores.

Even in the difficult conditions of the 1930s the chains had not killed off the independents. Indeed, the number of independent outlets had increased, rising from 38,506 to 43,506, and the independents' turnover had risen by 28 per cent in eleven years, so that the turnover per shop had clearly risen, and the independents' share of total turnover, 79 per cent in 1930 and 78.8 per cent in 1941, was essentially unchanged. Among the chains the commercial demography was very different. From 1930 to 1941 the number of chain outlets rose only 3.5 per cent, while turnover rose 32.3 per cent. Obviously turnover per outlet was rising very substantially, and one may suppose that the result was more economical operation. Among the independents, on the other hand, it is tempting to see some sign of 'crowding,' in that the population of independent stores somewhat outgrew the population of the province during the 1930s.

Although the development of chains is dramatic enough, one must not forget that the development of new goods – especially the new consumer durable goods that, by 1941, decorated so many of the garages and urban households of the province – made equally dramatic changes in retailing and wholesaling. Whether one looks at one or at the other, the impact is apparent at once, and it is concentrated in the automotive trades, the electrical trades, and petroleum. In 1871 there were thirteen dealers in oil, and naturally nobody dealt in the other goods: kerosene was widely sold through the ordinary channels of trade, but specialized dealers were few. Lovell records only three 'coal oil stores.' By 1941 there were 284 wholesalers in the automotive field, including fifteen manufacturers' sales offices, and there were 156 wholesalers of electrical goods, including thirty-nine manufacturers' sales offices; there were seventeen wholesalers of petroleum and its products. It will be noted that the manufacturers themselves were doing some of the wholesaling in all three groups of goods, but they were certainly not doing all of it. Within retail merchandise trade, there were over 7,000 establishments in the automotive group, including 4,627 filling stations, and in addition, as we saw above, there were 1,015 auto repair and service establishments, which, presumably, did not sell gasoline. Furthermore, although many of these enterprises were linked with larger entities through various dealership and franchising arrangements, the large corporations owned very few of them. Among filling stations, for instance, only 5.7 per cent of the establishments were the property of chains. In terms of total turnover, the automobile dealers, all by themselves, were larger than the department stores! As for retail appliances and electrical goods, it must be remembered that many of these items were sold in department stores and in variety stores, so that the specialized dealers had only part of the business. Still, in 1941 there were 1515 establishments in the 'furniture-household-radio' group of retailers;

in 1871, one can find only 118 furniture, music, and toy stores and dealers. Presumably at that time a substantial part of the populace would have made their own furniture, or would have ordered direct from craftsmen. Still, it is striking that in 1941 the specialized dealers in radios and household appliances, who numbered 707, were six times as numerous as the furniture dealers had been in 1871. In addition, in 1941 Ontario could boast 141 electrical supply stores, and 194 establishments that repaired appliances and radios. To some extent the rising automotive trades should be set against the declining horse-coping trades, even though the former were considerably larger than the latter had been in 1871. But the electrical trades were wholly new.

Entertainment, health, and recreation had also been transformed, and the results show vividly in the roster of retail services. In 1871 there was one theatre in Ontario, and in 1930 there were two, plus some amateur and 'little' theatres that the census enumerators did not count. During many of the intervening years Ontario certainly contained many more theatres, vaudeville houses, and theatre-like halls; there is plenty of qualitative evidence, though no numerical summary count, attesting to the fact. During those intervening decades, furthermore, the county and local histories provide glimpses of the birth of the movies – a new and very different economy of entertainment, and one that had nothing to do with the legitimate theatre and not much to do with vaudeville and the music halls, even though to some extent it shared auditoria with these older forms of entertainment.[96] Stories of local initiative and success could be told for many places, and the result was straightforward enough: By 1930 there were 324 motion picture houses in Ontario, and in 1941, 412, with an average turnover of $46,000.

In all, the Ontario of 1941 contained 2,170 'places of amusement and recreation,' whereas in 1871 one can identify only thirty-five. In addition, in 1941 there were 3,063 restaurants, cafeterias, and other eating places, whereas for 1871 only fifty-five can definitely be identified, presumably because the hotels and taverns provided most of what food services there were. Even in 1941 eating places were, on the whole, not large: average turnover was only $14,800. To anyone who recalls the typical Ontario eatery of 1941 – or 1961 – the memory is not likely to be attractive, except for reasons of sentiment or nostalgia. But growth there had certainly been. The same could be said of the pharmacists, who numbered 463 in 1871, 1,464 in 1930, and 1,720 in 1941. Expansion, in this trade, had been spurred by the prohibition arrangements of 1916–27; a contraction had then followed, but expansion on a sounder basis was resumed during the 1930s.

All these new fields presented ideal opportunities for the 'small man.' In spite of chain penetration, even in 1941 the chains had only 4.5 per cent of the restaurant outlets, and only 13 per cent of restaurant turnover. As for the movie houses, there are no usable summary data, and it is certainly true that many of the major city outlets were owned and managed by the great foreign-based firms, such as Twentieth-Century, Odeon, and Famous Players. On the other hand, there were plenty of owner-operated movie theatres, especially in smaller centres, linked though they generally were to the chains through rental and franchising arrangements.

The overall picture is quite striking. In 1941 Ontario contained 47,055 retail stores, and 17,612 purveyors of retail services, plus 1,762 hotels, totalling 66,429 retail establishments of all kinds. In merchandise trade, there were 3,385 chain establishments. There are no such figures for the other two categories, but the number of proprietors is known, and this information suggests that it would be reasonable to divide 3,385 by 47,055 and apply the result, 7.2 per cent, to the total, thus calculating that in 1941 there were some 61,600 independent small retail businessfolk in Ontario. This is triple the number that can possibly have existed in 1871. Now, it is no mean achievement for an economy, in what some have called the 'era of finance capitalism' or even the 'era of monopoly capitalism,' to triple the number of such entrepreneurs, when the population had barely doubled. Thus there were far more small businessfolk in the Ontario of 1941 than there had been in 1870–1 – not only more traders but more farmers as well.

Similarly, the extent of commercial growth and the increase in the range and variety of consumer goods and services must prompt some reflection on the question of living standards. It has been seen above that, at least in the long run, the chains and the department stores did not grow by squeezing out the wholesaler and the independents; there proved to be room both for the new sorts of merchandiser and for the old. In much the same way, except with respect to the horse-servicing trades the expansion of new retail businesses was not at the expense of the old trades; rather than squeezing out the food and apparel trades or the trade in building materials, the newer trades such as electricity and the movies expanded in parallel with the older ones. Even in horse-coping, where the number of establishments had fallen by 2,423 since 1871, the decline of the horse trades had been swamped by the rise of the automotive trades, whose establishments numbered 13,036 in 1941.

These results – new up-market trades, a great expansion not only of retail and wholesale trade but of trades purveying comforts, conveniences, and luxuries, and an enormous increase in the range and the quality of the goods available for retail sale even in traditional trades such as food – are broadly consistent with the hypothesis that in the long run per capita real incomes were tending to rise. If living standards had been falling, surely retail trade would have developed along very different lines.

18 *Financial Evolution*

It was in the years before 1914 that Ontario's financial structure evolved into a shape that late twentieth-century observers would recognize. Except for the credit unions, which were of little importance until long afterward, the financial system took on a form that the quite dramatic disturbances of the 1920s and 1930s would not disrupt. In this chapter, even more than in most other chapters, one cannot avoid reference to other parts of the world; indeed, because capital funds were so mobile both between regions and between countries, the idea of a 'provincial financial market' was and is an absurdity. To understand what was happening in Ontario one has to know something about developments in the dominion as a whole, and indeed in the wider world.

The Banks, 1867–1914

There were two kinds of bank in Ontario – the incorporated or 'chartered' bank, operating under dominion regulation, and the unincorporated or 'private' bank, operating under few restrictions of any sort. The former were much the most important, although the latter are also interesting.

At Confederation the Bank of Upper Canada had just suspended operations, and the Commercial Bank at Kingston would shortly do so. Following these two failures the Montreal chartered banks, especially the Bank of Montreal, dominated the Canadian financial scene. In Ontario there were only a few banks – the Niagara District, the Bank of Toronto, the Gore Bank of Hamilton, the Ontario Bank of Bowmanville, the Royal Canadian Bank, and the newly incorporated Canadian Bank of Commerce. The failures of 1866–7, combined with the insecure and fragile states in which the Gore and the Royal Canadian had survived, cleared the way for the creation of new Ontario chartered banks. The troubles also provided a Horrible Example of the damage that bad banking practice could wreak.

The result, in the period 1867–75, was a considerable wave of new foundations. Ontario capitalists, and especially those based in Toronto, were not slow to seize the opportunities that prosperous conditions and banking law jointly offered. To set up a new bank one's shareholders had to pay in at least $100,000, but one could then issue bank-notes to the full amount of the paid-in capital. The leverage was thus considerable: even if no deposits were attracted, each dollar of capital could support almost two dollars' worth of earning assets, and leverage was further increased in so far as deposits could be attracted and held.[1]

The most important new foundation was the Canadian Bank of Commerce, set up by William McMaster as a response to the policies of the Bank of Montreal. McMaster, a director of that bank, believed that it was following a policy of restriction in Canada West, while accumulating deposits there and lending the proceeds in Montreal or New York. Accordingly, in 1866 he bought the charter of a bank that had yet to open its doors, arranged for the bank to be renamed, and opened for business on 15 May 1867.[2] The new bank quickly opened branches in other Ontario centres; in 1872 it established a New York agency, and in 1875 it did the same in Chicago. Savings accounts were first taken in 1868.[3] In 1870, outbidding the Bank of Montreal, the Commerce bought the shaky Gore Bank of Hamilton.[4]

Another important new foundation of the period 1867–75 was the Dominion Bank, which opened in Toronto early in 1871. Originally promoted by barristers and building contractors, it shortly came under the direction of James Austin, who was president from 1871 to 1897. Austin, an industrialist and financier, had been one of the original directors of the Canadian Bank of Commerce, but had left its board because he thought it was expanding too rapidly. Branches were opened at once, but only in 1897–8, with the extensions to Winnipeg and Montreal, did the Dominion Bank venture outside Ontario.[5]

Both these banks seem to have been run, at first, on conservative lines. For the Commerce the financial troubles of 1873–5 were painful, because the lumber trade was in especial distress. But the bank weathered these troubles without any particular difficulty.[6] As for the Dominion Bank, the official historian writes, 'there was little room for innovation. There were comparatively few manufacturing plants to finance, and still less need for assisting company flotations or lending money on call. Exporters of the country's natural products, importers of dry goods and groceries, wholesale and retail merchants, were the chief seekers of credit.'[7] This pattern is not a surprising one. Dominion banking law forbade chartered banks to make mortgage-loans. Furthermore, as earlier chapters have suggested, in the Ontario economy of the early 1870s industry's capital needs were not great, while many businesses could and apparently did generate a large cash flow from the retention of earnings.

Other early foundations that had long and distinguished careers were the Standard, the Bank of Ottawa (1874), and the Imperial (1875), which absorbed the Niagara District Bank. However, during the period 1871–5 there were two other foundations that had much shorter lives. One, the Federal Bank, went into voluntary liquidation in 1888, aparently because it had made bad loans to American lumber firms.[8] The other, the St Lawrence Bank, merged with the Standard in April 1876. The Royal Canadian Bank, which had been active but insecure at Confederation, suspended in May 1869, re-opened in 1870, merged in 1876 with the City Bank of Montreal, and then failed with that bank in August 1879.[9]

From 1873 through 1879 there was considerable distress among Ontario financiers, chiefly because of the world-wide slump that has been noted in other connections. The slump depressed both prices and outlets for many of Ontario's export goods – especially forest products. Thus until 1882 there were no new chartered banks in Ontario, and few existing banks felt it necessary to raise their paid-in capitals, while one bank, the Ontario, was obliged by losses to write down its capital by more than half. In Oshawa, local worthies promoted the Western Bank in 1882. In 1883 the Central Bank of Toronto and the Bank of London in Canada were created, the former failing in November 1887 and the latter in August of the same year.[10] But these were very small banks, and their failures ruffled few feathers. In 1885 the Traders' Bank of Toronto was created. It enjoyed a modest prosperity until it was bought out in 1911.

The depression of the mid-1890s was no time to be floating a bank. But the Great Boom of 1896–1913 provided a more stimulating climate, so that there were several new Ontario ventures. In 1902 the Sovereign and the Metropolitan Banks were set up. In 1904–7 Toronto was decorated in quick succession by the Crown, the Home, the Northern, the Sterling, the United Empire, and the Farmers Banks. The Sovereign was in liquidation by 1909, and the Metropolitan was merged with the Bank of Nova Scotia in November 1914. The Farmers ceased to exist in 1914, the same year in which the Bank of Montreal absorbed the United Empire. The Northern and the Crown were merged in 1908, only to become part of the Montreal-based Royal Bank in July 1918. The Sterling and the Home lasted until the post-war slump, when the former was absorbed by the Standard and the latter became insolvent, ending messily in 1923 – Canada's last bank failure until 1985. This record suggests that some of these new foundations may have taken on more risky loans than the longer-established banks. For the Home Bank, at least, there is archival evidence that this was the case.

Of much greater long-term importance was the decision by the Bank of Nova Scotia, in 1900, to move its General Office from Halifax to Toronto. This shift symbolized the emergence of Ontario's capital as a major centre of finance. The bank was new to Ontario; only in November 1897 had it opened a Toronto branch, and it had no others in the province. The bank's historians report that the decision was really the work of the new cashier, Henry C. McLeod, who believed that to participate fully in the nation's new prosperity the bank would have to shift its centre of operations. Correspondence with Halifax involved delays, and from so remote a centre it would be hard to maintain close and direct control over operations in central and western Canada and in the American mid-west, where the bank was already active. In due course the Metropolitan Bank and the Bank of Ottawa were merged into the Bank of Nova Scotia.[11]

The older Toronto banks, meanwhile, had not been idle in the Great Boom. The Bank of Toronto, which dated from 1855 and was led by members of the Gooderham family of distillers, had an ongoing interest in mines and railways. Thus it set up branches at Rossland in 1899, Copper Cliff and Sudbury in 1901–2, and South Porcupine in 1910. Also, in 1900–6, four new branches were opened in Quebec, joining the Montreal branch that dated from well before Confederation. Only in 1905 did the bank open a Winnipeg office, but it then proceeded to buy up some Manitoba private banks and to compete some others out of business. New prairie branches were established, and in 1908 the bank opened a Vancouver office.[12]

As for the Bank of Commerce, it embarked on a career of quite remarkable entrepreneurial vigour. In 1886 William McMaster resigned from the presidency; in doing so he proposed that George Albertus Cox, of Peterborough, should join the board. Cox had begun life in Colborne, worked as a telegraph operator in Peterborough, risen to become president of the Midland Railway, and sold that line at a profit to the Grand Trunk. In 1890 he became president of the Bank of Commerce, while simultaneously presiding over the Canada Life Assurance Company and Central Canada Loan and Savings Company. Cox was a very different sort of bank president than McMaster had been. His connections were with railways and with the newly emerging heavy industries, not with wholesale trade; his approach to banking, and indeed to finance in general, was considerably more energetic. Under his presidency the Bank of Commerce extended its operations both through merger and through the setting-up of new branches. It became actively involved in the promotional activities of Peterborough and Toronto industrialists, and, as chapter 15 explains, with the Canadian Northern railway project.

In 1900 the Bank of Commerce was able to assimilate the Bank of British

Columbia, which had operated on the west coast of North America, but under British ownership and management, since 1862. There had been distressing losses in the aftermath of the panic of 1893, and although the bank was still entirely sound, there was doubt about London's ability to enforce prudent banking practices over so long a distance. The absorption gave the Commerce its first London branch, six branches in British Columbia, and offices in San Francisco and Portland, Oregon. It also converted the bank from a provincial institution into a national and even an international one.[13] The London connections, in particular, would prove important for the distribution of long-term securities in the British market. To round out its national network, the Bank of Commerce acquired the Halifax Banking Company in 1903, the Merchants Bank of Prince Edward Island in 1906, and the Eastern Townships Bank in 1912 – all sound, but none dynamic.[14] For the Commerce these operations would provide not only local business but also deposits.

Thus in 1914 the Ontario network of chartered banks had come to resemble the one with which later generations would be familiar. Twenty-four banks had operated in the province between 1870 and 1914, but many had had lives that were nasty, brutish, and short. Of those banks that had survived to the outbreak of World War One, eleven were based in Toronto, one in Hamilton, and one in Ottawa. Most of the banks were active across Canada, and the larger banks had New York or London establishments, while the Bank of Commerce and the Bank of Nova Scotia were active in the American mid-west, and the Bank of Nova Scotia had seven branches in the Caribbean area.[15] Such activities brought business, deposits, and the chance to circulate the banks' own notes. New York and London were important because the banks could hold transactions balances and extra reserves in interest-bearing forms and with almost no risk. London, furthermore, was a place where long-term funds might be raised on behalf of one's clients – provinces, municipalities, railways. Smaller or more timid banks maintained the necessary connections with the outer world through correspondent relationships with British banks, American banks, or even other Canadian banks.

What sorts of men were the bankers? Here it is useful to distinguish between the promoters and shareholders, on the one hand, and the clerks and managers, on the other. Admittedly, to some extent the two groups interpenetrated. A clever and diligent man could rise, as Edmund Walker did, from clerk to president and general manager of the largest bank in the province. Clerks were hired young, both in Canada and abroad; the junior staff often led a monastic existence under the guidance of the branch manager, who, in turn, often lived 'over the shop.' Bank work was not well paid, but it was eminently respectable, and by the end of the nineteenth century it was generally pensionable as well. Bank stock was widely held; indeed, until the end of the century it was one of the few items of trade on the not very active Canadian stock exchanges. And banking, if prudently conducted, was profitable.

The promoters, presidents, and leaders of the chartered banks came from a variety of backgrounds, although commerce and finance predominated. William McMaster was prominent in the wholesale dry-goods trade, but was also involved with railways. Other early directors of his bank ran hardware firms, paper, saw, and flour mills, as well as chemical mills. One man was a financier.[16] The Dominion Bank was first promoted by a railway builder from Whitby, but the actual raising of capital was soon taken in hand by Pellatt and Osler, the stockbrokers, while James Austin was a wholesale grocer who had also founded the Consumers Gas Company.[17] Other Dominion Bank directors represented various interests – piano manufacture, milling, banking, railways, public utilities. The distilling families of Gooderham and Worts were leaders in Toronto banking circles for many decades, controlling the Bank of Toronto for an extended period.[18] The Western Bank of Oshawa was floated by several local families who were active not only in commerce but in manufacturing. Henry Pellatt, who developed the Home Bank out of a pre-existing loan company that had specialized in the financing of the stock market, was a broker and financier whose family had been influential in Toronto financial circles since before Confederation. The Metropolitan Bank was the creation of A.E. Ames, stockbroker and private banker, Chester Massey, manufacturer of agricultural machinery, Samuel Moore, producer of business forms, the vice-president of Imperial Life, and the general agent of the Presbyterian Church in Canada.[19] The Bank of Ottawa was a project of the capital's great lumbering families – the Frasers, Gilmours, Blackburns, Brysons, and MacLarens.[20]

The public had enough confidence in the bankers, and in their banks, to let the established ones expand their operations and to make room for new ones, so that bank assets expanded at an impressive rate of 7.7 per cent per year between 1871 and 1913. The banks' deposit liabilities expanded more quickly still – at an average rate of 10.9 per cent per year. Furthermore, the system was becoming more sophisticated. Even in 1871 the banks' deposit liabilities were 60 per cent larger than their note liabilities, but at the end of 1913 the deposits exceeded the bank-note issue by a factor of eight. As the banking habit sank more deeply into the Canadian population the Ontario banks had also seen a dramatic expansion of their savings deposits, which grew much more rapidly than demand deposits. This development both permitted and encouraged the development of the branch-banking network.

So far as Ontario banks were concerned, on the whole the public confidence was more or less justified. From Confederation to World War One no large bank went under, and the depositors in many weak banks were saved by merger, while all the failed banks managed at least to redeem their notes.[21] However, for all their reassuring talk, Ontario bankers were not averse to risk. The Home Bank plunged heavily into the financing of British Columbia timber limits; the Bank of Commerce involved itself so heavily with the Canadian Northern that if the dominion had not first guaranteed and then acquired the railway and its obligations, the bank would have been in serious difficulty. Such developments were very largely concealed from public view. The last thing any banker wanted was to frighten the depositors and the note holders, who could, if they chose, demand payment in gold.

As chartered banks waxed, the unincorporated private banks of Ontario first waxed in parallel, for the same general reasons, and then waned, as the chartered banks expanded their branch networks into the rural areas where the private banks primarily came to operate.[22] According to *Lovell's Directory*, there were thirty-one private banks in the province in 1871. Toronto had seven, Hamilton six, and Kingston two, so that just after Confederation the rural areas were anything but well supplied. During the next two decades, however, the private banks expanded primarily outside the large towns. Virtually all the private bankers had other activities; some were stockbrokers or exchange dealers, while others were insurance or travel agents: one was a miller, one a notary, and one the secretary of a sewing machine company.

By 1885 in Ontario there were at least 114 private banks, with eight branches among them, and in 1890, 137. It thus appears that although private banks were forbidden to issue their own notes, private banking developed very rapidly between Confederation and the end of the century, only to decline after 1900. In 1890 there were still three private bankers in Toronto, Hamilton, and Kingston, and two in Ottawa; the remainder were scattered over the small towns and villages, from Brockville through Flesherton, Embro, and Tara to Amherstberg, and from St Thomas to Port Arthur and Rat Portage.[23]

Local historians occasionally mention private banks, suggesting that elements of over-optimism might often have been present in their foundation. For instance, one learns that about 1871 three private banks opened in Strathroy, where there were fewer than 5,000 inhabitants – plus two chartered-bank branches.[24] During the 1880s there was Steward's private bank in Trenton,[25] and in Oakville a private bank was set up in 1871 and wound up three years later.[26] Two other private banks had longer lives, but both failed disastrously in 1902, the winding-up disclosing large holdings of real property and buildings. In the not particularly prosperous county of Bruce there was what might almost be called a plague of private banks, all of which failed untidily between 1894 and 1898, exposing their depositors to serious losses.[27] The economist E.P. Neufeld[28] provides us with a list of failures, as noted by the *Monetary Times*, which might not be complete. Private banks were brought down by advances on real estate, shipping, or the stock of a liquidating chartered bank, by speculation in patent rights, prairie land and ranching, and 'bucket shops,' and by simple fraud and theft.

The chartered banks were obliged to confine themselves to certain kinds of financial business, as defined by the Dominion Bank Act. Private bankers, on the other hand, could hold what assets they liked, lend as they wished, and be run in addition to and along with a wide range of financial, agency, and even commercial activities. They did not have to file government returns, or to publish financial statements, and very few ever did so. Private banks generally seem to have offered somewhat higher interest rates on deposits, and presumably, even though they might charge a little more for their services, farmers would find it profitable to deal with them so as to avoid the cost of going to and from the nearest branch of a chartered bank. To provide financial services at a distance, most private banks had arrangements either with the chartered banks or with firms in New York. However, competition from the growing network of chartered-bank branches and from the dominion post office savings system gradually reduced the sphere for private banking. After 1900, also, the motor car allowed farmers to go farther for banking services. Gradually private banking vanished – erased by retirement, by failure, and by absorption into the networks of the chartered banks, which could and did take over private banks, sometimes retaining the private banker as local manager. Only a prohibition of incorporated branch banking, as in most parts of the United States, could have saved Ontario private banking.

Life Insurance, Mortgage Loan, and Trust Companies, 1867–1914

In the years between Confederation and 1914, there was in Canada a remarkable growth of financial institutions that in some respects paralleled and duplicated the work of the banks, but that in other respects were very different.[29] These were the insurance companies, the mortgage loan companies, and the trust companies. Ontario entrepreneurs were active in their promotion and management; by 1900 it was apparent that all such firms were useful things for men of spirit and enterprise to control.

For life companies, as for chartered banks, the years around 1870 saw several new formations – in 1870 Ontario Mutual Life, and in 1871 Sun

Life of Montreal, both of which would share the field with the still small but long-established Canada Life of Hamilton, and with a plethora of British and American companies. Thereafter growth was rapid. By 1915 there were twenty-six federally registered companies, and insurance in force rose from $36 million in 1869 to $1,760 million in 1915, while Canadian companies' assets rose from $2.6 million to $258 million. Ontario-based companies shared more than proportionately in this growth: by 1914 there were twenty-one, with assets of $196 million, while Canada Life held 38 per cent of all Canadian life assets, and the other Ontario firms had another 36 per cent. All the great Ontario life companies – Canada, Dominion, North American, Confederation, Imperial, London, Manufacturers, and Mutual – had come into existence by 1897. In addition there were the fraternal societies, one of which, the Independent Order of Foresters, led by an imaginative Iroquois physician, Dr Oronhyatekha, had become very large and prominent indeed. Operations quickly were extended abroad. Canada Life was the first firm to do so; in 1889 it began to sell in Michigan. Other Toronto firms, and Sun Life as well, followed this example, extending their activities first to the United States and then to the Caribbean, Latin America, Britain, and elsewhere in the British Empire.[30]

Throughout the English-speaking world the methods of doing insurance business were reasonably standard. New kinds of policy, developed elsewhere, were adopted by the Ontario firms. Because of urbanization and the increasing importance of wage- and salary-earning status the demand for life policies was tending to increase, and as life expectancies rose, the companies' positions automatically became stronger, because the life tables were infrequently revised. Indeed, there were no life tables for Canada, and the companies had to rely on British experience, which in general implied a shorter life expectancy than the Canadian or American pattern. Furthermore, once people became policy holders they were likely to remain so; they might borrow against their policies, but would cash in or surrender them only with reluctance. Thus the life companies, their assets expanding, became important lenders and buyers of securities. Well before Confederation Canada Life had become significant in the municipal securities market, and in the 1870s and 1880s it went on buying municipal bonds, while continuing to lend large amounts on mortgage and policy loans. This was the normal pattern until the 1890s, and for some conservative firms, such as Mutual Life in Waterloo and the Jaffray family's London Life, it continued long afterward. But the Toronto firms became much more adventurous in their investment policies during the 1890s. In this respect they were, to a large extent, following American example. Nor was entrepreneurial investment behaviour incompatible with growth. Canada Life's assets rose from $16 million in 1895 to $56 million in 1914.[31]

Life insurance in Canada was a regulated industry. At first there was some confusion as to the locus of the regulation, and until 1910 many companies enjoyed special power by virtue of their private incorporating acts, but it was clear by the mid-1870s that the dominion, not the provinces, would be the effective regulating body.[32] Between Confederation and 1941 only the smallest and most localized companies opted for provincial supervision. The dominion's general rules controlled company investment policies, but between 1890 and 1910 there was a noticeable tendency to relax these rules, largely in response to pressure from the insurance entrepreneurs. Some scandals occurred, and were revealed first by Toronto-based investigative reporting and then by a royal commission; the result was a general regulating statute that appeared to be stricter than earlier measures, but that in fact left the companies with broad powers of investment. Naturally it was the freedom to manage and invest the policy holders' funds that made life insurance companies so attractive to financial entrepreneurs, especially in Toronto.

Building societies had existed in Ontario since long before Confederation. In 1874 there were at least twenty-four, of which fourteen were in Toronto and thirteen had been founded since 1867. The three largest were the Trust and Loan Company of Canada, which was owned in Britain, Canada Permanent, and Western Canada Loan, both of Toronto. In the next two decades many firms were established, including Henry Pellatt's Home Savings (1877) and George Cox's Central Canada Loan (1884). Between 1872 and 1887 assets increased twelve-fold, and shareholders' equity quadrupled. The firms borrowed at home by taking deposits and by selling debentures, that they also peddled in the United Kingdom; only the Crédit Foncier franco-canadien, owned and controlled in Paris, obtained funds on the continent. Total mortgage lending seems to have risen from $13 million in the early 1870s to $82 million in the late 1880s.

Canada Permanent had been the first 'permanent building society' in the province. Managed for fifty years by J.H. Mason, the canny Cornishman who had conceived it in 1855, it had taken savings deposits from the beginning, and in the 1860s it had begun to lend in rural Ontario while trying unsuccessfully to borrow on debentures in Britain. In 1875, following the passage of an enabling dominion statute, Mason went to Britain again, appointing agents in Edinburgh, Aberdeen, and London.[33] Offering 5.5 per cent, he was able to raise over $300,000 the first year. British money helped the firm grow, and in 1887 it became larger than its great competitor, the Trust and Loan Company. In 1881 the Permanent extended its lending activities to Winnipeg; although it lost heavily when the Manitoba land boom collapsed, it persevered in western Canada, extending its activities to Vancouver in 1892. Other large and energetic

Ontario firms were doing likewise – borrowing in Britain through Scottish agents, and lending not only in Ontario but in western Canada as well.[34]

Important though rural lending was to the mortgage companies, one should not assume that they were restricting themselves to it. It is certain that all the town-based firms, especially the Toronto ones, were lending large amounts on urban real estate. Indeed, without such lending it would have been hard to finance the explosive urbanization of the 1880s, and it may well have been the end of the urban building boom, as well as the declining agricultural prices and stagnating population, that caused trouble for so many mortgage companies in the mid-1890s.

From 1893 to 1897 the prospects for new lending were so poor, and Canadian interest rates had fallen to such an extent, that the companies drew ever more of their funds from the domestic market.[35] The Huron and Erie Savings and Loan Company complained: 'The increase of nearly a quarter of a million dollars in Canadian debentures is a gratifying evidence of the high esteem in which the company is held, while the reduction in the amount of sterling debentures outstanding is not due to any unwillingness on the part of investors in Britain to lend money as in the past, but because capital in this country is rapidly accumulating, and all the debenture money the board is permitted to accept is now available from local sources on terms about as favourable as the prevailing rate on sterling debentures.'[36] Yields on mortgages, meanwhile, had fallen also, and the president of Canada Permanent asked for wider powers of investment: 'it is my opinion that the company should have enlarged powers of borrowing and investing. Experience has shown that restrictive legislation does not ensure good management, or immunity from disastrous losses. Real estate does not now afford that unlimited field for investment at remunerative rates that it formerly did, and it is desirable and necessary that companies should have power to purchase and lend on good easily convertible securities, which hitherto they have been excluded from.'[37]

Other mortgage lenders were also restive. An official of the Imperial Life later remarked that 'while the life companies ... did not suffer so severely in their mortgage investments as the loan companies, yet some of them experienced somewhat anxious and trying times' during the depression of the 1890s.[38] An official of Confederation Life claimed that 'we have certainly lost more on mortgage investments than upon any other class of securities.'[39] Other companies complained that the right sort of mortgage paper was in short supply, while foreclosures had created a justifiable suspicion that mortgage paper might no longer be the supremely safe security it had once appeared to be. Some of this caution survived into the early years of the new century, when both life and loan companies were tasting the joys of security speculation for the first time.

The loan companies responded to their difficulties by merging, thereby reducing expenses and perhaps competition too. In 1898 Canada Permanent merged with three other old-established Toronto firms, and after a year's planning the merger was actually consummated in April 1900.[40] Other mergers were planned and completed during the same period.

Soon, however, with the revival in world prices and the renewed development not only in western Canada but in Ontario, the mortage companies were able to renew the cultivation of their traditional business and once more had to draw sizeable funds not only from Canadian savers but also from British and French. Central Canada Loan and Savings also cultivated the bond business and, in 1901, gave birth to Dominion Securities Ltd; Home Savings cultivated the financing of securities transactions, and then, in 1903, was transformed into the Home Bank of Canada; other mortgage companies devoted themselves to their traditional businesses, both in Ontario and in the north-west.

By 1914 the situation of the mortgage companies was as follows. The British-owned Trust and Loan Company was no longer active in the province, yet the companies' total assets equalled $161 million, an increase of 50 per cent since 1895. About 25 per cent of the funds had come from overseas debentures and stock, and slightly more from dollar debentures and deposits; the balance represented owners' equity, almost all of which, except the Credit Foncier shares, was apparently held within Ontario.

The mortgage companies were now smaller than the insurance companies, which for twenty years past had been growing faster. The trust companies also, if one includes the assets they held under administration, were now larger, and certainly they were growing more quickly. Important though the mortgage companies had been, and still were, it was apparent by 1914 that the movement of change was not on their side, in spite of the fact that both dominion and provincial authorities regularly widened their powers of borrowing and investment, more or less on request. Thus in the 1890s, when the companies had some trouble finding suitable mortgage paper,[41] the Ontario legislature dramatically broadened their powers, first in 1897[42] and then in 1900.[43] In 1903[44] the regulatory regime became laxer still.

Having received all the investment powers they could possibly want, the mortgage companies then ceased to agitate; indeed, as was shown above, most of them resumed the cultivation of the more traditional fields during the Great Boom. Meanwhile, the province's trust companies were growing fast. Canada's first operating trust company was the Toronto General Trusts, chartered in 1872 but actually opening a decade later, in 1882. The entrepreneur and first manager was John Woodburn Langmuir, a provincial inspector of prisons and asylums, who presumably had seen at first hand what useful work a trust company might do. The firm's act of incorporation forbade it to engage in banking,[45] and Langmuir believed that this provision meant he could not take deposits, which, indeed, the firm did not accept until 1928. Other trust companies were less nice; by the turn of the century about a dozen firms had been set up, largely under the general companies legislation, and several of these were accepting deposits and allowing depositors to draw cheques.[46]

Some of the trust companies were created by banking interests. Among the most important of these was the National Trust Company, promoted in 1898 by men who were closely linked with the Bank of Commerce.[47] The firm sold guaranteed investment certificates that were indistinguishable from mortgage companies' debentures, and it was willing to act as a corporate trustee in matters such as the maintaining of share registers, the safeguarding of bond and debenture issues, and the distribution of dividends. It soon opened offices in Winnipeg, Edmonton, and Montreal.

Other firms came from other roots. Thus by 1900 Ontario had also acquired the Grey and Bruce Trust and Savings Company (1887), the Imperial Trust (1889), the Canada Trust of London (1893), the General Trust (1894), the London and Western Trusts (1896), and the Trusts and Guarantee Company of Toronto – later Crown Trust (1897).[48]

What did all these companies do? Some quickly developed real estate businesses. Most were prepared to manage estates and to perform a variety of kinds of trustee work, thus acquiring the power to manage large and increasing sums. Most behaved like mortgage companies in that they received deposits and issued investment certificates. Naturally they concentrated on long-term lending, both on mortgage and on other sorts of security, especially municipal bonds.

For trust companies, as for mortgage companies, western development offered new opportunities, and so did Ontario's own urbanization. To manage mortgage lending in the west, and perhaps to attract deposits, prairie offices were needed. These were acquired by branching, and by merging with western trust firms such as Winnipeg General. Thus by 1914 Toronto General possessed offices and agencies in the three prairie provinces and was contemplating a Vancouver office. Furthermore, some firms obtained funds in Britain, especially during the later years of the Great Boom. Trust deposits, mortgage certificates,[49] and 'guaranteed trust investment receipts' were all issued overseas at one time or another.[50] Neufeld believes[51] that at first the regulatory authorities meant to limit the competition between bank and trust company, but it is clear that the restrictions were more apparent than real,[52] while, as with the mortgage companies, regulation became less strict with time,[53] so that by 1914 the trust companies could freely borrow and take deposits, even though their placement powers were rather closely restricted.[54] As with the mortgage companies, dominion and provincial jurisdictions overlapped, and only in 1914 did the dominion produce its own general regulatory measure.[55] The new dominion act of 1914 said nothing about deposits; presumably the trust companies that it regulated – those incorporated by the dominion – could borrow by that route if they wished.[56]

By 1914 the stage was set for the process of assimilation that, in the 1960s, would produce a coalescence of mortgage and trust businesses. Both kinds of firm could take deposits and borrow on medium-term obligations; both specialized in mortgage lending and made short-term loans only in rather exceptional circumstances; both, as a natural side effect of their mortgage businesses, were becoming active as real estate brokers; both had the rudiments of a branch network, especially in western Canada. However, there were differences. The mortgage companies borrowed extensively in Britain and France, while the trust companies did not; the trust companies were becoming active in the distribution of securities both at home and abroad, while the mortgage companies were not; the trust companies actually did receive and administer trusts and estates, a business that the mortgage companies were not empowered to undertake. In the years between 1919 and 1939 there would be some steps toward assimilation, although that movement would not be complete for many decades to come.

The Capital Market before 1914[57]

In the years of the Great Boom, 1896–1913, the financial system of Canada, equally based in Montreal and in Toronto, matured and took the shape with which Canadians in the second half of the twentieth century would be familiar. In tracing these developments in the present section, the main emphasis will be placed on Ontario developments. But Canada's capital markets formed an integrated whole, and they were also well connected with external markets, especially those of London, where Canadian governments and businesses could freely borrow, and where Canadians could lend if they wished.

Canadian interest rates, therefore, moved in parallel with rates in Britain, rising when London's rates rose and falling when they fell. New York was also important, especially after 1900, because Canadian borrowers and lenders could move equally easily onto the American scene. Furthermore, because all three currencies were on the gold standard, exchange rates were effectively pegged and could move only within very narrow margins, so that it hardly mattered in what currency one's assets and liabilities were denominated.

Obligations, in turn, might be incurred for longer or shorter periods of time. It is customary to speak of the 'capital market' when one is talking of comparatively long-period obligations – say, those with a term of five years or more – or when one is speaking of common and preference stocks, which are evidences of ownership that naturally have no expiry date at all. The capital market, in turn, can be divided into the new-issue market, where bonds and stocks are first sold, and the mortgage market, in which mortgage funds are borrowed and lent.

A well-functioning new-issue market needs a way to distribute new issues, some arrangement for underwriting these issues so that the issuer – government or corporation – can be sure of getting his money, some system of organized trading, and some assurance that someone will 'make a market,' buying and selling securities so as to absorb excess supply or fill excess demand. Some elements in this list of requirements had appeared by Confederation.[58] Municipalities were already selling securities to financial institutions, and some of the large cities had begun to issue securities by calling for tenders. But there were no specialized investment dealers, and no underwriters, nor was the stock exchange active: The Toronto Stock Exchange had first been formed in 1852, but until 1875 or so its activity was intermittent at best. When it was reorganized in 1871 it contained only thirteen members, and it was incorporated only in 1878. In 1881 it moved into new permanent quarters, and at that time some brokers' offices acquired telegraphic ticker-tape machines that linked them to New York. In 1886 direct cable connections to Europe became available. In 1896–7 two supplementary exchanges, the Toronto Stock and Mining and the Standard, were created, only to merge in 1899. The Standard Stock and Mining Exchange remained separate from the Toronto Stock Exchange, merging with it only in 1934. Meanwhile, in 1874, the Bank of Montreal began to act as an overseas underwriter and issuer for Canadian municipal securities. Toronto had already become a marketing centre for smaller municipal issues.[59] Specialized bond dealers had begun to appear, such as G.A. Stimson in the 1890s and A.E. Ames in 1889. Thus in the course of the 1870s and 1880s some of the gaps in the institutional framework had begun to be filled: the stock market was a good deal more active, there were more specialized brokers who worked within it, and the financial institutions had become a great deal more involved, if only through the provision of 'call money' – loans to brokers and customers secured on the pledge of securities.

Before 1900 there was certainly some new-issue activity in Toronto: bank and mortgage company shares were issued in considerable quantity, especially during the 1870s and 1880s, while the market in mining stocks was active in the 1890s. It was even possible to float off new promotions, such as National Trust, and large mergers, such as the ill-fated Canada Cycle and Motor Company (CCM). But industrial issues were few, and it is safe to say that except for mining shares, where a meaningful measure of activity cannot be constructed, the new issue markets were quiescent until the new century had begun. Hence the picture that table 18.2 presents is not wholly misleading as a rough representation.[60]

A great deal of the outside finance in Canadian industry was bond-finance. While issues of ordinary and preference stock totalled $243 million between the end of 1900 and the end of 1914, bond sales totalled $260 million. These bonds came from all sorts of firms, and neither the firms nor the issues were particularly large. It was perfectly possible to dispose of a $50,000 issue, and for a closely held private company to obtain funds by a public offering of its bonds.[61] After 1900, and particularly after the wave of mergers that began in 1909, the specialized bond houses were hungry for inventory, and access to external debt-finance became much easier. With the development of a formal mechanism for the creating and selling of securities, and given the close connections between some banks and some bond houses, it must have been both increasingly easy and increasingly natural for the Canadian banks to push clients into the arms of the bond houses when the clients would have been just as happy to remain in the arms of the banks. On the other hand, some banks, of which the most imaginative and active seems to have been the Bank of Nova Scotia, were energetically developing their own bond holdings.

The merger movement of 1909 gained momentum in 1910 and continued in 1911 and 1912, contributing to the flow of new issues.[62] Between the beginning of 1900 and the end of 1914 there were seventy-three Canadian consolidations, capitalized at $444 million.[63] The public was asked to subscribe, between February 1909 and January 1913, for forty issues that summed to $57.3 million.[64] Before 1909 there had been some mergers,[65] but not until 1909, when credit was cheap and when Canadian financiers had observed their American mentors and had learned from them, did a concerted assault on the industrial structure begin. There were also many conversions and reorganizations by which bond dealers converted private companies into public corporations.[66] When the Canadian public was offered a chance to subscribe for a new issue it generally proved eager to do so;[67] undersubscription, and the resultant 'indigestion' among bond houses and underwriters, was rare.

Toronto financiers found other ways to improve themselves with the aid of the new issue market – utility promotions in Latin America, in Ontario, and elsewhere in Canada; railway and street railway promotions, especially the Canadian Northern project that was described in chapter 15. The Mackenzie-Mann railway project had a dismal end, but not all the two promoters' enterprises ended in this way. Among their domestic projects were fisheries, blast furnaces, mines, lumber companies, oil wells, and electric railways and power plants in Toronto and Winnipeg. Altogether, in 1914 Mackenzie and Mann were said to control some thirty-two companies,[68] most of which they had created, and many of which had been financed wholly or in part by Toronto's financial institutions.[69]

Canadian financiers sometimes complained that there were too few utilities to develop in Canada. Sensibly tracing this defect to a lack of cities, they went adventuring in Latin America and Spain, where cities were not unknown. When the Mexican Light and Power Company was formed in Toronto in 1903, eminent city capitalists subscribed readily;[70] already the Cox group had co-operated with F.S. Pearson of New York to float the Sao Paulo Traction, Light, and Power Company.[71] As Latin bond and stock issues flowed onto the market, Toronto capitalists provided much of the underwriting,[72] and Toronto financial institutions were quick to pick up those issues that appeared to come under their owners' sponsorship.[73] The Toronto life companies also assisted with interim finance.[74]

In later years the Brazilian utility enterprises and the other Latin projects turned to Europe for permanent long-term finance, so that by 1914 the *Monetary Times* could write that there was little Canadian money in these territories.[75] None the less, it is said that Brazilian Traction was always controlled in Toronto, and certainly Toronto finance had been critical at the beginning, the utility projects, like the Canadian Northern and many of the merger operations, having been launched by Toronto financiers with the willing co-operation of local financial institutions.

Activity did not centre only around such glamorous projects. Nor did the mining shares that were so important on the Toronto market after 1903 provide all that market's business. New funds were raised by firms that served the expanding agricultural economy – milling companies, meat packers, dairies, and Great Lakes shipping companies. And as the years passed, while the mechanism of the bond houses became more highly developed, it became easier for smaller companies to make new issues. The banks, too, were obliged by the Canadian Bank Act to make new issues from time to time:[76] there was a rigid link between the banks' paid-up capital and their power to issue and circulate their own bank-notes.[77] In the mid-1890s the banks possessed plenty of unused power of note-issue, their capitals being considerably larger than their note-circulations. But by October 1902 capital was only 108 per cent of circulation – dangerously low, since the practical limit of note-issue power was thought to be about 10 per cent below the legal limit.[78] Thereafter bank capital was rapidly expanded.

Who was buying this large and growing flow of new issues? As can be seen from table 18.3, 43 per cent of the flow was absorbed by institutions and 57 per cent by individual purchasers between 1901 and 1914. The trust companies and the life insurance companies were particularly important, especially after 1910, when the attractions of mortgage lending again captured the interest of the mortgage companies. Banks were obliged to offer new shares in the first instance to existing shareholders. Their response to repeated requests is not clearly known, and it was later suggested that the double liability on bank stock might have frightened purchasers.[79] The *Monetary Times* believed that considerable blocks of stock often came on the open market;[80] this occurrence might explain how blocks of Bank of Commerce stock came to be held in the United States. However, the manager of that bank thought that 'in practice the old shareholders usually take up the capital,'[81] and this was certainly the experience of the Dominion Bank, not only in 1911 but also in 1913.[82]

When a new bank was floated, the distribution of shares was not infrequently a private affair, but when public issue was attempted, especially after 1900, the bond houses were generally involved.[83] This is what happened when Toronto's Metropolitan Bank was floated by A.E. Ames and Co., who held the larger share of the bank's capital for some months.[84] Another example was the flotation of the Sterling Bank by the Ontario Securities Co. There were also large private placements of bank shares *en bloc*, not infrequently with foreigners.[85] Thus it seems likely that the southward migration of Bank of Commerce shares may reflect the operations of the Dominion Securities Corporation, the bond house that was so closely associated with that bank and with the Cox family.[86]

The development of the new issue market went hand in hand with the emergence of the bond houses. By 1909 there were about fifty in Canada, about half of which were based in Toronto. Virtually all the bond houses that were to be important in the twentieth century came into existence before 1914.[87] Some had grown out of brokerage firms,[88] as A.E. Ames had done; this firm had been founded in 1889, and was operating as a private bank and issue house by 1900.[89] In June 1903 the firm suspended payment, but it was reconstructed, and the successor firm continued to call itself an 'investment bank,' retaining its stock exchange seat.[90] A similar Toronto firm was Pellatt and Pellatt, headed by Sir Henry Pellatt. This firm also concerned itself with broking and promoting, not least with the promotion of the Home Bank; it maintained close relations with that bank until after the end of World War One.[91]

There were also bond houses that had grown out of other financial institutions. The Ontario Securities Company, for instance, was set up in 1902 by the directors of Continental Life Insurance Company.[92] A much more active firm was Dominion Securities, mentioned above. Originally a wholly owned subsidiary of the Central Canada Loan and Savings Company, it was set up in 1901 to take over the securities business in which Central Canada had been engaged for some years.[93] Since Central Canada was controlled by George Cox, Dominion Securities naturally worked in close association with Canada Life and with the Canadian Bank of Commerce. In the first thirteen years after its foundation it sold at least $100 million of industrial bonds and shares,[94] and also an indeterminate quantity of municipal bonds.[95]

In their role as domestic buyers and distributors of corporate securities the Toronto banks and bond houses developed overseas connections that were used to sell corporate securities in Britain and Europe. They also developed American connections, although these were used less intensively, partly because some Canadian borrowers formed their own links with American bond houses.

In Canada, and especially in Toronto, many of the commercial banks and bond houses acquired their initial experience by buying and reselling municipal bonds, adding industrial securities as opportunity presented itself. Close ties between bond houses and financial institutions were helpful for the marketing of the issues and for the interim financing of the inventories. The bond houses were the principal initial purchasers of municipal and industrial bonds in the years between 1895 and 1914. They supplied securities to Canadian banks, insurance companies, and individuals. Although their overseas sales were overshadowed by the London activities of the Bank of Montreal and the Canadian Bank of Commerce, they sold large blocks of Canadian bonds in Britain, both by public issue and by private negotiation. The dealers, and the promoters with whom they were allied, carried through most of the mergers and promotions whose bonds and stocks so radically widened the range of available domestic securities, and thereby helped attract British funds to Canada through the issue of new securities in London. Earlier their importance in the issue of municipal securities and provincial securities was noted. This steady flow of government issues, and the strong local market that existed for municipal issues in the absence of any significant dominion domestic funded debt, provided the bond houses with assured though limited income and with contacts through which industrial issues could be distributed and the bank credit for carrying them could be obtained.

As a group the Canadian banks took up a considerable volume of corporate securities during the period 1900–14, although securities holdings remained extremely small relative to discounts and advances.[96] The economist Kenneth Buckley is probably correct in stating that the 'chief activity of the Canadian banks was the financing of inventories and receivables,'[97] but some banks – most notably the Bank of Nova Scotia – certainly took an active interest in investment-banking, and through the financing of the bond houses' inventories the chartered banks were involved in flotations and new issues at one remove. They also had an extensive overseas securities business, and their local activities should not be denigrated. It has been seen that under George Cox's direction the Bank of Commerce developed close connections with domestic issuers of industrial securities. Unfortunately, for other Canadian chartered banks the evidence for such connections is much less clear. The smaller Ontario banks do not seem to have formed them. But the Bank of Nova Scotia was different. It bought large quantities of long-term bonds, both Canadian and American.[98] Early in the century it received subscriptions for Nova Scotia Steel bonds and cold storage company stock.[99] Later it set up a bond department, and it was generally willing to receive orders for a client's issues.[100] However, like the smaller Canadian banks and unlike the Bank of Commerce, it did not participate energetically[101] in the domestic distribution or creation of corporate issues.

The role of the life insurance companies was two-fold once they began to move into industrial securities after 1895. Their most obvious activity was certainly the purchase of securities, in growing quantities and of steadily more diverse sorts. This widening of the market for domestic securities, whatever its effect on the policy holders, certainly increased the flow of institutional funds to the industrial sector.

On the new-issue market the brokers were not much in evidence, except in so far as they converted themselves into bond houses. In earlier years – before the mid-1890s – the Toronto and Montreal brokers had been the principal channel through which new security issues were marketed. In the years 1901–7 it was still not uncommon to find individual brokers buying blocks of securities from provincial governments, issuing securities for corporations, and doing the things that were becoming the special activities of the bond houses.

The Ontario government was the only provincial government to make any regular domestic issues between 1895 and 1914. Entering the twentieth century with no net debt,[102] the province began to borrow to build the T&NO Railway, and then the Ontario Hydro distribution system; well before 1914, however, as the next chapter explains, it was also borrowing to finance itself. By the end of 1914 some 40 per cent of its funded indebtedness was domestic. Furthermore, as table 18.6 reveals, most of this borrowing was done when the domestic boom was at its height. Nor were domestic funds always more expensive than London finance: indeed, in 1911 and 1912 Ontario found it cheaper to borrow at home, and in 1909 domestic borrowing was no more costly than overseas. It is not clear who was buying Ontario bonds; the accounts of the insurance companies show very small holdings,[103] and, as table 18.7 shows, the banks did not purchase and hold any significant amounts.[104] Presumably some of the buyers were corporate trustees and cautious individuals, both in Canada and in the United States.

Municipalities, also, borrowed very large amounts, thanks largely to the help of the bond houses, which generally bought up municipal issues and resold them. Municipalities and other local authorities generally borrowed by offering debentures for public tender. The practice began well before 1895,[105] and seems to have been copied from the United States.[106] Even the largest cities habitually sold their bonds in this way. During the years for which statistics are available the total of Canadian municipal bond issues was $309 million, of that nearly 30 per cent had been taken up in Canada.[107] Even in 1913 – a year of 'stringency' and the beginning of recession – Canadians took up $25 million in new municipal bonds.

The elements of a municipal new-issue market had come into existence before 1870, largely through the copying of American techniques of advertisement, public tender, and block sale.[108] The chartered banks had conducted a bond business ever since Confederation, and perhaps since an earlier date;[109] Montreal and Toronto brokers had begun to act as bond dealers, buying and selling *en bloc*; several of the important bond houses had already been established by 1890,[110] although their early dealings were 'largely confined to ... municipal and government bonds.'[111] After 1895 there were many new firms, an avalanche of new business, but no institutional innovations. In 1909 a Canadian municipality could expect to receive about twelve bids for an offering of securities. There were then about fifty Canadian bond houses in the market, as well as some dozen Canadian banks, trust companies, and insurance companies.[112] In addition there were about eight New York and London houses that occasionally took part,[113] but contemporary reports indicate that their bids were rarely successful. Consider the following statement, tantalizingly equivocal, made by the general manager of the Bank of Commerce: 'As to municipal bonds, with so many branches we are often asked to help the municipalities in the negotiation of their bonds; sometimes we buy them out and out, or if the amount is large we purchase them in combination with others.'[114]

It is perhaps safe to say that before 1914 most Canadian banks made little active effort to develop their bond business, although the Bank of Nova Scotia certainly was an exception. After 1914 the situation was different: in the early 1920s the bond dealers were complaining of unwonted chartered-bank competition.[115] Before 1914 some banks probably bought most of their bond inventories from bond dealers, rather than from the issuing municipalities,[116] while there is little doubt that insurance and trust companies dealt principally with the bond dealers and only infrequently with the banks.[117] The only relevant statistics are ambiguous, partly because bond houses occasionally shared responsibility with banks, but chiefly because in the context the exact meaning of the figures is not at all clear. From 1900 through 1905 Dominion Securities, then the largest bond house in the country, 'purchased entire issues to the par value of $9,301,000, and participated in purchase of, and had the selling rights on the Canadian market, of $38,767,000, or a total of $48,077,000, while corporate issues in Canada handled by other dealers amounted to only $9,588,000 during the period.'[118] The speaker, Senator George Cox, knew better than anyone else what the flows of securities might be. But did he mean to include the banks with the 'other dealers'? Unfortunately he did not tell the Senate, and the other senators seem to have been too somnolent to seek clarification.

Whichever institution was responsible for the distribution of a Canadian municipal issue, the process was entirely a private one. Few Canadian municipal bonds were listed on any domestic exchange. Hence the dealer could not feed them gradually onto an impersonal market but had to sell each bond by personal negotiation. By 1900 this necessity had led to the growth of a nation-wide sales network[119] – and to the formation of close ties with life insurance companies.[120]

Although a Canadian municipality rarely sold its bonds directly to the final holder, some municipalities did begin to sell bonds over the counter.[121] These sales were quite successful: surprising sums were raised quickly, even in small towns.

Municipal securities mattered because so many towns and cities were incurring large capital outlays during the Great Boom. Many of these expenditures were connected with the building boom that was under way in Montreal, Toronto, and many other cities in Ontario and Quebec, as well as in the towns of western Canada, where, in addition, large outlays were occurring for the opening up of the Prairie wheat economy. Hence mortgage markets, like municipal securities, were of immense importance during the years of the Great Boom.

For the mortgage, trust, and insurance companies, mortgages were alternatives to government securities and to some extent corporate securities as well. In Toronto the same financial entrepreneurs were involved not only with banking but with the other financial institutions, including those that specialized in mortgage finance. The period 1895–1914 shows an interesting shift in emphasis, as these firms first concentrated on securities and then became increasingly interested in mortgages. Table 18.8 shows the position in 1914, while table 18.9 records the changing pattern of institutional mortgage-lending.

Money flowed into mortgages when the return became more favourable in comparison with returns on the alternatives. During the period 1901–5, the average difference between the yield on mortgages and the yield on other securities, as reported by Ontario trust and mortgage companies, was 0.4 per cent. For the period 1911–14 the difference was 0.9 per cent. This growing differential pulled funds away from securities and into urban and agricultural mortgage loans. Similarly, because western mortgage yields were consistently higher than yields in Ontario, mortgage funds were attracted to the west and north-west,[122] while after 1900 the volume of acceptable western paper grew rapidly as homesteaders established title to their properties.[123] To the trust, insurance, and loan companies, the yields were sufficiently attractive to draw funds westward in an increasing stream. The mortgage-loan and trust companies developed their own lending departments in prairie cities.[124] The insurance companies lent through various channels – resident inspectors of mortgages,[125] salaried agents,[126] and local real estate men.[127] Some companies were initially nervous about the 'speculative nature' of western development,[128] while others felt uncertain about the commitment of money so far away from the directors' surveillance. These reluctances proved less inhibiting as time passed. However, some smaller insurance and loan companies never overcame their suspicion: that the higher returns on western mortgage loans would not suffice to compensate for higher risk, and for the higher cost of administration that western lending entailed.[129]

All these developments can be traced through the accounts of individual Ontario firms.[130] It is clear that between 1900 and 1914 the great increase in mortgage-company resources was used almost exclusively to support prairie lending.[131] Only the very small companies kept away from the west, preferring to maintain their operations in the towns of Ontario.[132] For the Ontario trust companies the same pattern appears.[133] The bulk of western lending by trust companies came from a few firms – among them Toronto General Trusts.

After 1914

As in manufacturing, so in finance: the heroic days of economic transformation were over by 1914. This is not to say that nothing occurred thereafter, whether in Ottawa or on Bay Street. But so far as Ontario is concerned, the developments of the 1920s and 1930s can best be seen as evolutions from the pre-1914 days.

The war did have a considerable impact on the chartered banks. Before 1914 they had lent very little to the dominion, or to the provinces. In the course of the war their holdings of dominion and provincial securities rose from barely 10 per cent of total assets to 11.6 per cent of a very much larger total; more important, when the dominion floated its first domestic bond issue in many decades during 1915–16, the banks helped mightily, not only as subscribers but also as distributors and as the financiers for buyers who did not have enough cash to pay for the bonds they wanted. In addition, the banks began to buy dominion treasury bills and to provide loans to the Imperial Government on the security of United Kingdom treasury bills. Some of these advances were not paid off until 1922.

During the war there was a very considerable monetary expansion and inflation, in which the Ontario banks played their full part: total assets rose 85 per cent from December 1914 to December 1919, and the circulation of bank notes rose 126 per cent. Holdings of gold, meanwhile, rose only 31 per cent. The inflationary boom of the war period continued into 1920, then gave way to a worldwide recession as demand fell and the prices of primary products, especially wheat, also dropped. In the slump the Ontario banks' deposit liabilities shrank by 13.1 per cent, and assets declined by 16.1 per cent – the first such drop for many years and the sharpest until that time.

The result was difficulty for some banks, especially for those who had made unwise loans. In Ontario the most overtly troubled banks were the Standard, which survived until the Commerce absorbed it in 1928, and Sir Henry Pellatt's Home Bank, which collapsed in 1923. The Home, however, was a small fish: its total assets were only 2 per cent of Ontario banking assets, and less than 1 per cent of Canadian. A failure of the Standard, whose assets were three times as large, would have been a much more serious proposition. More covert were the troubles of the Bank of Commerce, mired as it was in the financial collapse of the Canadian Northern Railway. If the dominion had not taken over that railway and its debts, the Commerce would have been in desperate straits.

For the rest of the 1920s, although there were fewer Ontario banks than before 1914, both assets and deposit liabilities expanded quite considerably, so that by the peak in 1928–9, both were from 27 to 29 per cent higher than they had been in 1923 and somewhat higher than at the 1919–20 peak. Branches, too, were scattered far and wide. The banks were developing and expanding their businesses at home and abroad along the lines that had been laid down before 1914.

During the slump of the nineteen-thirties there were no failures or mergers among the Ontario banks, although both assets and liabilities declined sharply – the former by 18.1 per cent from 1929 to 1932 and the latter by 13.7 per cent. This decline was followed by a considerable recovery, since deposits rose by 40 per cent between 1932 and 1939 while assets rose by 35 per cent. By 1939 the five remaining Ontario banks –

Nova Scotia, Commerce, Dominion, Imperial, and Toronto – were larger than they had ever been.

The Bank of Commerce was now, as it had been for twenty years, the third-largest bank in the country – second to the Royal Bank and the Bank of Montreal. The Bank of Nova Scotia was the fourth largest. Relative to pre-war days, the Ontario banks were smaller than the Montreal-based banks: they owned 42 per cent of all bank assets in 1939, whereas in 1929 they had owned 41 per cent, and in 1913, 47.5 per cent. The reasons for this development are entirely obscure; because the banks certainly did not compete either on lending terms or on deposit rates, the usual explanation – some sort of competitive failure with respect to the terms of borrowing and lending – cannot apply. It is possible, as some observers have suggested, that with the departure of the pre-war generation of financial entrepreneurs and buccaneers a certain vitality and energy left the Ontario banks.

It is also far from clear just how the banks came through the Great Depression with so little apparent damage. They did maintain 'hidden reserves,' against which losses could be offset without any trace being left in the reports either to shareholders or to government. They certainly 'nursed' many loans – not only the debts of businesses but those of municipalities and governments – hoping that recovery would eventually make the loans 'good' again. A variety of dominion measures, especially some taken covertly in 1931–2, may have provided an artificial floor under the value of some financial assets, thus avoiding the pressure for the kind of general liquidation that both caused and spread trouble in the United States. Most important, perhaps, was the continuing public confidence in the banks, so that there were no important instances of the 'runs' – depositors demanding currency or gold – that destroyed so many American banks during the slump.

The banks, like the insurance companies and the other financial institutions, had to oblige governments in the 1930s by absorbing enormous quantities of dominion and provincial debt. Perhaps they were not reluctant to do so: the demand for ordinary advances was anything but buoyant, and many borrowers – both large and small – were anything but credit-worthy.

In the 1920s the Ontario mortgage companies were still growing, but slowly; also, they were replacing sterling indebtedness with dollar indebtedness, both by taking deposits and by issuing debentures. The trust companies were growing much more quickly. Indeed, two mortgage companies converted themselves into trust companies, and one of them, British Mortgage of Stratford, would have a career that would last into the mid-1960s. There was also a pronounced tendency for the smaller mortgage companies to be absorbed by the larger ones, or by trust companies. Thus the rapid growth of trust companies' equity and guaranteed funds is to some extent a result of such transformation and merger. But assets under administration also grew with remarkable speed.

Among the life insurance companies, as with the trust companies, the number of firms grew only slightly during the 1920s. Extra assets were accumulated chiefly by the old established companies, such as Canada Life and Manufacturers' Life. All the Ontario firms were growing swiftly, but not as rapidly as Sun Life of Montreal. Thus Ontario's share of life company assets was lower by 1929 than it had been in 1913. It will be remembered that the chartered banks had had a similar experience. Perhaps the banks and the insurance companies had the same problem: dynamic entrepreneurs of the pre-war years had gone to their rewards, to be replaced by salaried functionaries.

Canada's stock and bond markets were far more active in the 1920s than they had been before 1914. The volume of new issues, of both bonds and stocks, increased considerably. Yet Ontario's manufacturing industries financed their expansion to a remarkable extent without the use of the new issue market. Profits were ploughed back; new issues of shares were offered to old shareholders; bank loans were certainly used not only for working capital but to pay for longer-term investment; the network of interfirm debit and credit, both domestic and international, could often be helpful, and for foreign-owned firms the resources of the British and American financial markets, and often of parent companies, could be drawn upon. This is not to say that Ontario manufacturing firms did not use the Canadian new-issue market. In a few industries, of which the most important was pulp and paper, businesses raised large sums from the Canadian public. Mergers and corporate reorganizations, also, were often occasions for public issues that might bring some new funds into a business. And of course the development of manufacturing industry provided plenty of business for the banks. There were certainly some connections between industrial and financial development during the 1920s, but these links were far less close than one might expect, given the rapid and parallel expansion of finance and industry during that decade. So far as manufacturing was concerned the banks were essential, the non-bank financial intermediaries were of little importance, and the new-issue market was usually little more than a useful way to supplement other and more important sources of funds.

The 1930s were not pleasant for any financial institutions, and for those that concentrated on mortgage lending the atmosphere, if anything, was even more unpleasant than for the chartered banks. The mortgage loan companies actually contracted, reducing their mortgage lending in the process. The insurance companies, whose assets continued to grow because of the long-term nature of insurance contracts, reduced mortgage paper from 33 per cent of their portfolios to 18 per cent, directing most of their newly accruing funds into bonds and debentures. For trust companies the pattern is broadly the same. Meanwhile all these firms were absorbing government securities in considerable quantity, thus helping finance the large dominion and provincial government deficits.

Throughout the decade most firms tried to 'nurse' their urban and rural debtors. Nevertheless foreclosures and abandonments did occur, and many companies ended the decade with substantial amounts of 'real estate held for sale.'[134] If the dominion and the provinces had not provided for the adjustment of mortgage debt and for the delaying or preventing of seizures, doubtless there would have been more foreclosures. There were many measures, differing in detail from province to province; all were important for Ontario financial institutions, because in the 1920s so many of them had been lending, on mortgage and in other ways, throughout the country. Full details cannot be presented here.[135] It is enough to observe that in many instances the banks and the other financial intermediaries were prevented from enforcing the collection of principal, interest, or both, and that residential mortgages were no less protected than agricultural.

The effect was considerable. In 1938 the economic historian W.T. Easterbrook wrote, 'Although the final results cannot be appraised as yet, approximately $50,000,000 has been written off the farm indebtedness of the whole country to date, and a saving in interest charges made possible in many cases.'[136] But this was only part of the story. Residential mortgages, too, were often written down or in default; thanks to the interposition of provincial law, both principal and interest were quite often uncollectable even where the principal had not been reduced. In Saskatchewan there was even a general statutory reduction of interest rates and an extension of term, an arrangement that affected all mortgage debt in the province.

The troubles of the 1930s naturally affected the programs of provincial credit that had been set in train during and soon after the end of World War One. The government of Premier E.C. Drury had created three such programs. One plan provided funds for low-cost housing. This program, assisted by the dominion, did not survive the 1920s. Another program, mentioned in chapter 5 above, provided money under several headings for agricultural development in northern Ontario. Loans of various kinds were made between 1916 and 1937, when the Department of Northern Development was at last abolished. The third and most important program was embedded in three provincial statutes of 1921 – the Agricultural Development Act, the Farm Loans Associations Act, and the Agricultural Development Finance Act. These measures provided agricultural mortgage loans for up to twenty years at 5.5 per cent, and short-term loans of up to $2,000. Funds were to come from a network of Province of Ontario Savings Offices, first devised and opened specifically to provide for this new type of agricultural finance.

From 1922 through 1934, $62 million in government agricultural mortgage loans was actually paid out under the 1921 measures. However, in 1934, Easterbrook writes, 'Signs of weakness appeared, and lending operations ceased.'[137] By mid-1937, 16,059 Ontario farmers still owed $44.4 million to the province. And although the provincial government had discontinued the loan scheme, it retained the system of savings offices, whose deposit liabilities, during the 1930s, showed a distressing tendency to shrink.

During the war and in the 1920s there was a considerable expansion of stock-trading in Toronto, a great development of the bond business, and some rise in the level of financial sophistication. At the outbreak of war the Toronto Stock Exchange (TSE) had just occupied the new building in which it remained until 1937, at which time it moved to a new and elegant Art Deco structure on Bay Street. In 1914 the exchange listed 200 stocks, but by the end of World War Two there were 850 listed stocks, of which 357 were mines and oils – the affair, in 1914, of the Standard Stock and Mining Exchange. Until the merger with Standard in 1934 the TSE had fewer seats than Montreal, but its relative importance was certainly growing. Thus in 1939 Toronto handled 56.3 per cent of all the value of stock exchange trading in Canada, while Montreal handled only 41.5 per cent, and the remainder was shared by Vancouver, Calgary, and Winnipeg.[138]

As for the bond dealers, in 1916 they grouped themselves into the Bond Dealers' Asociation of Canada under the presidency of that eminent Torontonian, E.R. Wood. In succeeding years the association was closely involved in the planning of the later dominion war bond issues. It was the last three of these issues that really attracted mass subscription, laying the foundation for something that had not existed before 1914 – what Neufeld[139] calls a 'much more active *trading* market' in government bonds.

During the 1920s, although the nature of the work in the Toronto bond houses and on the stock exchange was not significantly different from what it had been before 1914, the scale and scope expanded enormously. The bond houses, especially Wood Gundy and Dominion Securities with considerable although more tentative assistance from A.E. Ames, were prominent in the underwriting, issuing, and distributing of new securities, both bonds and stocks. Naturally such firms did not escape the stimulus of the great stock-market boom of the late 1920s – or the painful reckoning that followed. But for the issuing houses there was work even in the 1930s. The dominion and the provinces were borrowing immense amounts; these issues had to be distributed and placed.

It was in the interwar decades that the Ontario government extended its network of protective legislation to cover the securities business. Although the dominion and Ontario companies legislation of the period 1877–1912 contained various provisons regarding the disclosure of information to shareholders, it was only in 1923 that the Ontario legislature actually passed a measure – An Act Respecting the Sale of Securities – that was designed to regulate the practices of issuers. However, before the act had been proclaimed the United Farmers lost power to the Conservatives, who never did proclaim it. There was more legislation in 1924, but the two acts of that year also remained unproclaimed. In 1928 the legislature passed the Securities Frauds Prevention Act,[140] a measure that actually did go into effect.

Under the 1928 act, a law that was widely imitated in other provinces, brokers and salesmen had to be registered, and issuers of securities had to register as brokers. Various practices – 'intentional omission of material facts, outlandish promises, fictitious trades, the gaining of unconscionable commissions, and violation of the Act or Regulations' – were explicitly defined to be fraudulent.[141] Also, under the Companies Information Act of 1928,[142] firms that established Ontario head offices, did business in the province, or issued securities in it, were required to file a prospectus, its contents to be specified in the regulations under that Act.[143] This provision was not new; for instance, since 1907 the Ontario companies legislation had specified that 'no subscription for stock, debentures, or other securities, induced or obtained by verbal representations, shall be binding on the subscriber, unless prior to his so subscribing he shall have received a copy of the prospectus.'[144] Now, however, companies and issuers were required not merely to give stockbuyers the prospectus but to file such documents with the provincial authorities.

These legislative developments obviously had something to do with the great stock-market boom of the late 1920s, and with the suspicions of fraud or evil-doing that clustered around the many company floatations that marked those years, not only in the United States but also in Canada. Legislative activity, however, did not end with the stock market crash of 1929, which afflicted Toronto as well as New York. In 1930 a new and more elaborate Securities Frauds Prevention Act was passed along with a measure by which directors became liable for any damage that might result from false statements in prospectuses.[145] In 1931[146] the legislature made explicit provision for a 'Board, commission, or body of persons, or any person' that would administer the laws against fraud on the new-issue market. In 1932 the various relevant statutes were collectively renamed the Securities Act.[147] In 1933 the statutes begin to refer to the Ontario Securities Commission,[148] which by that time had come into existence under the legislation of 1931. In 1937 that arrangement was confirmed: the commission received an extension of its investigative powers, and its membership and staff were confirmed by statute.[149] The province had acquired a new regulative agency, one of immense power and one that rapidly acquired considerable prestige as well.

Conclusion

This chapter has traced a financial evolution of great complexity. The Ontario financial institutions never contained in their number a German-style 'universal bank' or an overtly 'promotional bank,' nor would the observer claim that they detected all credit-worthy borrowers, never made mistakes, never failed, channelled no funds to friends and private promotions, or in all respects behaved as self-righteous journalists and politicians would have wished. Nevertheless, the overall impression is a favourable one. The local firms provided a valuable service to local savers and entrepreneurs, not only by offering finance from their own resources but by attracting it from the broader public at home and abroad. Indeed, the absence of a 'universal bank' may be taken as an indication that no such bank was needed: if anyone had wanted to set one up, there was little to prevent him from doing so. Nor would a 'promotional bank,' on the Franco-Teutonic-Russian model, have made much difference to the economic development of the province or to the ownership structure of its industry. The capital needs of Ontario were in some respects well covered by the retained profits of business, and in others they were such that capital inflow could not have been avoided. There were plenty of indigenous entrepreneurs in manufacturing, commerce, and public utilities, nor does it appear that they were hindered in any general way by shortages of finance. No matter what sort of financial structure the province might have had, foreign firms would have entered it to exploit opportunities not only in natural resources but in manufacture. Their presence does not prove, or testify to, a 'financial failure.'

In the process of economic transformation the financial institutions of the province rarely played an initiating role. They were of immense importance, but in their lending policies they followed developments in other sectors; they did not try to affect the course of economic change in any emphatic way. Thus they resembled the financial institutions of Britain more than those of France, Germany, or Russia. But given the rapidity with which the regional economy was transformed between 1870 and 1914, it is hard to believe that 'followership' was a costly policy.

Nevertheless, there could have been some problems with the branch banking networks and the other financial institutions, centred as they were in Toronto and Montreal. First of all, given that so many of the financiers were deeply involved with other sorts of economic activity, there must have been some tendency to direct funds towards those worthy projects that were personal or belonged to one's friends; the result might be a constriction of funds for other projects. The denial of funds might even be used as a weapon in some larger competitive game, as some have suggested was done with respect to the Sydney steel and coal complex in Nova Scotia. The result might be called corrupt, but it need not have been centralizing: indeed, it is apparent that Ontario industrialists and financiers had interests from coast to coast. Nor should it be assumed that 'predatory financing' was the product of centralization; it could have been used with equal or greater vigour if banking had been regionalized, because regionalization is much more likely to produce local semi-monopolies in the supply of loanable funds, at least through the banking system. Canadian manufacturing would in any event have tended to become centralized in the St Lawrence Valley, which had many natural advantages and contained so high a proportion of the nation's people. Nor is there much reason to think that local banks or local insurance companies would have produced local industrialization. In this respect the American scene is instructive. Wyoming has local unit banks and no financial centralization. Is Wyoming industrialized? New York has been a financial centre for generations. Has American manufacturing centralized itself in the New York area? Each question answers itself.

19 *The Provincial 'Exchequer'*[1]

Since 1945 the provincial government has bulked very large in the economic life of the province. Before 1939, and especially before 1914, it did not do so. Provincial taxing and spending were certainly important, but they mattered far more to legislators and to the dispensers and receivers of patronage than in the day-to-day economic life of the province's citizens. At Confederation Ontario acquired a relatively simple fiscal structure – no net debt, a rather narrow range of functions, a sizeable dominion subsidy, and the right to levy and collect licence fees, crown land revenues, and the very unpopular direct taxes. The provincial legislature and its 'creatures,' the munipalities, would finance and manage roads, education, relief, and such social services as they might choose to offer. Naturally the costs of the legislature and the provincial civil service had to be borne by the provincial authorities; so did some elements in the costs of prisons and the administration of justice. The province would also have to spend on agriculture and to administer the crown lands – no light task, and not an inexpensive matter. The provincial treasurer would collect interest on some municipal obligations, which dated from the old Municipal Loan Fund arrangements of the 1850s, and he would have to make some small interest payments, sometimes to Quebec and sometimes to the dominion, on account of certain 'common school lands.' The dominion subsidy was large in comparison with expected outlays. The simplicity of the 1867 arrangements continued with remarkably little basic change until the 1890s; thereafter change was rapid, with respect to both revenue and expenditure. Similarly, intergovernmental transfer payments were, if anything, simplified between 1867 and 1900, and it was only in the 1920s and 1930s that the thicket of intergovernmental payments with which we are familiar first grew on Ontario's soil.

In 1868, the dominion's subsidy had comfortably covered all Ontario's outlays, so that for a few years the province squirrelled away a large portion of its revenues. By 1914 the subsidy covered no more than 21 per cent; indeed, it hardly covered what Ontario was then spending on civil government, legislation, and the administration of justice. Admittedly, those may well have been the main provincial functions the Fathers of Confederation envisaged. But from the beginning the government of Ontario had larger visions; further, it inherited larger responsibilities, especially with respect to the subsidization of agriculture[2] and the common schools, which it never confided wholly to the municipalities.

Provincial finances were always interlocked with municipal finances, but in the period 1867–1914 the connections tended, if anything, to become fewer and weaker. At first the province made regular per capita payments to each municipality, but these later tailed away, falling to nothing, or almost nothing, by the early 1880s. As for the inherited Municipal Loan Fund, in the early years the treasurer collected considerable amounts as interest and amortization, but these receipts dropped off sharply, and in 1874 the province began a remarkable program of 'surplus distribution' by which the debts of the debtor municipalities were written off, while the non-debtor municipalities received large exchequer grants. In 1904 the province began to make statutory payments to municipalities under the Good Roads Act;[3] in and after 1906, furthermore, there were regular distributions to municipalities from the proceeds of the new corporations taxes. Also, there were regular but small and diminishing distributions to townships from the proceeds of crown lands sales. But only in 1938 did the province begin to make general unconditional grants to municipalities.

Getting and Spending

Revenue and expenditure grew more or less together, and rather gently, from the late 1860s until 1901, at which time there was a change in trend which appears in both the revenue series and the expenditure data.[4] Over the entire period 1868–1901 there were years of surpluses and years of deficits, and the cumulative result was a deficit of $1.4 million, which was only 1.3 per cent of total outlay during that thirty-four-year period. When one remembers that 'surplus distribution' had swallowed up $3.3 million and cost the province at least $200,000 per year in forgone interest and amortization, it is obvious that in all other respects the province was managing its finances in an extremely conservative way. On the other hand, the data suggest that even if the conditions and policies of the years before 1900 had continued unchanged, the situation was by no means as sound as it looked. Revenue was tending to rise less rapidly than outlay, and the two trend lines intersected about 1893. Thereafter deficits would be chronic unless something really dramatic were to happen. Hence it is hardly surprising that the 1890s proved to be a decade of fiscal innovation – in 1892, the first revenue from the succession duty; then, in 1899, the first funds from corporation tax.

The great changes of the 1890s were not well signposted in the contemporary press, on which one must depend for any idea of what went on in the legislature. In 1892 the *Globe* remarked that during 1889–90 the province was able to retire maturing railway aid certificates out of its operating revenues, and that hereafter it would issue terminable annuities to retire any outstanding railway aid certificates or to fund any new railway aid projects. Later that same year the *Globe* applauded the new succession duty, chiefly because it was a modest proposal whose yield would be spent on deserving charitable institutions. In 1899 the paper went on to remark that the inheritance duty was a 'Good Tax,' falling as it did on property that could readily bear it and that had probably escaped its due burden during the lifetimes of the decedents.[5]

Obviously the new and remarkably buoyant revenue source helped transform the fiscal situation after 1900 and accounted for the part of the change of trend[6] that the revenue series displays. But although revenues were tending to rise much more rapidly than before the turn of the century, expenditures were also rising much faster than before. Once more it was certain that surpluses would turn into deficits sooner or later, and in this new and more expansive period it happened sooner – in 1908. Although the revenue from the taxes was rising steadily, the revenue from that old mainstay, lands, forests, and mines, was simply fluctuating around the new and higher level to which it had suddenly jumped in 1903. Some help came from motor vehicle licences and fees, first collected in 1904. But gasoline would not be taxed until 1925.

These patterns of taxing, spending, and transferring produced patterns of lending and borrowing that were, for a modern government, unusual. During the first five years after Confederation the impression is given of a government that is gradually growing into its fiscal resources. The province did not need to borrow, in the usual sense, until after 1900; the *Public Accounts* first record payments on account of interest and sinking fund in 1906. Some funds were raised in the 1880s and 1890s by the sale of annuities, and some of the railway subsidies which began to be paid in 1872 took the form of railway aid certificates that the recipient companies could sell on the open market. But the new taxes of the 1890s ended these expedients, and when borrowing began again in 1905, it took new and more conventional forms – tap issues of dollar bonds from the treasurer's office in Toronto, and public floatations of sterling obligations through the Bank of Montreal in London. At that time the exchequer was still in surplus, but funds were needed to finance the construction of the Timiskaming and Northern Ontario Railway. Originally the provincial line was supposed to raise funds by selling its own bonds under provincial guarantee. But the market was unreceptive, and after a short period of emergency hand-to-mouth financing the province began to borrow for the purpose. Soon, however, it was borrowing to cover its own current and capital outlays, and after 1909 it began to borrow to finance Ontario Hydro.

It is natural to wonder just why the revenue and expenditure trends changed so dramatically in the years 1901–2. Perhaps the change may be thought to herald the end of 'Oliver Mowat's Ontario,' and to presage the Whitney era, which was certainly much more disposed both to spend and to borrow. The net cost of Ontario Hydro was almost zero, and none of the railway projects was directly charged to the provincial exchequer, while by 1914 railway earnings plus dominion subsidies had fully offset the interest on the railway's cost,[7] and municipal payments were doing the same for Hydro borrowings. The result was that, in spite of all the borrowings of the preceding eight years, in 1914 debt service was still only 3.5 per cent of total provincial outlays. Certainly new programs were introduced in the years after 1901. The most important were the 'good roads' system of subsidy to local governments, and much more generous spending on higher education – including, for the first time and at long last, regular statutory funding for the provincial university. But the new kinds of outlay account for less than 25 per cent of the new provincial outlays between 1900 and 1914. Obviously far more was being spent in traditional ways and on traditional programs. These latter programs are indeed characterized by dramatic increases both in current spending and in capital outlays; only railway subsidies tended to decrease.

Neither journalistic comments nor archival materials have, as yet, cast any useful light on this interesting development. Perhaps one might suggest the following hypothesis. As revenues were rising unexpectedly quickly, it was natural for government to respond to the emerging surpluses by spending more money in many directions, without fully counting the cost for future years. Once generous spending programs had been established it was possible to continue them even after deficits had begun, because, in the interim, through railway and Hydro borrowing the province had discovered that domestic and overseas markets were quite willing to absorb its bonds.

One can examine the growth of government spending more precisely by grouping the various sorts of outlay into six analytical categories and then comparing each category with total outlay and with the growth in spending.[8] The first category might be called 'maintaining the fabric of society,' or MFS for short. It includes civil government, legislation, justice, prisons, and the construction and repair of the relevant public buildings. The second category is education and welfare – the 'Infant Welfare State,' or IWS. The third is 'Economic Development,' or ED, which includes agriculture and in the earlier years mechanics' institutes, public works of a developmental sort, crown lands administration, technical education, colonization and immigration, drainage, railway and sugar-beet subsidies, and some minor outlays of a developmental kind. The fourth category is 'higher education' or HE. Fifth is 'roads,' including both colonization roads and the programs which came after 1900. Finally there is the 'other' category, which includes debt service, surplus distribution, and many miscellaneous items that vary unpredictably from year to year.

There are wild swings in the relative importance of the different elements. Developmental spending was of special significance during the period 1872–82, almost entirely because of railway subsidies and large outlays on colonization. Spending on MFS and IWS, on the other hand, marched inexorably upward, generally rising and never declining very much, except when some major public work such as the central prison or the new parliament building was completed. It might almost be said that after the 1870s the province had to cut back on ED and on municipal aid to accommodate the steady growth of MFS and IWS – expenditures that already by 1880 accounted for almost 70 per cent of total provincial spending, and that certainly accounted for the long-run financial problems that have already been described.

After 1901 the picture is very different. All the expenditure categories show dramatic increases, with the fastest growth rates in debt service, higher education, and road outlays. Because outlays on colonization, agriculture, and immigration increased substantially, the province found itself spending much more on ED. IWS and MFS increased, but less rapidly. Their joint share in outlay, which had been 70 per cent in 1901, was only 50 per cent in 1913. The government's priorities had certainly changed, but spending in traditional directions was definitely not stagnating.

Both on the revenue and on the expenditure side, the trends of 1902–14 continued until the middle of World War One. Thereafter the development both of revenue and of expenditure became much more erratic than before, and much more obviously sensitive to changes in government. The data clearly reveal a surge of revenue and especially of expenditure during the period of the United Farmers government, renewed growth at a slower rate after a cut-back in spending soon after the beginning of the Ferguson-Henry period, and stability in outlay combined with a surge in revenue following the election of 1934. Again, until 1932 the trend increase in expenditure was always very much greater than the trend increase in revenue. Except in 1917 there was always a deficit, and in many years that deficit was very large – 51 per cent of total outlays in 1923, 43 per cent in 1934, and 20 per cent in 1940. In absolute terms, of course, the deficits were growing all the time. In 1939, for example, the provincial deficit was more than double the total outlays of 1914. It is reasonably clear that, although when governments changed efforts were often made to reduce outlays and raise tax rates, the successive provincial governments cannot have been in control of spending or of the deficit. In these circumstances it is hardly surprising that the most rapidly growing outlay item was debt service, which took 20 per cent of government outlay in 1939 as compared with 9 per cent (gross of interest receipts) in 1914.

Outlays on roads grew almost as fast as outlays on the debt, and during the Drury years they increased especially quickly. During the same period there was a dramatic jump in IWS. In the 1920s, much of the upward propulsion came from new programs – mothers' allowances, superannuation for schoolteachers and public servants, and new initiatives in the field of labour – together with very much higher outlays for health care, and an upward drift in education spending. During the 1930s old age pensions were introduced, and the other outlays in IWS rose fairly steadily, although educational spending fluctuated and the growth in relief spending dominated the decade. As for MFS, after an upward spurt during the UFO period there was stagnation until World War Two, at which time such outlays were only 5 per cent of total outlays, as against 18 per cent in 1914. Outlays on ED also surged during the Drury period, were cut back in 1924–6, and then resumed a reasonably gentle expansion until after 1930, when they fell perceptibly; in 1939 Ontario was deploying only 6.7 per cent of its expenditure on ED. Higher education, clearly the stepchild of the exchequer, attracted a large increase in funding under the United Farmers, then slumped to an outlay of just under $3 million, a figure around which spending fluctuated until the late 1930s. In 1939 the province allocated 2.4 per cent of its outlay to higher education; in 1914 it had allocated 7 per cent. Spending on universities had increased by $2.4 million, while total provincial spending had jumped by $130 million.

Priorities had changed since pre-war days. Outlays for roads, education, welfare and debt service grew especially rapidly; presumably for the first items the income elasticity of demand[9] was comparatively high, and the rapid growth of debt service must be seen as the natural result of a disjunction between people's desire for government services and their willingness to pay taxes for them. As for higher education, and direct outlays on economic development, extra outlays were not demanded with equal vigour, and so spending grew relatively slowly. But for all kinds of spending – even higher education – per capita outlays seem to have outgrown income per capita. It is no wonder that the provincial treasurers had to raise some old tax rates and to invent as many new taxes as they could.

The tax history of twentieth-century Ontario has been well chronicled,[10] so that one need not detail all the adjustments here. The main changes were as follows. In 1914 there were increases in the rates of corporation tax and succession duty. In 1915 there was a special provincial war tax – a surcharge on municipal real property taxation. In 1916, when liquor prohibition was enacted, there were new amusement taxes. Mines tax rates rose in 1917. In 1921 succession and corporation tax rates went up again, and there were new taxes on real estate transfers and bank reserves. In 1924 new taxes were imposed on mines, and the province began to collect land tax in unorganized territories. Gasoline was taxed for the first time in 1925. In 1932, the province began to tax the profits of all corporations as well as their capitals; until that time, only utility profits had been taxable. Rates of tax, meanwhile, were drifting upward throughout the late 1920s and early 1930s, and the liquor trade was developing into an important source of revenue, especially after 'liquor control' replaced prohibition in 1927. Finally, in 1935, the province at last imposed its own tax on personal incomes. The retail sales tax, however, would not appear until long after World War Two.

In addition, through the 1920s and especially during the 1930s the authorities in Queen's Park were receiving large new subventions from the dominion. These were all 'conditional' grants: that is to say, they were connected with 'shared cost programs' – labour exchanges, roads, old age pensions, and, of course, relief. In 1939 total transfers from Ottawa to Queen's Park covered 13 per cent of provincial spending. Some of these receipts, especially those on pensions, involved the province in spending money from its own resources – outlays that it might not otherwise have made. But other receipts, especially those related to roads and relief, probably absolved the provincial exchequer from heavy burdens that it would otherwise have had to shoulder alone.

Deficit and Debt

In spite of new taxes, higher rates, and dominion subventions, the provincial debt moved relentlessly and inexorably upward. Debt-free in 1900, by 1914 the province owed $40.4 million, but the net debt was only $5 million, because so much of the gross debt was the result of borrowing for Ontario Hydro and the T&NO. Thereafter, fuelled by constant deficits, the net debt rose ever higher. In 1929 the figure was $186.7 million, and in 1940, $494.5 million. In addition, because in 1917 Hydro began to borrow on its own account, contingent liabilities rose from $9.6 million in 1914 to $134.7 million in 1940. Much of the increase reflected the relief outlays of the 1930s, which seem to have accounted for at least 55 per cent of the borrowing during those years. But there was, in addition, a structural problem of balancing ordinary outlay, whether current or capital, against regular and recurring revenue.

Naturally the provincial authorities noticed the growth of debt, and they worried about it. Premier Hepburn was perhaps more concerned than other premiers had been. But by 1940 there was no obvious solution in sight. The Ontario government tried to convince the Rowell-Sirois Commission that Ottawa should vacate the fields of income taxation and succession duties, leaving these to the provinces. This would have more or less balanced the Ontario budget. But of course as a solution it was 'not on:' the dominion, too, was running a deficit. Nor would the Rowell-Sirois Commissioners' solution, by which Ottawa would acquire certain revenues while financing some welfare activities, have helped: if the dominion were to take over all Ontario's welfare programmes while collecting all the corporation taxes, all the income taxes, and all the succession duties, the Ontario exchequer would have been worse off.[11]

So far as one can tell from the scanty press coverage of the legislature's financial proceedings, legislators and journalists remained as confused about the financial situation as the public must have been. In February 1923 the provincial treasurer told the legislature that the existing taxes would comfortably meet expenditures in the fiscal year just ending. But in the event the deficit was $40 million, or half of total outlay. In 1927 Howard Ferguson explained to the legislature that his government's taxation policy was to shift the burden to make it more equitable. Thus, for instance, the tax on motor vehicles would be reduced, but a policy of 'pay as you go, as far as you go, and as fast as you go,' was proper in regard to the financing of highways through gasoline taxation. In 1934 G.S. Henry defined Ontario's taxation policy in the following terms: his government was not a taxing body, but a seller of services; if a person did not care to use the services he would not have to buy – 'It is significant that we derive our revenue mainly from luxuries – we have no provincial income tax. Dominion subsidy, licenses, fees, liquor profits, payments for privileges, gasoline tax – that is roughly the picture of our sources of revenue.' Naturally Premier Henry did not mention the succession duty and the corporation taxes, inescapable levies that were then providing 16 per cent of Ontario's revenue, or the dominion contributions to pensions, roadbuilding, and relief, which provided another 23 per cent. The government of Mitchell Hepburn was very critical of the corporation tax, arguing that profits, not capital, should be taxed; the impost, Hepburn argued, was handed on to consumers in the domestic market, while it handicapped Ontario's exporters. Nuisance taxes, also, did not appeal to Hepburn, who abolished them when he could. But the Hepburn government could not afford to dispense with the corporation tax, whose coverage it proceeded to broaden. And although it claimed to be aiming at a balanced budget, it did not manage to close the budgetary gap, even while imposing an income tax of its own. In 1937 Hepburn had said that he was introducing a 'pay as you go' policy; by 1940 there was still some distance to go before the policy would pay.

Conclusion

These findings prompt some reflections about the nature of taxing and spending in democratic Ontario, especially during the twentieth century. So far as taxation was concerned, the authorities relied as long as possible, and as far as possible, on taxes that were almost self-administering, and on revenue sources wherein collection and administration costs would be small. This was most obviously true of the succession duty and the original corporation tax, but most of the later nuisance taxes and of course the gasoline tax produced revenue simply and almost costlessly. The same might be said of the drink trade. Not only were there interesting possibilities for patronage, but the 'rate of tax' did not have to be legislated at all; the political cost, therefore, was insignificant, although the government did have to operate the stores if it was to garner the loot. Certainly the province did not try to redistribute income or wealth through its taxing and spending. On the expenditure side, the Ontario pattern illustrates the paradox of the democratic exchequer. Everyone wants public service, and governments are elected by providing more and by promising still more, but legislatures, reflecting legislators' understanding of public attitudes, will not impose the taxes to pay for the services. The Hepburn income tax may illustrate the problem. If the premier had been serious about balancing the budget, why not impose income tax rates that would bring in sufficient revenue to make the budget balance? Of course from time to time an opposition may displace a government by crying about 'fiscal indiscipline,' 'squandering,' and the like, but a change of government does not dispose of the paradox, which soon reasserts itself. Meanwhile, the whole operation can continue so long as the financial environment is complaisant. In 1905 the provincial treasurer discovered that it is really quite easy to borrow. Thereafter he and his successors never looked back. The old nineteenth-century days of balanced budgets might have been good; the new twentieth-century ways to electoral success looked even better.

Statistical Appendixes

Appendix A: Northern Forestry Statistics

TABLE A1
Sales of Timber Limits, 1871–1903

Year	Location	Size (sq. miles)	Dues	Ground Rent	Bonus	Bonus (sq. miles)
1871	Muskoka-Parry Sound	487	0.75	2.00	117,672	241.62
1872	North Shore of Lake Huron	5,031	0.75	2.00	592,601	117.79
1877	Muskoka-Parry Sound	375	0.75	2.00	75,739	201.97
1881	South of Lake Nipissing and French River	1,379	0.75	2.00	733,675	532.00
1885	Nipissing and North Shore	1,054.25	0.75	2.00	318,645	302.73
1887	Muskoka-Petawawa	459	1.00	3.00	1,312,313	314.87
1890	Rainy River	376	1.00	3.00	346,256	919.00
1892	Nipigon	633	1.25	3.00	2,315.058	3,657.18
1897	Sudbury Rainy River	159.25	1.25	3.00	265,162	1,665.07
1899	Nipissing-Alogoma	287.75	1.25	3.00	698,080	2,426
	Rainy River	72.5	1.25	3.00	25,738	355
1903	Timiskaming	826.25	2.00	5.00	3,687,337	4,461.38

NOTE: All timber limits were sold for three separate payments:
1. Dues: Fixed by government and paid on wood cut
2. Ground Rent: Fixed by government and determined by land area in limit
3. Bonus: The basic competitive aspect of the bidding for limits; no fixed amount, the total amount often being not paid in one instalment

SOURCE: 'Annual Reports,' *Crown Lands* (Ont.) 1872–1905

TABLE A2
Pulp and Paper Mills, Northern Ontario, 1895–1930

North Shore of Lake Huron

1. Sault Ste Marie: founded c. 1895 as Sault Ste Marie Pulp and Paper, by F.H. Clergue, an American promoter. Bankruptcy in 1903.
2. Espanola: founded 1905 by Spanish River Company, a consortium of US and Canadian investors.
3. Sturgeon Falls: founded 1901 as Sturgeon Falls Company; taken over by Ontario Pulp and Paper Company (English investors) in 1905.
4. In 1911 the above three firms were acquired by the Backus-Brooks group, from Wisconsin. Sault became Lake Superior Pulp and Paper; Espanola and Sturgeon Falls operated as Spanish River Pulp and Paper. All three were absorbed by Abitibi in 1928.
5. Katawong (Manitoulin Island): founded 1925 by Manitoulin Pulp Company (American investors from Wisconsin). A small mill buying wood from local settlers.

Clay Belt

6. Iroquois Falls: founded 1912 as Abitibi Pulp and Paper Company (Pulp and Power Company after 1914). Canadian-owned, though originally with some American investors.
7. Smooth Rock Falls: founded 1917 as Mattagami Pulp and Paper Company. Taken over by Abitibi in 1927.
8. Kapuskasing: founded 1920 as Spruce Falls Power and Paper Ltd. Owned by Kimberly-Clarke; 49 per cent interest sold to *New York Times*
9. Haileybury: founded 1927 as Northern Ontario Light and Power Company, New Liskeard. Closed in 1934.

North-West Ontario

10. Dryden: founded 1911 as Dryden Pulp and Paper Company Ltd. T.A.G. Gordon first.
11. Fort Frances: founded in 1914 as Fort Frances Pulp and Paper Company; controlled by Minnesota and Ontario Paper Company, which was in turn controlled by Backus-Brooks
12. Port Arthur (Thunder Bay): founded in 1918 as Port Arthur Pulp and Paper Company Ltd; became Thunder Bay Paper Company Ltd. Second firm founded in 1924 as Provincial Paper Ltd.
13. Fort William (Thunder Bay): founded in 1911 as Fort William Paper. In 1927, taken over by Abitibi. Second firm founded in 1924 as Great Lakes Paper Company Ltd, controlled by Backus-Brooks; in receivership in 1930.
14. Nipigon: founded in 1923 as Nipigon Corporation Ltd; controlled by Canadian International Paper Company Ltd, subsidiary of International Paper and Power Co. of New York.
15. Kenora: founded in 1924 as Kenora Paper Mills Ltd, a subsidiary of Backus-Brooks's Minnesota and Ontario Paper Company.

Appendix B: The Industrial Statistics and the Problems They Pose

Between 1870 and 1914 one is dependent largely on the decennial censuses, which, as was observed in chapter 1, provide quite extensive information about Ontario industry. Regrettably, during the period 1870–1911 there were some changes in coverage with respect to industry, and these are sufficiently large to prevent one from using some of the census information without qualifications and adjustments, while some types of commodity – especially textiles and dairy products – were counted as industrial output only if they were not produced on farms, where household production was assessed only incompletely and in dissimilar ways. Similarly, the very considerable volume of industrial production that occurred in the railway company shops was not included in the census industrial data. Regrettably, also, there are almost no usable annual series on industrial production. The Ontario authorities attempted annual surveys in the early 1880s and after 1901, but coverage was so incomplete and so erratic that for historical purposes the data cannot be used.[1] Like the United Kingdom, Canada was slow to establish an annual census of production, and the Dominion Bureau of Statistics was set up only in 1918. Hence one must begin by addressing the problems that the census data pose. The decennial censuses systematically gathered information about 'industry' – capital employed, wage and salary earners, cost of raw material, and gross value of sales. In 1906 and 1916 there were, in addition, postal censuses of manufactures, which related to the calendar years 1905 and 1915. In 1918 the newly created Dominion Bureau of Statistics began the series of annual censuses of manufacturing that has continued until the present. The first such census covers the year 1917. With the creation of this annual census the decennial enumeration no longer tried to cover manufacturing industry, although after 1918 it came to treat various matters that in the 1870s, 1880s, and 1890s would have been included with 'industry.'

The early censuses recorded information on 'industrial establishments,' and published this information in great detail. The 1871 census, which reported industrial information for 1870, identified 140 separate 'industries'; later censuses retained this degree of detail, and indeed increased it. The enumerators counted the number of establishments, the number of employees, the capital employed, the annual outlays on wages and raw materials, and the value of output. In later censuses, such as those of 1901 and 1911, still more detail was gathered. However, no one knows how accurate the returns were. Most businesses were unincorporated, and many were extremely small; also, there was no personal income tax and no levy on corporation profits. Therefore, many business records must have been sketchy at best. It is reasonable to suppose that many firms had only the vaguest ideas about their annual receipts, payments, employment, and capital, even assuming that the notion of 'capital employed' can be given an unambiguous meaning. In the printed reports for individual industries in particular counties, where often only a single firm was present, there is commonly a suspicious roundness to the reported figures. Nevertheless, the economic historian cannot avoid using these materials, and one must simply hope that the reporting errors cancel one another. Perhaps for employment, costs, and sales, this hope is a reasonable one. But for 'capital employed' it is much harder to defend, because no one is sure how to measure capital. Hence the present study makes use without apology of census information on labour, raw materials, and outputs, but makes very sparing use of the census data on 'capital employed.'

In 1918 the newly established Dominion Bureau of Statistics began an annual census of manufacturing that it and its successor, Statistics Canada, have carried on until the present. It appears that no such census was carried out for the year 1931, and for 1940 only the most aggregative findings have ever been published; but with these two exceptions there is annual information on output, number of employees, costs of raw materials, and capitalization, from 1917 to 1941. However, what the statistician giveth he also taketh away. The Dominion Bureau of Statistics published far less detail on industrial structure and on the regional aspect of that structure than the census authorities had published for 1870–1915. The historian therefore finds gaps and can less readily rearrange the numbers to ensure consistency through time or to answer questions that did not occur to contemporary statisticians.

The annual census of manufacturing was published in a peculiar way. The main reportage consisted of an entry in the *Canada Year Book*. Only in the earliest years did the separately issued census report consist of more than a *Canada Year Book* reprint, and remarkably little information was published in other forms. Until the mid-1920s the reports on provincial manufacturing gave industrial information that the main entry did not begin to contain until the late 1920s. Some information, also, found its way into annual or irregular reports on particular industries. But these reports often contained no provincial breakdowns – a commentary on the ideological gulf that separates the dominion of the 1920s and 1930s from the federal state of the 1980s.

From 1867 until 1915 there was a steady increase in the number of separately identified 'census industries,' but thereafter the Bureau of Statistics was less interested in this aspect of the industrial structure. Normally it published information only on the forty largest industries, a gathering that customarily covered between 75 per cent and 80 per cent of all Ontario's industrial output. In certain years,[2] it does not appear to have published even this breakdown on a province-by-province basis.

The decennial enumerations and the postal census included with 'industry' many repair, service, and utilities activities that later enumerations would not define as 'manufacturing.' In 1870–90, for instance, blacksmithing was substantial; thereafter, because of changes in coverage definition, it first diminishes, and then, after the mid-twenties, vanishes entirely. Electric power generation and gas production and distribution counted as 'industry' up to 1936. Carpenters, painters, glaziers, dyers, cleaners, launderers, jewellers, furriers, and photographic galleries, were regularly counted with 'industry' in the nineteenth century, and were banished from the statistics for good only in the mid-1920s. The historian can rid the earlier data of these intrusions, standardizing more or less completely on the definitions of 1936–41. For certain years in the period 1917–35, when full data were not published, the DBS statisticians themselves effected the purgations in publications of the period 1936–41. Yet in the early census tabulations there remains a large amount of hand and repair work that would not have been counted after the mid-1920s but that is certainly embedded deeply and inextricably in the industrial statistics of 1870–1915. For some activities, such as blacksmithing, tailoring, and dressmaking, the situation is apparent, even though the numerical resolution is not. Thus one is left with the fact that on the basis of the definitions of the 1920s and 1930s, the published census statistics of 1870–1915 exaggerate the size of Ontario's manufacturing industry, while – because they omit certain categories of farm production and railway workshop activity – they understate the volume of commodity output that might as well have come from factories.

Regrettably, there is more to 'coverage' than the question of inclusion or exclusion by industry, or the question of handwork, repair work, or public utilities. Which establishments are to be enumerated?[3] During the census enumerations of 1870–90, the rule was to count every establishment, no matter how small. During the annual enumerations of 1917–41 the same rule applied, although because of a narrowing definition of 'industry' the coverage diminished. Unfortunately, in the decennial censuses for 1900–10 and the postal censuses for 1905 and 1915, other criteria were applied. In 1900–10 the idea was to count no establishment that employed fewer than five workers. In 1906 and 1916, establishments were excluded if they produced less than $2,500 worth of output per year. However, in some industries all establishments were counted, no matter how small: in 1901, all establishments producing butter, cheese, brick, and tile were included; in 1906, 1911, and 1916, these 'exceptions' were extended to include flour- and grist-mills, saw and shingle-mills, fish-curing plants, lime kilns, and electric light and power plants. This new discontinuity was certainly less drastic than that separating 1890 from 1900. Indeed, the census officials argued that it did not matter much: the new 'exceptions' from the 'five workers or more' rule added only 1.24 per cent to the value of production in 1905, and only 1.52 per cent in 1910.[4] Nevertheless, this additional break is bound to worry the purist. And the breaks between 1890 and 1900 and between 1915 and 1917 certainly cannot be ignored.

The 1906 postal census of manufactures will not be discussed here because its data are not needed. The next postal census, held in 1916, poses certain problems of its own. In this census an establishment was included only if it produced at least $2,500 worth of output in the census year – 1915 – unless it operated in one of the industries, such as flour-milling, which were fully enumerated in 1911 regardless of size. Also, although both postal censuses were very detailed, neither gathered all the information produced in the decennial enumerations. When publishing the results of the 1916 postal census, the statisticians included tables that excluded all establishments having fewer than five employees. The result, therefore, should be comparable with the 1911 data except in so far as some establishments may have produced less than $2,500 worth of output while employing at least five workers, but did not operate in one of the fully enumerated industries. It is reasonable to suppose that such establishments were few and, in the overall picture, utterly insignificant.

Exactly the same basic information on employment, wages and salaries, costs, capital, and output was gathered until the end of our period, although in some years from 1870 some items were omitted. Thus in 1906 there was no question about the cost of raw materials, and in 1915 the postal census gathered information about employment but did not publish any separate tabulation for employment in firms having five employees or more. Furthermore, although the 'cost of materials' was usually reported, the cost of fuel and power was not. It is therefore not possible to derive a correct measure of 'value added' – the work actually done in an establishment or in an industry.

Fortunately, two decades ago Gordon Bertram, in co-operation with the Bureau of Statistics, produced an adjusted series for the period 1870–1915, which appears to be reasonably consistent in coverage and definition; also it is designed to connect with later DBS calculations. First of all, Bertram purged the data from the early censuses so as to eliminate activities that were not defined as manufacturing in the Standard Industrial Classification, adopted by the bureau in 1948. Second, he made upward adjustments in the published census data for 1900, 1910, and 1915, so as to include estimated values for the small establishments for which results were not then compiled. These upward adjustments were made industry by industry, and for all Canada they added 15.7 per cent to the estimate of the dominion's manufacturing in 1900, 8.5 per cent in 1910, and 2.3 per cent in 1915. Regrettably, Bertram did not perform these calculations for Ontario. But since the province's recorded industrial output was half the dominion's in 1900, and even larger in 1910 and 1915, little can go wrong if Bertram's correction is applied to the Ontario data. Except where otherwise stated, we have therefore used Ontario data that have been derived from Bertram's Ontario figures by the application of his all-Canada correction factors for 1900, 1910, and 1915.

The calculations begin with 1870, a year of considerable prosperity. But where is one to end? Every year between 1930 and 1940 was depressed, and although we have totals for 1940, we have no information on individual industries. The best year to choose seems to be 1941, when wartime prosperity was well established but not yet hectic, and when various interesting developments in the industrial structure were well under way. However, an argument can also be made for stopping in 1929. Therefore, we have calculated compound rates of growth over several periods, any of which could be argued for. These appear in table 7.15. Also, so as to reveal the structural change in the industrial economy we have grouped all the industrial outputs in three categories – consumer goods, intermediate goods, and capital goods including consumer durable goods. Our findings are in table 7.15. The first group includes categories such as meat-packing, brewing, distilling, boots, clothing, and canning; the second contains cotton textiles, flour-milling, saw-milling, primary iron and steel, and pulp and paper; the third contains agricultural implements, cars, furniture, household appliances, and the entire range of machinery, equipment, and foundry production. The categorization is certainly not perfect, if only in that some census industries produced two or more sorts of output. In broad outline, however, it seems to make sense. And it is only for broad outline that we shall be using it. We also have calculated growth rates for thirty-two industries that we can trace throughout our period, or at least for large parts of it. These findings appear in table 7.16. The data in tables 7.15 and 7.16 are derived directly from published information, in some instances with adjustments of our own; thus they are not in all instances precisely comparable with Bertram's data. Divergences, however, are slight.

Bertram's set of rearranged census data yields table 7.1, which includes census data on output and value added, along with Bertram's estimates, further revised to approximate full coverage for 1900–15; it also includes the census information on employment, which Bertram did not calculate, and a calculation of output per worker that uses census information only. The comparison of Bertram's estimates for output and value added with census figures is revealing: it suggests that, in spite of the many changes in census coverage, it is reasonably safe to use the census data to trace industrial growth over long periods, even though for particular decades, as in the 1890s and after 1900, the adjusted data give a very different picture from the raw ones. This result, in turn, occurs simply because Bertram makes the largest adjustment for the year 1900, and a very small one for the year 1915. Nevertheless, no matter that series is used, it is obvious that the 1870s and 1880s were years of very considerable expansion, though not nearly as rapid as the first years of this century, while the 1890s was a period of comparatively slow growth in manufacturing.

Bertram also produced series for the outputs of seventeen main industry groups and for primary and secondary manufacturing; these are reproduced in table 7.2. Primary manufacturing is taken to include those activities that involve further processing of domestic resources, chiefly for sale in export markets; secondary manufacturing involves more processing, substantial dependence on domestic markets, and often a use of foreign as well as domestic inputs. The latter kind of production grew more rapidly, especially in the twentieth century.

The data of tables 7.1 and 7.15 are still rather unrefined. The employment figures have not been adjusted to take account of changes in the average number of hours worked per year. Regrettably, there seems to be no means of making this adjustment. Also, the output data have not been adjusted for deflation and inflation. Here some adjustments can be made, although the available price data are not really suitable. Thanks to Michell, there are wholesale price indexes for the period 1868–1925; these are organized by commodity groups, no one of which corresponds to the census definitions of 'industry.' The Bureau of Statistics and the compilers of the first edition of *Historical Statistics of Canada* have produced more sophisticated wholesale price indexes for the years since 1867, but their results have the same shortcoming. There is a wholesale price index for 'fully and chiefly manufactured goods' that ought to fit the data fairly well; regrettably, it begins only in 1890.

These price data show that prices moved in different ways for various goods. Thus iron and other metals became steadily cheaper, while textiles and chemicals fell in price up to 1900 and then rose slightly. It also seems that the prices of manufactures fell much more in the period 1870–1900 than the general price index, dominated as it was by primary products, while the increase in the early twentieth century was far less for manufactures than for other goods – a 7.3 per cent increase in the index for the prices of fully and chiefly manufactured goods, as against 27.7 per cent for raw and partly manufactured goods. The difference is even greater if measured from the bottom of the price trough in 1896 to 1913. The price level of raw and partly manufactured products rose by 57.9 per cent in that seventeen-year period, while for fully and partly manufactured products wholesale prices rose 19.1 per cent.

One must therefore conclude that the current-price data of table 7.1 involve a substantial understatement of physical growth during the period 1870–1900, and only a slight exaggeration of it for the period 1900–10. In the table, if census data are used, output increases by at least 405.3 per cent from 1870 to 1910, while employment grows by 173.6 per cent and output per employee rises by 84.7 per cent. In reality, both physical output and output per worker must have risen by substantially more. Although there does not seem to be any very good way in which the data for 1870 and 1880 may be properly deflated, one can get a rough idea by applying the Michell and DBS general price index while recognizing that this procedure understates the real growth in industrial output. For 1890–1910 the DBS index for 'fully and chiefly manufactured goods' may be used. The result is table 7.3.

No one should be surprised to find that if different deflators are used different 'real answers' are obtained for output, output per worker and growth. But it is obviously very important to use the deflator that is least likely to mislead, and to be aware of the biases in the statistical techniques. Thus, for instance, if one relied on the Michell or DBS general price deflators, one would pretty clearly be understating the growth of the Ontario industrial economy not only in the twentieth century but also in the 1890s; also, because of what is known about the particular price-movements in the 1870s and 1880s, one can be reasonably sure that outputs grew more rapidly in those decades than the data can disclose.

Appendix C: Tables

TABLE 2.1
Gainful Workers, Ontario

Gainful Workers (thousand persons)

1871	461	1901	755	1931	1,346
1881	630	1911	991	1941	1,455
1891	732	1921	1,118		

Percentage Increase		Gainful Workers as Per cent of Population	
1871–81	36.7	1871	28.4
1881–91	16.2	1881	32.7
1891–1901	3.1	1891	34.6
1901–11	31.3	1901	34.6
1911–21	12.8	1911	39.2
1921–31	20.4	1921	38.1
1931–41	8.1	1931	39.2
		1941	38.4; 41.4 (including active service)

SOURCE: derived from *Census* volumes

TABLE 2.2
Occupations of Ontario's Gainfully Employed, Census Years, 1871–1941 (thousands and percentages)
1891–1931: ten years and over; 1941: fourteen years and over; 1871–81: coverage uncertain

		1871		1881		1891		1901		1911		1921		1931		1941	
		No.	%	No.	%	No.	%	No.	%	No.	%	No.	%	No.	%	No.	%
Agriculture	M					332	52.2	303	46.9	301	36.0	290	29.2	299	27.2	265	23.2
	F					6	5.8	4	3.6	6	3.7	5	2.8	7	2.7	5	1.7
	T	229	49.6	304	48.4	338	46.2	307	40.7	307	31.0	295	26.4	306	22.7	270	18.6
Fishing, Logging	T	4	0.8			7	1.0	8	1.1	14	1.4	10	0.9	15	1.1	20	1.4
Mining, Quarrying	T	0.2	0.1			2	0.3	4	0.5	17	1.7	7	0.6	15	1.1	24	1.6
Manufacturing	M					89	14.0	146*	22.5*	129	15.5	150	16.3	182	16.6	264	23.2
	F					32	33.7	34*	31.1*	46	29.4	40	20.5	42	17.0	55	17.4
	T	65	14.1	130	20.7	121	16.5	180*	23.8*	175	17.7	190	17.0	224	16.6	319	21.9
Construction	T	23	5.0			40	5.5	*	*	54	5.4	64	5.7	77	5.7	72	4.9
Transportation	M					25	4.0	†	†	56	6.7	71	7.7	102	9.3	8	7.7
	F					0.5	0.5	†	†	2	1.6	7	3.5	7	3.0	6	1.8
	T	8	1.8			25.5	3.5	†	†	58	5.9	78	7.0	109	8.1	94	6.5
Trade and Finance	M					39	6.2	78†	12.1†	71	8.5	92	9.9	112	10.2	115	10.8
	F					4	3.8	5†	4.6†	14	9.0	21	11.0	23	9.2	34	10.7
	T	12	3.3	44	7.1	43	5.9	83†	11.0†	85	8.6	113	10.1	135	10.0	149	10.2

TABLE 2.2 (concluded)

		1871 No.	1871 %	1881 No.	1881 %	1891 No.	1891 %	1901 No.	1901 %	1911 No.	1911 %	1921 No.	1921 %	1931 No.	1931 %	1941 No.	1941 %
Service	M					40	6.3	37	5.7	49	5.9	69	7.4	97	8.8	118	10.4
	F					51	53.5	58	53.6	70	44.9	77	39.5	115	46.0	135	42.9
	T	47	10.1			91	12.4	95	12.6	125	12.6	146	13.1	212	15.8	253	17.4
Personal	M					15	2.4	14	2.1	24	2.8	24	2.6	44	4.0		
	F					42	43.6	47	43.5	52	33.6	45	23.3	76	30.5		
	T	28	6.0	33	5.3	57	7.8	61	8.1	76	7.7	69	6.2	120	8.9		
Professional	M					17	2.6			19	2.3	28	3.1	39	3.5		
	F					9	9.4			17	11.0	31	15.9	39	15.5		
	T	17	3.6	23	3.7	26	3.6			36	3.6	59	5.3	78	5.8		
Clerical	M					10	1.6	15	3.5	17	3.1	33	5.1	43	5.3	78	6.8
	F					2	2.1	8	7.0	17	11.3	44	22.4	54	21.8	75	23.6
	T	8	1.8	††	††	12	1.6	23	3.0	34	3.4	77	6.9	97	7.2	143	9.8
Labourers	T	62	13.5	94	15.0	51	7.0	51	6.8	117	11.8	117	10.5	143	10.6	97	6.7
Total	M					636		646		836		923		1,097		1,140	
	F					96		109		155		195		249		315	
	T	461		630		732		755		991		1,118		1,346		1,455	

NOTES: Data for male and female workers begin with 1891. These are tabulated separately in the table when there are enough female workers to make the tabulation interesting. Occupational data for 1891 through 1921 were rearranged on the basis of the 1931 classification, although some adjustment of the 1931 groupings was necessary. A blank means that data are not available. The following symbols appear:
 *manufacturing and construction occupations combined as 'manufacturing'
 †transportation combined with 'trade and finance'
 ††apparently included in 'trade'
 SOURCE: basic data from *Census*: 1871 and 1881. *Canada Year Book*, 1939, 77; 1943–4, 1068

TABLE 2.3
Occupational Distribution, Ontario; Main Groups (percentage)

Occupational Group	1871	1881	1891	1901	1911	1921	1931	1941
Agriculture	49.6	48.4	46.3	40.7	31.0	26.4	22.7	18.6
Other Primary	1.8	n.a.	1.3	1.6	3.1	1.5	2.2	3.0
Total Primary	51.4	48.4	47.6	42.3	31.1	27.9	24.9	21.6
Manufacturing, Construction, Labourers: 'Secondary'	32.6	35.7*	29.0	30.6†	34.9	33.2	32.9	33.5
Clerical, Trade, Finance, Service, Not Stated: 'Tertiary'	14.2	15.9	19.9	27.1	28.1	31.9	35.1	38.4
Transportation	1.8	n.a.	3.5	n.a.	5.9	7.0	8.1	6.5

*includes fishing, logging, mining, quarrying, transportation
†includes transportation
n.a.: not available
SOURCE: Derived from the several decennial *Census* volumes

TABLE 2.4
Ontario's Gainfully Employed: Distribution among Industries, 1911–41 (thousands and percentages)

Industry		1911		1931		1941	
		No.	%	No.	%	No.	%
Agriculture	T	307	31.0	304	22.6	279	17.7
Construction	T	83	8.4	91	6.8	84	5.3
Domestic and personal service	T	79	8.0	*	*	*	*
Forestry, fishing, hunting	T	19	1.5	16	1.2	23	1.5
Manufacturing	T	231	23.3	299	22.2	474††	30.1
Mining	T	17	1.7	19	1.4	34	2.2
Professional	T	45	4.5	*	*	*	*
Trade and merchandising	T	113	11.4	149	11.1	191	12.1
Transportation	T	76	7.7	105	7.8	90	5.7
Civil and municipal government	T	27	2.7	*	*	*	*
Finance, insurance, real estate	T	*	*	37	2.7	42	2.7
Electricity, gas, water	T	†	†	9	0.7	13	0.8
All service not elsewhere specified	T	151	15.2	269	20.0	292	18.6

*in 'service not elsewhere specified'
†apparently in 'manufacturing'
††including some repair activities
T: total
SOURCE: *Census*

TABLE 2.5
Geographical Distribution of Canada's Population, 1871–1941 (percentages)

Year	Maritimes	Quebec	Ontario	Central Canada	Western Canada
1871	20.8	32.3	43.9	76.2	1.7
1881	20.1	31.4	44.6	76.0	2.6
1891	18.2	30.8	43.8	74.6	5.2
1901	16.8	30.7	40.6	71.3	11.2
1911	13.0	27.8	35.1	62.9	23.8
1921	11.4	26.9	33.4	60.3	28.2
1931	9.7	27.7	33.1	60.8	29.4
1941	9.8	29.0	32.9	61.9	28.2

SOURCE: *Census*

TABLE 2.6
Gainfully Employed, Ontario, 1941, Classified by Years of Schooling Completed, 1941 (percentage distribution)

	Years of Schooling Completed			
Occupational Group	0–4	5–8	9–12	13 plus
Agricultural and other primary occupations	13.1	68.2	17.5	1.9
Labourers outside primary industry	14.6	56.3	26.0	2.1
Personal service	8.9	52.1	35.6	3.4
Transport and communication	6.4	51.1	37.2	4.3
Manufacturing	5.3	46.1	42.9	5.3
Clerical workers	0.1	14.5	64.5	20.4
Trade and finance	2.7	31.8	52.2	12.2
Professional and recreational service	–	6.7	34.4	56.7

SOURCE: Calculated from *Census*, 1941

TABLE 2.7
Status of Ontario Gainfully Employed, 1941 (percentage)

1. *In agriculture*
   Employers and those working on their own account   11.0
   Employees working for wages   3.9
   Unpaid family workers (exluding wives and children)   3.6

2. *In other sectors of the economy*
   Employers   1.9
   Those working on their own account   7.1
   Wage and salary earners   71.2
   Those working without pay   1.2

SOURCE: *Census*, 1941. 'Unpaid family workers' includes children over the age of thirteen.

TABLE 3.1
Ontario Acreages, 1870–1941 (thousands of acres)

	1870–71	1880–81	1890–91	1900	1910	1911	1920	1921	1930	1931	1940	1941
Human food												
Fall wheat	1,366	*1,189*	1,430	1,115	760	833	636	545	547	535	758	571
Durum wheat		1,930		372	110	130	214	147	12	15	6	8
Other spring wheat		*587*							13	83	25	32
Potatoes	175	181	179	176	158	157	156	166	142	171	132	123
Garden			1	1				19		66		68
Orchard	207	305	335	*339*	*298*	*288*	*216*	*187*	*212*	*153*	*180*	*96*
Small fruit				*271*	*13*	*25†*	*25*	*26†*	*20*	*22*	*23*	*10*
Vineyard				*11*	*11*				*12*	*15†*	*15*	*14†*
Total	1,748	2,416	1,947	1,936	1,315	1,409	1,247	1,090	958	1,060	1,139	909
Industrial inputs												
Barley		849	681	586	503	520	403	412	486	449	334	336
Flax for seed		6		6	9	9	8	5	4	6	9	11
Sugar beet	0	0	0	0	27		20			34	40	29
Tobacco				3	7	14		7	35	46	55	58
Hops		2		1	0.3	0.4			1	1	7	
Flax for fibre							9	3				11
Total		859	681	546	546	542	438	427	526	536	446	444

TABLE 3.1 (concluded)

	1870–71	1880–81	1890–91	1900	1910	1911	1920	1921	1930	1931	1940	1941
Livestock fodder												
Oats		*1,375*	2,053	2,707	2,871	2,806	2,761	2,851	2,291	2,362	2,035	2,004
Rye		*189*	152	152	92	97	104	111	48	57	92	79
Corn (husking)		*207**	90	332	275	298	190	211	85	125	219	251
Buckwheat		*50*	39	73	67	179	115	114	215	188	152	116
Beans		*20*		42	41	45	15	19	82	77	119	108
Dry peas		*557*	781	587	322	258	80	83	53	60	37	41
Mix grains				117	323	389	495	547	986	1,012	1,107	1,156
Cultivated hay	1,691	*1,795*	2,529	2,606	3,262	3,521	3,355	3,456	3,638	3,710	3,627	3,713
Corn (fodder)		***			245	243	366	354	267	271	318	295
Grain cut for hay				167 ⎱	26 ⎱	27 ⎱	25	12	44	29	37	26
Other fodder							11	16	48	50	14	15
Turnips, swedes		*79*	*14* ⎱	169 ⎱	76	81	67	62	58	55	45	42
Other roots		*28*			72	76	59	54	54	56	61	53
Other field crops				1	0.3	0.4	0.01	0.01	0.3	0.4	5	6
Subtotal		4,299	5,769	6,953	7,774	8,022	7,643	7,891	7,869	8,053	8,113	7,903
Cleared pasture	*2,089*		*2,542*	*2,695*	*3,160*	*3,117*	*3,482*	*3,041*	*3,149*	*2,943*	*2,712*	*3,238*
Total			8,311	9,648	10,934	11,139	11,125	10,932	11,018	10,996	10,825	11,141
All field crops	6,537	8,370	8,166	9,198	9,212	9,683		9,165	9,165	9,360		9,087
Total in use				*11,840*	*13,208*	*13,164*	*13,782*	*13,746*	*13,189*	*12,456*	*12,048*	

*all corn
†with 'orchard'

SOURCE: *Census* volumes; Ontario Bureau of Industries and Statistical Branch, Department of Agriculture (italicized in table); Sugar Beet data from *Historical Statistics of Canada.* Blanks in commodity entries indicate that data are not available and in summations that no meaningful totals can be constructed. Totals accumulate data from both sources; data on 'All Field Crops' and 'Total in Use' come direct from the primary sources.

TABLE 3.2
Changes in Acreages

	1870/1–1880/2	1880/2–1900	1870/1–1900	1900–11	1911–41	1880/2–1941
Human food	668,311	−479,967	188,344	−529,522	−498,039	−1,507,528
Wheat	564,123	−442,490	121,611	−525,785	−332,141	−1,318,966
Potatoes	6,394	−5,224	1,670	−19,188	−33,889	−58,301
Industrial inputs	n.a.	−311,334	n.a.	−3,927	−98,260	−102,187
Barley	n.a.	−262,607	n.a.	−66,090	−184,095	−512,792
Livestock fodder	n.a.	2,654,699	n.a.	1,068,694	−119,030	3,604,363
Oats	n.a.	1,331,942	n.a.	98,707	−802,531	628,118
Hay	105,465	810,351	915,816	914,386	191,975	1,916,712
Roots	n.a.	64,818	n.a.	−8,161	−63,514	−10,395
Cleared pasture	n.a.	n.a.	605,600	422,168	121,097	n.a.
All field crops	1,832,828	827,650	2,257,515	485,591	−596,225	716,816

n.a.: not available
SOURCE: Calculated from table 3.1

TABLE 3.3
Ontario 'Average Farm Prices,' Crop Years, Related to Acreages Lagged One Year, 1913/14–1920/1 (dollars per bushel; acreages in thousand acres)

	1913–14	1914–15	1915–16	1916–17	1917–18	1918–19	1919–20	1920–21
Wheat								
Price	0.85	1.08	0.93	1.55	2.09	2.06	1.87	1.05
Acreage	834	1093	865	770	714	981	1030	774
Barley								
Price	0.56	0.64	0.56	0.99	1.16	1.06	1.31	0.94
Acreage	461	449	326	361	660	569	484	462
Oats								
Price	0.38	0.49	0.39	0.64	0.72	0.78	0.91	0.58
Acreage	2840	3095	1991	2687	2924	2674	2880	3095
Rye								
Price	0.69	0.85	0.79	1.17	1.64	1.55	1.48	1.35
Acreage	78	78	69	68	113	140	133	123
Buckwheat								
Price	0.60	0.70	0.70	1.09	1.37	1.40	1.36	1.07
Acreage	176	169	175	162	224	179	143	148

TABLE 3.3 (concluded)

	1913–14	1914–15	1915–16	1916–17	1917–18	1918–19	1919–20	1920–21
Mixed grains								
Price	0.53	0.63	0.54	0.89	1.12	1.09	1.35	0.81
Acreage	344	345	286	295	619	629	582	618
Flaxseed								
Price	1.39	1.70	1.72	2.78	3.70	3.41	3.48	1.51
Acreage	5	5	4	4	16	14	21	8
Fodder corn								
Price	4.56	4.72	4.76	4.80	5.00	5.73	6.30	6.85
Acreage	267	287	248	265	381	400	449	438
Dry beans								
Price	1.79	2.24	3.05	5.34	6.79	4.66	3.60	3.10
Acreage	38	38	27	36	100	23	23	27

SOURCE: Dominion Bureau of Statistics, *Handbook of Agricultural Statistics*, part I, revised

TABLE 3.4
Utilization of Ontario Milk, 1920–40

	1920	1929	1933	1939	1940
Butter	18.2	13.1	10.0	5.4	5.4
Farm	18.2	13.1	10.0	5.4	5.4
Creamery	20.2	31.0	35.3	37.6	36.4
Cheese					
Cheddar	24.1	20.0	17.9	20.5	20.8
Farm	0.03	0.03	0.03	0.0	0.0
Concentrated whole milk products	4.3	3.6	2.2	4.9	5.6
Ice cream mix	1.3	1.5	0.9	1.2	1.5
Other whole milk, cream cheese	*	*	*	0.0	0.1
Fed on farms	6.1	5.1	4.5	4.3	4.3
Consumed on farms	12.5	12.5	8.6	4.0	3.8
Sold as fluid milk	13.2	13.2	20.6	22.1	22.0

*insignificantly small
SOURCE: Dominion Bureau of Statistics, *Handbook of Agricultural Statistics*, part VII, table 9

TABLE 3.5
Fruit Trees and Production, 1900–41

	1900	1901	1910	1911	1920	1921	1930	1931	1940	1941
Apples										
Trees of bearing age	572,513	1,990		2,074		994		631		747
Output			271,284		390,317		181,367		149,487	
Output per tree		288		131		393		287		200
Peaches										
Trees of bearing age	26,974	812		704		934		606		1,118
Output			30,009		48,233		32,057		59,956	
Output per tree		33.2		37.8		51.6		52.9		53.6
Pears										
Trees of bearing age	24,388	565		505		331		343		340
Output			21,178		16,180		18,344		15,249	
Output per tree		43.2		41.9		48.9		53.6		44.9
Plums										
Trees of bearing age	16,855	999		784		587		437		287
Output			17,347		23,706		14,218		10,136	
Output per tree		16.9		22.1		40.4		32.5		35.3
Cherries										
Trees of bearing age	6,609	447		507		422		355		269
Output			7,322		14,788		11,500		7,633	
Output per tree		14.8		14.4		35.0		32.4		28.4

NOTE: Fruit trees: thousands; output: thousands of pounds; output per tree: pounds
SOURCE: *Census*, 1941, vol. VIII, tables 13, 14

TABLE 3.6
Sources of Farm Cash Income, 1926–40 (per cent of total)

	1926	1929	1932	1940
Crops	22.7	22.9	24.0	23.5
Wheat	3.9	3.4	2.1	2.0
Fruit	2.5	3.3	3.6	2.5
Vegetables	2.6	3.0	4.2	4.9
Tobacco	3.0	1.9	4.4	3.5
Livestock and products	75.0	74.7	73.6	74.6
Forest and maple products	2.4	2.4	2.3	1.9

SOURCE: Dominion Bureau of Statistics, *Handbook of Agricultural Statistics*, part II, Revised

TABLE 3.7
Structure of Outlays, Ontario Farms, 1926–40 (per cent of total)

	1926	1929	1932	1940
Operating Costs				
Feed and seed	18.1	16.9	11.9	17.9
Hired labour	17.9	17.6	14.9	18.2
Fertilizer and lime	1.9	2.2	11.3	3.4
Fruit and vegetable supplies	1.9	1.9	1.3	2.2
Vehicles, engines	9.0	10.8	12.3	13.6
Machinery repair	1.7	1.7	1.8	2.2
Building repair	3.9	3.8	3.6	3.0
Total operating costs	60.0	60.1	61.6	65.7
Overhead costs				
Taxes	8.9	9.1	12.3	8.1
Gross rent	4.4	4.2	3.9	4.4
Interest	8.9	8.9	13.6	6.4
Depreciation (buildings, machinery)	18.2	17.8	18.9	15.2
Total overhead costs	40.0	39.9	38.4	34.1

SOURCE: Dominion Bureau of Statistics, *Handbook of Agricultural Statistics*, part II, Revised

TABLE 3.8
Gross and Net Farm Incomes, Ontario, 1926–41 (million dollars*)

Year	Cash Income	Cash Outlays	Net Cash Income	Depreciation Charges	Incomes In Kind	Total Net Income	Real Net Income		Real Net Income Per Occupied Farm
							Total	Cash	
1926	245.9	138.2	107.6	30.8	55.9	148.8	195.9	142.0	1,004.03
1927	266.4	143.1	142.8	32.4	55.4	154.3	207.1	191.7	
1928	259.6	149.9	149.7	32.3	55.0	155.6	208.8	200.1	
1929	256.8	150.7	108.1	32.7	55.7	150.2	198.5	143.2	
1930	213.5	142.6	71.1	30.2	53.0	128.5	170.8	94.6	
1931	171.0	121.2	49.8	27.6	42.0	80.5	118.8	73.5	618.19
1932	131.5	103.2	28.3	24.1	35.2	50.6	82.1	45.9	427.22
1933	135.9	100.7	35.2	23.5	35.3	50.2	85.6	60.0	445.43
1934	149.9	106.5	43.4	23.9	36.0	79.0	132.8	72.9	
1935	160.9	110.0	70.9	23.8	38.0	84.5	141.0	118.4	
1936	176.5	115.9	61.0	24.2	39.3	83.6	136.8	99.8	
1937	201.9	129.6	72.3	24.6	39.9	110.4	175.2	114.8	
1938	201.2	124.6	76.6	24.2	40.2	109.5	171.9	120.2	
1939	209.0	128.0	80.9	24.2	41.7	115.1	182.1	128.0	
1940	215.8	133.3	82.4	24.0	41.1	113.8	173.3	125.4	
1941	274.5	146.5	128.0	23.8	44.9	146.3	210.1	183.9	1,178.42

*Dollars: 1949 = 100.

SOURCE: Dominion Bureau of Statistics, Handbook of Agricultural Statistics, part II, Revised; real incomes calculated by applying Historical Statistics of Canada (first edition) series J147; number of occupied farms from Census, 1941, vol. VIII, table 19, and by interpolation (195,113 occupied farms calculated for 1926)

TABLE 3.9
Farm Equipment in Ontario, 1870–1941

	1871	1921	1931	1941
Number of Occupied Farms	172,258	198,053	192,174	178,204
Number of Farms Reporting				
Tractors	0	6,942	18,318	34,478
Automobiles or trucks	0	58,220	129,708	135,141
Gasoline engines	0	40,913	40,082	28,193
Telephones	0	99,182	103,932	90,171
Gas or electric light	0	12,845	32,294	68,064*
Automobiles	0	n.a.	115,833	118,829
Trucks	0	n.a.	13,875	16,312
Binders	n.a.	n.a.	116,994	n.a.
Combines	0	n.a.	0	786
Cream separators	0	n.a.	127,086	n.a.
Electric motors	0	n.a.	7,118	22,681
Headers	n.a.	n.a.	0	n.a.
Milking machines	0	n.a.	4,007	n.a.
Silos	n.a.	n.a.	33,269	n.a.
Threshing mills (1871) and machines	13,805	n.a.	8,278	8,795
Fanning mills	120,732	n.a.	n.a.	n.a.
Horse rakes	46,246	n.a.	n.a.	n.a.
Reapers and mowers	36,874	n.a.	n.a.	n.a.
Ploughs, harrows, cultivators	n.a.†	n.a.	n.a.	n.a.
Transport vehicles	n.a.†	n.a.	n.a.	n.a.
Light carriages	n.a.†	n.a.	n.a.	n.a.
Horses	n.a.†	172,108	157,582	114,396

*Of which 900 gas light
†The numbers of horses reported by farms for 1871 was 368,585; the farms contained 289,362 ploughs, harrows, and cultivators, 299,357 transport carriages, and 206,243 light carriages, so it is reasonable to suppose that 100 per cent of the farms possessed at least one of each of these pieces of equipment.
n.a.: not available
SOURCES: *Census*, 1870–1, vol. III, table XXII; 1921, vol. V, tables 38 and LXXII; 1931, vol. VIII, tables XXVI, XXVII, and XCIX; 1941, vol. VIII, part II, tables 47, 297, and vol. IX, table 13

TABLE 3.10
Amenities on Ontario Farms, 1931 and 1941
(percentages)

Occupied Farms Possessing	1931	1941
Water piped in kitched	10.5	
Inside running or pump water		31.3
Water piped in bathroom ·	6.3	
Private or shared flush toilet		9.8
Telephone	54.1	50.6
Radio	21.5	65.8
Electric or gas light	16.8	37.8
Electric light		37.3
Gas light		0.5
Kerosene or gasoline lamps		62.2
Mechanical refrigeration		9.3
Ice refrigeration		8.8
Other refrigeration		4.0
Bath or shower		11.1
Vacuum clearner		11.0
Steam, hot water, or hot air heat		12.5
Wood fuel		75.5
Cooking by electricity or gas		13.1
Cooking by coal oil		1.2
Farm on asphalt road	2.9	
Farm on concrete road	4.1	
Farm on macadam road	6.5	
Farm on gravel road	65.1	
Farm on improved dirt road	10.2	
Farm on unimproved dirt road	9.7	
Railway station within		
less than 5 miles	62.6	
5 to 9 miles	27.6	
10 to 14 miles	5.2	
15 to 24 miles	1.8	
25 and more miles	0.2	
not reported	1.9	

SOURCE: *Canada Year Book*, 1934–5, 301; *Census*,
1941, vol. IX. Where no entries appear, no comparable
data are available. No questions respecting amenities
were asked in 1921 or in earlier censuses

TABLE 3.11
Trend Equations: Bushels per Acre, 1882–1941

Spring wheat	$y = 15.25 + 0.07t$
Fall wheat	$y = 19.00 + 0.13t$
Oats	$y = 36.13 - 0.02t$
Barley	$y = 26.08 + 0.10t$
Rye	$y = 15.61 + 0.03t$
Buckwheat	$y = 21.14 - 0.0003t$

SOURCE: Calculated from data in Ontario
Department of Agriculture, Statistical Branch,
Reports, 1940 and 1941

TABLE 3.12
Trend Increases, 1882–1941

Crop	Increase Over Fifty-Nine years (bu)	Per cent of Actual 1882 Figure
Spring wheat	4.2	25.5
Fall wheat	7.8	29.7
Oats	−1.2	−3.3
Barley	6.0	21.0
Rye	1.8	9.6
Buckwheat	0.018	0.1

SOURCE: Calculated from trend equations, table 3.11

TABLE 3.13
Land Use in Ontario Regions, 1870/1–1941 (thousand acres)

Region	1870/1	1926	1941
The Old North			
Improved acreage	22.8	281.8†	206.1††
Under crops	20.4	187.0	160.0
In pasture	2.3	61.2	54.5
In gardens and orchards*	0.04	0.53	0.56
The Shield Fringe			
Improved acreage	895.8	1,247.3†	917.2††
Under crops	661.7	815.2	645.9
In pasture	218.8	307.2	252.1
In garden and orchard*	22.6	12.7	7.7
The East			
Improved acreage	1,504.5	2,784.0†	2,170.5††
Under crops	977.2	1,785.5	1,488.8
In pasture	484.7	722.7	664.0
In gardens and orchards*	16.4	10.9	12.6
The South			
Improved acreage	6,402.2	10,493.3†	8,222.1††
Under crops	4,879.1	7,412.7	6,142.2
In pasture	1,381.0	2,129.5	1,669.7
In garden and orchard*	167.8	222.4	191.9
The New North			
Improved acreage	7.3	309.0†	409.1††
Under crops	4.7	233.9	344.5
In pasture	2.4	38.6	60.8
In gardens and orchards	0.064	0.85	1.0

*'Orchards, small fruits, vineyards' in 1926 and 1941
†'Cleared'
††Sum of cropped, fallow, pasture, orchard, small fruits
SOURCES: *Census*, 1870/1; Statistical Branch, Ontario Department of
Agriculture, *Reports*, 1926 and 1941

TABLE 3.14
Provincial Government Spending on Agriculture, 1868–1940 (thousand dollars per fiscal year)

	Agriculture as Such	Colonization, Immigration	Colonization Roads	Agricultural College	Drainage Debentures	Land Improvement Fund	Veterinary College	North/NW Ontario roads	Northern Development	Rural bonus to HEPC
1868	66		37							
1869	68	18	35							
1870	67	46	50		46					
1871	74	30	55	47	78					
1872	80	58	76	4	31					
1873	81	159	146	2	84					
1874	86	135	91	39	54					
1875	94	94	104	31	137					
1876	97	45	86	33	24					
1877	97	46	77	17	61					
1878	97	32	85	36	35					
1879	106	40	115	26	87					
1880	107	53	97	44	62					
1881	107	35	97	53	42					
1882	131	30	111	51	37	11				
1883	140	48	123	55	31	17				
1884	145	43	188	59	68	7				
1885	130	19	121	38	40	5				
1886	92	17	145	61	28	98				
1887	101	12	123	48	30	4				
1888	107	8	112	42	59	4				
1889	107	7	103	65	27	3				
1890	128	6	125	51	86	3				
1891	150	7	98	63	63	50				
1892	167	8	104	87	44	2				

TABLE 3.14 (continued)

	Agriculture as Such‖	Colonization, Immigration	Colonization Roads	Agricultural College	Drainage Debentures	Land Improvement Fund	Veterinary College	North/NW Ontario roads	Northern Development	Rural bonus to HEPC
1893	170	8	112	66	62	1				
1894	130	8	117	67	45	7				
1895	181	8	117	73	45	3				
1896	140	7	103	80	18	3				
1897	134	10	93	68	14	3				
1898	158	7	107	57	10	2				
1899	172	7	90	60	7	2				
1900	157	6	134	64	6	2				
1901	154	5	139	90	13	2				
1902	171	7	196	106	7	3				
1903	179	8	159	165	13	3				
1904	212	20	175	195	34	3				
1905	286	32	178	137	24	2				
1906	300	35	220	187	53	2				
1907	342	52	317	213	25	2				
1908	385	34	460	183	56		14			
1909*	541	34	449	156	43		14			
1910	435	75	452	199	84		32			
1911	474	107	451	182	64		55			
1912	474	106	434	224	78		41	237		
1913	473	135	406	243	104		146	1,063		
1914	394	101	481	358	127		67	816		
1915	457	49	220	234	98		66	665	101	
1916	446	83	253	318	135		34	526	102	
1917	490	46	264	325	205		31	482	311	
1918	612	73	268	347	145		33	628	49	
1919	689	68	391	380	145		37	1,462	122	

TABLE 3.14 (concluded)

	Agriculture as Such‖	Colonization, Immigration	Colonization Roads	Agricultural College	Drainage Debentures	Land Improvement Fund	Veterinary College	North/NW Ontario roads	Northern Development	Rural bonus to HEPC
1920	766	100	451	513	145		40	1,224	406	
1921	706	117	506	634	199		35	1,409	342	
1922	884	112	671	931	319		34	1,695	406	
1923	1,171	187	828	746	201		37	2,688	436	769
1924	1,340	149	447	737	161		59	2,949	178	99
1925	1,473	124	474	645	288		57	3,381	147	223
1926	1,475	163	296	627	236		34	3,737	57	555
1927	1,509	167	508	680	187		30	3,943	105	1,100
1928	1,649	176	369	704	398		31	3,717	155	740
1929	1,686	181	415	887	508		46	4,819	188	1,070
1930	1,756	203	259	1,517	424		49	7,392	194	1,689
1931	1,798	156	238	1,535	441		53	6,489	203	1,414
1932	1,436	90	384	1,069	98		51	4,411	170	725
1933	1,627	12	209	749	116		46	1,512	321	297
1934	1,370	4	220	785	180		50	3,299	210	292
1935††	502		152	293	107		18	1,305	72	120
1936	1,159		326	671	51		45	4,322	219	330
1937	1,141		324	681	23		46	1,800	485	1,000
1938	1,295		†	776	62		51	†		1,800
1939	1,473			782§	146		46§			3,030
1940	1,446			770	299		63			2,050

*Nine months
†In this and later years, included with Highways Dept.
††Five months
§Net of fees
‖In earlier decades, excludes certain central administrative outlays on account of agriculture
SOURCE: Ontario *Public Accounts*

TABLE 4.1
Volume and Value of Production, Selected Metals, Ontario, 1890–1940

	Nickel		Copper		Platinum Group	
Year	Volume of Production (000 pounds)	Value of Production ($000)	Volume of Production (000 pounds)	Value of Production ($000)	Volume of Production (000 pounds)	Value of Production ($000)
1890	3,560	504	–	–	–	–
1891	4,310	610	4,024	241	–	–
1892	4,164	591	3,872	232	–	–
1893	3,306	455	2,862	115	–	–
1894	5,141	613	5,496	196	–	–
1895	4,632	405	4,731	161	–	–
1896	3,897	357	3,736	131	–	–
1897	3,998	392	5,500	200	–	–
1898	5,568	514	8,374	268	–	–
1899	5,744	526	5,668	176	–	–
1900	7,080	757	6,728	320	–	–
1901	8,882	1,410	8,444	551	–	–
1902	11,890	2,211	8,456	645	7	132
1903	13,996	2,499	14,462	717	5	95
1904	9,486	1,517	4,326	297	1	29
1905	19,086	3,364	9,050	689	2	28
1906	21,572	3,839	12,064	961	0	6
1907	21,270	2,272	13,750	1,046	0	0
1908	19,126	1,866	15,122	1,071	0	0
1909	26,282	2,791	15,865	1,127	0	0
1910	37,272	4,006	19,260	1,374	0	0
1911	34,098	3,664	18,042	1,282	0	0
1912	44,990	4,736	22,252	1,584	7	228
1913	49,910	5,251	25,883	1,840	0	0
1914	45,824	5,137	28,905	2,081	0	0
1915	68,235	17,042	39,255	3,925	0	0
1916	82,749	20,686	45,017	8,332	0	0
1917	83,787	21,042	42,928	7,961	0	0
1918	92,045	27,840	47,114	8,474	0	0
1919	43,329	11,925	24,546	3,610	2	200
1920	57,563	15,689	30,227	3,966	19	1,997
1921	16,531	4,051	10,503	1,102	13	862
1922	30,416	7,038	19,918	2,067	12	925
1923	53,545	9,563	28,109	3,456	16	1,419
1924	61,157	11,309	34,581	3,820	19	1,891
1925	73,857	15.947	39,660	4,738	17	1,676
1926	65,714	14,374	41,313	4,829	19	1,560
1927	66,799	15,262	45,341	4,947	23	1,271
1928	99,617	22,319	68,401	8,770	24	1,310
1929	113,794	27,115	88,881	14,623	30	1,646
1930	105,235	24,455	127,708	14,056	68	2,437
1931	65,666	15,267	112,883	8,907	92	2,813
1932	30,328	7,180	77,055	4,408	65	1,999
1933	83,265	20,130	145,505	10,119	56	1,501
1934	128,687	32,139	205,060	14,823	200	6,188
1935	138,563	35,350	252,028	19,296	190	5,407
1936	169,739	43,879	287,914	26,899	235	7,803
1937	224,791	59,470	313,266	40,565	259	9,932
1938	210,566	53,916	309,030	30,406	292	887
1939	226,110	50,923	328,430	32,637	284	9,421
1940	245,563	59,804	347,931	34,742	200	7,760

TABLE 4.1 (*concluded*)

Year	Gold Volume of Production (000 troy ounces)	Gold Value of Production ($000)	Silver Volume of Production (000 troy ounces)	Silver Value of Production ($000)	Cobalt Volume of Production (000 pounds)	Cobalt Value of Production ($000)
1890	–	–	–	–	–	–
1891	–	2	–	–	–	–
1892	–	7	–	–	–	–
1893	–	39	–	–	–	–
1894	–	33	–	–	–	–
1895	0	57	–	–	–	–
1896	–	122	–	–	–	–
1897	9	193	–	–	–	–
1898	14	265	87	52	–	–
1899	28	425	104	62	–	–
1900	19	298	161	96	–	–
1901	14	244	145	80	–	–
1902	9	230	97	58	–	–
1903	6	186	16	9	–	–
1904	1	16	207	112	58	37
1905	5	101	2,474	1,373	236	100
1906	3	66	5,434	3,689	642	81
1907	4	67	9,997	6,147	1,478	93
1908	3	60	19,444	9,137	2,448	111
1909	2	33	26,006	12,646	3,066	95
1910	4	68	30,901	15,624	2,196	55
1911	2	43	31,499	16,175	1,706	171
1912	102	2,134	30,721	17,699	1,872	316
1913	221	4,544	29,797	16,589	1,189	420
1914	268	5,545	25,173	12,831	644	547
1915	407	8,410	24,355	11,950	427	380
1916	498	10,333	19,959	12,673	1,020	762
1917	421	8,698	19,479	16,183	815	1,123
1918	412	8,502	17,414	17,414	882	1,615
1919	506	10,452	11,335	12,904	748	1,009
1920	566	13,068	11,066	10,859	737	1,604
1921	713	16,085	8,427	5,667	204	502
1922	996	20,789	10,912	7,794	508	1,081
1923	974	20,417	10,636	6,841	1,477	1,804
1924	1,242	25,873	10,288	6,939	1,280	1,663
1925	1,461	30,152	12,035	8,298	1,466	2,329
1926	1,497	30,952	10,389	6,343	665	1,136
1927	1,627	33,680	9,048	5,172	881	1,765
1928	1,578	32,632	7,218	4,190	955	1,672
1929	1,622	33,697	8,519	4,381	929	1,802
1930	1,736	35,923	10,566	4,027	694	1,144
1931	2,086	45,017	7,186	2,208	521	651
1932	2,287	53,418	5,768	1,755	491	588
1933	2,156	60,752	5,077	1,887	467	598
1934	2,105	72,808	5,285	2,486	595	592
1935	2,220	78,067	6,265	4,013	681	513
1936	2,390	83,308	5,133	2,294	888	804
1937	2,587	90,509	4,508	2,012	507	848
1938	2,896	101,945	4,403	1,915	459	791
1939	3,086	112,115	4,634	1,867	733	1,213
1940	3,262	125,580	5,084	1,852	794	1,235

NOTES: – Means no activity reported; 0 means reported or rounded value is zero.
SOURCE: All figures were obtained from *Ontario Metal Mining Statistics*, Mineral Policy Background Paper No. 16 (Toronto: 1983). Volume and value of production series are based on Ministry of Natural Resources data and have been rounded to the nearest thousand. Individual series are located on the following pages: Nickel, 37; Copper, 19; Platinum Group, 42; Gold, 235; Silver, 47; Cobalt, 15.

TABLE 4.2
Mining Revenue, Province of Ontario, 1891–1940 (thousands of dollars)

Year	Mining Land Sales	Mining Land Leases	Prospecting Activity	Mining Royalties	Mining Profits Tax	Acreage Tax	Sales of Goods and Services
1891	118	5	–	–	–	–	–
1892	15	13	–	–	–	–	–
1893	11	15	–	–	–	–	–
1894	8	10	–	–	–	–	–
1895	16	18	–	–	–	–	–
1896	22	19	–	–	–	–	–
1897	59	91	3	–	–	–	–
1898	40	57	3	–	–	–	–
1899	75	76	5	–	–	–	–
1900	69	36	7	–	–	–	–
1901	25	42	4	–	–	–	–
1902	8	39	3	–	–	–	–
1903	22	46	2	–	–	–	–
1904	18	25	2	–	–	–	–
1905	7	40	15	–	–	–	–
1906	118	47	70	15	–	–	–
1907	1,185	22	272	208	27	5	2
1908	23	21	138	218	101	10	24
1909	235	19	219	338	29	10	118
1910	327	29	194	247	121	15	1
1911	64	26	212	286	176	15	2
1912	52	33	107	250	156	16	1
1913	95	21	93	200	174	14	1
1914	41	16	64	75	273	10	0
1915	47	14	52	53	140	11	0
1916	37	16	67	15	141	13	1
1917	57	17	62	0	1,504	14	1
1918	34	14	52	0	864	29	2
1919	29	14	64	0	553	33	1
1920	39	22	59	0	713	71	1
1921	26	14	51	0	184	38	5
1922	28	13	87	81	161	35	18
1923	30	10	93	2	253	31	22
1924	84	12	95	–	192	37	33
1925	41	11	86	–	287	32	23
1926	39	11	172	–	411	33	29
1927	44	9	223	–	341	37	25
1928	74	7	257	–	356	81	26
1929	77	7	170	–	397	34	25
1930	28	5	97	–	503	31	29

TABLE 4.2 (*concluded*)

1931	33	5	103	–	480	31	29
1932	18	3	83	–	515	21	21
1933	38	6	116	–	680	31	7
1934	55	8	220	–	1,074	35	21
1935	49	9	176	–	1,401	43	27
1936	77	12	304	–	1,564	78	35
1937	71	12	189	–	1,802	49	26
1938	61	11	159	–	2,128	47	29
1939	74	13	109	–	1,907	45	30
1940	65	14	86	–	2,003	53	33

NOTES: Prospecting Activity includes miners' licences and recorders' fees. Sales of Goods and Services includes laboratory, sample, and assay fees; sales of record books, blueprints, and maps.
– Means no activity reported; 0 means reported or rounded value is zero.
SOURCE: All figures were obtained from *Ontario Metal Mining Statistics*. Series have been rounded to the nearest thousand. The individual series are located on the following pages: Mining Land Sales, 127; Mining Land Leases, 128–9; Prospecting Activity, 130; Mining Royalties, 131; Mining Profits Tax, 133; Acreage Tax, 133; Sales of Goods and Services, 135.

TABLE 4.3
Direct and Indirect Effects of Gold and Nickel-Copper Mines, Selected Years, 1907–42

	Gold Mines			Nickel-Copper Mines		
Year	Number Wage Earners	Wages Paid ($000)	Process Supplies, Fuel, and Electricity ($000)	Number Wage Earners	Wages Paid ($000)	Process Supplies, Fuel, and Electricity ($000)
1907	138	115	–	1,660	1,279	–
1912	955	1,023	–	2,859	2,361	–
1917	2,561	3,220	–	3,356	5,571	–
1922	3,919	5,286	–	1,497	2,016	–
1927	5,963	9,521	–	3,418	4,919	–
1932	8,460	13,510	–	2,569	3,706	–
1937	14,783	24,950	13,379	11,198	18,685	19,796
1940	18,738	33,423	18,480	11,443	20,586	21,976

NOTES: 1940 figures are a three-year average centred on 1940.
– Means not available.
SOURCE: Ontario, *Report of the Royal Ontario Mining Commission* (Toronto: 1944), 2–3

TABLE 4.4
Direct and Indirect Effects of Non-Ferrous Smelting and Refining Activity, Selected Years, 1925–40

Year	No. of Establishments	No. of Production Workers	Wages Paid ($000)	Cost of Fuel and Electricity ($000)	Cost of Materials ($000)	Value of Production ($000)	Value Added ($000)
1925	4	–	–	–	5,822	27,041	–
1930	7	3,482	5,182	–	19,890	47,736	27,846
1935	8	3,907	5,366	913	64,210	105,035	39,912
1940	7	5,594	8,864	8,629	94,257	150,476	47,590

NOTE: – Means not available.
SOURCE: All figures were obtained from *Ontario Metal Mining Statistics*, 86–9

TABLE 5.1
Development of Agriculture in Northern Ontario*

Year	Total Population	No. of Farms	Total of Farm Area (000s of acres)	Total Cultivated Area (000s of acres)	Ratio of Cultivated Area to Total Area
1880	20,320	2,756	375	52.6	0.14
1890	54,876	6,230	958	171.0	0.18
1900	100,401	7,191	1,096	230.9	0.21
1910	214,339	11,985	1,792	353.5	0.20
1920	266,900	15,248	2,425	538.6	0.22
1930	356,405	16,766	2,774	679.4	0.24
1940	456,011	17,007	2,760	770.3	0.28

*Includes Districts of Algoma, Cochrane, Kenora, Manitoulin, Nipissing, Rainy River, Sudbury, Thunder Bay, and Timiskaming
SOURCE: *Census* volumes

TABLE 5.2
Agricultural Development by Districts, 1920–40

District/Year	No. of Farms	Improved Area (000s of acres)	Farm Population
Algoma			
1920	2,424	89.6	–
1930	2,056	92.3	9,161
1940	1,836	94.6	7,351
Cochrane			
1920	–	–	–
1930	2,489	74.6	10,678
1940	3,061	116.7	13,548
Kenora			
1920	717	17.8	–
1930	945	27.3	3,333
1940	931	29.9	3,247
Manitoulin			
1920	1,394	67.6	–
1930	1,274	67.5	5,725
1940	1,151	65.0	4,728
Nipissing			
1920	1,937	80.9	–
1930	2,001	89.4	11,348
1940	1,735	93.7	9,358
Rainy River			
1920	1,644	52.1	–
1930	1,728	68.7	6,560
1940	1,858	84.3	6,981
Sudbury			
1920	2,267	88.3	–
1930	2,148	96.7	11,739
1940	2,045	98.8	9,686
Thunder Bay			
1920	1,590	45.6	–
1930	2,173	62.9	8,706
1940	2,389	72.8	8,564
Timiskaming			
1920*	3,275	96.8	–
1930	1,943	100.2	8,479
1940	1,863	114.9	8,035

*Includes Cochrane
SOURCES: *Census*, 1921, 1931, and 1941

TABLE 5.3
Provincial Government Expenditures on
Northern Development

A. Expenditures by Ontario Government
   under Northern and Northwestern
   Development Act, 1912–37

Period	Total Expenditure
1912–20*	$ 6,787,120
1921–30	35,812,237
1931–7	23,427,085
1912–37*	$66,626,442

*Figures are not available for 1919.
SOURCE: Ontario Department of Lands and
Forests, *Annual Reports*, 1912–24; Ontario
Department of Northern Development,
Annual Reports, 1925–37

B. Breakdown of Government Expenditures by Project, 1912–37

	Per Cent
Roads and bridges	96.2
Farms and seed grain	0.9
Kapuskasing settlement	1.7
Other*	1.2
	100.0

*Includes agricultural implements, cattle
purchases, school buildings, creameries,
saw-mills, and fire relief.
SOURCE: Ontario Department of Northern
Development, *Annual Report*, 1937, 18

TABLE 5.4
Abandoned Farms, Northern Ontario, 1940

	No. of Abandoned Farms	Abandoned Farms as Percentage of Total Occupied
Ontario	5,563	3.1
Algoma	333	18.1
Cochrane	1,130	36.9
Kenora	149	16.0
Nipissing	229	13.2
Rainy River	279	15.0
Sudbury	439	21.5
Thunder Bay	369	15.4
Timiskaming	268	13.4
Northern Ontario	3,196	20.2

SOURCE: *Census*, 1941, vol. VIII, part 2, table 50

TABLE 5.5
Farms by Type, Northern Ontario, 1940

	Total	Part-Time	Subsistence	Forest
Algoma	1,836	158	939	30
Cochrane	3,061	670	1,318	271
Kenora	931	139	368	175
Nipissing	1,735	136	986	57
Rainy River	1,858	277	778	163
Sudbury	2,045	213	1,087	41
Thunder Bay	2,389	394	915	220
Timiskaming	2,001	216	721	51
Ontario	178,204	7,075 (3.9)	24,812 (19.5)	2,543 (1.4)
Northern Ontario	15,856	2,203 (13.9)	4,930 (30.9)	1,008 (6.4)

NOTE: Figures in parentheses represent percentages.
SOURCE: *Census*, 1941, vol. VIII, part 2, table 46

TABLE 5.6
Gross Farm Revenues, Northern Ontario, 1940

	Sale of Agricultural Total	Sale of Forest Part-Time	Income from Outside Subsistence	Total
Algoma ($000)	1,174.9	56.5	397.5	1,628.9
(per cent)	72.1	3.5	24.4	
Cochrane ($000)	908.4	222.2	854.5	1,985.1
(per cent)	45.8	11.2	43.0	
Kenora ($000)	209.5	106.3	167.9	483.7
(per cent)	43.3	22.0	34.7	
Manitoulin ($000)	684.2	60.0	102.0	846.2
(per cent)	80.9	7.1	12.0	
Nipissing ($000)	808.8	85.4	219.5	1,113.7
(per cent)	72.6	7.7	19.7	
Rainy River ($000)	591.1	128.6	391.1	1,110.8
(per cent)	53.2	11.6	35.2	
Sudbury ($000)	871.8	68.8	464.7	1,405.3
(per cent)	62.0	4.9	33.1	
Thunder Bay ($000)	1,067.2	166.0	608.5	1,841.1
(per cent)	58.0	9.0	33.0	
Timiskaming ($000)	985.1	43.3	308.3	1,336.7
(per cent)	73.7	3.2	23.1	

SOURCE: *Census*, 1941, vol. VIII

TABLE 6.1
Petroleum and Natural Gas Production, Ontario, 1870–1939

	Petroleum		Natural Gas	
	Quantity Million Imp. Gal.	Value ($000)	Quantity Million cubic feet	Value ($000)
1870	13.0	n.a.	0	0
1880	15.5	n.a.	0	0
1891	30.23	1,209	n.a.	n.a.
1892	28.0	1,400*	n.a.	160
1893	34.0	2,116*	2,342	238
1894	34.9	2,146*	1,653	204
1895	22.3*	1,895*	3,320	283
1896	27.3	1,955*	n.a.	277
1897	25.6	1,777*	n.a.	308
1898	27.0	1,970*	n.a.	302
1899	23.6	1,747*	n.a.	441

TABLE 6.1 (*concluded*)

	Petroleum		Natural Gas	
	Quantity Million Imp. Gal.	Value ($000)	Quantity Million cubic feet	Value ($000)
1900	23.4	1,868*	n.a.	393
1901	21.4	1,468*	n.a.	342
1902	18.2	940	n.a.	199
1903	16.6	1,024	n.a.	197
1904	17.2	904	n.a.	253
1905	22.1	899	n.a.	316
1906	19.9	762	n.a.	533
1907	27.6	1,050	n.a.	746
1908	18.5	702	n.a.	989
1909	14.7	559	n.a.	1,188
1910	11.0	368	7,263	1,491
1911	10.1	354	n.a.	2,187
1912	8.4	345	12,414	2,268
1913	7.9	398	12,516	2,362
1914	7.4	337	14,063	2,347
1915	7.9	334	15,212	2,623
1916	7.4	403	17.953	2,404
1917	8.1	559	20,025	3,220
1918	9.5	782	13,075	2,499
1919	7.7	663	11,086	2,583
1920	6.3	724	10,545	3,163
1921	6.1	467	8,532	4,018
1922	5.8	467	8,568	4,025
1923	5.6	395	8,128	4,066
1924	5.4	390	7,371	4,076
1925	5.0	368	7,257	4,083
1926	4.7	377	7,776	4,416
1927	4.9	289	7,311	4,332
1928	4.5	284	7,633	4,535
1929	4.5	293	8,583	4,968
1930	3.9	294	7,943	5,062
1931	4.4	261	7,420	4,635
1932	4.7	290	7,386	4,719
1933	4.8	300	7,166	4,523
1934	4.3	275	7,683	4,741
1935	6.3	408	8,159	4,938
1936	5.7	577	10,007	6,054
1937	5.8	375	10,746	6,589
1938	5.9	373	10,953	6,461
1939	7.2	429	11,967	7,262

*Sum of unrefined products
n.a.: Not available
NOTE: Output of petroleum for 1891 estimated from output in Bbl.
SOURCES: 1870: *Census*, 1870–1, vol. III, table XXVI; 1880: *Census*,
1880–1, vol. III, table XXVIII; 1891–1939: Ontario Bureau of Mines and
Mines Department, *Annual Reports*

TABLE 6.2
Quantity and Value of Crude Petroleum
Imported to Ontario 1869–1900

	Quantity (in gallons)	Value ($)
1869	1,979	413
1870	5,383	1,126
1871	8,484	1,483
1872	13,777	1,973
1873	34,500	6,706
1874	57,990	8,256
1875	58,205	7,729
1876	59,220	9,319
1877	35,980	6,723
1878	5,713	1,305
1879	962	214
1895*	42	1
1896	0	0
1897	0	0
1898	0	0
1899	140,232	4,977
1900†	206,628	11,977

*From 1879 to 1895 there are no figures and no heading for imports of crude oil. They then reappear under the heading 'Oils, mineral: – Crude petroleum, fuel and gas oils (other than naptha benzine or gasoline) when imported by manufacturers (other than oil refiners) for use in their own factories for fuel purposes or for manufacture of gas.'
†After 1900, trade data were not reported by province of entry.
SOURCE: 'Tables of the Trade and Navigation of the Dominion of Canada for the Fiscal Year ending 30 June ... ,' *Sessional Papers of the Dominion of Canada*

TABLE 7.1
Output, Value Added, and Employment in Ontario Manufacturing 1870–1915 (current prices)

| Year | Output ($000) | | Value Added ($000) | | Employment | Output per Worker (dollars) |
	Census	Bertram	Census	Bertram	Census	Census
1870	114,706.8	112,778	49,592.0	48,323	87,281	1,314
1880	157,989.9	155,465	66,825.7	65,283	118,303	1,335
1890	239,781.9	232,861	111,639.5	107,373	166,326	1,441
1900	241,533.5*	270,500	103,303.1*	99,275*	166,619	1,449
1910	579,810.0*	603,000	282,230.1*	265,774*	238,817	2,427
1915	715,532.0†	702,600	304,862.0†	288,021†	n.a.††	n.a.

Quinquennial and Decennial Growth Rates

Year	Census	Bertram	Census	Bertram	Census	Census
1870–80	37.7	37.9	34.8	35.1	35.5	1.6
1880–90	51.7	49.8	67.1	64.5	47.3	7.9
1890–1900	0.7	16.2	-7.5	-7.5	0.1	0.6
1900–10	140.0	122.9	173.2	167.7	58.0	67.5
1910–15	23.4	16.5	8.0	8.4	n.a.	n.a.
1870–1910	405.5	434.7	469.1	450.0	173.6	84.7
1870–1915	523.5	522.9	513.9	496.0	n.a.	n.a.

*Excludes many firms having fewer than five employees
†Firms of $2,500 output and over
††Total employment in *all* enumerated establishments was 222,417.
n.a.: Not available
SOURCES: Decennial Censuses; *Postal Census of Canada*, 1916 (DBS 31-D054); Gordon W. Bertram, 'Historical Statistics on Growth and Structure of Manufacturing in Canada, 1870–1957', Canadian Political Science Association, J. Henripin and A. Asimakopulos, eds., *Conferences on Statistics 1962 & 1963* (Toronto: University of Toronto Press, 1964), tables 5, 7

TABLE 7.2
Gross Value of Production and Value Added*: Primary, Secondary, and Total Manufacturing in Seventeen Main Industry Groups, Ontario, 1870–1915

Industry Group	1870		1880		1890		1900††		1910††		1915††	
	Value of Product	Value Added	Value of Product	Value Added	Value of Product	Value Added	Value of Product	Value Added	Value of Product	Value Added	Value of Product	Value Added
1. Food and beverages												
Primary	31,938	5,590	37,762	6,578	49,316	10,465	56,562	8,679	107,658	30,031	161,793	29,812
Secondary	8,484	4,552	9,968	4,007	15,287	7,056	15,470	7,184	42,923	23,876	61,649	31,132
Total	40,422	10,142	47,730	10,585	64,603	17,521	72,032	15,863	150,581	53,876	223,442	60,944
2. Tobacco and tobacco products												
Secondary	693	269	1,186	685	1,664	981	2,736	1,768	5,974	4,202	5,843	4,223
3. Rubber products												
Secondary	7	5	2	1	331	199	1,134	396	5,686	2,729	14,087	7,173
4. Leather products												
Secondary	10,113	4,835	10,742	4,851	12,051	5,992	11,173	3,788	27,361	13,078	36,551	11,233
5. Textile products (except clothing incl. knitting mills)												
Secondary	6,037	2,410	8,912	3,900	13,113	6,671	11,870	5,691	19,120	8,330	24,998	10,081
6. Clothing (textile and fur)												
Secondary	7,488	3,207	13,737	5,882	23,932	12,230	21,234	10,542	51,104	25,788	53,149	24,124
7. Wood products												
Primary	14,943	6,904	22,114	10,087	36,173	16,924	31,950	14,580	56,348	24,960	38,131	20,221
Secondary	4,026	2,400	4,996	3,053	9,134	5,504	9,421	5,433	19,100	11,321	17,423	9,941
Total	18,969	9,304	27,110	13,140	45,307	22,428	41,371	20,013	75,448	36,281	55,554	30,162
8. Paper products												
Primary	488	251	1,135	458	1,142	656	2,587	1,366	7,490	3,640	16,649	7,359
Secondary	154	92	179	98	860	357	1,568	817	4,802	2,767	8,215	4,571
Total	642	343	1,314	556	2,002	1,013	4,155	2,183	12,292	6,407	24,864	11,930

TABLE 7.2 (continued)

Industry Group	1870 Value of Product	1870 Value Added	1880 Value of Product	1880 Value Added	1890 Value of Product	1890 Value Added	1900†† Value of Product	1900†† Value Added	1910†† Value of Product	1910†† Value Added	1915†† Value of Product	1915†† Value Added
9. Printing, publishing and allied industries												
Secondary	2,335	1,440	4,041	2,363	6,550	3,977	7,168	4,955	15,211	10,583	17,798	12,586
10. Iron and steel products												
Secondary	14,688	9,290	19,889	11,788	32,034	18,802	27,814	16,436	92,559	48,743	88,531	46,801
11. Transportation equipment												
Secondary	3,667	2,486	6,778	3,778	9,008	5,205	10,177	5,028	30,279	16,377	47,211	19,043
12. Non-ferrous metal products												
Primary	–	–	–	–	1,896	1,140	1,894	622	12,988	4,107	21,193	13,948
Secondary	445	286	1,970	1,076	2,107	1,196	2,588	1,400	6,699	3,759	11,001	4,689
Total	445	286	1,970	1,076	4,003	2,336	4,482	2,022	19,687	7,866	32,194	18,637
13. Electrical equipment and supplies												
Secondary	–	–	–	–	446	341	1,172	506	7,126	4,250	12,800	7,213
14. Non-metallic mineral products												
Primary	14	7	44	29	191	104	847	717	3,261	2,905	3,594	1,758
Secondary	1,851	1,434	3,322	2,313	6,518	4,284	4,128	3,397	9,963	8,383	10,786	6,678
Total	1,865	1,441	3,366	2,342	6,709	4,388	4,975	4,114	13,224	11,288	14,380	8,436

TABLE 7.2 (concluded)

Industry Group	1870		1880		1890		1900††		1910††		1915††	
	Value of Product	Value Added	Value of Product	Value Added	Value of Product	Value Added	Value of Product	Value Added	Value of Product	Value Added	Value of Product	Value Added
15. Products of petroleum and coal												
Secondary	2,846	1,579	3,667	1,734	2,108	663	3,116	1,079	6,348	3,083	10,508	3,368
16. Chemicals and allied products												
Primary	—		85	25	83	36	35	21	240	188	95	40
Secondary	1,441	610	2,116	985	4,261	1,874	3,881	1,780	13,045	6,679	17,122	7,661
Total	1,441	610	2,201	1,010	4,344	1,910	3,916	1,801	13,285	6,867	17,217	7,701
17. Miscellaneous industries												
Secondary	1,120	676	2,820	1,592	4,656	2,786	5,283	3,090	9,978	5,995	7,821	4,356
Total Primary	47,383	12,752	61,140	17,177	88,801	29,325	93,875	25,985	187,985	65,831	241,455	73,138
Total Secondary	65,395	35,571	94,325	48,106	144,060	78,048	139,933	73,290	367,278	199,943	445,493	214,833
Total†	112,778	48,323	155,465	65,283	232,861	107,373	233,808 270,500	99,275	555,263 603,000	265,774	686,948 702,600	288,021

*Value added is computed by subtraction of cost of raw material values from gross value of production; no allowance has been made for the costs of fuel or power.
†Total is adjusted to approximate full coverage.
††Firms of five and over employees
SOURCE: Bertram, 'Historical Statistics,' tables 5, 7

TABLE 7.3
Approximations to Output and Output per Worker in Constant Prices, 1870–1910 (Various Deflators)

Year	Output ($000)			Output per Worker ($000)		
	Deflated by Michell (1900 = 100)	Deflated by DBS General (1926 = 100)	Deflated by DBS Fully & Chiefly Manufactured (1926 = 100)	Deflated by Michell (1900 = 100)	Deflated by DBS General (1926 = 100)	Deflated by DBS Full & Chiefly Manufactured (1926 = 100)
1870	88,661	141,326	n.a.	1,180	1,812	n.a.
1880	136,253	216,525	n.a.	1,284	2,041	n.a.
1890	225,204	347,036	351,223	1,530	2,358	2,386
1900	270,500	433,893	460,034	1,449	2,323	2,465
1910	508,861	768,153	967,897	2,048	3,092	3,897
Year	Percentage Growth			Percentage Growth		
1870–80	53.7	53.2	n.a.	8.8	12.6	n.a.
1880–90	65.3	60.3	n.a.	19.2	15.5	n.a.
1890–1900	20.1	25.0	31.0	−5.3	−1.2	3.3
1900–10	88.1	77.0	110.4	41.3	33.1	58.0

SOURCE: Tables 7.1; *HSC*, series J1, 34, 46. Output data are Bertram's; outputs per worker are *Census*.

TABLE 7.4
Decennial Percentage Growth, Industry Groups, Current Prices, 1870–1910 (Percentage Increases)

	1870–80	1880–90	1890–1900	1900–10
Consumer Goods				
Employment	16.2	38.0	39.7	22.6
Output	41.2	53.6	63.0	106.7
Capital and Consumer Durables				
Employment	18.3	24.1	17.4	98.3
Output	41.1	41.9	13.9	230.6
Intermediate Goods and Services				
Employment	22.8	43.6	8.9	35.7
Output	26.8	47.1	6.1	132.5
Export Goods				
Employment	23.8	39.2	4.8	6.3
Output	30.1	33.7	−8.2	103.7

SOURCE: Calculated from *Census*. Data for 1870, 1880, and 1890 are adjusted to remove small firms so far as possible.

TABLE 7.5
Real Rates of Growth, Ontario Industry Groups, 1870–1910

Industry Group	1870–80	1880–90	1890–1900	1900–10
Consumer Goods				
Deflated by DBS General Index	5.3	64.2	75.2	64.2
Deflated by DBS Manufactures Index			83.9	95.1
Capital Goods				
Deflated by DBS General Index	50.8	72.2	18.1	298.1
Deflated by DBS Manufactures Index			28.4	212.0
Intermediate Goods				
Deflated by DBS General Index	44.8	67.2	−2.6	179.9
Deflated by DBS Manufactures Index			5.9	119.5
Export Goods				
Deflated by DBS General Index	22.7	26.2	−5.0	63.3
Deflated by DBS Manufactures Index			3.6	92.2

SOURCE: *Census*, calculated with 'adjusted' data from table 7.4 and with the use of price indexes from table 7.2

TABLE 7.6
Quantity and Value of Coal Imports at Ontario
Ports of Entry, 1869–1900

Year	Quantity (tons)	Value
1869	144,071	607,934
1870	146,464	656,139
1871	162,320	703,220
1872	230,491	1,001,103
1873	333,365	1,444,686
1874	523,525	2,372,250
1875	384,178	1,879,168
1876	472,721	2,055,331
1877	723,205	2,506,152
1878	593,725	2,179,305
1879	591,221	2,096,173
1880	669,874	2,017,323
1881	816,011	3,019,662
1882	921,000	3,482,356
1883	1,178,501	4,573,579
1884	1,531,114	5,707,254
1885	1,537,207	5,709,107
1886	1,531,733	5,296,033
1887	1,851,667	6,165,932
1888	2,939,506	7,112,306
1889	2,054,867	6,566,446
1890	2,195,436	6,496,525
1891	2,532,999	7,493,043
1892	2,674,882	7,987,549
1893	2,672,252	8,318,369
1894	2,441,800	7,500,558
1895	2,497,410	6,885,275
1896	2,735,551	7,162,145
1897	2,609,742	6,939,130
1898	2,839,300	7,046,921
1899	3,935,315	9,053,055

NOTE: Includes coal, coke, and coal dust
SOURCE: Canada, 'Tables of the Trade and
Navigation of the Dominion of Canada for the
Fiscal Year Ending in June ... ,' *Sessional
Papers*

TABLE 7.7
Ontario Brick Production, 1891–1939

Year	Millions of Bricks
1891	173.6
1892	197.0
1896	117.1
1901	272.1
1906	339.9
1907	343.7
1908	278.6
1913	490.0
1939	71.4

SOURCE: Ontario Bureau of Mines,
Reports. The figures include
common, face, pressed, and terra-
cotta bricks, but not sand-lime
bricks.

TABLE 7.8
Ontario Cement Sales, 1891–1913

Year	Natural Rock Cement*	Portland Cement*
1891	46.2	2.0
1895	55.2	58.7
1908	0	2,022.9
1913		3,802.3

*Million barrels of 350 pounds
SOURCE: Ontario Bureau of Mines, *Reports*. In early years
the *Reports* do not clearly distinguish between sales and
production.

TABLE 7.9
Ontario's Fifteen Largest Industries, Gross Values of Outputs, 1870 and 1910 ($ million)

1870		1910	
Flour and Gristmill Products	27.1	Log and Lumber Products	53.1
Log and Lumber Products	14.9	Flour and Gristmill Products	52.7
Foundry, Machine Shop	4.8	Clothing	30.2
Woollen Yarn and Goods	4.6	Foundry, Machine Shop	29.3
Clothing	4.1	Slaughtering, Meat Packing	28.1
Liquors, Distilled	3.9	Iron and Steel Products	22.0
Slaughtering, Meat Packing	3.2	Agricultural Implements	19.2
Carriages, Wagons	3.1	Butter and Cheese	18.1
Bread, Biscuits, Confectionery	3.0	Printing, Publishing, Bookbinding	15.0
Oils	2.8	Leather, Tanning, etc.	14.7
Furniture	2.3	Bread, Biscuits, Confectionery	14.4
Agricultural Implements	2.3	Smelting	13.0
Boots and Shoes	2.0	Hosiery and Knit Goods	10.1
Plumbing, Tinsmithing	2.0	Furniture	9.2
Printing, Publishing, Bookbinding	1.9	Boots and Shoes	9.1

Sum of Above as Percent of Total Gross Outputs in 'Industry'
81.4   60.0

SOURCE: *Census*

TABLE 7.10
Orders for Rolling Stock Placed by Canadian Railways in 1912

Railway	Freight Cars	Passenger Cars	Locomotives
CPR	28,403	473	493
CNR	5,384	100	104
CNOR	326	23	10
CNQR	420	23	10
GTR	3,350	67	140
ICR	2,104	16	28
PEIR	16	0	0
TNOR	4	0	0
THBR	1,514	0	4
QCR	100	0	6
ACHBR	70	4	5
AER	119	5	2
S&LR	75	0	2

SOURCE: *Canadian Engineer*, 30 January 1913, 231 ff

TABLE 7.11
Production of Certain Forest Products, 1870–1914

Year	Square Pine Cu. Ft	Other Square Timber Cu. Ft	Total Cu. Ft	Timber MFBM	Pine Logs Number	Logs for Lumber MFBM	Total Lumber Production MFBM
1870	16,305,901	17,180,894	33,496,795	167,484	5,713,204	n.a.	n.a.
1880	14,111,497	37,921,065	52,032,552	260,162	14,945,679	n.a.	n.a.
1890	7,480,683	12,346,636*	19,827,319*	99,136*	10,293,171†	n.a.	n.a.
1900	1,044,439††	2,746,219††	3,790,658††	18,953††	n.a.	1,334,622	1,353,575
1908							1,294,794
1909							1,519,080
1910							1,642,191
1911							1,716,849
1912							1,385,186
1913							1,101,066
1914							1,044,131

*Includes 'square and sided' timber
†Defined as 'census standard logs.' Besides pine, there were in 1890, 11,660,615 'spruce and other logs.'
††'Square and Waney' in 1900

NOTES

n.a.: not available

MFBM: Thousand feet board measure

Conversions: 200 cu. ft = one MFBM.

No units for pine logs, 1870

SOURCE: 1870, 1880, 1890, and 1900 from *Census*; 1908–14 data from Dominion Bureau of Statistics, *Canadian Forestry Statistics – Revised*

TABLE 7.12
Timber Production from Ontario Crown Lands, Fiscal years, 1868–1913–14

Fiscal Year	Saw Logs, Boom and Dimension Lumber (MFBM)						Pulpwood Cords	Square Timber (million cu. ft)				
	Pine	Other	Western	Belleville	Ottawa	Total	Total	Pine Western	Belleville	Ottawa	Other	Total
1913–14	381.2	77.3	353.6	14.2	90.7	458.5	104.5	0.1	0	0	0	0.1
1912–13	354.5	64.2	331.8	12.7	74.0	418.5	131.4	0.5	0	0	0	0.5
1911–12	482.5	69.2	435.2	16.6	99.9	551.7	140.3	0.4	0			0.4
1910–11	577.5	93.2	549.8	20.7	100.7	670.7	90.7	0.6				0.6
1909–10	606.6	95.7	557.1	32.7	112.5	702.3		0.3				0.3
10 mos 09	463.8	64.5	396.8	11.7	119.8	528.3		0.3				0.3
1908	618.2	94.9	561.4	24.8	126.9	713.1		0.8	0	0		0.8
1907	777.8	86.1	650.8	43.3	169.8	863.9		1.0	0	0		1.0
1906	704.3	75.4	571.1	43.3	165.3	779.7	72.5	0.6	0	0	0.017	0.617
1905	622.5	64.3	507.2	45.5	134.1	686.8		1.1	0			1.1
1904	663.2	47.3	529.8	34.8	145.9	710.5		1.7	0	0.3		2.0
1903	719.8	66.2	617.0	44.2	124.8	786.0		0.6	0	0.2		0.8
1902	654.3	43.4	548.5	51.9	97.3	697.7		1.1	0	0.4		1.5
1901	631.1	45.5	533.5	50.8	92.3	676.6		1.2	0	0.5		1.7
1900	678.2	41.1	495.0	80.6	143.7	719.3	65.1	1.5	0	0.4		1.9
1899	528.0	17.5	371.5	56.3	117.7	545.5		1.1	0	0.6	0.015	1.715
1898	570.0	9.5	419.1	69.2	91.2	579.5		1.1		0.3		1.5
1897	503.9	9.4	257.1	60.6	195.6	513.3		1.6		0.4		2.0
1896	938.7	16.4	701.0	50.3	203.8	955.1		1.0	0	0.1		1.1
1895	832.6	14.7	556.1	75.9	215.3	847.3		0.7	0	0.1		0.8
1894	630.8	7.6	439.4	41.8	157.2	638.4		0.6		0.6	*	1.2
1893	742.6	9.0	543.5	87.7	120.4	751.6		1.1		0.7		1.9
1892	648.5	10.2	440.2	81.0	137.5	658.7		2.9	0.1	1.0		4.0
1891	489.0	3.6	300.4	58.3	133.9	492.6			0.1	1.2		1.2
1890	552.9	3.4	291.2	63.5	201.5	556.3		1.7	0	1.6		3.3

TABLE 7.12 (concluded)

Fiscal Year	Saw Logs, Boom and Dimension Lumber (MFBM)						Pulpwood Cords	Square Timber (million cu. ft)				
	Pine	Other	Western	Belleville	Ottawa	Total	Total	Pine			Other	Total
								Western	Belleville	Ottawa		
1889	757.6	3.6	383.8	127.5	249.9	761.2		2.9		2.0		4.9
1888	740.8	2.8	281.4	143.0	319.2	743.6		2.0	0.2	1.1		3.3
1887	599.0	2.4	223.0	95.4	283.0	601.4		1.2	0.1	1.2		2.5
1886	563.4	3.8	170.4	116.6	280.2	567.2		3.2	0.1	1.8		5.1
1885	501.8	3.6	129.8	117.0	258.6	505.4		1.4	0.6	1.3		3.1
1884	376.0	2.6	145.2	73.0	160.4	378.6		1.5	0.2	5.0		6.7
1883	462.8	1.4	159.8	101.2	203.2	464.2		0.9	0.1	5.3		6.3
1882	540.8	2.2	192.4	125.0	225.6	543.0		1.1	0.2	5.4		6.7
1881	513.0	2.6	153.6	130.6	231.2	515.6		0.5	0.2	5.7		6.4
1880	389.2	3.0	129.8	72.8	189.6	392.2		0.4	0.4	3.5		4.3
1879	332.8	1.0	101.4	85.6	146.8	333.8		0.2	0.1	2.2		2.5
1878	224.4	0.6	101.2	67.2	56.6	225.0		0.2	0.2	4.9		5.5
1877	214.8	0.4	74.6	70.6	70.0	215.2		0.6	0.2	8.7		9.5
1876	237.4	0.6	101.6	55.4	81.0	238.0		0.2	0.1	9.4		9.7
1875	338.0	0.6	67.2	105.2	165.2	338.6		0.1	0.1	6.4		6.6
1874	323.4	1.6	65.6	94.8	164.6	325.0		1.2	0.2	7.4		8.3
1873	498.0	1.4	111.0	149.8	238.6	499.4		0.3	0.1	7.9		8.3
1872	1,620.1	3.0	144.1	479.0	1,000.0	1,623.1		0.3	0.3	6.4		7.0
1871	1,288.2	1.8	72.8	251.7	965.5	1,290.0		0.3	0.2	11.0		11.5
1870	287.2	1.0	45.2	90.4	152.6	288.2		0.2	0.4	7.6		8.3
1869	375.2	0	59.6	115.4	200.1	375.2		0.6	0.5	11.3		12.4
1868	177.0	40.0	73.8	81.8	61.4	217.0		0.2	0.5	5.4		6.1

*Not reported 1868–95
SOURCE: Ontario Crown Lands Commission/Department, Minister of Lands, Forests, Mines, *Reports*

TABLE 7.13
Ontario Production of Butter and Cheese, 1870–1910

Census year	Home-Made Butter (lb)	Home-Made Cheese (lb)	Cheese Factories			Butter Factories			Butter and Cheese Factories (producing both)			Total Provincial Output	
			No.	Employ-ment	Value of Output ($)	No.	Employ-ment	Value of Output ($)	No.	Employ-ment	Value of Output ($)	Butter (million lb)	Cheese
1870	37,623,643	3,432,797	323	828	1,454,702	n.a.	n.a.	n.a.					
1880	54,862,365	1,701,721	551	1,567	4,668,078	23	81	212,480					
1890	55,564,496	1,065,737	893	1,861	7,269,225	45	129	300,113					
1900	55,378,568	n.a.	1,061	2,035	10,597,630	103	248	1,227,159	172	450	3,144,133		
1910	63,253,444	295,886	1,007	1,826	12,596,852	120	319	2,741,689	121	305	2,761,648	78.1	127.4

n.a.: Not available
SOURCE: *Census*

TABLE 7.14

Annual Rates of Growth, Ontario Industry, 1870–1941

Period	Value of Output	Employment	Volume of Output
1870–1941	5.4	2.4	4.8+
1890–1941	5.2	2.3	4.7±
1870–1929	5.1	2.3	4.3±
1890–1929	5.8	2.1	5.1±
1915–1929	8.1	3.6	6.1−
1870–90	3.7	2.9	4.6+

SOURCES: Bertram, 'Historical Statistics,' table 5; decennial *Censuses*; *Postal Census* of 1916 (from Bertram for 1870–1915 output; otherwise from *Censuses*): prices from *HSC*, series J1, J34, J46

TABLE 7.15

Annual Rates of Growth, Ontario Industry, Main Groupings, 1870–1941

	Consumer Goods		Capital and Consumer Durable Goods		Intermediate Goods	
	Value of Output	Employment	Value of Output	Employment	Value of Output	Employment
I. All establishments: '1936 coverage' of industries*						
1870–1941	4.2	1.6	5.5	2.8	4.5	1.4
1890–1941	4.6	2.1	6.2	2.9	4.2	0.9
1870–1929	4.8	1.8	5.8	2.6	4.5	1.0
1890–1929	5.9	2.4	6.9	2.8	3.6	1.0
1915–1929	6.3		9.5		4.3	
1870–90	5.0	3.0	3.5	1.6	2.8	2.4
II. Establishments having five employees or more*						
1870–1910	5.4	4.2	5.2	3.1	3.4	2.2
1870–1915	5.3	n.a.	5.1	n.a.	3.2	n.a.
1870–1890	7.7	2.3	11.2	6.1	8.5	3.0
1900–15	6.4	n.a.	9.8	n.a.	6.2	n.a.
1890–1915	6.0	n.a.	6.4	n.a.	3.4	n.a.

*Except 1915 – establishments having value of output at least $2,500 in Panel I, and also having at least five employees in II. Industries not included in 1941 have been eliminated from data for 1870–1890 and from 1915 data.
SOURCES: Calculated from data in *Census*, *Canada Year Books*, and Dominion Bureau of Statistics, *Postal Census of Manufactures*, 1915

TABLE 7.16
Average Annual Rates of Growth, Certain Ontario Industries, 1870–1929

Industry	1870–1929		1890–1929	
	Value of Output	Employment	Value of Output	Employment
Consumer Goods				
Boots and shoes	3.0	2.7		
Bread, biscuits, confectionery	4.4	2.1		
Butter and cheese	5.2	2.2		
Clothing	3.5	1.0		
Canning			4.1	1.5
Hosiery etc.	6.2	2.6		
Distilleries	2.4	0.7		
Breweries	3.8	1.9		
Drugs and medicines	7.1	2.0		
Print, publ, bkbind, lithography	5.0	2.0		
Rubber and elastic			11.1	3.9
Slaughter, packing houses	4.8	1.5		
Soap	4.4	1.2		
Capital Goods and Consumer Durable Goods				
Agricultural implements	3.9	1.4	3.7	1.4
Automobiles				
Railway rolling stock	2.2*	1.9*		
Electrical apparatus			12.8	3.0
Castings and forgings	3.7	1.1	4.4	1.2
Furniture	3.7	1.1	4.3	1.0
Iron and steel products, machinery, sheet metal	5.7	2.5	10.7	4.0
Intermediate Goods				
Brass and copper	5.0	0.6		
Cottons	4.3	1.6		
Electric light			10.2	3.2
Flour and grist-mill products	1.9	0.2	2.1	−0.2
Gas light	5.7	1.7	6.7	2.3
Leather	2.6	0.5	3.9	0.7
Log and lumber products	2.1	−0.1	1.3	−0.9
Oils	4.0	1.5	6.7	2.5
Pulp and paper	6.8	2.4	9.2	3.3
Smelting (ferrous and non-ferrous)			7.1	3.2
Woollens	1.6	0.1		

*1870–1927
SOURCE: Calculated from *Census* data, and from annual censuses of manufacturing (Dominion Bureau of Statistics)

TABLE 7.17

Approximations to Real Increases in Output and Labour Productivity, 1870–1941 (percentage)

1870–90:	Increase in nominal output	3.7	
	Change in price level (J1)	−0.9	p.a. or more
	Increase in real output	4.6	p.a. or more
	Increase in employment	2.9	p.a.
	Increase in average output per worker	1.5	p.a. or more
1870–1941:	Increase in nominal output	5.4	p.a.
	Change in price level (J34)	+0.6	p.a. or less
	Increase in real output	4.8	p.a. or more
	Increase in employment	2.4	p.a.
	Increase in average output per worker	2.4	p.a. or more
1890–1941:	Increase in nominal output	5.2	p.a.
	Change in price level 0.5 to 1.0; best is J46	+0.5	p.a.
	Increase in real output	4.7	p.a.
	Increase in employment	2.3	p.a.
	Increase in average output per worker	2.4	p.a.
1890–1929:	Increase in nominal output	5.8	p.a.
	Change in price level 0.7 to 1.8; best is J46	+0.7	p.a.
	Increase in real output	5.1	p.a.
	Increase in employment	2.1	p.a.
	Increase in average output per worker	3.0	p.a.
1915–29:	Increase in nominal output less than	8.1	p.a.
	Change in price level 2 to 2.2; best is J46	+2.0	p.a.
	Increase in real output less than	6.1	p.a.
	Increase in employment less than	3.6	p.a.
	Increase in average output per worker	2.5	p.a.
1890–1915:	Increase in nominal output more than	4.5	p.a.
	Change in price level 0.2 to 1.3; best is J46	+0.2	p.a.
	Increase in real output more than	4.3	p.a.
	Increase in employment more than	1.2	p.a.
	Increase in average output per worker more than	3.1	p.a.

SOURCE: Bertram, 'Historical Statistics'; table 7.1; *HSC*, series J1, J34, J46

TABLE 8.1
Electric Power Plants, Ontario, 1880–1915

Year	Number of Establishments	Capital ($)	Value of Product ($)
1880	n.a.	n.a.	n.a.
1890	48	1,658,130	482,678
1900	27	7,148,826	904,328
1910	133	57,660,774	5,584,091
1915	155	102,184,941	11,027,256

n.a.: Not available
SOURCES: decennial *Censuses*; Dominion Bureau of Statistics, *Postal Census of Manufactures*, 1916

TABLE 8.2
Number of Establishments and Number of Lamps, as Reported by the Dominion Inland Revenue, Fiscal Years, 1895/6–1913/14

Fiscal Year	Number of Firms	Number of Arc Lamps	Number of Incandescent Lamps
1895–6	145	6,835	171,404
1899–1900	187	6,557	336,278
1902–3	203	7,973	557,154
1912–13	230	9,238	2,079,000
1913–14	262	11,161	3,213,000

SOURCE: Canada, *Returns, Statistics of the Reports, Internal Revenues of the Dominion*; *Canada Year Book*

TABLE 9.1
War Trade as a Percentage of Total Trade,
Ontario, 1915

Agricultural implements	5.6
Automobiles	2.6
Awnings, tents, sails	46.3
Boilers and engines	55.8
Brass castings	10.9
Iron and steel bridges	15.5
Carpets	26.0
Cars and car works	73.4
Clothing, men's, factory	17.8
Clothing, women's, factory	10.7
Cottons	11.6
Electrical apparatus, supplies	42.8
Evaporated fruit and vegetables	59.1
Drugs and chemicals	28.2
Explosives	86.0
Foundry, machine shop products	17.1
Furnishing goods, men's apparel	21.8
Furniture	10.5
Harness and saddlery	68.2
Hosiery and knit goods	25.8
Iron and steel products	44.2
Jams and jellies	21.7
Leather goods	28.5
Leather	24.3
Lock and gunsmithing	44.9
Plumbers' supplies	63.5
Rubber and elastic goods	4.7
Shoddy	38.2
Slaughtering, meat-packing	6.7
Smelting	4.3
Woollen goods	55.7
Woollen yarns	26.8

SOURCE: Dominion Bureau of Statistics, *Postal
Census of Manufactures*, 1916

TABLE 9.2
Employment and Output in Some Ontario Heavy Industries, 1919 and 1922

	1919		1922	
Industry	Number	$ Million	Number	$ Million
Foundry and machine shop products	16,032	51.6	6,096	22.2
Agricultural implements	9,930	34.5	5,759	17.2
Rolling mills and steel furnaces	6,796	34.4	2,931	15.6
Electrical apparatus	6,274	21.0	7,579	30.7

SOURCE: Dominion Bureau of Statistics, *Census of Manufacturing*, 1919 and 1922

TABLE 9.3
Contraction of Canadian External Trade, 1929–34 (million dollars)

Industry	Fiscal years ending 31 March of			
	1929	1930	1932	1934
Paper	142.3	145.6	103.0	73.0
Wood pulp	44.9	44.7	27.7	25.0
Automobiles	43.1	35.3	3.6	11.5
Copper	26.9	37.7	19.3	18.7
Cheese	25.2	18.3	10.6	8.2
Whisky	24.1	25.9	11.6	16.0
Nickel	23.9	25.0	12.0	28.2
Meats	19.2	15.0	5.0	15.5
Rubber tires	19.1	18.2	5.1	4.3
Farm implements	15.9	18.3	2.5	1.8
Pulpwood	14.2	13.9	8.2	4.9
Raw gold	12.4	34.4	13.7	2.6
Silver	11.8	11.5	5.2	—
Leather and hides	19.0	6.4	2.3	3.3
Rubber boots	8.6	10.0	3.6	3.2
Machinery	7.3	7.2	3.7	2.9
Beer	5.6	2.0	0.002	0.4
Electric apparatus	2.4	2.5	0.7	2.0
Auto parts	2.4	2.3	0.7	1.4
Butter	0.8	0.5	2.4	0.8

SOURCE: *Canada Year Book*

TABLE 9.4
Contraction in Some Ontario Heavy Industries, 1929 and 1933

Industry	Output ($ million)		Employment (persons)	
	1929	1933	1929	1933
Electrical apparatus	85.4	29.4	13,293	8,696
Machinery	46.2	13.0	7,690	4,214
Primary iron & steel	43.2	11.6	5,915	2,966
Various iron & steel products	63.4	28.4	15,701	11,385
Sheet metal	46.2	13.0	5,559	3,475

SOURCE: Dominion Bureau of Statistics, *Census of Manufacturing*, 1929, 1933

TABLE 10.1
Rural and Urban Population, Ontario, 1871–1941

		1871	1881	1891	1901	1911	1921	1931	1941
Ontario:	Total	1,620,851	1,926,922	2,144,321	2,182,947	2,527,292	2,933,662	3,431,683	3,787,655
	Male	828,590	978,554	1,069,487	1,096,640	1,301,272	1,481,890	1,748,844	1,921,201
	Female	792,261	948,368	1,044,834	1,086,307	1,226,020	1,451,772	1,682,839	1,866,454
Rural:	Total	1,264,854	1,351,074	1,295,323	1,246,969	1,198,803	1,227,030	1,335,691	1,449,022
	Male	652,053	697,291	671,180	650,206	641,787	650,379	719,975	773,220
	Female	612,801	653,783	624,143	596,763	557,016	576,651	615,716	675,802
Urban:	Total	355,997	575,848	818,998	935,978	1,328,489	1,706,632	2,095,992	2,338,653
	Male	176,537	281,263	398,307	446,434	659,485	831,511	1,028,869	1,147,981
	Female	179,460	294,585	420,691	489,544	669,004	875,121	1,067,123	1,190,652

SOURCE: *Census*, 1951, vol. I, table 13

TABLE 10.2
Pattern of Urbanization, Ontario, 1900–41

	1900–1	1910–11	1921	1930–1	1941
Population (1941 boundaries)					
Toronto (incl. incorp. suburbs)	219,150	383,892	529,761	656,895	710,293
Hamilton (incl. Burlington, Dundas)	56,926	89,093	121,838	163,619	175,428
London	37,976	46,300	60,959	71,148	78,264
Ottawa (incl. Eastview, Rockcliffe Pk.)	67,226	90,231	113,167	134,509	164,397
Motor Cities*	19,592	30,869	67,875	121,618	132,124
Northern Centres†	12,450	34,048	47,270	77,974	104,742
Northern Centres†					
Excl. Sudbury, Timmins, Copper Cliff	7,923	26,816	32,209	42,083	40,017
Industrial Employment					
Toronto	42,500	63,500	66,708	94,754	133,099
Hamilton	10,200	21,100	28,192	31,053	45,421
London	5,700	9,400	7,384	9,366	12,016
Ottawa	6,900	9,200	5,841	8,255	9,974
Motor Cities*	1,700	4,800	8,448	19,369	38,805
Value of Manufacturing Output ($ million)					
Toronto	58.4	154.3	371.1	521.5	756.9
Hamilton	17.1	55.1	109.8	166.9	283.6
London	8.1	16.3	35.0	45.5	68.6
Ottawa	7.6	19.9	41.9	33.1	43.5
Motor Cities*	2.6	10.1	69.8	142.0	397.7

*Oshawa, Windsor Ford City, East Windsor, Walkerville
†Cobalt, Cochrane, Copper Cliff, Dryden, Englehart, Fort Frances, Haileybury, Hearst, Iroquois Falls, Kapuskasing, Kenora, New Liskeard, Rainy River, Sioux Lookout, Sturgeon Falls, Sudbury, Timmins
SOURCES: Dominion Bureau of Statistics, *Census of Manufacturing*, 1921–41, as reported in *Canada Year Book*; *Census*, 1901, vol. III, table xx; *Census*, 1911, vol. III, table xi; *Census*, 1941, vol. III

TABLE 10.3
Manufacturing in Some Northern Centres, 1939

Centre	Employment	Value of Product ($000)
Kapuskasing	1,014	8,314
Fort Frances	705	4,339
Kenora	470	3,933
Sudbury	540	2,225
Timmins	438	1,393

SOURCE: Dominion Bureau of Statistics, *Census of Manufacturing*, 1939 as reported in *Canada Year Book*

TABLE 11.1
Material and Labour Costs of Iron Smelting, 1899–1916

	Input Prices: Dollars Per Unit			
	Per Man Day	Per Ton Ore	Per Ton Fuel	Per Ton Flux
Deseronto				
1899–1902	1.42	3.40	4.36	0.90
1913–16	2.28	4.11	7.51	1.05
Hamilton				
1899–1902	2.00	3.68	3.81	0.76
1913–16	2.74	3.24	4.42	1.04

	Input Requirements: Per Ton of Iron			
	Labour (man-day)	Ore (tons)	Fuel (tons)	Flux (tons)
Deseronto				
1899–1902	0.90	1.63	0.72	0.04
1913–16	0.87	2.04	0.98	0.13
Hamilton				
1899–1902	0.73	1.71	1.15	0.48
1913–16	0.31	1.81	1.01	0.56

	Material and Labour Costs: Dollars Per Ton of Iron				
	Labour	Ore	Fuel	Flux	All Variable
Deseronto					
1899–1902	1.28	5.50	3.16	0.04	9.98
1913–16	1.99	8.40	7.36	0.14	17.89
Hamilton					
1899–1902	1.46	6.32	4.37	0.36	12.51
1913–16	0.84	5.83	4.49	0.58	11.74

SOURCE: The data are found in the Public Archives of Canada, RG 87, v. 18, with minor interpolation to fill lacunae. All tons are short tons of 2,000 pounds. A bushel of charcoal is assumed to weigh twenty-one pounds (see the Deseronto reports for 1906 and 1911).

TABLE 11.2
Ontario Pig Iron Output, Net Tons Annually, by Site 1896–1920

Year	Hamilton	Deseronto	Midland	Sault Ste Marie	Port Arthur	Port Colborne
1896	14,560	0	0	0	0	0
1897	26,115	0	0	0	0	0
1898	48,254	0	0	0	0	0
1899	51,739	13,010	0	0	0	0
1900	49,170	13,138	1,636	0	0	0
1901	67,512	12,513	42,208	0	0	0
1902	69,123	10,895	36,590	0	0	0
1903	43,152	9,979	33,873	0	0	0
1904	66,007	10,462	35,716	15,660	0	0
1905	73,408	11,220	31,956	136,285	0	0
1906	79,015	11,061	27,213	158,269	0	0
1907	89,554	3,474	27,168	146,825	8,436	0
1908	116,805	2,273	37,902	114,504	0	0
1909	164,929	12,233	39,851	180,891	9,108	0
1910	182,451	13,927	46,821	186,736	17,338	0
1911	175,706	20,101	67,324	247,090	16,414	0
1912	174,082	21,701	98,742	295,068	0	0
1913	180,712	23,696	70,027	345,135	0	29,329
1914	127,756	9,380	0	327,050	0	91,926
1915	165,870	13,692	0	219,724	0	94,214
1916	194,863	17,304	0	379,679	0	107,356
1917	204,228	14,092	0	351,112	0	121,802
1918	196,357	15,415	9,297	414,802	0	111,779
1919	190,251	20,731	30,073	256,567	0	127,371
1920	185,639	0	8,354	450,974	0	104,101

NOTE: The output of specialty ferro-alloys produced in electric furnaces is excluded.
All iron is made from coke fuel except at Deseronto in most years and at Sault Ste Marie
in 1905 (when charcoal comprised 12 per cent of the fuel). In 1913 the Standard Iron
Company of Deseronto erected at Parry Sound a second furnace, which produced only
in 1913 and 1919 accounting for 20 per cent and 65 per cent of the joint output. All other
output was from Deseronto. A small portion of the firm's fuel, was coke in 1906 and 1917;
almost all fuel was coke 1907–8 and 1918–19. Otherwise, charcoal was used. The Parry
Sound furnace in 1919 may have been operated by an independent firm known as the
Parry Sound Iron Company.
SOURCE: Public Archives of Canada, RG 87, vol. 18

TABLE 11.3
Ontario Steel Ingot Output, Net Tons Annually, by Site, 1901–20

Year	Stelco	Sault Ste Marie	DOFASCO	Canada Steel Foundries*	Other Firms†
1901	14,470	0	0	0	0
1902	18,921	49,881	0	0	0
1903	15,229	0	0	0	0
1904	11,529	47,878	0	0	0
1905	26,987	132,858	0	0	0
1906	41,125	222,891	0	0	0
1907	61,511	253,086	0	0	0
1908	37,170	174,227	0	3,281	0
1909	75,976	266,799	0	633	0
1910	89,558	299,740	0	844	0
1911	92,603	323,888	0	0	0
1912	89,600	368,474	0	0	0
1913	157,148	491,853	0	3,414	0
1914	100,346	392,654	n.a.	0	n.a.
1915	193,875	283,858	n.a.	n.a.	450
1916	238,411	419,131	58,946	n.a.	10,635
1917	375,724	526,344	94,000	40,885	28,012
1918	304,252	576,260	142,696	n.a.	101,418
1919	289,587	325,437	24,700	642	448
1920	301,050	405,525	30,440	0	1,121

n.a.: Not available
*The Ontario Iron and Steel Co. at Welland was merged with the Montreal Steel Works at the end of 1910 to form Canadian Steel Foundries, Ltd., which was associated with the Canadian Car and Foundry Co. The output reported here is that of the Welland works only.
†Electric Steel and Metals (Welland) was the only firm to produce in all years 1915–20 (accounting for 30 per cent of output in that period). Canadian Atlas Crucible (Welland) produced a small quantity of ingots in 1920 only, as had Dillon Crucible Alloy (Welland) 1919 and Swedish Crucible Alloy (Windsor) in 1916. William Kennedy and Sons of Owen Sound and Collingwood produced 4,185 tons in 1916 and 21,280 tons in 1918 at its Collingwood steel plant, which likely was the old Cramp works. The British Forgings plant was built in Toronto in 1917 by the Imperial Munitions Board to use light scrap steel turnings from shell production, which could not be remelted in ordinary furnaces. About 45 per cent of the steel used in shells was removed as scrap turnings (Carnegie, chapter 19). In 1917 11,472 tons were produced and in 1918 69,560 tons. The factory was acquired in 1920 by Baldwin's Canada Steel Co., which also purchased the Collingwood plant and removed it to Toronto.
SOURCE: Public Archives of Canada, RG 87, vol. 18. Ingot steel output is reported in the table but direct steel castings are not

TABLE 11.4
Canadian Iron Output, by Province, 1870–1939

Year	Ontario (net tons)	Quebec	Nova Scotia	Canada	Ontario (percentages)	Quebec	Nova Scotia
1870	0	7,896	1,501	9,397	0	84	16
1871	0	7,605	1,602	9,206	0	83	17
1872	0	7,403	896	8,299	0	89	11
1873	0	7,202	1,904	9,106	0	79	21
1874	0	3,685	1,602	5,286	0	70	30
1875	0	5,398	2,106	7,504	0	72	28
1876	0	4,301	403	4,704	0	91	9
1877	0	4,402	11,200	15,602	0	28	72
1878	0	2,397	14,560	16,957	0	14	86
1879	0	1,299	14,560	15,859	0	8	92
1880	0	2,800	21,840	24,640	0	11	89
1881	0	4,603	16,240	20,843	0	22	78
1882	0	8,702	19,040	27,742	0	31	69
1883	0	5,802	30,240	36,042	0	16	84
1884	0	3,898	25,872	29,770	0	13	87
1885	0	4,603	20,720	25,323	0	18	82
1886	0	8,702	23,520	32,222	0	27	73
1887	0	5,507	19,320	24,827	0	22	78
1888	0	4,243	17,556	21,799	0	19	81
1889	0	4,632	21,289	25,921	0	18	82
1890	0	3,390	18,381	21,772	0	16	84
1891	0	3,051	20,840	23,891	0	13	87
1892	0	8,049	34,393	42,442	0	19	81
1893	0	9,475	46,472	55,947	0	17	83
1894	0	8,623	41,344	49,967	0	17	83
1895	0	7,262	35,192	42,454	0	17	83
1896	28,302	6,615	32,351	67,268	42	10	48
1897	26,115	9,392	22,500	58,007	45	16	39
1898	48,253	7,134	21,627	77,015	63	9	28
1899	64,748	7,094	31,100	102,943	63	7	30
1900	62,387	6,055	28,133	96,575	65	6	29
1901	116,371	6,875	151,131	274,376	42	3	55
1902	112,688	7,970	237,244	357,902	31	2	66
1903	87,004	9,635	201,246	297,885	29	3	68
1904	127,845	11,122	164,488	303,454	42	4	54
1905	256,704	7,588	261,014	525,306	49	1	50
1906	275,558	7,844	315,008	598,410	46	1	53
1907	275,460	10,048	366,456	651,963	42	2	56
1908	271,484	6,709	352,642	630,834	43	1	56
1909	407,011	4,770	345,380	757,161	54	1	46
1910	447,273	3,237	350,287	800,797	56	0	44
1911	526,635	659	390,242	917,535	57	0	43
1912	589,593	0	424,994	1,014,587	58	0	42

TABLE 11.4 (*concluded*)

Year	Ontario (net tons)	Quebec	Nova Scotia	Canada	Ontario (percentages)	Quebec	Nova Scotia
1913	648,899	0	480,068	1,128,967	57	0	43
1914	556,112	0	227,052	783,164	71	0	29
1915	493,500	0	420,276	913,776	54	0	46
1916	699,201	0	470,055	1,169,256	60	0	40
1917	684,641	13,691	472,147	1,170,480	58	1	40
1918	747,650	32,030	415,871	1,195,551	63	3	35
1919	624,992	7,700	285,087	917,780	68	1	31
1920	749,069	8,833	332,493	1,090,396	69	1	30
1921	494,901	683	169,504	665,088	74	0	25
1922	293,662	0	135,261	428,923	68	0	32
1923	674,428	0	310,972	985,401	68	0	32
1924	465,888	0	198,327	664,215	70	0	30
1925	413,248	0	226,010	639,258	65	0	35
1926	567,928	0	280,267	848,195	67	0	33
1927	515,366	0	279,495	794,861	65	0	35
1928	823,168	0	339,087	1,162,254	71	0	29
1929	861,682	0	348,097	1,209,779	71	0	29
1930	598,687	0	238,152	836,839	72	0	28
1931	356,882	0	113,560	470,443	76	0	24
1932	127,045	0	34,381	161,426	79	0	21
1933	121,859	0	132,736	254,595	48	0	52
1934	304,231	0	149,363	453,594	67	0	33
1935	438,898	0	232,962	671,860	65	0	35
1936	471,613	0	288,006	759,619	62	0	38
1937	647,961	0	358,756	1,006,718	64	0	36
1938	519,200	0	270,879	790,078	66	0	34
1939	556,186	0	290,232	846,419	66	0	34

SOURCES: Kris Inwood, *The Canadian Charcoal Iron Industry* (New York, Garland, 1986), 105–6; *Halifax Herald*, 16 January 1890; Dominion Bureau of Statistics, *Iron and Steel and Its Products*, 1939

TABLE 12.1
Percentage Share of Industry Output Consumed by the American
Automobile Industry, 1929

Steel	18.0	Lead	31.2
Iron	52.9	Nickel	26.0
Rubber	84.2	Tin	23.6
Plate glass	73.0	Hardwood lumber	17.7
Upholstery leather	57.8	Copper	15.7
Gasoline	80.0	Zinc	5.5
Aluminum	37.4		

SOURCE: C.E. Fraser and G.F. Doriot, *Analyzing Our Industries*
(New York, 1932), 23

TABLE 12.2
Canadian-Owned Ontario Automobile Manufacturers

Make	Years	Location
Canadian Motor Syndicate (CMS)	1897–9	Toronto
McLachlan	1899	Toronto
Still	1899–1900	(see CMS)
LeRoy	1899–1907	Kitchener
Canadian Motors Ltd	1900–2	(see CMS)
Massey-Harris	1900–2	(see Russell)
Queen	1901–3	Toronto
Redpath	1903–7	Kitchener and Toronto
Ivanhoe	1903–5	(see Russell)
Russell	1905–16	Toronto
Chatham	1906–9	Chatham
Menard	1908–10	Windsor
Tudhope	1908–13	Orillia
McLaughlin	1908–22	Oshawa
Kennedy	1909–10	Preston
Dominion	1910	Walkerville
Swift	1910	Chatham
Guy	1911	Oshawa
Canada	1911	(see Galt)
Galt	1911–13	Galt
Superior	1911–12	Petrolia
Harding	1911–12	London
Jules	1911	Toronto and Guelph
Brockville '30'	1911	(see Brockville Atlas)
Every Day	1911–13	Woodstock
Martin	1911	Chatham
Sager	1911	Welland
Peck	1912–13	Toronto
Brockville Atlas	1912–14	Brockville
Amherst 40	1912	Amherstburg
Tate	1912–14	Walkerville
WelDoer	1913	Kitchener
Bartlett	1914–17	Toronto and Stratford
Dart	1914	Toronto
Fisher	1914–15	Walkerville and Orillia
Galt	1914–14	Galt
Regal	1915–17	Kitchener
Gray-Dort	1915–25	Chatham
Bell	1916–18	Barrie
La Marne	1921	Toronto
Brock Six	1921	Amherstburg
Roberts Six, Mercury Six	1921	Lachine
Glen	1921–2	Toronto
London Six	1921–5	London
Canadian	1922	Walkerville
Gilson	1922	Guelph
Orton	1922	Petrolia
Fleetwood-Knight	1923	Kingston
Brooks	1924–9	Stratford
Frontenac	1931–3	Toronto

SOURCE: Durnford and Baechler, *Cars of Canada*, 68 and 71

TABLE 12.3
American-Owned Ontario Automobile Manufacturers

Manufacturer and Make	Years in Canada	Location
*National Cycle and Automobile	1899–1900	Hamilton
Locomobile		
*Ford	1904–	Windsor, St Catharines
*Packard Electric		
Oldsmobile	1905–7	
*Reo Motors		St Catharines
Reo	1909–15	
Reo (Dominion Motors)	1931–3	Toronto
*Canadian Regal Motors		Kitchener
Regal	1915–17	
*Hupp Motors		Windsor
Hupmobile	1911–14	
Hupmobile	1933–6	
*E–M–F		Walkerville
E–M–F	1909–12	
Flanders		
*Studebaker		Walkerville
(E–M–F)	1912	
(Flanders)		
Studebaker	1913–36	
Pierce-Arrow	1928–34	
Studebaker	1948–66	Hamilton
*Packard Motors		Windsor
Packard	1931–9	
*Schacht		Hamilton
Schacht	1911–13	
*Holden Morgan Company		Toronto
Imp	1913	
*Keeton Motors		Brantford
Keeton	1913–15	
*Willys-Overland		Hamilton
Willys-Overland	1914–15	
(Overland)	1915–18	Toronto
(Russell)		
Overland	1919–25	
Whippet	1926–30	
Willys Knights	1926–33	
*Canadian Crow Motors		London
Crow-Elkhart	1915–18	
*Canadian Briscoe Motors (Tudhope)		Brockville
Briscoe	1916–21	
*General Motors	(1907–18)	Oshawa
*Durant Motors		Toronto
Durant Star	1922–28	
Durant Frontenac	1928–31	

TABLE 12.3 (*concluded*)

Manufacturer and Make	Years in Canada	Location
*Chrysler Canada		Walkerville
(Chalmers Motor) T	(1916–17)	
(Maxwell Motor) T	(1916–25)	
Chrysler Canada	1925–	
(Dodge Brothers)	(1925–28)	Toronto
*Graham-Paige Motors		Toronto
Graham-Paige	(1931–35)	
*American Motors		
(Hudson-Essex of Canada) T	1932–41	Tilbury
(Nash Motors)	1950–56	
American Motors	1956–	Brampton

*Indicates manufacturer
NOTE: Firms in parentheses were absorbed by the main entry firm
SOURCE: Compiled from Durnford and Baechler, *Cars of Canada*, 222–7

TABLE 12.4
Canadian Automotive Production, Exports, Imports, and Employment, 1917–39

Year	Production			Average No. of Employees	Exports			Imports		
	Cars	Trucks	Total		Cars	Trucks	Total	Cars	Trucks	Total
1904–16	n.a.	n.a.	135,000	n.a.	n.a.	n.a.	n.a.	n.a.	n.a.	n.a.
1917	n.a.	n.a.	93,810	5,919	n.a.	n.a.	9,492	15,825	831	16,656
1918	75,089	7,319	82,408	5,362	n.a.	n.a.	10,361	9,190	1,622	10,812
1919	79,936	7,899	87,835	6,771	19,597	3,352	22,949	9,637	2,113	11,750
1920	83,970	10,174	94,144	8,281	18,070	4,942	23,012	7,191	1,954	9,145
1921	61,098	5,148	66,246	5,475	9,305	1,421	10,726	6,319	951	7,270
1922	92,838	8,169	101,007	7,344	35,396	2,564	37,958	10,705	886	11,591
1923	127,976	19,226	147,202	9,305	57,481	12,439	69,920	10,467	1,355	11,822
1924	114,537	18,043	132,580	9,277	43,883	12,772	56,655	8,344	957	9,301
1925	135,573	26,397	161,970	10,301	58,005	16,146	74,151	13,486	1,146	14,632
1926	166,887	37,840	204,727	11,905	53,628	20,696	74,324	26,345	2,199	28,544
1927	146,421	32,633	179,054	11,063	39,900	17,514	57,414	32,826	3,804	36,630
1928	197,848	44,206	242,054	16,749	55,732	23,656	79,388	40,226	7,182	47,408
1929	203,307	59,318	262,625	16,435	64,863	36,848	101,711	39,446	5,278	44,724
1930	121,337	32,035	153,372	12,541	28,841	15,712	44,553	19,683	3,550	23,233
1931	65,072	17,487	82,559	9,545	9,282	4,531	13,813	7,492	1,246	8,739
1932	50,694	10,095	60,789	8,810	9,800	2,734	12,534	1,160	289	1,449
1933	53,849	12,003	65,852	8,134	15,828	4,575	20,403	1,098	683	1,781
1934	92,647	24,205	116,852	9,674	31,274	12,094	43,368	1,988	917	2,905
1935	135,562	37,315	172,877	13,095	47,592	16,738	64,330	3,133	978	4,111
1936	128,369	33,790	162,159	12,933	42,351	13,219	55,570	8,053	1,950	9,903
1937	153,046	54,417	207,463	14,946	43,801	22,066	65,867	17,267	2,802	20,069
1938	123,761	42,325	166,086	14,872	40,368	17,382	57,767	13,445	1,709	15,154
1939	108,369	47,057	155,426	14,427	38,548	19,955	58,503	16,585	1,699	18,284

n.a.: Not available
SOURCE: Dominion Bureau of Statistics, *Automobile Statistics*, 1931 and 1939

TABLE 12.5
Percentage Distribution, by Occupation, of Ford Car
Purchasers in Canada, 1920

Agents and salesmen (non-Ford employees)	9.3
Agriculturists	33.5
Government bodies	2.6
Manufacturers	5.2
Jobbers	3.6
Retail merchants	14.2
Professionals	8.8
Public services corporations	0.5
Transportation companies	3.2
Public institutions	0.1
Sundry trades	6.7
Personal users	9.4
Women	1.9
Unclassified purchasers	1.2
Total	100.0

SOURCE: Public Archives of Canada, *Tariff Commission Transcripts, 1920*, vol. 8, file no. 23, 4327

TABLE 13.1
Equipment and Amenities in Ontario Households, 1941

	Heating System			Refrigeration				Equipment			
	Steam Hot Water	Hot Air	Stove	Mechanical	Ice	Other	None	Radio	Telephone	Vacuum	Car
Farm areas	1.8	16.7	81.5	9.3	8.8	4.0	77.9	66.2	50.9	11.1	69.6
Rural non-farm	11.6	26.0	62.4	24.5	25.0	1.9	48.6	77.2	38.7	25.9	50.7
Urban areas	25.6	44.8	29.6	40.8	35.1	0.6	23.5	90.9	57.0	44.8	42.5
Ottawa	38.2	41.7	20.1	49.9	40.9	0.8	8.4	92.5	74.0	48.7	40.4
Kingston	34.3	31.4	34.3	52.7	18.4	0.6	28.3	92.9	72.9	43.9	47.5
Toronto	43.7	49.9	6.4	44.4	44.0	0.1	11.5	93.1	73.2	50.3	38.4
Hamilton	23.9	53.6	22.5	49.5	39.3	0.4	10.3	94.6	47.6	49.9	43.1
St Catharines	21.7	55.4	22.9	55.4	33.0	0.4	11.2	94.3	55.9	54.4	50.2
Brantford	12.7	44.7	42.6	42.9	35.3	0.8	21.0	89.9	49.1	47.9	40.2
Kitchener	37.1	57.9	5.0	49.0	21.3	0.3	29.4	91.6	60.2	55.0	44.7
London	14.7	61.0	24.3	47.2	32.4	0.7	19.7	93.4	59.6	53.5	41.4
Windsor	17.8	52.6	29.6	41.8	50.5	0.2	7.5	92.7	38.8	50.1	47.7
Sudbury	32.2	27.7	40.1	36.7	24.9	—	38.4	87.2	50.7	26.2	32.6
Fort William	13.9	43.1	43.0	29.4	8.4	0.5	61.7	93.8	64.0	38.9	37.0

TABLE 13.1 (*continued*)

	Rooms per Dwelling (percentages)				Housing Density		
Number of Rooms	Total	Farm	Rural Non-Farm	Urban	Toronto	Hamilton	Ottawa
1	1.2	0.9	2.5	0.9	1.0	0.6	0.8
2	3.2	2.8	5.1	2.7	2.7	1.8	2.8
3	7.0	4.3	9.3	7.2	7.5	6.8	8.9
4	11.1	7.4	15.8	10.8	8.7	10.3	12.7
5	15.7	10.6	18.2	16.6	13.3	20.1	15.3
6	26.2	16.4	21.6	30.9	34.9	34.5	26.0
7	15.1	18.9	12.2	14.7	11.3	14.1	16.5
8	10.5	17.8	8.1	8.9 ⎫	15.8	8.7	11.6 ⎫
9	4.9	10.3	3.5	3.6 ⎭			
10	2.8	6.0	2.1	1.9 ⎫	4.8	3.1	5.4 ⎫
11+	2.3	4.6	1.6	1.8 ⎭			

Number of Persons	Persons per Dwelling (percentages)			
	Total	Farm	Rural Non-Farm	Urban
1	5.4	5.2	6.8	5.0
2	20.4	7.1	22.5	20.8
3	21.2	20.8	21.5	21.5
4	19.3	19.4	18.6	19.5
5	13.5	14.6	12.6	13.4
6	8.4	9.2	8.0	8.3
7	5.0	6.0	4.4	4.8
8	2.8	3.0	2.7	2.7
9	1.6	2.0	1.2	1.6
10	1.0	1.2	0.8	0.9
11+	1.4	1.5	0.9	1.5

TABLE 13.1 (concluded)

Amenities

	Farm	Rural Non-Farm	Urban
Toilets			
Private flush	9.5	37.5	80.9
Shared flush	0.3	2.6	9.2
Chemical	2.4	2.5	0.4
Outside privy	87.8	57.4	9.5
Bathing			
Private	10.7	35.9	75.0
Shared	0.4	1.6	8.8
No bath or shower	88.9	61.5	16.2
Water			
Inside running	14.0	46.1	94.3
Inside pump	17.3	11.3	1.5
Outside	68.9	42.6	4.2

	Farm	Rural Non-Farm	Urban
Cooking Fuel			
Coal	5.3	7.0	4.1
Wood	80.4	48.5	15.1
Electricity } Gas	13.1	42.7	80.0
Coal oil, other	1.2	1.8	0.8
Lighting			
Gas	0.5	0.3	0.2
Electricity	37.3	70.9	98.4
Coal oil, other	62.2	28.8	1.4
Heating			
Coal	19.7	46.4	67.0
Wood	75.5	42.3	11.6
Electricity	0.2	0.4	0.2
Gas	2.2	3.1	5.7
Coke	1.8	5.7	12.6
Fuel oil	0.6	2.1	2.9

SOURCE: *Census*, 1941, vol. IX, tables 6B, 7B, 10–18

TABLE 13.2
Money and Real Earnings in Ontario Industry, 1870–1910

Year	Total Wage Bill ($)	Earnings Per Worker ($)	Wholesale Consumer Goods	Family Budget	Fifteen Foodstuffs (Wholesale)	Bertram-Percy 1913 = 100	Real Earnings Per Worker ($)	
							(a)	(b)
1870	21,415,700	245	n.a.	n.a.	122	n.a.	200.8	n.a.
1880	30,604,000	259	n.a.	n.a.	117	n.a.	221.4	n.a.
1910	117,645,784	492	58.8	91.2	131	92.2	348.94	401.28

NOTES: Real earnings per worker: (a) deflated by fifteen-foodstuffs index; (b) deflated by Bertram-Percy. Wage bill figures include salaries, which were separately tabulated for 1900 and 1910; wage and employment figures for 1870, 1880, and 1890 come directly from Census tabulation.

n.a.: Not available

SOURCE: Census; HSC, series J62, 128, 165; Gordon W. Bertram and Michael B. Percy, 'Real Wage Trends in Canada, 1900–1926,' Canadian Journal of Economics, 12 (1979) 306

TABLE 13.3
Structure of Employment, Toronto, 1911 (percentages of totals)

	Males	Females	Both Sexes
Agriculture	1.1	0.1	0.8
Building trades	15.6	0.1	11.7
Domestic and personal service	5.3	27.1	10.8
Fishing, hunting, forestry	–	–	–
Manufacturing, mechanical industries	34.9	35.2	35.0
Mining	0.3	–	0.3
Professional	4.9	13.2	7.0
Trade, merchandising	23.8	10.9	23.1
Transportation	8.6	2.7	7.1
Total	100	100	100

SOURCE: *Census*, 1911, vol. VI; 262ff

TABLE 13.4
Wages, Raw Materials, and 'Surplus Value' in Ontario Industry, 1870–1910 (percentages)

Year	Wages and Salaries	Raw Materials	'Surplus Value'*	Marxian 'Rate of Profit'
1870	18.7	56.7	24.6	74.4
1880	19.4	57.7	22.9	44.7
1890	20.7	53.4	25.9	35.1
1900	23.4	57.2	19.4	21.7
1910	20.2	51.3	29.5	27.6

*'Surplus value' is a balancing item, in that from this item must be paid taxes, capital
charges, and depreciation, as well as dividends and retained earnings. It is therefore
much larger than 'profit,' as conventionally defined. Marx's rate of profit, however, divides
surplus value by the value of capital employed, so that the 'Marxian rate of profit'
is naturally a great deal higher than a more conventionally defined rate of profit on capital.
Marx himself would have deducted depreciation charges from 'surplus value,' as presented
here, adding it and the cost of raw materials so as to determine the non-labour costs
of production, which he called 'constant capital.' The 'Marxian rate of profit' in the table,
therefore, is higher than the rate Marx himself would have derived.
SOURCE: *Census*, 'Unadjusted data'

TABLE 14.1
Labour Relations and Labour Organization in the 1880s, as Reported by the Ontario Bureau of Industries

	1885	1886	1887	1888	1889	1890	1891	1892
Number of strikes	5	20	24	7	11	4	3	3
Number of Knights of Labour local assemblies		54	95	20	47			
Number of other locals		53	65	85*	106††			
Membership of Knights of Labour local assemblies		3,630	8,731	625†				
Membership of other locals			4,449					
Memberships in Toronto		12,000	8,500	4,500*				
Memberships in Hamilton			3,000					
Memberships in St Catharines		1,000	1,023					
Total memberships reported		18,830	16,180					

*Excludes Toronto membership in the Knights of Labour, reported only as 'thousands'
†Includes totals for Hamilton, Oshawa, and St Catharines, for which the collectors did not segregate Knights of Labour assemblies from other local unions
††Includes totals for Hamilton, where collectors did not segregate Knights of Labour assemblies
SOURCE: Ontario Bureau of Industries, *Reports*. Data for 1890, 1891, and 1892 are from mailed questionnaires

TABLE 14.2
Unions and Union Memberships, Ontario, 1911–40

| Year | Unions | | Memberships Reported | | | | | | |
	Total	Reporting Membership	Province	Hamilton	Kingston	London	Ottawa	Toronto	Windsor and Oshawa
1911	702	419	34,530	3,198	361	1,608	2,447	15,177	640
1912	756	427	41,371	3,166	421	2,350	2,765	16,415	924
1913	807	470	45,261	3,847	405	2,418	3,089	18,184	766
1914	805	396	38,235	2,684	394	1,587	3,262	14,781	248
1915	757	427	34,856	2,907	360	1,725	2,658	13,273	763
1916	753	524	41,654	3,539	405	2,411	3,714	13,025	849
1917	803	556	52,478	3,451	796	2,637	3,906	15,546	842
1918	926	670	62,605	3,596	1,304	3,613	5,048	18,834	983
1919	1,201	821	87,105	5,253	978	5,053	9,271	24,822	2,271
1920	1,221	812	89,954	5,184	1,910	5,009	11,143	25,478	
1921	1,099	735	66,771	4,538	756	3,954	6,377	22,507	
1922	1,044	704	62,500	3,763	454	3,189	6,409	22,091	
1923	1,032	727	61,410	4,291	563	3,910	5,073	20,441	
1924	1,005	765	62,405	4,031	502	3,547	5,118	21,619	
1925	1,006	760	63,251	2,237	657	3,570	4,192	22,246	

TABLE 14.2 (concluded)

	Unions		Memberships Reported						
Year	Total	Reporting Membership	Province	Hamilton	Kingston	London	Ottawa	Toronto	Windsor and Oshawa
1926	991	739	59,443	3,423	584	3,723	4,433	21,772	1,488
1927	1,014	792	64,082	3,991	483	3,694	4,163	23,931	2,236
1928	1,024	794	68,252	4,534	697	4,467	4,043	25,384	2,376
1929	1,055	838	71,889	5,306	611	4,052	4,253	27,512	2,736
1930	1,076	862	78,336	5,351	628	4,000	4,544	31,592	2,192
1931	1,046	811	66,317	4,726	654	3,788	4,592	25,626	1,913
1932	1,022	789	57,743	3,274	389	3,334	4,076	23,498	1,554
1933	1,012	772	52,906	3,353	187	3,026	3,279	20,191	1,396
1934	1,054	810	61,057	3,779	451	3,938	3,692	23,402	1,731
1935	1,026	853	64,989	4,010	538	4,549	3,099	25,340	2,254
1936	1,093	932	79,831	4,281	523	4,294	3,866	31,302	2,795
1937	1,205	1,040	112,074	6,039	447	5,782	5,017	38,352	9,812
1938	1,214	1,089	105,353	4,640	475	5,274	4,709	36,950	10,963
1939	1,184	1,066	109,257	4,692	528	4,905	4,735	42,517	6,231
1940	1,176	1,041	110,497	5,733	755	5,224	4,475	39,843	6,692

SOURCE: Dominion Department of Labour, Annual Reports on Labour Organization

TABLE 15.1
Ontario Railway Mileages,
1867–1939

1867	1,275
1901	7,933
1910	8,230
1916	11,320
1918	11,057
1920	11,001
1930	10,938
1939	10,570

NOTES:
1867 and 1901: 'miles of track
laid'
1910, 1916, and 1918: steam
mileage at 30 June; apparently
single track
1920, 1930, and 1939: steam
mileage at 31 December, single
track; industrial sidings not
included, and double-track line
not double-counted
SOURCE: *Canada Year Book*

TABLE 15.2
Shipping on the Ontario Register, 1874–1939

Year	Number of Vessels	Registered Net tonnage
1874	815	113,008
1880	1,042	137,481
1900	1,610	141,112
1915	2,111	312,971
1925	1,667	317,850
1932	1,761	419,828
1939	1,318	398,161

SOURCE: Dominion Department of Marine
Reports, *Supplements, Sessional Papers* 11b of
1900 and 21b of 1913; *Canada Year Book*

TABLE 18.1
Assets of Ontario Financial Institutions, 1874–1939 (millions of dollars)

	1874	1895	1914	1919	1929	1939
Chartered Banks –						
Dominion Chartered						
Assets	50.6	114.7	734.9	1,356.5	1,443.5	1,590.4
Deposit Liabilities	18.0	72.2	485.8	803.7	939.6	1,137.4
No. of Banks	9	10		9	5	5
Mortgage Loan Cos –						
Ontario Registered						
Assets	14	107	161	155	174	164
Mortgages	13	97	120	99	132	115
Sterling Debentures and						
Stock	0.01	44*	41	35	18	16
Dollar Debentures	0	10	25	19	66	68
Deposits	4	18	22	26	37	35
No. of Cos	23	86	49	44	22	15
Trust Companies –						
Ontario Registered						
Guaranteed Funds	0	n.a.	2	34	85	114
Deposits	0	0.4	0.5	0	31	60
Assets – Co. and Guaranteed	0	6	20	53	121	148
Mortgages	0	5.5	7	31	84	76
Bonds ⎱	0	0.7	14	14	25	41
Stocks ⎰					2	2
Assets-Estates, Trusts,						
Agencies	0	6	161	229	564	753
No. of Cos	0	3	14	17	23	21
Insurance Companies –						
Dominion Registered						
Assets	2	30	196	234	712	1,241
Mortgages	0.3+	10	93	69	235	227
Bonds and Debentures ⎱	1.2+	8	54	106	282	696
Stocks ⎰	nil		10	8.6	25	57
Policy Loans	0.2+	3	27	28	110	135
No. of Cos	4	9	21†	15	18	19
Province of Ontario Savings						
Office						
Deposits				1.5††	23	40

*Appears to exclude debenture stock.
†Includes IOF and three assessment companies.
††1922
NOTE: The table includes only financial institutions whose head offices are in Ontario;
it includes total assets and total liabilities of such institutions, without regard to location
SOURCES: Dominion Department of Insurance, *Reports*; Ontario Registrar of Loan
Corporations, *Reports*; Ontario Bureau of Industries, *Reports*; *Canada Gazette* for
chartered banks and for 1874 data on 'permanent building societies'; Ontario *Public
Accounts*

TABLE 18.2
Public Issues of Corporate Securities, Canada, 1901–14 (Mining Issues Excluded)
(thousands of dollars)

Year	Ordinary	Preference	Bank Stock	Total	Bond Sales*	Grand Total
1901–5	31,662	7,025	25,362	64,038	80,000	144,038
1906–10	57,895	23,215	26,924	106,033	95,700	203,733
1911–14	87,163	32,828	29,941	149,931	85,000	234,931
1901–14	176,720	63,066	82,227	312,002	260,700	672,702
1900–14	179,129	63,553	67,677	320,346	280,000	600,346

*Wood's series for issues in Canada, with municipal and provincial issues eliminated
SOURCE: Drummond, 'Capital Markets,' appendix

TABLE 18.3
Net Purchases of Canadian Securities of All Sorts, 1901–14 (thousands of dollars)

	1901–5	1906–10	1911–14	1901–14	1896–1900
Banks*	5,100	10,500	8,840	18,440	5,600
Canadian Life Cos†	27,877	29,933	15,630	73,440	12,587
Foreign Life Cos	12,533	6,503	10,874	28,910	10,448
Canadian Fire Cos	1,947	2,612	956	5,516	820
Foreign Fire Cos	356	11,582	(6,927)	(18,865)	1,686
Montreal Savings Bank	3,243	−1,404	13,100	14,939	n.a.
Ontario Trust Cos††	12,629	73,112	80,584	166,325	n.a.
Ontario Load Cos	2,689	5,982	1,071	9,742	8,178
Total purchases by					(1897–1900)
Institutions	66,374	137,820	131,982	336,232	
Stock Sales in Canada	64,038	106,033	149,931	322,002	
Bond Sales in Canada	124,000	162,382	165,729	462,111	
Loan Co. Debentures	4,553	2,076	1,470	8,099	
Total increase in stock					
of securities	192,591	272,491	317,130	782,212	
Securities not sold to					
financial institutions	126,377	134,671	185,148	446,196	
Per cent of total					
issues absorbed by					
institutions	35	51	42	43	
Per cent of total issues					
not absorbed by					
institutions	65	49	58	57	

NOTES
The calculations for 1896–1900 have not been attempted, because there appear to be no
reliable data on the volume of securities issued.
*One-third of increase in security holdings, as suggested by Viner
†Includes purchases of American securities
††'Other' securities; includes some call loans and some real estate
SOURCE: Drummond, 'Capital Markets,' appendix. Constructed from balance-sheet
figures, without adjustment for any change in valuation of old assets that companies
may have made in their balance sheets.

TABLE 18.4
Annual Estimates of the Flow of New Issues, Canada, 1900–14 (thousands of dollars)

Year	Ordinary Shares	Preference Shares	Bank Stock	Total Shares	Bonds
1900	2,409.1	485.0	5,450.0	8,344.1	5,000
1901	1,105.9	2,915.0	1,772.0	5,792.9	20,000
1902	9,502.0	2,660.0	600.0	12,762.0	20,000
1903	8,473.0	840.0	11,424.0	20,737.0	20,000
1904	9,004.5	75.0	2,333.3	11,412.8	24,235
1905	3,576.3	525.0	9,233.2	13,334.5	39,996
1906	12,257.4	2,337.5	13,615.0	28,707.9	23,305
1907	8,381.0	2,257.8	2,075.0	12,713.8	14,762
1908	8,741.6	750.0	1,573.2	10,864.8	24,585
1909	16,267.1	8,432.4	3,981.2	28,680.7	60,434
1910	12,448.0	9,437.1	5,680.0	27,565.1	39,296
1911	15,526.8	12,495.0	17,691.5	45,713.3	49,390
1912	27,966.4	14,753.5	7,125.0	49,844.9	37,735
1913	36,276.6	3,832.6	5,125.0	45,234.2	45,604
1914	7,392.5	1,746.9	0	9,139.4	33,000

SOURCE: Drummond, 'Capital Markets,' appendix

TABLE 18.5
Domestic Security Issues in Canada as Per Cent of London Issues on Canadian Account, 1904–13

1904	1905	1906	1907	1908	1909	1910	1911	1912	1913
163	104	112	75	23	49	38	44	46	28

SOURCE: Drummond, 'Capital Markets,' appendix, and Jacob Viner, *Canada's Balance of International Indebtedness, 1900–1913* (Cambridge: Harvard University Press, 1924), table XXXIII

TABLE 18.6
Ontario: Sales of Provincial Securities, 1907–14

Year	In London Amount ($000)	Coupon Rate	Price of Issue	In Canada Amount ($000)	Coupon Rate	Price of Issue
1906 1907	1,200	4	n.a.	3,000,000	3½	n.a.
1908	nil			nil		
1909	820	4	102	2,070	4	102
1910	nil			1,430	4	102
1911	500	4	101	290	4	102
1912	200 100	4 4	101.375 100	1,438.3	4	102
1913	20.5	4	101.125	1,770.3	4	99.5
1914	817.3	4½	100	1,205.0	5	100

n.a.: Not available
SOURCE: Ontario *Public Accounts*

TABLE 18 7
Government Securities Held by Canadian Chartered Banks
at 31 December, 1895–1914

Year	$'000	Per Cent of Bank Assets	Per Cent of Dominion Funded Debt
1895	2,830	0.8	1.3
1899	4,779	1.1	2.0
1901	9,760	1.7	2.1
1910	13,103	1.0	5.0
1913	10,950	0.7	4.0
1914	11,234	0.7	3.7

SOURCE: Curtis, *Statistical Contributions to Canadian
Economic History* (Toronto: Macmillan, 1932), 47, 65

TABLE 18.8
Mortgage Loans Outstanding in 1914

	$'000	Percentage of Assets	Percentage of Total
Home life insurance companies	94,765	34.5	26
Foreign life insurance companies	27,593	22	7
Mortgage companies*	160,600	82	43
Trust companies*	76,937	25	20
⌠Fire insurance companies	3,169	18	1
⌡Foreign fire insurance companies	14,696	14	4.5

*Ontario-registered companies only
NOTE: All the several institutions did not end their financial years on the same dates;
local mortgage brokers, attorneys, and private banks provided some intermediation that is
not recorded here; farmers could and did borrow from implement companies; chartered
banks lent to farmers on the borrowers' credit, with, in the background, some idea of
the worth of the land, even though such loans were not formally mortgages (see
H.M.P. Eckhardt, *Manual of Canadian Banking* (Toronto: *Monetary Times*, 1913), 136)
SOURCES: Balance sheets; Ontario Registrar of Loan Corporations *Reports*; Dominion
Superintendent of Insurance, *Reports*

TABLE 18.9
New Mortgage Loans in Canada, 1895–1914, through Institutional Channels (thousands of dollars)

	Life Insurance Companies	Foreign Life Insurance Companies	Fire Insurance Companies	Foreign Fire Insurance Companies	Mortgage Companies	Trust Companies	Total
1895–1900	5,197	3,760	−86	2,584	n.a.	n.a.	32,302
1901–5	8,365	720	215	2,416	7,060	13,526	90,281
1906–10	26,457	−19	630	6,738	21,750	34,725	135,397
1911–14	41,605	14,730	2,281	884	35,192	40,705	257,980
1901–14	76,427	15,431	3,126	10,038	64,002	88,956	

n.a.: Not available
SOURCE: Balance Sheets; Superintendent of Insurance and of Ontario Registrar of Loan Corporations, *Reports*

TABLE 18.10
Sources of Funds, Ontario Loan Companies, 1897–1914 (thousands of dollars)

Year	From Shareholders	Deposits	Canadian Debentures	Sterling Debentures	Sterling Debenture Stock	Total Canadian* Funds	Total Overseas Funds
1897–1900	2,932	1,506	4,911	−6,923	−55	9,359	−6,978
1901–5	0	1,837	4,553	−1,994	−8,895	6,390	−3,889
1906–10	5,200	−1,054	2,076	19,335	720	7,222	20,055
1911–14	13,900	2,514	1,470	24,621	−1,529	17,884	23,092
1901–14	20,100	3,297	8,099	41,962	−2,704	31,496	39,258
1897–1914	23,032	4,803	13,010	35,039	−2,104	40,845	32,935

*Includes all the increase of shareholders' funds in Credit Foncier Franco-Canadien
SOURCE: Ontario Registrar of Loan Corporations, *Reports*

Notes

1 See K.J. Rea, *The Prosperous Years: The Economic History of Ontario 1939–75* (Toronto: University of Toronto Press, 1985)
2 See Christopher Armstrong, *The Politics of Federalism* (Toronto: University of Toronto Press, 1981)
3 The information about agriculture and industry in this section is drawn almost entirely from the various volumes of this *Census.*
4 The coverage corresponds neither to the 'labour force' nor to the 'gainfully employed,' as later censuses and statisticans would define these terms, because it includes a few groups – most obviously, pensioners and gentlemen of leisure – that would nowadays not be counted as 'workers.' For more on the definitional problems see chapter 2.
5 Strictly speaking, the census reported the difference between the value of output and the reported 'cost of materials.' In so far as some costs – interest, municipal taxes, and the cost of fuel – were not included in the latter figure, value added was less than it seems from the census returns. The difference, however, must have been small in the early 1870s.
6 See below, chapter 2, and table 2.2.
7 Dominion *Sessional Papers,* 1870, No. 4
8 Economists normally personalize economies, sectors, and even industries. But this is no more than a convenient shorthand; economists are not ignorant of the fact that all the relevant decisions come from individuals, business firms, and governments.
9 See, for instance, Harold Innis, 'An Introduction to the Economic History of Ontario from Outpost to Empire,' *Papers and records of the Ontario Historical Society* xxx, reprinted in Harold A. Innis, *Essays in Canadian Economic History* (Toronto: University of Toronto Press, 1956), 118–22; W.T. Easterbrook and Hugh G.J. Aitken, *Canadian Economic History* (Toronto: Macmillan of Canada, 1956); William Marr and Donald Paterson, *Canada: An Economic History* (Toronto: Macmillan of Canada, 1982), 383–403, 520–2.
10 O.J. Firestone, *Canada's Economic Development* (Cambridge: Bowes and Bowes, 1958; Kenneth Buckley, 'The Role of Staple Industries in Canada's Economic

Development,' *Journal of Economic History,* 18:4 (December 1958), 439–52; Robin Neill, 'The Politics and Economics of Development in Ontario,' *Ontario History,* 70:4 (December 1978), 281ff; Bryan D. Palmer, *A Culture in Conflict* (Montreal: McGill-Queen's University Press, 1979), xi–34; Gregory S. Kealey, *Toronto Workers Respond to Industrial Capitalism 1867–1892* (Toronto: University of Toronto Press, 1980)

11 The patterns have been traced by Simon Kuznets, *Modern Economic Growth: Rate, Structure, Spread* (New Haven: Yale University Press, 1965), Andrea Boltho, *The European Economy* (London: Oxford University Press, 1982), and many other scholars. Attention was first drawn to the pattern by Colin Clark, in *The Conditions of Economic Progress* (London: Macmillan, 1940).

12 For a contrary view see Tom Naylor, *The History of Canadian Business* (Toronto: James Lorimer, 1975).

13 For an elaboration of these themes see H.V. Nelles, *The Politics of Development* (Toronto: McClelland and Stewart, 1972).

CHAPTER 2 *What People Did*

1 That is, persons who earn money or assist in the production of marketable goods. For a fuller discussion, see *Census,* 1941, vol. VII, xii–xvii. More recent statistical practice uses the concept of 'labour force,' by which is meant those who were at work, who had jobs from which they were temporarily absent, or were looking for work. Both definitions are meant to include paid workers, own-account workers, and most though not all unpaid family workers. Both the 'gainful worker' and the 'labour force' definitions exclude students, housewives, and the retired, as well as all those below the age of ten (in 1911, 1921, and 1931), or below the age of fourteen (in 1941 and thereafter). In the present chapter the evasive term 'workforce' is sometimes used as a synonym for 'gainful workers.'

2 The statistics appear in table 2.1. They are derived from raw data which appear in decennial censuses, extensively rearranged and re-processed. It is possible to adjust the early census reports so as to generate consistent series of data. Occupational data are available only for census years.

3 Economists call this proportion the 'participation rate.'

4 For most occupations, the published census tabulations first distinguished between men and women workers only in 1891.

5 See below, chapter 13.

6 I owe this point to Dr Tanis Lee, of Queen's University.

7 It has been argued that in certain places and industries, especially in Hamilton iron and steel, there was a 'de-skilling' of the work force between 1900 and 1930. This means that smaller numbers of certain skilled tradesmen were required, and that less was demanded of them in terms of skill. This development, in so far as it occurred, is compatible with the present set of numbers, which lump together a wide range of skilled and semi-skilled occupations, treating only common labour separately.

8 See below, chapters 15 and 16.

9 Of course, a great deal of the local transport work was then done by farmers, and it

was only with increasing specialization of occupation in later decades that this unidentified and unidentifiable transport work became detectable as the activity of particular transport occupations.

10 These industries, as defined by the national-income statisticians, are transportation, storage, communication, utilities, wholesale and retail trade, finance, insurance, real estate, public administration and defence, and personal and professional service.

11 Industrial data differ from occupational data chiefly because various white-collar workers are distributed among the industries which employ them. Industrial data are available only from 1911, and only for census years. It will be noticed that in 1911 the census statisticians provided rather more data about the service industries and about fishing and hunting than their descendants in 1931 and 1941. In the 1941 data, men and women on active service are distributed so far as possible among the industries in which they last worked. The same was done for the unemployed in 1931.

12 See Kuznets, *Modern Economic Growth*, tables 3.2, 3.8, and 4.4 for international comparisons of occupational and industrial patterns.

13 See below, chapter 3.

14 The dominion first gathered data on the educational level of the work force in the 1941 census: table 2.6 records the results of that enquiry.

15 First from the province itself, and then, starting in 1919, from a dominion-provincial shared-cost program.

16 For the estimates of wholesale and retail trade, see below, chapter 17; for agriculture, see chapter 3. Many but not all of the 1871 artisans are included in chapter 17's estimates for 'trade.'

17 See below, chapter 14.

CHAPTER 3 *Agriculture, 1867–1941*

1 *Census of Canada*, 1941, vol. VIII, table 1

2 In 1921–41 just over 80 per cent of all Ontario farm operators had been born in the province, while roughly 2.5 per cent came from Quebec. A few had come from the United States, and rather more from Britain, while Germany, Finland, and Poland had contributed as well. Ibid., table 2.

3 In 1921 only 32.7 per cent of Ontario farm operators were less than forty years old, while 20 per cent were sixty or older. In 1941 the former percentage was 25.1 per cent, and the latter was 27 per cent.

4 Marvin McInnis, 'The Changing Structure of Canadian Agriculture 1867–1897,' *Journal of Economic History*, 42: 1 (1982), 191–8; D.A. Lawr, 'The Development of Ontario Farming 1870–1919,' *Ontario History*, 64:4 (1972), 239–51; John Isbister, 'Agriculture, Balanced Growth, and Social Change in Central Canada: An Interpretation,' *Economic Development and Cultural Change*, 25:4 (July 1977), 673–97. For a somewhat longer-run view, see William Norton, 'Some Comments on Late Nineteenth Century Agriculture in Areas of European Overseas Expansion,' *Ontario History*, 74:2 (June 1982), 113–7.

5 Statistical data come from the decennial censuses, from the Ontario Bureau of

Industries and its successors, and, after 1900, from the Dominion Department of Agriculture and the Dominion Bureau of Statistics.

6 The developments with respect to land use are summarized in table 3.1.

7 More detail on fruit can be found in J.A. Archibald, 'Our Horticultural Heritage,' in T.A. Crowley, ed., *First Annual Agricultural History of Ontario Seminar Proceedings, Saturday, October 16, 1976* (Guelph: Office of Continuing Education, University of Guelph, 1977), 63–74. Archibald notes that spraying became important from 1868, when the discovery of Paris Green staved off a very serious threat from the Colorado potato beetle. Spraying experiments for orchards were begun in 1878, and Bordeaux Mixture began to be recommended as a fungicide in 1882.

8 See tables 3.1 and 3.1.

9 McInnis, 'Changing Structure,' esp. 192–7

10 Ian A. McKay, 'A Note on Ontario Agriculture: The Development of Soybeans, 1893–1952,' *Ontario History,* 75:2 (1983), 175–86

11 See McInnis, ' Changing Structure,' esp. 192.

12 William Marr, 'The Wheat Economy in Reverse: Ontario's Wheat Production 1887–1917,' *Canadian Journal of Economics,* 14:1 (1981), 133–45; Robert E. Ankli and Wendy Millar, 'Ontario Agriculture in Transition: The Shift from Wheat to Cheese,' *Journal of Economic History,* 42:1 (1982), 207–15

13 William L. Marr and Peter W. Sinclair, 'Trends in Wheat Production in Southern Ontario, 1885–1914,' paper presented to the Economic History Workshop, University of Toronto, October 1985

14 Isbister, 'Agriculture,' 678–81

15 See below, chapter 15.

16 Cf. McInnis, 'Changing Structure,' 197. For the cheese industry, see below, chapter 7.

17 Table 3.3 gives some data on prices and acreages, the latter lagged by a year. Naturally the fit is less than precise, but some relationship can surely be detected.

18 Data from Ontario Statistical Branch

19 See below, chapter 17.

20 Johnson tells us that small farmers were forced off the land by debt in periods of depression such as 1867–9, and he writes of a social crisis, complete with rural depopulation, in the decade of the 1870s. But he presents no data on debt, immiserization, outmigration, living standards, or any other relevant matter. Furthermore, the census data show that there was no rural depopulation during the 1870s: the number of occupied farms rose from 172,251 to 206,989 in Ontario as a whole, and from 4,837 to 5,386 in Ontario County itself. See Leo Johnson, *History of the County of Ontario 1615–1875* (Whitby: Corporation of the County of Ontario, 1973).

21 Norman Robertson, *History of the County of Bruce* (Toronto: William Briggs, 1906), 121; Watson Kirkconnell, *County of Victoria Centennial History* (Lindsay: Victoria County Council, 1967), 76. See also Humfrey Michell, *The Grange in Canada* (Kingston: Jackson Press, 1914).

22 See Ramsay Cook, 'Tillers and Toilers: The Rise and Fall of Populism in Canada in the 1890s,' in Canadian Historical Association, *Historical Papers,* 1984, 1–20.

23 See tables 3.7 and 3.8.

24 See table 3.8.

25 *Census,* 1941, vol. VIII, table 48

26 *Census,* 1870–1, table XXII

27 W. Riddell, 'Farming in Northumberland County, 1833–1895,' *Ontario Historical Society Papers and Records,* 30 (1934), 146–7

28 Jean Kirkby, *Morris Township: Past to Present* (Clinton: Clinton Commercial Printers, 1981), 147; T.H.B. Symons and others, *A History of Peel County* (Brampton: The Corporation of the County of Peel, 1967), 34

29 Ross W. Irwin, 'Energy: from Man to Machine,' in Crowley, ed., *First Annual Agricultural History of Ontario Seminar,* 39–55, esp. 50–3

30 Kirkby, *Morris,* 150; Symons, *Peel,* 39

31 Royce MacGillivray and Ewan Ross, *A History of Glengarry* (Belleville: Mika, 1979), 435

32 John Craig, *Simcoe County: The Recent Past* (n.p.: Corporation of the County of Simcoe, 1977), 244; MacGillivray and Ross, *Glengarry,* 391; Harry and Olive Walker, *Carleton Saga* (Ottawa: Carleton County Council, 1968), 21

33 MacGillivray and Ross, *Glengarry,* 392

34 For details about some innovative products around the time of Confederation see Irwin, 'Energy,' esp 42–9; see also Riddell, 'Farming,' 143–9.

35 See table 3.9.

36 See *Census,* 1941, vol. IX, for details on amenities in rural farm and non-farm districts.

37 W.T. Easterbrook, *Farm Credit in Canada* (Toronto: University of Toronto Press, 1938), chs II, III

38 Table 3.11 summarizes the information on yields by fitting trend-equations to annual data.

39 Table 3.13 presents data on land use in the six agricultural regions of the province.

40 J.C. Hopkins, *Historical Sketch of the Ontario Department of Agriculture,* (Toronto: William Briggs, 1912), 1–5

41 Florence G. Partridge, 'An Overview of Popular Education in 19th-Century Ontario,' *First Annual Agricultural History of Ontario Seminar, Proceedings,* 14–25

42 *Canada Year Book,* 1934–5, 247–8

43 *Canada Year Book,* 1930, 200–1; Ontario Minister of Agriculture, *First Report* (1910)

44 Ibid.

45 Analysts sometimes divide tariff revenue by import value so as to derive an average rate of duty collected. This measure, however, is biased downward as a measure of protection, because the volume and value of imports vary directly with the height of the duty; prohibitive duties, which give the most protection, generate neither revenue nor trade.

46 Margaret Dunrabin, *History of Canadian Agricultural Tariffs 1906–1955* (Ottawa: Dominion Department of Agriculture, 1955), passim

47 See below, chapter 17

48 See Ian M. Drummond, 'Marketing Boards in the White Dominions,' in D.C. Platt

and Guido di Tella, eds, *Argentina, Australia, and Canada: Studies in Comparative Development 1870–1965* (London: Macmillan, 1985), 194–207

49 1 Geo VI c 23
50 Provincial agricultural spending is summarized in table 3.14.
51 See below, chapter 18.

CHAPTER 4 *Ontario's Mining Industry, 1870–1940*

1 Ontario became Canada's most important metal-producing province because it contains a large, accessible part of the Canadian Shield, one of the world's richest mineral-producing areas. Brief accounts of these mineral resources are presented by Elwood S. Moore, *The Mineral Resources of Canada* (Toronto: Ryerson, 1933), 21–4, 73–4, 110–21, and 127–34, and by E.W. Miller, 'Mineral Regionalism of the Canadian Shield,' *The Canadian Geographer*, 13 (1959), 17–30.

2 For the metals considered here, Northern Ontario accounts for practically all Ontario's output.

3 D.M. LeBourdais, *Metals and Man: The Story of Canadian Mining* (Toronto: McClelland and Stewart, 1957) gives an excellent review of the historical development of the Canadian mining industry, including that of Ontario. Another informative survey is Thomas W. Gibson, *Mining in Ontario* (Toronto: King's Printer, 1937).

4 Mining in the pre-1880 period is briefly described by Miller, 'Mines and Mining,' 616–24, Nelles, *Politics*, 20–4, and Thomas W. Gibson, *The Mining Laws of Ontario and the Department of Mines* (Toronto: King's Printer, 1933), 1–6. Diane C.E. Newell, 'Technological Change in a New and Developing Country: A Study of Mining Technology in Canada West – Ontario, 1841–1891,' unpublished PH D thesis, University of Western Ontario, 1981, chs 3, 4, 5, is a more detailed account.

5 Silver Islet's brief but spectacular history has been recounted several times. See, for example, the article by Archibald Blue, 'The Story of Silver Islet,' in Ontario Bureau of Mines, *Annual Report 1896*, 125–58, and Beryl H. Scott, 'The Story of Silver Islet,' *Ontario History*, 55 (1963), 193–204.

6 Morris Zaslow, *The Opening of the Canadian North 1870–1914* (Toronto: McClelland and Stewart, 1971), 149–52

7 See Morris Zaslow, *Reading the Rocks: The Story of the Geological Survey of Canada 1842–1972* (Ottawa: Macmillan in association with the Department of Energy, Mines and Resources, and Information Canada, 1975), passim, and Nelles, *Politics*, 122–9.

8 The essential history of nickel- and copper-mining in the Sudbury district is found in LeBourdais, *Metals*, chs. 6, 14, and in D.M. LeBourdais, *Sudbury Basin: The Story of Nickel* (Toronto: Ryerson, 1953), passim; O.W. Main, *The Canadian Nickel Industry* (Toronto: University of Toronto Press, 1955), passim; and Gibson, *Mining*, 71–105. The sequence of ore discoveries and early attempts at mining are summarized in Royal Ontario Nickel Commission, *Report* (Toronto: King's Printer, 1917), chs 2, 3.

9 The INCO merger was masterminded by J.P. Morgan, who also engineered the

creation through merger of US Steel. The formation of INCO is discussed in Main, *Nickel Industry*, 45, and Royal Ontario Nickel Commission, *Report*, 67.

10 The controversy over the location of INCO's refining capacity is discussed below.

11 See Main, *Nickel Industry*, esp. chs 8 and 9 for a discussion of market structure in the nickel industry.

12 This section is based largely on LeBourdais, *Metals*, ch. 7, Gibson, *Mining*, 42–90, and H.A. Innis, *Settlement and the Mining Frontier*, vol. IX of W.A. Mackintosh and W.L.G. Joerg, eds, *Canadian Frontiers of Settlement* (Toronto: Macmillan, 1936), ch. 7.

13 Gibson, *Mining*, 57

14 This point is emphasized by Innis, *Settlement*, 336–9. But the increased capital-intensity of production brought with it some human costs. It was at Cobalt that the first attempts were made to unionize the mine labour force, by the Western Federation of Miners in 1906, and that labour unrest erupted in 1907 in the first serious labour disputes.

15 The standard treatments of gold mining are LeBourdais, *Metals*, chs 8, 9, 13, Gibson, *Mining*, 1–41, and Innis, *Settlement*, ch. 8. S.A. Pain, *Three Miles of Gold: The Story of Kirkland Lake* (Toronto: Ryerson, 1969), and L. Carson Brown, 'The Golden Porcupine,' *Canadian Geographical Journal*, 74 (1967), 4–17, are specific to Kirkland Lake and Porcupine, respectively.

16 From Larder Lake and Kirkland Lake prospectors also investigated eastwards into Quebec. Indeed, the Ontario mining industry took the primary initiative in developing mining in the adjacent territory of Quebec. The formation of Noranda Mines Ltd, a large producer of copper and gold in the Rouyn-Noranda area of that province, dates from 1922. See LeBourdais, *Metals*, ch. 10.

17 The mechanization of all phases of gold-mining – the use of the cyanide mill, shrinkage-stope mining techniques, the central shaft and electric haulage, and machine drills – and their implications for the scale of mining and the social structure of the labour force are discussed for the Porcupine camp by James Otto Petersen, 'The Origins of Canadian Gold Mining: The Part Played by Labour in the Transition from Tool Production to Machine Production,' unpublished PH D thesis, University of Toronto, 1977, chs 8, 9, 10, 14. Also see Innis, *Settlement*, 354–69, and F.A. Knox, *Gold Mining in Ontario: Report of the Committee of Enquiry into the Economics of the Gold Mining Industry* (Toronto: Government of Ontario, 1955), ch. 2.

18 Ontario Ministry of Natural Resources, *Metal Mining Statistics*, Mineral Background Paper no. 16 (Toronto: Queen's Printer, 1983), 120–1

19 Nelles, *Politics*, 24

20 Gibson, *Mining Laws*, 1–80, provides an exhaustive enumeration of changes in mining legislation and regulations. Warren Jestin, 'Provincial Policy and the Development of the Metallic Mining Industry in Northern Ontario, 1845–1920,' unpublished PH D thesis, University of Toronto, 1977, usefully surveys the pre-1920 period.

21 Ontario, *Report of the Royal Commission on the Mineral Resources of Ontario and Measures for their Development* (Toronto: Queen's Printer, 1890), passim

22 Gibson, *Mining Laws*, 11–15

23 The origins and early responsibilities of the Bureau of Mines and the subsequent
establishment of the Department of Mines are described in Gibson, *Mining Laws*,
83–7. The bureau's published *Annual Reports* (after 1919, Department of Mines
Annual Reports) contain a great amount of material on mining developments and
operating mines in the province.

24 Gibson, *Mining Laws*, 16

25 Ibid., 27–30

26 In 1906 the interpretation of 'valuable mineral' was tightened to mean 'a vein, lode,
or other deposit of mineral or minerals in place, containing such quantity of
mineral or minerals *as to make it probable that the said vein, lode or deposit was
capable of being developed into a working mine*' (Gibson, *Mining Laws*, 27,
italics supplied). In the Act of 1908 this already-strict interpretation of 'discovery'
was narrowed even further to stipulate that the deposit be 'capable of being
developed into a producing mine *likely to be workable at a profit*' (Ibid., 32 [italics
supplied]).

27 See below, under 'Policy Issues in Mining.'

28 Gibson, *Mining Laws*, 7

29 This is the essential thesis in Nelles's superb analysis of the role of the provincial
government in the development of Ontario's resource base. See Nelles, *Politics*,
109.

30 R.M. Burns, *Conflict and its Resolution in the Administration of Mineral Resources
in Canada* (Kingston: Centre for Resource Studies, Queen's University, 1976),
15–22

31 The chronological development of Ontario's tax legislation affecting the mining
industry is outlined in Gibson, *Mining Laws*, 30, 45–51. J. Harvey Perry reports
the principal features of Ontario's tax policy in *Taxes, Tariffs, and Subsidies*
(Toronto: University of Toronto Press, 1955), vol. I, 118, 172, 236–7, and in
Taxation in Canada, 3d edition (Toronto: University of Toronto Press, 1961), ch. 13.

32 Gibson, *Mining Laws*, 30, 49

33 Ibid., 47; Royal Ontario Nickel Commission, 512–13

34 Gibson, *Mining Laws*, 50–1; Perry, *Taxes*, vol. I, 236–7

35 Perry, *Taxes*, vol. II, table 16, 648–51. Only in 1918 did mining profits tax receipts
exceed timber dues and bonuses, a result of the increased rate of tax on nickel
mines and their high wartime profits.

36 Royal Ontario Nickel Commission, 5, 62

37 Royal Commission on Mineral Resources, xxi–xxiii

38 Royal Ontario Nickel Commission, 8–9

39 Ibid., 11

40 Ibid., 13. Blue's memorandum argued that Ontario's case for extending the 'manufacturing condition' to nickel should be based on the employment-generating
effects of local refining, since there was a significant imbalance between wages and
salaries paid in New Jersey and the value of the ore mined at Sudbury. Reported
in Nelles, *Politics*, 92

41 Royal Ontario Nickel Commission, 13–15

42 Ibid., 17–18; Gibson, *Mining Laws*, 79–80. A good discussion of the refining of
Cobalt ores at Deloro is contained in Bowles, 'Metallurgical Developments.'

43 Royal Ontario Nickel Commission, 19
44 Ibid., xxxv. Main, *Nickel*, ch. 6, and Nelles, *Politics*, ch. 9, are good discussions of
    wartime events.
45 P.E. Nickel, I.R. Gillies, T.J. Henley, and J.O. Saunders, *Economic Impacts and
    Linkages of the Canadian Mining Industry* (Kingston: Centre for Resource Studies,
    Queen's University, 1978) contains a useful survey of recent studies assessing the
    impact of mining, both nationally and provincially. All the relevant studies relate
    to the post-World-War-Two period. They share a common reliance on input-output
    analysis, in which the system is exposed to an exogenous change in demand for
    the output of the industry under examination, and then the direct, indirect, and
    induced effects on other sectors are traced out. No such studies exist for Ontario
    for our period.
46 This is best documented for Sudbury. See, for example, Noel Beach, 'Nickel
    Capital: Sudbury and the Nickel Industry 1905–25,' *Laurentian University Review*,
    6 (1974), 55–74; and Gilbert A. Stelter, 'The Origins of a Company Town: Sudbury
    in the Nineteenth Century,' *Laurentian University Review*, 3 (1971), 3–37, and
    'Community Development in Toronto's Commercial Empire: The Industrial Towns
    of the Nickel Belt, 1883–1931,' *Laurentian University Review*, 6 (1974), 3–54.
47 Innis, *Settlement*, 403
48 Demand shifts also put pressure on metallurgical technology. The growing demand
    for nickel alloys, for example, prompted a continuing search for low-cost pro-
    cesses that would separate the metal from its complex ores; improved chemical and
    mechanical processes for treating such complex ores allowed further recovery of
    joint products such as nickel, copper, and the platinum group of metals.
49 Nickel et al., *Impacts*, 18
50 Cited in Royal Commission on Mining, 1944, 5. The Mining Association of Canada
    claimed, in 1975, that one job in mining supported seven jobs elsewhere in the
    Canadian economy (see Nickel, *Impacts*, 2). However, Nickel reports a province-
    wide figure of 2.41 for Ontario in 1977 (ibid., 72).
51 Noel Beach, 'Nickel Capital,' presents an interesting analysis of the changing
    composition of Sudbury's work force. Around 1905 not many persons living in
    Sudbury were directly employed in mining; most mine workers lived in smaller
    hamlets around Sudbury, which served as a distribution centre for these communi-
    ties. By 1931, however, there had been a significant change: more mine and
    smelter workers were Sudbury residents, and the city had acquired its single-
    enterprise, resource-based identity. Similarly, Haileybury served as the distribution
    centre for Cobalt and the later fields of the Timiskaming Mining Division. See
    T.D. Tait, 'Haileybury: the Early Years,' *Ontario History*, 55 (1963), 193–204.
52 See E.S. Moore, *American Influence in Canadian Mining* (Toronto: University of
    Toronto Press, 1941), passim, and Herbert Marshall, Frank Southard Jr, and
    Kenneth W. Taylor, *Canadian-American Industry: A Study in International Invest-
    ment* (New Haven: Yale University Press, 1935; reprinted Toronto: McClelland
    and Stewart, 1976). The Royal Commission on Mineral Resources (*Report*, 208–9)
    acknowledged Ontario's early dependence on American investment and technical
    expertise.
53 See Newell, 'Technological Change,' passim, for an account of technological

borrowing in copper, silver, petroleum, and salt in the pre-1890 period, and James Otto Petersen, 'Origins,' passim, for illustrations drawn from gold-mining.

54 Marshall, Southard, and Taylor, *Canadian-American Industry*, 89, 92–4

55 Moore, *American Influence*, 84–9, gives data on the proportion of shares and bonds held by Canadians, residents of the United States, the United Kingdom, and other countries. By the mid-1930s some 56 per cent of all mining dividends were paid to Canadians, 37 per cent to Americans, and 6 per cent to UK residents (ibid., 89).

56 Ibid., 92–7

57 Royal Ontario Mining Commission, 1944, I

58 Newell, 'Technological Change,' and Petersen, 'Origins,' represent important contributions to the study of technological change in Ontario mines.

59 Among recent studies are Wallace Clement, *Hardrock Mining: Industrial Relations and Technological Change at INCO* (Toronto: McClelland and Stewart, 1981), Brian F. Hogan, *Cobalt: Year of the Strike, 1919* (Cobalt: Highway Bookshop, 1983), and Laurel Sefton MacDowell, *'Remember Kirkland Lake': The History and Effects of the Kirkland Lake Gold Miners' Strike, 1941–42* (Toronto: University of Toronto Press, 1983). Petersen, 'Origins,' ch. 12, also speculates on the implication of mechanization in the Kirkland Lake mines for changes in the social structure of the labour force, especially underground.

60 For the mining industry occupational health and safety were given prominence by the report of the Royal Commission on the Health and Safety of Workers in Mines in 1976. See also below, chapter 14, for some information about the development of the mining safety codes both before and after the Great War.

61 Stelter, 'Origins,' 28, cites some early, contemporary reflections on the 'very abomination of desolation' created by the heap-roast yards, where preliminary processing of ores took place.

CHAPTER 5 *The North and the North-West*

1 A. White, 'The Forest Resources of Ontario,' in Ontario Ministry of Lands and Forests, *Annual Report, 1908*, Appendix 46

2 Nelles, *Politics*, 64–5

3 This discussion of lumbering relies heavily on A.R.M. Lower, *The North American Assault on the Canadian Forest* (Toronto: Ryerson, 1936).

4 For details, see Department of Crown Lands, *Annual Reports*, 1892–7, and Nelles, *Politics*, 62–80.

5 Lower, *Assault*, 154–6

6 Ibid., 156–7

7 *Census of Canada*, 1911, vol. 3, tables I and VII. The comparison slightly exaggerates the growth of the industry, because in 1901 the census enumerators omitted mills that employed fewer than five people, while in 1911 they counted all saw-mills, no matter how small. See below, chapter 7 and appendix B.

8 Lower, *Assault*, 195

9 Ibid., 195–7

10 Ibid., 195, 199

11 *Canadian Manufacturer*, 1 June 1883, 398; see below, chapter 7.

12 N. Reich, *The Pulp and Paper Industry in Canada* (Toronto: Macmillan, 1926), 13–17

13 J.A. Guthrie, *The Newsprint Paper Industry* (Cambridge: Harvard University Press, 1941) chs 1, 2, 13

14 'Agreement between Her Majesty ... and the Spanish River Pulp and Paper Co., 1899,' in Ontario *Sessional Papers*, XXXII, part 10, 1900

15 Nelles, *Politics, 81–7*

16 Department of Crown Lands, Annual Report, 1905: vii

17 T.O. Dick, 'Canadian Newsprint, 1913–1930,' *Journal of Economic History*, 42:3 (1982), 659–87, explains the importance of underlying demand and supply factors.

18 Dominion Bureau of Statistics, *Canadian Forestry Statistics – Revised 1959* (Ottawa: Queen's Printer, 1960), 106

19 *Variations in Business and Economic History (Research in Economic History, Supplement 2, 1982)* (Greenwich, Ct.: JAI Press, 1982), 8–10 and passim. Prices are FOB Iroquois Falls. Slightly different figures appear in A.E. Safarian, *The Canadian Economy During the Great Depression* (Toronto: University of Toronto Press, 1959), 162–6.

20 V.W. Bladen, *An Introduction to Political Economy* (Toronto: University of Toronto Press, 1941), 162–6

21 For information on the output-restriction plans see Bladen, *Introduction*, 170–82, and Nelles, *Politics*, 443–64.

22 J.H. Dales, *The Protective Tariff in Canada's Development* (Toronto: University of Toronto Press, 1966), esp. chs 2, 3, 6; Nelles, *Politics*, esp. chs 2, 3, 12

23 A.R.M. Lower, *Settlement and the Forest Frontier in Eastern Canada* (Toronto: Macmillan, 1936)

24 For a survey of the geography see J.L. Robinson, *Resources of the Canadian Shield* (Toronto: Methuen, 1969), ch. 6.

25 Ontario Commissioner of Crown Lands, *Annual Reports*, 1879–1900.

26 R.S. Lambert, *Renewing Nature's Wealth* (Toronto: 1968), ch. 6

27 Ontario Department of Lands and Forests, *Annual Reports*, 1916–17, viii, 1924–5, 7, and 1942, 39

28 On the T&NO – now the Ontario Northland Railway – see below, chapter 15; see also Temiskaming and Northern Ontario Railway Commission, *Annual Reports;* R. Tennant, *Ontario's Government Railway* (Halifax: the author, 1972); and O.T.G. Williamson, *Ontario Northland Railway* (North Bay: Ontario Northland Railway Commission, 1959).

29 On Kapuskasing, see W. Kirkconnell, *Kapuskasing: An Historical Sketch* (Kingston, Ontario: Bulletin of the Departments of History and Political and Economic Science, Queen's University, 1921).

30 The *Globe*, 11 April 1932, 1–2, and 19 April 1932, 1

31 Relief and Land Settlement Committee, *First Report*, (1932–33); Ontario Department of Lands and Forests, *Annual Report*, 1933–4, 9

32 Ontario Archives, Prime Ministers' Papers, *Hepburn Collection:* memorandum, Cain to Hepburn, 4 April 1935. See also the *Globe*, 18 April 1935, 11.

33 For example, Ontario Department of Lands and Forests, *Annual Report* (1929), 17,

gives the cut of pulpwood as 659,868 cords on settler land and 461,992 cords on crown lands.

34 Lower, *Settlement*, 131–3
35 Ibid., 131; G. McDermott, 'Advancing and Retreating Frontiers of Settlement in the Clay Belts,' doctoral dissertation, Department of Geography, University of Wisconsin, 1959; Peter W. Sinclair, 'Colonization in Ontario and Quebec,' in *Canadian Papers in Rural History*, 5 (1986), 104–20
36 V.C. Fowke, *Canadian Agricultural Policy* (Toronto: University of Toronto Press, 1978), 272: 'Assistance to agriculture has been consistently recognized as a function of government at all times ... The clearest and most significant uniformity regarding Canadian agricultural policy has been its deliberate and consistent use as a basis for economic and political empire.'

CHAPTER 6 *The Oil and Gas Industry*

1 Michael O'Meara, *Oil Springs: The Birthplace of the Oil Industry in North America* (Oil Springs, 1958), 13
2 Edith G. Firth, ed., *Profiles of a Province* (Toronto: Ontario Historical Society, 1967), 159
3 'Early History of Oil Springs,' *Western Ontario Historical Notes* (1950), 15; E.S. Phelps, 'The Canadian Oil Association,' ibid. (1963), 35
4 R.B. Harkness, 'Ontario's Past in the Petroleum Industry,' *Canadian Oil and Gas Industries* (February and March 1951), 3
5 Ibid., 5
6 Jean Elford and Edward Phelps, 'Oil Then to Now,' *Canadian Geographical Journal*, 77:5 (November 1968), 170
7 *Profiles*, 160–2; 'Canadian Oil Association,' 35
8 *Canada Year Book*, 1869, 31
9 Ontario Royal Commission on the Mineral Resources of the Province, *Report* (Toronto: Queen's Printer, 1890), 161
10 *The Yearbook and Almanac of Canada* (Montreal: John Lowe, 1870), 59
11 Charles Whipp and Edward Phelps, *Petrolia 1866–1966* (Petrolia: Petrolia *Advertiser-Topic* and Centennial Committee, 1966), 24, 31. Note that in the nineteenth century the town was normally called ' Petrolea.'
12 Ibid., 14, 24
13 'The First Seventy-Five Years,' *Imperial Oil Review*, 39:4 (September 1955), 10
14 Fergus Cronin, 'North America's Father of Oil,' *Imperial Oil Review*, 39:4 (September 1955), 23
15 Whipp and Phelps, *Petrolia*, 30
16 'First Seventy-Five Years,' 13–15
17 *Canadian Engineer* (hereafter *CE*), November 1899, 185
18 *CE*, October 1899, 161
19 John T. Saywell, 'The Early History of Canadian Oil Companies: A Chapter in Canadian Business History,' *Ontario History*, 53 (1961), 70–2
20 *CE*, October 1904, 291
21 Ontario Department of Mines, *Annual Report*, no. 48 (1939), part 5, 65

22 Ibid., no. 38 (1939), part 5, 35
23 Ibid., no. 41 (1932), part 5, 55
24 Victor Lauriston, *Blue Flame of Service* (Chatham: Union Gas of Canada, 1961), 12–13
25 Ontario Bureau of Mines, *Annual Report,* no. 10 (1901), 19
26 Ibid., no. 28 (1919), 212–14
27 D.A. Coste, 'History of Natural Gas in Ontario,' Welland County Historical Society, *Papers and Records* (1926), 96
28 Idem.
29 Lauriston, *Blue Flame,* 18
30 Ontario Bureau of Mines, *Annual Report,* no. 28 (1919), part 1, 209
31 Lauriston, *Blue Flame,* 19
32 Bureau of Mines, *Report,* (1919), part 1, 209
33 Lauriston, *Blue Flame,* 49
34 8 Geo v c 12; Gibson, *Mining Laws,* 55
35 Ontario Department of Mines, *Annual Report,* no. 34 (1925), part 5, 18

CHAPTER 7 *Ontario's Industrial Revolution, 1867–1914*

1 O.D. Skelton, *General Economic History of the Dominion, 1867–1912* (Toronto: Publishers' Associates, 1913)
2 H.A. Innis, *Essays in Canadian Economic History* (Toronto: University of Toronto Press, 1956), 108–22
3 Ontario Bureau of Mines, *Report,* 1895, 18
4 Ibid., 1902, 28–9
5 The point has been developed in somewhat different terms by a variety of scholars within the past decade, although no one appears to have made the argument in print, or in public, until the present time.
6 Michael Bliss, *A Living Profit* (Toronto: McClelland and Stewart, 1974)
7 See in particular the many writings of Alexander Gerschenkron, especially *Economic Backwardness in Historical Perspective* (Cambridge: The Belknap Press of Harvard University Press, 1962), chs 1, 2, 3.
8 W.G. Phillips, *The Agricultural Implement Industry in Canada* (Toronto: University of Toronto Press, 1956), 38–9
9 See Ontario Royal commission on Forestry, *Report* (Toronto: King's Printer, 1947), 9
10 Ontario Minister of Lands, Forests and Mines, *Report,* year ending 31 October 1912, x–xi
11 M.C. Urquhart and K. Buckley, eds, *Historical Statistics of Canada,* first edition (Toronto: Macmillan, 1965), (hereafter cited as *HSC*), series J26, J39, J56
12 Department of Lands, Forests and Mines, *Report* for year ending 31 October 1913, xii
13 See, for instance, Lower, *Assault*
14 *CE,* 16 January 1913, 187; Carl Wiegman, *Trees to News: A Chronicle of the Ontario Paper Company's Origin and Development* (Toronto: McClelland and Stewart, 1953)

15 Felicity L. Leung, *Grist Mills and Flour Mills in Ontario: From Millstones to Rollers, 1780s-1880s* (Ottawa: National Historic Parks and Sites Branch, 1981), part IV, esp. 184ff

16 Ibid., 187

17 Ibid., 190

18 *CE,* August 1899, 115; October 1899, 174

19 *CE,* April 1902, 166

20 *CE,* February 1903, 47; May 1904, 130

21 *CE,* October 1905

22 *CE,* January 1905, 22

23 *CE,* February 1897, 292

24 *CE,* April 1899, 354; Public Archives of Canada, RG 28 III 26, *Bronson Papers,* vol. 709: Letter, E.H. Bronson to Frank Bronson, 24 August 1907

25 *CE,* 10 April 1914, 593ff

26 *CE,* June 1905, 22

27 *CE,* May 1907

28 J.T.H. O'Connor, 'A Note on Sulphuric Acid Production in Victorian Ontario,' *Ontario History,* 65:3 (1973), 290–7

29 Ontario Bureau of Mines, *Report,* 1905, 136

30 *CE,* January 1894, 256

31 *CE,* January 1897, 272; May 1897, 30

32 *CE,* October 1897, 174; November 1897, 211

33 *CE,* October 1898, 173

34 *CE,* February 1898, 48, citing Ontario Bureau of Mines

35 *CE,* February 1902, 44

36 *CE,* July 1905, 226

37 *CE,* 7 February 1908, 88

38 *CE,* 10 September 1909, 1

39 *CE,* 3 December 1909, 1

40 *CE,* 23 May 1911, 468

41 *CE,* 13 November 1913, 702

42 Michael Bliss, *A Canadian Millionaire* (Toronto: Macmillan, 1978)

43 Ibid., 34

44 Ibid., 39

45 Ibid., 50

46 Ibid., 192

47 J.A. Ruddick, 'The Development of the Dairy Industry in Canada,' part II of H.A. Innis, ed., *The Dairy Industry in Canada* (Toronto: Ryerson Press, 1937), 15–126

48 Ibid., 118

49 Ibid., 44

50 Ibid., 275–6

51 Ibid., 64

52 Ibid., 65

53 *Census,* 1911, vol. 3 table I, vol. 4, table XI

54 *HSC,* series J9, J18

55 Ruddick, 'Development,' 70
56 Ibid., 71–2

CHAPTER 8 *The Electrification of Ontario*

1 J.T. Saywell, *One More River: An Essay on the History of Hydro-Electric Construc-tion,* Economic Council of Canada Discussion Paper No. 20 (Ottawa: 1975), 4
2 *Canadian Manufacturer,* 20 January 1882, 1
3 Ibid., 6 April 1883, 252
4 *History of the County of Peterborough, Ontario* (Toronto: C.B. Robinson, 1884), 352–60
5 Merrill Denison, *The People's Power* (Toronto: McClelland and Stewart, 1966), 20
6 *CE,* February 1898, 324
7 *CE,* November 1894, 200
8 *CE,* 18 November 1894, 199; on electric power development in Ottawa generally, see John H. Taylor, *Ottawa: An Illustrated History,* (Toronto: Lorimer, 1986), 80–1, 164.
9 *CE,* August 1902, 201
10 *CE,* September 1902, 231–2
11 See Robert Belfield, 'Technology Transfer and Turbulence, the Emergence of an International Energy Complex at Niagara Falls, 1896–1906,' *HSTC Bulletin,* s.2 (May/mai 1981) 69–98; Christopher Armstrong and A.V. Nelles, 'Contrasting Development of the Hydro-Electric Industry in the Montreal and Toronto Regions 1900–1930,' *Journal of Canadian Studies,* 18:1 (Spring 1983), 5–27.
12 *CE,* February 1896, 265
13 *CE,* December 1896, 245; November 1897, 209
14 *CE,* June 1897, 55
15 *CE,* December 1898, 217
16 *CE,* February 1900
17 *CE,* October 1899, 176
18 *CE,* November 1902, 292
19 *CE,* September 1904, 277
20 *CE,* June 1904, 157. See also Saywell, *One More River,* 11–12, and Nelles, *Politics,* 222–37.
21 Nelles, *Politics,* 237ff
22 Ibid., 258
23 Ibid., 274
24 Ibid., 286
25 Ibid., 286
26 *CE,* 6 March 1908, 146–7
27 *CE,* 8 June 1911, 803
28 *CE,* 29 May 1911, 749
29 *CE,* July 1899, 82; June 1902, 54; December 1902; September 1903, 318
30 *CE,* 31 July 1893, 252
31 See, for instance, the examples reported by Ian M. Drummond, 'Canadian Life

Insurance Companies and the Capital Market, 1890–1914,' *Canadian Journal of Economics and Political Science,* 28:2 (1962), 204ff.

CHAPTER 9 *Manufacturing, 1914–1941*

1 Numerical data for the late wartime and post-war years are much more comprehensive and reliable than for earlier years, because of the establishment of the Dominion Bureau of Statistics. In 1916 there was a postal census of manufactures, which was more comprehensive than that of 1906. An annual census of manufactures was regularly conducted in and after 1918. In addition, the bureau gathered and tabulated other sorts of data that had not been available before. Hence the compilers of *HSC,* first edition, could present far more individual production series for the 1920s and 1930s than for earlier periods. Long afterward, furthermore, the bureau constructed national income and expenditure estimates on modern principles. These data begin in 1926.
2 See above, chs 1, 2, 8.
3 See Bliss, *Millionaire,* ch. 14
4 *HSC,* series R149
5 *HSC,* Series Q290
6 Kenneth Buckley, *Capital Formation in Canada 1896–1930* (Toronto: University of Toronto Press, 1955), tables B, C, D; Statistics Canada, *National Income and Expenditure Accounts 1926–75,* table 2
7 See below, chapter 11, and Duncan McDowall, *Steel at the Sault* (Toronto: University of Toronto Press, 1984), ch. 4.
8 Public Archives of Canada, RG 28 III: *Beach Papers,* vol. 1, file 1 and vol. 10, file 2
9 *The Canadian Economy in the Great Depression* (Toronto: University of Toronto Press, 1959)
10 The data on outputs and prices in this paragraph come from *HSC.*
11 *HSC,* series J41
12 *HSC,* series J39
13 *HSC,* series J39

CHAPTER 10 *The Development of Industrial Cities*

1 *HSC,* 5
2 John C. Weaver, *Hamilton* (Toronto: James Lorimer, 1983); J.M.S. Careless, *Toronto to 1918* (Toronto: James Lorimer, 1984); James Lemon, *Toronto since 1918* (Toronto: James Lorimer, 1985); John Taylor, *Ottawa* (Toronto: James Lorimer, 1986)
3 George Nader, *Cities of Canada* (Toronto: Macmillan of Canada and the Maclean-Hunter Press, 1976), 202, 210
4 *The Urban Development in South-Central Ontario* (Assen: Van Gorcum and Comp., 1955)
5 Ibid., 126
6 Ibid., 117
7 Ibid., 132

8 Ibid., 119, 132

9 Ibid., 117; for comment see Nader, *Cities*, 191–9

10 Gregory S. Kealey, *Toronto Workers Respond to Industrial Capitalism 1867–1892* (Toronto: University of Toronto Press, 1980), 25

11 Ibid., 20

12 Ibid., 4

13 Ibid., 33

14 Ibid., 34

15 Karl Marx, *Capital* (Modern Library Edition), vol. 1, 686

16 John C. Weaver, *Shaping the Canadian City*, table 5; Buckley, *Capital Formation*, ch 11

17 Ibid., 41

18 *HSC*, series R179

19 Buckley, *Capital Formation*, 43

20 Peter Goheen, *Victorian Toronto* (Department of Geography, University of Chicago, 1970)

21 Careless, *Toronto*, 147

22 Piva, *Condition*, ch. 5

23 John T. Saywell, *Housing Canadians*, Economic Council of Canada Discussion Paper No. 24 (Ottawa: the council, 1975), 147–9

24 *Globe* supplement, 9 November 1907, cited in Saywell, *Housing*, 123

25 Frederick H. Armstrong, *Toronto: The Place of Meeting* (Toronto?: Windsor Publications, 1983), 141

26 M.J. Doucet, 'Mass Transit and the Failure of Private Ownership: The Case of Toronto in the Early Twentieth Century,' *Urban History Review*, 3–77 (1978), 3–33

27 'Mass Transit and Private Ownership: An Alternative Perspective in the Case of Toronto,' *Urban History Review*, 3–78 (1979), 60–98

28 Ibid., 88–90

29 Ibid., 91. See also Christopher Armstrong and H.V. Nelles, *Monopoly's Moment* (Philadelphia: Temple University Press, 1986).

30 Weaver, *Hamilton*, chs 3 and 4

31 Bryan Palmer, *A Culture in Conflict* (Montreal: McGill-Queen's University Press, 1979), 15

32 See also Naylor, *Canadian Business*, II, 41, 62, 181–4, 237.

33 Palmer, *Culture*, 16

34 Ibid., 17

35 William Kilbourn, *The Elements Combined* (Toronto: Clarke Irwin, 1960), 34

36 Ibid., 42

37 Ibid., 50

38 *Hamilton Spectator*, 15 July 1946

39 Nader, *Cities*, II, 167–8

40 Elizabeth Bloomfield, 'Building the City on a Foundation of Factories: The "Industrial Policy" in Berlin, Ontario, 1870–1914,' *Ontario History*, 75: 3 (1983), 207–445; 'City-Building in Berlin/Kitchener and Waterloo, 1870–1930,' unpublished PHD thesis, University of Guelph, 1981

41 Joseph D. Lindsey, 'Water and Blood: The Georgian Foundry, Hydraulic Technology, and the Rise and Fall of a Family Firm in Small Town Ontario,' and Richard
Reid, 'The Rosamond Woollen Company of Almonte: Industrial Development in
a Rural Setting,' both in *Ontario History*, 75:3 (1983), 266–89
42 *Strathroy Centennial 1860–1960* (n.p., n.d.)
43 See Donald M. Wilson, *Lost Horizons: The Story of the Rathbun Railway and the
Bay of Quinte Railway* (Belleville: Mika, 1983)
44 Archie Bremner, *City of London, Ontario* (n.p., 1897), 74, 81, 89, 91, 93, 96, 114;
London: Its Men of Affairs (n.p., 1914?), 126
45 See below, chapter 15; see also McDowall, *Steel*, chs 1, 2.

CHAPTER 11 *The Iron and Steel Industry*

1 Early but still useful authorities on nineteenth-century iron and steel are J. Bartlett,
*The Manufacture, Consumption and Production of Iron, Steel and Coal in the
Dominion of Canada* (Montreal: Dawson Bros, 1884) and W.J. Donald, *The
Canadian Iron and Steel Industry* (Boston: Houghton Mifflin, 1915). More recent is
Kris Inwood, *The Canadian Charcoal Iron Industry, 1870–1914* (New York:
Garland, 1986).
2 The investors included Peter McGill and Alex Simpson of the Bank of Montreal and
several figures from the important Montreal merchant houses of Gillespie, Moffat
and Company and Anderson, Evans and Forsyth; see Inwood, *Charcoal*, 276–7.
3 Rita Michael, 'Ironworking in Upper Canada,' *Bulletin of the Canadian Institute of
Mining and Metallurgy*, 76 (1983), 132–4; W.H. Smith, *Canada: Past, Present
and Future* (Toronto: Legislature, 1851), 246–9; *Montreal Gazette*, 5 November
1829; Ontario Bureau of Mines, *Report*, 1892, 14ff; Public Archives of Canada,
MG 24, D28
4 *Census of Canada*, 1870–71, vols III, 336 and IV, 199; Gordon Bertram, 'Economic
Growth in Canadian Industry 1870–1915,' *Canadian Journal of Economics and
Political Science* 29:2 (1963), 162–84
5 Adam Shortt, 'Railway Construction and National Prosperity,' *Transactions of the
Royal Society of Canada*, 8 (1914)
6 Public Archives of Canada, MG 29, B15, V. 53, 'Iron in Ontario and Nova Scotia'
7 This and the following discussion are based on Inwood, *Charcoal*, 113–16, 275–8
and 376–7.
8 Royal Commission on the Mineral Resources of Ontario, *Report*, 1890, 393, 481
9 Inwood, *Charcoal*, 163–295, esp 275–8
10 D. Hogarth, *Pioneer Mines of the Gatineau Region* (Ottawa: Beaver, 1975),
'Edward Haycock and His Gatineau Mine,' *Bulletin of the Canadian Institute of
Metallurgy*, 75 (1982), and 'The Hull Iron Ranges, 1801–1977,' ibid., 76
(1983), no. 854
11 Catalan forges produced wrought-iron in a single metallurgical process. Far more
common was the two-step process of smelting pig iron and then refining it into
wrought-iron in an independent operation that involved the puddling furnace.
12 The MacLarens also supported Sam Ritchie in his attempts to develop the Coe Hill
deposit (see below in text) and an 1882 attempt to manufacture with petroleum

fuel in Montreal; see *Canadian Manufacturer* (1882), 100 and *Monetary Times* (1881–2), 371, 979, 1043. Petroleum smelting had been tried in Ontario as well – to the amusement of American observers; see *Engineering and Mining Journal* (1875), 401–2.

13 *Canadian Manufacturer* (1882), 17 and 117; *Journal of the U.S. Association of Charcoal Iron Workers* (1883), 339

14 *Iron Age*, 4 June 1885, 13; *Iron Trades Review*, 11 July 1889, 2; *Canadian Manufacturer* (1890–91), 265; Ontario Bureau of Mines, *Report*, 1910, 159

15 Ontario Bureau of Mines *Report*, 1892, 89 and 1910, 154–72; Public Archives of Canada, MG 26A, v. 45, 17624–8; G. May and V. Lemmer, 'Thomas Edison's Experimental Work with Michigan Iron Ore,' *Michigan History*, 53 (1969), 109–29; J. Jeans, *American Industrial Conditions and Competition* (London: British Iron Trades Association, 1902), 406–8

16 *Iron Trades Review*, 11 July 1889

17 Royal Ontario Nickel Commission, *Report*, 1917, 253–423

18 R. Hessen, 'The Transformation of Bethlehem Steel,' *Business History Review*, 46 (1972), 339–60, esp. 347

19 Main, *Canadian Nickel Industry*, 18–69; Nelles, *Politics*, 90; Royal Commission on the Mineral Resources of Ontario, *Report* (1890), 405; Ontario Bureau of Mines, *Report*, 1892, part 2, 110–11; Public Archives of Canada, MG 26A, v. 45, 17607–17821, v. 257, 116410–76; *CE*, March 1900, 308; House of Commons, *Journals*, 1910, appendix 5, evidence of John Patterson

20 Productivity lagged, even though advanced mining technology was used; see Newell, 'Mining Technology,' 118–34.

21 Geological Survey of Canada, *Report*, 1887–1888, 62–64s; 1895, A49–A61; and 1899, I. Royal Commission on the Mineral Resources of Ontario, *Report*, 1890, 234, 345 and 474. Ontario Bureau of Mines *Report*, 1908, 209; 1910, 159. *Canadian Manufacturer*, 1890–91, 224; *CE*, 8 (1901), 205; *Iron Age*, 14 December 1882, 11; *Iron Trades Review*, 15 Augst, 1889, 2; *Journal of the Iron and Steel Institute*, 1887, 220. About one-third of all iron ore raised in Ontario had to be dumped; see Ontario Bureau of Mines, *Report*, 1892, 238.

22 *Monetary Times*, 14 March 1890, 595; *Canadian Manufacturer*, 1896, 288; *Journal of the U.S. Association of Charcoal Iron Workers*, 1884, 48; Jeans, *American Industrial Conditions*, 236; Peter Temin, *Iron and Steel in Nineteenth Century America* (Cambridge: MIT Press, 1964), 112; Royal Commission on the Mineral Resources of Ontario, *Report*, 1890, 234

23 *Iron Age*, 23 September 1895. See also Inwood, *Charcoal*, 124–5; *Journal of the U.S. Association of Charcoal Iron Workers*, 1883, 341; *Canadian Manufacturer*. 1891, 288; Toronto *Mail and Empire*, 20 December 1900

24 Temin, *Iron*, 153–93

25 Bertram, 'Economic Growth'

26 Ibid.

27 Buckley, *Capital Formation*

28 I distinguish the extraordinary investment and export boom 1900–13 from cyclical recovery from a depression during the mid-1890s. Prairie homesteading and railway construction increased during the late 1890s, but their levels were not yet

unusual by the standards of earlier decades The contemporary press did not
report unusually strong demand for metal until after the turn of the century; see *CE,*
January 1902, 14.

29 Albert Fishlow, 'Productivity and Technical Change in the Railroad Sector, 1840–
1910,' *National Bureau of Economic Research Studies in Income and Wealth,* 30
(1966), 583–646

30 Robert C. Allen, 'The Peculiar Productivity History of American Blast Furnaces,'
Journal of Economic History, 37 (1977), 605–33; W. Isard, 'Some Locational
Factors in the Iron and Steel Industry since the Early Nineteenth Century,' *Journal of
Political Economy,* 56 (1948), 207–17; Temin, *Iron,* ch. 3

31 *Iron Age,* 17 March 1879; Kris Inwood, 'Effective Transport and Tariff Protection in
Nineteenth Century Canada: The Case of the Iron Industry,' Saint Mary's University Economics Working Paper 85–24, autumn 1985

32 Inwood, 'Effective'

33 B. Forster, 'Tariffs and Politics: The Genesis of the National Policy,' unpublished
doctoral dissertation, University of Toronto, 1982, 107, 328–30; House of
Commons, *Debates,* 24 February 1881, 1109 and 28 April 1882, 1225

34 *Iron Age,* 3 August 1882 and *Journal of the U.S. Association of Charcoal Iron
Workers,* 1882, 27. Although such statements may sound far-fetched to modern
ears, they were taken seriously in the nineteenth century. Indeed, it has not been
very long since Canadians were told that the iron industry is 'the ne plus ultra of
the developed industrial state' and 'indispensable in the life of any progressive
community;' see O. McDiarmid, *Commercial Policy in the Canadian Economy*
(Cambridge: Harvard University Press, 1949), 191; T.W. Gibson, *Mining in Ontario*
(Toronto: Ontario Bureau of Mines, 1937).

35 *Iron Age,* 26 May 1887; see also House of Commons, *Debates,* 24 April 1879,
1531, and 19 April 1883, 717; Public Archives of Canada, *Laurier Papers,*
72011, Laurier to Dandurand, 10 April 1903.

36 In response to the secessionist threat Charles Tupper returned from London to help
his fellow Conservatives carry Nova Scotia in the 1887 federal election. Tupper
then became minister of finance and promptly delighted the Nova Scotia iron lobby
by increasing support for iron production. See A. MacIntosh, 'The Career of Sir
Charles Tupper in Canada, 1864–1900,' unpublished doctoral dissertation, University of Toronto, 1960, 288; *Iron Age,* 26 May 1887, 17. Tupper's intervention to
promote the iron industry was reminiscent of bold moves to assist railway
construction during his tenure as minister of railways and canals 1879–84. See P.
George, 'Rates of Return in Railway Investment and Implications for Government Subsidization of the Canadian Pacific Railway,' *Canadian Journal of
Economics* 1 (1968), 740–62.

37 MacIntosh, 'The Career,' 292–301

38 Public Archives of Canada, RG 19, v. 3720–1, #1, 14 May 1887: correspondence of
the Ontario Rolling Mills

39 Inwood, 'Effective'

40 References to this concern are numerous: Dominion Board of Trade *Report,* 1873,
44–7 and 1874, 68, 72, 85; *Iron Age,* 17 October 1878 and 1 June 1882;
Monetary Times, 13 June 1879 and 1881–2, 14, 97, 305; House of Commons,

Debates, 28 April 28, 1882, 1225 and 19 April 1883, 714, 717; Public Archives of Canada, RG 19, file C, 1887, P.H. Griffin of the St Thomas Wheel Company; *Canadian Manufacturer,* 1891a, 408 and 1891b, 340; Ontario Bureau of Mines, *Report,* 1892, 105; *CE,* 1894, 340, and 1896, 289; *Canadian Mining Review,* 1898, 97; reminiscences of W. A. Child in the Hamilton *Spectator,* 15 July 1926; Kilbourn, *Elements,* 43.

41 *CE,* March 1898, 366; Deseronto *Tribune,* 8 June 1897, 22 October 1897, 4 February 1898, 18 March 1898, 15 April 1898, and 29 July 1898

42 T.S. Ashton, *Iron and Steel in the Industrial Revolution* (Manchester: Manchester University Press, second edition, 1951)

43 F.K. Hyde, *Technological Change and the British Iron Industry* (Princeton: Princeton University Press, 1977)

44 Inwood, *Charcoal,* ch. 3

45 The late persistence of charcoal iron in Canada paralleled the experience of the 'land-abundant' regions of northern and eastern Europe; see ibid.

46 Ibid., ch. 8

47 Ibid., ch. 9; R. Schallenberg, 'Evolution, Adaptation and Survival,' *Annals of Science,* 32 (1975), 341–58

48 K. Inwood, 'Productivity Change in Obsolesence: Charcoal Iron Revisited,' *Journal of Economic History,* 45 (1985), 293–8

49 Inwood, *Charcoal,* 311–12; Ontario Bureau of Mines, *Report,* 1893, 20; Public Archives of Canada, RG 87, v. 18. The figures assume a weight of fifteen pounds per bushel in Quebec and twenty pounds elsewhere; see Inwood, *Charcoal,* 364 n 14.

50 This and the following two paragraphs rely extensively on Inwood, *Charcoal,* ch. 10.

51 About one-half of all US charcoal iron in 1889 was estimated to have been used for railway wheels; see *Iron Trades Review,* 31 October 1889. The purchase of rolling stock equipped with charcoal iron wheels allowed the government to assist the new iron company. The government-owned Intercolonial Railway, for example, ordered a large number of boxcars from the Rathbuns in 1899, just as the Deseronto blast furnace was blown in; see *CE,* 1899a, 298.

52 Royal Commission on the Mineral Resources of Ontario, *Report,* 1890, 329 and *CE,* 1894–5, 329; Nov. 1906, 428.

53 Victor S. Clark, *History of Manufactures in the U.S.* (New York: McGraw-Hill, 1929), vol. 2, 250

54 Royal Commission on the Mineral Resources of Ontario, *Report,* 1890, 329; *Iron Trades Review,* 2 April 1903, 78–9. *Canadian Manufacturer,* 1888, 16; 1889, 13; 1891, 16. *CE,* 1894–5, 357; 1895–6, 76; 1903, 112; 1904, 74; 1907, 33; 19 July 1907. The Walkerville foundry was quite large; see *CE,* February 1901, 214. The Toronto, Oshawa, and Smiths Falls foundries served implement makers. The oldest malleable foundry, the Burrow, Stewart and Milne works in Hamilton, was built during the early 1860s and is described in *Canadian Manufacturer,* 15 June 1883, 441.

55 Standard Chemical, Iron and Lumber Company, *Annual Report,* 1916. Acetone, which found its way into the production of cordite, was manufactured at several

Canadian sites during the war. The output of other firms was purchased by the Imperial Munitions Board; only Standard Chemical bypassed the board to export directly to Britain. See Peter Rider, 'The Imperial Munitions Board,' unpublished doctoral dissertation, University of Toronto, 1974, 141–2.

56 Demand changes may have reinforced the effect of production costs. Metallurgical progress made it increasingly easy to approximate the qualities of charcoal iron using coke iron.

57 Standard Chemical declared no dividends between 1914 and 1917; see *Canadian Chemical Journal*, 1918, 220.

58 Allen, 'Peculiar'

59 Inwood, *Charcoal*, 382–3

60 *Chemical Trades Journal*, 56 (1915), 315; *Canadian Chemical Journal*, May 1917, 11–13; 1918, 220; 1919, 372. P. Dumesny and J. Noyer, *Wood Products* (London: Scott Greenwood, 1921), 150; H. French and J. Withrow, 'The Hardwood Distillation Industry in America,' *Journal of Industrial and Engineering Chemistry*, 7 (1915), 49–63; M. Klar and A. Rule, *The Technology of Wood Distillation* (London: Chapman and Hall, 1925), 73–4; C. Warrington and R. Nicholls, *A History of Chemistry in Canada* (Toronto: Pitman, 1949), 242; A. Wilson, *The Development of the Chemical, Metallurgical and Applied Trades in Relation to the Mineral Industry* (Ottawa: Department of Mines, 1924), 10–11, 127

61 Kilbourn, *Elements*, 50; D. Middleton and D. Walker, 'Manufactures and Industrial Development Policy in Hamilton, 1890–1910,' *Urban History Review*, 8 (1980), 20–40

62 *CE*, 1893, 60; May 1895, 23; June 1895, 48. Initially, the company had hoped to rely upon Canadian ore *(CE*, May 1894, 30). Unfortunately, the quality of the Canadian ores caused problems *(Iron Age*, 4 June 1896, 1306 and *Iron and Coal Trades Review*, 1898, part 2, 278). As a result 60 per cent of the ore charged to the furnace in its first ten years was imported; see Public Archives of Canada, RG 87, v. 18. The Deseronto furnace also limited its use of Ontario ores because of quality problems; see Ontario Bureau of Mines, *Report*, 1901, 24 and 74 and 1908, 314ff.

63 John Weaver, 'The Location of Manufacturing Enterprise: The Case of Hamilton's Attraction of Foundries, 1830–1890,' 197–217 in R.A. Jarrell and A.E. Roos, eds, *Critical Issues in the History of Canadian Science, Technology and Medicine* (Thornhill and Ottawa: HSTC, 1983); Kilbourn, *Elements*, 49; Inwood, *Charcoal*, 269–72; *Engineering and Mining Journal*, 61 (1896), 36

64 Kilbourn, *Elements*, 50; *CE*, 7 (1899), 206–7 and July 1900, 46–7

65 *CE*, September 1902, 250 and April 1907, 155

66 Kilbourn, *Elements*, 56–96

67 Ibid., 93–5

68 Donald Kerr, 'The Location of the Iron and Steel Industry in Canada,' in R. L. Gentilcore, ed., *Geographical Approaches to Canadian Problems* (Scarborough: Prentice-Hall, 1971), 59–69; Weaver, 'Location;' Kilbourn, *Elements*, 126–7

69 Weaver, 'Location'

70 Ibid.; Anonymous, *Hamilton and Its Industries* (Hamilton: Spectator, 1884); Kilbourn, *Elements*, ch. 3

71 D. Fletcher, 'Railways and the Iron Industry, 1876–1900,' unpublished BA thesis, Queen's University, 1978; M. Grier, 'Railways and the Canadian Iron Industry,' unpublished MA thesis, Queen's University, 1980

72 House of Commons, *Journals,* 4 April 1910, 163–4 and 183–7; Tom Traves, *The State and Enterprise: Canadian Manufacturers and the Federal Government, 1917–31* (Toronto: University of Toronto Press, 1979), 126. For a more general discussion of the point see Alfred D. Chandler Jr, *The Visible Hand* (Cambridge: Harvard University Press, 1977) and Temin, *Iron,* ch. 7.

73 Frank Jones, General Manager of the Dominion Iron and Steel Company, Public Archives of Canada, RG 36, series 17, v. 7, 433

74 Temin, *Iron,* ch. 10. In 1890 US manufacturers produced one-half ton of steel for every ton of iron produced; by 1920 there were one and a quarter tons of steel for every ton of iron. See *Iron Trades Review,* 3 January 1924, 4.

75 Kilbourn, *Elements,* 117

76 Sample cost structures may be found in the *Iron and Coal Trades Review,* 15 April 1898; *Iron Age,* 4 October 1888, 498; *Journal of the Iron and Steel Institute,* 1890, 795–6; I.L. Bell, *The Iron Trades of Great Britain* (London: British Iron Trades Association, 1886), 131. The same information is conveyed by the ratio of Bessemer pig to rolled steel billet prices; see Temin, *Iron,* 285.

77 Public Archives of Canada, RG 87, v. 18 is the data source for table 11.1, which provides market values of inputs and output at the furnace.

78 The dominion government paid a production subsidy of $2 on iron made from imported ore and $3 on iron made with domestic ore. In addition, the provincial government paid $0.50 per ton of Ontario ore used. Because the Hamilton firm used Ontario and imported ore in roughly equal measures 1899–1902, the average subsidy was about $3 per ton.

79 The Hamilton furnace was similar in many ways to small American coke blast furnaces. Data describing US blast furnaces in 1899 (*1900 US Census of Manufactures,* 'Iron and Steel Manufacturing,' table 28) indicate miscellaneous costs of $0.45 per ton and capital valued at $9 per ton. It is conventional to view the annual cost of capital as composed of depreciation and interest paid on funds needed for investment. Interest and depreciation rates combined are unlikely to have exceeded 15 per cent. As an upper-bound estimate a combined interest and depreciation charge of 17 per cent may be imputed. This implies an annual capital cost of $1.53, which in turn suggests that an average American furnace incurred about $2 in capital and miscellaneous costs. This figure is applied in the text to the Hamilton furnace.

80 Public Archives of Canada, RG 87, v. 18

81 Kilbourn, *Elements,* 140, 147

82 Ibid., 119

83 Ibid., 143

84 Ibid., 142

85 L. Morgan, *The Canadian Primary Iron and Steel Industry* (Ottawa: Royal Commission on Canada's Economic Prospects, 1956), 68

86 The figure for 'disposable' profit, which is revenue net of operating costs as well as bond and mortgage payments, totalled $5.1 million 1911–14, of which only $1.6

million was paid out as dividends. Successful steel companies typically financed a large portion of their improvements from net earnings; see Jeans, *American*, 301.

87 Kilbourn, *Elements*, 94; Inwood, *Charcoal*, 269–72

88 Between 1911 and 1914 fiscal years retained earnings totalled $3.5 million and debt expansion $3.2 million.

89 C. Heron, 'Hamilton Steelworkers and the Rise of Mass Production,' Canadian Historical Association, *Historical Papers* 1982, 103–31

90 Kilbourn, *Elements*, 308; Dominion Department of Mines, *Report*, 1908, 338

91 Public Archives of Canada, RG 87, v. 18; see also Kilbourn, *Elements*, 122.

92 G. Bertram and M. Percy, 'Real Wage Trends in Canada, 1900–1926: Some Provisional Estimates,' *Canadian Journal of Economics*, 12 (1979), 299–312. See also below, ch. 13.

93 Ibid.

94 Heron, 'Hamilton;' *CE*, April 1900, 332 and October 1904, 291

95 *CE*, March 1902, 74

96 Nelles, *Politics*, 136; McDowall, *Steel*, 46–54

97 Ibid., 53

98 Ibid., chs 4, 6. The loss, which includes depreciation for the period 1919–1930, is reported by Traves, *State*, 127. Another calculation placed the firm's operational losses at $100,000 per year 1913–23; see McDowall, *Steel*, 71.

99 McDowall, *Steel*, ch. 6

100 D. Eldon, 'The Career of Francis H. Clergue,' *Explorations in Entrepreneurial History*, 3 (1950–1), 264

101 D. Eldon, 'American Influence in the Canadian Iron and Steel Industry,' unpublished doctoral dissertation, Harvard University, 1954, 310; Main, *Nickel*, 122; *Iron and Coal Trades Review*, 18 November 1898, 863; *CE*, January 1899, 265; 1900–1, 109, 145 and 39; 1903, 15

102 The discovery is thought to have been at least partly accidental, since the iron deposit was encountered as a by-product of a gold rush in the Michipicoten region; the Klondike discoveries in 1896 appear to have stirred the gold exploration activity north of Lake Superior. The annual reports of the Ontario Bureau of Mines ably chronicle these events.

103 *CE*, November 1899, 207

104 Technical explanations are given by J.F. Thompson and N. Beasley, *For the Years to Come* (Toronto: Longmans, 1960), 128; C. Warrington and R. Nicholls, *A History of Chemistry in Canada* (Toronto: Pitman and Sons, 1949), 56, 343 and testimony reported in House of Commons, *Journals*, 1910, appendix 5, 33.

105 Jeans, *American*, 46, and *Canada's Resources and Possibilities* (London: British Iron Trades Association, 1904), 142–7; F. Popplewell, *Iron and Steel Production in America* (Manchester: Manchester University Press, 1906), 51–2; *Transactions of the Canadian Institute of Metallurgy 1901*, 191–5

106 Ontario Bureau of Mines, *Reports*, 1902, 170; 1904, 168 and 188; 1905, 70; 1906, 188–189; 1907, 167; 1913, 106; 1915, 206. Eldon, 'American Influence,' 54; Public Archives of Canada, MG A51, v. 313, 'Helen' file

107 Public Archives of Canada, RG 87, v. 18

108 Ontario Bureau of Mines, *Report*, 1908, 291; *Transactions of the American Institute*

of Mining Engineers, 1908, 228. The Algoma region was at the northern limit of hardwood growth; see C. Jones, 'The Hardwood Industry of Canada,' unpublished BCOM thesis, University of Toronto, 1928, 5.

109 Jeans, *American,* 337; Kilbourn, *Elements,* 126

110 Traves, *State,* 128–31

111 Public Archives of Canada, RG 87, v. 18

112 Jeans, *Canada's Resources,* 118–19; Public Archives of Canada, MG 31, B3, 13–14. The obsolete and inexpensive nature of the steel plant helps account for its establishment before blast furnaces were erected, to which McDowall (*Steel,* 34) draws attention.

113 McDowall, *Steel,* 36

114 Public Archives of Canada, RG 87, v. 18

115 Traves, *State,* 126–8

116 K. Inwood, 'Steel Manufacturers at the Margin in Nova Scotia,' *Business and Economic History, Proceedings of the Business History Conference,* Second Series, vol. 13 (1984), 61–74 and K. Inwood, 'Corporate Structure, Strategy and Regional Development: The Case of the Nova Scotia Steel and Coal Company,' Saint Mary's University Economics Department Working Paper 85–29, Winter 1985–6

117 Bartlett, *Manufacture,* 59–99; annual reports of the Department of Mines

118 Canada, Dominion Bureau of Statistics, *Iron and Steel and Their Products,* 1939; Department of Trade and Commerce, *The Trade of Canada,* various years

119 Traves, *State,* ch. 7; McDowall, *Steel,* 40 and 64–6; Sault *Star,* 24 July 1902; House of Commons, *Journals,* 1910, appendix 5, 4

120 House of Commons, *Journals,* 1910, appendix 5, 51; McDowall, *Steel,* 88

121 Lake Superior Corporation, *Annual Reports* for the years ending 30 June 1917 and 1918.

122 This was a much greater increase than that experienced in Great Britain, the United States, or the world in total. See Rider, 'Imperial,' 135, 412; D. Carnegie, *The History Of Munitions Supply in Canada* (London: Longman's, 1925), 133, 281.

123 Carnegie (*Munitions,* 127) reports the number of shells produced annually in Canada; an average 70 lbs per shell may be assumed (Carnegie, *Munitions,* 134 and Rider, 'Imperial,' 131). I adjust for the share of shell steel that was imported (25 per cent: Rider, 'Imperial,' 131) and the export of ingots and blanks not yet fully processed (Carnegie, *Munitions,* 107). The result is an estimate of 160,000 net tons for shells in 1915, rising to 600,000 and 720,000 tons in 1916 and 1917, respectively falling to 490,000 in 1918.

124 Ibid., 26

125 McDowall, *Steel,* 144–50; Traves, *State,* ch. 7

126 Canada, Dominion Bureau of Statistics, *Iron and Steel and Their Products,* 1939

127 Eldon, 'American,' 150

128 McDowall, *Steel,* 127–8. The company's assets had been pledged to secure short term loans as early as 1903; see McDowall, *Steel,* 45–6, 65; Nelles, *Politics,* 136; Eldon, 'American,' 92ff; Public Archives of Canada, MG 30, A51, v.11, T-2, September 1902.

129 McDowall, *Steel,* 145–9, 157–8

130 Ibid., ch . 6 (esp. 126)

131 Ibid., 169

132 Ibid., 172. This was not the first sheet- and plate-mill to have been attempted without success in the Canadian market; a tin-plate-mill operated briefly at Morrisburg before World War One. See *CE*, June 1906, 238, and December 1906, 463.

133 T. Navin and M. Sears, 'The Rise of a Market for Industrial Securities,' *Business History Review*, 39 (1958), 105–38

134 Eldon, 'Career,' 264

135 Eldon, 'Career;' McDowall, *Steel*, ch. 2

136 *CE*, 1903, 321

137 McDowall, *Steel*, 34–56, 78–80, 144–50

138 Traves, *State*, ch. 7; McDowall, *Steel*, 40–42, 56–9, 63–5, 76–94

139 Nelles, *Politics*, 122ff; McDowall, *Steel*, ch. 2

140 A. Dyment, Liberal MP for the Soo, cited in McDowall, *Steel*, 36

141 Eldon, 'Career,' 264

142 F. Redlich, 'The Role of Theory in the Study of Business History,' *Explorations in Entrepreneurial History*, 4 (1951), 135–44

143 *CE*, January 1901, 190

144 *CE*, 1893, 51

145 *Canadian Manufacturer*, 1891a, 244. A description of the furnace may be found in *CE*, January 1901, 188–90.

146 Ontario Bureau of Mines, *Report*, 1898, 6; 1900, 30, 300; *Canadian Mining Manual*, 1900, 65; *Canadian Mining Review*, 1900, 161 and 213; Montreal *Daily Star*, 19 December 1900; Donald, *Canadian*, 223

147 W.R. Williams, 'The Midland Blast Furnace,' *Inland Seas*, 19 (1963), 308–10; Donald, *Canadian*, 214, 217; Eldon, 'American,' 79, n77; *CE*, 8 (1901), 188

148 The furnace was not erected until 1913, although the municipality was known to be ready to pay a cash subsidy as early as 1900; *CE*, May 1900, 38, July 1900, 63.

149 A description of the furnace may be found in *CE*, 26 March 1909, 425–7.

150 *CE*, May 1894, 28 and 8 March 1907; Canada, Department of Mines, *Report*, 1890, 83s and 1908, 332; Canadian Northern Railway, *Annual Reports*, 1907 and 1909; *Journal of the U.S. Association of Charcoal Iron Workers*, 1885, 335; *Canadian Manufacturer*, 1890b, 375; Port Arthur *Herald*, 22 March 1890 and 24 Feburary 1893; Ontario Bureau of Mines, *Report*, 1892, 236; Toronto *Advocate*, 28 November 1893; *CE*, 1893, 45, April 1899, 332, Oct. 1899, 174; Toronto *Mail and Empire*, *20 December 1900*

151 *CE*, 1906, 112, 427, 26 July and 18 October 1907, 22 February 1912

152 *CE*, March 1900, 307, 331; June 1900, 36, 43; Feb. 1901, 204–5; May 1902, 138; 1903, 83, 255; 1904, 74, 244, 291

153 Public Archives of Canada, RG 87, v. 18, William Kennedy and Sons, 1918

154 *CE*, January 1905, 219, February 1907, 72; January 1916, 192

155 H. Bruce, *Frank Sobey* (Toronto: Macmillan, 1985), 221–2; Kilbourn, *Elements*, 132

156 *CE*, 1899, 174–6; 1903, 317; 1904, 256; 1906, 389; 1912, 154. L.G. Denison, 'Canadian Steel Foundries,' *Canadian Machinery*, 8 (1912), 325–30; *Report of*

the Mining and Metallurgical Industries (Ottawa: Department of Mines, 1908), 322, 335–6. The large steel companies at Hamilton and the Soo also produced small quantities of steel castings for their own use.

157 Forster, 'Tariffs,' 224–5; *Canadian Manufacturer,* 1882, 181, 322; 1883, 136–137, 219; 1891b, 385–6; 1892a, 240

158 *Monetary Times,* 1881–2, 277; *Canadian Manufacturer,* 1891b, 386; *Iron Age,* 5 December 1878, 3 September and 1 October 1885, 8 April 1886; *Iron and Coal Trades Review,* 1898/1, 853

159 Jeans, *American,* 169, 173, 240, 310ff

160 *CE,* 1901, 140, 170, 212, 221, 250, 397; 1904, 150–151; 1905, 269, 383; 1907, 4, 14–15, 44. A. Stansfield, 'The Electric Furnace,' *Transactions of the Canadian Mining Institute,* 12 (1909)

161 D.Cooper, 'History and Financial Analysis of DOFASCO, Ltd.,' unpublished B COM dissertation, Queen's University, 1958; R. Storey, 'Unionization vs Corporate Welfare,' *Labour/le travailleur,* 12 (1983), 7–42

CHAPTER 12 *The Development of the Ontario Automobile Industry to 1939*

1 Emma Rothschild, *Paradise Lost: The Decline of the Auto-Industrial Age* (New York: Random House, 1974)

2 *Industrial Canada,* October 1925, 59, 75

3 *Canada Year Book,* 1942, 370–1, 405–6

4 C.H. Aikman, *The Automobile Industry of Canada* (Montreal: McGill University, 1926), 26; D. Michael Ray, 'The Location of United States Manufacturing Subsidiaries in Canada,' *Economic Geography,* 47 (1971), 389–400

5 'Branch plant' is a slippery term that can mean various things. In this chapter it is applied to Canadian firms that, regardless of ownership, had close connections with American firms. Thus some 'branch plants' in the auto industry began with Canadian initiative, operated for some time with substantial Canadian ownership interest and under effective Canadian management, and passed only later into American ownership; others were, from the start, wholly owned subsidiaries of American parent firms. On a narrower application of the 'branch plant' label, only the latter would qualify.

6 *HSC,* 550

7 Mira Wilkins and Frank E. Hill, *American Business Abroad: Ford on Six Continents* (Detroit: Wayne State University Press, 1964), 6

8 See ibid., 1–19.

9 The following discussion is based on R.S. McLaughlin, *My Eighty Years on Wheels,* as told to Eric Hutton. Reprinted from *Maclean's Magazine,* 15 September, 1 October, and 15 October, 1954.

10 Herbert Marshall, F.A. Southard, and K.W. Taylor, *Canadian-American Industry* (New Haven: Yale University Press, 1935), 65; Arthur Pound, *The Turning Wheel* (New York: Doubleday Doran, 1954), 236

11 MacLaughlin, *Eighty Years*

12 H. Durnford and G. Baechler, *Cars of Canada* (Toronto: McClelland and Stewart, 1973), 102–11

13 Ibid., 84–98
14 Robert E. Ankli and Fred Frederikson, 'Canadian Automobile Production Prior to 1930,' paper presented to the Canadian Historical Association Annual Meeting, 1982; idem, 'The Dodge Brothers in Canada,' *Vintage Vehicles of Canada*, 2:2 (September/October 1980), 7–10
15 Durnford and Baechler, *Cars*, 151–63
16 Public Archives of Canada, *William Gray Papers*, as quoted by Ankli and Frederiksen, 'Canadian Automobile Production'
17 Ibid.; Durnford and Baechler, *Cars*, 259; McLaughlin, *Eighty Years*
18 To sample the negative or pessimistic view see Canada, *Foreign Direct Investment in Canada* (Ottawa: Information Canada, 1972), and Robert Laxer, *Canada's Unions* (Toronto: James Lorimer, 1976), 82–91. Not all observers, however, have been equally pessimistic, and the question remains an open one.
19 Aikman, *Automobile Industry*, 36; Sun Life Assurance Company, *The Canadian Automotive Industry*, Study prepared for the Royal Commission on Canada's Economic Prospects (Ottawa: Queen's Printer, 1956), 10 and table IV
20 *Financial Post*, 25 November 1921
21 Public Archives of Canada, *Tariff Commission Transcripts*, 1920, v. 8, file 23, 4327: testimony of W.R. Campbell. In 1920, Ford sold 31,805 cars in Canada. See Wilkins and Hill, *Ford*, 422 and appendix 6.
22 J.B. Rae, *The American Automobile: A Brief History* (Chicago: University of Chicago Press, 1965), 104; Wilkins and Hill, *Ford*, 43
23 John Manley, 'Organize the Unorganized: Communists and the Struggle for Industrial Unionism in the Canadian Automobile Industry, 1922–36,' paper presented at the Canadian Historical Association Annual Meeting, 1981
24 Durnford and Baechler, *Cars*, 353–4
25 W.T. Hogan, *Economic History of the Iron and Steel Industry in the United States* (Lexington: Heath, 1971), III, 1004–6
26 Aikman, *Automobile*, 20; R.P. Thomas, 'Style Change and the Automobile Industry during the Roaring Twenties,' in L.P. Cain and P.J. Uselding, eds., *Business Enterprise and Economic Change* (Kent State University Press, 1973)
27 McLaughlin, *Eighty*; Hogan, *Economic History*, 1005
28 Sun Life, *Canadian Automotive Industry*, 37; *HSC*, 549; Perry, *Taxes, Tariffs, and Subsidies*, 238, table 18; also below, chapter 16.
29 Quoted in Wilkins and Hill, *Ford*, 43
30 T.C. Byrnes, 'The Automotive Industry in Ontario,' MA thesis, University of Toronto, 1951, 68–9; O.J. McDiarmid, 'Some Aspects of the Canadian Automobile Industry,' *Canadian Journal of Economics and Political Science*, 12 (1948), 261, n3; Ian M. Drummond, *British Economic Policy and the Empire 1919–1939* (London: Allan and Unwin, 1972), ch. 2
31 Sun Life, *Automotive Industry*, 11
32 Aikman, *Automobile Industry*, 35–6; Wilkins and Hill, *Ford*, appendix 6; General Motors of Canada Ltd, Domestic and Export Production 1908–31 (December 1972). I have used Aikman's figures but I suspect that they may be a little high.
33 Aikman, *Automobile Industry; Financial Post*, 7 October 1921
34 Wilkins and Hill, *Ford*, 120–30; Canada, Advisory Board on Tariffs and Taxation

(ABTT), Record of Public Sittings, *Iron and Steel,* Hearings of 12 December 1929 and 22–23 January 1930, vol. 3, Automobiles and Parts, 79–80; Aikman, *Automobile Industry,* 31–6

35 Public Archives of Canada, *W.L.M. King Papers,* 'Papers and Correspondence,' vol. 123, no. 104622: T.A. Russell, President of Automotive Industries of Canada, to King, 10 June 1925; no. 104625: Russell to King, 17 July 1925.

36 The tariff issue is discussed more fully in Traves, *State,* ch. 6.

37 *Industrial Canada,* May 1926, 39; *King Papers,* 'Diaries,' vol. 21, 23 April 1926, and 'Papers and Correspondence,' vol. 128, no. 109943–6: G.H. Boivin, Minister of Customs and Excise, to King, 1 May 1926; Toronto *Globe, 24 April 1926; London Free Press,* 28 April 1926

38 Traves, *State*

39 *King Papers,* 'Memoranda and Notes,' vol. 135, file 1086, C98509; ABTT, *Iron and Steel,* 22, 31, 44, 47; Sun Life, *Automotive,* 16, table 7; Dominion Bureau of Statistics, *Automobile Statistics;* ABTT *Papers,* vol. 48, file 134–43: data prepared by Prof. H.R. Kemp, University of Toronto

40 A.D. Chandler Jr, *Strategy and Structure,* (Cambridge: Harvard University Press, 1962), *Giant Enterprise* (New York: Harcourt Brace and World, 1964), and, with Stephen Salsbury, *Pierre S. DuPont and the Making of the Modern Corporation* (New York: Harper and Row, 1971); Hogan, *Economic History,* 1019, table 29–16; J.C.S. Grimshaw, 'Problems and Policies of Labour and Management in the Automobile Industry in Relation to Prices, Competitive Conditions, and Industrial Structure,' MA thesis, University of Toronto, 1946; Wilkins and Hill, *Ford,* 442, Appendix 6: G.M.

41 ABTT, *Iron and Steel,* 15, 53–5, 90, 94–5; 'Papers,' vol. 49, 134–6: Memo re: 12 December 1929; memo re: 22 January 1930; E.R. Musselman, Ford Motor Co., to W.H. Moore, 11 June 1929; file 134–7: Prof. J. A. Coote to Moore, 20 August 1929; 134–8, memo from General Motors, 12 December 1929

42 Dominion Bureau of Statistics, *Automobile Statistics;* General Motors, 'G.M. in Canada,' mimeo

43 Public Archives of Canada, *R.B. Bennett Papers,* v. 734, file T-100A, 449077–341; 450787–8: E.B. Ryckman, Minister of National Revenue, to Bennett, 9 February 1931; 449999: T.A. Russell to Bennett, 20 February 1931; 450791, Bennett to Russell, and 449961, Bennett to J.H. Fortier, both 18 February 1931; Motor Vehicle Manufacturers' Association, 'Background on the Canada-U.S.A. Automotive Products Agreement,' mimeo

44 Ibid.; Sun Life, *Automotive,* 7–8

45 Ibid., 4–5; Motor Vehicle Manufacturers' Association, *Background,* 20–2; Canada, Royal Commission on the Automotive Industry, Report, (Ottawa: Queen's Printer, 1961), 8–10

46 Sun Life, *Automotive,* 13, table v, 16–18; Motor Vehicle Manufacturers' Association, *Background,* 22

47 Irving Abella, 'Oshawa, 1937,' in *On Strike* (Toronto: James Lorimer, 1975), 95

48 The following discussion is based on Manley, 'Organize the Unorganized.'

49 Ibid.; see also below, ch. 14.

50 The following discussion is based on Abella, 'Oshawa, 1937.'

51 David Moulton, 'Ford Windsor 1945,' in Abella, *On Strike*
52 Sun Life *Automotive*, 6–8, 18
53 Tariff Board of Canada, *Report of the Tariff Board in Reference No. 91, The Automotive Industry, 1939* (Ottawa: King's Printer, 1939), 1; *Canada Year Book*, 1942, 405–6

CHAPTER 13 *Labour and Capital*

1 J. Williamson, *Did British Capitalism Breed Inequality?* (London and Boston: George Allan and Unwin, 1985).
2 Ontario began the registration of births, deaths, and marriages in 1869, but registration was incomplete for many years. It was thought that in the first full year of registration, 1870, perhaps 20 per cent of the deaths were registered; by the early twentieth century the figure had risen to some 85 per cent (See the *Reports* of the registrar-general, for the calendar year 1870 and for the year ending 31 December 1898 in Ontario *Sessional Papers*; title varies slightly.) It was also thought (ibid., year ending 31 December 1876, 24, 95) that registration was far more complete in urban areas, and that by the mid-1870s a reasonable approximation to full registration of deaths had been attained. The dominion has collected vital statistics only since 1921, although, with the aid of census data, life tables have been calculated for the years 1871, 1881, and 1921. *Canadian Abridged Life Tables, 1871, 1881, 1921, 1931* (Ottawa: Queen's Printer, 1939), and *HSC*, 32, and series B65–B74.
3 For twenty-year-old males the life expectancy in 1871 is said to have been 47.9 years, in 1881, 48 years, in 1921, 49.1 years, and in 1941, 49.57 years; for twenty-year-old females the figures are 47.3 years, 47.8 years, 49.2 years, and 51.76 years. See ibid., series B67, B68.
4 All these data come from the Ontario Registrars-General, *Reports*.
5 In Canada as a whole, the years before World War One saw a considerable reduction in the population per physician (−22 per cent, 1871–1911), per dentist (−70 per cent, 1871–1911), and per nurse (−93 per cent, 1891–1911) (see *HSC*, series B83, B88, B91). The data for Ontario, which can be constructed from census materials, show the same pattern.
6 *Census of Canada*, 1941, vol. IX. This was the first general housing census that had been conducted in or by the dominion. The tabulations distinguish three dwelling locations – farm areas, rural non-farm areas, and urban areas; they also give information about the various sizes of urban areas and about the larger cities and towns. For Ontario, eleven cities and towns are separately identified.
7 A dwelling was defined to be the equivalent of a home or household; rooms occupied by boarders or lodgers were not defined as dwellings. Such persons, therefore, were counted as inhabitants of the dwellings in which they lived.
8 As usual, there is no perfect way to adjust money earnings for changes in the price level. The only available index that covers the forty-year period 1871–1911 is a very unsatisfactory one, in that it covers only fifteen items, all foodstuffs. Also, its weighting system is obscure. As the prices of non-foodstuffs tended, in general, to fall in relation to the prices of foodstuffs, this index understates deflationary

tendencies in living costs and overstates inflationary ones. It is, however, the only available published index that covers the entire period, and the results of applying it are in the right-hand column of table 13.2.

9 Ontario Bureau of Industries, *Report,* 1886, 193.

10 Ibid., table v.

11 Ibid., table xi.

12 A wholesale index of consumer goods prices rises by 17.6 per cent; the Department. of Labour cost of living index rises by 30.8 per cent; Michell's index of fifteen foodstuffs, which may well overstate consumer price movements because foods were rising in price relative to manufactures while perhaps declining in relation to rents, rises by 41 per cent; the Bertram-Percy index, much more sophisticated and conceptually satisfactory, rises by only 22 per cent; Chambers' index rises by 41 per cent from 1891 to 1914, and 50 per cent from 1900 to 1914. See Gordon Bertram and Michael J. Percy, 'Real Wage Trends in Canada 1900–1926,' *Canadian Journal of Economics,* 12 (1979), 307, and Edward Chambers, 'New Evidence on the Living Standards of Toronto Blue Collar Workers in the Pre-1914 Era,' paper presented to the Fourteenth Canadian Quantitative Economic History Conference. 1985. Things are rendered still more complicated because in the cities, especially in Toronto, some elements of living cost did not move in parallel with the province or the country as a whole.

13 Michael J. Piva, *The Condition of the Working Class in Toronto 1900–1921* (Ottawa: University of Ottawa Press, 1979); Board of Enquiry into the Cost of Living, *Report* (Ottawa: King's Printer, 1915)

14 For instance, Piva studied only Toronto and built up his earnings data from a variety of unsatisfactory and unreliable sources, while we are reporting calculations resting on census data that cover the whole province; Piva treated workers both in construction and in manufacturing, while our findings relate only to manufacturing; Piva's cost of living index appears to be less satisfactory than ours.

15 This is the standard that Piva employs.

16 Ontario Bureau of Industries, *Report,* 1887, part iv.

17 These years are in broad respects comparable years in that both were war-time years of considerable but not hysterical prosperity. An average of, say, 1917–20 compared with, say, 1939–41 would reveal the same broad tendency.

18 When businessmen decide to invest more, national output rises. This rise induces an increase in consumption, but this in turn is less than the rise in income. Because almost all wages are spent on consumption and because most profits are not consumed, the 'room' for the increase in investment has to turn up chiefly as an increase in profits, while the increase in wages turns up as an increase in income. Hence in a boom the profit-share is likely to go up, and the wage-share to go down, even though total wages and average wage per worker may be rising strongly. See Ian M. Drummond, *Economics: Principles and Policies in an Open Economy* (Georgetown: Irwin-Dorsey, 1976), 532–8.

19 It will be remembered that because the capital figures come from the *Census of Canada,* they are available only for census years.

20 Coverage as in 1936 census of manufacturing. Beginning in 1917 there are annual

data on capitalization in manufacturing. For the appropriateness of a comparison between 1917 and 1941, see above, n17.

21 There was no upward movement in the general price level between 1917 and 1941. Indeed, the best available price-index (*HSC*, series J65) reports a figure of 120.6 in 1917 and 83.6 in 1941 for 'producers' goods,' a category roughly corresponding to capital goods. Hence these comparisons, if anything, understate the actual changes in real capital and real capital per employee. Sad to say, there is no satisfactory way to adjust the figures for price change; indeed, economists cannot agree as to what 'real capital' might mean. The problem arises in part because the data reflect the reporting practices of businessmen, who may not have been valuing their buildings, equipment, and inventories on a replacement-cost basis. This fact, plus the numerous differences in data-coverage, make it hazardous to infer anything from the magnitudes of apparent changes in capital growth-rates over long periods of time. It is not useful, for instance, to calculate and compare capital growth rates before and after 1914. But it is clear that real capital and capital per employee were moving upward both before and after that date. For the purposes of this chapter that fact is sufficient.

CHAPTER 14 *Protecting the Workers*

1 Commission on the State of the Manufacturing Industries in Ontario and Quebec, *Report, 1885 (Dominion Sessional Paper* 37 of 1885); Royal Commission on the Relations of Labour and Capital in Canada, *Report, 1889*

2 See in particular the various writings of Greg Kealey, Bryan Palmer, and Craig Heron.

3 Eugene Forsey, *Trade Unions in Canada, 1812–1902* (Toronto: University of Toronto Press, 1982), chs 2, 3

4 First, Ottawa adopted an English statute which had the effect of making union activity legal. Then it amended the master and servant statutes so that no employer could bring criminal action against a striker. These changes followed pressure from unions, and the latter change followed from the actions of the Grand Trunk Railway, which, in 1877, arranged for the criminal prosecution of its striking engine drivers.

5 30 Vic c 26. The measure provided for the arbitration of non-wage matters in a fashion that could be both cheap and simple, keeping such disputes out of the ordinary courts. The model, obviously enough, was the common provision for the arbitration of contractual disputes between or among businesses. Under the statutes the awards of a board were 'final and conclusive'; they could not be appealed, but they could be enforced like any other arbitrative judgment. See in particular sections 2, 11, 12.

6 Ontario Bureau of Industries, *Report,* 1886, 230, 24–8

7 57 Vic c 42, sections 21, 22 and form F. Unions helped elect the employee members of these bodies, and in various aspects of the arrangements a union might represent employees, but the law gave no special status to unions, nor did it provide for collective bargaining or for union-recognition. Nothing was said about strikes or lock-outs. In 1897, however, mayors were told to notify the registrar when a strike

or lockout occurred, and the arbitrators were told to try to communicate with both parties to bring such disputes to an end. It should be observed that under the 1894 statute the province was perfectly willing to arrange for conciliation or arbitration on the railways, even though these were within the dominion's sphere of jurisdiction. This fact illustrates the obscurity that long surrounded the question of jurisdiction in labour matters. When the dominion set up its own Labour Department in 1900, Ontario had already had a registrar of councils of conciliation and arbitration for more than five years. Indeed, William Lyon Mackenzie King, who is often credited with having invented conciliation in Canada, was still a Toronto undergraduate when Ontario passed the relevant statute in 1894.

8 69 Vic c 25, and 2 Edw VII c 22

9 10 Edw VII c 74

10 H.D. Woods and S. Ostry, *Labour Policy and Labour Economics in Canada* (Toronto: Macmillan, 1962), 22. The dominion's 1927 measure covered 'any work, undertaking, or business which is within the legislative authority of the Parliament of Canada,' but defined this coverage to include 'works, undertakings, or businesses of any company or corporation incorporated by or under the authority of the Parliament of Canada' – a much broader coverage than in 1907, apart altogether from the provisions by which provinces could opt in.

11 There were still no provisions to ensure that workers could organize themselves into unions without facing harassment from employers, nor were employers yet required to bargain in good faith. There was no arrangement for the orderly choice of a bargaining agent. Woods and Ostry (ibid., 23) may give some readers the erroneous impression that the Ontario Industrial Standards Act did or said something useful about collective bargaining.

12 37 Vic 34, 57 Vic c 48

13 See *Revised Statutes of Ontario, 1897*, c. 157, incorporating amendments of 1886. This measure of 1873 provided that employers could not make arbitrary or unilateral changes in the terms of employment, and that with specified exceptions contracts made with non-residents would not be binding on such employees. Furthermore, if wages were not paid, employees were offered comparatively cheap justice before a police magistrate, who could make an order not only for the payment of wages but also for costs. In such cases, if no specific rates of wages had been agreed, the magistrate could fix the wage rate. Employees could not waive the protection of the act; verbal contracts could not bind for more than a year, or written contracts for more than nine. In the same year the Mechanics' Lien Act established that everyone who worked on construction projects or installations of any sort should have a 'lien or charge for the price or value of such work' for a period of ninety days.

14 In 1885 wage and salary obligations were given priority in any assignment for the benefit of creditors, and at the winding-up of a joint-stock company. In 1891 woodsmen's wages, and in 1985 street railwaymen's wages, were given similar protection and priority. In 1896 there were special measures to protect the wages of people who worked on the execution of provincial projects, and in 1899 came a measure to secure wage claims against the estates of deceased persons. In later years such provisions were extended and repeated in various statutes. See 36 Vic c

27, 54 Vic c 22; *Revised Statutes of Ontario, 1897*, c 156, 208; 59 Vic c 27; 62 Vic(2) c 17; 10 Edw VII c 71.

15 The measure established that all workmen except domestic or menial servants had the right to compensation whenever employer negligence caused injury. But the measure did not apply to certain railways that had made provision through provident societies for compensation, and it required the injured workers to sue in the ordinary courts. See 49 Vic c 28.

16 62 Vic(2) c 18

17 The measure, 4 Geo v c 25, created a board that was to distribute benefits in accord with detailed statute specifications, providing for burial, surviving widows, and dependent children, as well as for disability whole or partial. There could be no appeal from the board's judgments; an accident fund was to be accumulated; industrial diseases, deaths, maimings, and incapacity temporary or permanent, total or partial, were all covered. The measure, which repealed the 1886 statute, did not cover farm labourers or domestic servants, and it applied only to those manufacturing and mining industries specified in it. None the less, the coverage was broad enough to include all the hazardous trades, as well as many that were reasonably save. On the background to the measure see R.C.B. Risk, '"This Nuisance of Litigation": The Origins of Workmen's Compensation in Ontario,' in David H. Flaherty, ed., *Essays in the History of Canadian Law* II (Toronto: University of Toronto Press for the Osgoode Society, 1983), 418–491.

18 In 1916 injured employees lost all remaining rights to bring action against employers in the ordinary courts, but at the same time the Board acquired the power to require deposits from employers; later measures provided for medical care, forbade employee contributions, extended coverage to sufferers from silicosis, and made for further provision for extra-Ontarian accidents.

19 Ontario Bureau of Industries, *Report*, 1886, 249–50

20 Forsey, *Trade Unions*, 438

21 47 Vic c 33. The measure applied only to places that employed more than twenty people and that used mechanical power. It forbade the employment of 'any child, young girl, or woman' in any way such that the 'the health of such child, young girl or woman is likely to be permanently injured'; it prohibited the employment of any boy under twelve years of age, or any girl under fourteen, in any factory; it insisted that no child, young girl, or woman should work more than sixty hours per week, not including a statutory hour at midday for meals, and it prohibited the use of child, teenage, and female labour for certain tasks in connection with moving machinery and cleaning equipment. Exceptions were possible, as required by the 'customs or exigencies of certain trades,' or by accident or breakdown, but in no circumstances was any woman, young girl, or child to work more than 71.5 hours per week for more than six weeks per year, nor was work to begin before six a.m. or to continue after nine p.m. Factories were to be clean, well ventilated, and sanitary; there were to be a 'sufficient number and description of privies,' grouped by sex. Every factory was to fence its moving parts, shafts, and wells. There was to be fire-extinguishing equipment.

22 51 Vic c 33. Again there were limitations on the hours of work for young people; local councils received the authority to regulate hours of opening and closing.

23 58 Vic c 50

24 22 Geo v c 35

25 53 Vic c 10; 19 Geo v c 15; 20 Geo v c 8. As with the factory and shop acts, there were numerous amending statutes not noted here.

26 10–11 Geo v c 87

27 The board specified minimum weekly wages, in the first instance, for women in Toronto laundries, dry-cleaning, and dye works. The scale distinguished between women on the bases of age and experience. Next came minimum wages for females in Toronto manufacturing and retailing. Outside Toronto there was soon a scale – a rather lower one – for laundresses and retail clerks. The minima, which were always differentiated according to the size of the city or town, were extended year by year to cover additional industries, smaller cities, and various service trades.

28 25 Geo v c 28

29 Ontario *Sessional Papers*, LXIX, part III, 1937, 47, for early proceedings under the act; for the general power to fix minimum wages, 1 Geo VI c 43, and for the further extension of the Industrial Standards Act, 1 Geo VI, c 32.

30 See in particular Craig Heron, 'The Crisis of the Craftsman: Hamilton's Metal Workers in the Early Twentieth Century,' in Michael Cross and Gregory S. Kealey, eds., *The Consolidation of Capitalism, 1896–1929: Readings in Canadian Social History*, VI (Toronto: Lorimer, c. 1983).

31 As in Gregory S. Kealey and Bryan Palmer, *Dreaming of What Might Be* (Oxford University Press, 1982), and 'The Bonds of Unity and the Knights of Labour in Ontario, 1880–1900,' *Histoire Sociale/Social History*, 14: 28 (November 1981), 369–411. See also Forsey, *Trade Unions*, Ch. 7, Desmond Morton, 'The *Globe* and the Labour Question: Ontario "Liberalism" in the "Great Upheaval," May 1886,' *Ontario History*, 73:2 (March 1981), 19–39.

32 Forsey, *Trade Unions*, 141

33 Kealey and Palmer, 'Bonds,' 382. The Kealey-Palmer calculations respecting the number of Knights, and their quantitative significance, have been criticized by Michael J. Piva, in ' "The Bonds of Unity:" A Comment,' *Histoire Sociale/Social History*, 16:31 (May 1983), 169–74; in rebuttal, Kealey and Palmer admitted that they used category titles carelessly and that they mildly exaggerated the quantitative significance of the order, but they continued to maintain that the Knights were very important. See ' "Bonds," Some Further Comments,' in idem, 175–89.

34 Forsey, *Trade Unions*, 146; Kealey and Palmer, ' "Bonds",' 388; Morton, 'Globe,' 20

35 This method of calculation is essentially that of Piva. For Kealey-Palmer's criticisms of it, which do not appear to be persuasive, see the works cited above, n33.

36 As Kealey-Palmer claim for St Thomas, Kingston, and the Lincoln, Niagara, and Welland region. See 'Bonds,' 389–90.

37 Forsey, *Trade Unions*, 144–5

38 Ibid., 144–6

39 Ontario Bureau of Labor [sic], *Report*, 1903

40 We have assumed that the average membership of each non-reporting union is the same as the average membership of each union that did report its membership. In 1911–13 only 58 per cent of identified unions reported membership, but in 1927–9

the percentage was 83, and in 1938–40, 93. Adjustment, therefore, is urgently required if the membership series is to be at all useful.

41 In 1919, 39,375 Ontarians were involved in strikes. Thus the chance of a city worker being on strike was roughly 5 per cent. In 1937, 24,073 Ontarians went on strike, but by 1941 the province's non-agricultural labour force was 1,185,000; thus the chance of strike-involvement in 1937 was roughly 2 per cent – much lower than in 1919. In 1891 the number of days lost per non-agricultural Ontario worker was 0.863, while in 1921 it was 0.668, in 1931, 0.061, and in 1939, 0.054. Interpolating between census years we can estimate that for 1919 the figure is 1.286, for 1929, 0.83, and for 1937 – the peak year for days lost in the late 1930s – 0.222.

42 It is never quite clear whether the working folk would remember these events if the labour historians did not enjoy writing about them.

43 The 1872 strike of Toronto printers is said to have hastened the passage of the Dominion Trades Union Act of the same year. In the 1880s there were numerous strikes, largely orchestrated by the Knights of Labour (see above, n31). The 1891 strike of Ottawa saw-mill and lumber-yard workers kept 2,400 men off work for more than six weeks, accounting for 83 per cent of all the days lost through strike action in Ontario that year. There were extended but unsuccessful strikes among Toronto building tradesmen in the 1890s, and the construction workers at Niagara Falls struck with greater success. In 1907 there was extensive strike activity among mining and quarry workers, where 3,000 men were on strike, while in Toronto the Bell telephone operators struck to defend their schedule of working hours. In 1908 there was a nation-wide strike of CPR shop employees, and in 1910 1,500 Toronto painters from 150 firms struck successfully for higher wages, and 1,500 builders' labourers struck less successfully to the same end. Thus the building trades accounted for 91 per cent of the days lost through strike action in 1910; the nation-wide Grand Trunk strike, by comparison, involved few Ontarians and little lost labour. In 1912–13 there were extended strikes among garment workers in Toronto and Hamilton. In 1917 Toronto's street railway employees struck for increased wages. In 1918 there was a dramatic increase in strike activity among miners, the metals trades, shipbuilders, garment workers, meat packers, and street railway employees, among many other trades and industries. These strikes, which pushed time lost to exceptionally high figures, were generally related to questions of wages and hours; they were often but by no means always successful. The same general patterns continued in 1920–1, although strikes were fewer and far less time was lost. In 1923 – harbinger of things to come after 1960 – there was a widespread strike of postal workers, which accounted for more than a quarter of the days lost through strike action in that year. In 1925–6 there was trouble among clothing workers, and in 1926–9, among paper and lumber workers, most noticeably among pulpwood cutters, whose strike action was significantly more successful in 1926–8 than in 1929. Given the movement of the business cycle, 14 October 1929 was not an auspicious date on which to begin strike action! In 1930–2, as the Depression deepened, strikes became comparatively rare, and little time was lost through them. Nevertheless, in 1931 there were major strikes among Toronto clothiers and hatters. They accounted for 87 per cent of all the time lost through strikes in that year. The workers wanted higher wages and shorter hours; not

surprisingly, given the general economic conditions of the time, their success was only partial. The same was true in 1933, when another wave of strikes occurred in the Toronto and Hamilton clothing trades. In 1933–5 there were important strikes among pulpwood cutters and loggers, and also in the garment trades, these two groups accounting for most of the strike activity. In 1936–8 textile workers became restive, accounting in 1936 for 67 per cent of the time lost through strikes, and in 1937 for 48 per cent – a higher proportion than could be assigned to the famous General Motors strike of the same year. And although most strikes were still about wages, in 1934–8 24 per cent of all Ontario strikes were about the granting of a union agreement or about union recognition – a strong indication that there would soon have to be some change in the inherited voluntarist legal framework.

44 See, for instance, James A. Pendergast, 'The Attempt at Unionization in the Automobile Industry in Canada, 1928,' *Ontario History*, 70 (1978), 245–62, and James D. Leach, 'The Workers' Unity League and the Stratford Furniture Workers: The Anatomy of a Strike,' *Ontario History*, 60 (1968), 39–48.

CHAPTER 15 *The Older Means of Transport and Communication: Rail, Water, and the Early Electric Media*

1 On the development of the national trunk lines see: H.A. Innis, *A History of the Canadian Pacific Railway* (London: King, 1923); W.Kaye Lamb, *A History of the Canadian Pacific Railway* (New York: Macmillan, 1977); A.W. Currie, *The Grand Trunk Railway of Canada* (Toronto: University of Toronto Press, 1957); G.R. Stevens, *Canadian National Railways* (Toronto: McClelland and Stewart, 1960–2); G.B. de T. Glazebrook, *A History of Transportation in Canada* (New Haven: Yale University Press, 1938).

2 The story of this line has been told by T.D. Regehr, *The Canadian Northern Railway: Pioneer Road of the Canadian Prairies* (Toronto: Macmillan of Canada and the Maclean-Hunter Press, 1976).

3 William John Wilgus, *The Railway Interrelations of the United States and Canada* (New Haven: Yale University Press, 1937), 165–74

4 See above, chapters 4, 5.

5 Employment data are from *Census* volumes. For the industrial activities of the railways, see Paul Craven and Tom Traves, 'Canadian Railways as Manufacturers, 1850–1880,' Canadian Historical Association, *Historical Papers*, 1983, 254–81.

6 Regehr, *Canadian Northern*, chs 1,2, 13, 14

7 Peat, Marwick, Mitchell and Co., *Canadian Northern Railway System: Investigation of Accounts as at 30 June 1916*, prepared at the request of the Minister for Railways and Canals (mimeographed and blueprinted) (Ottawa: the Department, 1916)

8 See above, chapter 5, and below, chapter 17.

9 See chapter 11 above, and McDowall, *Steel*, for more discussion of the career of Clergue. Discussion of the railway is at 33ff.

10 O.S. Nock, *Algoma Central Railway* (Sault Ste Marie: the company, 1975), 24–39, 57, 62

11 Albert Tucker, *Steam into Wilderness: Ontario Northland Railway, 1902–1962*

(Toronto: Fitzhenry and Whiteside, 1978), 2–10, 14, 33, 36, 84, 87–9; Patrick Hughes, 'Ontario Northland Railway: Root of a Mini-Empire,' *Laurentian University Review*, 13:2 (February 1981), 81–93

12 See below, chapter 19.

13 Data on railway mileage are to be found in various issues of the *Canada Year Book*. See also table 15.1.

14 For the plan see R. Louis Gentilcore and C. Grant Head, *Ontario's History in Maps* (Toronto: University of Toronto Press, 1983), map 6.31.

15 Information on the Ontario register of shipping comes from the Dominion Department of Marine *Supplements* for the period 1874–1911, and from the *Canada Year Books* for later years. It should be remembered that Ontario-registered ships did not have a lake monopoly. Montreal-registered ships could and did ascend the St Lawrence canals, while American ships were involved in traffic between the ports of the two countries even though Canadian law excluded them from Canada's own 'coasting trade.'

16 E.B. Ogle, *Long Distance, Please* (Toronto: Collins, 1979), esp. 27–8, 37, 41; Graham D. Taylor, 'Charles Sise, Bell Canada, and the Americans: A Study of Managerial Autonomy, 1880–1905,' Canadian Historical Association, *Historical Papers*, 1982, 11–30; Christopher Armstrong and H.V. Nelles, *Monopoly's Moment* (Philadelphia: Temple University Press, 1986), esp. part two

17 Canada, House of Commons, Select Committee on Telephone Systems, *Proceedings* (1905), 404–541

18 Dominion *Sessional Paper* 20d of 1913

19 See Armstrong and Nelles, *Moment*, esp. parts three and four.

20 Ibid., ch. 2

21 *Canada Year Book*, 1915, 485

22 John F. Due, *The Intercity Electric Railway Industry in Canada* (Toronto: University of Toronto Press, 1966), 47, 61–95

CHAPTER 16 *Roads, Airways, and Airwaves: Changing Modes of Communication in the Twentieth Century*

1 For instance, in the mid-1870s it was provided that dung-carts could pass over toll roads without paying. See 57 Vic c 46 and 58 Vic c 31. Other legislation appears in 30 Vic c 41, 35 Vic c 33, and 3 Edw VII c 14.

2 H.V. Nelles and C. Armstrong, *The Revenge of the Methodist Bicycle Company* (Toronto: Peter Martin Associates, c. 1977), 169

3 *HSC*, series s231

4 2 Geo v c 11,12

5 Regularized by statute in 1915, under 5 Geo v c 18

6 5 Geo v c 17, esp. section 28

7 7 Geo v c 16

8 Ontario Department of Highways, *Report*, 1920, 47

9 Ontario Department of Highways, *Reports*, various years; *HSC*, series s231

10 One such is reproduced in Gentilcore and Head, *Ontario's History in Maps*, map 6.11.

11 See Statistics Canada, *Aviation in Canada, 1971*, esp. 17, 24; *Canada Year Books;* C.A. Ashley, *Trans-Canada Air Lines* (Toronto: Macmillan, 1965), and Robert Bothwell and William Kilbourn, *C.D. Howe* (Toronto: Macmillan, 1977).

12 Frank Peers, *The Politics of Canadian Broadcasting* (Toronto: University of Toronto Press, 1969), 18–21

13 See K.J. Rea, *Prosperous Years,* 80

14 A precise number can be provided, because each owner of a receiving set was supposed to pay a licence fee. In so far as they did not do so, there were even more radios than the figures suggest.

CHAPTER 17 *The Revolution in Ontario Commerce*

1 See Careless, *Toronto,* ch. 4, and Weaver, *Hamilton,* chs 2, 3.

2 Public Archives of Canada, *Henry Elliott Papers,* vol. 6, 5963–86

3 Ibid., vol. 8, 6379, 6382, 6410–6472

4 *Canadian Grocer* (hereafter cited as *CG*), 5 October 1894, 29

5 *CG,* 7 October 1892, 8

6 *CG,* 17 October 1890, 3; 2 October 1891, 10

7 As at Sarnia; see *CG,* 18 September 1891, 16.

8 Careless, *Toronto,* 115

9 Ibid., 133

10 Brenda Newall, 'From Cloth to Clothing,' MA thesis, Trent University, 1984, 87

11 *Hamilton,* 96–7

12 Newall, 'Cloth,' 87

13 Careless, *Toronto,* 115–7

14 William Stephenson, *The Store that Timothy Built* (Toronto: McClelland and Stewart, 1969), 43

15 *Golden Jubilee 1869–1919: A Book to Commemorate the Fiftieth Anniversary of the T. Eaton Co.* (Toronto: the company, 1922?), 184–98

16 Newall, 'Cloth,' passim

17 Ibid., 18, 24–5, 32, 49, 95–9; *Golden Jubilee,* 57

18 *CG,* 1 July 1898, 38

19 Newall, 'Cloth,' 142

20 *Golden Jubilee;* C.L. Burton, *A Sense of Urgency* (Toronto: Clarke Irwin, 1952), 160

21 Stephenson, *Store,* 44, 84

22 The Freiman family has deposited a large mass of material in the Public Archives of Canada, but in that material there is nothing respecting the early history of the business.

23 *CG,* 1 February 1895

24 Canada, Royal Commission on Price Spreads, *Minutes of Proceedings and Evidence* (hereafter cited as *RCPS*), 590–4, 607–9; John P. Nichols, *Skyline Queen and the Merchant Prince: The Woolworth Story* (New York: Trident Press, 1973), 73–8; James Brough, *The Woolworths* (New York: McGraw Hill, 1982), 5–12

25 *RCPS,* 707

26 Ibid., 681

27 *CG*, 13 April 1928, 57; 9 November 1928, 35; 29 March 1929, 33
28 Canada, House of Commons, *Special Committee on Price Spreads and Mass Buying, Proceedings and Evidence* (hereafter *SCPS*), 2741, reports that the purchase took place in 1904.
29 Burton, *Sense*, 155–60
30 *CG*, 10 August 1917, 24–5
31 *SCPS*, 3053; *RCPS*, 1360–1
32 *SCPS*, 3068
33 *SCPS*, 3056
34 *SCPS*, 3053
35 *CG*, 15 March 1929, 42; C.H. Cheasley, *The Chain Store Movement in Canada* (Orillia: Packett-Times Press, 1930), 66–77
36 *SCPS*, 3056
37 Cheasley, *Chain Store*, 72
38 *SCPS*, 2743–5
39 Bliss, *Millionaire*, 391, 443–4, 490–4
40 Burton, *Sense*, 230–1
41 *SCPS*, 3091, 3104, 3476, 3130–1, 3380, 3476
42 *SCPS*, 2754–5, 2773
43 *RCPS*, 1197–99
44 Alan Wilson, *John Northway: A Blue Serge Canadian* (Toronto: Burns and MacEachern, 1965), 62–75
45 Bliss, *Millionaire*, 34, 111ff
46 Weaver, *Hamilton*, 91
47 *CG*, 15 October 1909, 83
48 *CG*, 19 March 1909, 27; 17 November 1916, 21
49 *CG*, 19 March 1920, 29ff
50 *CG*, 7 May 1920, 165
51 Canada, House of Commons, *Proceedings of the Special Committee appointed for the Purpose of Enquiring as to the Prices ... (Journals of the House of Commons,* vol. LV, part 2: appendix, no. 7, 1919 (Ottawa: King's Printer, 1919) (hereafter cited as *COL*), 908, 911
52 *COL*, 203–9, 277–83, 394–441
53 *COL*, 125, 138, 145, 151–2, 168–71, 203–9, 243–75
54 *COL*, 260–72, 436–7, 446, 668–9, 674–6, 772, 899, 908, 911
55 Bertram T. Huston, 'The Chain Store,' *Queen's Quarterly* (Spring 1929), 314–5
56 *CG*, 1 February 1918, 25
57 *CG*, 26 December 1919, 28–9
58 *CG*, 9 December 1929, 37; 30 January 1931, 17; 13 February 1931, 32; 8 May 1931, 26
59 *CG*, 30 August 1929, 32; 11 October 1929, 16; 22 November 1929, 29
60 Data compiled from *CG*. Carroll incorporated only in 1931; the corporate and financial history of Arnold and Stop and Shop formed one of the more dramatic financial sagas of the late 1920s. See *RCPS*, 941, 991.
61 *RCPS*, 789, 874, 941
62 It is not possible to mention all the buying groups of the period, but it may be useful

to refer to a few of the largest, most influential, and best known. In 1919 sixty Toronto retailers formed the York Trading Company, and those firms took stock in the concern, calling themselves Superior Stores. In 1924, Adanac Stores was formed by twenty-five Toronto retail grocers who wanted to make bulk purchases once a week; by 1927 most of Adanac supplies came through one wholesaler, Jas Lumbers Co. The next year forty Toronto grocers set up the Leader Group. Meanwhile, in 1925, there was a merger of twenty-five wholesale grocery houses to form National Grocers Company, which was said to handle 70 per cent of the province's wholesale grocery business. The new firm quickly became a power in the provisioning of the buying groups: by 1928 it controlled Leader, Supreme, Maple Leaf, and Red and White, and in 1930 it had 549 outlets with a turnover of $16.5 million. York Trading, for its part, had also expanded greatly: in 1930 it had 892 outlets with a turnover of $18.5 million. *CG*, 13 October 1922, 27; 4 April 1924, 36; 20 March 1925, 19; 14 August 1925, 1; 21 August 1925, 1; 28 August 1925, 1; 9 October 1925, 25; 24 June 1927, 18–19; 25 May 1928, 40; 26 April 1929, 98

63 *CG*, 19 March 1920, 29
64 *CG*, 10 March 1933, 14; 21 April 1933, 25; 15 September 1930, 42; 1 January 1940, 24; 1 January 1939, 26
65 *CG*, 13 November 1936, 29
66 H.H. Hannam, *Pulling Together for Twenty-Five Years: A Brief Story of Events and People in the United Farmers' Movement in Ontario During the Quarter Century 1914–1939* (Toronto: United Farmers of Ontario, 1940)
67 *CG*, 20 February 1915, 19–20; for a subscription co-op, *CG*, 26 October 1923, 17
68 Hannam, *Pulling*, 51–2
69 See *CG*, 5 September 1902, 44, for information about the Grocers' Wholesale Company which several prominent Hamilton retailers assembled.
70 *RCPS*, 1243, 1357
71 *RCPS*, 1405, 1413–4
72 *COL*, 260–72, 436–7, 446, 668–9, 674–6, 772, 899, 908, 911
73 *RCPS*, 3570, 3366
74 Huston, 'Chain Store,' 313; Cheasley, *Chain Store*, 20
75 Huston, 'Chain Store,' 319–20
76 Lloyd Reynolds, 'Some Notes on the Distributive Trades in Canada,' *Canadian Journal of Economics and Political Science*, 4:4 (1938), 545–7; see also Huston, 'Chain Store,' 321.
77 Huston, 'Chain Store,' 313–4
78 *RCPS*, 2725
79 *RCPS*, 2851
80 Figures compiled from *Lovell's Province of Ontario Directory for 1871 containing Names of Professional and Business Men ...* (Montreal: Lovell, 1871)
81 *CG*, 14 March 1890, 1; 7 October 1892, 8
82 Ontario, *Report on the Operation of the Liquor Licensing Acts*, 1916, schedule G
83 *CG*, 14 March 1890, 1
84 The data regularly appeared, on an all-Canada basis, in the *Canada Year Book*.
85 Some months later the dominion would use its wartime powers to effect a more

stringent prohibition, but nation-wide prohibition was a wartime expedient which would lapse soon after the end of hostilities, having lasted less than two years.

86 6 Geo v 1916 c 50
87 10–11 Geo v c 80
88 24 Geo v c 26, part IIIA, s 69a
89 Compiled from *Lovell's Directory* and from Dominion Bureau of Statistics, *Censuses of Distribution,* 1930 and 1941
90 Dominion Bureau of Statistics, *The Control and Sale of Liquor in Canada* (Ottawa: Queen's Printer, 1942), 14, 19
91 *Census,* 1941, vol. x, 88
92 Consumption data from Dominion Bureau of Statistics, *Control and Sale,* 19
93 Dominion Bureau of Statistics, *Control and Sale,* 19
94 The statistical material in this section has been assembled from Canada, *Census* of 1870–1; *Lovell's Directory;* Dominion Bureau of Statistics, *Census of Trading Establishments 1924* (data apply to 1923), tables 13, 14, 15, 19; *Census of Merchandising and Service Establishments, 1931* (data apply to 1930), tables 1, 1A, 2, 10; *Census of Merchandising and Service Establishments, 1941* (data apply to 1941), tables 1, 3, 5, 13.
95 It will be remembered that blacksmiths, harness makers, and boot and shoemakers have already been counted in retail merchandising, but they can properly be included here as well, so long as one does not add the figures from this paragraph to the preceding one.
96 For example, in Brantford the first 'flicker' was shown in Bertram Allan's general store; the next year Allan built a 'Theatorium,' and in 1908 he opened the Lyric Theatre. C.M. Johnston, *Brant County: A History 1784–1945* (Toronto: Oxford University Press, 1967), 131. In 1919 the Brant Theatre, which cost $250,000, was opened. F. Douglas Revile, *History of the County of Brant* (Brantford: Hurley Printing Company, 1920), 172.

CHAPTER 18 *Financial Evolution*

1 Under the Dominion Bank Act of 1870. For the transitional arrangements immediately following Confederation see R. Craig McIvor, *Canadian Monetary, Banking, and Fiscal Development* (Toronto: Macmillan, 1958), 67–9.
2 Victor Ross, *History of the Canadian Bank of Commerce* (Toronto: Oxford University Press, 1920), II, 17
3 Ibid., II, 54ff
4 Ibid., I, 237–45
5 *The Dominion Bank* (Toronto: privately printed, 1922), 32–37–8, 56. The commercial backgrounds of the several founders, and the complex negotiations respecting the creation of the new bank, are told in somewhat more detail by Joseph Schull, *One Hundred Years of Banking in Canada* (Toronto: Copp Clark, 1958), ch. 5. The Dominion Bank opened in Vancouver in 1907, in London, England, in 1911, and in New York, only in 1919, while it extended its branch network to the Maritime provinces only in 1922.
6 Ross, *History,* II, 76–78

7 *Dominion Bank,* 45; Ross, *History,* II, 76–7

8 Naylor, *Canadian Business,* II, 243

9 The Standard was absorbed by the Bank of Commerce after World War One, and the Imperial, in the 1950s, followed the same path, while the Bank of Ottawa was acquired in 1919 by the Bank of Nova Scotia. On the 'flickering existence' of the Royal Canadian Bank, and the unsuccessful attempt to merge it with the Dominion Bank, see *Dominion Bank,* 32.

10 *Garland's Banks, Bankers, and Banking in Canada* (Ottawa: Methuen, 1890), 42

11 Joseph Schull and J. Douglas Gibson, *The Scotiabank Story* (Toronto: Macmillan, 1982), 19. The Metropolitan was absorbed in 1914 and the Bank of Ottawa in 1919.

12 Schull, *100 Years,* 89–114

13 Ross, *History,* I, 345–9

14 Ibid., I, 119–20, 158, 309–404

15 Naylor, *Canadian Business,* II, 240, 254

16 Ross, *History,* II, 19–25

17 *Dominion Bank,* 32–8

18 Schull, *100 Years,* 39–44, 71

19 Schull and Gibson, *Scotiabank,* 115

20 Ibid., 123

21 McIvor, *Canadian Monetary,* 77; B.E. Walker, *A History of Banking in Canada* (Toronto: privately printed, 1909), 100

22 E.P. Neufeld, *The Financial System of Canada* (Toronto: Macmillan, 1972), ch. 6. See also McIvor, *Canadian Monetary,* 86–101.

23 *Garland's Banks,* 43–5

24 *Strathroy Centennial 1860–1960* (n.p., n.d.)

25 Nick and Melma Mika, *Trenton, City of Promise* (Belleville: Mika, 1979), 55

26 Hazel C. Mathews, *Oakville and the Sixteen* (Toronto: University of Toronto Press, 1953), 432–3

27 Norman Robertson, *History of the County of Bruce* (Toronto: William Briggs, 1906), 139–40.

28 Neufeld, *Financial System,* 173–4. The adventures of Joseph C. Graham may not be unique or untypical. In 1891 he opened the first bank in Tiverton, but in 1897 he suddenly closed the bank and absconded with the money. See Tiverton Centennial Book Committee, *A Historic Album of Tiverton* (Tiverton: the committee, 1979).

29 *Financial System,* chs 3, 7, 9

30 Ibid., 242–6, 257

31 Drummond, 'Canadian Life Insurance Companies,' 204–24

32 Neufeld, *Financial System,* 233

33 G.R. Stevens, *The Canada Permanent Story* (Toronto: privately printed, 1955), 18–19; Basil Skodyn, *The Permanent Story* (Toronto: privately printed, 1980), 14

34 See Easterbrook, *Farm Credit.*

35 Ibid., 29–30

36 Annual Report of the Company, as reported in *Monetary Times,* 1899–1900, 1118

37 Annual Report, as reported in *Monetary Times,* 1898–99, 1127

38 Canada, Royal Commission on Insurance, *Minutes of Evidence* (Ottawa: King's Printer, 1906), 1126–7
39 Ibid., 906–7
40 Skodyn, *Permanent,* 19
41 Easterbrook, *Farm Credit,* 29–30
42 60 Vic c 38
43 63 Vic c 27, s 6(c)
44 3 Edw VII c 16 s 2
45 35 Vic c 83
46 Skodyn, *Permanent,* 40–1
47 Bliss, *Millionaire,* 60ff
48 Neufeld, *Financial System,* 294–5
49 *Canada Today, 1911,* 190, 194, 197; *The Times* (London, England), 25 March 1914, for a prospectus
50 *Stock Exchange Yearbook,* 1915, 784
51 Neufeld, *Financial System,* 297ff
52 60 Vic c 36, esp. section 12
53 2 Geo v c 34
54 Neufeld, *Financial System,* 298
55 *Monetary Times,* 13 March 1914, 37
56 4–5 Geo v c 55; see also Neufeld, *Financial System,* 299. Only in 1922, by 12–13 Geo v c 31, 51 were the rules of the 1914 statutes extended to cover all trust and mortgage companies.
57 This section incorporates material from and relies upon the author's unpublished doctoral dissertation, 'Capital Markets in Canada and Australia 1895–1914,' Yale University, 1959.
58 Neufeld, *Financial System,* 470
59 Ibid., 485
60 For a detailed account of the data and their compilation see Drummond, 'Capital Markets,' appendix. The flows are understated rather than overstated, especially with respect to common stock.
61 See detailed lists in *Canada Today,* 1910 and thereafter.
62 Canada, Royal Commission on Price Spreads, *Report* (Ottawa: King's Printer, 1935), 32. Of eighty-seven consolidations between 1900 and 1920, 22 per cent had to liquidate or reorganize within four years.
63 Ibid., 28, 331. The figure refers to paid-up capital based on par values.
64 From F. Field's compilation in *Monetary Times Annual Review,* January 1913, 76, 206. It appears that in most years some two-thirds of all mergers' public issues were floated abroad.
65 On Canadian Cycle and Motor see *Monetary Times,* 4 April 1902, 1296, and 13 November 1903, 612; on Toronto trams and utilities, ibid., 28 March 1908, 1643, and *Stock Exchange Year Book,* 1913, 570; on mergers in the electrical industries, J. Castell Hopkins, *Canadian Annual Review* (Toronto: Annual Review Publishing Co.), 1910, 40–4, and H. Marshall et al., *Canadian-American Industry,* 72; on fish-packing, where the Bank of Commerce assisted the merger activities of R. Bell-Irving, see United Kingdom, Dominions Royal Commission, *Evidence* (Cd. 8459), 1343.

66 For instances see *Monetary Times,* 21 May 1910, 2120, and 9 January 1914, 155. One affected firm was Ogilvie Flour Mills, which had large Ontario operations.

67 This was true of the first Electrical Development Company bond-issue in 1903, of the Canada Cement issue in 1909, and of an issue of American traction securities that A.E. Ames brought to Toronto. See *Moody's Magazine,* 8 (August 1909), 152, and (November 1909), 317.

68 Compiled from *Stock Exchange Year Book* and *Annual Financial Review, Canadian.*

69 Ibid., 339–40; *Monetary Times,* 30 September 1904, 422, and 30 December 1904, 850. Among the purchasers were Canada Life and Manufacturers Life, the creatures, respectively, of Cox and Mackenzie.

70 Hopkins, *Canadian Annual Review,* 1903, 500

71 Royal Commission on Insurance, *Evidence,* 124–5

72 Ibid., 1032

73 Examples in ibid., 161–2, 339, 1189

74 Examples in ibid., 320–1, 1164

75 *Monetary Times,* 24 April 1914, 9

76 Excess issue was permitted between 10 October and 31 January, so as to assist in crop-moving, but this excess was limited in amount.

77 J.F. Johnson, *Canadian Banking System* (Washington: Government Printing Office, 1910), 65–6

78 For information about the pressure on circulation and the motives that lay behind new issues see the annual reports of the principal banks, especially the Bank of Commerce and the Bank of Montreal.

79 Superintendent of Insurance, in House of Commons Select Standing Committee on Banking and Commerce, *Proceedings,* 1924, 188

80 26 April 1913, 761

81 Select Standing Committee on Banking and Commerce, *Proceedings,* 1913, 489

82 Annual Reports of Dominion Bank, 1911 and 1913

83 Between 1900 and 1910, $3.6 million was raised by private placement, and $2.2 million by public issues of bank stock.

84 Hopkins, *Canadian Annual Review,* 1902, 316; Dominion Department of Finance, *Lists of Shareholders in Chartered Banks* at 31 December 1902 and 31 December 1903, in Dominion *Sessional Papers.*

85 For instance, after its chartering in 1901 the Sovereign Bank raised $1 million by selling shares to J.P. Morgan and to the Dresdner Bank. See *Monetary Times,* 25 January 1908, 1213, and 18 July 1908, 112–3.

86 Union Trust Company of Detroit held large blocks of shares in the Bank of Commerce, the Metropolitan Bank, and the Imperial Bank. Some American individuals also held large amounts. Department of Finance, *Lists of Shareholders.*

87 Benjamin Haggott Beckhart, *Foreign Banking Systems* (New York: Holt, 1929), 320

88 As noted in the Dominion Royal Commission on Banking, *Report* (Ottawa: King's Printer, 1933), 27.

89 In the *Canadian Year-Book,* 1903, 254, the Ames advertisement mentions both bond-broking and banking.

90 On the Ames collapse, and on the securities-dealings which had been financed by the taking of deposits, see *Monetary Times,* 15 January 1904, 912.

91 Royal Commission to Enquire into and Report upon the Affairs of the Home Bank of Canada, *Report* (Ottawa: King's Printer, 1924)

92 Royal Commission on Insurance, *Evidence*, 1397, 1402, and *Report*, 95–7

93 Royal Commission on Insurance, *Evidence*, 970

94 Its owner believed (ibid., 984–5) that from its foundation in 1905 it had sold over $31 million in corporate securities. Presumably it did at least as much business in each succeeding year of the Great Boom.

95 $11.5 million in the period 1900–5 alone (ibid., 985).

96 Data on bank assets from C.P. Curtis, *Statistical Contributions to Canadian Economic History* (Toronto: Macmillan, 1932)

97 Buckley, *Capital Formation*, 67

98 I owe this observation to Dr Neil Quigley, of Victoria University, Wellington, New Zealand.

99 Bank of Nova Scotia, *Circular Book No. 2*, 12 April 1888 to 11 March 1902, Nos 674 and 867

100 *Rules and Regulations of the Bank of Nova Scotia*, 1917 edition, Rules 7:162, 7.168. The rule book of 1902 had nothing to say about a bond department or about the reception of share-applications.

101 Ibid., Rule 7:163

102 Ontario *Public Accounts; Morang's Annual Register*, 1901, 185

103 Dominion Department of Insurance, *Reports*

104 See table 18.2

105 Neufeld, *Financial System*, 479–90

106 Investment Bankers Association of America, *Proceedings of Second Annual Meeting*, 1913, 62–3

107 Calculated from E.R. Wood, *Annual Surveys of the Bond Market* (Toronto: *Monetary Times*, annual)

108 Investment Bankers Association, *Proceedings*

109 Dominion Parliament, Standing Committee on Banking and Commerce, 13–14 Geo V, 1923, *Proceedings*, 513–4: evidence of Sir Edmund Walker

110 A.E. Ames and Co. was founded in 1889, and Central Canada Loan, in 1884.

111 Royal Commission on Banking, *Report*, 27

112 From the beginning of 1900 through 1906 Canada Life obtained 38 per cent of its securities directly from the original issuers. Royal Commission on Insurance, *Evidence*, 972

113 *Monetary Times*, 10 April 1909, 1831

114 U.S. National Monetary Commission, *Interviews*, 127–8

115 Standing Committee, 1923, *Proceedings*

116 Standing Committee, 1913, *Proceedings*, 235–9

117 Royal Commission on Life Insurance, *Evidence*, 984–5; Superintendant of Insurance, *Reports*, 1910–14: 'List of Securities Bought and Sold'

118 Canada, Senate, *Debates*, 3d Session, 10th Parliament, 1906–7, 551ff

119 Idem; Royal Commission on Life Insurance, *Evidence*, 971

120 Ibid., 972: from 1900 through the first half of 1906, 12 per cent of Canada Life's new securities were bought from Central Canada Loan and 32 per cent from Dominion Securities, two companies controlled by George A. Cox, the President of Canada Life.

121 Toronto was willing to sell its own securities over the counter, although few people knew about the fact (*Securities Magazine,* June 1913, 7). Chatham, Oakville, and St Thomas did the same thing in the same year (*Monetary Times,* 20 December 1913, and other issues of that year).

122 Coats, *Enquiry,* 730ff

123 United Kingdom, Royal Commission on the Dominions (Cd 8458), *Report,* 401ff

124 By 1903 Canada Permanent had branches at Winnipeg and Edmonton.

125 London Life; Royal Commission on Life Insurance, *Evidence,* 1525

126 Excelsior Life; ibid., 1293–4

127 Northern Life; ibid., 1560

128 Ibid., 1425: evidence of G.B. Woods of Continental Life

129 Ibid., 906–7: mortgages 'yield a good rate of return but they are very much more cumbersome than other classes of securities and entail a good deal more expense in attending to investments of that class.'

130 Ontario Registrar of Loan Corporations, *Report,* 1900

131 Ibid., 1905–15

132 Ibid., and Quebec Registrar of Trust Companies, *Report,* 1913

133 Skodyn, *Permanent,* 30–1, 45

134 For a more complete account see Easterbrook, *Farm Credit,* 138–57.

135 Ibid., 139

136 On the background see Neufeld, *Financial System,* 423–5.

137 Easterbrook, *Farm Credit,* 89

138 Neufeld, *Financial System,* 495–500

139 Ibid., 507

140 18 Geo v c 34

141 J. Peter Williamson, *Securities Regulation in Canada* (Toronto: University of Toronto Press, 1960), 22

142 18 Geo v c 33

143 Williamson, *Securities,* 21

144 7 Edw vii c 34, s 97(c); cited by Williamson, *Securities,* 10

145 20 Geo v c 29; 20 Geo v c 38

146 21 Geo v c 48

147 22 Geo v c 53, s 36

148 23 Geo v c 59, ss 33, 34

149 1 Geo vi c 69

CHAPTER 19 *The Provincial 'Exchequer'*

1 This chapter is a compression of a longer paper in which detailed time series are presented, and the perplexities of the *Public Accounts* data are discussed, along with the methodology that underlies the calculations which the chapter presents only in summary form.

2 See above, chapter 3.

3 See above, chapter 16.

4 Trend equations were fitted to the corrected and homogenized series for revenue and

for expenditure; the former has a slope of 0.0588 and the latter, 0.0789, for the period 1868–1901.

5 Toronto *Globe*, 20 February 1892; 14 March 1892, 4; 11 February 1899, 24; 14 February 1899, 6.

6 For 1902–14 the slope of the revenue function is 0.5972, while that of the expenditure function is 0.99126.

7 This relationship would not continue; by the mid-1930s the railway was a considerable net burden in that it kept its own profits, while the province serviced the relevant debt.

8 The data for this discussion have been compiled from the provincial *Public Accounts*, which require extensive 'processing' before they can be used for this or for any other analytical purpose.

9 The percentage increase in demand for a service, divided by the percentage increase in aggregate real income within the community

10 See Perry, *Taxes, Tariffs, and Subsidies,* appendix A.

11 Ibid., 313; David Fransen, 'Unscrewing the Inscrutable,' unpublished PH D dissertation, University of Toronto, 1984

APPENDIX B

1 Ontario: Bureau of Industries, *First Report;* Bureau of Labor, *Reports*

2 1917, 1918, 1920, and 1921

3 Gordon W. Bertram, 'Historical Statistics on Growth and Structure of Manufacturing in Canada, 1870–1957,' in J. Henripin and A. Asimakopulos, eds, Canadian Political Science Association Conferences on Statistics, 1962 and 1963, *Papers* (Toronto: University of Toronto Press, 1964), 93–146

4 *Census,* 1911, vol. III, vii

Index